The Hidden ~~Power~~
of ~~Law~~

Imogen Goold
St Anne's College
Oxford

The Hidden Gender of Law

Second Edition

Regina Graycar
Faculty of Law, University of Sydney

Jenny Morgan
Faculty of Law, University of Melbourne

Foreword
Justice Mary Gaudron
High Court of Australia

THE FEDERATION PRESS
2002

Published in Sydney by

The Federation Press
PO Box 45, Annandale, NSW, 2038.
71 John St, Leichhardt, NSW, 2040.
Ph (02) 9552 2200. Fax (02) 9552 1681.
E-mail: info@federationpress.com.au
Website: http://www.federationpress.com.au

First edition 1990
Second edition 2002

National Library of Australia
Cataloguing-in-Publication entry
    Graycar, Regina
    The hidden gender of law

    2nd ed
    Bibliography
    Includes index
    ISBN 1 86287 340 2

    1. Women – Legal status, laws, etc, – Australia. 2. Sex discrimination against women –
Law and legislation – Australia. I. Morgan, Jenny. II. Title.

342.940878

©   The Federation Press
This publication is copyright. Other than for the purposes of and subject to the conditions prescribed under the Copyright Act, no part of it may in any form or by any means (electronic, mechanical, microcopying, photocopying, recording or otherwise) be reproduced, stored in a retrieval system or transmitted without prior written permission. Enquiries should be addressed to the publisher.

Typeset by The Federation Press, Leichhardt, NSW.
Printed by McPherson's Printing Group, Maryborough, Vic.

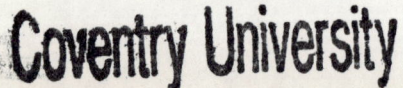

Praise for the first edition:

The Hidden Gender of Law is, quite simply, a *tour de force*. ... It shatters the idea of traditional legal course boundaries by adopting a new analytical framework.
          Mary Jane Mossman, *Canadian Journal of Women and the Law*

[T]ruly international ... It successfully presents feminist legal theory as a dynamic set of ideas, moving and changing with the times, neither static nor unitary ... It remains true to the central critical aspiration of relating theory to practice and it does this both by contextualising the theory it presents ... and practically, by exploring the problems women commonly confront and the law's response to them. ... [Graycar and Morgan] have produced a book which deserves considerable credit and attention, for its fine blend of creativity and practicality.
          Joanne Conaghan, *Feminist Legal Studies (UK)*

This is a well researched book of international relevance. ... It is its tight theoretical framework which makes the book a success. ... It successfully presents us with a student text, and an introduction to feminist legal studies, while simultaneously managing to be an important contribution to feminist legal theory. ... What makes this book special is that the authors have drawn together an impressive array of primary and secondary material that exposes the gendered nature of the barriers and of law generally, while simultaneously breaking them down.
          Belinda Bennett, *International Journal of the Sociology of Law (UK)*

A starting point for becoming a new sort of practitioner.
          Marian Evans and Robin MacKenzie, *New Zealand Universities Law Review*

An excellent starting point for researchers, students and practitioners alike ... One of the most interesting aspects of this book is the diversity of thought and theory it presents. The reader is not spoonfed a particular viewpoint ... This extensive resource is for those not afraid of having their beliefs and assumptions challenged.
          Amanda Gorely, *Law Institute Journal (Victoria)*

An original critical analysis focused on breaking down the doctrinal categories which underpin the gendered nature of law.
          Josephine Shaw, *International and Comparative Law Quarterly*

The underlying themes and messages are well-written, forceful, thought-provoking and very universal.
          Stephen Digby, *The Legal Executive Journal (UK)*

In my view, this book is a *tour de force* – an outstanding contribution.
          Christine Boyle, *Dalhousie Law Journal (Canada)*

[A] lively and challenging work replete with fascinating cases.
          Queensland Bar Association

Foreword

'Equality' is an elusive concept, not least because people differ from one another, with different aptitudes, abilities and experiences. The concept of 'equal justice' is more easily stated: 'equal justice' is justice that is blind to differences that don't matter but is appropriately adapted to those that do.

Equal justice requires, as a first step, the analysis of rules and practices predicated on difference so as to ascertain whether the difference, if any, justifies the rule or practice in question. The second and more difficult step is to recognise differences that bear on the justice of the situation. The third and most difficult of all is to articulate those differences and to advocate appropriately adapted measures which take them into account.

In their second edition of *The Hidden Gender of Law*, Graycar and Morgan pose fundamental questions as to the impact of the law on women and their participation in society. They are questions to which every lawyer should attempt an answer. Many of the questions do not permit of a single correct answer, but an understanding of the problems posed by Graycar and Morgan is a most important step along the road to equal justice for women and, ultimately, to equal justice for all.

Justice Mary Gaudron
High Court of Australia
January 2002

Foreword to the First Edition

There is a certain inevitability in the commitment which women have to law reform, and in their distrust of common law which took away their legal personality on marriage. This distrust continues, even though the more obvious discriminations against women have been removed from the law. Legal institutions have always strongly resisted change, and they remain under suspicion of deeply entrenched and insidious gender bias, hard to identify and even harder to eradicate.

Australian lawyers can thank Reg Graycar and Jenny Morgan for exploring these hidden areas of gender bias in the law and exposing them for our attention. Sometimes no more is needed than to expose what judges have actually said about women. For example:

> Many a married woman seeks work. She does so when the children grow up and leave the house. She does it, not solely to earn money, helpful as it is: but to fill her time with useful occupation, rather than sit idly at home waiting for her husband to return. The devil tempts those who have nothing to do.[1]

They also introduce us to the writings of feminist jurists who have thrown new light on old concepts and revealed clearly the failure of the legal system to acknowledge, let alone accept, that there could be another way to see things.

This analysis brings to light a society permeated by gender bias, a society in which women's role, women's work, and women's contribution are not given their full value, and which has failed to protect women from male violence and oppression. The message is that the legal system incorporates this bias and helps to perpetuate it. Some examples will illustrate this.

A liberating force for women has been access to safe contraception and abortion. Greater control over fertility, fewer children and less time spent in child rearing and in domestic work have opened up choices for women, and enabled them to have some economic independence and a greater opportunity to participate in public life. If equity and independence for women were highly valued, access to fertility control, to contraceptive and abortion services at reasonable cost, would also be a high priority. And yet it has been a continuing struggle for women to gain and to keep the right to choose freely whether and when to have children. The denial of this right, in any society, falls hardest on the most vulnerable, the young and the poor.

The generally limited aspirations of girls in education and training are compounded by a gender structured workforce in which many women lack career and promotion opportunities, and in which their earning levels are far lower than those of men. If women have family responsibilities they carry the double burden of work and the costs of child care. They have to compete in a workforce which assumes, despite the facts, that a worker is a male breadwinner in full time employment, a workforce which is not structured for workers with family responsibilities and makes few concessions to them. If they choose the homemaker role this is not regarded as 'work' and their contribution to the family is not given full recognition in matrimonial property law. In many ways the law reinforces women's dependency role. For example, our social security laws assume that a

---

1   *Langston v AUEW* [1974] 1 All ER 980 at 987 (per Lord Denning).

woman living in a relationship with a man is or should be a dependant of that man, even though she has no right to claim support from him or to a share in property. To qualify for support a woman living with a man may have to prove that there is not a 'marriage-like' relationship, even though it is clear that the legal consequences of marriage do not apply.

The extent of male violence towards women, and the high level of acceptance of this violence are compounded by rape laws which focus on the male offender's belief about consent rather than on the question whether the victim did in fact consent. In some States the law still presumes a wife's consent to sexual intercourse, regardless of the facts. The feminist assertion that sexual intercourse should be seen as criminal unless consent is proved will be seen in a very different light by women than by men. But it is the male view which prevails.

Australia is not the only country whose institutions are shaped by gender bias. It is not surprising that the UN Convention on the Elimination of all Forms of Discrimination against Women puts sex stereotyping high on its 'hit list'. The Convention calls on states to change social and cultural patterns of conduct and to eliminate prejudices and practices based on the idea of the inferiority or the superiority of either of the sexes or on stereotyped roles for men and women.

To respond to this call major social reform is necessary to reshape society so that it more clearly reflects the needs of women as well as men. Law reform is an essential part of this process. The law can liberate and protect, put right wrongs, as well as inflict them. The Courts, though constrained by precedent, procedure and hidden bias, can be enlightened as well as reactionary. Judicial decisions on equal pay, discrimination, sexual harassment, and abortion have recognised the realities of women's lives. The Parliament, though limited by the pressures of political expedience, and by its traditional prejudices, has responded to the claims of women by legislating against discrimination and violence. While legal categories are often confusing and apparently irrelevant, they are not closed. New categories and new remedies can be introduced, such as privacy protection, class actions, sexual harassment.

The women's movement has already generated much necessary law reform in Australia. Getting down to the entrenched bias, however, is no easy task. While it is hard to change the system from outside, operating inside it causes a dilemma for women who are called on to act in accordance with the established rules and hierarchies of that system, to compete with and behave in the same way as men, and to take part in the essentially combative approach of the legal process. The twin dangers of either absorbing the culture and ignoring its bias, or of totally rejecting its insensitivity have to be overcome if a genuine attempt is to be made to bring about a fundamental change in the institution and its values.

Another problem is that women do not necessarily share the same values and attitudes about these issues. Women may have completely different views about such things as economics, social policy, the environment, peace, war, disarmament and military service, poverty, housework, parenting. Where women are united they can influence the political process (as the Women's Electoral Lobby showed in 1972). But many law reform issues are controversial. It is not necessary to agree or to disagree with every point of view that is presented in the material. The important thing is that these issues be considered and discussed. Where opinions differ, the problem of the reformer is to convince lawmakers of the justice and equity of the changes necessary to overcome their own prejudices.

The challenge presented by this book is to step beyond the goals of formal equality and affirmative action and to remake our political, legal and social institutions in a way which gives full human value to women. As such it is a valuable resource for the law reformer as he or she attempts to uncover the underlying policy and values of the law, to consider what the policies should be, and how best to achieve them. When choices are made in our legal system, the message is that women of every viewpoint should participate in the process on a basis of equality. If women's experience and outlook differ from those of men, if they speak with 'another voice', their insights are essential in framing legal policies and in deciding what is relevant and what is reasonable.

While the idea of a gender-neutral law has its attractions, there are important aspects of life, such as conception, childbirth, sex and sexual violence, in which women's experience is quite different from that of men. The law can not readily be gender neutral in areas where the specific experience of women needs recognition, or where there is continuing disadvantage. It is only in the hazy future that we might think of replacing the reasonable man not with the reasonable woman, but with the reasonable person, able to present an integrated and balanced view of human experience.

Justice Elizabeth Evatt AO
President
Australian Law Reform Commission
July 1990

Contents

Foreword *Justice Mary Gaudron*	vii
Foreword to First Edition *Justice Elizabeth Evatt*	viii
Authors' Note	xv
Acknowledgements	xvi
Table of Cases	xviii
Table of Statutes	xxiv

Chapter One: Introduction

Introduction	1
Legal categories and constructing women's lives	1
Towards a new doctrinal framework: The structure of this book	3
How is this edition different?	5
A book about possibilities	7

Part One
Recurring Theoretical Themes

Chapter Two: The Public/Private Dichotomy

Introduction	10
The construction of 'the private': An example from the law of contract	15
Complicating the public/private dichotomy	17
'Intervention and non-intervention'	17
Is privacy always 'bad'?	20
What is 'public'?	22
A legal right of privacy?	24

Chapter Three: Gender (In)Equality

Introduction	28
Equality models applied	32
The example of pregnancy	33
Challenges by men to women-only programs	35
The 'presumption of advancement'	44
Equality for whom? Differences amongst women	48

Chapter Four: Methodologies and Epistemologies

Introduction	56
Legal methodologies	56
Claims to objectivity	56
Claims to truth	65
Feminist methodologies	71
Consciousness raising	71
Legal storytelling	74
'Truth' claims and claims on behalf of undifferentiated women	78
Privacy, equality and method: The Hindmarsh Island Bridge dispute	81

CONTENTS

Part Two
Women and Economic (In)dependence

Chapter Five: Work in Families

Money and relationships	87
Women's unpaid work	87
Women's work in the home and in the market: An empirical introduction	88
Changes in the paid workforce	89
Marriage and family	90
The legal consequences of marriage: A brief historical account	91
Family law?	96
Financial aspects of family law	98
The current legal framework in Australia	98
Debates about 'equality'	99
Who gets what? The economic consequences of marriage breakdown	101
The relevance of violence	108
The marriage 'contract': The move to private ordering	111
Relationship debt or 'sexually transmitted debt'	114
Women's work in the home: Personal injury damages	126
The valuation of a woman's loss of capacity to work in the home	126
Whose loss?	129
Housework as hobby: Economic or non-economic loss?	130
Damages for the costs of care	133

Chapter Six: Out to Work

Introduction	139
Constructing women's work: Personal injury damages	139
Wages for women	145
Introduction	145
The 'family wage'	147
The 'equal pay' cases	150
Anti-discrimination laws	151
Affirmative action laws	156
Comparable worth and job evaluation	159
Labour market institutions	163
Conclusion	165

Part Three
Women and Connection

Chapter Seven: Constructing Relationships

A doctrinal introduction from tort law	173
Nervous shock	173
Wrongful birth/wrongful conception	183
Pregnant tribunals: Biology as destiny?	192
A connection thesis?	194

Chapter Eight: Controlling Reproductive Bodies

Introduction	199
Abortion	199
A brief legal survey	200

Criminal law	200
Using constitutional law	202
Legislative amendment	204
The language of claims	208
Privacy	208
Equality	209
Morality	212
Abortion in practice	213
Public funding	213
'Hospital autonomy' and 'free speech'	215
Public opinion and abortion	217
Who decides whether a woman can have an abortion?	218
'Foetal rights'	222
Policing women	223
Civil actions	228
Wardship	228
Court-ordered treatment	236
Revisioning the relationship between a woman and the foetus she is carrying	243
A UK example	244
A Canadian example	245
Assisted reproduction	249
Conclusion	257

Chapter Nine: Losing Children

Introduction	258
Australian child custody law	258
A brief history	258
The *Family Law Act* 1975 (Cth)	259
Gender neutrality in custody law	260
The primary caregiver: A feminist alternative?	267
Child custody: A narrow white heterosexual perspective?	277
Indigenous families and family law	277
Lesbians as mothers in the family law system	287
Losing children: Criminal and tort law perspectives	292
An Australian cause celebre: The story of Lindy Chamberlain	293
Tortious death to children: The law's response	298

Part Four
Gendered Harms

Chapter Ten: Violence: An introduction

The incidence of violence against women	303
Attitudes to violence against women	306
Gender neutrality and the language of domestic violence	308
Violence against women and legal categories	314
The forfeiture rule	315
Traditional legal responses to violence against women	316
'Special laws' to respond to violence against women	317
The victim-agency debate	322
Conclusion	326

Chapter Eleven: Invading Women's Bodies
Medical and other injuries to women   328
    Eugenic sterilisation of women   328
    Dangerous products and dangerous drugs   334
    The 'unfortunate experiment'   337
Rape   343
    'Real rape'   343
    The construction of heterosexuality   348
    Proving rape   354
    Neutralising rape   364
    Moving beyond consent?   365
Civil actions for sexual assault   369
    Introduction   369
    Tort law and equality   373
    Conclusion   379

Chapter Twelve: Sexual Harassment and Pornography
    Introduction   381
Sexual harassment   381
    Tort or discrimination law?   381
    The development of a legal doctrine   385
    Whose perspective?   388
    The 'reasonable victim/person/woman/employee'   390
    Gender neutrality   397
    Sexual harassment beyond the workplace: Feminists create 'victims'?   399
Pornography   403
    An obscenity approach   403
    Pornography and equality   405
        The United States: The ordinance approach   405
        Canada: Interpreting obscenity law   407
    The role of law?   418
    Conclusion   419

Part Five
An Agenda for Gender?

Chapter Thirteen: Strategies in Law
    Introduction   422
    Is there any point engaging with law?   422
    Adding women (and stirring): Will more women make a difference?   422
    Intervening in litigation   428
    Initiating litigation   431
    Creating new legal claims   434
        Sexual harassment   434
        The Violence Against Women Act   435
    Developing evidentiary strategies: The example of 'battered woman syndrome'   438
    Legislative initiatives/law reform   442
    An alternative feminist process? The Grandview agreement   445
    Is there any point engaging with law?   448

Bibliography   450
Index   476

Authors' Note

There are a number of people who have assisted us in a variety of ways. Thanks to: Hilary Astor, Connie Backhouse, Susan Boyd, Sally Brown, Hilary Charlesworth, Michael Chesterman, Suzanne Christie, Graeme Coss, Annie Cossins, Michael Crommelin, Margie Cronin, Martin Davies, Brettel Dawson, Lisa De Ferrari, John Dewar, Elizabeth Evatt, Belinda Fehlberg, Peter Hanks, Margaret Harrison, Rosemary Hunter, Isabel Karpin, Miranda Kaye, Andrew Kenyon, Harold Luntz, Lisa Maher, Ian Malkin, Jo Manning, Veronique Maury, Thérèse McCarthy, Jenni Millbank, Wayne Morgan, Mary Jane Mossman, Anne Orford, Di Otto, Rosemary Owens, Sundhya Pahuja, Sarah Pritchard, Helen Rhoades, Merrilee Robb, Danny Sandor, Lisa Sarmas, Cheryl Saunders, PJ Schwikkard, Liz Sheehy, Miranda Stewart, Julie Stubbs, Maureen Tehan, Michael Thomson, Julia Tolmie, Richard Vann, Amy Veitch, Kris Walker, Jane Wangmann, John Waugh, Claire Young, and Melanie Young. We especially want to thank the eagle-eyed and extremely diligent Sarah Richardson who worked with us on the last stages of the book and found more references and more typos than we knew existed.

We also could not have completed this book without the invaluable assistance of the staff at the Law Library, University of Sydney; the Law Library/Legal Resource Centre, University of Melbourne and the Attorney General's Department (NSW) Library. We are also indebted to the IT staff of the Attorney General's Department (NSW) and of the Faculties of Law, University of Sydney and University of Melbourne. The Australian Research Council and the Faculty of Law, University of Sydney, provided support that enabled us to employ research assistants at various stages.

It has been 12 years since the first edition of this book was published. We thank our publishers, Federation Press, for their patience.

As we were finishing the book, we received the sad news of the death of Marlee Kline on 29 November 2001, after a long and courageous battle with illness. Marlee, a colleague from the University of British Columbia, inspired a pointed reconsideration of whether the claims made by feminist legal scholars excluded the interests of First Nations or Indigenous women and men. She will be sorely missed.

Reg Graycar and Jenny Morgan
January 2002

Acknowledgments

The authors wish to thank the following authors and publishers for permission to reprint extracts from the copyright works listed below. All rights in the copyright works are reserved by each author and publisher giving permission to reprint. Efforts have been made to contact and obtain permission from the copyright holder prior to publication. Any copyright holder who has not been correctly acknowledged is invited to contact The Federation Press, and any oversight will be corrected at the first opportunity.

Chapter 2
Butterworths Tolley, for Katherine O'Donovan, *Sexual Divisions in the Law*, Weidenfeld & Nicholson (1985).

Chapter 3
Commonwealth of Australia, for Australian Law Reform Commission, *Equality Before the Law: Women's Equality*, Report No 69, Part II (1994).
Lisa Sarmas and Melbourne University Law Review, for Lisa Sarmas, 'A Step in the Wrong Direction' (1994) 19 *Melbourne University Law Review* 758.

Chapter 4
Joanna Bourke and University of New South Wales Law Journal, for Joanna Bourke, 'Women's Business: Sex, Secrets and the Hindmarsh Island Affair' (1997) 20 *University of New South Wales Law Journal* 333.

Chapter 5
Grania Sheehan, Jody Hughes and Australian Institute for Family Studies, for Grania Sheehan and Jody Hughes, *Division of Matrimonial Property in Australia*, Research Paper No 25, AIFS, March 2001.
Grania Sheehan, Bruce Smyth and Butterworths, for Grania Sheehan and Bruce Smyth, 'Spousal Violence and Post-separation Financial Outcomes' (2000) 14 *Australian Journal of Family Law* 102.
Refractory Girl, for Regina Graycar, 'Hoovering as a Hobby: The Common Law's Approach to Work in the Home' (1985) 28 *Refractory Girl* 22.

Chapter 6
Barbara Pocock and Blackwell Publishing, for Barbara Pocock, 'Equal Pay Thirty Years On: The Policy and the Practice' (1999) 32 *Australian Economic Review* 279.
Wexdev, for Rosemary Hunter, *The Beauty Therapist, the Mechanic, the Geoscientist and the Librarian: Addressing the Undervaluation of Women's Work*, ATN, Wexdev, University of Technology, Sydney, 2000.

Chapter 7
Bronwyn Naylor and the Alternative Law Journal, for Bronwyn Naylor, 'Pregnant Tribunals' (1989) 14 *Legal Service Bulletin* 41.
Lawbook Co for Reg Graycar and Jenny Morgan, '"Unnatural Rejection of Womanhood and Motherhood": Pregnancy, Damages and the Law: A Note on CES v Superclinics (Aust) Pty Ltd' (1996) 18 *Sydney Law Review* 323

Chapter 8
Kris Walker and the Alternative Law Journal, for Kris Walker, 'Equal Access to assisted reproductive services: The effect of *McBain v Victoria*' (2000) 25 *Alternative Law Journal* 287.
Temple University Press, for Laura Gomez, *Misconceiving Mothers: Legislators, Prosecutors and the Politics of Prenatal Drug Exposure*.

Chapter 9
Susan Boyd, Helen Rhoades, Kate Burns and Butterworths, for Susan B Boyd, Helen Rhoades and Kate Burns, 'The Politics of the Primary Caregiver Presumption: A Conversation' (1999) 13 *Australian Journal of Family Law* 233.

ACKNOWLEDGMENTS

HREOC, for *Bringing Them Home*: Report of the National Inquiry into the Separation of Aboriginal and Torres Strait Islander Children from Their Families, Commonwealth of Australia, Sydney, 1997.

Refractory Girl, for Adrian Howe, 'Chamberlain Revisited: The Case Against The Media' (1989) 31-32 *Refractory Girl* 2.

Jenni Millbank and the Family Court, for Jenni Millbank, 'Same Sex Couples and Family Law', (1998) Paper presented at Family Court conference, October 1998, available at <http://www.familycourt.gov.au/papers/html/millbank.html>.

Chapter 10

Columbia Law Review, for Kathryn Abrams, 'Sex Wars Redux: Agency and Coercion in Feminist Legal Theory'. This article originally appeared at 95 *Columbia Law Review* 304 (1995). Reprinted by permission.

Women Against Violence, for Dale Bagshaw and Donna Chung, 'Gender Politics and Research: Male and Female Violence in Intimate Relationships' (2000) 8 *Women Against Violence: An Australian Feminist Journal* 4.

Chapter 11

Alison Young and Melbourne University Law Review, for Alison Young, 'The Wasteland of the Law' (1988) 22 *Melbourne University Law Journal* 442.

British Medical Journal, for Charlotte Paul, 'The New Zealand cervical cancer study: Could it happen again?' (1988) 297 *British Medical Journal* 533.

Northeastern University Press, for Lucinda Finley, 'The Pharmaceutical Industry and Women's Reproductive Health: The Perils of Ignoring Risk and Blaming Women', From *Corporate Victimization of Women*, edited by Elizabeth Szockyj and James G Fox. Copyright 1996 by Northeastern University Press, Boston, 1996. (Reprinted with permission of Northeastern University Press.)

Bruce Feldthusen, for Bruce Feldthusen, 'The Civil Action for Sexual Battery: Therapeutic Jurisprudence?' (1993) 25 *Ottawa Law Review* 203.

Palgrave, for Liz Kelly, 'The Continuum of Sexual Violence', in Jalna Hanmer and Mary Maynard (eds), *Women, Violence and Social Control*, Macmillan Press, London, 1987. (Reproduced with permission of Palgrave.)

Catharine A MacKinnon and University of Chicago Press, for Catharine A MacKinnon, 'Feminism, Marxism, Method, and the State: Toward Feminist Jurisprudence' (1983) 8 *Signs: Journal of Women in Culture and Society* 635.

Yale Law Journal, for Susan Estrich, 'Rape' (1986) 95 *Yale Law Journal* 1087.

Chapter 12

Catharine A MacKinnon and Yale University Press, for Catharine MacKinnon, *Sexual Harassment of Working Women*, Yale University Press, New Haven, 1979.

Chapter 13

Bruce Feldthusen, Olena Hankivsky, Lorraine Greaves and Cancopy, for Bruce Feldthusen, Olena Hankivsky and Lorraine Greaves, 'Therapeutic Consequences of Civil Actions for Damages and Compensation Claims by Victims of Sexual Abuse' (2000) 12 *Canadian Journal of Women and the Law* 66.

Catharine A MacKinnon, for Catharine A MacKinnon, 'Sexual Harassment: Its First Decade in Court' in *Feminism Unmodified*, Harvard University Press, Cambridge MA, 1987, and for Catharine A MacKinnon, 'Disputing Male Sovereignty: On United States v Morrison' (2000) 114 *Harvard Law Review* 135.

Law Book Co, for Elizabeth Sheehy, Julie Stubbs and Julia Tolmie, 'Defending Battered Women on Trial: The Battered Woman Syndrome and its Limitations' (1992) 16 *Criminal Law Journal* 369.

Cases

Incorporated Council of Law Reporting for England and Wales, for cases reported in the Law Reports (AC, KB, QB) and Weekly Law Reports.

CCH, for cases reported in the Australian Torts Reports and the Australian Sales Cases.

Lawbook Co, for cases reported in Commonwealth Law Reports and New South Wales Law Reports.

Table of Cases

A v B (unreported, NZ HC Auckland, Young J, 19 March 1999): 342
A v Bottrill (unreported, NZ CA 75/00, 13 June 2001): 341-343
A and J (1995) 19 Fam LR 260: 289-290
AC, Appellant, In Matter of 539 A 2d 203 (1988): 238
AC, Appellant, In re 573 A2d 1235 (1990): 236-238, 240, 242-244
AIS Pty Ltd v Najdovska (1988) EOC ¶92-223: 151-152
Akins v National Australia Bank (1994) 34 NSWLR 155: 121, 125
Akron v Akron Center for Reproductive Health, Inc 462 US 416 (1983): 219
Alcock v Chief Constable of South Yorkshire Police [1992] 1 AC 310: 173
Aldridge v Booth (1988) EOC ¶92-222: 397
Allen v Bloomsbury [1993] 1 All ER 651: 186
Allison v Rank City Wall Canada Ltd (1984) 45 OR (2d) 141: 317
American Bookseller Association, Inc v Hudnut, Mayor, City of Indianapolis 771 F 2d 323 (1985): 406-407
Angelopoulos v Rubenhold (unreported, SASC, FC, 3 April 1991): 144
Armstrong v Commonwealth Bank of Australia [1999] NSWSC 588: 124-125
Associated Provincial Picture Houses Ltd v Wednesbury Corporation [1948] 1 KB 223: 194
Attorney-General v Harris (unreported, VCCA, 11 August 1981): 347
Attorney General v X (1992) 15 BMLR 104: 2
Attorney-General (Qld) (ex rel Kerr) v T (1983) 57 ALJR 285: 219, 221-222
Attorney-General's Ref No 3 of 1994 [1996] QB 581: 244
Australian Iron and Steel Pty Ltd v Banovic (1989) 168 CLR 165: 151
B and R and Separate Representative (1995) 19 Fam LR 594; (1995) FLC ¶92-636: 64, 284, 285
Baby Doe, In re 632 NE 2d 326 (1994): 241-242
Baby F, Re (1987) 9 RFL 415: 229
Baby R, Re (1988) 15 RFL 225: 229, 236
Bagias v Smith (1979) FLC ¶90-658: 128
Baker v Bolton (1808) 1 Camp 493: 298
Balfour v Balfour [1919] 2 KB 571: 15-17
Barclay's Bank plc v O'Brien [1994] 1 AC 180: 121, 124

Barker v City of Hobart et al (unreported TASSC jury decision; reported in Sunday Tasmanian, 11 July 1993): 384-385
Barrett v Enfield London Borough Council [1999] 3 All ER 193: 377
Baumgartner v Baumgartner (1987) 164 CLR 137: 87
Bazley v Curry [1999] 2 SCR 534: 446
BCCI v Aboody [1989] 1 QB 923: 124
Becin v GEC Australia (unreported, QSC, 13 May 1993): 144
Bellotti v Baird 443 US 622 (1979): 219
Best v Fox [1952] AC 716: 128
Biddle v The Queen [1995] 1 SCR 761 (Supreme Court of Canada): 425
Bird v Free (1994) 126 ALR 475: 59, 423
Bird v Volkers (unreported, FCA, 20 October 1994): 59
Blank v Sullivan and Cromwell 418 F Supp 1 at 4 (SDNY 1975): 60
Bliss v Attorney-General (Canada) [1979] 1 SCR 183: 34
Bondin v Lamaro (unreported, NSWCA, 14 October 1994): 144
Box Hill College of Technical and Further Education v Fares (1992) EOC ¶92-464: 52
Braschi v Stahl Associates Co 544 NYS 2d 784 (1989): 97
Breen v Williams (1996) 186 CLR 71: 371
Brennan v NSW Fire Brigades (1996) EOC ¶92-845: 38
Brisbane South Regional Health Authority v Taylor (1996) 186 CLR 541: 372
Brodie [1962] SCR 681: 408
Brooks v Canada Safeway Ltd [1989] 1 SCR 1219: 34
Brown v Brown (1993) 31 NSWLR 582: 45, 47, 107
Bruno v Davies (1988) 144 LSJS 226: 137, 316
Bryson v Bryant (1992) 29 NSWLR 188: 48
Buck v Bell 274 US 200 (1927): 329, 331
Burchard v Garay 229 Cal Rptr 800 (1986): 260, 264
Burnicle v Cutelli [1982] 2 NSWLR 26: 129-130
C v S [1987] 1 All ER 1230: 219
California Federal Savings and Loan Association v Guerra 479 US 272 (1987): 33
Calverley v Green (1984) 155 CLR 242: 46
Canadian Newspapers Co v Canada (A-G) [1988] 2 SCR 122: 21

TABLE OF CASES

Carmichele v Minister for Safety and Security and Minister of Justice and Constitutional Development, Constitutional Court of South Africa, CCT 48/00, 16 August 2001: 378-379
Carrick v Commonwealth [1983] 2 Qd R 365: 134
Cartledge v Jopling [1963] AC 758: 372
CES v Superclinics (Aust) Pty Ltd (1995) 38 NSWLR 47: 3, 183-189, 202, 429-431
Chamberlain v The Queen (No 2) (1984) 153 CLR 521: 296
Chan v Minister for Immigration and Ethnic Affairs (1986) 169 CLR 379: 194
Chapman and Barton v Tickner (1995) 133 ALR 74: 82
Chapman v Luminis Pty Ltd (No 5) [2001] FCA 1106: 82
Cherry (Guardian ad Litem of) v Borsman (1990) 75 DLR (4th) 668: 183
Chester v Waverley Corporation (1939) 62 CLR 1: 174-178
Chief General Manager, Department of Health v Arumugam (1987) EOC ¶92-195: 389
Cleaver v Mutual Reserve Fund Life Association [1892] 1 QB 147: 315
Collins, Ex parte (1899) 9 LR (NSW) 497: 403
Commonwealth v Tasmania (Tasmanian Dams Case) (1983) 158 CLR 1: 397
Commonwealth Bank v HREOC (1998) EOC ¶92-908: 153
CP, In re (1997) 21 Fam LR 486: 198, 283, 285
Crowe v Graham (1968) 121 CLR 375: 403, 408
Cubillo and Gunner v Commonwealth (2000) 174 ALR 97: 433, 446
D, In re (unreported, Family Court, 1996): 270
Dahl v Purnell (1992) 15 Qld Lawyer Reports 31: 186
Daniels v Thompson [1998] 3 NZLR 22: 373
Darrach v R [2000] 2 SCR 443: 431
Dawood v Minister of Home Affairs (2000) 3 SALR 936 (Constitutional Court): 97
Dietrich v R (1992) 177 CLR 292: 432
Diprose v Louth (No 1) (1990) 54 SASR 438 (King CJ): 74
Diprose v Louth (No 2) (1990) 54 SASR 450 (FC): 74
Dixon v Davies (1982) 17 NTR 31: 198
Djokic v Sinclair (1994) EOC ¶92-643: 52, 395
Dobson (Litigation Guardian of) v Dobson (1997) 148 DLR (4th) 332 (NBCA): 232
Dobson (Litigation Guardian of) v Dobson [1999] 2 SCR 753: 232, 233, 235
Doe v Bolton 410 US 179 (1973): 202

Donselaar v Donselaar [1982] 1 NZLR 97: 341
Dothard v Rawlinson 433 US 321 (1977): 29
Douglas/Kwantlen Faculty Association v Douglas College (1990) 77 DLR (4th) 94: 215
Dudgeon v United Kingdom (1981) 4 EHRR 149: 77
Dulieu v White [1901] 2 KB 669: 173
Ebner v Official Trustee in Bankruptcy; Clenae Pty Ltd v ANZ Banking Group [2000] HCA 63: 58
EEOC v Sears, Roebuck and Co 628 F Supp 1264 (1986): 77, 153, 155
Eldridge v Attorney General of British Columbia and Medical Services Commission [1997] 3 SCR 624: 23, 215
Elizabeth, Re (1989) 13 Fam LR 47: 329
Emeh v Kensington Area Health Authority [1985] 1 QB 1012: 186, 189
Epperson v Dampney (1976) 10 ALR 227: 259
Ettingshausen v Australian Consolidated Press Ltd (1991) 23 NSWLR 443: 385
Eve, Re [1986] 2 SCR 388: 332
F, In Marriage of (1989) 13 Fam LR 189: 3, 220-222
F (In Utero), In re [1988] 2 WLR 1288: 228, 230, 236
Fares v Box Hill College of TAFE (1992) EOC ¶92-391: 52-53
Federated Clothing Trade v JA Archer (1919) 13 CAR 647: 148
Ferraro, In Marriage of (1992) 16 Fam LR1: 104, 126
Finance Sector Union v Commonwealth Bank (1997) EOC ¶92-889: 153
Fisher v Toler 194 Kan 701; 401 P 2d 1012 (1965): 95
Fitzpatrick v Sterling Housing Association Ltd [2001] 1 AC 27: 97
Formosa v Formosa [1962] 3 All ER 419 at 421-2: 94
Garcia v National Australia Bank Ltd (1998) 194 CLR 395: 121-122, 124-125
Gardiner v AH Robins Co 747 F 2d 1180 (1984): 336
Gardiner v Mounfield (1989) 5 BMLR 1: 183
Geduldig v Aiello 417 US 484 (1974): 34, 209
Gibbs v Commonwealth Bank (1997) EOC ¶92-877: 153
Gillick v West Norfolk and Wisbech Area Health Authority [1986] AC 112: 17, 330
Goudge, Marriage of (1984) FLC ¶91-534: 286
Gough v Commonwealth Bank of Australia (1994) ASC ¶56-270: 116
Grant, In Marriage of (1994) FLC ¶92-506: 109, 271

TABLE OF CASES

Great Atlantic and Pacific Company of Canada Ltd v Ontario (Human Rights Commission) (1993) 109 DLR (4th) 214: 58
Green v Matheson [1990] NZAR 49: 341
Griffiths v Kerkemeyer (1977) 139 CLR 161: 133, 137-138, 316
Gronow v Gronow (1979) 144 CLR 513: 166, 260
Group Four Industries v Brosnan (1991) 9 ACLC 1181 (SASC): 125
GTB Nominees Pty Ltd v Uniting Church Property Trust in Australia and City of Kew (unreported, VSC, 25 January 1989): 193
H (1995) 81 A Crim R 88: 346
Hall, Oliver and Reid v Sheiban (1988) EOC ¶92-227: 392, 398
Hall, Oliver and Reid v Sheiban Pty Ltd (1989) EOC ¶92-250: 393
Halliwell v Stephens (1998) EOC ¶92-914: 38
Hambrook v Stokes Brothers [1925] 1 KB 141: 173, 177-178
Harper v Bangalow Motors Pty Ltd (unreported, NSWCA, 24 July 1990): 144
Harris v McRae 448 US 297 (1980): 3, 214, 333, 347-348
Harvester Case see HV McKay, Ex parte
Haynes (Edith), In re (1904) 6 WAR 209: 42
Hill v Chief Constable of West Yorkshire [1989] AC 53: 376-377, 379
HL v Matheson 450 US 398 (1981): 219
Hollis v Vabu [2001] HCA 44: 446
Horne and McIntosh v Press Clough Joint Venture and the Metals and Engineering Workers' Union (WA) (1994) EOC ¶92-556: 390
HREOC v Mt Isa Mines (1992) EOC ¶92-420: 29, 329
HREOC v Mt Isa Mines (1993) 46 FCR 301: 35, 37
HV McKay, Ex parte (1907) 2 CAR 1 (Harvester judgment): 147-149
International Union v Johnson Controls 499 US 187 (1991): 29, 329
Irvine, In Marriage of (1995) 19 Fam LR 374: 109, 271
Jaeger, In Marriage of (1994) 122 FLR 209; 18 Fam LR 126: 109, 271
Jaensch v Coffey (1984) 155 CLR 549: 173, 178
Jane Doe v Police Board of Commissioners (1989) 58 DLR (4th) 396: 376-377
Jane Doe v Metropolitan Toronto (Municipality) Commissioners of Police (1998) 160 DLR (4th) 697: 317, 373, 376-377, 379, 431, 433
Jane, Re (1988) 12 Fam LR 662: 329
Janzen et al v Platy Enterprises Ltd [1989] 1 SCR 1252 (Canada): 386-387

Jarman v Lloyd (1982) 8 Fam LR 878: 287
Jayatilake v Federal Commissioner of Taxation (1991) 22 ATR 125: 18
JEB v Alabama ex rel TB 511 US 127 (1994): 58, 425
Jefferson v Griffin Spalding County Hospital 274 SE 2d 457 (1981): 240, 242
JG and BG, In Marriage of (1994) 18 Fam LR 255: 109, 271, 276
JM v QFG [2000] 1 Qd R 373: 255
JM v QFG, GK and Queensland (Anti-Discrimination Tribunal, Decision of RG Atkinson, 31 January 1996): 254, 288
Johnson v Kelemic (1979) FLC ¶90-657: 134
Johnson v State 602 So 2d 1288 (1992): 225
K v Domestic Violence Crisis Service Inc (1999) EOC ¶93-021: 38
K v Minister for YACS [1982] 1 NSWLR 311: 202, 219
Kais v Turvey (1994) 17 Fam LR 498: 197
Kaycliff Pty Ltd v Australian Broadcasting Tribunal (1989) 90 ALR 310: 58, 194
Kealey v Bereszowski (1996) 136 DLR (4th) 708: 183, 188
Kealley (JK) v Jones; PM Kealley v Jones [1979] 1 NSWLR 723: 126, 128
Keitley, Re [1992] 1 VR 583: 315
Kelson v Transport Accident Commission (unreported, VSC, 5 May 1994): 144
Kennon v Kennon (1997) FLC ¶92-757: 95
Kolavo v Ainsworth Nominees (1994) EOC ¶92-576: 52
Koowarta v Bjelke-Petersen (1982) 153 CLR 168: 397
Koppen v Commissioner for Community Relations (1986) 67 ALR 215: 59
Kovac v Kovac [1982] 1 NSWLR 656: 133-134, 137
Kroeker v Jansen [1995] BCJ No 724: 129
L and GM and MM and the Director General, Department of Family Services and Aboriginal and Islander Affairs (Re Sarah) (1994) FLC ¶92-449: 330
L and L (1983) FLC ¶91-353: 287, 289
Langston v AEUW [1974] 1 All ER 980 at 987: 144
Law Society of British Columbia v Andrews et al [1989] 1 SCR 143: 32, 42
Law v Canada (Minister of Employment and Immigration) [1999] 1 SCR 497: 32
Lee v Swan [1996] BCJ No 259 (BCCA) [1996] 19 BCR (3d) 21: 145
Lindon v Kerr (1995) 57 FCR 284: 60
Lister v Hesley Hall Limited [2001] UKHL 22: 446
Little Sisters Book and Art Emporium v Canada (Minister of Justice) [2000] 2 SCR 1120: 412, 415-416
Livesey v NSW Bar Association (1983) 151 CLR 288: 58, 193

TABLE OF CASES

Lodge v Commissioner of Taxation (1972) 128 CLR 171: 18
Longman v Queen (1989) 168 CLR 79: 356, 361
Louth v Diprose (1992) 175 CLR 621: 74, 197
Lynch v Lynch (1991) 25 NSWLR 411: 231-233, 235
M and M (1988) 166 CLR 69: 263
M v H [1999] 2 SCR 3: 433
M(K) v M(H) [1992] 3 SCR 3: 371
McBain v Victoria [2000] FCA 1009: 40, 250-253
McCrostie v Boral Resources (1999) EOC ¶92-994: 153
McFall v Shimp 127 Pitts Leg J 14 (1978): 242
MacFarlane v Tayside Health Board [2000] 2 AC 59: 183, 189-191
McKay v Essex Area Health Authority [1982] QB 1166: 190
McKinney v University of Guelph (1990) 76 DLR (4th) 545: 215
McLoughlin v O'Brian [1983] 1 AC 410: 173
Macmillan and Jackson (1995) FLC ¶92-610: 264
Madyun, In re 114 Daily Wash L Rptr 2233 (1986): 236, 242
Maiward v Doyle [1983] WAR 210: 130
Malott [1998] 1 SCR 123: 441
Mara [1997] 2 SCR 630: 417
Marion's Case see Secretary, Department of Health and Community Services v JWB and SMB
Marsh v Marsh (1994) 17 Fam LR 289: 95, 317
Martin v Federal Commissioner of Taxation (1984) 2 FCR 260: 18
Mayor, Councillors and Citizens of the City of Moe v Pulis (1988) EOC ¶92-243: 39
MB (Medical Treatment), Re [1997] 2 FLR 426: 238-241
Melchior v Cattanach [2001] QCA 246: 191-192
Meritor Savings Bank v Vinson 477 US 57 (1986): 386, 388
Metal Manufacturers Ltd v Lewis (1988) 13 NSWLR 315: 125
Mills v Mills (unreported, Fam CA, FC, 10 September 1996): 59
Mitchell, In Marriage of (1995) 19 Fam LR 44: 106, 129
Moffa v R (1977) 138 CLR 601: 67-69, 197-198
Moge v Moge [1992] 3 SCR 813: 105-106, 129
Morgan v GK [2001] QADT 10: 254-255
Morgentaler v The Queen [1988] 1 SCR 30: 2, 23, 203-204, 215
Morrow v DPP [1994] Crim LR 58: 215
Mt Isa Mines v Marks (1992) 35 FCR 96: 35, 37
Muir v Alberta (1996) 132 DLR (4th) 695: 331-332
Murphy v Brentwood District Council [1991] 1 AC 398: 189
Muschinski v Dodds (1985) 160 CLR 583: 87
MW, DD, TA and AB v Royal Women's Hospital [1997] HREOCA 6: 249
NAB Ltd v Garcia (1996) 39 NSWLR 577: 121
Najdovska v AIS (1985) EOC ¶92-140: 151-152
Namala v Northern Territory (1996) 131 FLR 468: 198, 299
Napaluma v Baker (1982) 29 SASR 192: 198
National Australia Bank v Maher [1995] 1 VR 318: 48
National Coalition for Gay and Lesbian Equality v Minister for Justice (1999) 1 SALR 6: 26
Neilsen v City of Kamloops [1984] 2 SCR 2: 377
Nelson v Nelson (1995) 70 ALJR 47: 48
Nguyen v Nguyen (1990) 169 CLR 245: 298
Norberg v Wynrib [1992] 2 SCR 226: 370
Nova Scotia (Minister of Community Services) v SMS (1992) 110 NSR (2d) 91: 63
NSW Insurance Ministerial Corporation v Rayner (unreported, NSWCA, 19 March 1993): 145
NSW Insurance Ministerial Corporation v Wynn (1994) Australian Torts Rep ¶81-304 (NSWCA): 139
O'Brien v O'Brien (1983) FLC ¶91-316: 137
O'Callaghan v Loder (1984) EOC ¶92-023; (1984) EOC ¶92-024: 386, 388, 390
Olugboja [1982] QB 320: 239
Osland v R (1998) 197 CLR 316: 440
Osman v United Kingdom (1998) 29 EHRR 245: 377
P (A minor), Re (1982) 80 LGR 301: 219
P v P (1994) 181 CLR 583: 331
Paramasivan v Flynn (1998) 160 ALR 203: 372
Park v Hobart Public Hospitals (unreported, TASSC, 12 December 1991): 145
Partridge v GIO (unreported, NSWSC, 5 May 1993): 144
Paton v Trustees of BPAS [1978] 2 All ER 987: 219, 221-222
Paton v UK (1980) 3 EHRR 408: 229
Patsalou, In Marriage of (1995) 18 Fam LR 426: 109, 271, 275
Pearce v South Australian Health Commission (1996) 66 SASR 486: 249
Pennsylvania v Local Union 542, International Union of Operating Engineers 388 F Supp 155 (1974): 60
Planned Parenthood v Ashcroft 462 US 476 (1983): 219

TABLE OF CASES

Planned Parenthood v Casey 505 US 833 (1992): 219
Planned Parenthood v Danforth 428 US 52 (1976): 219
Popiw v Popiw [1959] VR 197: 17
President of the Republic of South Africa v Hugo (1997) 4 SALR 1: 43
Proudfoot v ACT Board of Health (1992) EOC ¶92-417: 36, 38-39
Public Trustee v Evans (1985) 2 NSWLR 188: 315
Public Trustee v Kukula (1990) 14 Fam LR 97: 197
Q v Minto Management (1985) 49 OR (2d) 531: 317
QFG and GK v JM [1997] QSC 206: 254
Question of Law Reserved on Acquittal Pursuant to Section 351(1A) Criminal Law Consolidation Act (1993) 59 SASR 214: 361
R v A [2001] UKHL 25: 60
R v Bayliss and Cullen (1986) 9 Qld Lawyer Reps 8: 200, 202
R v Biddle [1995] 1 SCR 761: 58
R v Bourne [1939] 1 KB 687: 202
R v Butler [1992] 1 SCR 452: 407-412, 414-417
R v Clarence (1888) 22 QBD 23: 13
R v Close [1948] VLR 445: 408, 411
R v Commonwealth Conciliation and Arbitration Commission; Ex parte Angliss Group (1969) 122 CLR 540: 60
R v Davidson [1969] VR 667: 201-202
R v Equal Opportunity Board; Ex parte Burns (1984) EOC ¶92-122: 386
R v Ewanchuk [1999] 1 SCR 330: 427-428
R v F (1996) 89 A Crim R 250: 244
R v Hakopian (unreported, VCC, 8 August 1991): 346-348
R v Hakopian (unreported, VCCA, 11 December 1991): 347-348
R v Henry and R v Manning (1968) 53 Cr App R 150: 355
R v Hickey (unreported, NSWSC, 14 April 1992): 53-54, 442
R v Hicklin (1868) LR 3 QB 360: 403
R v Judge of District Courts and Shelley; Ex parte Attorney-General [1991] 1 Qd R 170: 58
R v K (unreported, VCC, September 1996): 359-360
R v L (1991) 174 CLR 379: 13, 94
R v Lavallée [1990] 1 SCR 852: 440-441
R v Lewis (1996) 139 DLR (4th) 480: 215
R v McMinn [1982] VR 53: 93
R v Moffa (1976) 13 SASR 284: 68
R v N-T (unreported, VCC, November 1996): 357, 360
R v O (unreported, VCC, February 1997): 358, 360
R v O'Connor [1995] 4 SCR 411: 362
R v Osolin [1993] 4 SCR 595: 374, 376
R v P (unreported, VCC, April 1997): 357, 360
R v Pahuja (1987) 49 SASR 191: 362
R v Parks (1993) 15 OR (3d) 324: 63-64
R v Red Hot Video Limited (1985) 45 CR (3d) 36: 409
R v Runjanjic, R v Kontinnen (1991) 53 A Crim R 362: 438-440
R v Seaboyer; R v Gayme [1991] 2 SCR 577: 428-431
R v Sherrin (No 2) (1979) 21 SASR 250: 356
R v Smith (1991) 109 NSR (2d) 394: 63
R v Sullivan and Lemay [1991] 1 SCR 489: 210, 246
R v Wald (1971) 3 DCR (NSW) 25: 201
R v West (1848) 2 Cox CC 500: 244
R and S v Queensland (2001) Aust Tort Reports ¶81-626: 317
R, In re (unreported, Family Court, 1996): 271
Rabidue v Osceola, 584 F Supp 419 (1984): 390
Rabidue v Osceola, 805 F 2d 611 (1986): 391
Randall v Dul (1994) Aust Torts Reports ¶81-307: 144
Rasmus v GIO (unreported, NSWCA, 22 December 1992): 145
RDS v R [1997] 3 SCR 484: 61-65
Reece v Reece (unreported, NSWCA, 28 February 1994): 145
Refugee Review Tribunal, Re; Ex parte H [2001] HCA 28: 58
Retail, Wholesale and Department Store Union, Local 580 v Dolphin Delivery Ltd [1986] 2 SCR 573: 22
Riggs v Palmer 115 NY 506; 22 NE 188 (1889): 315
Roe v Wade 410 US 113 (1973): 2, 23, 200, 202, 206, 209, 213, 218
Roller v Roller 37 Wash 242; 79 P 788 (1905): 95
Ross v University of Melbourne (1990) EOC ¶92-290: 38
Royal Bank of Scotland plc v Etridge (No 2) [1998] 4 All ER 705 (CA): 124
Royal Bank of Scotland plc v Etridge (No 2) [2001] UKHL 44 (HL): 124
Rural Workers' Union v Mildura Branch of Australian Dried Fruits Association (1912) 6 CAR 62: 148
S v S (unreported, NSWCA, 17 July 1998): 379
S, In re (1989) 13 Fam LR 660: 329
Sanders v Sanders (1976) FLC ¶90-078: 286
Sciuriaga v Powell (1979) 123 Sol J 406: 183
Secretary, Department of Health and Community Services v JWB and SMB ('Marion's Case') (1992) 175 CLR 218: 14, 211, 330-331
Semaynes Case (1604) 77 ER 194: 12

TABLE OF CASES

Sharman v Evans (1977) 138 CLR 563: 131
Singer v Berghouse (No 2) (1994) 181 CLR 201: 88
Skinner v Oklahoma 316 US 535 (1942): 329
Smith v Smith (unreported, ACTSC, 8 July 1991): 145
Spence v Percy [1992] 2 Qd R 299: 182-183
St George's Healthcare NHS Trust v S; R v Collins; Ex parte S [1998] 3 All ER 673: 238, 241, 244
Standard Chartered Bank v Antico (1995) 13 ACLC 1381: 125
Statewide Tobacco Services v Morley (1990) 2 ACSR 405: 125-126
Stekovic v City Group Pty Ltd (unreported, ACTSC, 2 November 1994): 144
Stubbings v Webb [1991] 3 All ER 949 (CA): 372
Stubbings v Webb [1993] AC 498 (HL): 372
Sullivan v Gordon (1999) 47 NSWLR 319: 130
Sun Zhan Qui v Minister for Immigration and Ethnic Affair (1997) 151 ALR 505: 425
Sunday Times v United Kingdom [1979] 2 EHRR 245: 336
Swaney v Ward (1988) FLC ¶91-928: 264
Symes v Canada [1993] 4 SCR 695: 18
T v C (unreported, Family Court, 1997): 271
Tasmanian Dams case *see* Commonwealth v Tasmania
Teachers Health Investments P/L v Wynne (1996) ASC ¶56-356: 121, 125
Teed v Mount Alexander Hospital (1987) EOC ¶92-211: 389
Teenager, In re a (1988) 13 Fam LR 85: 13, 329-330
Thake v Maurice [1984] 2 All ER 513: 183, 185
Thompson v Thompson 218 US 611 (1910): 95
Tickner v Bropho (1993) 40 FCR 183: 83
Tickner, Minister for Aboriginal and Torres Strait Islander Affairs v Chapman (1995) 133 ALR 226: 82
Tremblay v Daigle [1989] 2 SCR 530: 221
Tucker v Westfield Design and Construction Pty Ltd (unreported, FCA, 5 April 1993): 143
Tully v Cole (unreported, QSC, 13 October 1993): 145
Udale v Bloomsbury Area Health Authority [1983] 2 All ER 522: 2, 183-184, 186-187, 189
United States v Morrison 120 S Ct 1740 (2000): 435-438
Uren v John Fairfax and Sons (1966) 117 CLR 118: 341
V v Australian Red Cross (WA) (unreported, HREOC, 18 February 1999): 52

Van Druten v Sheraton Pacific Hotels (1996) EOC ¶92-855: 153
Van Gervan v Fenton (1991) Aust Torts Reports ¶81-103 (TASSC): 133
Van Gervan v Fenton (1992) 175 CLR 327 (HCA): 133-137
Vancouver General Hospital (1990) 76 DLR (4th) 700: 215
Veivers v Connolly [1995] 2 Qd R 326: 187
Veselinovich v Thorley [1988] 1 Qd R 191: 137
Victorian Railways Commissioner v Coultas (1888) 13 App Cas 222: 173
Vriend v Alberta [1998] 1 SCR 493: 428
W v D and Royal Women's Hospital (unreported, HREOC, 24 December 1999): 249
W v W [1999] 2 NZLR 1: 373
W v W; R and G (by their next friend P), intervener (1994) FLC ¶92-475: 317
Wakim, Re; Ex parte McNally (1999) 198 CLR 511: 95
Wallen v Hird (unreported, QSC, 4 October 1993): 144
Ward and Ward (unreported, Fam CA, 7 October, 1987): 263
Wardley v Ansett Transport Industries (1984) EOC ¶92-002: 34-35, 37
Ware v Secretary, Commonwealth Department of Family and Community Services (2000) EOC ¶93-093: 38
Webster v Reproductive Health Services 294 US 490 (1989): 207
Western Australia v Minister for Aboriginal and Torres Strait Islander Affairs (unreported, FCA, Carr J, 7 February 1994): 83
Whiteley, In Marriage of (1993) FLC ¶92-335: 104
Williams v Minister Aboriginal Land Rights Act (1994) 35 NSWLR 497: 372
Williams v Minister Aboriginal Land Rights Act 1983 [2000] NSWCA 255: 446
Williams v Williams (1984) FLC ¶91-541 (Fam CA, FC); (1985) FLC ¶91-628 (HCA): 137
Winnipeg Child and Family Services (Northwest Area) v G(DF) [1997] 3 SCR 925: 229, 231, 235
Woods v Lowns (unreported, NSWSC, 9 February 1995): 179, 182
Woods v Lowns (1995) 36 NSWLR 344 (NSWSC): 179
Woods v Lowns (1996) Aust Torts R 81 (NSWCA): 179
Wynn v NSW Ministerial Corporation (1995) 184 CLR 485: 125, 139, 141-142
Yerkey v Jones (1939) 63 CLR 649: 121-122
Zecevic v DPP (1987) 162 CLR 645: 438

Table of Statutes

Constitution
s 51: 94, 259, 397
s 109: 250

Commonwealth
Aboriginal and Torres Strait Islander Heritage Protection Act 1984: 82
Administrative Decisions (Judicial Review) Act 1977
   s 5: 194
Affirmative Action (Equal Opportunity for Women) Act 1986: 151, 156-158
Classification (Publications, Films and Computer Games) Act 1995: 404
   s 11: 404
Corporations Act 2001
   s 201A: 125
Corporations Law
   s 588G: 125
Customs (Prohibited Imports) Regulations 1956: 404
   reg 4A: 404
Domicile Act 1982: 94
Equal Opportunity for Women Act 1999: 151, 156-158
   s 2A: 158
   s 3: 157
Family Law Act 1975 (FLA): 87, 94, 98-99, 103, 106, 109, 112-113, 259, 263, 266, 275-276, 285-288, 316, 330, 444
   Pt VII: 109
      Div 11: 276
   Pt VIIIA: 113, 124
   s 4: 220
   s 43: 109, 276
   s 60B: 276
   s 60D: 110-111
   s 63E: 259, 274
   s 64B: 259
   s 65E: 260, 330
   s 68F: 263, 271, 276-277, 285
   s 68K: 271, 276
   s 68R: 276
   s 68T: 276
   s 68T: 271
   s 72: 106, 148
   ss 73-74: 106
   s 75: 98, 106, 109
   s 79: 98, 104, 109
   s 81: 105
   s 114: 220, 222
   s 119: 93, 95

Family Law (Amendment) Act 2000: 17, 112
Family Law Legislation Amendment (Superannuation) Act 2001: 108
Family Law Reform Act 1995: 259, 269, 275, 276
Family Law Amendment Bill 1999: 114
Health Insurance Act 1973: 214
Income Tax Assessment Act 1997
   s 8: 19
Income Tax Assessment Act 1936: 123
   s 51: 18, 19
Jurisdiction of Courts (Cross-Vesting) Act 1987: 95
Privacy Act 1988: 24
Sex Discrimination Act 1984 (SDA): 23, 29, 36-41, 151, 153, 250, 253-254, 384, 397-398
   s 5: 37
   s 7D: 38
   s 22: 251
   s 28: 397
   s 28A: 386, 392
   s 31: 37
   s 32: 40, 251-252
   s 33: 37
Social Security Act 1991: 38, 123
   s 4: 14, 15
Superannuation Guarantee (Administration) Act 1992: 147
Workplace Relations Act 1996: 160
   s 170BC: 160

New South Wales
Adoption Act 2000: 292
   s 26: 292
Anti-Discrimination Act 1977: 151, 386
   s 22A: 386, 392
Compensation to Relatives Act 1897: 298
Contracts Review Act 1980: 115, 120
Crimes Act 1900
   Pt 15A: 365
   s 22: 297
   ss 82-83: 201
   s 409B: 443-444
   s 562AC: 365
   s 562AF: 319
   s 562AK: 319, 320
   s 578C: 404
Criminal Procedure Act 1986
   s 105: 443
De Facto Relationships Act 1984 *see* Property (Relationships) Act 1984

Evidence Amendment (Confidential Communications) Act 1997: 362
Factories, Shops and Industries Act 1962: 152
Guardianship Act 1987
　s 45: 330
Law Reform (Marital Consortium) Act 1984: 128
Motor Accidents Act 1988: 145
Property (Relationships) Act 1984: 87, 93, 106, 114, 291, 316
　s 4: 15
　s 5: 106
Property (Relationships) Legislation Amendment Act 1999: 106, 291, 433
Testators Family Maintenance and Guardianship of Infants Act 1916: 258
Victims Support and Rehabilitation Act 1996: 369

Queensland

Anti-Discrimination Act 1991
　s 7: 254
　s 10: 254
　s 11: 254, 256
　s 118: 23
　s 119: 392
Classification of Computer Games and Images Act 1995: 404
Classification of Publications Act 1991: 404
Criminal Code
　s 224: 201
　s 225: 201, 219
　s 226: 201
　s 282: 202
Law Reform Act 1995
　s 13: 128
Property Law Amendment Act 1999: 87

South Australia

Criminal Law Consolidation Act 1935: 204
　ss 81-82: 201, 204, 205
De Facto Relationships Act 1996: 87
Equal Opportunity Act 1984
　s 87: 392
Evidence Act 1929
　s 34I: 361
Evidence (Confidential Communications) Amendment Act 1999: 362
Reproductive Technology Act 1988
　s 13: 249
Reproductive Technology (Code of Ethical Clinical Practice) Regulations 1995: 256
　cl 11: 256
　cl 14E: 256
Wrongs Act 1936
　s 23: 298
　s 33: 128

Tasmania

Common Law (Miscellaneous Actions) Act 1986: 128
Criminal Code 1924
　ss 122-123: 24
　ss 134-135: 201
　s 165A: 297
De Facto Relationships Act 1999: 87
Evidence Act 1910
　s 103AB: 21
Sex Discrimination Act 1994
　s 17: 384

Victoria

Administrative Appeals Tribunal Act: 193
Classification (Publications, Films and Computer Games) Enforcement Act 1995: 404
　s 6: 404
Crimes Act 1958
　s 6: 297
　ss 65-66: 200-201
Equal Opportunity Act 1995
　s 66: 39
　s 85: 387, 392
　ss 86-95: 387
Equal Opportunity Act 1984: 38, 249, 251
　s 39: 38, 39
Equal Opportunity Act 1977: 34
Evidence (Confidential Communications) Act 1998: 362
Judicial Proceedings Reports Act 1958: 21
　s 4: 21
Infertility Medical Procedures Act 1984: 249, 254
Infertility Treatment Act 1995: 249, 251
　s 7: 251
　s 8: 250
Infertility Treatment (Amendment) Act 1997: 249
Limitation of Actions Act 1958: 372
Property Law Act 1958: 87
Statute Law Amendment (Relationships) Act 2001: 291-292
Victims of Crime Assistance Act 1996: 369

Western Australia

Acts Amendment (Abortion) Act 1998: 205, 206
Criminal Code: 205
　s 199: 205
Health Act 1911: 205
　s 334: 206
Human Reproductive Technology Act 1991
　s 23: 249
Legal Practitioners Act 1893: 42

Australian Capital Territory

Crimes Act 1900: 206
Discrimination Act 1991
    s 58: 392
Domestic Relationships Act 1994: 87, 291
Forfeiture Act 1991: 316
    s 3: 316
Health Regulation (Maternal Health Information) Act 1998: 206
    s 4: 206
    ss 7-8: 206
    s 10: 206
    s 14: 206
Law Reform (Miscellaneous Provisions) Act 1955: 128, 130
    Pt 10: 131
Law Reform (Miscellaneous Provisions) (Amendment) Act (No 2) 1991
    ss 32-33: 128

Northern Territory

Anti-Discrimination Act 1992
    s 4: 249
    s 22: 392
Community Welfare Act 1993: 287
Compensation (Fatal Injuries) Act 1974
    s 10: 128, 298
De Facto Relationships Act 1991: 87

New Zealand

Accident Compensation Act 1972: 340
Accident Compensation Act 1982: 132
    s 27: 341
Accident Insurance Act 1998
    s 394: 341
    s 396: 373

Canada

Access to Abortion Services Act 1995 (British Columbia): 216
    Preamble: 215
Canadian Charter of Rights and Freedoms: 23, 379, 408-409, 428
    ss 1-2: 216, 409
    s 7: 203-204, 376
    s 15: 373, 375
Criminal Code: 23, 407, 410
    s 163: 407-409, 411
Divorce Act 1985
    s 16: 262
    s 251: 204

Individual's Rights Protection Act 1980 (Alberta): 428
Juvenile Delinquents Act: 447
Sexual Sterilisation Act RSA 1955 (Alberta): 331-332
Quebec Charter of Rights and Freedoms: 221-222

South Africa

Bill of Rights: 378
Child Care Act: 426
Constitution (interim)
    s 8: 43
Guardianship Act: 426

United Kingdom

Abortion Act 1967: 205, 207, 211
    s 1: 207
Children Act 1989: 266
Congenital Disabilities (Civil Liability) Act 1976: 231, 233
Guardianship of Minors Act 1971: 229
Human Rights Act 1998: 379
Mental Health Act 1983: 239
Rent Act 1977: 97

United States of America

Bill of Rights: 33
Civil Rights Act 1964
    Title VII: 33, 388
Constitution
    Amendment 1: 406
    Amendment 14: 203
Pregnancy Discrimination Act 1978: 33
Violence Against Women Act (VAWA): 435-438

International

Convention on the Elimination of All Forms of Discrimination Against Women 1979 (CEDAW): 41, 252, 397
    Article 15: 397
International Covenant on Civil and Political Rights (ICCPR): 41, 252
    Article 2: 24, 41
    Article 17: 24
    Article 26: 25, 41
    Optional Protocol: 24

Chapter One

Introduction

Introduction

The first edition of this book, published in 1990, opened with the observation that in 1988 the Index to Legal Periodicals had added an index entry for feminist jurisprudence. At the time, this was a landmark: after all, it was only in 1985 that Kathleen Lahey had described feminist legal scholarship as 'an uncatalogued item'.[1] We noted the growth in courses on 'women and the law' or 'law and gender' and the development of monographs and journals devoted to feminist legal scholarship.[2] Since the first edition was published, the growth has been exponential.[3] It seems almost unimaginable to us now that feminist legal theory, or law and gender, was once an unrecognised field of legal endeavour.

It is clear that we have moved a considerable distance from the time when 'women and the law' might have been understood as involving violence against women and family law, but no attention was paid to the gendered nature of damages assessment,[4] or of equitable doctrines such as undue influence.[5] We have also moved some distance from the days when jurisprudence remained impervious to 'feminist' jurisprudence (the one with the adjective): this is manifest most clearly in Margaret Davies' 1994 monograph *Asking the Law Question*.[6]

In this chapter, we outline some of the ideas that inform this book and question whether gender is any less 'hidden' in the law than it was in 1990 when we published our first edition. We articulate the structure we have used in the book and point out where the two editions differ.

Legal categories and constructing women's lives

When we first wrote this book, one of our key aims was to place women's lives at the centre of legal analysis and see to what extent, if any, the law could or would

---

1 Kathleen Lahey, 'Until Women Themselves Have Told All That they Have to Tell ...' (1985) 23 *Osgoode Hall Law Journal* 519 at 519.
2 For some of those published in Australia since the first edition, see, for example, Ngaire Naffine and Rosemary J Owens (eds), *Sexing the Subject of Law*, LBC, Sydney, 1997; Margaret Thornton (ed), *Public and Private: Feminist Legal Debates*, Oxford University Press, Melbourne, 1995. The *Australian Feminist Law Journal* was launched in 1993.
3 In this context, it is salutary to compare the bibliography published by Susan Boyd and Elizabeth Sheehy, 'Feminist Perspectives on Law: Theory and Practice' (1986) 2 *Canadian Journal of Women and the Law* 1 with Josée Bouchard, Susan B Boyd, and Elizabeth A Sheehy, 'Canadian Feminist Literature on Law: An Annotated Bibliography' (1999) 11 (1&2) *Canadian Journal of Women and the Law*. See also Joanne Conaghan, 'Reassessing the Feminist Theoretical Project' (2000) 27 *Journal of Law and Society* 351.
4 Graycar, 'Hoovering as a Hobby and Other Stories: Gendered Assessments of Personal Injury Damages' (1997) 31 *University of British Columbia Law Review* 17.
5 See Belinda Fehlberg, *Sexually Transmitted Debt*, Clarendon Press, Oxford, 1997, and the discussion in Chapter 5.
6 *Asking the Law Question*, LBC, Sydney, 1994.

adapt to respond effectively to women's problems and concerns. This remains our aim in this second edition. That is, we have maintained our aim of challenging the categories that have been used to define legal problems since those categories themselves might have played a role in the relegation of women's concerns to the margins of the legal terrain and, indeed, to the subordination of women: 'The starting point of feminist work must be found in women's lives and not in legal definitions'.[7] Or, as Christine Littleton put it, feminist jurisprudence must take 'women's experience as central and legal categories or doctrines as merely raw material – to be cut and pasted, stretched, arranged, and sewn together to fit that experience'.[8]

Feminist legal scholars are not the only ones to have questioned the categories and definitions used to structure legal problems. Practising lawyers have always known that people's lives do not readily fit into legal categories, yet this has not often been reflected in a legal system that fragments its treatment of people's problems into categories such as tort, crime, family law, etc. This fragmentation into narrowly bounded categories is supported by the structure and practice of law, and by the textbooks and law school courses that replicate and reinforce those divisions. While the narrowness of doctrinal categories can serve to exclude a wide range of problems from legal analysis, simply because they do not fall into a recognised cause of action, women have been particularly vulnerable to this form of exclusion, given that legal doctrines were largely developed without any reference to women's lives. And the problem, of course, is more complex than one of absence. Where women *are* (re)present(ed), legal texts are replete with images of 'the bad mother',[9] the 'hapless company director',[10] 'the slut'[11] or the 'good mother': 'nice looking but rather overweight'.[12] That is, through both presence and absence, law constructs women (and men) rather than merely operating upon pre-existing naturally occurring categories of people.

In order to illustrate the inadequacy of legal categories, consider the issue of abortion.[13] It is obviously a legal issue, if only because abortion is a frequent matter of litigation and is the subject of regular debates about the appropriate form of legal regulation. But to which category of law does it belong? In Australia, abortion is a criminal law issue since all States and Territories criminalise abortions in certain circumstances. In other jurisdictions, where there are written Bills of Rights, such as the United States and Canada, legal debates about abortion are also played out as questions of constitutional law.[14] Or, as we saw in a case from the Republic of Ireland, the ability of a woman to travel freely to another country in order to secure an abortion may raise an issue of public international law or human rights law (freedom of movement).[15] Abortion is a 'family law'

---

7 'Introduction' (1986) 14 *International Journal of the Sociology of Law* 233.
8 Christine A Littleton, 'Book Review; Feminist Jurisprudence: The Difference Method Makes' (1989) 41 *Stanford Law Review* 751 at 766, note 3.
9 See, for example, the discussion of Australia's most famous 'bad mother', Lindy Chamberlain, in Chapter 9.
10 See the discussion of sexually transmitted debt in Chapter 5.
11 For discussions of the sexualisation of women, see especially the discussion of rape in Chapter 11, and sexual harassment and pornography in Chapter 12.
12 *Udale v Bloomsbury Area Health Authority* [1983] 2 All ER 522 at 526, discussed in Chapter 7.
13 This is discussed in detail in Chapter 8.
14 For the US, see *Roe v Wade* 410 US 113 (1973); for Canada, see *Morgentaler v The Queen* [1988] 1 SCR 30.
15 *Attorney General v X* (1992) 15 BMLR 104, Supreme Court of Ireland. For a comment, see Ailbhe Smyth, 'The "X" Case: Women and Abortion in the Republic of Ireland, 1992' (1993) 1 *Feminist Legal Studies* 163.

issue, as demonstrated by attempts by men to prevent women from having an abortion.[16] These actions raise related questions most usually classified as 'remedies' issues. And, abortion can be a tort law issue, as *CES v Superclinics* indicates.[17] Criminal law texts may tell us about prosecutions of doctors or women, but will not assist in understanding the law's response to men's role in abortion decision-making. Remedies texts may tell us about injunctions and how these may be used by men wishing to control women's decision-making, but are unlikely to cover the criminal law issues nor concern themselves with the jurisdiction of the Family Court of Australia nor with the role of the medical profession in abortion decision-making. None of these texts will tell us about the public funding of abortion, a crucial issue for women.[18] In other words, it is not possible to consult a traditional legal text, look up the topic 'abortion', and find gathered together all the relevant legal rules and regulatory practices.

What we have tried to do is to make connections between different areas of legal doctrine by making issues in women's lives the central organising principle. At the same time, we have linked these issues through three persistent theoretical themes which we explore at length in the next three chapters: the meaning of equality, the playing out of the public/private dichotomy and, underlying all, questions of epistemology or methodology. We also use and analyse primary legal materials (that is, cases and statutes) extensively. To that extent, we see this as a 'law book' just as much as it is a 'book about law'[19] and an exercise in applied legal theory. How we engage in that exercise is described in the next section.

Towards a new doctrinal framework: The structure of this book

This edition of the book, like the first, is divided into parts, each of which deals with a particular issue in women's lives or raises questions about how feminists have engaged with law, rather than dealing with a discrete area of legal doctrine. We have deliberately eschewed using any of the conventional legal subject headings. So, for example, there is no chapter on criminal law, nor on tort, nor on family law, though we cover each of these in the book. Rather, as we noted above, we have focused on issues in women's lives, informed by a series of theoretical themes to assist in organising the material we have covered.

The first main part of the book, **Recurrent theoretical themes**, contained in Chapters 2, 3 and 4, explores in depth the three major theoretical themes we have drawn on throughout the book. We examine and critique a series of dichotomies that have structured liberal legalism. Chapter 2 explores the public/private dichotomy, where women are identified with the private and men with the public sphere; and the creation by legal discourses of a public and a private sphere. We review some of the critiques of a simplistic use by some feminist scholars of the public/private dichotomy, and examine ways in which the dichotomy might remain useful as a tool for critically analysing aspects of the legal system. Chapter 3 examines the meanings of equality. Gender equality in legal decision-making

---

16   See, for example, *In Marriage of F* (1989) 13 Fam LR 189.
17   See *CES v Superclinics (Aust) Pty Ltd* (1995) 38 NSWLR 47. Aspects of this case are discussed in Chapters 7 and 8. See also Graycar and Morgan '"Unnatural rejection of womanhood and motherhood": Pregnancy, damages and the law – A note on *CES v Superclinics (Aust) Pty Ltd*' (1996) 18 *Sydney Law Review* 323; and Jane Swanton, 'Damages for "wrongful birth" – *CES v Superclinics (Aust) Pty Ltd*' (1996) 4 *Torts Law Journal* 1.
18   See *Harris v McRae* 448 US 297 (1980).
19   Cf Katherine O'Donovan, *Sexual Divisions in Law,* Weidenfeld and Nicolson, London, 1985 at x; and Richard Abel, 'Law Books and Books About Law' (1973) 26 *Stanford Law Review* 175.

has often been seen as a dichotomous choice between treating men and women in exactly the same way or treating them differently. We explore the purchase of these understandings of equality and consider whether it is possible, or desirable, to promote other understandings. The last chapter in this part, Chapter 4, is concerned with methodological or epistemological questions. We investigate some of the ways in which legal method makes a claim to both objectivity and to truth. We also consider aspects of feminist methodologies that have been used in law. In particular, we examine both consciousness raising and legal storytelling, raising questions about the extent to which these methodologies might also make claims to truth. The themes in this part of the book are central to our investigations in the remainder of the book and are woven throughout our more explicit attempts to apply these theoretical concepts to concrete issues in women's lives, and to reconstruct legal categories.

The second part of the book, **Women and Economic (In)dependence**, is directed towards scrutiny of women's access to economic resources. This part of the book has two chapters. In the first of these, Chapter 5, *Work in Families*, we look at aspects of women's work that arise out of their involvement in family relationships, especially through marriage and marriage-like relationships. After setting the scene with a detailed empirical introduction, we use three case studies: marriage and family (where we explore some of the financial aspects of 'family law', at the same time as we question the narrow way in which that term is used); relationship debt or 'sexually transmitted debt'; and, in the third, we consider some of the ways in which women's unpaid work is treated when it arises for evaluation in the context of personal injury damages assessment. In the second chapter of this part, Chapter 6, *Out to Work,* we focus more closely on some issues that particularly affect women's participation in paid work, exploring the perennial question of why women earn less than men. While we have separated out these two aspects of women's work in discrete chapters for ease of exegesis, in Chapter 6 we also attempt to 'close the circle' and point out some of the connections between women's work in the home and in the paid workforce.

The third part of the book, **Women and Connection,** is an opportunity to survey the ways in which women have been, and continue to be, dealt with in legal discourses in terms of their relationships with others rather than as independent actors. Most of the areas surveyed in this part concern women's construction as mothers or would-be mothers. The part commences, in Chapter 7, with constructions of 'good mothers' in both nervous shock and wrongful birth cases; it goes on to consider some attempts to theorise 'connection' and concludes by briefly contrasting the construction of men's relationships to others in legal doctrine. Chapter 8, *Controlling Reproductive Bodies,* focuses attention on three important aspects of potential motherhood – abortion, foetal rights and access to assisted reproduction services. For lesbians, it is often the desire to have access to safe sperm that brings them into contact with sometimes draconian state regulation that limits their access. For heterosexual women, the concern may be to terminate an unwanted pregnancy safely. Pregnant women may also come into conflict with other forms of restrictive state regulation. The material on foetal rights examines state attempts, particularly in North America, to mediate women's relationship with the foetus they are carrying by enforcing some form of medical treatment or intervention for the foetus over the wishes of the woman concerned. This examination encourages us to explore the legal construction of the relationship between a woman and the foetus she is carrying. Chapter 9 returns us to the situation of women who have had children and considers how relationships with them can be curtailed or severed, both through the actions of individual men and via the direct actions of the state, especially for indigenous women whose children were taken away as part of the 'stolen generations'.

The next part of the book, Part Four, **Gendered Harms**, considers an array of injuries that happen overwhelmingly to women and therefore may usefully be characterised as gendered harms. That is, we are trying to conceptualise injuries to women as revealing some pattern, as having some regularity. In Chapter 10 we commence with a detailed analysis of available empirical data on the incidence of violence against women and attitudes towards that violence. We are concerned to ensure not only that injuries traditionally recognised by the criminal law are adequately conceptualised (hence, in Chapter 11, we consider in some depth the law's treatment of rape or sexual assault), but also that other forms of violence beyond the criminal law are recognised. Thus, we also consider in Chapter 11 the issue of medical abuses of women, including eugenic sterilisation and the cervical cancer 'experiment' in New Zealand. Chapter 12 explores the harms of sexual harassment and pornography. In relation to the former, we investigate the array of legal responses that might be available to respond to sexual harassment and the attempts to conceptualise the harm caused. The section on pornography raises questions about whether law is the most appropriate way to respond to the issue of pornography. In some ways this is the hardest section of the book to conceptualise; after all, could not everything we have canvassed in the rest of the book be conceived as about injuries to women? At one level our response to this question is pragmatic: many issues that some feminist writers would or could conceptualise as social or gendered harms are dealt with elsewhere in the book and therefore we do not need to deal with them in this part. At another level, our response is conceptual: if all things that happen to women are conceptualised as injuries, there is a real danger of an endless depiction, and creation, of women as always already victims. This is not to suggest that women are not injured or are not subordinated to men, but rather that there are some real risks in the relentless depiction of women as victims, risks and responses which we discuss at the end of the introductory chapter to this part, Chapter 10.

The final part of this book, **An Agenda for Gender?**, is a brief conclusion that explicitly addresses questions of feminist strategies in law. We look at the perennial question of whether more women in law will make a difference and address some of the possibilities of using litigation to effect social change. We also consider the legislative arena and institutional law reform as well as canvassing some laws and processes that have been designed to respond specifically to gendered harms. One central theme in this chapter is the very broad question of whether there is any point engaging with law.

How is this edition different?

In the first edition, our second chapter called 'Feminism Comes to Law School' surveyed the impact of feminist scholarship on law books and on law curriculum and teaching, trying to convey a flavour of the extent of feminist work in doctrinal areas not elsewhere covered in the book. That work is now enormous. In our view, any attempt to cover it in detail would be not only impossible, but also unnecessary as it is now widely accessible. In the second main part of the book, women and economic (in)dependence, we have omitted the chapter previously included called 'Dependence on the State'. This is because, when using the first edition, we found this chapter quickly went out of date. However, where relevant, we have included some of the issues raised in it in the two chapters that now comprise that part. These are probably the major omissions.

There are also other omissions, as well as changes in emphasis, at the level of detail. One such example is the use of Carol Gilligan's work.[20] In 1990, law journals were replete with then recent publications using the phrase 'in a different voice' in their titles,[21] endeavouring to reconstruct rights so that they recognised 'connection'.[22] While not wishing to detract from the enormous influence that Gilligan's work had in law, it is no longer seen as so central as it seemed to be in 1990 and we touch on it only briefly in this edition. We also no longer discuss surrogacy and the feminist attempts to outlaw it: the issue does not raise the controversy it did in the 1980s. We have omitted the case study on legal responses to domestic violence, expanding instead the empirical information on violence, including the evaluation of 'special' remedies to respond to violence against women in the home. The potential of law, **or** the different ways law might respond to gendered violence, is explored throughout this part of the book, including in our examination of rape, sexual harassment and pornography.

The book does not purport to deal with all areas of doctrine that affect women. Nor could it. One particularly obvious omission is that of international law. While we very occasionally mention international treaties, we have largely omitted this field of legal work.[23] This is not because it is unimportant, but rather because it is well canvassed elsewhere: see, in particular, Hilary Charlesworth and Chris Chinkin, *The Boundaries of International Law*.[24] Moreover, in the areas of doctrine that the book does examine, it does not purport to be doctrinally comprehensive: it is not the aim of this book to teach 'black letter law'. Thus, we do not usually provide a jurisdiction-by-jurisdiction survey of the legal doctrines we address. When we published our first edition in 1990, we tried to be comprehensive about feminist scholarship, for example, we included lengthy bibliographies on particular topics. One of the consequences of the explosion of feminist legal scholarship is that we no longer feel the need to use this book as a reference tool in the same way.

In relation to what is new, we have considerably expanded the introductory theoretical section, which has grown from one chapter into three. While the areas covered are similar, they are dealt with in much more depth and detail. We have also radically changed the section on women's economic (in)dependence, with an extensive discussion of the effect of heterosexual women's relationships on their unpaid work through a variety of legal doctrines. We also have a more sustained

---

20 Notably, *In a Different Voice: Psychological Theory and Women's Development*, Harvard University Press, Cambridge MA, 1982. Gilligan, a psychologist, re-examined the work on the moral development of children, arguing that girls and boys reasoned about moral issues in different ways. Boys (and men) were said to reason through a hierarchy or ladder of rights, while girls (and women) through a web of connection.

21 See, for some discussions of Gilligan's work, Carrie Menkel-Meadow, 'Portia in a Different Voice: Speculations on a Woman's Lawyering Process' (1985) 1 *Berkeley Women's Law Journal* 39; Kenneth Karst, 'Woman's Constitution' [1984] *Duke Law Journal* 447; Suzanna Sherry, 'Civic Virtue and the Feminine Voice in Constitutional Adjudication' (1986) 72 *Virginia Law Review* 543; Paul J Spiegelman, 'Integrating Theory and Practice in the Law School Curriculum: The Logic of Jake's Ladder in the Context of Amy's Web' (1988) 38 *Journal of Legal Education* 243.

22 See Morgan, 'Feminist Theory as Legal Theory' (1988) 16 *Melbourne University Law Review* 743.

23 Note, however, for an illustration of the impact of feminist jurisprudence, the Human Rights Committee has recently published a general comment on equality: see UN Human Rights Committee, 'Equality of Rights Between Men and Women', General Comment No 28, 68th Session, March 2000.

24 Hilary Charlesworth and Christine Chinkin, *The Boundaries of International Law: A Feminist Analysis*, Manchester University Press, Manchester, 2000.

focus on why women earn less than men when they engage in paid work and, as noted above, we discuss access to assisted reproduction services for lesbians and single heterosexual women. More broadly, we have endeavoured to make the book more responsive to the critiques of both feminist writers in the post-modern tradition, who have questioned the 'foundational tones' in which much feminist legal work is often couched, and those of indigenous women, women of colour, culturally and linguistically diverse women, and lesbians, who have argued that much early feminist legal work spoke only of white, English-speaking heterosexual women and their needs.

While we have largely followed the structure in the first edition, the vast majority of the content of this book is new. The period of some 12 years since the previous edition was written has thrown up not only new cases and legislation, but new ways of thinking about legal issues. Hence, even when material that was canvassed in the first edition is included here, we have usually asked different and more complex questions of it.

A book about possibilities

This is a book about possibilities, about exploring new ways to construct legal doctrines and categories. While the section explicitly on 'theory' (Part One) has expanded considerably, it will become clear that it is still not our intention to present a single 'grand theory' of feminist legal scholarship. Since a critical aspect of this project is exposing law's partiality, it would be particularly ironic were feminist legal theory to propose a new partiality to replace the old one.

Does the expansion in feminist legal scholarship mean, as some colleagues have suggested to us, that we need to rename our book – that the gender of law is no longer hidden? Our own view is that, while feminist legal scholarship has grown exponentially, many of the questions we raised in our first edition about the legal system's responses to women and about its gendering processes remain as pertinent today as they were in 1990. While so much may have changed, so much also remains the same.

PART ONE

RECURRING THEORETICAL THEMES

In this part, we discuss some of the key theoretical issues that have engaged legal theorists working on feminist approaches to law. The themes outlined in this part inform our treatment of many of the substantive issues raised in the remainder of the book. We have gathered them in this section for sustained analysis, not to suggest that theory is separate from the issues we deal with in later chapters, but to provide a concentrated focus for some of the main ideas and arguments that have informed so much of feminist work in law.

We deal in this part with several separate, but connected, ideas or themes. Those we discuss in detail are the 'public/private distinction'; understandings of 'equality'; and issues of epistemology and methodologies. A common thread that runs through the central themes we have identified is the way in which Western thought is characterised by dichotomies, and by dichotomised systems of meaning. As Margaret Davies has summarised it: 'Words do not have essential meanings: meaning is constructed through systems of oppositions'.[1] Joan Scott has suggested, summarising Derrida's approach to discerning meaning:

> The Western philosophical tradition ... rests on binary oppositions: unity/diversity, identity/difference, presence/absence, and universality/ specificity. The leading terms are accorded primacy; their partners are represented as weaker or derivative. Yet the first terms depend on and derive their meaning from the second to such an extent that the secondary terms can be seen as generative of the definition of the first terms.[2]

A number of scholars have drawn out the particular resonances a focus on binary oppositions has for feminist analyses. Scott points out that:

> [S]exual difference (the contrast masculine/feminine) serves to encode or establish meanings that are literally unrelated to gender or the body. In that way, the meanings of gender become tied to many kinds of cultural representations, and these in turn establish terms by which relations between women and men are understood.[3]

Frances Olsen lists a series of dichotomies that recur in liberal discourses: 'rational/irrational; active/passive; thought/feeling; reason/emotion; culture/ nature; power/sensitivity; objective/subjective; abstract/contextualized; principled/ personalized'.[4] She points out that these dichotomies are both hierarchised and sexualised: the side of the dichotomy accorded lesser value is identified with the

---

1   Margaret Davies, *Asking The Law Question*, Law Book Co, Sydney, 1994, at 215.
2   Joan Scott, 'Deconstructing Equality-Versus-Difference: Or the Uses of Poststructuralist Theory for Feminism' (1988) 14 *Feminist Studies* 33 at 37. Scott applies this approach to an analysis of the terms 'equality' and 'difference' and we come back to that issue in Chapter 3.
3   *Ibid.*
4   Frances Olsen, 'Feminism and Critical Legal Theory: An American Perspective' (1990) 18 *International Journal of the Sociology of Law* 199 at 199.

female. Hence, the 'private' is associated with women, and the 'public' with men: 'the association of men and women with public and private respectively is one of the few assertions that can be categorically made about the nature of the dualism'.[5] Gender equality in legal decision-making has often been seen as a dichotomous choice between treating men and women in the same way, or treating them differently. Legal discourses are replete with deference to the values of reason, objectivity and neutrality, which contrast with the lesser and 'feminine' values of emotion or passion, subjectivity and perspective or partiality.[6] In the final chapter of this part, dealing with epistemologies and methodologies, we show how refusing to see reason as in part defined by and containing passion, objectivity as encompassing subjectivity, and neutrality as depending on perspective, and the overvaluation of the primary term in these binary oppositions, has silenced those identified with the so called lesser values. But before we deal with epistemologies and methodologies, we explore in Chapter 2 the particular dichotomy between the 'public' and 'private' and whether analysing legal doctrines through this prism remains a useful feminist strategy. Chapter 3, in turn, focuses on the ways in which (gender) equality might be understood.

---

5   Margaret Thornton, 'The Public/Private Dichotomy: Gendered and Discriminatory' (1991) 18 *Journal of Law and Society* 448 at 449.

6   Olsen states: 'Law is identified with the hierarchically superior, "masculine" sides of the dualisms. "Justice" may be depicted as a woman, but, according to the dominant ideology, law is male, not female. Law is supposed to be rational, objective, abstract and principled ... like men; it is not supposed to be irrational, subjective or personalized like women' ('Feminism and Critical Legal Theory', at 201). The rational, objective claim of law is returned to below in Chapter 4 on epistemology and methodology.

Chapter Two

The Public/Private Dichotomy

Introduction

Feminist legal scholars have taken seriously the feminist slogan, 'the personal is the political' and explored how the dichotomy between the public and the private has been constructed and supported by the legal system, to the detriment of women. In the following extract, Katherine O'Donovan explores how the legal system has constructed the family as 'private' – as a zone of 'non-intervention', yet demonstrates the extent to which the law actually, if indirectly, intervenes in the family and, indeed, constructs the family.

Katherine O'Donovan, *Sexual Divisions in Law*
Weidenfeld & Nicolson, London, 1985
"Divisions and Dichotomies"

[2] "The realm of life and work in *Gemeinschaft* is particularly befitting to women; indeed, it is even necessary to them. For women, the home and not the market, their own or a friend's dwelling and not the street, is the natural seat of their activity."

FERDINAND TÖNNIES

Dichotomies
... In liberal philosophy privacy is central to individualism as an area of life not subjected to the power of society. ... Steven Lukes, in his review of privacy as a core idea of individualism, concludes that

> the idea of privacy refers to a sphere that is not of proper concern to others. It implies a negative relation between the individual and some wider "public", including the state – a relation of non-interference with, or non-intrusion into, some range of his thoughts and/or action. ... [Lukes, *Individualism,* Basil Blackwell, Oxford, 1973, p 66]

[3] An outcome of this is that law as regulator or non-regulator is a crucial expression of the limits of state intervention. ...

This book [*Sexual Divisions in Law*] uses the concepts of private and public to distinguish between areas of activity and behaviour unregulated or regulated by law, as in the classical liberal fashion. In legal discourse privacy is more often used as a concept concerned with the protection of individuals from an overly intrusive corporate state prying into personal secrets. ... Further difficulties of definition arise because in recent writings the concepts private and public stand for a variety of referents. "Public" may be used to denote state activity, the values of the market-place, work, the male domain or that sphere of activity which is regulated by law. "Private" may denote civil society, the values of family, intimacy, the personal life, home, women's domain or behaviour unregulated by law. The confusion is increased in legal discourse which calls legal relations between state and citizens public and those between individuals private.

If the private is identified as the unregulated zone of life this poses problems which are neither discussed nor recognised in liberal political philosophy. Those areas such as the personal, sexuality, biological reproduction, family, home, which are particularly identified socially as women's domain, are also seen as private. It can be argued that social differentiation between women and men in the gender order has its counterpart in the general social distinction between private and public. A simple summary is: "the public sphere is that sphere in which 'history' is made. But the public sphere is the sphere of male activity. Domestic activity becomes relegated to the [4] private sphere and is mediated to the public sphere by men who move between both. Women have a place only in the private sphere." [D Smith, 'Women, the Family and Corporate Capitalism' in M Stephenson, *Women in Canada,* New Press, Toronto, 1974, p 6.] This argument raises issues about power in personal relations and in the organisation of the private; ....

The importance of the distinction between private and public lies in its influence on our perception of the social world and the maintenance of the distinction in law. ...

[7] A deliberate policy of non-intervention by the state may mask a passing of control to informal mechanisms. For instance the legal doctrine of the unity of spouses serves as a justification for state policy of non-intervention in marriage. ... Who then controls the family? It can be argued that non-intervention by law may result in the state leaving the power with the [8] husband and father whose authority it legitimates indirectly through public law support for him as a breadwinner and household head. A deliberate policy of non-intervention does not necessarily mean that an area of behaviour is uncontrolled.

The Distinction Between Private and Public in Legal Discourse
The idea that private and public can be distinguished is imbued in legal philosophy and informs legal policy. ... This division is not confined to distinguishing relations between individual and state from relations between individuals. It also draws a line dividing the law's business from what is called private. Although this boundary between the private and public shifts over time, the existence of the distinction and the notion of boundary are rarely questioned. ...

[9] The Wolfenden Committee Report on Homosexual Offences and Prostitution provides an excellent example of the implementation in law of the liberal view of the distinction between public and private. The committee accepted as unproblematic the idea of "private lives of citizens". It stated that the function of criminal law in relation to homosexuality and prostitution was "to preserve public order and decency, to protect the citizen from what is offensive and injurious, and to provide sufficient safeguards against exploitation and corruption of others". [1957, para 13] ...

The elaboration in legal discourse of a private domain of subjectivity, morality and the personal as "not the law's business" has inevitably led to non-intervention in domestic life. ... One implication is that those confined to the domestic sphere need not look to law to rectify any power imbalance resulting from the division of labour.

The Unregulated Family
... [*O'Donovan discusses here the 'retreat of the family' into a 'zone of private life', from the eighteenth century onwards and continues:*] [11] Men who pass [12] freely between public and private, but who are primarily located in the public, are socially expected to act as rational, calculating, economic individuals, whose actions are guided by self-interest. Women, who are seen primarily in the context of reproduction, home and family are expected to retain the values of

Gemeinschaft. The private, regarded in legal ideology as unsuitable for legal regulation, is ordered according to an ideology of love.

... [I]deas of privacy established in legal decisions preclude intervention in the family. The common law assumption that "the house of everyone is his castle" [*Semaynes Case* (1604) 77 ER 194] is an early and useful bulwark in the defence of civil liberties. But it may also conceal a power struggle within the family. ... [I]t also masks physical abuse and other manifestations of power and inequality within the family.

In discussions of the privacy of marital relations or of the boundaries of state intervention, the home, the family and the married couple remain an entity that is taken for granted. The couple is a unit, a black box, into which the law does not purport to peer. What goes on inside the box is not perceived as the law's concern. The belief is that it is for family members to sort out their personal relationships. What this overlooks is the power inequalities inside the family which are of course affected by structures external to it. This ideology of privacy and non-intervention has been articulated by legislators, by the judiciary and by legal scholars. ...

[14] **State Intervention**
It is a standard liberal view that intervention by the state in family life is to be avoided if at all possible. ... Family law continues to be imbued with a belief in non-intervention. But discussions of non-interference whether expressed in legal ideology or in state policy usually refer only to direct intervention. What is overlooked is that structures external to the family have a significant effect on it, and that state policy in areas such as employment, taxation and social security affects what goes on in the family. Furthermore, informal mechanisms of intervention through education, medicine, psychiatry and welfare policies have existed since the Tudor Poor Laws. ...

[A]lthough the state is reluctant to intervene directly, policies in areas which impinge on the family and which are expressed in legislative, judicial and administrative provisions construct a particular family form. The nuclear family in which there is a division of labour between wife and husband is an expression of these policies. ...

[15] ... An ... omission in the analysis of direct state intervention as unmitigatedly bad is that it ignores the influence of state policy in areas which impinge on the private. Policies on employment, welfare, housing, education, medicine, transport, production, planning, crime, in fact on almost everything, influence family life. How could it be otherwise? The whole fabric of the personal life is imprinted with colours from elsewhere. Not to acknowledge this, and to pretend that the private is free, leads to a false analysis.

Notes

1. Police and state inaction against male violence in the home were often justified on the basis of 'preserving family unity and stability'.[1] That is, such behaviour was 'private' and thus not a matter for state intervention. This sort of rhetoric, and its practical effects, have been targets of feminist activism over the past few decades. As O'Donovan suggests, to deem what happens in

---

1 Jennifer Koshan, 'Sounds of Silence: The Public/Private Dichotomy, Violence, and Aboriginal Women' in Susan B Boyd (ed), *Challenging the Public/Private Divide: Feminism, Law, and Public Policy*, University of Toronto Press, Toronto, 1997, at 90. For an Australian description of these attitudes, see Women's Policy Co-ordination Unit, Department of Prime Minister and Cabinet, *Criminal Assault in the Home: Social and Legal Responses to Domestic Violence Discussion Paper*, Victoria, July 1985.

the traditional heterosexual nuclear family unit as 'private' tends to mask gendered structures of power. Indeed, violence by men against women in the heterosexual family and the desire to provide a way to challenge traditional thinking about such violence remain central to analyses of the public/private dichotomy in feminist work within and outside law.

The resort to privacy in legal doctrine crosses a wide array of subject areas. For example, the criminal law, perhaps the most quintessentially 'public' area of law, nonetheless resorted to privacy in the construction of, or at least the justification for, the marital rape exemption (now abolished in all Australian States).[2] In essence, this provided married men with a legal immunity from liability for raping their wives. Brett and Waller, in a leading criminal law textbook published in 1977, used the doctrine of privacy to argue for an *extension* of the marital rape immunity to de facto spouses.[3]

Brett and Waller argued:

> From the standpoint of sexual relations, a couple living in concubinage are in the same situation as a married couple. Sexual transactions are a part of their ordinary living, and it is no more appropriate to subject each transaction to legal scrutiny as regards consent than it is to subject the sexual transactions of married couples to such scrutiny. Consent to intercourse may properly be made a matter of enquiry when the persons involved are not living in an intimate relationship. In *Clarence* (1888), Wills J lucidly expounded the reasons why the criminal law declines to enquire into the ordinary sexual transactions which are part of one intimate relationship, ie marriage.
>
> In our view, what our time demands is recognition of the fact that what is important in an intimate relationship is its privacy from the outside world, not whether it is based on a formal and valid marriage ceremony.[4]

2. In the 1980s there was considerable debate and litigation about who should have responsibility for decisions on sterilisation of minors with intellectual disabilities (and, indeed, whether they should occur at all). In *In re a Teenager*,[5] Cook J considered whether the parents of a 14-year-old girl with a severe intellectual disability could authorise her sterilisation. He used the doctrine of family privacy to justify the non-intervention of the Family Court into the parents' decision:

> [T]he matter of unwarranted or undue interference with or invasion of, the family's operations as a unit, by outsiders including, not the least, the Court. ...
>
> ... One could only predicate [*sic*], as already mentioned, a marked resentment and a marked weakening of confidence in the discharging of the

---

2   See *R v L* (1991) 174 CLR 379.
3   Peter Brett and Louis Waller, *Criminal Law: Text and Cases,* 4th ed, Butterworths, Sydney, 1977. However, this was not repeated in later editions.
4   Brett and Waller, at 93-94. Wills J was overturning a man's conviction for assault and inflicting grievous bodily harm. He had had intercourse with his wife while he knew, but she did not, that he had gonorrhea. Wills J stated: 'a wide door will be opened to inquiries not of a wholesome kind, in which the difficulties in the way of arriving at truth are often enormous, and in which the danger of going wrong is as great as it is by people in general inadequately appreciated. A new field of extortion may be developed, and very possibly a fresh illustration afforded of the futility of trying to teach morals by the application of the criminal law to cases occupying the doubtful ground between immorality and crime, and of the dangers which always beset such attempts': *R v Clarence* (1888) 22 QBD 23 at 32-3.
5   (1989) FLC ¶92-006; (1988) 13 Fam LR 85.

THE HIDDEN GENDER OF LAW

role of parents if they ... would be compelled to implement or resist Court proceedings in respect of decisions which are so intimate, so private and so dependent upon a very close knowledge and understanding of a child.[6]

3. One other central theme in O'Donovan's analysis is her argument that the traditional liberal suggestion that the family is private and unregulated leads to a failure to recognise the many ways in which the law in fact indirectly regulates the so-called private sphere. One example of this is the so-called 'cohabitation rule' in Australian social security law. Australian social security law determines rates of benefit, or in some cases eligibility, for a particular payment by reference to whether a person is living in a 'marriage-like' relationship. If they are found to be in such a relationship, their income and assets for the purposes of setting a rate of pension will be assessed by including the income and assets of their partner; they will be eligible for (half of) the 'married rate' of pension or benefit (that rate being lower than the single rate), and they will be completely ineligible for income support as a sole parent. In order to assess whether a man and a woman[7] are living in a 'marriage-like' relationship, a decision-maker is enjoined to examine:

(a) the financial aspects of the relationship, including:
  (i) any joint ownership of real estate or other major assets and any joint liabilities; and
  (ii) any significant pooling of financial resources especially in relation to major financial commitments; and
  (iii) any legal obligations owed by one person in respect of the other person; and
  (iv) the basis of any sharing of day-to-day household expenses;
(b) the nature of the household, including:
  (i) any joint responsibility for providing care or support of children; and
  (ii) the living arrangements of the people; and
  (iii) the basis on which responsibility for housework is distributed;
(c) the social aspects of the relationship, including:
  (i) whether the people hold themselves out as married to each other; and
  (ii) the assessment of friends and regular associates of the people about the nature of their relationship; and
  (iii) the basis on which the people make plans for, or engage in, joint social activities;
(d) any sexual relationship between the people;
(e) the nature of the people's commitment to each other, including:
  (i) the length of the relationship; and
  (ii) the nature of any companionship and emotional support that the people provide to each other; and
  (iii) whether the people consider that the relationship is likely to continue indefinitely; and

---

6   (1989) ¶FLC 92-006 at 77,223-4. It should be noted that this view has not prevailed: See *In re Jane* (1989) ¶FLC 92-007; *Secretary, Department of Health and Community Services v JWB and SMB (Marion's Case)* (1992) 175 CLR 218. In *Marion's Case*, the High Court held that only a court could authorise sterilisation of a young woman. This issue is discussed further in Chapter 11.

7   Note that the definition only applies to a man and a woman. Thus the *Social Security Act* 1991 (Cth) is profoundly heterosexist: Section 4(2)(b)(i) provides that one of the criteria of being in a 'marriage-like' relationship is that the parties are of opposite sex.

(iv) whether the people see their relationship as a marriage-like relationship.[8]

Is it possible to sustain an argument that the family is 'private' in the face of legislation of this nature?[9]

In another section omitted from the principal reading, O'Donovan discusses the well-known case of *Balfour v Balfour* which is extracted below.

The construction of 'the private': An example from the law of contract

In *Balfour v Balfour,* a woman sued her husband in an attempt to enforce a verbal agreement that he pay her 30*l* a month. The agreement had been made before his departure for Ceylon, and subsequently Ms Balfour sought a divorce.

Balfour v Balfour
[1919] 2 KB 571

[578] ATKIN LJ. The defence to this action on the alleged contract is that the defendant, the husband, entered into no contract with his wife, and for the determination of that it is necessary to remember that there are agreements between parties which do not result in contracts within the meaning of that term in our law. The ordinary example is where two parties agree to take a walk together, or where there is an offer and an acceptance of hospitality. Nobody would suggest in ordinary circumstances that those agreements result in what we know as a contract, and one of the most usual forms of agreement which does not constitute a contract appears to me to be the arrangements which are made between husband and wife. It is quite common, and it is the natural and inevitable result of the relationship of husband and wife, that the two spouses should make arrangements between themselves – agreements such as are in dispute in this action – agreements for allowances, by which the husband agrees that he will pay to his wife a certain sum of money, per week, or per month, or per year, to cover either her own expenses or the necessary expenses of the household and of the children of the marriage, and in which the wife promises either expressly or impliedly to apply the allowance for the purpose for which it is given. To my mind those agreements, or many of them, do not result in contracts at all, and they do not result in contracts even though there may be what as between other parties would constitute consideration for the agreement. The consideration, as we know, may consist either in some right, interest, profit or benefit accruing to one party, or some forbearance, detriment, loss or responsibility given, suffered or undertaken by the other. That is a well-known definition, and it constantly happens, I think, that such arrangements made between husband and wife are arrangements in which there are mutual promises, or in which there [579] is consideration in form within the definition that I have mentioned. Nevertheless they are not contracts, and they are not contracts because the parties did not intend that they should be attended by legal consequences. To my mind it would be of the worst possible example to hold that agreements such as this resulted in legal obligations which could be enforced in the Courts. It would mean this, that when the husband makes his wife a promise to give her an allowance of 30*s* or 2*l* a week, whatever he can afford to give her, for

---

8 *Social Security Act* 1991 (Cth) s 4(3).
9 A similar list is included in s 4 of the *Property (Relationships) Act* 1984 (NSW) to guide decision-makers when there is an issue as to the existence of a de facto relationship (same or opposite sex).

the maintenance of the household and children, and she promises so to apply it, not only could she sue him for his failure in any week to supply the allowance, but he could sue her for non-performance of the obligation, express or implied, which she had undertaken upon her part. All I can say is that the small Courts of this country would have to be multiplied one hundredfold if these arrangements were held to result in legal obligations. They are not sued upon, not because the parties are reluctant to enforce their legal rights when the agreement is broken, but because the parties, in the inception of the arrangement, never intended that they should be sued upon. Agreements such as these are outside the realm of contracts altogether. The common law does not regulate the form of agreements between spouses. Their promises are not sealed with seals and sealing wax. The consideration that really obtains for them is that natural love and affection which counts for so little in these cold Courts. The terms may be repudiated, varied or renewed as performance proceeds or as disagreements develop, and the principles of the common law as to exoneration and discharge and accord and satisfaction are such as find no place in the domestic code. The parties themselves are advocates, judges, Courts, sheriff's officer and reporter. In respect of these promises each house is a domain into which the King's writ does not seek to run, and to which his officers do not seek to be admitted. The only question in this case is whether or not this promise was of such a class or not. For the reasons given by my brethren it appears to me to be plainly established that the promise here was [580] not intended by either party to be attended by legal consequences. I think the onus was upon the plaintiff, and the plaintiff has not established any contract. The parties were living together, the wife intending to return. The suggestion is that the husband bound himself to pay 30*l* a month under all circumstances, and she bound herself to be satisfied with that sum under all circumstances, and, although she was in ill-health and alone in this country, that out of that sum she undertook to defray the whole of the medical expenses that might fall upon her, whatever might be the development of her illness, and in whatever expenses it might involve her. To my mind neither party contemplated such a result. I think that the parol evidence upon which the case turns does not establish a contract. I think that the letters do not evidence such a contract, or amplify the oral evidence which was given by the wife, which is not in dispute. For these reasons I think the judgment of the Court below was wrong and that this appeal should be allowed.

[*Lord Justice Warrington and Lord Justice Duke wrote judgments in similar terms.*]

Notes

1. *Balfour v Balfour* is often cited as authority for the proposition that the law or the state is reluctant to intervene in domestic relations, constructing them as 'private'.[10] In 'The Decline of Privacy in Private Law', Hugh Collins has offered an alternative reading of *Balfour:*

    > Far from deliberately leaving the relation unregulated, thus putting the wife at the husband's mercy, the court viewed its decision as one which preserved the paternalist framework of rights accorded to the deserted spouse.[11]

---

10 See, for example, HK Lücke, 'The Intention to Create Legal Relations' (1967-70) 3 *Adelaide Law Review* 419; O'Donovan, *Sexual Divisions in Law* at 11, 13 and 108-9.

11 (1987) 14 *Journal of Law and Society* 91 at 100. He cites in support of his conclusion a statement from Duke LJ's judgment: 'In order to establish a contract there ought to be something more than mere mutual promises having regard to the domestic relations of the parties. It is required that the obligations arising out of that relationship shall be displaced before either of the parties can found a contract upon such promises': *Balfour v Balfour* [1919] 2 KB 571 at 577.

In other words, there was a clear difference between what 'family law' and the law of contract would provide to Ms Balfour. Does Collins' analysis illustrate another of O'Donovan's themes: that the law does regulate the private, though often indirectly?

There are a number of aspects to the relationship between contract law and family law, aside from the issue of 'intention to create legal relations'. In Australia, family law has become increasingly 'privatised' culminating in the enactment of the *Family Law (Amendment) Act* 2000 (Cth) under which agreements made before, during and after the breakdown of marriages will be legally binding so long as they satisfy the legislative requirements. This is discussed further in Chapter 5.[12]

2. Even if Collins' view of this case is correct, *Balfour* clearly illustrates the proposition for which it is frequently cited: the law's avowed reluctance to intervene in the private. Whether this reluctance is primarily at the level of rhetoric rather than reality, as Collins argues, the rhetoric is both colourful and powerful and is part of the law's role in creating the zone of the private. As Atkin LJ said, 'each house is a domain into which the King's writ does not seek to run, and to which his officers do not seek to be admitted'. It is also worth noting that the law has always been less reluctant to intervene in domestic relationships when the relationship is 'over', at the same time, of course, determining when it is legally 'over'. So, for example, in *Popiw v Popiw*,[13] the court did enforce an agreement between a husband and wife (that he would transfer a half interest in the home to her, if she would return to live with him) because that agreement had been made after she had left the matrimonial home and the relationship had 'broken down'.

Complicating the public/private dichotomy

'Intervention and non-intervention'

While feminist critique of the law's role in creating the family as a private zone is relatively well developed, as is the analysis of the way in which the law, whilst purporting to stay out of the family, indirectly regulates its functioning, attempts to break out of this dichotomous way of thinking are less advanced. One of the obvious difficulties occurs in the formulation of the argument: if one defines the private as that which remains unregulated by law, as O'Donovan does, it is difficult to sustain the parallel important insight that the private is in fact indirectly regulated by law.[14] Frances Olsen has pointed out the problems with using the language of intervention and non-intervention to refer to the state's role in the family.[15] She argues that this terminology is incoherent: it depends very much on one's perspective whether a particular law will be characterised as intervention or non-intervention. For example, she asks whether a law that required family planning agencies to notify a young woman's parents that she was taking contraceptives is really intervention or non-intervention in the family.[16] Some

---

12 Cf Michael Freeman, 'Contracting in the Haven: *Balfour v Balfour* Revisited' in Roger Halson (ed), *Exploring the Boundaries of Contract*, Dartmouth, Aldershot, 1996.
13 [1959] VR 197 at 198.
14 See Graycar, 'Review of Katherine O'Donovan, *Sexual Divisions in Law*' (1987-88) 26 *Journal of Family Law* 265.
15 Frances Olsen, 'The Myth of State Intervention in the Family' (1985) 18 *University of Michigan Journal of Law Reform* 835.
16 See, in this context, *Gillick v West Norfolk and Wisbech Area Health Authority* [1986] AC 112.

would support a law of this nature on the ground that it was reducing state intervention in the family; on the other hand, it could be seen as a form of state intervention in that it was 'intrud[ing] into the parent-child relationship and pass[ing] along information that the parents have neglected to obtain in the old-fashioned way – by talking to their children'.[17]

Is Olsen's argument about the incoherence of the language of intervention and non-intervention a way of moving away from dichotomous thinking and/or a demonstration of the way in which the state indirectly regulates the private?

Notes

1. Nicola Lacey has argued that a traditional feminist examination of violence against women in the home through a critique of the public/private dichotomy is of only limited assistance. On one analysis, it could be argued that violence has always been regulated in the sense that we have always had laws against assault. Yet it is notorious that these laws were not used by state agencies (for example, the police) to provide women with proper protection from violence in the home.[18] So if something is regulated by 'law' but unregulated in practice, how do we analyse it within the terms of regulation and non-regulation or intervention and non-intervention? Or, to put it in another way, how useful is it to persist in a presentation of violence against women in the home as a culturally private issue which must be made a culturally public issue?

2. In the past three decades there was a series[19] of decisions that rejected the argument that the costs incurred in relation to child care by a woman (or a man)[20] who was engaged in paid work could be considered as tax deductible. The High Court in *Lodge v Commissioner of Taxation*[21] explained:

> To qualify as an allowable deduction under s 51(1) of the *Income Tax Assessment Act* 1936-1971 (Cth) it must appear that the item of expenditure was "incurred in gaining or producing assessable income" or was

---

17   Olsen, 'The Myth of State Intervention in the Family', at 860.
18   Nicola Lacey, 'Theory into Practice? Pornography and the Public/Private Dichotomy' (1993) 20 *Journal of Law and Society* 93 at 96.
19   Apart from the decision of the High Court discussed below, see *Jayatilake v Federal Commissioner of Taxation* (1991) 22 ATR 125, where the Full Federal Court refused to allow a tax deduction for child care expenses incurred by a taxpayer while she was engaged in part-time study; see also *Martin v Federal Commissioner of Taxation* (1984) 2 FCR 260.
20   Though note that women living in heterosexual relationships and engaging in paid work still remain overwhelmingly responsible for care of the children of the relationship: this is discussed in detail in Chapter 5.
21   (1972) 128 CLR 171. And for Canada, see *Symes v Canada* [1993] 4 SCR 695. Although the majority of the Supreme Court of Canada reached the same conclusion as the Australian High Court, L'Heureux-Dubé and McLachlin JJ (the two women on the court) dissented. L'Heureux-Dubé J in discussing the concept of an allowable business expense, stated: '[I]t is clear that this area of law is premised on the traditional view of business as a male enterprise and that the concept of a business expense has itself been constructed on the basis of the needs of business*men*. ... [W]hen only one sex is involved in defining the ideas, rules and values in a particular domain, that one-sided standpoint comes to be seen as natural, obvious and general. As a consequence, the male standard now frames the backdrop of assumptions against which expenses are determined to be, or not to be, legitimate business expenses. Against this backdrop, it is hardly surprising that child care was seen as irrelevant to the end of gaining or producing income from business but rather as a personal non-deductible expense' (at 798, emphasis in original).

necessarily incurred "in carrying on a business for the purpose of gaining or producing" such income.[22]

Margaret Lodge was a single parent who worked from home doing costings on solicitors' files. In order to do this work she found she needed to place her child in child care. The court held:

> The expenditure was incurred for the purpose of earning assessable income and it was an essential prerequisite of the derivation of that income. Nevertheless its character as nursery fees for the appellant's child was neither relevant nor incidental to the preparation of bills of cost, the activities or operations by which the appellant gained or produced assessable income. The expenditure was not incurred in, or in the course of, preparing bills of cost.[23]

The relevant section of the *Income Tax Assessment Act* also provided that expenditure was not deductible if it was of a 'private or domestic' nature. The court went on to find that expenses incurred for child care were 'private or domestic'.[24] A straightforward feminist critique of this decision might argue that encouraging tax deductibility of child care expenses 'facilitates the movement of women from the private sphere (the family) into the public sphere (the workplace)'.[25] However, as Claire Young points out:

> The problem is that, at the same time, the deduction has a privatizing effect with respect to the child care services that are intended to reduce the impediment to women's participation in the paid labour force. Put simply, public funds allocated to childcare are, through a combination of factors, being directed towards financing child care in the private sphere, that is, the family or the private market. Unlike direct subsidies paid in the form of operating or capital grants to non-profit childcare facilities, tax subsidies are received by individuals and may be in respect of any child care expense. ... [I]t is irrelevant for tax purposes whether the child care is provided by the private sector (through the family or other in-home care-givers) or the public sector (through licensed day care facilities) or, indeed, in unlicensed day care facilities that may run for profit or not. This method of funding may serve to privatize child care and is one example of the general trend towards privatizing the costs of social reproduction.[26]

Young emphasises that a system of tax deductions for child care expenses benefits only those who earn an income and pay income tax. It also benefits higher income earners more than lower income earners.[27] Given Young's

---

22 *Lodge*, at 174. See now *Income Tax Assessment Act* 1997 (Cth) s 8(1) in the same terms.
23 *Lodge*, at 176.
24 *Ibid*. And cf L'Heureux-Dubé J's dissent in *Symes*: 'If we survey the experiences of many men, it is apparent why it may seem intuitively obvious to some of them that child care is clearly within the personal realm. This conclusion may ... reflect men's experience of child care responsibilities. ... [T]he evidence before the Court indicates that, for most men, the responsibility of children does not impact on the number of hours they work, nor does it affect their ability to work. Further, very few men indicated that they made any work-related decisions on the basis of child-raising responsibilities. The same simply cannot be said for women. For women, business and family life are not so distinct and, in many ways, any such distinction is completely unreal, since a woman's ability to even participate in the workforce may be completely contingent on her ability to acquire child care. The decision to retain child care is an inextricable part of the decision to work, in business or otherwise' (at 800).
25 Claire FL Young, 'Public Taxes, Privatizing Effects, and Gender Inequality' in Boyd (ed), *Challenging the Public/Private Divide,* at 310.
26 *Ibid.*
27 Cf L'Heureux-Dubé J in *Symes*, at 823-5.

criticisms of a tax deduction for child care costs, can you think of other ways in which the cost of child care might be dealt with? Would different state action in this field lead to a more comprehensive challenge to the public/private dichotomy?[28]

The wages of child care workers are notoriously low. Young argues that a system of payment for child care through the tax system, that is, by way of tax deductions (as opposed to, say, the direct state provision of child care services), contributes to the low wages of child care workers. Why do you think this might be the case?[29]

Is privacy always 'bad'?

As noted above, traditional feminist arguments raise concerns about the private sphere as notionally unregulated, for example, in suggestions that 'the legal system' has traditionally failed to respond to violence against women in their homes. Not only has this approach meant an over-reliance on an analytical tool that fails to encompass the experiences of many women, particularly those from indigenous communities, but Lacey suggests that some feminist critiques imply that privacy as a value 'has nothing to recommend it to women'.

> [T]he value of privacy is contextual – it depends on the particular area of life we are thinking of, and the circumstances which prevail. This means that an approach to protecting privacy which operates by delineating a relatively concrete *sphere* seems inappropriate. But ... it is far from clear that a critique of the public/private dichotomy should bring with it a total rejection of the notion that privacy can be valuable and ought sometimes to be protected by the state and other powerful institutions. Indeed, given the double burden inherent in current social arrangements, privacy is one of the many things which women tend to lack.[30]

For example, in Australia, indigenous women's relationships with their children were far from 'private', as the history of the 'stolen children' recounted in *Bringing Them Home*, makes clear.[31] In Chapter 9 we summarise the findings of this report, indicating the various methods and justifications used by the state through the 19th and 20th centuries to remove indigenous children from their parents. In this context, the invocation of the rhetoric of the right to family privacy may have provided some protection to indigenous families from the predations of the state.

---

28   Young, 'Public Taxes, Privatizing Effects', at 311-12.
29   *Ibid.* For further discussion of child care expenses and tax deductibility, see Claire Young, 'Child Care and the Charter: Privileging the Privileged' (1994) 2 *Review of Constitutional Studies* 20 and 'Child Care – A Taxing Issue?' (1994) 39 *McGill Law Journal* 539.
30   Lacey, 'Theory into Practice?', at 100.
31   HREOC, *Bringing Them Home: National Inquiry into the Separation of Aboriginal and Torres Strait Islander Children from Their Families*, Commonwealth of Australia, Sydney, 1997. For similar observations in Canada see Susan B Boyd, 'Challenging the Public/Private Divide: An Overview' in Susan Boyd (ed), *Challenging the Public/Private Divide*, at 13; Marlee Kline, 'Child Welfare Law, "Best Interests of the Child" Ideology, and First Nations' (1992) 30 *Osgoode Hall Law Journal* 375 and 'Complicating the Ideology of Motherhood: Child Welfare Law and First Nation Women' (1993) 18 *Queen's Law Journal* 306; and Patricia Monture, 'A Vicious Circle: Child Welfare and First Nations' (1989) 3 *Canadian Journal of Women and the Law* 1.

Notes

1. Jennifer Koshan has also urged some caution in simplistically using a feminist critique of the public/private dichotomy to respond to violence against indigenous women (in Canada):

    The public/private dichotomy may be a useful starting point for feminist theorizing around issues of male violence against women, as it describes the historical treatment of such violence by the Euro-Canadian state. The analysis breaks down, however, when it leads to assumptions about the causes and sites of violence against women that ignore factors such as racialization, class, disability, and sexual orientation. Feminist critiques must be broadened to recognize that public/private analysis may be of limited use in some cases. ... To assume that patriarchal gender relations are the primary cause and to locate the family as the primary site of women's oppression, does not accord with the analysis of these issues by Aboriginal women, or, indeed, by many non-Aboriginal women.

    When the public/private dichotomy becomes the framework for feminist law reform efforts in the context of male violence against women, as it did in the early 1980s, these difficulties may be further entrenched. It is overly simplistic, and perhaps harmful, to equate 'public' with a response that results in survivors' forced engagement with the criminal justice system via police and prosecution policy directives. Whereas initially it was thought that these policies may be useful as both symbols of and vehicles for state action around issues of intimate violence, time has shown that any such initiatives must be more responsive to the needs and concerns of survivors of violence, in all their diversity.[32]

    We return to this issue in Chapter 10.

2. In March 2000, *The Age* pleaded guilty to contempt of court and a breach of s 103AB of the *Evidence Act* 1910 (Tas).[33] The Tasmanian legislation prohibits absolutely (unless the court has so ordered) the public identification of sexual assault victim/survivors. Equivalent legislation in Victoria, the *Judicial Proceedings Reports Act* 1958 (Vic), provides that where the victim/survivor gives permission for public identification, there is no breach of the Act.[34] The newspaper was publicising the conviction of Steve Randall, a former test cricket umpire, for '15 counts of indecent assault between 1981 and 1982 ... committed on ... girls when [he] was a teacher'. In doing so they published a photo, identifying and telling the story of one of his victims. She had apparently given permission for this, and the editor of the paper was quoted as saying 'the woman saw the story and photograph as an "incredible process of healing" and that she had been on a crusade'. Similar legislation restricting the media from publishing material that would identify survivors of sexual assault in Canada has been challenged as a breach of news media's right to freedom of expression.[35] Do you think such legislation should allow victim/survivors to waive their right to anonymity? Can you think of a way to justify the protection against identification of rape victim/survivors which does not rely on privacy?[36]

---

32 Koshan, 'Sounds of Silence', at 100. See also Mary Eaton, 'Abuse by Any Other Name: Feminism, Difference, and Intralesbian Violence' in Martha Albertston Fineman and Roxanne Mykitiuk (eds), *The Public Nature of Private Violence: The Discovery of Domestic Abuse*, Routledge, New York, 1994, at 214-15.
33 Steve Butcher, 'Age pleads guilty on contempt count' *The Age*, 3 March 2000, at 2.
34 *Judicial Proceedings Reports Act* 1958 (Vic) s 4(1B)(b)(ii).
35 *Canadian Newspapers Co v Canada (A-G)* [1988] 2 SCR 122.
36 See Christine Boyle, 'Publication of Identifying Information About Sexual Assault Survivors: *R v Canadian Newspapers Co Ltd*' (1990) 3 *Canadian Journal of Women and the Law* 602.

What is 'public'?

Susan Boyd, in the introduction to a collection of (largely) Canadian writing on the public/private divide, has noted how the public/private dichotomy as a 'conceptual tool' has come under increasing scrutiny by feminist scholars and activists, leading some to abandon it as no longer useful.[37] She suggests that most authors in her collection have continued to use it as a conceptual tool, but the questioning has led to a more critical approach which 'determin[es] more precisely how the divide operates in relation to different groups and issues and in different periods and locations'.[38] The previous discussion on Aboriginal children is an attempt to complicate the more traditional feminist analyses of the public/private dichotomy by looking at a particular group at a particular time.

Nicola Lacey has also drawn attention to some of the difficulties with the (traditional feminist) use of the public/private dichotomy. She argues that, when the term is used descriptively, it '"reifies" spheres which cannot be clearly identified by means of careful concrete sociological analysis'.[39] Similarly, Boyd points out:

> [G]eographic imagery delineating separate spheres, with paid work mainly occurring in the market, fails to apply to the lives of many women. ... [I]n many women's lives, the home is not set apart from the market. Some immigrant women, for example, work for pay as domestic workers in other women's homes. ... For others, the market moves into the home: homework, or paid work done in the home, is not uncommon for immigrant women, ...[40]

Lacey argues that when the public/private divide is used analytically, it tends to obscure the connection between the two spheres:

> [T]he state is not monolithic; it is rather a set of diverse institutions. This gives rise to further complexities in identifying regulation or non-regulation. ... Once we incorporate non-state power, and acknowledge the difficulty of distinguishing between state and non-state bodies in a world where 'public' and 'private' power are inextricably linked with each other, the picture threatens to disintegrate.[41]

The difficulties, and absurdities, of creating a division between state or public and non-state or 'private' actors plays itself out in some countries' constitutional laws. In many of the jurisdictions that have constitutional Bills of Rights, such as the USA and Canada, their operation is confined to 'State action' (in the USA),[42] or 'government action' (in Canada).[43]

Hester Lessard describes a series of Canadian decisions which have defined various bodies, including hospitals which receive a large amount of government funding, as 'private' or at least not as government actors, and thereby not subject

---

37 Boyd, 'Challenging the Public/Private Divide: An Overview', at 12.
38 *Ibid.*
39 Lacey, 'Theory into Practice?', at 100.
40 Boyd, 'Challenging the Public/Private Divide: An Overview', at 14.
41 Lacey, 'Theory into Practice?', at 96.
42 See Frances Olsen, 'Constitutional Law: Feminist Critiques of the Public/Private Distinction' (1993) 10 *Constitutional Commentary* 319.
43 See *Retail, Wholesale and Department Store Union, Local 580 v Dolphin Delivery Ltd* [1986] 2 SCR 573; and see more broadly Hester Lessard, 'The Construction of Health Care and the Ideology of the Private in Canadian Constitutional Law' (1993) 2 *Annals of Health Law* 121.

to the restrictions on their actions contained in the Canadian Charter of Rights and Freedoms.[44] As Lessard says:

> [A] number of notions became entrenched: the notion of a limited state; the notion of power as coercion; and the notion of a state power as juridical and concentrated within a circle of identifiable officials, rather than ideological and diffused throughout a system of actors, structures, and relationships.[45]

This classification of hospital boards has had particular implications for the availability of abortion in Canada. In 1988 the Supreme Court of Canada in *Morgentaler* struck down the *Criminal Code* provisions which rendered abortion unlawful as an unconstitutional interference with women's 'life, liberty and security of the person'.[46] Since then, no new criminal provisions have been enacted. However, as Lessard notes, '*Morgentaler* simply removed the most visible manifestation of state coercion in abortion decision making, namely the Criminal Code prohibition'.[47] She describes the decision of a hospital board in Manitoba in Canada to refuse to provide abortion services and shows how, once it was decided that such a body is 'private', even if its services are provided largely through the provision of government funding, its decisions as to which services to make available are not subject to constitutional or Charter challenge. Instead, it is left to bodies such as the local hospital board to make such decisions. So while *Morgentaler* may have got rid of the most obvious legal barrier to abortion, it has done nothing to guarantee access to safe and affordable provision of those services (a similar situation to that following *Roe v Wade*[48] in the US).[49]

Notes

1. What criteria would you use to identify something as 'government action'? Obviously the very asking of this question accepts the dichotomy between government and non-government action and implies it is both possible and desirable to make this distinction. Can you engage with law in countries where such a distinction is entrenched and not do this? Which has more power: the (non-government) corporation News Limited or the local government of the shire of Pearl Bay?
2. Australian anti-discrimination or human rights laws such as the *Sex Discrimination Act* 1984 (Cth) and the various State and Territory counterparts generally proscribe discrimination only in defined areas of 'public' life, such as employment, education, accommodation and the provision of goods and services.[50] So although the areas where discrimination is proscribed cover a much wider base than 'state action', the focus of anti-discrimination laws is

---

44 But see now *Eldridge v Attorney General of British Columbia and Medical Services Commission* [1997] 3 SCR 624. See also Isabel Grant and Judith Mosoff, 'Hearing Claims of Inequality: *Eldridge v British Columbia (A-G)*' (1998) 10 *Canadian Journal of Women and the Law* 229; and Margot Young, 'Change at the Margins: *Eldridge v British Columbia (A-G)* and *Vriend v Alberta*' (1998) 10 *Canadian Journal of Women and the Law* 244.
45 Lessard, 'The Construction of Health Care', at 139.
46 *Morgentaler, Smoling and Scott v The Queen* [1988] 1 SCR 30.
47 Lessard, 'The Construction of Health Care', at 138.
48 410 US 113 (1973).
49 This is discussed further in Chapter 8.
50 See Margaret Thornton, 'The Public/Private Dichotomy: Gendered and Discriminatory' (1991) 18 *Journal of Law and Society* 448 and compare with s 118 *Anti-Discrimination Act* 1991 (Qld) which outlaws sexual harassment simpliciter, with no restriction as to areas of operation.

clearly demarcated and quite limited. Why don't anti-discrimination laws concern themselves with who does the washing up in a household?

3. Lacey also asks us to question whether, even as we identify many sources of regulatory power beyond those clearly identified as 'the state', we too easily assume that power is only, or mainly, wielded by institutions:

> The very idea of power as something which is deliberately exercised by identifiable agents, as opposed to, or at least also, subsisting in discourses and practices spreading throughout the social body – including those other 'publics' ignored by the traditional public/private distinction – misses important aspects of how subjects' positions are constituted and maintained in the social world.[51]

Does this mean that there is no point analysing the role of the state?[52]

A legal right of privacy?

While there is little or no recognition of a right to privacy in Australian domestic law,[53] there is explicit recognition of such a right in international law. The International Covenant on Civil and Political Rights (ICCPR) in Art 17 provides:

1. No one shall be subject to arbitrary interference with his privacy, family, home or correspondence, nor to unlawful attacks on his honor or reputation.
2. Everyone has the right to the protection of the law against such interference or attacks.[54]

This provision was used by the Tasmanian Gay and Lesbian Rights Group (TGLRG) in the early 1990s to attack Tasmania's 'unnatural sex' laws.[55] Until 1997, the *Criminal Code* (Tas) provided:

> **122** Any person who –
> (a) has sexual intercourse with any person against the order of nature;
> (b) has sexual intercourse with an animal; or
> (c) consents to a male person having sexual intercourse with him or her against the order of nature,
> is guilty of a crime.
> Charge: Unnatural sexual intercourse.
>
> **123** Any male person who, whether in public or private, commits any indecent assault upon, or other act of gross indecency with, another male person, or procures another male person to commit any act of gross indecency with himself or any other male person, is guilty of a crime.
> Charge: Indecent practice between male persons.

In 1991 Australia signed the Optional Protocol to the ICCPR. This allows individuals who have exhausted domestic remedies to complain to the United Nations Human Rights Committee that Australia has breached its international

---

51 Lacey, 'Theory into Practice?', at 96.
52 See Boyd, 'Challenging the Public/Private Divide: An Overview', at 16 and '(Re)Placing the State: Family, Law and Oppression' (1994) 9 *Canadian Journal of Law and Society* 39.
53 There are, of course, various statutory forms of protection for the use by government of details about individuals: see, for example, *Privacy Act* 1988 (Cth). See also, NSWLRC, *Surveillance: An Interim Report*, Report No 98, Ch 1, 2001.
54 This needs to be read in conjunction with Art 2(1) which provides that rights in the ICCPR are respected 'without distinction of any kind, such as race, colour, sex, language, religion, political or other opinion, national or social origin, property, birth or other status'.
55 The term Wayne Morgan uses in his article 'Identifying Evil for What It Is: Tasmania, Sexual Perversity and the United Nations' (1994) 19 *Melbourne University Law Review* 740.

obligations. After the Tasmanian upper house repeatedly refused to repeal these laws, the TGLRG approached the Human Rights Committee. The TGLRG, as well as arguing that the laws breached gay men's and lesbians' right to privacy, also argued that the laws breached their right to equality, as contained in Art 26 of the ICCPR. This provides that:

> All persons are equal before the law and are entitled without any discrimination to the equal protection of the law. In this respect, the law shall prohibit any discrimination and guarantee to all persons equal and effective protection on any ground such as race, colour, sex, language, religion, political or other opinion, national or social origin, property, birth or other status.

The TGLRG argued that the Tasmanian laws violated the right to privacy by bringing private activity into the realm of government scrutiny and by authorising police to enter private homes if they had a suspicion that two consenting homosexual adult men might be engaging in a criminal offence. Such interferences were arbitrary because society gained nothing from the enforcement of these laws.[56] The TGLRG described the breach of equality in the following way:

> Further, the Communication [*the name of the document submitted to the UN Human Rights Committee explaining the alleged breach*] alleges that the impugned laws violate the author's rights to equal protection of the law and his right to live free from discrimination. The Communication argues that in so far as the criminal laws do not prohibit private, consensual sex between adult heterosexuals and lesbians, they make gay men 'unequal before the law and unable to claim the equal protection of the law'. The TGLRG then attempts to draw a direct link between the existence of unnatural sex laws and acts of discrimination and violence against gay men and lesbians.[57]

Although the Committee was presented with arguments about both privacy and equality, the majority chose only to deal with the privacy arguments in accepting the claims of the TGLRG.[58] Wayne Morgan has argued:

> The feminist critique of the public/private dichotomy should sound warning bells for any decision maker who attempts to base 'rights' on the shifting and uncertain grounds of privacy. ... The Committee's decision, based on the right to privacy (with its attendant metaphors of freedom and non-regulation) obscures the link between legal discourses on homosex and 'private' acts of discrimination and violence.
>
> By naming sexuality as an issue of *privacy*, the Committee's decision reinforces the popular view that sexual difference is a matter not to be spoken of, something which is intimate and *no-one else's business*. Such a view disempowers gay men and lesbians: our sexuality has no public face. ...
>
> What needs to be pointed out here is that the *privacy* of homosex does not mean that there is *no* public discourse about it, but it does mean that voices which contradict the views expressed by institutional voices (like law) are usually silenced. Thus, legal actors continue to produce their stories about the *dangerous otherness* of homosex, whilst silencing other views by naming them *private*. In Foucauldian terms, privacy jurisprudence is part of the explosion of institutional discourse about sex, which defines, scrutinises and controls those who are labelled with a gay or lesbian identity. ... Homosex is private, secret, silenced. Heterosex is public, acceptable, normal.[59]

---

56 *Ibid*, at 743.
57 *Ibid*.
58 One member of the Committee did consider and accept the equality argument.
59 Morgan, 'Identifying Evil', at 753-4.

Wayne Morgan suggests that a decision based even on a limited understanding of equality as mere formal equality (see below) would have been preferable to one based on privacy. An equality discourse would have 'provid[ed] gay men and lesbians with better rhetorical arguments in their struggle against homophobia'.[60]

Instead, by analysing unnatural sex laws within the paradigms and ideological limits set by the juridical discourse of 'privacy', decision-makers, like the Committee members, restrain and contain 'deviant' sexual identities within a sphere constructed as powerless. In gay and lesbian terms, the sphere of the 'closet'. As long as contested sexual identities are kept closeted, secret, private; as long as gay men and lesbians appear as straight, no damage is done to the unitary, hegemonic construction of heterosexuality dominant in popular and institutional discourse.[61]

Note

1. The Constitutional Court of South Africa was much more willing to rely on the right to equality as the basis for overturning that country's sodomy laws.[62] The court also considered that the law in question breached gay men's right to privacy. In doing so, the court indicated its awareness of the sort of critique Morgan has made of seeing sodomy laws as a breach of privacy rights.[63] In his separate concurring judgment, Sachs J engaged with this issue in some depth. He summarised the critique of the Coalition for Gay and Lesbian Equality of the discourse of privacy:

> [P]rivacy analysis is inadequate because it suggests that homosexuality is shameful and therefore should only be protected if it is limited to the private bedroom; it tends to limit the promotion of gay rights to the decriminalisation of consensual adult sex, instead of contemplating a more comprehensive normative framework that addresses discrimination generally against gays; and it assumes a dual structure – public and private – that does not capture the complexity of lived life, in which public and private lives determine each other, with the mobile lines between them being constantly amenable to repressive definition.[64]

Although Sachs J described these concerns as 'valid' he continued:

> I consider that they arise from a set of assumptions that are flawed as to how equality and privacy rights interrelate and about the manner in which privacy rights should truly be understood; in the first place, the approach adopted by the applicants subjects equality and privacy rights to inappropriate sequential ordering. ...
> ... The fact is that both from the point of view of the persons affected, as well as from that of society as a whole, equality and privacy cannot be separated, because they are both violated simultaneously by anti-sodomy laws. In the present matter, such laws deny equal respect for difference, which lies at the heart of equality, and become the basis for the invasion of

---

60 *Ibid*, at 756.
61 *Ibid*.
62 *National Coalition for Gay and Lesbian Equality v Minister for Justice* (1999) 1 SALR 6 (Constitutional Court).
63 *Ibid*, at paras 29-32. The court referred extensively to an article by Edwin Cameron, 'Sexual Orientation and the Constitution: A Test Case for Human Rights' (1993) 100 *South African Law Journal* 450.
64 *Ibid*, at para 110.

privacy. At the same time, the negation by the state of different forms of intimate personal behaviour becomes the foundation for the repudiation of equality. Human rights are better approached and defended in an integrated rather than a disparate fashion. This requires looking at rights and their violations from a person-centred rather than a formula-based position, and analysing them contextually rather than abstractly. ...

[T]he impact of these [*anti-sodomy*] laws on the group is of such a nature that a number of different protected rights are simultaneously infringed. In these circumstances it would be as artificial in law as it would be in life to treat the categories as alternative rather than interactive. In some contexts, rights collide and an appropriate balancing is required. In others, such as the present, they inter-relate and give extra dimension to the extent and impact of the infringement. Thus, the violation of equality by the anti-sodomy laws is all the more egregious because it touches the deep, invisible and intimate side of people's lives.[65]

Does Sachs J's analysis of the interaction of equality and privacy help us move away from a dichotomised understanding of these two rights?

The next chapter looks in some detail at notions of equality.

---

65   *Ibid*, at paras 112-14. Sachs J also explains that he thinks there may be an impoverished understanding of privacy rights (see paras 115-19).

Chapter Three

Gender (In)equality

Introduction

There are a number of different ways to understand what gender equality might mean. In its 1994 report, *Equality Before the Law*, the Australian Law Reform Commission (ALRC), drawing on the analysis of Canadian Liz Sheehy,[1] describes two of these understandings in the following way:

> **Australian Law Reform Commission, *Equality Before the Law: Women's Equality***
> Report No 69, Part II, Commonwealth of Australia, 1994
>
> **Formal equality or gender neutral treatment**
> 3.8 *Treating everyone the same.* One approach, known as formal or rule equality, sees equality as a matter of gender neutral treatment. Formal equality requires simply that women and men be treated exactly the same in all circumstances. This approach denies that there are any important, immutable differences between women and men. It assumes that the creation of a level playing field, of itself, will achieve equality. It has been useful in combating some of the most overt examples of discrimination against women, such as denying women the right to vote or barring women from entry to professions or excluding married women from permanent employment. It is simple to understand and apply: no law may validly distinguish between women and men in any way.
> 3.9 *Deficiencies.* The formal equality or gender neutral treatment approach has some important deficiencies in areas where women have been subjected to long term disadvantage.
> - First, women and men have not historically been treated identically. Treating them exactly the same now may only reinforce the disadvantage that has flowed to women from past different treatment.
> - Second, this approach takes the treatment of men as the yardstick for equality. It ignores difference even where it is relevant. It uses male experience and a male perspective as the benchmark without questioning that standard. This disadvantages women who do not conform to male-defined norms or who, for example, cannot or do not pursue career paths that resemble those of men. Women risk losing further ground when they fail to live up to the male standard.
> - Third, this model has nothing to offer where there is no comparable male experience on which to base women's claim to identical treatment. It cannot respond to structural disadvantages faced by women. Indeed, it may further

---

[1] Elizabeth A Sheehy, *Personal Autonomy and the Criminal Law: Emerging Issues for Women*, Background Paper, Canadian Advisory Council on the Status of Women, Ottawa, September, 1987.

entrench those disadvantages. Unequal gender relations thrive when the rhetoric of gender neutrality denies their existence.
- Finally, this model cannot accommodate the notion of indirect discrimination, recognised, for example, in the *Sex Discrimination Act 1984* (Cth) (the SDA). Indirect discrimination occurs when a rule or practice appears to apply to women and men in the same way but has the effect of imposing on women a burden that men do not face or an unreasonable requirement that men can meet more readily. In other words, proscribing indirect discrimination recognises that sometimes treating women and men identically can result in discrimination against women.

Anti-discrimination legislation on the whole takes a formal equality approach. However, it implicitly recognises the limitations of this approach and the need to move beyond it, for example, to prohibit indirect discrimination. ...

The differences approach

3.11 ***Women's experiences are different.*** A second approach to equality recognises that women do not necessarily have the same experiences as men. It acknowledges women's differences from men. This approach suggests that women and men should not be treated identically in all circumstances and that women's differences from men need particular recognition. This differences approach legitimises laws and policies which apply specifically to women because of biological or socially constructed differences. Recognising differences between women and men, such as the capacity to bear children, can sometimes promote women's equality; for example, it assists in the provision of employment-related benefits such as maternity leave.

3.12 ***Deficiencies.*** While the difference approach has been of some benefit to women in some areas, it has also operated to entrench their inequality.
- First, differences between women and men have often been used to justify less favourable treatment for women. The difference approach seems to assume that differences between women and men will always justify different rules. In this way, women can be further disadvantaged because discriminatory practices will be justified by resort to women's differences from men. For example, this approach has been used to exclude women from certain jobs, such as in the lead industry [see *HREOC v Mt Isa Mines* (1992) EOC ¶92-420 discussed further below and *International Union v Johnson Controls* 499 US 187 (1991)] or as a prison guard [see *Dothard v Rawlinson* 433 US 321 (1977)].
- Second, the differences approach can be used as little more than a variant of the formal equality or gender neutrality approach. Both approaches use men as the benchmark. One requires women to be the same as men while the other stresses women's differences from men. Neither challenges male experience or characteristics as the standard from which women are measured. Emphasising women's similarity to or difference from men has the effect of distracting attention from the major issue of systemic inequality between women and men. It can entrench the dependency notion.

What the ALRC describes as 'formal equality or gender neutral treatment' is also often known as the 'strict equal treatment approach'; what is described as the 'differences approach' is often known as 'special treatment'. These terms – 'strict equal treatment' or 'special treatment' describe what are seen as the appropriate responses of law – law should either treat women and men in exactly the same way, with formal equality, or it should give women 'special treatment' because of their differences to men. The ALRC stated: 'Difference as such has not led to inequality for women but, rather, differences between women and men have been relied on to disadvantage women. The disadvantage to which legal recognition of gender difference has led is the focus of the third approach, the subordination or dominance approach'.²

The strict equal treatment model of equality, and the related differences or special treatment model, predominated in academic and legal discourses until Catharine MacKinnon articulated the subordination approach. (Though it must be said the two earlier models, perhaps particularly that of formal equality, continue to have a strong purchase in judicial understandings of equality, as we explore below.) MacKinnon has been one of the strongest critics of equality models that support identical treatment *and* models which opt for different treatment (both of which she places under the rubric of the 'difference approach').³ The following two short passages from her work address both aspects.

> One question that feminism poses is: "What is gender a question of?" I see two answers. The first answer has historically been the politically dominant, legally and conceptually: The gender question is a question of difference. There are two options under it. The first option I call the "male standard": Women can be the same as men. In law it is called gender neutrality. The other option I call the "female standard": You can be *different* from men. In law, it is called special protection. These bear a remarkable resemblance to the masculine and the feminine.
>
> The other answer to the question, a dissident view from the dominant mainstream legal and political position and discourse, is that gender is a question of dominance. In this answer, the issue of discrimination or inequality is not centrally one of accurate categorization, as it is in the first. It is one of hierarchy, the top and the bottom of a hierarchy are different all right, but that is hardly all. One part of the distinction is dominant, and the other part of the distinction is subordinate.
>
> From this second standpoint – which is my answer to the gender question – we see that the two standards in the first answer are two different versions of the male standard. If you see gender as a hierarchy – in which some people have power and some people are powerless, relatively speaking – you realize that the options of either being the same as men or being different from men are just two ways of having men as your standard. Men are set up as a standard for women by saying either: "You can be the same as men and then you will be equal," or "You can be different from men, and then you will be women".⁴

Or, as she has described the subordination approach elsewhere:

> In this approach, an equality question is a question of the distribution of power. Gender is also a question of power, specifically of male supremacy and female subordination. The question of equality, from the standpoint of what it is going to take to get it, is at root a question of hierarchy, which – as power succeeds in constructing social perception and social reality – derivatively becomes a categorical distinction, a difference. ... Gender might not even code as difference, might not mean distinction epistemologically, were it not for its consequences for social power.⁵

---

2   ALRC, *Equality Before the Law: Women's Equality*, Report No 69, Part II, Commonwealth of Australia, 1994, at para 3.12.
3   Catharine A MacKinnon, 'Difference and Dominance' in *Feminism Unmodified,* Harvard University Press, 1987, at 34. See also Catharine A MacKinnon, *Sexual Harassment of Working Women,* Yale University Press, New Haven, 1979, at 4-5 and 101-41; and Catharine A MacKinnon, *Toward a Feminist Theory of the State*, Harvard University Press, 1989, at 215-34.
4   Ellen Du Bois et al, 'Feminist Discourse, Moral Values and the Law – A Conversation' (1985) 34 *Buffalo Law Review* 11 at 20-1.
5   MacKinnon, 'Difference and Dominance', at 40.

Notes

1. Sheehy has raised one practical difficulty with the use of MacKinnon's dominance or subordination approach in law: judges may fail to understand the subordinating effect of a particular legal policy; but she suggests that the subordination analysis provides a clearer standard for law-makers to use than either the sameness or the difference standard.[6] Do you think that the subordination analysis could be used as a guide by law-makers in assessing law reform across a wide variety of areas? Is it an appropriate test of the adequacy of a theoretical framework that it can be easily used by law-makers? Do you agree with MacKinnon that the subordination analysis directs itself to questions of power, whereas the equal treatment/special treatment standards ignore power questions? If so, is Sheehy correct when she suggests that this makes it likely to be resisted vigorously?[7] Does the subordination analysis pose a threat to law's claim to neutrality?

2. MacKinnon first articulated her approach to equality in her book *Sexual Harassment of Working Women*. There she noted that, in some situations, use of what she calls the 'difference approach' to sexual inequality (that is, the equal treatment and special treatment approaches) and the dominance or subordination analysis can lead to the same result. MacKinnon argued that sexual harassment could be envisaged as a form of sex discrimination under both the difference and dominance approaches.[8] Under the difference approach, sexual harassment can be seen as either unequal treatment of women: 'sexual harassment singles out a gender-defined group, women, for special treatment in a way which adversely affects and burdens their status as employees';[9] or as having an unequal impact on their employment conditions – if an employer has a policy of tolerating sexual harassment this will have a differential burden on women. Under the subordination approach, sexual harassment is clearly sex discrimination:

> [F]irst, the exchange of sex for survival has historically assured women's economic dependence and inferiority as well as sexual availability to men. Second, sexual harassment expresses the male sex-role pattern of coercive sexual initiation toward women, often in vicious and unwanted ways. Third, women's sexuality largely defines women as women in this society, so violations of it are abuses of women as women.[10]

However, she suggested that a difference approach probably would not find there was discrimination if an employer sexually harassed both women and men, since they are receiving the same treatment.[11] How would you analyse this form of sexual harassment under a subordination approach?

Obviously, in other situations, the subordination approach leads to an entirely different analysis and different legal solutions. How would you deal with the issue of maternity leave under a subordination approach?

---

6 Elizabeth A Sheehy, *Background Paper, Personal Autonomy and the Criminal Law: Emerging Issues for Women*, Canadian Advisory Council on the Status of Women, Sept 1987, at 8.
7 *Ibid*.
8 And see our more detailed discussion of sexual harassment in Chapter 12.
9 MacKinnon, *Sexual Harassment of Working Women*, at 193.
10 *Ibid*, at 174.
11 *Ibid*, at 203.

3. In its final report, the ALRC adopted a model of equality based upon a subordination approach. They recommended that there should be an Equality Act and that that Act

> should require that in assessing whether a law, policy, program, practice or decision is inconsistent with equality in law regard must be had to:
> - the historical and current social, economic and legal inequalities experienced on the ground of gender
> - the historical and current practices of the body challenged and the extent to which those practices have contributed to or perpetuate the inequalities experienced
> - the history of the rule or practice being challenged.[12]

While this model may work to discourage a decision-maker from applying an equal treatment or special treatment approach when there is an alleged breach of equality rights, how relevant is the adoption of a particular model of equality to assessing, say, reforms to criminal law?[13]

4. What is the connection between the debates about the appropriate model of equality and the analysis of the public/private dichotomy? The ALRC recommended that:

> [T]he proposed Act should apply the right to equality to acts done:
> - by the legislative, executive or judicial arms of the Commonwealth, States or Territories; or
> - in the performance of any public function, power or duty conferred or imposed on any person or body by law.[14]

Is this understanding of what is a 'public' responsibility broader than the Canadian 'governmental action' doctrine discussed in Chapter 2? The Commission specifically rejected an approach that would allow the Act to apply to 'private' actors:

> The Equality Act should give rise to a new cause of action only in relation to acts of government and the performance of public functions, powers and duties. Its availability would turn on whether the power, function or duty is a government one. It should only arise in private litigation to support or oppose a claim under an existing cause of action.[15]

Why do you think the Commission might have recommended in this way? How would you argue for a broader application of such a principle of equality to Australian law?[16]

Equality models applied

There is now an enormous body of jurisprudence considering the meaning of 'equality' between women and men. Much of this has arisen in Canada and the

---

12   ALRC, *Equality Before the Law: Women's Equality*, Recommendation 4.5, at para 4.23. This approach drew heavily on the Supreme Court of Canada's decision in *Law Society of British Columbia v Andrews et al* [1989] 1 SCR 143; and Diana Majury, 'Equality and Discrimination According to the Supreme Court of Canada' (1991) 4 *Canadian Journal of Women and the Law* 407. See also now *Law v Canada (Minister of Employment and Immigration)* [1999] 1 SCR 497.
13   Compare Christine LM Boyle et al, *A Feminist Review of Criminal Law*, Minister of Supply and Services, Ottawa, 1985.
14   ALRC, *Equality Before the Law: Women's Equality*, Recommendation 6.1, at para 6.14.
15   *Ibid.*
16   Compare with ALRC, *Equality Before the Law: Women's Equality*, Ch 16, Minority View, especially at paras 16.20-16.21, extracted below.

USA where 'equality' is enshrined in those countries' constitutional Bills of Rights.[17] Australia does not, as yet, have any explicit guarantee of equality in its Constitution. But many of the same issues about the meaning of equality have arisen in Australia, most obviously in the context of anti-discrimination laws but also throughout more 'traditional' and familiar legal doctrines. Equality and its meaning remains central to all the areas of law discussed throughout this book. We have chosen to focus here on some of the ways in which the meaning of equality has been understood in legal discourses by illustrating the issue via three short case studies. The first concerns aspects of the ways in which pregnancy in the workplace has been treated within the legal system.[18] The second focuses on a challenge to a women-only health service by three men while the third interrogates a 'black letter' legal doctrine – the 'presumption of advancement'.

The example of pregnancy

Much of the legal discourse on the meaning of gender equality developed in the United States and Canada in the 1980s mostly through discussion and litigation about pregnancy, in particular, maternity leave provisions. Only a few States in the US had enacted special maternity leave laws.[19] In the 1980s these came under challenge as being in violation of federal US anti-discrimination laws (Title VII and the *Pregnancy Discrimination Act* 1978)[20] on the grounds that they treated pregnant women better than non-pregnant workers who were unable to work for other reasons.[21] Such challenges were supported by 'equal treatment' or 'strict identical treatment' feminists who argued that 'pregnancy can or should be visualized as one human experience which in many contexts, most notably the workplace, creates needs and problems similar to those arising from causes other than pregnancy, and which can be handled adequately on the same basis as other physical conditions of employees'.[22]

Special treatment supporters, on the other hand, argued that pregnancy *was* unique and required particular laws which were different from those for general sickness and disability leave.[23] Some of the attraction of this view lay in the inadequate nature of sick leave provisions in the US generally – if pregnant women were forced to rely on general disability provisions, the amount of leave allowed would be inadequate for pregnant women's needs and thus they would, effectively, be back in the old position of losing their jobs because of pregnancy.[24] Relying on 'sick' leave also involves treating pregnancy as an

---

17 See also, since 1996, the developing jurisprudence of the Constitutional Court of South Africa.
18 The case study by no means exhausts the ways in which pregnancy is constructed throughout the law's treatment of women. Some of these are explored explicitly in Part 3.
19 See Wendy S Strimling, 'The Constitutionality of State Laws Providing Employment Leave for Pregnancy: Rethinking *Geduldig* After *Cal Fed*' (1989) 77 *California Law Review* 171.
20 Title VII of the *Civil Rights Act* 1964 (42 USC 2000e and following) is the federal law concerned with discrimination in employment.
21 See, for example, *California Federal Savings and Loan Association v Guerra* 479 US 272 (1987).
22 Wendy W Williams, 'Equality's Riddle: Pregnancy and the Equal Treatment/Special Treatment Debate' (1984-85) 13 *New York University Review of Law and Social Change* 325 at 326.
23 See, in particular, Ann Scales, 'Towards a Feminist Jurisprudence' (1980-81) 56 *Indiana Law Journal* 375.
24 Lucinda Finley, 'Transcending Equality Theory: A Way Out of the Maternity and the Workplace Debate' (1986) 86 *Columbia Law Review* 1118 at 1147-8. Cf Linda J Krieger and Patricia N Cooney, 'The Miller-Wohl Controversy: Equal Treatment, Positive Action and the Meaning of Women's Equality' (1983) 13 *Golden Gate University Law Review* 513 at 569. Williams, an equal treatment advocate, maintained that the equal treatment approach can accommodate this argument: if a practice has the effect of creating a disparate impact on women, it should be found discriminatory under Title VII: Williams, 'Equality's Riddle', at 365-6, 378.

illness. Some have questioned, in turn, whether it was appropriate for women unionists to campaign in a piecemeal way, that is, to have as their first priority the needs of pregnant women and then to improve the disability leave provisions for all workers.[25] If women workers were considered 'normal', was pregnancy leave really 'special treatment'?[26]

It is worth noting the historical context of this battle. In *Geduldig*,[27] the exclusion of pregnancy from a disability insurance program was challenged, the argument being that this amounted to discrimination on the grounds of sex, that is, a failure to accord equal protection of the laws. The Supreme Court concluded that this was not sex discrimination; rather, it merely constituted a distinction between 'pregnant and non-pregnant persons' or, as Scales has described it, 'no discrimination exists if pregnant women and pregnant men are treated the same'.[28] The Supreme Court of Canada in *Bliss*,[29] decided in 1978, had adopted the analysis used by the US Supreme Court in *Geduldig*, stating: 'Any inequality between the sexes in this area is not created by legislation but by nature'.[30] However, in 1989, the Supreme Court of Canada overruled itself and accepted that discrimination because of pregnancy was discrimination on the ground of sex concluding 'how could pregnancy discrimination be *anything other than* sex discrimination'?[31]

Note

1. The most obvious area in Australia in which legal understandings of equality are considered is that of anti-discrimination or human rights laws. Australian equal opportunity tribunals, when first addressing these issues, appeared to realise that 'pregnant persons' were women. In one of our earliest, and arguably still most famous, discrimination cases, Deborah Wardley challenged Ansett Airlines' refusal to employ her as a pilot, arguing that it had breached the *Equal Opportunity Act* 1977 (Vic). The evidence included a letter from the General Manager of Ansett to the Secretary of the Women's Electoral Lobby which stated that:

   > We ... have adopted a policy of only employing men as pilots. This does not mean that women cannot be good pilots, but we are concerned with the provision of the safest and most efficient air service possible. In this regard we feel that an all male pilot crew is safer than one in which the sexes are mixed.

   The letter concludes:

   > I am sure you will be pleased to know that I have met Mrs Wardley and find her a very nice person, highly intelligent and undoubtedly a good pilot, but that is not quite what we are talking about.[32]

---

25 Krieger and Cooney, 'The Miller-Wohl Controversy', at 570-2.
26 See Finley, 'Transcending Equality Theory' at 1147-8; Scales, 'Towards a Feminist Jurisprudence' (1980-81) 56 *Indiana Law Journal* 375 at 427-35. And see Williams' refutation of this argument, 'Equality's Riddle', at 366-8.
27 *Geduldig v Aiello* 417 US 484 (1974).
28 Ann Scales, 'The Emergence of Feminist Jurisprudence: An Essay' (1986) 95 *Yale Law Journal* 1373 at 1399.
29 *Bliss v Attorney-General (Canada)* [1979] 1 SCR 183.
30 *Ibid*, at 190.
31 *Brooks v Canada Safeway Ltd, Allen et al v Canada Safeway Ltd; Women's Legal Education and Action Fund (LEAF), Intervener* [1989] 1 SCR 1219 at 1242, emphasis in original.
32 *Wardley v Ansett Transport Industries* (1984) EOC ¶92-002 at 75,260. The case was in fact decided in 1979, though not reported until 1984.

The Board found that what Ansett *was* talking about was excluding Ms Wardley because she indicated an intention to have children and therefore airline regulations would have required her to be out of the workforce for substantial periods of time. The Board accepted an argument, contrary to the earlier US and Canadian cases, that discrimination because of (potential) pregnancy was discrimination because of sex, that is, that Ms Wardley was a target of sex discrimination. Given that a requirement of the legislation was that discrimination against a woman could only occur if she was treated differently to a man who was 'in the same or similar circumstances', the Board in this decision clearly rejected the proposition that Wardley's capacity to become pregnant placed her in a materially different situation from that of a man.

This approach can be contrasted with that of a single judge of the Federal Court in *Mt Isa Mines*.[33] Davies J upheld a challenge by Mt Isa Mines to regulations on employment in the lead industry proposed by the National Occupational Health and Safety Commission (NOHSC). The lead industry had traditionally excluded women from employment on the basis of evidence suggesting that high levels of lead can interfere with reproductive capacity, and damage foetuses or breastfeeding babies.[34] The NOHSC had worked quite closely with the Human Rights and Equal Opportunity Commission to ensure that the regulations protected the safety of *all* workers, without discriminating against women. In *Mt Isa Mines*, without mentioning any case law, Davies J rejected the view that discrimination because of pregnancy, or potential to become pregnant, was discrimination against women. Instead, he decided that any attempt to exclude women from the lead industry would be 'discrimination on the basis of health', and therefore did not constitute unlawful discrimination. Specifically, he found that 'a woman who was seeking to become pregnant or a woman who was pregnant or a woman who was breastfeeding a child'[35] was not in the same or similar circumstances to a man in the lead industry. This appears to be quite contrary to the earlier decision made in *Wardley*. Indeed, this aspect of Davies J's decision was rejected by the Full Federal Court.[36]

Challenges by men to women-only programs

One persistent feature of equality jurisprudence in both Canada and the USA, where 'equality' is a right enshrined in their Constitutions, has been the use of these equality provisions by men to challenge what they argue is discrimination

---

33 *Mt Isa Mines v Marks* (1992) 35 FCR 96.
34 See Chris Winder and Neil Gunningham, 'Protective Legislation and Discrimination in Employment in the Australian Lead Industries: The Reproductive Effect of Inorganic Lead' (1988) 4 *Australian and New Zealand Journal of Occupational Health and Safety* 9. There is also evidence that men's reproductive health may be affected by exposure to lead: see *ibid*; and Sally Kenney, 'Reproductive Hazards in the Workplace: The Law and Sexual Difference' (1986) 14 *International Journal of the Sociology of Law* 393; and Sally Kenney, *For Whose Protection? Reproductive Hazards and Exclusionary Policies in the United States and Britain*, University of Michigan Press, Ann Arbor, 1992.
35 (1992) 35 FCR 96 at 103.
36 Although the appeal was dismissed on other grounds: *HREOC v Mt Isa Mines* (1993) 46 FCR 301 (per Black CJ at 307, per Lockhart J at 327).

against them.[37] This move has had its echo in Australia with some high-profile challenges under Australian equal opportunity laws to programs designed to redress discrimination against women.

In April 1989, the then Prime Minister announced the establishment of a National Women's Health Program. The ACT had two specific women's health initiatives, the Canberra Women's Health Centre which provided education and information, but no clinical services, and the Canberra Women's Health Service which provided clinical services on a part-time basis from two Canberra locations. In 1990, three men – Dr Proudfoot, Mr Smith and Dr Henderson challenged these women's health programs as discriminating against them and, indeed, against all men in the ACT.[38] They argued that the provision of these services was unlawful under the *Sex Discrimination Act* 1984 (Cth).

The model of equality relied on by the challengers is somewhat difficult to discern. It appears that their challenge was not to programs directed to services women need because of their 'distinctive physiology'.[39] Rather, Dr Proudfoot challenged any health service directed to only one sex, whilst Dr Henderson appeared to be complaining about the failure to direct sex-specific services to men or 'the alleged imbalance between the [health] services provided for women and those provided for men'.[40] Perhaps the complainants' approach can best be characterised as a strict equal treatment approach – unless the services provided to men are exactly the same as the services provided to women, then there is discrimination against men.

It was argued that the male complainants suffered no disadvantage because the ACT Board of Health provided a generalist medical service for women and men at eight locations in the ACT, where the waiting time for an appointment was considerably less than the six-week waiting period at the Women's Health Service. The Human Rights and Equal Opportunity Commission (HREOC) decided that the health care services provided especially for women *did* discriminate against men. Even if there were no detriment to the men, the mere denial of a benefit was enough to attract a finding of discrimination. Wilson P found that:

> [T]he mere fact that one person is refused a service while another person of a different sex is provided that service necessarily identifies less favourable treatment in respect of the provision of that service.[41]

If the provision of specialist women's health services constitutes discrimination against men, there appears to be an assumption that women and men are in the same situation. However, the Commission found that women and men were not in the same situation: women had particular needs that were not met by generalist health services because the model used in medical teaching and practice was a male one (presumably in part reliant on the nature of medical research) and because of the current unequal situation of women in relation to access to money, exposure to male violence and responsibility for children which had a direct effect on their health.[42] These findings did not lead to the conclusion that to provide 'special' services for women in order to redress these inequalities escaped the

---

37 See Gwen Brodsky and Shelagh Day, *Canadian Charter of Rights and Freedoms: One Step Forward or Two Steps Back?* Canadian Advisory Council on the Status of Women, Ontario, 1989.
38 *Proudfoot v ACT Board of Health* (1992) EOC ¶92-417.
39 Ibid, at 78,979.
40 Ibid.
41 Ibid.
42 Id, at 78,981-2 and 78,984.

label of discrimination. Instead it was decided that, in order to assess whether women and men were in 'circumstances that are the same or are not materially different' as required by the legislation, differences which were 'referable to gender', which arose from the mere fact of being a woman (or a man), had to be excluded.[43]

The Commission decided that this analysis was required because otherwise the provisions in the Act which allowed for 'special measures' to redress inequality would be irrelevant. And it went on to find that both women's health programs were exempt under these 'special measures' provision (under s 33 of the SDA they were services designed 'to ensure that persons of a particular sex have equal opportunities'). The clinical service was also exempt under s 31 as a service which could only be provided to members of one sex.

Notes

1. The Commission may well be technically correct, given the structure of the sex discrimination legislation, but is this the understanding of equality which should inform a more general understanding of equality in law? We are implying that the Commission should have adopted an understanding of equality that encompassed the context of inequality between women and men (in health services) when considering the threshold question of whether there was discrimination. However, there are clear dangers in such an analysis, dangers that the Commission recognised. The federal *Sex Discrimination Act 1984*, like the State equivalents, broadly defines direct discrimination as having occurred when women and men are treated differently in circumstances which are the same or not materially different. Our critique of the way this challenge to women-only programs was handled requires that a contextualised assessment of the actual needs of women and men should occur at the initial assessment of whether 'discrimination' has taken place, an analysis which would have found that there was no discrimination in the provision of women-only health services because of the inequalities in women's and men's health needs and the services provided. However, our analysis may not work so well when women are challenging discrimination against them. If we set up a hurdle requirement that discrimination does not occur unless men and women are in the same or similar circumstances, women are going to find it extremely difficult to mount a discrimination claim – they may never be in the same or similar circumstances as men.

   The early decision in the *Wardley v Ansett* case discussed earlier is a clear indication that Australian equal opportunity tribunals can recognise that a mere ability to become pregnant, and even an intention to do so, do not justify discriminating against women in employment situations. It would seem to follow from *Wardley* that taking account of biological difference does not mean that women and men cannot be found to be in the same or similar circumstances for the purposes of anti-discrimination laws. But the decision of the single judge of the Federal Court in *Mt Isa Mines*, also discussed above, suggests that such an understanding is not universal.

---

43 Wilson P stated: 'I therefore conclude that a difference to be material cannot be referable to the prohibited basis for less favourable treatment, namely sex. The purpose of s 5(1) is to identify less favourable treatment of one sex than the other in essentially the same circumstances, which circumstances are external to the question of sex' (*ibid*, at 79,980). This view was endorsed by the Full Federal Court in *HREOC v Mt Isa Mines* (1993) 46 FCR 301.

The *Sex Discrimination Act* 1984 (Cth) was amended in 1994 to provide that, if a person takes special measures in order to ensure equality between women and men, a person is taken not to have discriminated.[44] Does this adequately address the problem we have identified? Would it be more satisfactory to draft equal opportunity legislation that directly dealt with the issue of context within the basic meaning of 'discrimination'? Would the ALRC's approach to defining equality, noted earlier, more adequately address the problem?

2. While *Proudfoot* is probably the best known challenge to specific services designed to respond to women's needs, it is by no means the only one.[45] In *Ross v University of Melbourne*,[46] the Equal Opportunity Tribunal upheld a claim by two men[47] that they were Victorian unlawfully discriminated against by the University of Melbourne when it offered some five hours a week of women-only time in the Light Weight Room at the University's Sports Union. The University then had two weight rooms, known as the 'Main Weight Room' and the 'Light Weight Room'. In upholding the claim, the Tribunal found that, unless the two rooms had exactly the same equipment[48] and offered men similar exclusive access at the same times, they had been treated less favourably than women because of their sex. While Dr Gold wanted access to the Light Weight room at the time it was closed to him because he wanted access to the lighter equipment due to injury, Mr Ross did not in fact want to use the Light Weight Room, but participated in the case because he believed that the limitation on access discriminated against him.[49]

The University Union claimed that it was 'correct[ing] a disadvantage that women had experienced in accessibility [sic] to exercise facilities'.[50] The judgment notes briefly that the decision was made because women had experienced 'difficulties in access'. It will be recalled that the Commission in *Proudfoot* 'saved' women-only health services by finding that they fell within exemptions within the *Sex Discrimination Act* 1984 (Cth) – they were either services that could only be provided to persons of one sex or were designed to redress inequality. The Victorian *Equal Opportunity Act* 1984 contained some similar provisions, including s 39(b) which provided that:

---

44   Section 7D.
45   See also *Brennan v NSW Fire Brigades* (1996) EOC ¶92-845 (discrimination to refuse to allow a man to stand for election in the Spokeswoman's program); *Halliwell v Stephens* (1998) EOC ¶92-914 (discrimination to refuse entry to men to a lesbian nightclub); *K v Domestic Violence Crisis Service Inc* (1999) EOC ¶93-021 (possible discrimination by domestic violence crisis service in assumption that woman rather than man was victim of domestic violence); *Ware v Secretary, Commonwealth Department of Family and Community Services* (2000) EOC ¶93-093 (specific provisions in *Social Security Act* 1991 (Cth) allowing that certain age-related benefits be paid to women at the age of 60 and men not until the age of 65 did not offend *Sex Discrimination Act* 1984 (Cth) as the more specific provisions of the former Act overrode the more general provisions of the latter and there was a specific exemption from the operation of the SDA for the SSA).
46   *Ross v University of Melbourne* (1990) EOC ¶92-290.
47   Although originally there had been some 26 complainants.
48   It is unclear from the reported decision whether the two rooms had precisely the same equipment.
49   *Ibid*, at 77,933-4. Mr Ross's lack of interest in using the light weight room must raise serious questions about his standing to bring the complaint.
50   (1990) EOC ¶92-290 at 79,933.

This Act does not render unlawful: ...

(b) the exclusion of persons of one sex from participation in any sporting activity ...[51]

But the Tribunal found that s 39(b) did *not* justify women-only times in the Light Weight Room. According to the Tribunal, s 39(b) did not apply because what women were doing was not 'sport'. It was 'toning', 'rehabilitation' and 'general recreational use', or preparation for 'other' sporting activity.[52]

The Tribunal also refused to find that the women-only time was a bona fide plan or arrangement to reduce disadvantage.[53] According to the Tribunal, in order to attract the protection of this general affirmative action provision something more than mere closure of the Light Weight Room to men for the specified times was required:

> If, in fact, the respondent had conducted specially organised beginners classes in light weight lifting designed for women at a specific time, and had then undertaken a program to promote these to women within the university area, to encourage women to come along to these classes to learn to use weights, then it may be that this could be said to be a bona fide arrangement within sec 39(f). The mere fact that the rationale behind the closure was to increase the use of the Light Weight Room by women is not enough to constitute an appropriate arrangement pursuant to sec 39(f).[54]

Is it likely that women would not use the 'Main Weight Room' because it was seen as a male space? Given that there was evidence presented before the Tribunal that school girls dropped out of sport at a much greater rate than boys and that they do not receive their fair share of sporting resources,[55] could it be argued that the Tribunal ignored the context of the weight rooms and women's participation in weight training in deciding that a mere closure of the rooms to men at particular times was not an 'arrangement' designed to reduce disadvantage? What other arguments can you suggest to support the conclusion that the minimalist response of setting aside times for women-only use of the light weight room amounted to a bona fide plan to reduce the disadvantage of women? What (or whose) notion of 'sport' is contained in the Tribunal's findings?

3. It will be recalled that in *Proudfoot* the women-only clinical service was exempt from the operation of the SDA because it was a service that could

---

51 This exemption was itself subject to a series of exceptions: the coaching (s 39(b)(i)) or administration (s 39(b)(ii)) of any sporting activity or any prescribed sporting activity (s 39(b)(iii)). No sporting activities have been prescribed for the purposes of the Act. See now *Equal Opportunity Act* 1995 (Vic) s 66(1).

52 (1990) EOC ¶92-290 at 77,935. The Tribunal also relied on the Victorian Supreme Court's decision in *Mayor, Councillors and Citizens of the City of Moe v Pulis* (1988) EOC ¶92-243 where it rejected a Friday evening women-only swimming time. In order to accommodate the numbers of women who attended and given the visibility of the pool to the rest of the sporting arena, the men's change rooms were utilised and men were effectively excluded from the whole of the Moe Council's sporting complex for one evening. The court held that, because men were not just excluded from a sporting activity but from a place, this was an exclusion not covered by the legislative exemption.

53 Section 39(f), while arguably drawn more narrowly than the equivalent provision in the Commonwealth legislation, stated: 'This Act does not render unlawful ... (f) the exclusion of any person from a bona fide programme, plan or arrangement designed to prevent or reduce disadvantage suffered by a particular class or disadvantaged person'.

54 (1990) EOC ¶92-290 at 77,936.

55 This was argued before the Tribunal, but no formal findings were made (*ibid*, at 77,934).

only be provided to members of one sex (see s 32). This section was used in 2000 by the Australian Catholic Bishops Conference to argue that infertility treatment services were not governed by the SDA as they were services that could only be provided to women.[56] This argument was rejected by Sundberg J in the Federal Court:

> [T]he nature of these treatments is such that they are capable of being provided to both sexes. The service is the "treatment procedure" – the artificial insemination of a woman with sperm from a man who is not her husband, or a fertilisation procedure. The reason for undertaking either of these procedures may be because of some physical feature of a man or a woman. ... The fact that for biological reasons the embryo is placed in the body of a woman is but the ultimate aspect of the procedure.[57]

If the Catholic Church's argument had been successful, it would have had the effect of removing infertility treatment services from the purview of the Act, thus allowing continuing discrimination against lesbians and single women wanting access to assisted reproductive services.[58]

4. In recommending that the Commonwealth should enact an Equality Act, the majority of the ALRC recommended that the Act should ensure the equality of both women and men: 'Although the main objective of the Equality Act should be to advance women's equality, the very nature of equality is that it includes everyone, women and men. It should not be guaranteed for women alone'.[59] By contrast, the minority[60] argued that the Commonwealth Parliament should enact a Status of Women Act. This would be expressly directed toward ensuring the equality of women:

> 16.23 ... One way to respond to ... gender bias in our legal system is to propose the creation of a legislative guarantee of women's equality. This would have greatest impact if it clearly defined the problem to be dealt with: women's inequality in the legal system. It would make a strong symbolic statement about the imbalanced nature of the legal system and the government's determination to redress it. Practically, it would provide a remedy for women in particular cases of inequality.
>
> 16.24 *Consistency with the subordination approach.* Legislation that unequivocally recognises that the central issue in gender equality is the power imbalance between women and men, rather than mere differences between them, is most consistent with the subordination approach to equality outlined ... [above].
>
> 16.25 *The importance of accurate naming.* If the problem of women's lack of equality in law is recognised by name in the title and body of the legislation, we not only accurately label the problem but allow it to be properly addressed. Naming a problem accurately assists in its resolution. For example, the development of a legal remedy for sexual harassment contributes to the recognition of the problem, in the community discussion of what the problem was, and in the development of both legal and non-legal strategies to address it. As has been pointed out, 'sexual harassment, the event, is not new to women. It is the law of injuries that it is new to' [MacKinnon, *Feminism Unmodified*, at 103]. In our view, the identification

---

56 *McBain v Victoria* [2000] FCA 1009.
57 *Ibid*, at [15].
58 This issue is discussed in more detail in Chapter 8, including the attempt to change the SDA in order to allow such discrimination.
59 ALRC, *Equality Before the Law: Women's Equality*, at para 4.28.
60 Hilary Charlesworth, Regina Graycar and Jenny Morgan.

of the problem of inequality for women in the law will increase our capacity to address it.

16.26 *Other forms of discrimination experienced by men.* While men may be discriminated against in some circumstances, this is in almost all cases not because of their gender or sex, but because of some other characteristic that manifests disadvantage in our society. For example, Aboriginal men are disproportionately likely to be imprisoned. However, this is not because they are men – as is demonstrated, if by nothing else, by the fact that Aboriginal women are also much more likely than white women to be imprisoned – but because of their race.

16.27 *Existing remedies available.* To the limited extent that men are discriminated against because of their sex (rather than, say, their race or their disability), they are able to make a claim under the Sex Discrimination Act (SDA). Although the ALRC has suggested in Final Report Part 1 that this Act embodies only a limited understanding of equality, and applies in limited areas (largely the so-called public spheres of work, accommodation, provision of goods and services), the ALRC argued that it remains an important tool for individuals to pursue claims of discrimination. Some of these individuals will be men.

16.28 Indeed, if a gender-neutral approach is to be pursued, as the majority recommends, it would seem more appropriate to amend the Sex Discrimination Act (SDA), rather than to introduce new legislation. This could contain the new, contextualised definition of equality, and further efforts could be made to remove or appropriately limit the exemptions under that Act. However, if our focus is on women's inequality, we need a different, more specific, legislative response.

16.29 *Consistency with international obligations.* Women's experience of inequality in law has been recognised by the international community. CEDAW was adopted in recognition of the fact that women's interests could not be dealt with without especially drawing attention to them. Articles 2 and 26 of the International Covenant on Civil and Political Rights (ICCPR) deal with non-discrimination on the basis of sex, but, as the preamble to CEDAW makes clear, they have not been adequate to address women's inequality. CEDAW, then, is a recognition of the particular nature of discrimination against women. The success of the Convention is based on its sex-specificity; its force would be totally dissipated if it were gender-blind or gender-neutral. The majority of the Commission recognise that CEDAW was designed to respond to 'the specific problem of women's inequality and discrimination against women'. However, they note that it was enacted in the context of a general (and gender-neutral or gender-inclusive) recognition of equal rights contained in the ICCPR. In our view, Australia is in a precisely parallel situation. As noted above, the SDA gives a cause of action to both women and men who have been discriminated against because of their sex. In our view, it is now appropriate to have an equality right directed solely to women; to those people in our society who are overwhelmingly more likely to experience inequality because of their sex than men.

16.30 *An unnecessary additional platform for challenges to women's programs.* One disadvantage of a gender-neutral Act, applying equally to women and men, is that it would allow and indeed encourage further legal challenges to women-only programs or services that were designed in order to address some of the well-documented legal disadvantages experienced by women.

16.31 ***A women-only Act is likely to be interpreted broadly.*** It is argued by the majority of the Commission that a women-only equality guarantee could lead to 'a limited and narrow interpretation of equality'. It is difficult to find evidence for this proposition. The risk that a women-only guarantee would be interpreted narrowly seems no greater a risk than that a gender-neutral Act would be used to attack programs designed to redress women's disadvantage.

16.32 ***Gender-neutral provisions do not necessarily work for women.*** The majority of the Commission argue that sex-based distinctions do not necessarily work in favour of women. We cannot disagree. But we can equally assert that gender-neutral provisions also do not necessarily work for women. The 'persons cases' illustrate well how gender-neutral provisions can be interpreted in ways that do not benefit women. Earlier this century, a series of cases involved attempts by women to participate in a variety of forms of public activity such as the professions (including law) and their entitlement to be elected to public office. In Western Australia, for example, the *Legal Practitioners Act* 1893 entitled a 'person' to apply to be admitted to legal practice. But when Edith Haynes applied to be admitted to practice, after passing her examination in 1904 (and serving a period of time as an articled clerk, with the permission of the Barristers Board), that board refused to admit her. She then applied for a writ of mandamus to compel the Board to do so but the WA Supreme Court decided that she was not a 'person' within the meaning of the Act. [*In re Edith Haynes* (1904) 6 WAR 209] And, ... much of the gender bias that still exists in law arises from (or under) gender-neutral provisions. In any event, the proposed Status of Women Act bears no resemblance to sex-based distinctions that were designed to exclude women.

16.33 ***Will women intervening in 'men's cases' be of use to women?*** It is argued by the majority that the Women's Legal Education and Action Fund (LEAF), a Canadian feminist litigation organisation, was able to intervene in *Andrews*, the case in which the Supreme Court of Canada developed a contextualised understanding of equality. The Court relied on LEAF's argument, and the majority suggests that this demonstrates the value of a generally applicable equality guarantee. As the majority notes, *Andrews* was not a case about sex discrimination or discrimination against men on the ground of sex. Rather, it was a case about discrimination on the ground of citizenship/residence. A feminist litigation organisation in Australia, provided it was granted standing, could as easily intervene in such a case whether there was a gendered or a gender-neutral Act. Indeed, under an equality guarantee that applies to men as well as women, such organisations may well be required to intervene in 'men's cases' to defend programs specifically designed to redress women's disadvantage.

16.34 ***Who can use a Status of Women Act?*** The majority of the Commission state that '[i]f men could not make direct use of an equality guarantee, they would be less likely to advocate for equality for women'. We disagree. As we have argued above, naming the problem – that women, because of their sex, experience inequality – on the face of any equality guarantee is more likely to lead to an increased recognition of the real harm to which the legislation is addressed, and therefore lead both women and men to advocate for women's equality. Under our proposed legislation, men or groups of men, provided they were concerned with equality for women, would have standing in the same way that women or groups of women would have standing.

What other arguments could be used to support, or criticise, an Act that enshrined equality for women only? How likely is it that the federal government would enact a Status of Women Act that could be used by women only? Should a law reform commission, in formulating its recommendations, take into account the political likelihood of those recommendations being adopted by the government of the day?

5. In 1994, the President of South Africa, Nelson Mandela, declared a remission of sentence for all mothers in prison who had children under the age of 12 who were in prison on the date of his inauguration, 10 May 1994. This declaration was challenged by a male prisoner, whose wife had died and who had a child under 12. He argued that this unfairly discriminated against him on the ground of his sex or gender (and against his son) and was therefore unconstitutional.[61]

O'Regan J, concurring with the majority decision which upheld the remissions program, stated:

> I ... see no reason to doubt that as a matter of fact in South African society, mothers not only bear a considerably greater proportion of the burdens of child rearing than fathers, but also that mothers, as a general rule, do have a special role in relation to the nurturing and care of children. There are, of course, some fathers who share fully in the responsibility of child rearing.
>
> The responsibility borne by mothers for the care of children is a major cause of inequality in our society. Being responsible for the rearing of children is a great privilege, but also a great strain. Many women rear children single-handedly with no help, financial or otherwise, from the fathers of the children. The need to support children financially is one of the reasons for women seeking work outside the home. However the responsibility for child rearing is also one of the factors that renders women less competitive and less successful in the labour market. The unequal division of labour between fathers and mothers is therefore a primary source of women's disadvantage in our society.
>
> ... Even where discrimination in a particular case arises from reliance upon a stereotype or generalisation, the focus of the section 8(2) determination must remain whether the impact of the discrimination was unfair.
>
> To determine whether the discrimination is unfair it is necessary to recognise that although the long-term goal of our constitutional order is equal treatment, insisting upon equal treatment in circumstances of established inequality may well result in the entrenchment of that inequality. There are at least two factors relevant to the determination of unfairness: it is necessary to look at the group or groups which have suffered discrimination in the particular case and at the effect of the discrimination on the interests of those concerned. The more vulnerable the group adversely affected by the discrimination, the more likely the discrimination will be held to be unfair. Similarly, the more invasive the

---

61 *President of the Republic of South Africa v Hugo* (1997) 4 SALR 1 (Constitutional Court of South Africa). Section 8(1) of the interim Constitution provided that 'every person shall have the right to equality before the law and to equal protection of the law'. Section 8(2) provided that 'no person shall be unfairly discriminated against, ... on one or more of the following grounds ... : race, gender, sex, ethnic or social origin, colour, sexual orientation, age, disability, religion, conscience, belief, culture or language'. Section 8(3) further provided that 'this section shall not preclude measures designed to achieve the adequate protection and advancement of persons or groups or categories of persons disadvantaged by unfair discrimination, in order to enable their full and equal enjoyment of all rights and freedoms'.

nature of the discrimination upon the interests of the individuals affected by the discrimination, the more likely it will be held to be unfair. In determining the effect of the discrimination, the reasons given by the agency responsible for the discrimination, will be only of indirect relevance. However, should the discrimination in any particular case be held to be unfair, the reason for the discriminatory act may well be central to an investigation into whether the discrimination is nevertheless justified ....

In this case, mothers have been afforded an advantage on the basis of a proposition that is generally speaking true. There is no doubt that the goal of equality entrenched in our constitution would be better served if the responsibilities for child rearing were more fairly shared between fathers and mothers. The simple fact of the matter is that at present they are not. Nor are they more likely to be more evenly shared in the near future. For the moment, then, and for some time to come, mothers are going to carry greater burdens than fathers in the rearing of children. We cannot ignore this crucial fact in considering the impact of the discrimination in this case. With respect, therefore, I cannot agree with Kriegler J [*one of the dissenting judges in the case*] that it is a "profound and troubling" disadvantage for women when the President says that mothers play a special role in nurturing children. The profound disadvantage lies not in the President's statement, but in the social fact of the role played by mothers in child rearing and, more particularly, in the inequality which results from it. Putting an end to that inequality is a major challenge for our society. There can be no doubt that where reliance upon the generalisation results in greater disadvantages for mothers, it would almost without question constitute unfair discrimination. On the other hand, were we to establish the rigid rule proposed by Kriegler J that reliance upon that generalisation even to afford some advantage to mothers, except in very narrow circumstances, be unfair, we may well make the task of achieving the equality desired by the Constitution more difficult. On the facts of this case, I conclude that the President's reliance upon the fact of women's greater share of child rearing responsibilities in order to afford an advantage to some women has not caused any significant harm to other women.[62]

Is O'Regan J's judgment an example of adopting a subordination approach to inequality? Does it successfully negotiate the conflict between the entrenchment of inequality and the process of change?

The 'presumption of advancement'

Although equality issues may seem most obviously raised in anti-discrimination laws, or by way of constitutional challenge in jurisdictions with Bills of Rights, in fact understandings of equality are central to a wide variety of legal situations. The following example concerns the rules developed to determine ownership of a piece of real property. Generally, it is presumed that parties intended to hold property in proportion to their respective financial contributions. However, the general rule that financial contribution determines ownership (a presumption of resulting trust) can be displaced by the 'presumption of advancement'. The presumption of advancement assumes that certain transactions are intended as gifts, although this presumption can be rebutted with evidence that no such gift was intended. The presumption has traditionally applied to contributions by husbands and fathers to

---

62   *Ibid*, at paras 109-13.

property in the name of their wives or children; that is, even though, say, a father has paid for a particular piece of property which is in his daughter's name, the presumption that the property belongs to the father because he paid for it is displaced by a presumption that the father intended to advantage the daughter. She is then the real (or beneficial) owner. This presumption can be rebutted by evidence that the father really meant to continue as owner. This 'presumption of advancement' did not traditionally apply to gifts from mothers to their children (or wives to their husbands). In *Brown v Brown*,[63] the NSW Court of Appeal held unanimously that the presumption should now also be applied where a mother makes a contribution to property in the name of her children (although a majority held that the presumption was rebutted on the facts in that case). Should the presumption apply in exactly the same way to mothers and wives as it applies in relation to fathers and husbands?

Lisa Sarmas, 'A Step in the Wrong Direction: The Emergence of Gender "Neutrality" in the Equitable Presumption of Advancement'
(1994) 19 *Melbourne University Law Review* 758

[759] The rationale underlying the Court's decision was based on the notion that women and men are 'equal', and that the application of different presumptions merely on the basis of gender is therefore inappropriate. ...

[761] *BROWN v BROWN*: TOWARDS A GENDER 'NEUTRAL' PRESUMPTION OF ADVANCEMENT

In 1958 Mrs Alice Brown contributed approximately half of the purchase price of a property in Gladesville. The legal title was put into the joint names of her two adult sons, who contributed the rest of the funds. Mrs Brown also had two daughters.

Mrs Brown and three of the children moved into the house at Gladesville. When two of the children eventually moved out, she remained there with her son, Jack, and his family until she moved to a nursing home in 1987.

In 1990 Mrs Brown commenced proceedings seeking a declaration that she had a beneficial interest in the Gladesville property. She claimed that the sons held the Gladesville land on resulting trust for herself and themselves in proportion to their respective contributions to the purchase price. She died during the course of the trial. Her daughters were the beneficiaries under her will.

There was some dispute as to the nature of the arrangements with respect to the purchase of the property in 1958. The sons claimed that there was an oral agreement that in return for her contribution to the purchase price, Mrs Brown was entitled to live in the house rent and rate free for the rest of her life. They also gave contradictory evidence suggesting that her contribution was a loan. They claimed that there was no intention that she was to have a beneficial interest in the property.

Mrs Brown claimed that before 1987 she did not even know that her name was not on the title to the property, and that she never agreed that she would have no interest in it. Her evidence was given in affidavits because she was not well enough to attend the hearing. As a result she was not available for cross-examination.

The trial judge, Bryson J, decided the case in her favour on the basis of the presumption of resulting trust. His Honour found that there was no agreement made in 1958 about the terms on which the property was to be held. He accepted

---

63 *Brown v Brown* (1993) 31 NSWLR 582.

Mrs Brown's evidence that she did not intend to make a gift or loan of her contribution.

... [762] The sons appealed, and the appeal was dismissed by a majority in the New South Wales Court of Appeal (Gleeson CJ and Cripps JA, Kirby P dissenting). ...

[*Gleeson CJ concluded that the presumption of advancement should apply to mothers as well as fathers:*]

> In the social and economic conditions which apply at the present time the drawing of a rigid distinction between male and female parents, for the purposes of the application of the presumptions of equity with which we are concerned, may be accepted to be inappropriate. I would be prepared, although with rather less conviction, to say the same about conditions in 1958. I would, therefore, not decide this case upon the basis that, Mrs Brown being a mother rather than a father, the presumption of advancement did not apply [(1993) 31 NSWLR 582 at 591].

His Honour found, however, that any presumption of advancement was rebutted by 'the facts as found by Bryson J, and the objective circumstances':

> [Bryson J] found that Mrs Brown did not intend to make a gift (or a loan) to her sons. Moreover, where a widowed mother, of modest means, makes a payment of substantially the whole of her assets to contribute to the purchase of real estate, and legal title to the real estate is vested in her adult, able-bodied sons, the facts seem to me to point against an intention of advancement. Mrs Brown had no moral obligation to make such provision for her sons at the expense of her estate [*ibid*].

Kirby P preferred the approach of Murphy J in *Calverley v Green* [(1984) 155 CLR 242], that is, that the presumptions be abolished altogether. His Honour considered himself bound, however, to follow the majority in that case and apply the relevant presumptions. In so doing, he went even further than Gleeson CJ in advocating a gender 'neutral' presumption of advancement. In contrast to Gleeson CJ's negatively expressed formulation ... Kirby P positively affirmed the application of the presumption to 'gifts' by mothers and also extended its application to 'gifts' by wives:

> I would have no hesitation in supporting the principle that the presumption of advancement, if it is still to be applied, must be applied equally to gifts by [763] mothers and wives as by fathers and husbands [*ibid*, at 598-9].

His Honour examined the relevant case law and concluded that there was no binding authority dictating that the presumptions be applied in a gender-specific way. His Honour stated that:

> [A] compelling reason for releasing the presumption of advancement from its earlier gender-based discrimination ... [is that] it should be grounded not in the gender of the parties ... but in the relationship which exists between them [*ibid*, at 598].

He also noted that there were reasons of legal principle and legal policy for 'terminating the gender distinction accepted by earlier judges'. These included:

> [T]he general desirability that the law should not be expressed in terms which differentiate between people on the ground of their gender unless the differentiation is firmly based upon rational grounds supported by fact, not mere prejudice, stereotype or history received from earlier times when attitudes to women were different [*ibid*, at 599]. ...

The Court's approach to the issue was based on the supposed 'equality' between women and men which apparently necessitated 'equal' or 'identical' treatment before the law. Kirby P thought that such 'equality' had come about sufficiently by 1958 to make distinctions in respect of gifts [by mothers and fathers] completely unacceptable. Moreover, his Honour invoked the principles of 'gender neutrality' and 'equality' to thwart the respondents' argument that the distinction should be maintained on the basis that it is favourable to women:

> It is true that the principle of gender neutral application of the law will normally [764] involve the removal of legal rules which have disadvantaged women ... However, it would be an impermissible approach to the development of either common law or equitable principle to accept the removal of stereotypes only where this resulted in advantages to women ... In the operation of the presumptions, so long as they endure, their content should be, and is, gender neutral. In this respect, the rules reflect the egalitarian nature of modern Australian society, including as between the sexes [*ibid*, at 600].

Notes

1. Sarmas is critical of both a 'sameness' and a 'difference' approach to the resolution of the legal issues in *Brown v Brown*. She argues that the traditional approach of not applying the presumption of advancement to mothers but only to fathers (a 'difference' approach) assumes not only that the legal obligations of each are different when they are not, but seems to assume 'that a mother is less likely than a father to intend to make a gift of property to her children. This approach devalues the role of mothering by failing to acknowledge the substantial contribution women make as providers for children'.[64] Assuming sameness (that mothers and fathers should be treated in the same way), Sarmas argues, does at least recognise that women do financially contribute to their families and 'works against the stereotype of women as dependent wives and mothers'.[65] However, she argues such an approach has other problems. Sarmas is particularly critical of Kirby P's approach which rejects the relevance of the practical effects of his decision. She argues instead that:

   > In the context of women's disadvantaged economic position relative to men, any change that contributes to their further dispossession should be viewed with suspicion. This is particularly so in the case of property dealings between wives and husbands, where legal title is often placed in the husband's name for reasons associated with traditional notions about the man's role as the head of the family.[66]

   Can you suggest any justifications for Kirby P's approach?
2. Sarmas also emphasises the importance of considering relationships outside the traditional nuclear family in the context of the extension of the 'presumption of advancement' to mothers (and wives). If the rationale for the presumption is some observed pattern of altruism, why does this same presumption not apply to same-sex couples, close friendships or heterosexual de facto relationships?
3. Sarmas argues that '[w]hat is needed in this area of the law is not 'different' treatment nor gender 'neutrality' but an approach which does not disadvantage women or privilege a particular family form'.[67] She considers and rejects as inadequate the mere abolition of all presumptions. Why might she consider this

---

64 Lisa Sarmas, 'A Step in the Wrong Direction: The Emergence of Gender 'Neutrality' in the Equitable Presumption of Advancement' (1994) 19 *Melbourne University Law Review* 758 at 764.
65 *Ibid*.
66 *Ibid*, at 765.
67 *Ibid*, at 766.

an inadequate response? Are women more likely to be viewed as acting altruistically (thus as more giving) than men are, if presumptions are abandoned?[68] Should we treat payments by women to their husbands differently to payments by mothers for the benefit of their children?[69]

Equality for whom? Differences amongst women

Probably the most profound critique of understandings of equality in feminist legal theory has come from women of colour, especially in North America. A particular target of this critique has been the work of Catharine MacKinnon. For example, Angela Harris suggests that MacKinnon's work, 'though powerful and brilliant in many ways',

> relies on what I call gender essentialism – the notion that a unitary, "essential" women's experience can be isolated and described independently of race, class, sexual orientation, and other realities of experience. The result of this tendency towards gender essentialism ... is not only that some voices are silenced in order to privilege others (for this is an inevitable result of categorization, which is necessary both for human communication and political movement), but that the voices that are silenced turn out to be the same voices silenced by the mainstream legal voice of "We the People" – among them, the voices of black women.[70]

Harris was concerned that, where black women were included in the work of MacKinnon and other white feminist legal scholars, 'black women become white women only more so'.[71] That is, it was implied that disadvantages could be added together – the disadvantage becomes the sum of being black and a woman.

> The result of essentialism is to reduce the lives of people who experience multiple forms of oppression to addition problems: "racism + sexism = straight black women's experience" or "racism + sexism + homophobia = black lesbian experience" [Deborah K King, 'Multiple Jeopardy, Multiple Consciousness: The Context of a Black Feminist Ideology' (1988) 14 *Signs* 42, at 51]. Thus, in an essentialist world, black women's experience will always be forcibly fragmented before being subjected to analysis as those who are "only interested in race" and those who are "only interested in gender" take their separate slices of our lives.[72]

Or in Grillo's words:

> Race and class can never be just "subtracted" because they are in ways inextricable from gender. The attempt to subtract race and class elevates white, middle-class experience into the norm, making the prototypical experience. As Elizabeth Spelman says ... such essentialism "makes the participation of other

---

68 See *Bryson v Bryant* (1992) 29 NSWLR 188.
69 See *National Australia Bank v Maher* [1995] 1 VR 318; and compare *Nelson v Nelson* (1995) 70 ALJR 47.
70 Angela Harris, 'Race and Essentialism in Feminist Legal Theory' (1990) 42 *Stanford Law Review* 581 at 585. Or in Trina Grillo's words, 'An essentialist outlook assumes that the experience of being a member of the group under discussion is a stable one, one with a clear meaning, a meaning constant through time, space, and different historical, social, political, and personal contexts': Trina Grillo, 'Anti-Essentialism and Intersectionality: Tools to Dismantle the Master's House' (1995) 10 *Berkeley Women's Law Journal* 16 at 19.
71 Harris, 'Race and Essentialism', at 595.
72 *Ibid*, at 588-9. Harris also cites the expressively titled chapter of Elizabeth Spelman's 'Gender & Race: The Ampersand Problem in Feminist Thought': Elizabeth V Spelman, *Inessential Women: Problems of Exclusion in Feminist Thought*, Beacon Press, Boston, 1988.

women inessential to the production of the story. How lovely: the many turn out to be one and the one that they are is me." [*Inessential Women*, at 159].[73]

Harris applies her analysis to feminist examinations of rape, central to MacKinnon's work and that of other feminist legal theorists and activists. When the history of rape in the US is considered, Harris notes that black women were 'uniquely vulnerable' to sexual abuse in their work in the homes of white men (and women) and slaves were legally unrapeable. Furthermore, 'for black people, male and female, "rape" signified the terrorism of black men by white men, aided and abetted, passively (by silence) or actively (by "crying rape"), by white women'.[74] She argues that if this history is not part of the analysis of rape law, there is a failure to understand the rape of African-America women.

Larissa Behrendt makes a similar point for Australian indigenous women:

> Writers like MacKinnon are telling Aboriginal women not to see what they see: that their position in society is defined by their gender rather than their race, that the push for rights by white women will empower black women, that we are aligned with white women in the battle against oppression and that white women are as oppressed as we are. We do not believe any of these white lies. The experiences of black women are trivialised when viewed as merely an extension of the experiences of white women.
>
> MacKinnon speaks the truth when she says that it is because men treat us differently that we know what it means to be a woman. In the same way, it is because the white dominant culture treats us differently, that we know what it means to be an Aborigine. The fact that we can feel our Aboriginality more strongly than our gender is a reflection that the repercussions of racism in Australia are often greater than those of sexism. ...
>
> Aboriginal women and non-Aboriginal women in Australia do not have a shared experience. This is due to a potent combination of racism and sexism in the lives of black women.
>
> Aboriginal women feel excluded from the women's movement because it is concerned only with the struggle for power between white men and white women. Its goals are not those of Aboriginal women and gains made by the women's movement have rarely trickled down to benefit Aboriginal women. Aboriginal women are in a position where they need to create their own organisations and political strategies rather than work within white women's organisations to attempt to improve their position in society.
>
> MacKinnon and other white feminists see the world in terms of "male" and "female" and the struggle for power fought only between these two spheres. But the world is also divided into "white" and "black", "indigenous" and "non-indigenous", "rich" and "poor", "heterosexual" and "homosexual". The failure of the feminist movement to meet the needs of minority women shows that just as men in our society will never know what it is like to be a woman, a white woman will never know the reality of living as a black woman.[75]

Many activists and scholars, overseas and in Australia, have echoed these concerns.[76] The critique which started with the concern that MacKinnon's work, in

---

73 Trina Grillo, 'Anti-Essentialism and Intersectionality', at 19.
74 Harris, 'Race and Essentialism', at 599.
75 Larissa Behrendt, 'Aboriginal Women and the White Lies of the Feminist Movement: Implications for Aboriginal Women in Rights Discourses' (1993) 1 *Australian Feminist Law Journal* 27 at 41-4.
76 See, for some Australian examples, Jackie Huggins, 'A Contemporary View of Aboriginal Women's Relationship to the White Women's Movement' in Norma Grieve and Ailsa Burns (eds), *Australian Women: Contemporary Feminist Thought*, Oxford University Press, Melbourne, 1994; and Aileen Moreton-Robinson, *Talking Up to the White Woman: Indigenous Women and Feminism*, University of Queensland Press, Brisbane, 2000.

its focus on gender, neglected race has extended to a broader critique of the essential category 'woman'. For example, lesbian legal scholars have questioned the presumptions of heterosexuality in much feminist legal theory[77] and similar concerns have been raised about issues of ethnicity, class and disability.[78] Some of these concerns are evident in Sarmas' work on the presumption of advancement discussed above.

Notes

1. One area in which the equality claims of 'minority' women have been dealt with – or might be thought to be dealt with – is anti-discrimination law. These laws proscribe discrimination on a series of grounds – for example, sex, race or disability. What happens when someone is discriminated against because of, say, both her race and her sex? In 1989, Kimberlé Crenshaw, a US legal scholar, argued that in 'race discrimination cases, discrimination tends to be viewed in terms of sex- or class-privileged Blacks; in sex discrimination cases, the focus is on race- and class-privileged women'.[79]

   Through a careful analysis of a series of cases involving African-American women, Crenshaw demonstrates how they lost discrimination cases because courts found it impossible to say that they were victims of race discrimination (that is, white people/women would not be treated that way) or sex discrimination (men, white or African-American would not be treated that way). Her point was that the law as presently structured was unable to comprehend a situation where a woman was discriminated against because of her race and sex.

   Crenshaw describes African-American women's experience as one of 'intersectionality', that is, their experience is at the intersection of a number of categories of experience. This analysis can be contrasted with an approach which recognises that Black women may have a different

---

77   See Ruthann Robson, 'Lesbian Jurisprudence?' (1990) 8 *Law and Inequality* 443: 'Feminist jurisprudence certainly has failed to incorporate lesbian visions, and to that extent it is heterosexist' (at 448); and Ruthann Robson, *Lesbian (Out)Law: Survival Under the Rule of Law*, Firebrand Books, Ithaca, New York, 1992 and *Sappho Goes to Law School: Fragments in Lesbian Legal Theory*, Columbia University Press, New York, 1998; Didi Herman and Carl Stychin (eds), *Legal Inversions: Lesbians, Gay Men and the Politics of Law*, Temple University Press, Philadelphia, 1995; Carl Stychin and Didi Herman (eds), *Sexuality in the Legal Arena*, Athlone Press, London, 2000.

78   See, for example, Elizabeth V Spelman, *Inessential Women: Problems of Exclusion in Feminist Thought*, Beacon Press, Boston, 1988; Michele Barrett, *Women's Oppression Today: Problems in Marxist Feminist Analysis*, Verso, London, 1986; Jan Pettman, *Living in the Margins: Racism, Sexism and Feminism in Australia*, Allen and Unwin, Sydney, 1992; Ruthann Robson, 'To Market, To Market: Considering Class in the Context of Lesbian Legal Reforms' (1995) 5 *Review of Law and Women's Studies* 173; Ruth Fincher, 'Women, immigration and the state: Issues of social difference and justice' in Anne Edwards and Susan Magarey (eds), *Women in a Restructuring Australia: Work and Welfare*, Allen and Unwin, Sydney, 1995; cf Susan Boyd, 'Family, Law and Sexuality: Feminist Engagements' (1999) 8 *Social and Legal Studies* 369.

79   Kimberlé Crenshaw, 'Demarginalizing the Intersection of Race and Sex: A Black Feminist Critique of Antidiscrimination Doctrine, Feminist Theory and Antiracist Politics' [1989] *University of Chicago Legal Forum* 139 at 140, reprinted in Frances E Olsen (ed), *Feminist Legal Theory I: Foundations and Outlooks*, Dartmouth, Aldershot, 1995, at 443. See also Kimberlé Crenshaw, 'Mapping the Margins: Identity Politics, Intersectionality, and Violence Against Women' (1991) 43 *Stanford Law Review* 1241.

experience (of discrimination) to that of white women, but sees this as a matter of addition – what Harris described, as noted above, as 'white women only more so'. Lise Gotell has been critical of early work by Canada's LEAF (Women's Legal Education and Action Fund) for adopting this sort of additive approach:

> LEAF has acknowledged particularity; but this does not mean a rejection of the notion that all women share an essential experience of subordination. Instead, LEAF has articulated the issue of differences through a discourse of 'double disadvantage': '... in addition to being disadvantaged by sex, women are also subject to discrimination on the basis of race, religion, material, status, age, disability, sexual orientation, economic status or other grounds' [Gotell here is quoting from *LEAF: Litigation Works: A Report on LEAF Litigation Year Two*, Toronto, 1987]. In many ways, this discourse of double disadvantage is deceptive. While appearing to acknowledge the complex condition of women's lives, it in fact stresses commonality. Although 'double disadvantage' allows for some differences among women of different classes, races, sexual orientation and so on, it construes these as subsidiary to more basic similarities.[80]

Do you think seeing particularity as intersectional rather than additive would change the agenda of feminist legal work in other ways? How likely is it that legal discourses will develop effective ways to respond to intersectional disadvantage?

2. Nitya Duclos (Iyer), in response to Crenshaw's article, examined the adequacy of the Canadian human rights jurisdiction's treatment of racial minority women.[81] She examined all Canadian cases of race or sex discrimination in a 10-year period and noted that it was often extremely difficult to identify complaints from minority women and rather than an exclusion of their claims, as Crenshaw found, 'there ... [was] little realization that racial minority women even exist as a group'.[82]

She concluded:

> The most fundamental error in current antidiscrimination jurisprudence lies in its location of difference in the individual complainant rather than in his or her relationship with others. It treats difference as an intrinsic characteristic of the individual – the discrimination is due to his or her race or sex – rather than as arising out of the relationship between that individual and others. ... The possibility that the dominant group and its institutions are as much a cause of discrimination by their determination of who is labelled different and who is not, is ignored.[83]

---

80 Lise Gotell, 'Litigating Feminist 'Truth': An Antifoundational Critique' (1995) 4 *Social and Legal Studies* 99 at 112.
81 Nitya Duclos, 'Disappearing Women: Racial Minority Women in Human Rights Cases' (1993) 6 *Canadian Journal of Women and the Law* 25. This was reprinted, under the name Nitya Iyer, in Sanda Rodgers and Caroline Andrew (eds), *Women and the Canadian State*, McGill/Queens University Press, Montreal, 1996, at 241.
82 Nitya Duclos, 'Disappearing Women' (1993) 6 *Canadian Journal of Women and the Law* 25 at 30.
83 *Ibid*, at 47.

It is similarly difficult in Australia to trace instances of intersectional discrimination.[84] There are certainly cases where a complainant has alleged both race and sex discrimination and these allegations have been treated separately (see, for example, *Djokic v Sinclair*,[85] discussed in Chapter 12), and cases where race *or* sex discrimination was alleged but the intersectional nature of that experience was ignored.[86] However, in *Fares v Box Hill College of TAFE*,[87] Fares successfully alleged that she was discriminated against because she was a non-English speaking background (NESB) woman, described as discrimination on the grounds of sex and ethnicity.[88] Fares worked as a teacher in the Clothing Industry Studies Department of a Technical and Further Education (TAFE) college. The Tribunal accepted:

> The evidence of Mr O, the [*only*] NESB male in the ... Department, regarding the situation which he alleges to the present time, that there were four groupings within the Department; the students, teachers of NESB, teachers of ESB [*English speaking background*] and himself.[89]

It found that the head of the Department, Ms B, had an antagonistic attitude to Ms Fares:

> B's attitude can be seen to emanate from her perception of Ms Fares as a NESB woman who approached her job and the Department in a way very different to the way in which B saw as appropriate and, because of the difference, B reacted towards her in a way that was different to her reaction to English speaking male and female members of staff and to the one male NESB member of staff and her treatment of the Complainant in this regard was less favourable.[90]

It concluded that 'there was in fact within the Department ... an underlying atmosphere of discrimination against NESB women and this manifested itself in the attitude of the other members of the Department towards each of them and, particularly, towards Ms Fares'.[91] They found she had been discriminated against, on the ground of her sex and ethnicity, or because she was a NESB woman, by a selection committee in its decision on her application for

---

84 See Hilary Astor, 'A Question of Identity: The Intersection of Race and Other Grounds of Discrimination' in Race Discrimination Commission, *Racial Discrimination Act 1975: A Review*, AGPS, Canberra, 1995. See also Aileen Moreton-Robinson, 'Masking Gender and Exalting Race: Indigenous Women and Commonwealth Employment Policies' (1992) 15 *Australian Feminist Studies* 5: Moreton-Robinson examined the employment policies of the Aboriginal and Torres Strait Islander Commission (ATSIC) and argued 'because race has tended to become the marker for identifying discriminating practices in employment, this has tended to mask gender-based discrimination' (at 5). She continues 'indigenous people are not genderless. They are subject to gender relations which overtly impact on each sex which means that indigenous men and indigenous women will experience disadvantage in the labour market differently' (at 9).
85 (1994) EOC ¶92-643.
86 See, for example, *Kolavo v Ainsworth Nominees* (1994) EOC ¶92-576.
87 *Fares v Box Hill College of TAFE* (1992) EOC ¶92-391 (Equal Opportunity Board). The decision was appealed to the Supreme Court and was partially overturned on matters not relevant here: see *Box Hill College of Technical and Further Education v Fares* (1992) EOC ¶92-464.
88 Cf *V v Australian Red Cross (WA)* (unreported, HREOCA, 18 February 1999), where the tribunal recognised racial and sexual harassment, concluding that some comments were made because the complainant was an Aboriginal woman.
89 *Fares* (1992) EOC ¶92-391 at 78,782.
90 *Ibid*, at 78,782-3. The Tribunal describes the attitude as 'a belief that NESB women are generally more emotional, highly strung, demanding and overly conscientious in the work, long winded and unable to be concise, holding undue regard for academic qualifications as opposed to practical experience and thus ambitious for themselves' (at 78,782).
91 *Ibid*, at 78,783.

promotion, in the arrangements made for her teaching and in a letter sent to her after she went on sick leave due to the discrimination she had experienced.

Has the Tribunal understood discrimination as relational as suggested by Duclos and as intersectional as suggested by Crenshaw? At the procedural level, there was no equivalent case in the *Fares* situation alleging discrimination against NESB men. Do you think this made it easier for the Tribunal to find discrimination against NESB women?[92]

3. One powerful Australian example of the use of an intersectional approach in dealing with a legal doctrinal issue is an analysis of a homicide case involving an Aboriginal woman.[93] Cynthia Hickey was an Aboriginal woman who killed her partner, an Aboriginal man. She had visited him on the night of the murder, so that he could see their child. He attacked her and Hickey stabbed him when he was sitting on the bed with his back to her. The court accepted evidence of 'battered woman syndrome'[94] and she was found not guilty as she was seen to be acting in self-defence. Stubbs and Tolmie argue that 'Cynthia Hickey's behaviour [w]as intelligible and explicable in the circumstances in which she found herself'.[95] It could have been recognised as action in self-defence, without the need to invoke the battered woman syndrome, if the intersectional nature of her experience had been understood. They argued that such an analysis required the recognition of the history of colonisation, including:

> The loss of traditional lands, the dispersal of families, the stripping of identity, the disintegration of traditional culture and authority structures and the resulting despair that manifests in excessive alcohol consumption.[96]

They also remind us that, given the role of the state in the oppression of Aboriginal communities and the continuing racism experienced in the criminal justice system, Aboriginal women may be more wary than non-Aboriginal women of calling on state authorities to respond to violence against them. They point also to the extreme economic inequality experienced by Aboriginal women, as well as loyalty to kin and family and note that leaving a violent situation also involves leaving 'the physical and emotional support of their extended families and of their communities'.[97] Stubbs and Tolmie criticise the way in which Hickey's actions were recounted to and understood by the court, largely through the use of expert evidence which failed to take account of aspects of her identity as an Aboriginal woman. After detailing ways in which the evidence of the expert witness, whose role was to assist the court in understanding Hickey as a 'battered woman' suffering from 'battered woman syndrome', failed to locate her within her community, they conclude by suggesting a number of alternative ways that Hickey's story can be read. A feminist reading, uninformed by race, applauds her acquittal while expressing some 'disquiet about the manner in which women who are battered are constructed by courts'.[98] However, '[a] second, more sobering

---

92 Note, however, that the Tribunal relied on the evidence of the only NESB man in the workplace to find that there were four groupings in the organisation: students, NESB women, ESB men and women, and him. Given that he classified himself as a separate grouping, might there also have been discrimination against him?
93 Julie Stubbs and Julia Tolmie, 'Race, Gender and the Battered Woman Syndrome: An Australian Case Study' (1995) 8 *Canadian Journal of Women and the Law* 122.
94 This is discussed in more depth in Chapter 13.
95 Stubbs and Tolmie, 'Race, Gender and the Battered Woman Syndrome', at 131.
96 *Ibid*, at 132.
97 *Ibid*, at 133.
98 *Ibid*, at 157.

reading, is that her acquittal comes as a consequence of a racist criminal justice system not valuing the life of an Aboriginal man'.[99] They go on to suggest that, by acknowledging both 'the simultaneous and inseparable operation of race and gender':

> [A]n alternative reading is possible that acknowledges the complexity of her life, her connectedness to others and her agency in the face of extreme violence. ... Such a reading attempts to acknowledge ... Hickey's particular experience, an experience informed by being both Aboriginal and a woman ....[100]

How do you think this sort of intersectional analysis could be presented in a courtroom? How could you encourage a court to respond positively to a structural analysis of this nature in the context of the assessment of liability of an individual accused?

4. One way that has been suggested to respond to the exclusion of indigenous, Black and other women marginalised by traditional feminist discourse, has been the notion of multiple consciousness.[101] This notion is described by Trina Grillo:

> Each of us in the world sits at the intersection of many categories: She is Latina, woman, short, mother, lesbian, daughter, brown-eyed, long-haired, quick-witted, short-tempered, worker, stubborn. At any one moment in time and in space, some of these categories are central to her being and her ability to act in the world. Others matter not at all. Some categories, such as race, gender, class, and sexual orientation, are important most of the time. Others are rarely important. When something or someone highlights one of her categories and brings it to the fore, she may be a dominant person, an oppressor of others. Other times, even most of the time, she may be oppressed herself. She may take lessons she has learned while in a subordinated status and apply them for good or ill when her dominant categories are highlighted. For example, having been mistreated as a child, she may be either a carefully respectful or an abusive parent.[102]

Grillo's analysis emphasises that all women's experience can be analysed as 'intersectional'. How important is that understanding in challenging essentialism?

5. The analysis of Harris, and many of the other writers we have cited, raises the question of the utility of using the category 'women' to structure our legal claims. However, it should be emphasised that Harris, for example, is not arguing for the abandonment of all categorical claims. She begins her article by describing the Jorge Luis Borges character, Ireneo Funes, from *Funes the Memorious*.[103] Funes had a life of 'infinite unique experiences';[104] for example, he had developed his one unique numbering system, replacing numbers with words that reflected no known counting system. 'In the teeming world of Funes, there were only details, almost immediate in their presence'.[105] As Harris describes him:

---

99 *Ibid*.
100 *Ibid*, at 157-8.
101 See Mari Matsuda, 'When the First Quail Calls: Multiple Consciousness as Jurisprudential Method' (1989) 11 *Women's Rights Law Reporter* 7; and Harris, 'Race and Essentialism'.
102 Grillo, 'Anti-Essentialism and Intersectionality', at 17.
103 Jorge Luis Borges, *Labyrinths: Selected Stories and Other Writings*, at 59 (cited by Harris, 'Race and Essentialism', at 581).
104 Harris, 'Race and Essentialism', at 582.
105 Borges, at 66 (cited in Harris, 'Race and Essentialism', at 582).

For Funes, language is only a unique and private system of classification, elegant and solipsistic. The notion that language, made abstract, can serve to create and reinforce a community is incomprehensible to him.[106]

Harris concludes that unless we all want to be as 'autistic' as Funes, 'terrorised by the sheer weight and particularity of the experience',[107] we do need categories:

> No categories at all, moreover, would leave nothing of the women's movement, save perhaps a tepid kind of "I've got my oppression, you've got yours" approach.[108]

But she cautions against seeing this as a dichotomous choice between no categories and those that are traditionally used.[109]

Or, in Matsuda's words:

> Categories count in calling attention to social facts, in organizing for social change. They count tragically, in determining who gets shot in the back while running from the police in the night in Louisville, Kentucky.
>
> Categorisation is not antithetical to recognising movement either within a structure or within a category. ...
>
> [The] ... dynamic quality of intragroup and intergroup relations does not necessarily destroy the intellectual power of group categorization. In fact, it can reinforce it. A category of analysis becomes useful when, understood in its full complexity and revealed in its exceptions and counterexamples, it helps to know more than we would have known otherwise.
>
> To clarify, a category like "women of colour" is useful if thinking about that category tells us more about the workings of racism and patriarchy than we would know if we did all our thinking without that category. A pragmatic approach to the problem of group identity might be to say that, even if we do not know how useful a group analysis will be, we can consider the classification provisionally, asking what it adds to our thinking. ...
>
> ... We must conceptualize, albeit with provisional humility, the structures of subordination.[110]

Duclos, in her analysis of anti-discrimination law discussed above, suggests:

> The error in the current approach lies not so much in the use of categories, which may well be intrinsic to the way we think, but in the assumption that the particular categories we are using now are natural, objective and permanent. We can continue to use the categories we have, in this case the grounds of discrimination, but we should strive to make them flexible, dynamic and relational. ... We need to abandon the current approach where identification of one ground becomes an excuse to put on blinkers, to slot the case into a prefabricated and narrowly defined category of discrimination with standardized, universal indicia of a successful claim.[111]

Are Harris, Iyer/Duclos' and Matsuda's approaches consistent with each other?

We return to this issue at the end of the following chapter, after we have discussed some issues of epistemology, or ways of knowing.

---

106 Harris, 'Race and Essentialism', at 582.
107 *Ibid*, at 607.
108 *Ibid*.
109 *Ibid*.
110 Mari Matsuda, 'Pragmatism Modified and the False Consciousness Problem' (1990) 63 *Southern California Law Review* 1763 at 1773-6.
111 Duclos, 'Disappearing Women', at 50.

Chapter Four

Methodologies and Epistemologies

Introduction

Lorraine Code, in an overview of 'Epistemology' for *A Companion to Feminist Philosophy* in 1998, stated that, despite the fact that feminist work had made inroads into political and moral philosophy in the late 1960s and 1970s, it was still 'outrageous' for her to ask in 1981: 'is the sex of the knower epistemologically significant'?[1] She continued:

> Knowledge, science, and logic seemed, virtually by definition, to stand secure as the repositories and guardians of truth and objectivity, occupants of a space isolated and protected from the vagaries of politics and of gendered specificities.[2]

In our view, 'law' could be inserted into her list of sites of epistemic privilege, for it too makes claims to both truth and objectivity.

In this section we explore some of the ways in which legal methods make this claim to both objectivity and truth. In the course of doing so we examine the meaning of 'impartiality' and 'objectivity', the way in which 'facts' are found in litigation, and the relationship between law and facts. We then go on to consider aspects of feminist methodologies which have been used in law. In particular, we examine both consciousness raising and legal storytelling, raising questions about the extent to which these methodologies in turn also make claims to truth.

Legal methodologies

Claims to objectivity

Mary Jane Mossman has argued that legal method is particularly resistant to feminist challenge. By legal method, she means the process of defining boundaries – law's tendency to separate out a 'legal issue' from a 'political' or 'moral' question; its notion of 'relevance', of determining that only certain facts will be considered and others dismissed as irrelevant (usually those outside the experience of the judges); and, finally, the fact that there are always choices available to common law courts in selecting precedents and hence no guarantee that those which might benefit, rather than harm, women will be used.[3]

Other writers have emphasised the way legal methods make claims to 'objectivity'. Catharine MacKinnon has drawn attention to the gendered nature of claims to objectivity:

---

1   Lorraine Code, 'Epistemology' in Alison M Jaggar and Iris Marion Young (eds), *A Companion to Feminist Philosophy*, Blackwell Publishers, Malden, MA, 1998, at 173.
2   Ibid.
3   Mary Jane Mossman, 'Feminism and Legal Method: The Difference it Makes' (1986) 3 *Australian Journal of Law and Society* 30 at 44-5.

[M]ale dominance is perhaps the most pervasive and tenacious system of power in history, ... it is metaphysically nearly perfect. Its point of view is the standard for point-of-viewlessness, its particularity the meaning of universality.[4]

And earlier in the same article:

> If the sexes are unequal, and perspective participates in situation, there is no ungendered reality or ungendered perspective. And they are connected. In this context, objectivity – the nonsituated, universal standpoint, whether claimed or aspired to – is a denial of the existence or potency of sex inequality that tacitly participates in constructing reality from the dominant point of view. Objectivity, as the epistemological stance of which objectification is the social process, creates the reality it apprehends by defining as knowledge the reality it creates through its way of apprehending it.[5]

And MacKinnon points out that '[o]bjectivity is a stance only a subject can take. ... [I]t is men socially who are subjects, women socially who are other, objects'.[6] As Margaret Davies emphasises, MacKinnon is not here arguing that:

> "objectivity" is of necessity male. If that were the case there would be nothing we could do about it. Rather, the position of the "knower", and thus of objectivity (since modern knowledge is regarded as good only insofar as it is objective), has been socially and philosophically male. It is one of the political tasks of feminism not only to ensure that women get access to the position of the subject, but also that the non-situated, non-subjective, paradigm of knowledge is challenged. Such a challenge is important because the ideal of objective knowledge has ... worked to silence or stigmatise as "subjective" views which do not reflect the orthodox epistemological order.
>
> MacKinnon says that objectivity "is a stance only a subject gets to take", which is a very succinct way of saying that in any case there has to be a subject of knowledge (not a subject matter, but a person who knows), and in this sense, subjectivity is an unavoidable element of knowledge. The further argument ... is that in the ideal of objective knowledge, the existence of the subject position is minimised, and usually erased altogether. For something to qualify as "objective knowledge" the subjects of it must be interchangeable: the idea is that anyone could do the knowing. Knowledge is "out there", and the content is the same no matter who is doing the knowing – except that it is the male position which is seen to be position-less (and hence interchangeable with other similarly neutered beings) while as subjects women are visibly sexed, and therefore never neutral enough to be objective. None of this alters the fact that knowledge is not in itself neutral, since it always exists within a particular social and philosophical context. "Neutrality" is only the position which is culturally enabled to deny its positionality – it is the position which is empowered to know.[7]

Notes

1. One of the ways within legal discourse in which challenges to the objectivity of legal decision-makers arise is in challenges for 'bias'.[8] The doctrine of 'natural justice' or procedural fairness provides that a party has the right to be heard, and the right to be heard by a person who is not biased or, more

---

4   Catharine MacKinnon, 'Feminism, Marxism, Method and the State: Towards Feminist Juris-prudence' (1983) 8 *Signs* 635 at 638-9.
5   *Ibid,* at 636.
6   Catharine MacKinnon, *Feminism Unmodified*, at 55.
7   Davies, *Asking the Law Question*, at 176-7.
8   See Graycar, 'The Gender of Judgments: Some Reflections on "Bias"' (1998) 32 *University of British Columbia Law Review* 1.

accurately, the bias rule is infringed if there is a reasonable perception of bias.[9] There have been a series of challenges to women and people of colour, alleging that they are biased. For example, a Melbourne solicitor sought judicial review of a planning tribunal decision on 'the novel ground that the tribunal was five months pregnant'.[10] He argued that 'the proposition seemed absurd that a tribunal would purport to exercise wide discretions while pregnant'.[11] He alleged that the tribunal member, 'suffered from the well known medical condition ('placidity') which detracts significantly from the intellectual competence of all mothers to be'.[12] He also lodged an affidavit from a well-regarded medical expert that a pregnant woman 'no longer has the clarity of mind and precision of thought she had before pregnancy'.[13] Somehow, this amounted to a claim that the tribunal was biased. The action did not ultimately proceed. In a criminal trial in Queensland in 1990, a District Court judge agreed to a request from a man charged with a criminal offence that no women jurors be empanelled since, '[a]s a Christian man it's against my religious beliefs to be judged by women, as is specified in the Bible. It's an abomination of God. Man has been given the responsibility, and therefore I need men to sit on the jury for me'.[14]

In 1989, the chair of the (then) Australian Broadcasting Tribunal was challenged under the bias ground of the rules of procedural fairness, on the basis that she may have discussed a matter with her husband, also a lawyer.[15]

In 1993, Canadian law professor Constance Backhouse, who held a part-time appointment as a human rights adjudicator, was successfully removed from a sex discrimination case for bias because she had been one of 120 complainants in a systemic discrimination case against a university.[16] Most problematically, comments in the decision suggest that her experience in the area of sex discrimination law might constitute sufficient grounds for removal.[17] In that sense,

---

9   *Livesey v NSW Bar Association* (1983) 151 CLR 288. See also *Ebner v Official Trustee in Bankruptcy; Clenae Pty Ltd v ANZ Banking Group* [2000] HCA 63; and *Re Refugee Review Tribunal; Ex parte H* [2001] HCA 28.
10 Bronwyn Naylor, 'Pregnant Tribunals' (1989) 14 *Legal Service Bulletin* 41 at 41.
11 *Ibid.*
12 *Ibid.*
13 *Ibid*, at 42.
14 *Sydney Morning Herald*, 20 April 1990, at 5. The Attorney-General subsequently successfully sought to have this decision quashed: *R v Judge of District Courts and Shelley; Ex parte Attorney-General* [1991] 1 Qd R 170. Compare the decision of the US Supreme Court in *JEB v Alabama ex rel TB* 511 US 127 (1994) and that of the Supreme Court of Canada in *R v Biddle* [1995] 1 SCR 761.
15 *Kaycliff Pty Ltd v ABT* (1989) 90 ALR 310. The Full Federal Court rejected the challenge, endorsing the view of the primary judge who said: 'it would be wrong to conclude that a casual statement by a husband of his views on a matter under consideration by a tribunal of which his wife is a member gives rise to a reasonable apprehension that the husband's views might have been formed after discussion with his wife, or might be communicated to his wife' (cited at 320).
16 See *Great Atlantic and Pacific Company of Canada Ltd v Ontario (Human Rights Commission)* (1993) 109 DLR (4th) 214. See also Constance Backhouse, 'Bias in Canadian Law: A Lopsided Precipice' (1998) 10 *Canadian Journal of Women and the Law* 170.
17 'During the course of argument, we advised counsel that we did not think it necessary to decide whether Miss Backhouse's public advocacy in favour of the same position advanced before her by the Commission in relation to systemic sex discrimination went so far as to create a reasonable apprehension of bias in relation to this case': *ibid*, at 223. There have subsequently been a series of challenges to decision-makers with feminist backgrounds, none of which has been successful: see the cases referred to in The Honourable Maryka Omatsu, 'The Fiction of Judicial Impartiality' (1997) 9 *Canadian Journal of Women and the Law* 1 at 10-12; and see the discussion in Richard Devlin, 'We Can't Go On Together With Suspicious Minds: Judicial Bias and Racialised Perspective in *R v RDS*' (1995) 18 *Dalhousie Law Journal* 408.

the case has some resonance with an Australian case in which an Aboriginal woman who had been appointed a human rights commission conciliator in a small community was found to have been 'biased' for commenting at a preliminary conference that her daughters had also been refused service at an establishment which was the subject of a race discrimination complaint. She was successfully challenged.[18] The case clearly raises the issue of the relevance of knowledge and experience to decision-making. Commenting on this case Margaret Allars has pointed out: 'Where individuals are appointed as members of tribunals by virtue of their expertise, their very expertise may expose them to claims of an appearance of bias'.[19] If the conciliator had said nothing about the experience of her daughters in the conciliation conference, would she still have been biased? Does the previous question assume that a decision-maker who has ever experienced discrimination of the same or similar kind to that which is argued before them cannot make an unbiased decision? Does this mean that women, indigenous people or people with disabilities can never be appointed to bodies that hear and determine discrimination cases?

Martha Minow has suggested that bias can arise both where a person is too close to a dispute *and* where they are too distant from it.[20]

> Is it possible to risk actual bias, or its appearance, by having a total absence of experience or knowledge of the issue or evidence at hand? To be able to evaluate statements of witnesses a jury [or a judge] needs sufficient knowledge of the witnesses' world to place their statements in context. Moreover, to be able to render judgment, jurors need sufficient knowledge of the life experiences of those before them to make sense of testimony and motivations. Even when women were excluded from jury service, for example, Anglo-American tradition provided for the use of midwife juries on occasions in which knowledge of pregnancy or childbirth would be critical to a reliable judgment.[21]

And later Minow states: 'Prejudice interferes with impartiality. Prior knowledge may assist impartiality, however, if coupled with a willingness to be surprised, rather than always confirmed'.[22] Would it be possible to develop a legal test for bias which recognised prior knowledge as an asset and assessed 'willingness to be surprised'?

2. In Australia, in late 1994, a then newly appointed Federal Court judge in Queensland was asked to remove herself from hearing a case on the ground that she was a woman and also that the applicant suspected she might be Jewish.[23] In September 1996, a man asked the Full Family Court in Australia to remove a judge from hearing a case on the grounds of bias: he alleged that the judge was 'anti-man' or 'anti-father' or both and too set in her ways to put his case in her hands.[24] It would, he argued, be like 'sending the Ku Klux Klan to judge a black man'. In his application he stated:

---

18   *Koppen v Commissioner for Community Relations* (1986) 67 ALR 215.
19   Margaret Allars, *Introduction to Australian Administrative Law*, Butterworths, 1990, at para 6.84 (at 272-3).
20   Martha Minow, 'Stripped Down Like a Runner or Enriched by Experience: Bias and Impartiality of Judges and Jurors' (1992) 33 *William and Mary Law Review* 1201.
21   *Ibid*, at 1205.
22   *Ibid*, at 1214.
23   *Bird v Volkers* (unreported, FCA, 20 October 1994); *Bird v Free* (1994) 126 ALR 475.
24   *Mills v Mills* (unreported, Fam CA, Full Court, 10 September 1996).

> I have abused the judge on two separate occasions. I have written an abusive affidavit and an abusive letter which she has read. I have also written a 38 page letter to the Attorney General with more abuse of her. ... I don't believe the judge can after all this abuse be impartial and even if she feels she can ... there is no way she can be seen to.

With one or two exceptions, we know of no challenge for bias to male decision-makers on the ground of their maleness.[25] Judy Scales-Trent, who has looked at bias challenges against Black American judges, has suggested that the process of reasoning involved in these challenges to women and people of colour for bias is as follows: while women are women and blacks are blacks, white men are just 'regular people'. Therefore, it is possible for them to imagine, and argue, that women and black men are biased, while white males are not.[26] As one male African-American judge who was asked to stand aside from a discrimination case commented, 'black lawyers have litigated in the federal courts almost exclusively before white judges, yet they have not urged that white judges should be disqualified on matters of race relations'.[27] Or, as an African-American woman judge commented, when asked to recuse herself from hearing a sex discrimination case against a prominent New York law firm, 'if background or sex or race of each judge were, by definition, sufficient grounds for removal, no judge on this court could hear this case, or many others, by virtue of the fact that all of them were attorneys, of a sex, often with distinguished law firm or public service backgrounds'.[28]

Martha Minow has argued that what these judges were doing in their comments was questioning the baseline from which bias is adjudged. That is, not only may bias arise when one is too close to a situation, and when one is too distant, but there is the equally important question of what is neutrality. She argues that the two judges 'mean to expose the assumption that the neutral baseline against which to evaluate bias is the vantage point of a white male. They mean to show that even whites and males have a vantage point that can and should be evaluated for bias'.[29] How central to the reconsideration of what we mean by saying a decision-maker is biased is an examination of what we mean by 'neutrality'? Does this sort of questioning

---

25 An Australian exception is *Lindon v Kerr* (1995) 57 FCR 284 (Full Federal Court). Here the (male) applicant asked that the court disqualify itself on the grounds of gender bias because it was constituted by male judges only. The court rejected the applicant's argument, citing as reasons the doctrine of necessity (no women judges were available) and their view that no gender issue was raised by the facts. This last point is of course debatable: the Federal Court judges did not elaborate on what would constitute a 'gender issue'. See also *R v Commonwealth Conciliation and Arbitration Commission; Ex parte Angliss Group* (1969) 122 CLR 540 where an industrial decision-maker, making a decision on an equal pay claim, was (unsuccessfully) challenged for bias because he had earlier indicated support for equal pay for women. See also, *The Times*, 21 March 2001, reporting on an argument by the Fawcett Society that the House of Lords in a rape appeal case should not be constituted by men only. The case concerned was *Reg v A* [2001] UKHL 25, but the bias challenge is not addressed in the final decision of the court, which rejected the challenge. (There are currently no women law lords.)
26 Judy Scales-Trent, 'Women in the Lawyering Process: The Complications of Categories' (1990) 35 *New York Law School Law Review* 337.
27 *Pennsylvania v Local Union 542, International Union of Operating Engineers* 388 F Supp 155, at 177 (ED Pa, 1974) per Higginbotham J.
28 *Blank v Sullivan and Cromwell* 418 F Supp 1 at 4 (SDNY 1975) per Motley J.
29 Martha Minow, 'Stripped Down Like a Runner or Enriched by Experience: Bias and Impartiality of Judges and Jurors' (1992) 33 *William and Mary Law Review* 1201 at 1207.

resonate more closely with traditional legal understandings of bias than a focus on the role of 'prior knowledge' in impartial decision-making?

3. The following extract comes from a recent consideration of the doctrine of bias by the Supreme Court of Canada.[30] It arose when a trial judge in Nova Scotia was dealing with the arrest of a 15-year-old black youth who was alleged to have interfered with the arrest of another youth. He was charged with unlawfully assaulting a police office and resisting a police officer. While delivering an oral judgment, dismissing the case, the judge stated:

> The Crown says, well, why would the officer say that events occurred the way in which he has relayed them to the Court this morning. I am not saying that the Constable has misled the Court although police officers have been known to do that in the past. I am not saying that the officer overreacted, but certainly police officers do overreact, particularly when they are dealing with non-white groups. That to me indicates a state of mind right there that is questionable. I believe that probably the situation in this particular case is the case of a young police officer who overreacted. I do accept the evidence of [RDS] that he was told to shut up or he would be under arrest. It seems to be in keeping with the prevalent attitude of the day.[31]

The Crown successfully argued that these comments gave rise to a reasonable apprehension of bias, a decision confirmed by a majority of the Nova Scotia Court of Appeal.[32] The Supreme Court of Canada overturned this decision.[33] The following extract is from the judgment of L'Heureux-Dubé and McLachlin JJ:

I. Introduction

We have read the reasons of our colleague, Justice Cory, and while we agree that this appeal must be allowed, we differ substantially from him in how we reach that outcome. As a result, we find it necessary to write brief concurring reasons. ...

In our view, the test for reasonable apprehension of bias established in the jurisprudence is reflective of the reality that while judges can never be neutral, in the sense of purely objective, they can and must strive for impartiality. It therefore recognizes as inevitable and appropriate that the differing experiences of judges assist them in their decision-making process and will be reflected in their judgments, so long as those experiences are relevant to the cases, are not based on inappropriate stereotypes, and do not prevent a fair and just determination of the cases based on the facts in evidence.

We find that on the basis of these principles, there is no reasonable apprehension of bias in the case at bar. Like Cory J we would, therefore, overturn the findings by the Nova Scotia Supreme Court (Trial Division) and the majority of the Nova Scotia Court of Appeal that a reasonable apprehension of bias arises in this case, and restore the acquittal of RDS. This said, we disagree with Cory J's position that the comments of Judge Sparks were unfortunate, unnecessary, or close to the line. Rather, we find them to reflect an entirely appropriate recognition of the facts in evidence

---

30   *RDS v R* [1997] 3 SCR 484.
31   *Ibid*, at 494, cited by Major J, his emphasis omitted.
32   (1995) 145 NSR (2d) 284.
33   Cory and Iacobucci JJ allowed the appeal, though Cory J wrote a separate judgment in which Iacobucci J joined; La Forest and Gonthier JJ endorsed the joint reasons of L'Heureux-Dubé and McLachlin JJ; Lamer CJ, Sopinka and Major JJ dissented.

in this case and of the context within which this case arose – a context known to Judge Sparks and to any well-informed member of the community.

II. The Test for Reasonable Apprehension of Bias

... In order to apply ... [*the test for bias*], it is necessary to distinguish between the impartiality which is required of all judges, and the concept of judicial neutrality. [They referred to the work of Cardozo, *The Nature of the Judicial Process* (1921)] ... where he affirmed the importance of impartiality, while at the same time recognizing the fallacy of judicial neutrality. ...

Cardozo recognized that objectivity was an impossibility because judges, like all other humans, operate from their own perspectives. As the Canadian Judicial Council noted in Commentaries on Judicial Conduct (1991), at p 12, "[t]here is no human being who is not the product of every social experience, every process of education, and every human contact". What is possible and desirable, they note, is impartiality: ...

True impartiality does not require that the judge have no sympathies or opinions; it requires that the judge nevertheless be free to entertain and act upon different points of view with an open mind. ...

A. The Nature of Judging

As discussed above, judges in a bilingual, multiracial and multicultural society will undoubtedly approach the task of judging from their varied perspectives. They will certainly have been shaped by, and have gained insight from, their different experiences, and cannot be expected to divorce themselves from these experiences on the occasion of their appointment to the bench. In fact, such a transformation would deny society the benefit of the valuable knowledge gained by the judiciary while they were members of the Bar. As well, it would preclude the achievement of a diversity of backgrounds in the judiciary. The reasonable person does not expect that judges will function as neutral ciphers; however, the reasonable person does demand that judges achieve impartiality in their judging.

It is apparent, and a reasonable person would expect, that triers of fact will be properly influenced in their deliberations by their individual perspectives on the world in which the events in dispute in the courtroom took place. Indeed, judges must rely on their background knowledge in fulfilling their adjudicative function. ...

[N]otwithstanding that their own insights into human nature will properly play a role in making findings of credibility or factual determinations, judges must make those determinations only after being equally open to, and considering the views of, all parties before them. The reasonable person, through whose eyes the apprehension of bias is assessed, expects judges to undertake an open-minded, carefully considered, and dispassionately deliberate investigation of the complicated reality of each case before them. ...

Judicial inquiry into the factual, social and psychological context within which litigation arises is not unusual. Rather, a conscious, contextual inquiry has become an accepted step towards judicial impartiality. ...

An understanding of the context or background essential to judging may be gained from testimony from expert witnesses in order to put the case in context, ... from academic studies properly placed before the Court; and from the judge's personal understanding and experience of the society in which the judge lives and works. This process of enlargement is not only consistent with impartiality; it may also be seen as its essential precondition.

A reasonable person far from being troubled by this process, would see it as an important aid to judicial impartiality.

B. The Nature of the Community

The reasonable person ... is an informed and right-minded member of the community, a community which, in Canada, supports the fundamental principles entrenched in the Constitution by the Canadian Charter of Rights and Freedoms. Those fundamental principles include the principles of equality set out in s 15 of the Charter and endorsed in nation-wide quasi-constitutional provincial and federal human rights legislation. The reasonable person must be taken to be aware of the history of discrimination faced by disadvantaged groups in Canadian society protected by the Charter's equality provisions. These are matters of which judicial notice may be taken. In Parks, ... [*R v Parks* (1993) 15 OR (3d) 324 (CA)] at p 342, Doherty JA, did just this, stating:

> Racism, and in particular anti-black racism, is a part of our community's psyche. A significant segment of our community holds overtly racist views. A much larger segment subconsciously operates on the basis of negative racial stereotypes. Furthermore, our institutions, including the criminal justice system, reflect and perpetuate those negative stereotypes.

The reasonable person is not only a member of the Canadian community, but also, more specifically, is a member of the local communities in which the case at issue arose (in this case, the Nova Scotian and Halifax communities). Such a person must be taken to possess knowledge of the local population and its racial dynamics, including the existence in the community of a history of widespread and systemic discrimination against black and aboriginal people, and high profile clashes between the police and the visible minority population over policing issues: Royal Commission on the Donald Marshall Jr Prosecution (1989); *R v Smith* (1991), 109 NSR (2d) 394 (Co Ct). The reasonable person must thus be deemed to be cognizant of the existence of racism in Halifax, Nova Scotia. It follows that judges may take notice of actual racism known to exist in a particular society. Judges have done so with respect to racism in Nova Scotia. In *Nova Scotia (Minister of Community Services) v SMS* (1992), 110 NSR (2d) 91 (Fam Ct), it was stated at p 108:

> [Racism] is a pernicious reality. The issue of racism existing in Nova Scotia has been well documented in the Marshall Inquiry Report (sub. nom. Royal Commission on the Donald Marshall, Jr, Prosecution). A person would have to be stupid, complacent or ignorant not to acknowledge its presence, not only individually, but also systemically and institutionally.

We conclude that the reasonable person ... endorsed by Canadian courts is a person who approaches the question of whether there exists a reasonable apprehension of bias with a complex and contextualized understanding of the issues in the case. The reasonable person understands the impossibility of judicial neutrality, but demands judicial impartiality. The reasonable person is cognizant of the racial dynamics in the local community, and, as a member of the Canadian community, is supportive of the principles of equality.

Before concluding that there exists a reasonable apprehension of bias in the conduct of a judge, the reasonable person would require some clear evidence that the judge in question had improperly used his or her perspective in the decision-making process; this flows from the presumption of impartiality of the judiciary. There must be some indication that the judge was not approaching the case with an open mind fair to all parties. Awareness of the context within which a case occurred would not constitute such evidence; on the contrary, such awareness is consistent with the highest tradition of judicial impartiality.

> [*McLachlin and L'Heureux-Dubé JJ then applied this test to the facts concluding:*]

> Judge Sparks' oral reasons show that she approached the case with an open mind, used her experience and knowledge of the community to achieve an understanding of the reality of the case, and applied the fundamental principle of proof beyond a reasonable doubt. Her comments were based entirely on the case before her, were made after a consideration of the conflicting testimony of the two witnesses and in response to the Crown's submissions, and were entirely supported by the evidence. In alerting herself to the racial dynamic in the case, she was simply engaging in the process of contextualized judging which, in our view, was entirely proper and conducive to a fair and just resolution of the case before her. ...
> In the result, we agree with Cory J as to the disposition of this case.
> We would allow the appeal, overturn the findings of the Nova Scotia Supreme Court (Trial Division) and the majority of the Nova Scotia Court of Appeal, and restore the acquittal of the appellant RDS.[34]

Does this judgment recognise both that prior knowledge is part of impartiality and at the same time question the baseline definition of neutrality? Note that the judgment refers to an Ontario Court of Appeal judgment in *R v Parks* where that court referred to the existence of racism. In *B and R and Separate Representative*,[35] the Full Family Court canvassed the history of disadvantage of indigenous Australians and paid detailed attention to the policy of taking children away from their families that was later documented by the HREOC in *Bringing Them Home*.[36] Can you suggest why such discussions have gone without challenge on the ground of bias?

4. In his dissent Major J stated:

> The life experience of this trial judge, as with all trial judges, is an important ingredient in the ability to understand human behaviour, to weigh the evidence and to determine credibility. It helps in making a myriad of decisions arising during the course of most trials. It is of no value, however, in reaching conclusions for which there is no evidence. The fact that on some other occasions police officers have lied or overreacted is irrelevant. Life experience is not a substitute for evidence. There was no evidence before the trial judge to support the conclusion she reached.[37]

He continued:

> If a judge instructed the jury ... that because the complainant was a prostitute he or she probably consented, or that prostitutes are likely to lie about such things as sexual assault, the decision would be reversed. Such presumptions have no place in a system of justice that treats all witnesses equally. Our jurisprudence prohibits tying credibility to something as irrelevant as gender, occupation or perceived group disposition'.[38]

---

34 *Ibid*, at paras 27-60.
35 (1995) FLC ¶92-636.
36 HREOC, *Bringing Them Home: National Inquiry into the Separation of Aboriginal and Torres Strait Islander Children from their Families*, Commonwealth of Australia, Sydney, 1997.
37 *Ibid*, at para 13.
38 *Ibid*, at para 16.

Is the parallel Major J draws between a judge's comments on lying prostitutes and the judge's comments in *RDS* on policing and racism an apt one?[39]

For further discussion of this case, see Christine Boyle, Brenna Bhandar, Constance Backhouse, Marilyn MacCrimmon and Audrey Kobayashi, '*R v RDS*: An Editor's Forum' (1998) 10 *Canadian Journal of Women and the Law* 159.

5. It was noted earlier that Professor Backhouse in Canada was removed from hearing a sex discrimination case on the grounds that she had been a participant in one (and note the court's suggestion about the relevance of her general expertise in the area). Would a solicitor who had worked for 10 years as a practitioner in the area of discrimination law, acting only for plaintiffs, be considered to be 'biased' if subsequently appointed to hear discrimination cases? Or suppose he or she worked for an employer's law firm, acting only for defendants? What of a law academic who specialised in discrimination law and had written extensive critiques of the jurisprudence? And if a solicitor with a women's legal service (who therefore acted only for women) were to be appointed a human rights hearing commissioner, would she be considered 'biased' if she presided over sex discrimination cases? Could a woman who had been raped preside over a sexual assault trial? What if her daughter had been the victim? What if the judge is a man and his daughter had been the victim? How about if a prominent feminist law academic was appointed to the bench and she had published extensive critiques of the law dealing with sexual assault: should she be excluded from hearing such cases? What if the late English Professor Glanville Williams, who wrote at length about the fact that women falsely accuse men of rape, had been appointed to the bench? Would a judge in a personal injury damages case have to recuse him or herself if they had been involved in a car accident? What if the judge was on the Family Court and had been divorced? By what criteria would we decide whether any of these decision-makers warranted removal on the ground of bias?

Claims to truth

Carol Smart has argued that not only do legal processes claim objectivity, they also make a claim to 'truth':

> [L]aw sets itself above other knowledges like psychology, sociology, or common sense. It claims to have the method to establish the truth of events. ... A more public version of this claim ... is the criminal trial which, through the adversarial system, is thought to be a secure basis for findings of guilt and innocence. Judges and juries can come to correct legal decisions; the fact that other judges in higher courts may overrule some decisions only goes to prove that the system ultimately divines the correct view.
>
> Law's claim to truth is not manifested so much in its practice, however, but rather in the ideal of law. ...
>
> If we accept that law, like science, makes a claim to truth and this is indivisible from the exercise of power, we can see that law exercises power not simply in its material effects (judgements) but also in its ability to disqualify other knowledges and experiences. Non-legal knowledge is therefore suspect and/or secondary. Everyday experiences are of little interest in terms of their meaning for

---

39 The trial judge was Judge Corinne Sparks who, at the time of the trial, was the only Black judge in Nova Scotia: Devlin, 'We Can't Go On Together With Suspicious Minds', at 410.

individuals. Rather these experiences must be translated into another form in order to become 'legal' issues and before they can be processed through the legal system ... . For the system to run smoothly ... the ideal is that all parties are legally represented and that the parties say as little as possible ... . The problem for the lawyer is that the litigant may bring in issues which are not, in legal terms, pertinent to the case, or s/he might inadvertently say something that has a legal significance unknown to her/him. So the legal process translates everyday experience into legal relevances, it excludes a great deal that might be relevant to the parties, and it makes its judgement on the scripted or tailored account. Of course parties are not always silenced but ... how they are allowed to speak, and how their experience is turned into something that law can digest and process, is a demonstration of the power of law to disqualify alternative accounts.

Law sets itself outside the social order, as if through the application of legal method and rigour, it becomes a thing apart which can in turn reflect upon the world from which it is divorced.[40]

Notes

1. Do you agree that law does make a claim to truth? Can you think of other aspects of legal method that make a claim to either truth or objectivity?
2. Richard Delgado has coined the term 'stock story' to describe the truth-claiming function of traditional legal decision-makers:

   > [M]uch of social reality is constructed. We decide what is, and, almost simultaneously, what ought to be. Narrative habits, patterns of seeing, shape what we see and that to which we aspire. These patterns of perception become habitual, tempting us to believe that the way things are is inevitable, or the best that can be in an imperfect world. Alternative visions of reality are not explored, or, if they are, rejected as extreme or implausible.[41]

Delgado explains this concept of the stock story, a concept used by both critical race scholars and feminist scholars to explore our narrative assumptions, in the following story, concerning the failure to hire a Black academic. He uses an imagined dialogue between a student member of the advisory appointment committee, and a white male tenured law teacher, with the latter justifying the non-appointment. Delgado states:

> [*His*] account represents the stock story – the one the institution collectively forms and tells about itself. This story picks and chooses from among the available facts to present a picture of what happened: an account that justifies the world as it is. It emphasises the school's benevolent motivation ("look how hard we're trying") and good faith. It stresses stability and the avoidance of risks. It measures the black candidate through the prism of pre-existing, well-agreed-upon criteria of conventional scholarship and teaching. Given those standards, it purports to be scrupulously meritocratic and fair; [*the candidate*] would have been hired had he measured up. No one raises the possibility that the merit criteria employed in judging [*the*

---

40 Carol Smart, *Feminism and the Power of Law*, Routledge, London, 1989, at 10-11; cf Smart, 'Law's Truth/Women's Experience' in Graycar (ed), *Dissenting Opinions: Feminist Explorations in Law and Society*, Allen and Unwin, Sydney, 1990, and 'Law's Power, the Sexed Body, and Feminist Discourse' (1990) 17 *Journal of Law and Society* 194.

41 Richard Delgado, 'Story-Telling for Oppositionists and Others: A Plea for Narrative' in Richard Delgado (ed), *Critical Race Theory: The Cutting Edge*, Temple University Press, Philadelphia, 1995, at 65-6.

candidate] are themselves debatable, *chosen* – not inevitable. No one ... calls attention to the way in which merit functions to conceal the contingent connection between institutional power and the things rated.

... The account is highly procedural – it emphasizes that [*the candidate*] got a full, careful hearing – rather than substantive: a black was rejected. It emphasises certain "facts" without examining their truth ... .

The dominant fact about this first story, however, is its seeming neutrality. It scrupulously avoids issues of blame or responsibility.[42]

Delgado goes on to say 'Naturally, the stock story is not the only one that can be told. By emphasising other events and giving them slightly different interpretations, a quite different picture can begin to emerge'.[43] The role of 'counter-stories', as he names them, is returned to below.

3. Judges also often use 'common sense' or 'experience' in their fact-finding – in the stories they tell.[44] For example, Judge Bland of the Victorian County Court, in instructing a jury in a rape case, stated 'it does happen, in the common experience of those who have been in the law as long as I have anyway, that no often subsequently means yes'.[45]

And in yet another case, Justice O'Bryan, in the Victorian Supreme Court, in the course of sentencing a man to eleven years' jail, commented that a seventeen-year-old girl who was bashed, raped and had her throat slit was 'not traumatised' by the rape because she was 'probably comatose at the time', having been knocked unconscious by the offender.[46]

These examples 'illustrate the belief of judges in a pre-existing body of "knowledge" on which they can, at least in part, base their judgments'.[47] Is it possible to intervene in these discourses? If the intervention is with other 'stories' – contingent, hesitant and questioning stories – can these judicial stories which claim truth be adequately challenged? We return to this question below.

4. The methodologies used in fact-finding also influence the way legal doctrine develops:

[C]ourts don't first settle on the interpretation of the facts and *then* figure out what the law means. The practice of judging simultaneously engages both in an ongoing process of meaning-making, producing a single opinion in which fact and law are woven together in one coherent whole. Constructing the facts and constructing the law are not two separate enterprises, but are mutually implicated in the same project.[48]

One example of the way law and facts are intermeshed is provided by the High Court's decision in *Moffa*.[49] The case concerned the availability of the defence of provocation, a partial defence to murder, which reduces the offence to manslaughter (and therefore warrants a lower sentence). The accused killed his wife by hitting her with a piece of pipe. He argued he was

---

42 *Ibid*, at 68.
43 *Ibid*, at 68-9.
44 See Graycar, 'The Gender of Judgments: An Introduction' in Thornton (ed), *Public and Private: Feminist Legal Debates*.
45 As quoted in *The Age*, 6 May 1993.
46 Graycar, 'The Gender of Judgments', at 271.
47 *Ibid*, at 272.
48 Kim Lane Scheppele, 'Facing Facts in Legal Interpretation' (1990) 30 *Representations* 42 at 60.
49 *Moffa v R* (1977) 138 CLR 601. See Morgan, 'Provocation Law and Facts: Dead Women Tell No Tales, Tales Are Told About Them' (1997) 21 *Melbourne University Law Review* 237.

provoked by her. The accused had visited Italy for a month and when he returned he said his wife was 'indifferent to him'. He said she had told him she was not interested in sexual intercourse with him and was planning to leave him. He said she had told him she no longer loved him and that she had 'been enjoying [herself] screwing with everybody on the street'.[50] He said she showed him photos of herself in the nude saying, '[i]f you want to look at me, look at the pictures'.[51] And he also said she called him a 'black bastard' and threw a telephone at him. This behaviour was described by Barwick CJ in the following way:

> The totality of the deceased's conduct on that occasion, according to that account [*the account extracted above*], was that there was *vituperative* and *scornful* rejection of the applicant's connubial advances, a *contemptuous* denial of any continuing affection, a *proclamation of finality* in the termination of their relationship coupled with an expression of pleasure in having had intercourse *promiscuously* with neighbouring men. This statement of enjoyment in that course of conduct might reasonably be thought, particularly if coupled with the manner of her rejection of the applicant, to contain an assertion, *contemptuously* expressed by the deceased, of sexual inadequacy on the part of the applicant.[52]

This can be contrasted with the description of the facts in the judgment of Gibbs J:

> [T]he deceased repeated what she had previously been saying, that she did not love her husband and intended to leave him; she admitted that she had promiscuously committed adultery, and she uttered some vulgar abuse.[53]

The appellate judges are, of course, describing the same story that Moffa told about what he said she said, it's just that the 'facts' are somehow different.[54]

And the judges describe some other 'facts' in different ways. For example, Stephen J says 'she threw at him photographs of herself which the jury might have understood to have been taken, unknown to the applicant, by another man, and to be obscene'.[55] Only Gibbs J explains that most of these photos had in fact been taken by the accused – this 'fact' is not mentioned in any other judgment.[56]

The basic test in common law jurisdictions in Australia for the defence of provocation is, broadly, whether the accused was provoked by the actions of the victim to lose his (or her) self-control and whether an ordinary person

---

50   *Moffa*, at 614-15.
51   Ibid.
52   *Moffa*, at 606, emphasis added.
53   *Moffa*, at 617.
54   See Kim Lane Scheppele, 'Just the Facts Ma'am: Sexual Violence, Evidentiary Habits, and the Revision of Truth' (1992) 37 *New York Law School Law Review* 123. Note also the way the facts are presented in the headnote to the *Moffa* decision: 'On the morning of the killing, she had rejected his advances in a scornful and abusive way; she had contemptuously denied his continuing affections and said that their marriage had ended; and she had boasted of promiscuous sexual conduct with men in the neighbourhood' (at 601).
55   *Moffa*, at 618.
56   *Moffa*, at 615. The Full Bench of the South Australian Supreme Court in their consideration of *Moffa* stated that the appellant eventually admitted having taken the photos himself (*R v Moffa* (1976) 13 SASR 284 at 287). Gibbs J is also the only judge who makes clear the connection between the deceased's illness and her refusal of intercourse. The South Australian Supreme Court's appeal judgment makes this even clearer – she was suffering vaginal bleeding and thought she had cancer, though she subsequently found out she did not ((1976) 13 SASR 284 at 286).

could have also lost self-control and acted in the way the accused did. If both these aspects of the test are found to be satisfied (or, more accurately, if the Crown fails to negative them), the offence is reduced from murder to manslaughter. These are ultimately questions for the jury; however, a trial judge should withdraw the issue from the jury if there is no evidence that the accused was so provoked or 'if the evidence could not reasonably support the conclusion that the provocation was of such a character as could have deprived a reasonable [*or ordinary*] person of the power of self-control to such an extent as to lead him to do what the accused did'.[57] The majority of the High Court in *Moffa* (including Barwick CJ) concluded that provocation should have been left to the jury. Gibbs J dissented. What is the relevance of the various factual readings, the various tales, to this conclusion?[58]

5. Kim Lane Scheppele has not only questioned the separation in legal method between law and fact but has analysed the methods courts use to find facts in an analysis of a non-judicial fact 'finding' process. She examined the United States Senate Judiciary Committee hearings into Anita Hill's accusations that Clarence Thomas, then a nominee for the Supreme Court (and now a judge on that court), sexually harassed her while he was her boss at the Equal Employment Opportunity Commission.[59] She notes courts' reliance on physical evidence (what she calls the 'smoking gun') and goes on to discuss the physical evidence available to Hill and to Thomas:

> In the absence of torn clothes, weapons at the scene, or bruises and cuts from physical struggle – evidence that courts prefer because these are signs of "real" violence – the only available physical evidence was records written at the time. And Anita Hill didn't have any written records specifically about Thomas's actions.[60]

Hill had not kept contemporaneous records of his behaviour, but Thomas by virtue of his position did have such records – the records of his phone logs kept by his secretary:

> The phone logs revealed that Anita Hill had called Clarence Thomas a number of times after she had left the EEOC, leaving messages that included her room number at a hotel in Washington, and one congratulating Thomas on his marriage. Of course, Thomas's notes could not show that he didn't do what Hill said he did. Instead, they were believed as evidence in his favour because they showed conduct on her part that would be inconsistent with the way most people believed that a sexually harassed women would behave. Though the notes were portrayed as speaking for themselves, it was not the notes per se that convinced people; it was the notes *in conjunction* with their culturally acceptable interpretation that provided the necessary evidence.
>
> But what else could these phone records be taken to be saying? The phone logs only showed incoming calls. Outgoing calls were not recorded. Only Hill's messages were kept; Thomas's replies were not part of that record. Given the recordkeeping practices of powerful people who have staffs to work for them, those with full-time secretaries will have better records (however one-sided) than those who do not.[61]

---

57 *Moffa*, at 613 (per Gibbs J).
58 See Morgan, 'Provocation Law and Facts: Dead Women Tell No Tales'.
59 Kim Lane Scheppele, 'Manners of Imagining the Real' (1994) 19 *Law and Social Inquiry* 995.
60 *Ibid*, at 1001.
61 *Ibid*, at 1002.

Scheppele goes on to examine the process of decontextualisation in fact finding. She argues that Hill was attacked by the Senate because she had not told the full story to the FBI on initial investigation, but rather added details as she told the story again and again:

> Question after question cut Hill's story into tiny bits, where one slightly discrepant factlet was compared with another. Hill's story had been compelling to those who believed her precisely because it was so detailed and coherent, but Specter's [*Arlen Specter, a Republican Senator*] strategy involved undercutting both the detail (by insinuating that it had been recently invented) and the coherence (by breaking the story up into pieces, each decontextualised).[62]

Hill's response to this was to urge that her statement should be looked at as a whole.[63] The Republican senators expressed scepticism that she could remember so many details implying that her 'testimony was overly specific and coherent' which 'operated to undermine precisely what had made the story seem most real'.[64] Scheppele argues:

> Stories that present familiar tales, laced with enough detail to be distinctive but not so much as to feel contrived, are the most credible. But the people who can produce such stories must know the narrative conventions, which may not be widely available or widely shared in a culturally divided society. And the people who produce such stories must be able to rely on a dominant cultural repertoire of familiar plot lines. Since those culturally familiar plot lines are likely to benefit the privileged, the stories of the subordinated seem particularly susceptible to inversions.[65]

Furthermore:

> Republican senators piled on suspicions that Anita Hill had invented her story by noting how long she had delayed in talking about it. She said nothing at the time to her co-workers; she made no formal complaint. ...
> Delayed stories, stories growing out of a silence that has gone before, are disbelieved precisely because they are delayed.[66]

Thirdly, Scheppele argues:

> To be credible, witnesses' narratives need to be close enough to culturally available stories to be recognizable as something that could happen but possessed of enough distinguishing information to be recognizable as the narrative of a distinct event. Another strategy used by Republican senators to discredit Hill's account involved portraying her story as stereotyped and therefore not genuinely experienced, borrowed from other accounts of sexual overtures.[67]

Thomas confirmed that there were racialised stereotypes of black male sexuality, which implicitly Hill was drawing on, thus 'mak[ing] Hill into the injuring aggressor and Thomas into the helpless victim'.[68] Thomas drew on one of the most powerful images of racial oppression in the US, describing the

---

62 *Ibid*, at 1004.
63 *Ibid*.
64 *Ibid*, at 1005.
65 *Ibid*, at 1022.
66 *Ibid*, at 1005-6.
67 *Ibid*, at 1006.
68 *Ibid*.

Senate committee investigation as 'a high-tech lynching for uppity blacks'.[69] In Delgado's terms, Hill was being accused of using a 'stock story' imbued with racial stereotypes, while Thomas used a 'stock story' himself.

Scheppele argues:

> Anita Hill lost her fight. But in this, at least, she is not alone. Disadvantaged people, those not backed by official power, class privilege, insider status, gender and racial credibility, and deep knowledge of the rules of the game, often have trouble making their stories heard as fact in formal settings because of the way in which informal rules of evidence work against the background of cultural interpretation.[70]

Feminist methodologies

Consciousness raising

Catharine MacKinnon has identified a feminist methodology, a methodology she calls 'consciousness raising' which she describes in the following passage.[71]

> Feminism ... is the theory of women's point of view. ... Consciousness raising is its quintessential expression. ... Consciousness raising not only comes to know different things as politics; it necessarily comes to know them in a different way. Women's experience of politics, of life as sex object, gives rise to its own method of appropriating that reality: feminist method. ...
>
> Through consciousness raising, women grasp the collective reality of women's condition from within the perspective of that experience, not from outside it. The claim that a sexual politics exists and is socially fundamental is grounded in the claim of feminism *to* women's perspective, not from it. Its claim to women's perspective *is* its claim to truth. In its account of itself, women's point of view contains a duality analogous to that of the marxist proletariat: determined by the reality the theory explodes, it thereby claims special access to that reality. Feminism does not see its view as subjective, partial, or undetermined but as a critique of the purported generality, disinterestedness, and universality of prior accounts. These have not been half right but have invoked the wrong whole. Feminism not only challenges masculine partiality but questions the universality imperative itself. Aperspectivity is revealed as a strategy of male hegemony.[72]

A Feminist Dictionary defines consciousness raising as 'Talk in small, supportive groups about women's experiences' and in the late 1960s and 1970s consciousness raising groups were extremely common.[73] Of course, MacKinnon did not invent consciousness raising. But, according to Christine Littleton, MacKinnon was responsible 'for the introduction of feminist method into *law* and public discourse about law'.[74]

---

69 Clarence Thomas, 11 October 1991, cited in Emma Coleman Jordan, 'The Power of False Racial Memory and the Metaphor of Lynching' in Anita Fay Hill and Emma Coleman Jordan (eds), *Race, Gender and Power in America: The Legacy of the Hill-Thomas Hearings*, Oxford University Press, New York, 1995, at 37.
70 *Ibid*, at 1009.
71 See also Catharine A MacKinnon, *Toward a Feminist Theory of the State*, Harvard University Press, Cambridge, MA, 1989, especially Chapter 5.
72 Catharine A MacKinnon, 'Feminism, Marxism, Method and the State: An Agenda for Theory' (1982) *Signs* 515 at 535-7.
73 Cheris Kramarae and Paula A Treichler, *A Feminist Dictionary*, Pandora Press, Boston, 1985, at 105.
74 Christine A Littleton, 'Book Review; Feminist Jurisprudence: The Difference Method Makes' (1989) 41 *Stanford Law Review* 751 at 752.

The identification of consciousness raising as *the* feminist methodology in law has been widely criticised. For example, Anne Bottomley et al argue:

> While we recognise the value of consciousness raising for the empowerment of individual women, and the significance of this in raising feminist theory, we cannot accept that it is, or should be, the entire or only methodology. ...
>
> ... [W]e see consciousness raising as primarily a method of empowering individual women. If we are right that patriarchy is constituted in more than the sum of individual lives, then the response to it must be more than the sum of articulated individual experience.[75]

Similarly, Ruth Colker says:

> We can only engage in consciousness raising with a limited number of people; thus, we can never be fully exposed to all the possibilities for ourselves. Who we are exposed to influences how we see ourselves.[76]

Littleton suggests that these critics have misunderstood MacKinnon's notion of consciousness raising. She argues that MacKinnon is not restricting her notion of feminist method to these consciousness raising groups:

> Rather, in the expanded meaning that MacKinnon seems to use, it still embodies feminist method. Taking women seriously, on our own terms – the essence of CR [consciousness raising] – *is* feminist method.[77]

Littleton notes that this feminist epistemological stance 'reverses the traditional academic privileging of the "disinterested observer"' and, for Littleton, not only is feminism 'a theory *of* women, not a theory *about* women' but it can only be a theory created by women: 'women's experience [is] a necessary prerequisite for doing feminism'.[78]

Thus, Littleton describes feminist jurisprudence as 'feminist method applied to law'.[79]

> Thus "feminist jurisprudence" includes all attempts to explain, critique, and change law on behalf of, and *from the perspective of*, women. While it may be practiced in many forms, all forms must start in the same place, ie, by taking women's experience as central, and legal categories or doctrines as merely raw material – to be cut and pasted, stretched, arranged, and sewn together to fit that experience.[80]

Notes

1. Is MacKinnon making a claim that the adoption of a feminist methodology will lead to discovering 'the truth'? In the extract quoted above MacKinnon says consciousness raising's 'claim to women's perspective *is* its claim to truth'. For Ruth Colker, this means that MacKinnon 'validates women's cries

---

75 Anne Bottomley, Susie Gibson and Belinda Meteyard, 'Dworkin; Which Dworkin? Taking Feminism Seriously' (1987) 14 *Journal of Law and Society* 47 at 56.
76 Ruth Colker, 'Feminism, Sexuality, and Self: A Preliminary Inquiry into the Politics of Authenticity' (1988) 68 *Boston University Law Review* 217 at 245.
77 Christine Littleton, 'Book Review', at 765.
78 *Ibid*, at 765, particularly note 72, where Littleton refers to Christine Littleton, 'Reconstructing Sexual Equality' (1987) 75 *California Law Review* 1279 which more fully expounds the thesis that only women can create feminist theory. Littleton suggests that MacKinnon does not take this latter view, accepting that men can have the experience of being feminised, for example when they are raped.
79 *Ibid*, at 766.
80 *Ibid*, at 766, note 73.

of pain or humiliation within traditional sexuality but not women's cries of freedom or authenticity'.[81] Similarly, Robin West suggests that some women do get pleasure from the 'eroticisation of submission' and to ignore those descriptions of pleasure or, as she suggests MacKinnon does, to see them as manifestations of false consciousness is to abandon feminist method.[82] Or, according to Carol Smart:

> If we do not elevate consciousness-raising to the dubious status of a scientific method, we may still find that it has value. Lahey (who does treat it as a method) talks of consciousness-raising as a process of reordering understanding and as a way of creating moments-of-knowing. However, she does not elevate this to a truth. I see this as more fruitful, as long as experience is not given any inherent essential meaning (Weedon, 1987). This is because consciousness-raising allows for the possibility of alternative accounts, ones which recognise that 'things can be different'. Hence women come to recognise that they can change themselves and their circumstances (within limits). Consciousness-raising links knowledge with strategy, breaking down isolation and constructing alternatives. Rather than being a method to reveal Truth, consciousness-raising is part of a struggle over meaning. Hence what was natural (eg male violence) becomes defined as political and change is then potentiated. Consciousness-raising is about creating knowledge which can be liberating, once it becomes a feminist truth it becomes another mode of disqualifying women who do not conform to that version of events. It is in this respect that MacKinnon's espousal of consciousness-raising as a method is so suspect.[83]

2. Is it necessary to make claims to truth in order to engage with law? Gotell has been particularly critical of the way LEAF, the Canadian feminist litigation organisation, has made foundational claims about women in the course of participating in litigation. By this she means that LEAF claimed to be speaking the (one and only) truth about women, even where the women it talked about have become more than just white middle-class women. She argues that '[t]o engage within legal discourse, feminists need not speak from essential foundations but they must speak from a position of "Truth"'.[84] However, she suggests that 'even though the claim to "Truth" may have the effect of empowering feminist claims in law, this foundationalist strategy is not without its strategic perils for feminist politics'.[85]

> By conceiving feminist politics as being about an opposition between feminism and its external enemies, foundationalism denies that feminism itself is a site of legitimate political differences. In this manner it encourages an assertion of feminist 'Truth' against feminist politics and discourages democratic debate within feminism.

---

81 Colker, 'Feminism, Sexuality and Self', at 250.
82 Robin West, 'The Difference in Women's Hedonic Lives: A Phenomenological Critique of Feminist Legal Theory' (1987) 3 *Wisconsin Women's Law Journal* 81 at 118. Note that West also claims that consciousness raising reveals the truth (at 128).
83 Carol Smart, *Feminism and the Power of Law*, Routledge, London, 1989, at 80. The article by Lahey referred to is Kathleen Lahey, '"...until women themselves have told all that they have to tell..."' (1985) 23 *Osgoode Hall Law Journal* 519 and the book by Weedon is Chris Weedon, *Feminist Practice and Post-Structuralist Theory*, Blackwell, Oxford, 1987.
84 Lise Gotell, 'Litigating Feminist "Truth": An Antifoundational Critique' (1995) 4 *Social and Legal Studies* 99 at 114.
85 *Ibid*, at 123.

For feminist legal actors, like LEAF, these considerations are at once unsettling and at the same time critical. Law as it currently exists rests on foundations; but perhaps feminist legal strategy should seek to unsettle these foundations. As Smart ... has argued, feminists must attempt to disrupt law at its heart, including its privilege of objectivity and abstraction, in order to make way for multiple and diverse feminist discourses. At the level of practice, perhaps this means that feminist litigators must make it explicit that legal arguments are always the product of politics and normative assertion, rather than 'Truth'. Perhaps it means that feminist legal discourse must reflect complexity, contingency and contending feminist positions. Perhaps it also means that we should encourage multiple and sometimes competing feminist interventions in law. Coherent subject positions and 'Truth' do enable feminist uses of law but foundational claims may also inhibit legal recognition of the full texture and complexities of social relations.[86]

Some of Gotell's article is directed towards LEAF's failure to engage in appropriate consultation before reaching the position it put forward, as *the* feminist position, in litigation. Part of its 'authority', she argues, 'has rested ... on an assertion of legal expertise'.[87] What does this suggest about the way legal actors should engage with non-legal actors in pursuing legal interventions?

There is no equivalent to LEAF in Australia and we have very different rules about standing.[88] Hence, even if an Australian court were to allow a feminist organisation to intervene in litigation, it is highly unlikely to permit two or more such organisations, representing different feminist perspectives on an issue.

Legal storytelling

As well as a critical focus on the 'stock stories' legal decision-makers draw on, which we have averted to above, many legal scholars have also turned their attention to how alternative stories can be told, in particular how, as Matsuda describes them, 'outsider voices' can be heard.[89] One Australian example that examines both stock stories and counter stories is Lisa Sarmas' analysis of the infamous High Court decision in *Louth v Diprose*.[90]

In this case, Diprose, a male solicitor who had given a house to a woman, Mary Louth, managed to have the gift set aside on the ground that it would be unconscionable for her to maintain her interest in the house. It was considered 'unconscionable' because he was infatuated with her and it was held she had manipulated him into giving her the house. Through an imagined discussion between students discussing the case and relying on the formal decisions by the various judges and (in a move surprisingly rare in legal scholarship) using the trial transcript – the verbatim transcript of what was actually said by all parties in the

---

86 Ibid.
87 Ibid, at 114.
88 See ALRC, *Standing in Public Interest Litigation*, Report No 27, AGPS, Canberra, 1985; and *Equality Before the Law: Women's Equality*, Report No 69, Part II, Chapter 7.
89 Mari Matsuda, 'Affirmative Action and Legal Knowledge: Planting Seeds in Plowed-Up Ground' (1988) 11 *Harvard Women's Law Journal* 1.
90 Lisa Sarmas, 'Storytelling and the Law: A Case Study of *Louth v Diprose*' (1994) 19 *Melbourne University Law Review* 701; *Louth v Diprose* (1992) 175 CLR 621 (HCA) (and *Diprose v Louth (No 1)* (1990) 54 SASR 438 (King CJ); *Diprose v Louth (No 2)* (1990) 54 SASR 450 (Full Court)).

original litigation – Sarmas problematises how 'the facts' were found in this case. In describing the way the parties in this case were portrayed by the majority judges, Sarmas states:

> There is nothing subtle about this story. It stands out for its vivid characterisations of both parties, the ample use of metaphor, and generally, the presence of an explicit 'narrative' flavour. When the powerful image of the 'damned whore' is juxtaposed with that of the 'love-struck knight in shining armour', we know immediately that Louth must lose the case.[91]

Although the minority dissenting judges decided that Mary Louth should keep the gift of the house, Sarmas is equally concerned about their characterisation of Louth. For them Louth 'deserves our pity. She is a single mother, after all, and she is poor. Sick, emotionally unstable, suicidal, victim of rape, oppressed former wife'.[92] Louis Diprose, on the other hand, is:

> A romantic man of limited assets, he showered her with gifts. But he is not entitled to take those gifts back just because he regrets giving them. He is a grown professional man who knew what he was doing. He is not a fool, and he must have been getting something out of the relationship. Louth and he were on relatively *equal* terms.[93]

Sarmas concludes that:

> [B]oth of the stories told in the case are stock stories. Whether it's whore or victim, kindly gentleman or romantic fool, these images not only fail to capture the complex nature of human subjectivity, but they also reinforce dominant stereotypes about women, particularly poor women, and about men.[94]

Sarmas suggests another reading of the case that is sensitive to both gender and class inequality through one of her imaginary students (Tran Scripts) who goes back to the trial transcript to look for other 'facts'. She suggests, for example, that Louth might have seen the behaviour of Diprose as sexual harassment (as Sarmas points out, he had sent Louth 91 'love poems').[95] She also argues that their economic positions were quite disparate, a disparity not recognised by any of the judges. Again in the words of the 'student' Tran:

> All of the judgments suggested that Diprose was not a wealthy man. His assets were described as 'limited' and reference was made to the fact that he was living in 'rented accommodation' and 'had to work as an employee solicitor for a living'. The trial judge referred to the following assets owned by Diprose: mortgage money worth '$91,000, an old car, an aeroplane of the value of $25,000/$30,000 ... interest worth about $15,000 or $20,000 and a house owned with other members of his family ... [and] debts of about $15,000'.
>
> Compared with Louth, who was on the supporting parents' benefit at the time, and who appears to have owned no significant assets at all, it seems to me that Diprose was very well off indeed.[96]

Sarmas is somewhat sceptical 'about the potential of counternarratives to change the views and actions of insiders':

---

91   Sarmas, 'Storytelling and the Law', at 719.
92   *Ibid.*
93   *Ibid.*
94   *Ibid*, at 720.
95   *Ibid*, at 716-17. One of these poems included the following lines: 'I feel you biting my neck, our intertwined tongues,/Your awakening nipples under my busy hands;/And take you and f... you deeply in my thoughts' (cited in *ibid*, at 716).
96   *Ibid*, at 717-18.

Reservations have been expressed about the ability of judges (in particular) to empathise with outsider groups given that they do not share the same experiences and understandings. It has also been pointed out that because dominant narratives are seen as the 'natural' state of affairs, because they have the power of 'truth', then it is unlikely that counternarratives will persuade people to think otherwise. They are more likely to generate resistance rather than conversion, particularly amongst those who have a stake in the status quo.[97]

However, she argues:

> The telling of outsiders' stories in and out of court might not achieve change overnight, but it may assist in the gradual process of fracturing dominant narratives and creating larger spaces in the gaps which appear. It can also help create a viable opposition through community building and consciousness raising within outsider groups.[98]

Notes

1. Sarmas points out that her presentation of Louth's counterstory is not in fact Louth's story. It was created from reading trial transcripts which are already a filtered version of what happened and who she was. That is, Sarmas is not claiming that Sarmas' story is Louth's story as Louth would have told it or wanted it presented. What effect does this concession have on the strength of Sarmas' argument?
2. Hilary Astor raises another of the hazards or limitations of the legal storytelling method – the accusation that the teller is engaged in special pleading.[99] She describes using a storytelling method to raise the issues of violence in mediation at a general conference of legal academics. She told the fictitious story of Elizabeth, a lawyer, who was severely bashed by her husband and who left him after his violence had caused her to have a miscarriage. She wanted to get the audience to reflect on whether Elizabeth might end up in mediation in the resolution of her disputes with her husband about property and access and how Elizabeth might fare in a mediation process. The second part of her published article reflects on the reaction to her paper by that audience. One part of that reaction was that the paper was unlike others at the conference: 'It was emotional! The author must have a barrow to push – perhaps she is talking about herself!'.[100]

   > One does wonder whether, when an academic gives a paper on bankruptcy, there is speculation about whether that academic has personal experience of bankruptcy. Or whether, if one used a storytelling method to illustrate the dilemmas faced by a bankrupt in the legal system, one would be seen as pushing a "barrow". Speculations that Elizabeth's story was polemic motivated by autobiography are disturbing in that they do not do justice to the issues raised, which are an important part of legal scholarship and the law school curriculum.[101]

---

97 *Ibid*, at 725.
98 *Ibid*, at 726.
99 See Hilary Astor, 'Elizabeth's Story: Mediation, Violence and the Legal Academy' (1997) 2 *Flinders Journal of Law Reform* 13.
100 *Ibid*, at 27.
101 *Ibid*, at 29. See also Christine Boyle, 'Sexual Assault and the Feminist Judge' (1986) 1 *Canadian Journal* 93 at 102, note 39, who notes that she appeared in a graduate seminar course outline 'under the heading of 'Legal Scholarship for a Cause', while a male tax lawyer spoke under the heading 'Conventional Legal Research'.

To what extent do you think it is reliance on a storytelling method that led to the accusation of barrow pushing? Or is it still the case (as Astor suggests)[102] that what we said in the first edition of this book (in 1990) — that '[f]or some time there has been a tendency toward characterising feminist scholarship on law as critical, polemical, and having a "viewpoint" (suggesting, of course, that other forms of scholarship are viewpoint neutral)' — remains true? In other words, was it the feminist label Astor wore rather than her use of storytelling that encouraged some participants to see her paper as 'special pleading'? Is the use of a storytelling methodology within feminist and other critical scholarship more likely to lead to its being described as 'emotional' than more traditional feminist scholarship?

3. In the chapter on the public/private dichotomy we drew attention to the TGLRG's challenge to Tasmania's 'unnatural sex laws' before the UN's Human Rights Committee. In their representations before that Committee, the TGLRG also used stories to make their argument:

> The legal arguments are short. Little time is taken in outlining the distinctions made in law between homos and heteros. There are no arguments that gay men and lesbians deserve the same rights because we are as good as them. Instead, the communication concentrates on telling stories about the lives of gay men and lesbians in Tasmania. ... Stories of discrimination in employment and access to services, and stories of violence are told involving eight gay men and three lesbians. In each of these stories, the perpetrators justified their actions by reference to the 'illegality' of homosex in Tasmania.[103]

Morgan argues that the focus on gay and lesbian lives was connected to the methodology used in drafting the submission/Communication to the Human Rights committee: 'Although primarily drafted by one person, it was subject to agreement, editing and approval by a successful coalitionist group of lesbians and gay men (the TGLRG)'.[104] Is a storytelling methodology particularly useful where it is important to recognise and represent a diversity of interests in a legal submission?

Morgan also suggests that '[t]he Committee's decision speaks of gay and lesbian lives in a more positive way than is usually the case in legal texts'.[105] Although Morgan does not explicitly argue this, do you think it is likely that the inclusion of the stories of actual women and men may have encouraged the court in its more positive expression?[106]

---

102 Astor, 'Elizabeth's Story', at 29.
103 Wayne Morgan, 'Identifying Evil for What It Is: Tasmania, Sexual Perversity and the United Nations' (1994) 19 *Melbourne University Law Review* 740 at 748.
104 *Ibid*.
105 *Ibid*. Morgan contrasts this with the equivalent decision in the *Dudgeon* case (*Dudgeon v United Kingdom* (1981) 4 EHRR 149), a decision of the European Court of Human Rights. There, he suggests, 'the dissenting judgments amount to vilification and even the majority decision is flavoured with distaste and speaks in the subordinating language of toleration' (*ibid*).
106 See also the discussion of the *Sears* litigation in Chapter 6.

'Truth' claims and claims on behalf of undifferentiated 'women'

In the chapter on equality, we raised the challenge to feminist work in law by indigenous women and women of colour in North America. This work has argued that much feminist analysis has addressed the needs of white middle class able-bodied women and ignored the needs and interests of 'other' women. The critique by women of colour and other women excluded by white feminism has been echoed in theoretical work by those explicitly embracing a postmodern or post-structuralist theoretical position.[107] Chris Weedon states:

> Poststructuralist analysis ... assumes that identity in Western cultures is not something given, it is rather a precarious and temporary effect of difference. The relations of difference involved are historically and socially specific, and they change. For example, men define themselves in relation to women. In this process, women become the Other, that is, what men are not. Whiteness is defined in a relationship of difference from blackness. ... Difference in this model is always a relationship and – more often than not – a hierarchical one. [There is a commitment to] the idea that identity is both temporary and precarious, without a firm grounding in natural gender difference, for example, in 'being a woman'....[108]

This critique clearly has connections with the criticisms we have noted above made by Gotell of feminist work in law that insists on making claims to 'truth'. If identity is both 'temporary and precarious', it is difficult to speak of it in 'foundational tones' – to claim it represents a foundation of truthful experience. Wendy Brown makes this connection in the following statement:

> In fact, postmodern decentering, disunifying, and denaturalizing of the subject is far more threatening to the status of feminism's well of truth than to feminism's *raison d'etre*. While often cast as concern with retaining an object of political struggle, feminist attachment to the subject is more critically bound to retaining women's experiences, feelings, and voices as sources and certifications of post-foundational political truth. When the notion of a unified and coherent subject is abandoned, we not only cease to be able to speak of woman or of women in an unproblematic way, we forsake the willing, deliberate, and consenting "I" that liberalism's rational-actor model of the human being proffers, and we surrender the autonomous, rights-bearing fictional unity that liberalism promises to secure. Yet each of these terms and practices – woman, willing, deliberate, consenting, an "I", rational actors, autonomy and rights – has been challenged by various *modernist* feminisms as masculinist, racist, ethnocentric, heterosexist, culturally imperialist, or all of the above. Moreover, dispensing with the unified subject does not mean ceasing to be able to speak about our experiences as women, only that our words cannot be legitimately deployed or construed as larger or longer than the moments of the lives they speak from; they cannot be anointed as "authentic" or "true" since the experience they announce is linguistically contained, socially constructed, discursively mediated, and never just individually "had".[109]

---

107 We do not make a distinction between these positions for the purposes of this book. For explorations of the differences (and similarities and connections), see, for example, Davies, *Asking the Law Question*; and Chris Weedon, *Feminism, Theory and the Politics of Difference*, Blackwell, Oxford, 1999, especially Chapter 5.
108 Weedon, *Feminism, Theory and the Politics of Difference*, at 104.
109 Wendy Brown, *States of Injury: Power and Freedom in Late Modernity*, Princeton University Press, New Jersey, 1995, at 40-1.

Notes

1. We have suggested that this postmodern or poststructural analysis of identity 'echoes' that of indigenous, Black and other women who have criticised feminist theory for making global claims which exclude their experience. *Is* this critique an 'echo'? Is it 'the same as', 'similar to' or completely different from the critique presented by Harris and Behrendt discussed earlier in this chapter?
2. This postmodern challenge has encountered resistance from some feminist theorists.[110] Weedon refers to the work of Nancy Hartsock who has argued:

   > Somehow it seems highly suspicious that it is at the precise moment when so many groups have been engaged in "nationalisms" which involve redefinitions of the marginalised Others that suspicions emerge about the nature of the "subject", about the possibilities for a general theory which can describe the world, about historical "progress". Why is it that just at the moment when so many of us who have been silenced begin to demand the right to name ourselves, to act as subjects rather than objects of history, that just then the concept of subjecthood becomes problematic?[111]

   While Hartsock is here being sceptical about the usefulness of the postmodern project for feminist work, does her scepticism also mean that she is discounting the challenge from indigenous and 'Other' women to feminist theory? Smart suggests that postmodern work in feminism has been subject to a much stronger critique from other (white) feminists than earlier anti-essentialist work which directly exposed the exclusion of indigenous, Black, lesbian and Other women from much feminist theory:

   > The women who attacked the Women's Movement and Feminist Theory for the presumption that there was a 'We' being properly represented and who pointed out that such representation was spurious and that gender should not obliterate race or ethnicity, or sexuality and so on, received none of the opprobrium that Butler and others have received for saying virtually the same thing.[112]

   Assuming that Smart is correct, why might postmodern work seem more unsettling than the more explicit challenges from women who have been or felt excluded from much traditional feminist work?
3. Some writers have suggested that law may be particularly resistant to postmodern insights. Smart appears to be taking this view where she discusses the use of social constructionist insights in the context of rape law:

   > The idea that the category of woman is constructed does not mean that "real" women (as historically constituted) do not walk the social landscape. As Butler argues:

---

110 See Weedon who suggests that the notion that identity has no 'firm grounding in natural gender difference ... has proved controversial within feminism, especially among those writers who see identity as the precondition for effective political action' (at 104).
111 Nancy Hartsock, 'Foucault on Power: A Theory for Women' in Linda Nicholson (ed), *Feminism/Postmodernism*, Routledge, London, 1990, at 163. See also, for example, Susan Bordo, 'Feminism, Postmodernism, and Gender-Scepticism' in Nicholson (ed), *Feminism/Postmodernism*; Diane Bell and Renate Klein (eds), *Radically Speaking: Feminism Reclaimed*, Spinifex Press, Melbourne, 1996; Catharine MacKinnon, 'Points Against Postmodernism' (2000) 75 *Chicago-Kent Law Review* 687.
112 Carol Smart, 'Law, Feminism and Sexuality: From Essence to Ethics?' (1994) 9 *Canadian Journal of Law and Society* 15 at 23.

> To claim that gender is constructed is not to assert its illusoriness or artificiality, where those terms are understood to reside within a binary that counterposes the "real" and the "authentic" as oppositional. [Judith Butler, *Gender Trouble*, Routledge, London, 1990, at 32].

Thus *we* are not natural, but *we* are real. *We* are also constituted as more than just women: we have more than our gender. Whilst there is still a need to avoid falling back into what Butler calls the totalising gesture of feminism, it does still mean that in struggle with powerful discursive mechanisms, such as the law on rape, we can continue to operate with the category of woman – but in the recognition that certain political situations require the articulation of apparently naive categories which have greater significance/depth when subjected to a feminist reading or which should not be presented so naively outside the confines of legal "engagement".[113]

Gayatri Spivak coined the notion of strategic essentialism to describe the need, on occasion, to engage in the language of universalism:

> [I]t's absolutely on target to take a stand against the discourses of essentialism .... But *strategically* we cannot. ... You pick up the universal that will give you the power to fight against the other side and what you are throwing away by doing that is your theoretical purity.[114]

4. It is also the case that there are connections between postmodern feminist work and that of Catharine MacKinnon, as Margaret Davies has demonstrated.[115] According to Davies, one of the fundamental elements of MacKinnon's work, like much postmodern work, 'concerns the analysis of social meanings. ... [P]ower is associated with the definitions through which we create the world. Men have the power to create the world in their own image, to define what counts as truth'.[116] She argues that the feminist project of placing women's experience as central, not marginal, also parallels the general deconstructionist project of showing that the dominant term in a binary pair only gets its meaning from the marginalised term:

> One of the central ways in which the association of power with truth appears in both radical feminism and postmodernism is the idea that meaning is constructed through exclusion and hierarchy.[117]

Finally, Davies argues that the central tenet of MacKinnon's radical feminism that '[w]omen are constructed according to masculine images, because men have the power to define reality' is 'also the basis for the postmodern critique of masculinist ideals of femininity.[118]

---

113 *Ibid*, at 29.
114 Elizabeth Grosz and Gayatri Spivak, 'Criticism, Feminism and the Institution: An Interview with Gayatri Chakravorty Spivak' (1984/85) 10/11 *Thesis Eleven* 175 at 184. However, see also her reconsideration of her position in Gayatri Chakavorty Spivak (with Ellen Rooney) 'In a Word, Interview' (1989) 1(2) *Differences* 124, especially at 126-30. Here she suggests that one of the reasons strategic essentialism became popular was that it provided 'an alibi' for essentialism (at 128). She proposes instead a strategy of 'noting how ourselves and others are what you call essentialist, without claiming a counter-essence disguised under the alibi of strategy' (*ibid*). However, she also argues that 'the critique of essentialism' should be 'understood not as an exposure of error, our own or others, but as an acknowledgement of the dangerousness of what one must use' (*ibid*, at 129).
115 Davies, *Asking the Law Question*, at 214-18.
116 *Ibid*, at 214.
117 *Ibid*, at 215.
118 *Ibid*, at 218.

Davies is not, however, arguing that postmodernism and radical feminism are the same. For example, she points out that the postmodern critique of MacKinnon's work – that she has an overdetermined view of female sexuality – has led to work that sees female sexuality as more than is accounted for by patriarchal definitions of it, and a focus on multiple female (and male) sexualities.[119] At the same time she says radical feminism and postmodernism 'are not mutually exclusive approaches because the questions being tackled, and the level at which they are addressed, differ: although the theories intersect in various ways, the terrain being covered is never identical'.[120]

5. Davies concludes her comparison of postmodernism and radical feminism by focusing in on some of the difficulties of engaging with law:

> There is a tension between envisaging fundamental social and conceptual change and the necessity of negotiating with a system of oppression which just keeps on reasserting itself.[121]

This last comment suggests to us a certain theoretical eclecticism; one's choice of a theoretical modality may depend on how one is engaging with the legal system. That is, there may be different answers to the issues and questions we have raised depending on the way in which one is engaging with law. For example, the theoretical and strategic tools may be different depending on whether one is engaging in litigation, drafting a submission to a parliamentary committee or writing an academic article. This is not meant to imply that one should be willing to forget the limitations of the categories we use, but to suggest that the willingness of that particular legal institution to listen, and an assessment of what is to be achieved by that engagement, may be relevant to how those methodologies and categories are used. Lorraine Code suggests:

> [I]t is as important to be objective in order to contest oppression with well-established facts as it is to be strategically skeptical in order not to allow closure that could erase experiences and differences under an assimilationist rubric. It is as important to affirm identities and allegiances as politically informed, active thinkers as to acknowledge the falsely essentializing, solidifying tendencies of identity politics and political categories to impose premature structure on events and circumstances that need to be open to transformative intervention.[122]

Privacy, equality and methodology: The Hindmarsh Island Bridge dispute

The Hindmarsh Island Bridge dispute, discussed by Joanna Bourke,[123] brings together a number of the major theoretical themes in this part of the book, themes that inform the remainder of the book. In 1989, Binalong Pty Ltd proposed a large tourist development on Hindmarsh Island, off the coast of South Australia, and the proposal included building a bridge from the Island to the mainland. The South Australian government agreed to its construction. However, before work

---

119 *Ibid.*
120 *Ibid*, at 214.
121 *Ibid*, at 218.
122 Code, 'Epistemology', at 183.
123 Joanna Bourke, 'Women's Business: Sex, Secrets and the Hindmarsh Island Affair' (1997) 20 *University of New South Wales Law Journal* 333.

commenced, the Aboriginal Legal Rights Movement sought heritage protection for the area under the *Aboriginal and Torres Strait Islander Heritage Protection Act 1984* (Cth). In 1994, Professor Cheryl Saunders was appointed to conduct an inquiry under the Act. In her report to the Minister, she noted that the area was sacred to the Ngarrindjeri people and she enclosed an envelope which was only supposed to be seen by women, documenting the secret women's business of the local women. On the basis of this report the Minister, without examining the contents of the envelope,[124] declared that the bridge should not be built, at least for 25 years. This decision was successfully challenged in the Federal Court.[125] A group that came to be described as the 'dissident women', and some Aboriginal men,[126] challenged the notion that the area was sacred. The State government then set up a Royal Commission to inquire into the veracity of the women's beliefs.[127] Bourke argues:

> Aboriginal people, more than almost any other group within Australian society, have been the objects of legal examination, discipline and normalisation. This legal control has been extended to encompass nearly every sphere of Aboriginal life, so that even decisions not to intervene are informed by the legal system and its fixed concepts of harm and relevance. The legal regulation of Aboriginal sacred knowledges can be looked at using the analytical tool of ... the public/private division ... .
>
> Several important issues are raised by the public control of religious or spiritual knowledges, an area which has been regarded as one of the most private realms of human existence. The legislative framework designed to protect Aboriginal heritage is based on the assumption that Aboriginal people will, and should, rely upon the state for the 'preservation and protection' of their culture. Importantly, the protection of Aboriginal sacred sites has been positioned within legal discourse as forming part of 'the public interest'. This placement has had the effect of opening such knowledges up to public scrutiny in a way that the 'private interests' of developers frequently are not. ...
>
> The underlying assumption in the case of the Hindmarsh Island Royal Commission was that as such knowledge is already in the 'public domain' as part of the 'public interest', there should be no objection to subjecting this knowledge to the legitimatising process of legal examination. The questions of whether the private spiritual life of Aboriginal women is a suitable subject for legal scrutiny, or whether such knowledge should be regarded as 'public property', remain unasked.
>
> ... The 'public's interest' in the preservation of cultural knowledge might be better served if this knowledge was kept privately by its custodians.[128]

Bourke goes on to suggest that the claims in the Hindmarsh case were subject to much more scrutiny than equivalent claims by indigenous men have been:

---

124 Note that the envelope was by mistake delivered to the Opposition Minister, Ian McLachlan, who read the secret documents. He resigned from Cabinet soon after (*ibid*, at 350).

125 See *Chapman and Barton v Tickner, Minister for Aboriginal and Torres Strait Islander Affairs* (1995) 133 ALR 74 (per O'Loughlin J) and, on appeal, *Tickner, Minister for Aboriginal and Torres Strait Islander Affairs v Chapman* (1995) 133 ALR 226.

126 Bourke notes that 'Doug Milera, whose story of fabrication was seized upon as "the truth" by sections of the media, told his story whilst intoxicated, to a journalist who had offered to provide him with a bed for the night as well as free food and alcohol' (Bourke, 'Women's Business', at 348, note 82.

127 The chronology is taken from an appendix to Bourke, 'Women's Business', at 350-1. Subsequent to the publication of Bourke's article, the bridge was in fact built and the developers were unsuccessful in their case suing for damages (*Chapman v Luminis Pty Ltd (No 5)* [2001] FCA 1106) (though they have appealed the decision).

128 Bourke, 'Women's Business', at 336-7.

This legacy of 'cultural invisibility' has meant that although the claims being made by Ngarrindjeri women in relation to Hindmarsh Island are no different in character from those discussed in the cases concerning the knowledge of Yawuru [*Western Australia v Minister for Aboriginal and Torres Strait Islander Affairs* (unreported, Federal Court, Carr J, 7 February 1994] or Waugyl [*Tickner v Bropho* (1993) 40 FCR 183] men, they have been treated in a very different manner. It is suggested that the reason the sacred knowledges relating to Hindmarsh Island have proved controversial enough to require scrutiny by two separate Commissions of Inquiry, is that they are not assertions of an 'ungendered' (male) Aboriginal secret life, but are claims being made by Aboriginal women. ...

The processes of the cultural imperialism which accompanied white invasion had the effect of destroying much Aboriginal sacred knowledge. Alongside this trivialisation of Aboriginal religion was the assumption that the patriarchal structure of Anglo-Australian culture was also the norm in Aboriginal societies. This 'two-pronged' operation successfully made the ritual life of Aboriginal women culturally invisible and, as a consequence, this knowledge became even more vulnerable to destruction and desecration than the sacred knowledges of Aboriginal men.[129]

Bourke compares the situation of the treatment of Aboriginal men's and women's beliefs in the 'Junction Hole mediation'[130] and suggests that '[t]he fact that the Arrernte women were subject to intense scrutiny, while the Arrernte men (asserting very similar knowledges) were not, suggests that the media's preoccupation with secrets will be even greater if they belong to women and therefore become imbued with an "eroticism" not found in "men's business"'.[131]

Note

1. Is it possible for indigenous women (or men) to engage with state attempts to protect indigenous heritage while keeping their religious beliefs 'private'? Bourke concludes her article in the following way:

   > The belief that Aboriginal knowledge is 'public property' and the reification of the procedural aspects of law have actively worked against the interests of Aboriginal people in the protection of their sacred sites. Aboriginal women in heritage claims have become the victim of 'single axis thinking'. The same colonial processes which have left women such as the Ngarrindjeri most vulnerable to 'spiritual dispossession' have been reinvented in order to deny the legitimacy of their claims. The uncertainties and contradictions surrounding the 'women's business' in this case have been used as 'proof' that the women are lying, rather than as proof of the dislocating effect of colonisation on such knowledges. The adoption of the Anglo-Australian patriarchal model of gender relations by Aboriginal communities has also meant that Aboriginal men will, at certain times,

---

129 *Ibid*, at 340-1.
130 Bourke cites Hal Wootten, 'The Alice Springs Dam and Sacred Sites' (1993) 65 *Australian Quarterly* 8.
131 Bourke, 'Women's Business', at 343. Note that Bourke (*ibid*) also quotes Wootten, in his report on the Alice Springs dam proposal saying: 'I can assure the curious that the confidentiality of the site is not because the information would be found titillating, shocking or even particularly interesting by Western standards. It simply lacks significance in Western culture, and I could not claim to appreciate its significance to Aborigines'. Bourke also goes on to examine the credibility of Aboriginal women, suggesting that they are doubly incredible as both Aboriginal and women (*ibid*, at 347).

actively oppose the interests of Aboriginal women in preserving their sacred beliefs. The claims of the Ngarrindjeri women in relation to Hindmarsh Island have been rendered illegitimate through socially constructed definitions of 'credibility' and the workings of a truth/ knowledge hierarchy which devalues the kind of knowledge these women are asserting. In order to encompass the knowledge and the experiences of Aboriginal women, the current paradigm of administrative law needs to be reconceptualised along the lines proposed by Donna Haraway:

> I am arguing for politics and epistemologies of location, position and situating, where partiality and not universality is the condition of being heard to make rational knowledge claims. These are claims on people's lives; the view from a body, versus the view from above ... [Haraway, *Simians, Cyborgs and Women: The Reinvention of Nature*, Free Association Books, 1991, at 195].

Given the material on 'bias' earlier in this chapter, do you think it is likely that administrative law will be reconstructed in the way Haraway advocates? How would you go about that reconstruction?

The remainder of the book uses the theoretical themes we have introduced here to explore a range of legal doctrines that impact on women's lives, that create women as legal objects (and much less frequently legal subjects). However, the rest of the book is not organised by legal categories but in a way that takes account of the diversity of women's lives. Hence the next part examines women's participation in work, commencing with unpaid work in the home, and moving, in Chapter 6, to paid work. The following part looks at women's relationships, particularly relationships with children, examining the decision to have children, the 'rights' of foetuses and the loss of children. The fourth part, gendered harms, considers an array of injuries – or what might be constructed as injuries – to women, looking at medical abuses, domestic violence, rape, sexual harassment and pornography. The final chapter of the book considers a series of strategic questions about feminist engagement with law.

PART TWO

WOMEN AND ECONOMIC (IN)DEPENDENCE

In this part of the book, we look broadly at the issue of women's work. There is a tendency to assume that when we use the word 'work' in a legal context, we are speaking about labour law. In fact, there are many different ways in which women work, some for money, and some unpaid, and many of these are affected by forms of legal regulation.

This part of the book has two chapters. In the first, *Work in Families*, we look at aspects of women's financial situation that arise directly out of their involvement in family relationships, generally through marriage and other close personal relationships. In the second chapter, *Out to Work,* we focus on some issues that particularly affect women's participation in paid work.

Although for ease of treatment we divide these chapters into separate discussions, the issues are intimately and often inextricably connected. In 1984, the late Norwegian Professor of Women's Law, Tove Stang Dahl, published a pioneering discussion called 'Women's Rights to Money' in which she argued that women have access to money in three main ways: through paid work, through dependence on men (usually marriage) and through dependence on the state.[1] As we noted in the introductory part of this book, traditional legal categories rarely accurately capture the ways in which women's lives are organised and, perhaps more importantly, the ways in which they experience legal problems. When loosely translated into the legal categories we use in Australia, Stang Dahl's approach would emphasise labour law, family law and social security law. Importantly, she demonstrated through the use of the following diagram how these three sources are interconnected and how women move between and amongst them at various times in their lives.

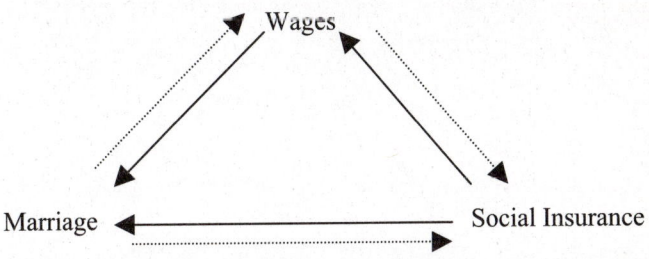

Figure 1. Sources of maintenance

---

1 Tove Stang Dahl, 'Women's Rights to Money' (1984) 12 *International Journal of the Sociology of Law* 137.

In this part of the book, we build upon her analysis, looking at some of the areas of law she identified as well as others that affect women's economic situation. For example, building upon her category 'dependence on men' we look not only at 'family law' as it has traditionally been understood (generally, as the law of marriage and divorce) but also at a range of legal doctrines that assume women's economic dependence based upon some aspect of relationship or status. In the second chapter, *Out To Work*, in addition to looking at women's participation in the paid work force via the vehicle of labour law, we look at some issues from doctrinal areas outside labour law that also contribute to the construction of women's relationship with the paid labour market, and we refer to some of the state policies that impact on women's economic lives, for example, superannuation and child care.

Chapter Five

Work in Families

Money and relationships

This chapter looks at a number of legal issues that arise because of women's participation in family life. To some extent, we might refer to this broadly as 'family law', but that terminology is usually reserved for the laws that govern marriage and, more particularly, relationship breakdown (divorce and related matters such as matrimonial property and children's issues). While a part of this chapter does deal expressly with some of the economic aspects of 'family law', we also consider some other legal consequences of women's participation in family life. This helps us to broaden our understanding of how the law impacts on women's lives in the family beyond those laws governing marriage and divorce. Another aim is to expand our understanding of 'work' beyond that encompassed by the terminology of 'labour law'. An underlying theme of this chapter is that many of the ways in which law affects women's family life involve their work, albeit work outside the paid labour market. By looking at aspects of law not usually associated with 'work', we see more clearly some of the many ways that women contribute to the economic wellbeing of their communities and their families, often through forms of unpaid work rarely recognised or accorded value. And, as much of women's unpaid work is undertaken in the home, by focusing on the value of women's work in a variety of legal doctrines, we also question the dichotomy between the public and the private, which, as we discussed in Part 1, might be said to keep the domestic sphere beyond the scrutiny of law, though regulated by it.

Women's unpaid work

Where might women's unpaid work feature in legal regulation? In addition to being central to the assessment of personal injury damages, which we examine both in this chapter and the next, it may also be an issue in family property proceedings. Claims based on a woman's contribution as homemaker and parent may be made under the *Family Law Act* 1975 (Cth) or under a State or Territory Act dealing with other relationships.[1] In equity, a woman can make a claim for a share in her partner's property if it would be unconscionable, upon the breakdown of a relationship, to disregard her work as a homemaker.[2] Similar issues of the

---

1   See *Property (Relationships) Act* 1984 (NSW); *De Facto Relationships Act* 1991 (NT); *Domestic Relationships Act* 1994 (ACT); *De Facto Relationship Act* 1999 (Tas); *Property Law Amendment Act* 1999 (Qld); *De Facto Relationships Act* 1996 (SA); *Property Law Act* 1958 (Vic). Some of these now extend to women in same sex or other close personal relationships (for example, NSW, ACT, Qld and Victoria): this is discussed further below.
2   See *Baumgartner v Baumgartner* (1987) 164 CLR 137; *Muschinski v Dodds* (1985) 160 CLR 583.

undervaluing of women's caring work are also raised when looking at family provision or testator's family maintenance issues within the law of succession.[3]

In this chapter, we use three case studies to illustrate some of the ways in which women's economic contributions are evaluated, either directly or indirectly, in legal contexts outside the arena of labour law. These three examples are 'family' law, sexually transmitted debt or relationship debt in the context of guarantees for other people's debts, and the assessment of personal injury damages. Before going on to consider these examples, we locate them in empirical data about women's work, both unpaid and paid.

Women's work in the home and in the market: An empirical introduction

There is a plethora of research showing that women in Australia remain primarily responsible for domestic work (eg cleaning, childcare, cooking, shopping etc).[4] Despite profound social and economic changes in Australia in the latter part of the 20th century, men still spend markedly less time than women on domestic work. Figures from 1997[5] show that married women spent an average of almost two hours more per day on household work than their husbands and were also more likely than their partners to participate in such work on an average day.[6] Where both partners worked similar hours in paid work, the difference was less marked though women still averaged one hour and 16 minutes more time than their husbands. The statistics also reveal 'a high degree of segregation in the specific types of domestic work [*men and women*] undertook',[7] with women focusing on tasks such as food preparation and cleaning up, laundry work and general housework, and men on grounds and animal care and general home maintenance.[8] Unless the task involved 'fixing something', men were generally occupied outside the home and women inside it.

When it comes to caring for children, a similar trend emerges. In 1992, mothers spent more than twice as much time as fathers on child care activities and though over the five years to 1997 women were spending slightly less time on child care, there was little change in the amount of time fathers spent caring for their children.[9] On the 1997 figures, where both parents worked full time, mothers spent about twice as much time as fathers caring for children and spent more time than fathers on all types of child care activities, for children of all age groups. Further, in families where fathers worked, mothers spent progressively less time with their children as their own hours of work increased. However:

---

3 See Graycar, 'Legal Categories and Women's Work: Explorations for a Cross-Doctrinal Feminist Jurisprudence' (1994) 7 *Canadian Journal of Women and the Law* 32. See also the judgment of Gaudron J in *Singer v Berghouse (No 2)* (1994) 181 CLR 201.
4 See, for example, Michael Bittman, *Juggling Time: How Australian Families Use Their Time*, OSW, Department of the Prime Minister and Cabinet, 1991; Australian Bureau of Statistics, *Women in Australia*, Cat No 4113.0, 1993; and Australian Bureau of Statistics, *How Australians Use Their Time*, Cat No 4153.0, 1994; Michael Bittman and Jocelyn Pixley, *The Double Life of the Family*, Allen and Unwin, Sydney, 1997.
5 See ABS, *Australian Social Trends 1999*, Cat No 4102.0, 1999; and *Time Use Survey, 1997*, Cat No 4150.0, 1997.
6 *Ibid*, at 119. Women averaged one hour and 47 minutes more.
7 *Ibid*, at 120.
8 *Ibid*.
9 *Ibid*, at 39. This is based on data from the 1992 and 1997 Time Use Surveys.

[F]or fathers in such families, the time spent with their children bore little relationship to the mother's hours of work. In fact, men spent slightly less time with their children, on average, when women worked full-time than when they worked part-time.[10]

ABS data published in 2000, based on information collected in the 1997 Time Use Survey, estimates the total value of unpaid work to the Australian economy to be about $261 billion. Of that, $237 billion (or 91%) consisted of unpaid household work of which women's contribution was two-thirds, while men's made up one-third.[11] Women were also over-represented amongst the participants in volunteer and community work.[12]

While most of the research that looks at the distribution of unpaid work in the household, particularly in Australia, has been undertaken in households where the adults are a married couple, recent research that compares married couples with those living in heterosexual cohabiting relationships found that, while the division of labour was less marked for those in de facto relationships, nonetheless 'women do a much larger proportion of child care and routine indoor housework tasks than men, regardless of marital status'.[13] And while there is still very little empirical work on the distribution of housework in lesbian households, there are indications from some studies in other countries that, where lesbian couples have had children together:

> Lesbian couples, by and large, reported being able to negotiate their division of labour equitably. In addition, lesbian nonbiological mothers were consistently described as more involved than heterosexual fathers with their children.[14]

Another United States study found that the majority of those lesbian couples who had jointly planned and conceived their child(ren) reported that parenting and domestic work were equally shared between the partners.[15] Though there is no comparable Australian research, it seems fair to speculate (if cautiously) that the lack of balance in the distribution of unpaid work in the home is a function of the nature of heterosexual (particularly marital) relationships.

Changes in the paid workforce

Unlike patterns of unpaid household labour, which show that the burden of this work continues to fall more heavily on women, the past few decades have seen significant changes take place in the paid labour force. These include an increase in part-time employment for women and a decrease in full time employment for men.[16] 1996

---

10   ABS, *Australian Social Trends 1999*, at 40.
11   See *Unpaid Work and the Australian Economy*, ABS at Cat No 5240.0 at 40, 2000. The estimated amounts vary according to which method of calculation is used: see chapter one of the report.
12   *Ibid*, at 10. Men contributed 44%, women 56%.
13   Janeen Baxter, 'Marital Status and the Division of Household Labour: Cohabitation vs Marriage' (2001) 58 *Family Matters* 16 at 18. See also Jo Lindsay, 'Diversity but not Equality: Domestic Labour in Cohabiting Relationships' (1999) 34 *Australian Journal of Social Issues* 267.
14   Charlotte Patterson and Raymond Chan, 'Families Headed by Lesbian and Gay Parents' in Michael Lamb (ed), *Parenting and Child Development in 'Nontraditional' Families*, Erlbaum, New Jersey, 1999, at 203.
15   Maureen Sullivan, 'Rozzie and Harriet: Gender and Family Patterns of Lesbian Co-Parents' (1996) 10 *Gender and Society* 747 at 756.
16   See *Australian Women's Year Book 1997*, at 70 (based on Labour Force Survey, unpublished data, showing figures for 1986-1996). There was also an overall increase in part-time employment for men over this period. For both men and women the increase was 3-4%. Further, for women in the 25-44 age group, there was a shift of 2.6% away from part-time hours and of 1.2% away from usual full-time hours towards long full-time hours (3.8%). See *Australian Social Trends 1999*, at 106.

figures show that the labour force participation rate has remained higher for men (73%) than women (53%), with the latter's participation dropping off particularly for married women in the 25-34 year age group (the prime child-bearing ages).[17] Further, the proportion of women who worked part time, either on a permanent or casual basis, was significantly higher than the proportion of men, reflecting men's greater participation in full-time work.[18] Added to this, women were more likely than men to hold a second job and, for both men and women, there was a decrease in the number of people working a standard working week of 35-40 hours.[19]

Women's labour force participation is significantly affected by having children to care for. For example, in 1996, in 34% of families consisting of couples with at least one child, the wife was not in the labour force and in another 31% of them, the wife worked part time and the husband full time.[20] Where women headed single-parent families, in 14% of cases the mother worked full time and in 21% part time.[21] It is interesting to compare the figures of women who did and did not have children to care for. Of women in the 35-44 age group with husbands in the labour force, where there were no dependants, 59% of women worked full time, compared to 29% of those with dependants of any age.[22] And [t]he proportion of mothers not in the labour force decreased as the age of the children increased'.[23] For married women aged 15-34 years who also had young children, only 17% worked full time compared to 71% with no dependants. It is often assumed that sole parents are more likely than those in two parent households to be in paid work, yet the opposite is in fact the case.[24] To give an overall picture, '[a]lmost half of women with children aged 0-9 years were not in the labour force, over five times the proportion of those with no dependants'.[25]

MARRIAGE AND FAMILY

In the introduction to this Part, we referred to Tove Stang Dahl's model of the three (sometimes interconnected) sources of income for women. One of these was income from participation in family life. Heterosexual women, by marrying, are assumed to have access to their partner's financial resources and this is why Stang Dahl refers to this particular source as being based on their 'economic dependence

---

17   See *Australian Women's Year Book 1997*, at 71 (source: ABS, *Labour Force, Australia*, Cat No 6203.0). However, in the 16-19 age group there was less than one percentage point difference between men and women due largely to the high numbers of young women working part time while studying full time.
18   17.3% of women worked permanent part time and 23.6% worked casual part time compared to the respective figures of 2.2% and 7.6% for men. See *Australian Women's Year Book 1997*, at 72, table, Employees, August 1995. (Source: *Working Arrangements*, Australia, Cat No 6342.0)
19   See *Australian Women's Year Book 1997*, at 73.
20   These figures are for married women aged 35-44 years whose husbands were in the labour force.
21   See *Australian Women's Year Book 1997*, at 75.
22   *Ibid*, at 75-6. The percentages in this extract are for married women aged 35-44 years whose husbands were in the labour force.
23   See *Australian Women's Year Book 1997*, at 76.
24   According to Australian Bureau of Statistics figures on labour force participation (June 2000), of women in couples with children under four years, 48.0% are employed (16.1% full time and 31.9% part time). As the child reaches school age (5-9), the figure rises to 66.7% (25.9% full time and 40.8% part time). For female sole parents with children under four, 28.5% are employed (9.0% full time; 19.5% part time). As the child reaches school age, 52.3% of female sole parents are employed (22.2% full time, 30.0% part time): ABS, *Labour Force Status and Other Characteristics of Families Survey*, June 2000, Cat No 6224.0.
25   See *Australian Women's Year Book* 1997, at 76. Issues related to women's participation in the paid labour force are explored further in Chapter 6.

on men'. In this part of the chapter we examine some aspects of the laws that affect family relationships (including, though not limited to, marital relationships), focusing especially on the impact on women's financial circumstances. We start by looking at some of the historical consequences of marriage for women, before going on to consider some of the assumptions that underpin the term 'family law' as it has tended to be used in law school courses and broader legal discourses. Traditional treatments of 'family law' rarely acknowledge the complex role of law in regulating relationships, but instead tend to focus on divorce and its consequences: ie, 'family' life after marriage breakdown.[26] In the remainder of this case study, we focus also on these aspects of family law (relationship breakdown and its consequences) in relation to how they affect women and their economic situation. The discussion in this part of the chapter relates closely to issues dealt with in Part 1, particularly the public/private distinction, and the models of equality we discussed there. We also consider some current policy issues in family law, such as the increasing recognition of the importance of superannuation in the context of family law property, the relevance of violence to property division and the implications of the trend toward private ordering in family law. As mentioned in the introduction, since much of the law that deals with 'families' presumes particular types of familial relationship, there is a clear presumption of heterosexuality in many of the issues raised here that should be borne in mind as you read this chapter.

The legal consequences of marriage: A brief historical account

There is a long history of the law's treatment of women as the dependants of men, most usually their husbands, though in the case of unmarried women, this role could be occupied by the father. However, the most significant disabilities were those attached to married women who, at common law (with infants and lunatics), had no legal capacity. The following extract documents the situation for married women under the common law prior to the enactment of the Married Women's Property Acts in Britain and the Australian States in the late 19th and early 20th centuries.

Lee Holcombe, *Wives and Property*
Martin Robertson, Oxford, 1983

[18] 'In law husband and wife are one person, and the husband is that person.' This popular saying, generally ascribed to the great eighteenth-century jurist Sir William Blackstone, aptly summed up the common law relating to marriage. Where matters of property were concerned, the unity of husband and wife meant that the law recognized the husband as the family's sole arbiter. Under the common law the property that a woman possessed or was entitled to at the time of her marriage and any property she acquired or became entitled to after marriage became her husband's to control.

... Historians of the law have speculated about the origins of the legal fiction of the identity of husband and wife, with its corollary that married women were [19] deprived of property rights. Some have argued that the common law sought to embody the sacramental view of marriage held by the medieval Church – that

---

26 Compare Graycar, 'Law Reform by Frozen Chook? Family Law Reform for the New Millennium?' (2000) 24 *Melbourne University Law Review* 737.

marriage made two persons one flesh, and gave the husband dominion over the wife, meaning control of her person and property. Other historians have maintained that the common law, embodying the idea that marriage was for husbands a profitable guardianship of their wives' person and property, merely reflected the economic and social realities of the position of women in the middle ages, when the law developed. This seems the more persuasive argument as to the law's origins and purpose, especially in view of the fact that the extent of a husband's control over his wife's property depended upon the nature of that property. ...

[25] Despite the complexity of the legal rules relating to married women's rights in different categories of property, one fact stood out clearly and consistently – during marriage women had no property at their disposal; instead, their husbands assumed ownership or at least control of their property. Unlike single women and widows, who had the same property rights as men, except the right to vote, married women had legally no rights over property. Since property and status went hand in hand in English law, wives were reduced to a special status, subordinate to and dependent upon their husbands. In the words of Sir William Blackstone, 'By marriage the very being or legal existence of a woman is suspended, or at least it is incorporated or consolidated into that of the husband, under whose wing, protection and cover she performs everything, and she is therefore called in our law a *feme covert*.'

Notes

1. Holcombe goes on to describe a variety of legal disabilities that flowed from the fact that a wife's 'legal existence' was incorporated into that of her husband. For example, a woman could not sue or be sued in her own right – her husband was required to sue for her or was sued in her place where she would otherwise have been liable for a tort; a husband was responsible for all contracts and debts entered into by the wife before the marriage. A husband could also sue for damages for abrogation of his marital rights in actions of criminal conversation or loss of consortium (discussed in the next case study in this chapter). And, husband and wife could not sue each other in tort nor could they contract with one another (see the discussion of *Balfour v Balfour* in Chapter 2). The unity of husband and wife was also reflected in the law of evidence where husband and wife could not give evidence against one another as this would have been considered equivalent to self-incrimination. In addition to a number of consequences for the wife's treatment under the criminal law, there were rules concerning agency and partnership, which severely restricted married women's capacity to engage in commerce. Holcombe goes on to point out:

> The husband's guardianship of his wife, and his legal responsibility for her, entailed the right to control her actions and to chastise her to keep her within the bounds of wifely duty. Since the late seventeenth century, courts had held that chastisement did not extend to physical punishment but meant only admonition of the wife and her confinement to the house. Yet older interpretations lingered on, and it was generally believed that a man could beat his wife, although not in a violent or cruel manner – not with a stick bigger than his thumb.[27]

---

27 Lee Holcombe, *Wives and Property: Reform of the Married Women's Property Law in Nineteenth Century England*, Martin Robertson, Oxford, 1983, at 29-30.

Holcombe concludes the chapter with the comment: 'Such facts justified the feminist claim that marriage, or at least the married women's property law, reduced women to a state of "virtual slavery"'.[28]

2. The Court of Chancery in Britain developed a number of equitable doctrines to lessen the harshness of the common law rules concerning ownership of property. Through these devices, most particularly the trust, married women unable to own property at common law could hold beneficial interests in property. Some of these trust devices (for example, the constructive trust) are still used in property disputes arising out of de facto and other relationships where there is no statutory scheme dealing with these issues, as there is in NSW.[29] However, equity protected only those women who had separate property. As AV Dicey put it: 'There came ... to be not in theory but in fact one law for the rich and another for the poor. The daughters of the rich enjoyed, for the most part, the considerate protection of equity, the daughters of the poor suffered under the severity and injustice of the common law'.[30] Even after the passage of the Married Women's Property Acts, a number of restrictions on married women's legal status remained. For example, while married women were gradually able, after the Married Women's Property Acts, to own property and to sue and be sued in tort, they were still unable to sue their spouses. This incapacity, or interspousal immunity as it has been called, was removed at different times in the various States and not finally abolished until the enactment of the *Family Law Act* 1975 (Cth) s 119. We discuss this in more detail below.

3. One particular aspect of the old fiction that husband and wife are one person (which still survives in some jurisdictions) is the husband's immunity from prosecution for rape of his wife. The common law's protection for this form of abuse is said to derive from Lord Hale, who, in his *Pleas of the Crown*, stated that 'by their mutual matrimonial consent and contract the wife hath given up herself in this kind to her husband, which she cannot retract'.[31] Nineteenth century liberal theorist, John Stuart Mill, described a wife as the 'actual body-servant of her husband: no less so, as far as legal obligation goes, than slaves commonly so called'. Mill suggested that, unlike a slave (at least in theory) a wife has no right 'to refuse to her master the last familiarity ... [she can be] made the instrument of an animal function contrary to her inclinations'.[32] The rationales given for protecting husbands from liability include the law's respect for the 'privacy' of the family; the implied consent notion as outlined by Lord Hale, and the difficulty of securing convictions given the unlikelihood of witnesses being available.

---

28 *Ibid*, at 35.
29 See *Property (Relationships) Act* 1984 (NSW); and see Holcombe, *Wives and Property*, Chapter 3.
30 AV Dicey, *Lectures on the Relation between Law and Public Opinion in England During the Nineteenth Century*, London, Macmillan, 1920, at 383, cited by Holcombe, *Wives and Property*, at 47.
31 Hale's *Pleas of the Crown*, volume 1, at 629. This passage is frequently cited by courts and commentators alike: see for example, the recent Victorian case of *R v McMinn* [1982] VR 53 at 57; and see Jennifer Temkin, *Rape and the Legal Process*, London, Sweet and Maxwell, 1987, at 45; Michael Freeman, 'Doing his best to sustain the sanctity of marriage' in Norman Johnson (ed), *Marital Violence*, Routledge, London, 1985.
32 John Stuart Mill, 'The Subjection of Women' in JS Mill and Harriet Taylor, *Essays in Sex Equality* (A Rossi ed), University of Chicago Press, Chicago, 1970, at 158, 160 (cited in Carole Pateman, 'The Marriage Contract' in Norma Grieve and Ailsa Burns (eds), *Australian Women: New Feminist Perspectives*, Oxford University Press, Melbourne, 1986, at 175.

While the States at various times abolished or limited this immunity, it was not until the High Court's decision in 1991, in *R v L*,[33] that it was finally removed entirely from Australian law. In their judgment, Mason CJ, Deane and Toohey JJ commented: 'Whatever the scope of the power of the Parliament to make laws with respect to marriage, s 51(xxi), it is apparent that the Commonwealth Act [the *Family Law Act*] does not attempt comprehensively to regulate the rights and obligations of the parties to a marriage and in particular says nothing to express or imply an obligation to consent to sexual intercourse by a party to a marriage'.[34] What law, if any, *does* regulate the 'rights and obligations' of parties to a marriage?

4. Another way in which legal doctrine created and reinforced the notion of married women's lack of legal capacity was through the doctrine of dependent domicile. Domicile is a private international law notion which, broadly speaking, defines a person's legal home. It is customary to describe a person's domicile as being where he is actually residing, so long as he also intends to make that place his permanent home.[35] The choice of pronoun in this last sentence is quite deliberate: neither minors nor, until recently, married women had legal capacity to acquire a domicile of choice. Instead, their domiciles were deemed by law to be those of their fathers and husbands respectively. As Lord Denning pointed out in 1962, the consequences for women could be 'severe':

> [I]n point of law, when [a woman's] husband deserts her, she is still bound by his domicil ... with all the legal consequences which follow from it, not only on her marriage, but on her will and many other things.[36]

It was not until the *Domicile Act* 1982 (Cth) that the bar on married women's acquisition of a domicile of choice was finally removed in Australia.

5. Another consequence of married women's loss of legal status was their inability to sue their husbands for injuries perpetrated by them. This flowed from the common law doctrine of interspousal immunity.[37] Lucinda Finley has graphically documented the way in which this immunity has been relied upon in the United States in cases where women brought actions against abusive spouses.[38]

> Interspousal immunity was originally based on the notion that husband and wife merged into one being – the husband – upon marriage. Intrafamilial immunity was additionally based on the principle that the husband and father was the equivalent of the absolute monarch within the family [see Blackstone, *Commentaries*, *430]. In its early days, the doctrine was often developed and applied in suits brought by battered wives against their husbands, and operated to close off tort law as a route for compensation for victims of domestic violence and sexual abuse. The principal rationale

---

33 (1991) 174 CLR 379. Note that the High Court reached this decision without making any reference to the extensive feminist work that had called for the immunity to be abolished over many years.
34 *Ibid*, at [9].
35 See, for a general discussion of domicile, Edward I Sykes and Michael C Pryles, *Conflict of Laws: Commentary and Materials*, Law Book, Sydney, 3rd ed, 1988, Chapter 8.
36 *Formosa v Formosa* [1962] 3 All ER 419 at 421-2.
37 For a clear exposition of this doctrine, and a discussion of responses to it in Canada, Britain and Australia, see Law Reform Commission of British Columbia, *Report on Interspousal Immunity in Tort*, LRC 62, Vancouver, 1983.
38 Lucinda M Finley, 'A Break in the Silence: Including Women's Issues in a Torts Course' (1989) 1 *Yale Journal of Law and Feminism* 41.

offered for the immunity in early cases was that litigation might disrupt family harmony or the sanctity of the conjugal bond. ...

[*Finley notes that in some jurisdictions, the immunity has been removed.*] Some [*US*] jurisdictions, however, have retained intrafamilial immunity for intentional torts, while abrogating immunity for negligent actions. Others wholly retain immunity. Thus, it is still easier for someone injured in a car accident occasioned by the negligence of a family member to recover in tort than for a woman injured physically and emotionally by the blows of her husband.[39]

In Australia, the *Family Law Act* 1975 (Cth), s 119, removed the last vestiges of any such immunity. However, there are other impediments to the use of tort remedies to deal with interpersonal violence.[40] In particular, the cost of legal action precludes many survivors of violence from pursuing such remedies. Nor is it likely that damages would be payable in the event of a court determination of liability since the tort system is, in a practical sense, dependent on the widespread use of liability insurance, resulting in the fact that the overwhelming majority of tort actions in the courts are motor vehicle or industrial accident cases.[41] Despite these constraints, for a (brief) period after the enactment of the *Jurisdiction of Courts (Cross-Vesting) Act* 1987 (Cth), it was possible for the Family Court to hear and determine actions for damages arising out of marital violence as part of the other proceedings following the breakdown of a marriage (eg, with the property action).[42] However, after the decision of the High Court of Australia in *Re Wakim*[43] this is no longer possible and a damages claim would have to be heard by a State court separately from any proceedings that might take place in the Family Court. What factors might militate against women using the State courts, which have jurisdiction to hear tort claims, to bring actions for damages against their (former) partners for assault?

6. What other areas of legal doctrine are constructed around assumptions of women's lack of legal capacity? For a detailed historical discussion of some of the common law restrictions on married women's legal capacity and details of the modifications to some of these doctrines in each of the Australian jurisdictions, see Henry Finlay and Alastair Bissett-Johnson, *Family Law in Australia*, Butterworths, Sydney, 1972, Chapter 5, 'The

---

39 *Ibid*, at 45, 47-8. Cases Finley discusses in the text include *Thompson v Thompson* 218 US 611 (1910), where the immunity was used by the US Supreme Court to deny a remedy to a battered wife who sought damages against her husband for repeated assaults, on the grounds that litigation would disrupt family harmony; *Roller v Roller* 37 Wash 242; 79 P 788 (1905), where a daughter sought damages against her father because he had raped her; and *Fisher v Toler* 194 Kan 701; 401 P 2d 1012 (1965). In the latter case, while a divorce action was pending, the husband repeatedly rammed his car into his wife's car, in an attempt to kill her. She was seriously injured and brought a tort action. Even though the marriage was dissolved by the time of the action, the court ruled that because they had been legally married when the assault took place, the interspousal immunity statute barred the wife's action.

40 We discuss violence more extensively in Chapter 10 and in Chapter 11, we also look at the use of civil actions to respond to sexual assault.

41 Most personal liability policies, which operate in a large number of households, are designed to deal only with negligent, rather than intentional, injury. They also usually exclude members of the household of the liable person from recovery: see Comment, 'Litigating Incest Torts Under Homeowner Insurance Policies' (1988) 18 *Golden Gate University Law Review* 539.

42 See, for example, *Marsh v Marsh* (1994) 17 Fam LR 289; *Kennon v Kennon* (1997) FLC ¶92-757. See also Juliet Behrens and Kim Bolas, 'Violence and the Family Court: Cross Vested Claims for Compensation' (1997) 11 *Australian Journal of Family Law* 164.

43 *Re Wakim; Ex parte McNally* (1999) 198 CLR 511.

Legal Effect of Marriage' (discussing such matters as interspousal immunity; contractual capacity; competence and compellability of spouses to give evidence etc); and see also, for what was almost certainly the first Australian discussion of these issues, Enid Campbell, 'Legal Appendix' in Norman Mackenzie, *Women in Australia: A Report to the Social Science Research Council of Australia*, Cheshire, Melbourne, 1962, containing a comprehensive account of the legal status of women in a number of areas of 'public' and 'private' life.

Family law?

The most common way in which 'family law' is understood is as the law concerned with the breakdown of family relationships, rather than with the regulation of subsisting domestic arrangements. This construction has been the subject of a number of compelling critiques.[44] The law's apparent disregard for what transpires during the course of a marriage is of great concern to a number of the issues discussed in this book, including marital rape and domestic assault and battering.

In his essay, 'Towards a Critical Theory of Family Law', Michael Freeman referred to the classic statement of Otto Kahn-Freund that 'the normal behaviour of husband and wife or parents and children towards each other is beyond the law – as long as the family is healthy. The law comes in when things go wrong'.[45] Freeman describes this as the 'pathological' view of the law, a view he believes is common.[46] And it will be recalled that Katherine O'Donovan, in her critique of the public/private distinction, discussed in Chapter 2, also suggests that the construction of the family as a private sphere, unregulated by law, is a false analysis.[47]

As we discussed in Chapter 2, Frances Olsen has taken issue with the concept of 'intervention' in the family. She argues that the notions of intervention and non-intervention are 'largely meaningless' and 'indeterminate' and draws an analogy with arguments about intervention and non-intervention in the free market. She describes her argument about the indeterminacy of these phenomena as the 'incoherence argument'.[48] For Olsen, because the 'state defines the family and sets roles within the family; it is meaningless to talk about intervention or non-intervention, because the state constantly defines and redefines the family and adjusts and readjusts family roles. Non-intervention is a false idea because it has no coherent meaning'.[49]

---

44 See, for some American examples, Frances E Olsen, 'The Myth of State Intervention in the Family' (1985) 18 *Journal of Law Reform* 835; Frances E Olsen, 'The Family and the Market: A Study of Ideology and Legal Reform' (1983) 96 *Harvard Law Review* 1497. See also Katherine O'Donovan, *Sexual Divisions in Law*, Weidenfeld and Nicolson, London, 1985, some of which is extracted in Chapter 2.

45 Otto Kahn-Freund, preface to John Eekelaar, *Family Security and Family Breakdown*, Penguin, Harmondsworth, 1971, at 7; cited by Freeman, at 158. See also Frances Olsen, 'The Myth of State Intervention in the Family' (1985) 18 *Journal of Law Reform* 835 at 841.

46 See also Michael DA Freeman, 'Family Values and Family Justice' (1997) 50 *Current Legal Problems* 315.

47 Katherine O'Donovan, *Sexual Divisions in Law*, at 15.

48 Olsen, 'The Myth of State Intervention' (1985) 18 *Journal of Law Reform* 835 at 842.

49 *Ibid*.

Notes

1. To illustrate this last point, Olsen gives the following example:

    > [S]uppose a good-natured, intelligent sovereign were to ascend the throne with a commitment to end state intervention in the family. Rather than being obvious, the policies she should pursue would be hopelessly ambiguous. Is she intervening if she makes divorces difficult, or intervening if she makes them easy? Does it constitute intervention or nonintervention to grant divorce at all? If a child runs away from her parents to go live with her aunt, would nonintervention require the sovereign to grant or to deny the parents' request for legal assistance to reclaim their child?[50]

    How would you respond to these questions?

2. There are a number of ways in which the law impacts upon the family that might as readily be described as 'family law' as the law of marriage and divorce. For example, in 1999, the House of Lords had to consider who was a 'member of a tenant's family' for the purpose of deciding whether the surviving partner of a deceased gay man could succeed to his tenancy after the tenant's death.[51] The *Rent Act* 1977 (UK) provides that either a surviving spouse (which was defined to include someone who had been living with the tenant at the time of the tenant's death 'as his or her wife or husband'), or a member of the original tenant's family, can succeed to a statutory tenancy on the death of the original tenant. By majority, the House of Lords held that while the meaning of 'spouse' under the Act did not include same sex partners, a same sex partner could be a member of the original tenant's family for the purposes of the *Rent Act* 1977.[52]

    As Lord Nicholls commented: '[T]he expression 'family' does not have a single, readily recognisable meaning. ... [T]he meaning of family depends upon the context in which it is being used'.[53] And in a decision of the Constitutional Court of South Africa, O'Regan J said:

    > [F]amilies come in many shapes and sizes. The definition of the family also changes as social practices and traditions change. In recognising the importance of the family, we must take care not to entrench particular forms of family at the expense of other forms.[54]

    If the meaning of 'family' can vary so much, what does this say about our understanding of family law? Is who can inherit when someone dies without a will an issue of 'family law'? How does (or should) the law decide who is to be consulted when a person needs emergency medical treatment? If these are all questions about what is a family, or who is a member of one, given they involve legal consequences for those included or excluded within the notion of 'family', would we (or should we) describe these as issues of 'family law'?[55] Keep these questions in mind as you read the remaining part of this case study which narrows its focus to the unit with which we are most familiar: the married couple and some other couple relationships, while looking at financial issues that arise following the breakdown of those relationships.

---

50 *Ibid*.
51 *Fitzpatrick v Sterling Housing Association Ltd* [2001] 1 AC 27.
52 In its decision, the House of Lords applied an earlier decision of the New York Court of Appeals, *Braschi v Stahl Associates Co* 544 NYS 2d 784 (1989) (NY Ct of Apps) that had dealt with an analogous statutory provision.
53 *Fitzpatrick v Sterling Housing Association Ltd* [2001] 1 AC 27 at 45.
54 *Dawood v Minister of Home Affairs* (2000) 3 SALR 936 (Constitutional Court), at para 31.
55 See Graycar, 'Concept of "Family" under Review' (2001) 39(3) *Law Society Journal* 64.

Financial aspects of family law

The current legal framework in Australia

In their examination of the economic consequences of marriage breakdown, Grania Sheehan and Jody Hughes describe the basic legal framework that governs the division of matrimonial property in the following way:

> **Legal Framework**
> The Australian system for dividing the matrimonial assets on divorce is a 'separate' property regime. On separation, the starting point when dividing property is that each spouse retains ownership of the property legally theirs. This is, however, only a starting point. Under the financial provisions of the *Family Law Act 1975*, the Family Court has the discretionary power to alter parties' property interests on marriage breakdown if it is satisfied that, in all the circumstances, it is just and equitable to make the order. Exercising this power requires the court to consider the parties' respective contributions to the property and other factors under s 75(2) including their future financial needs. Where spousal support is sought in addition to a property order, it becomes the final stage in the process.
>
> More specifically, when dividing the property, the court is directed to take account of the financial and non-financial contributions made to the property and to the welfare of the family. Non-financial contributions in particular include any labour that may have increased the value of the property as well as contributions made to the welfare of the family through unpaid work at home and care of the children (FLA s 79(4)).
>
> ... [T]here are clear difficulties involved in comparing contributions which are fundamentally different from one another. In the case of non-financial contributions, there are also difficulties involved in placing a monetary value on the contributions made. ...
>
> Having determined the respective shares of property based on these contributions, the court is directed to make an adjustment to take account of other factors including the future needs of each of the parties. The estimation of future need is based on factors or circumstances of a broadly financial nature such as the age and health of the parties, employment prospects and financial resources, responsibility for the care of children post-separation and divorce, the duration of the marriage and the extent to which it has affected the future earning capacity of the parties. ... (the factors are set out in FLA s 75(2)).[56]

Sheehan and Hughes point out that one of the main purposes of their research paper was to revisit the economic consequences of marriage breakdown which had been the subject of detailed empirical research by the Australian Institute of Family Studies (AIFS) in the 1980s.[57] This was considered particularly timely as the Federal Government was in the process of considering reforming the system of dealing with property after relationship breakdown and more than a decade had passed since research that covered both privately negotiated and judicially determined settlements was conducted.[58] One of the particular issues that has been on the reform agenda was whether to replace the discretionary system with a less

---

56 Grania Sheehan and Jody Hughes, *Division of Matrimonial Property in Australia*, Research Paper No 25, AIFS, March 2001, at 1-2.
57 Peter McDonald (ed), *Settling Up: Property and Income Distribution on Divorce in Australia*, AIFS and Prentice-Hall of Australia, Melbourne, 1986; Kathleen Funder, Margaret Harrison and Ruth Weston, *Settling Down: Pathways of Parents After Divorce*, AIFS, Melbourne, 1993.
58 Sheehan and Hughes, *Division of Matrimonial Property in Australia*, at 4.

flexible statutory framework for the division of matrimonial property.[59] There have been suggestions that the discretionary system leads to considerable uncertainty and indeed, that it is unfair.[60] In 1999, a government discussion paper had proposed two alternative models. The first would have retained the discretion, but with a presumptive starting point of equal sharing based on the assumption that each party had contributed equally. The second option was to establish a 'community property' scheme, under which property acquired during the marriage would be treated as 'equally owned' with only limited scope for departure to take account of future needs or to compensate for loss of income or earning capacity arising from the marriage.[61] While neither of the options canvassed ultimately received support, the debate over how to reform the laws governing matrimonial property is one that rarely leaves the policy agenda. It is of interest here since it directly raises questions about understandings of equality and how discourses of equality are played out in reform debates.

Debates about 'equality'

The *Family Law Act* 1975 (Cth) came into effect in 1976 and has therefore been in operation for a relatively short time. Yet it has been the subject of a significant number of reviews,[62] the first of which, by a 1980 Parliamentary Committee[63] considered replacing the discretionary system with a community of property scheme. However, the Committee recommended that before this happened there should be a comprehensive survey of community attitudes, coupled with a detailed law reform commission study of the implications of such a scheme and a comparative assessment of similar regimes overseas.[64] This led to the ALRC's inquiry into matrimonial property and to assist the Commission, the Australian Institute of Family Studies (AIFS) conducted an exhaustive empirical study of the economic consequences of divorce. The AIFS 1986 study[65] demonstrated starkly the gross disparities in post-divorce living standards between women and men. Women living alone or as single parents experienced a vast decline in their standards of living, while men, including those who became sole parents, experienced considerable improvement. Significantly, women, especially those who were custodial parents, were likely to receive more than 50% of the basic assets,[66] usually somewhere around a 60-40 division in their favour[67] and this often enabled

---

59 See, for example, John Dewar, 'Reducing Discretion in Family Law' (1997) 11 *Australian Journal of Family Law* 309.
60 Some of these arguments are canvassed in Attorney General's Department, *Property and Family Law: Options for Change*, Commonwealth of Australia, Canberra, 1999.
61 See Attorney General's Department, *Property and Family Law: Options for Change* (July 1999) and see also Sheehan and Hughes, at 3.
62 There are constant calls for review by those dissatisfied with the 'system': for some discussions of that phenomenon, see Graycar, 'Law Reform by Frozen Chook: Family Law Reform for the New Millennium?' (2000) 24 *Melbourne University Law Review* 737; Miranda Kaye and Julia Tolmie, 'Fathers' Rights Groups in Australia' (1998) 12 *Australian Journal of Family Law* 19; Kaye and Tolmie, 'Discoursing Dads: The Rhetorical Devices of Fathers' Rights Groups' (1998) 22 *Melbourne University Law Review* 162.
63 Joint Select Committee on the Family Law Act (the 'Ruddock Committee'), *Family Law in Australia*, AGPS, Canberra, 1980.
64 *Ibid*, at para 5.158.
65 See *Settling Up* (1986).
66 It should be stressed that the AIFS used the term 'basic assets' to mean only those assets, such as the matrimonial home, closely associated with the marriage. This excluded other assets (where they existed) such as business assets.
67 *Settling Up*, at 184.

women who were custodial parents to stay in the matrimonial home with their children. Research in California had suggested that a strict regime of equal division led more often than not to the house being sold and the proceeds being divided down the middle, leaving neither party, particularly a woman with limited or non-existent work experience or skills, in a position to purchase another property.[68]

After reviewing various overseas jurisdictions, notably New Zealand and Ontario, the ALRC indicated that it did not favour the establishment of a community of property regime, but rather one of 'result equality' in which:

> Recognition of the different economic effects of the presumptively equal contributions made by the spouses to the marriage partnership may require unequal division of their property at the end of the marriage.[69]

The Commission rejected the enactment of an 'equality' regime, because it considered that while such a regime might notionally appear to be an advance for women, it would in practice aggravate the economic inequality that often arises from the differing effects of marriage and childrearing on the spouses primarily to the detriment of custodial parents and women whose earning capacity has been impaired by their marriage.

> All the evidence leads to the conclusion that equal sharing of property at the end of a marriage is not necessarily fair sharing. A just sharing of property should be based upon a practical rather than a merely formal, view of the equal status of husbands and wives within marriage. ... Thus, a just sharing of property should take into account any disparity arising from the marriage in the standards of living reasonably attainable by the parties after separation.[70]

The ALRC report was never implemented but, as noted at the beginning of this section, the 'reform of family law' is rarely off the political agenda and there have been several other inquiries since then.[71] In the remaining part of this case study we look at some more recent data on the economic consequences of marriage breakdown, briefly discuss the role of superannuation, then consider the relevance of violence to family law decision-making before concluding this case study with a discussion of private ordering or the role of private contracts in regulating family law.

Note

1. Why is 'equal shares' or 'community of property' such a recurring theme in family law reform discourses? Why is there so much recourse to the discourses of equality by those involved with the family law system?

---

68 See Lenore Weitzman, *The Divorce Revolution: The Unexpected Social and Economic Consequences for Women and Children in America*, Free Press, NY, 1985. For some comments on this work, which has generated a vast body of literature (including considerable criticism), see Martha Fineman, 'Illusive Equality: On Weitzman's *Divorce Revolution*' (1986) *American Bar Foundation Research Journal* 781; Fineman, 'Implementing Equality: Ideology, Contradiction and Social Change. A Study of Rhetoric and Results in the Regulation of the Consequences of Divorce' (1983) *Wisconsin Law Review* 789; and Martha Minow, 'Consider the Consequences' (1986) 84 *Michigan Law Review* 900. See also reviews of Weitzman by Katherine O'Donovan, (1987) 14 *Journal of Law and Society* 273; Carol Smart, (1987) 26 *Journal of Family Law* 261; Mary Jane Mossman, (1986) 5 *Canadian Journal of Family Law* 341 and Belinda Meteyard (1986) 14 *International Journal of the Sociology of Law* 435.
69 ALRC, *Matrimonial Property*, Discussion Paper 22, 1985, at para 146.
70 ALRC, *Matrimonial Property*, Report No 39, at para 273.
71 For some examples, see Joint Select Committee, The *Family Law Act 1975: Aspects of its Operation and Interpretation*, 1992; ALRC, *Equality before the Law: Justice for Women?* Report No 69, Part I, 1994, especially Chapter 9.

For example, the Attorney General's 1999 Discussion Paper on Property promoted the idea that, since women are now 'equal', therefore a change in the way we deal with property might be warranted. This was supported by propositions such as the one that concludes the chapter called, 'Australia: The Changing Social Context' with the statement: 'T[he] evidence supports the claim that, due to increased workforce participation, women are making an economic as well as nurturing contribution to marriage'.[72] How does this square with the data outlined earlier in this chapter (and see also the next chapter for some further information about workforce participation and its economic consequences)? What is the nature of women's increased workforce participation? What effect, if any, has that had on women's unpaid work in the home?[73]

Who gets what? The economic consequences of marriage breakdown

In the late 1990s, the AIFS revisited the earlier work done to accompany the ALRC inquiry as part of its Australian Divorce Transitions Project (ADTP).[74] The researchers noted that, in addition to proposals for overcoming the wide area of discretion in family law, there had been several significant changes in the social and economic context since the earlier work had been undertaken. Specifically, they referred to the establishment of the Child Support Scheme,[75] the continued growth in women's workforce participation (though note that much of this is part time or casualised);[76] as well as changes in fertility and the nature of relationships (for example, an increasing tendency for couples to live together before marriage and to have fewer children and have them later). Yet as Sheehan and Hughes point out, drawing on data from the Australian Divorce Transitions Project, Ruth Weston and Bruce Smyth had found that 'sole mothers, and women from long term marriages who live alone are still more likely than men to experience financial hardship after divorce, and the hardship they experience is considerable'.[77]

---

72 Attorney General's Department, *Property and Family Law: Options for Change* (July 1999), at para 4.11.

73 For some discussions of the rhetorical devices used in family law reform debates, see Kaye and Tolmie, 'Discoursing Dads: The Rhetorical Devices of Fathers' Rights Groups'; Graycar, 'Matrimonial Property and Models of Equality: Discourses in Discord?' (1995) 25 *Victoria University of Wellington Law Review* 9; Graycar, 'Law Reform by Frozen Chook'.

74 For a discussion of the ADTP, see 'About the Institute's Australian Divorce Transitions Project' in (2000) 55 *Family Matters* at 6-7.

75 For some background discussions of this scheme, see Margaret Harrison, Patricia Harper and Meredith Edwards, *Child Support – Public or Private?* Paper presented to Family Law Conference, Hobart, 1984; Cabinet Sub-Committee on Maintenance, *Child Support: A Discussion Paper on Child Maintenance*, AGPS, Canberra, 1986; Graycar, 'Family Law and Social Security: The Child Support Connection' (1989) 3 *Australian Journal of Family Law* 70; and for discussion of recent changes, see Margaret Harrison, 'Recent Issues and Initiatives' (1999) 52 *Family Matters* 61; and Linda Hancock, 'Reforming the Child Support Agenda: Who Benefits?' (1998) *Just Policy* No 12, March 1998, 20.

76 Statistics from the Australian Bureau of Statistics reveal that the difference in earnings between low and high income earners in full-time jobs has been increasing and that women's hourly earnings fell as a proportion of men's hourly earnings between 1994 and 1998: ABS, 'ABS releases latest social trends in Australia' (4 July 2000); ABS, A*ustralian Social Trends 2000*, Cat No 4102.0, Canberra, 2000; and see ABS, 'Casual Employment' in *Australia Now – A Statistical Profile*, ABS, Labour Force Australia, July 1999, Cat No 6203.0.

77 Sheehan and Hughes, *Division of Matrimonial Property*, at 5 (referring to Ruth Weston and Bruce Smyth, 'Financial Living Standards After Divorce' (2000) 55 *Family Matters* 10).

In a related discussion, Sheehan and Smyth point out:

> Historically, women have tended to experience greater economic vulnerability across the life course than men. This vulnerability is clearly evident upon marital separation. Research by the Australian Institute of Family Studies suggests that women are at a considerable disadvantage compared to men in terms of their financial circumstances following marital dissolution. Women's greater economic vulnerability post-separation can be attributed to a combination of social and economic factors, many of which operated independently of marriage. These factors include women's weaker position in, and attachment to, the labour market and their relatively lower earnings compared with similarly aged men. Other factors, by contrast, relate more specifically to the role some women adopt during and after marriage, and in particular to the time they spend out of paid work to have and care for children.[78]

It was in this context that they made the following findings.

Grania Sheehan and Jody Hughes, *Division of Matrimonial Property in Australia*
Research Paper No 25, AIFS, March 2001

[30] The chief findings of this research are as follows

Nature and value of the assets on divorce

The asset wealth of a large minority is insufficient to meet the immediate needs and longer-term financial needs of both parties and the children on separation and divorce. In particular:

- For a large minority (46%) of women and men, the assets owned at separation consist primarily of 'basic' assets (such as the family home and contents, car(s), savings and private loans) and superannuation (usually the husband's).
- In general, the most valuable asset is the family home, followed by superannuation. Few couples had ready cash available at the time of settlement.
- [31] The estimated median value of net asset wealth as reported by women and men (excluding superannuation) was $124,101. In addition, the median value of women's superannuation at divorce was $5,590 compared with $22,361 for men.
- Respondents from 'low asset' marriages differ from those from 'high asset' marriages in that they are less likely to own non-basic assets; and to have equity in the family home.

Shares of property at distribution

The current discretionary system allows for substantial variation in settlement outcomes. [*The authors note that despite that variation, there is*] a high degree of consistency in the share of basic and of non-basic assets the wife receives. The wife receives on average two thirds of the couple's basic assets and one fifth of the couple's non-basic asset wealth. [*They also emphasise the fact that while women from 'low asset' marriages are more likely to get a majority share of the assets given the limited amounts involved, in actual money terms this does little to assist those from low asset marriages after separation and divorce.*]

---

78 Grania Sheehan and Bruce Smyth, 'Spousal Violence and Post Separation Financial Outcomes' (2000) 14 *Australian Journal of Family Law* 102 at 113.

Factors of influence
The factors related to the financial provisions of the Family Law Act that predict share received are:
- The wife's share of assets is *reduced*, and the husband's share *increased*, in cases where non-basic assets (ie investments, businesses and farms) comprise a high proportion of the couple's asset wealth.
- Both the husband's and wife's share of assets is *increased* in cases where they are the resident parent.
- Other factors not included in the financial provisions also predicted share received. In particular, the share to the husband increased when he remained in the family home post-separation.

[*In light of these findings, and the recurring debates about equal shares, Sheehan and Hughes went on to consider what would be the implications of a change to 'equal shares':*]

Impact of equal share
The equal division of property acquired during marriage may both improve the position of women from 'high asset' marriages and disadvantage women from 'low asset' marriages. In particular:
- A 50:50 split produces an increase in the percentage share of assets received by the wife in 'high asset' marriages and a shift away from the wife in 'low asset' marriages.
- The shift in the dollar value of these assets is, however, marginal for women from 'low asset' marriages and substantial for women from 'high asset' marriages.

Notes

1. In their discussion of these findings, Sheehan and Hughes draw attention to the differences between those from 'high asset' and those from 'low asset' marriages. Women from the latter group receive well over half of (what may be the very meagre) property available, but this is not the case where 'financial resources' are included (ie, in cases of women from high asset marriages). They found that, consistent with the findings from *Settling Up* and *Settling Down*, non-basic assets, such as businesses, farms and investments, were allocated to the husband as were financial resources such as superannuation.

    > [N]on-financial contributions made to these assets, particularly the domestic activities performed by one spouse that free the other spouse to work directly for financial reward, may have been undervalued by parties when they divided the property.
    > The apparent under-recognition of women's non financial contributions to the non-basic asset wealth of the marriage is not, however, supported by empirical evidence of a reduction in the contribution women actually make. The entry of mothers in unprecedented numbers into the labour force ... has done little to alter the gender-based distribution of responsibility for work in the family home.[79]

    The failure to give economic and legal recognition to women's work is, of course, a problem much wider than its manifestations within the *Family Law Act*, as the two other case studies in this chapter make clear. However, 'family law' is the one area of law where the statutory provisions spell out expressly that caring work and homemaker contributions have economic value: see

---

79 Sheehan and Hughes, *Division of Matrimonial Property*, at 32.

s 79(4)(b) and (c). Can you suggest ways in which courts might be encouraged to value that work more appropriately?

2. In other AIFS work (discussed below), the authors make the point that most discussions of issues of family law are based either on anecdotal evidence[80] or on the reported cases.[81] For a variety of reasons, reported cases represent only a tiny fraction of family law disputes – most cases settle without going to a contested hearing, and the small amounts of money involved in the majority of cases that involve only 'basic assets', combined with the lack of legal aid,[82] means that most of the property decisions that are actually litigated and reported involve substantial amounts of money. There is a considerable body of case law involving such matters: cases such as *In Marriage of Ferraro*,[83] and *In Marriage of Whiteley*[84] all involve amounts of several million dollars. *Ferraro* is well known as a case dealing with the issue of 'special skill' and business acumen and it was in that case that the trial judge had commented:

> The parties' property empire blossomed because the husband had the innate drive, skills and abilities to enable him to succeed in his chosen occupation, whereas the wife's contribution was neither greater nor less than when the husband had been a carpenter. To equalise the parties' contributions is akin to comparing the contributions of the creator of Sissinghurst Gardens, whose breadth of vision and imagination, talent, drive and endeavours led to the creation of the most beautiful garden in England, with that of the gardener who assisted with the tilling of the soil and the weeding of the beds.[85]

Why do you think the 'Sissinghurst Gardens' analogy has become so well known?[86] The Full Court in *Ferraro* expressly rejected the use of the Sissinghurst Gardens analogy and said that the homemaker's contributions should be valued in a substantial and not token way 'rather than paying lip-service to it'.[87] The court acknowledged that:

> [A]n assessment of the quality of a homemaker contribution to the family is vulnerable to subjective value judgments as to what constitutes a competent homemaker and parent and cannot be readily equated to the value of assets acquired. This leads to a tendency to undervalue the homemaker role.[88]

Yet, despite this, the Full Court confirmed that the husband's business skills in cases such as this were 'special skills' entitled to recognition as an extra or 'special' contribution.[89] The court also acknowledged that the wife 'virtually conducted the homemaker and parent responsibilities without assistance from the husband (other than financial), particularly in the latter years'[90] but they

---

80 Cf Graycar, 'Law Reform by Frozen Chook' (2000) 24 *Melbourne University Law Review* 737.
81 Grania Sheehan and Bruce Smyth, 'Spousal Violence and Post Separation Financial Outcomes' (2000) 14 *Australian Journal of Family Law* 102 at 103.
82 See Rosemary Hunter et al *Legal Services in Family Law*, Law and Justice Foundation, 2001; John Dewar, Barry Smith and Cate Banks, *Litigants in Person in the Family Court of Australia*, Family Court of Australia, Research Report No 20, 2000.
83 (1992) 16 Fam LR 1.
84 (1993) FLC ¶92-335.
85 (1992) 16 Fam LR 1 at 28.
86 For a discussion of this issue that includes a detailed account of the creation of the Sissinghurst Gardens (by Vita Sackville-West), see Lisa Young, 'Sissinghurst, Sackville-West and Special Skill' (1997) 11 *Australian Journal of Family Law* 268.
87 (1992) 16 Fam LR 1 at 47.
88 *Ibid*, at 38.
89 (1992) 16 Fam LR 1 at 50.
90 *Ibid*.

were not equal to her husband's contribution. If a homemaker contribution is 'outstanding' or 'special' should it also be able to tip the balance as 'special' business contributions do when property is being divided?[91]

3. In 1999, the National Network of Women's Legal Services released a report it had commissioned that surveyed community legal centre lawyers about their experiences of property disputes in family law.[92] Not surprisingly, it showed that most of the clients of those surveyed had very little in the way of property. Significantly, not one of the solicitors surveyed who advise and act for women in family law cases favoured a move to a less discretionary system. They all considered that, despite problems in the exercise of the discretion, their clients would be rendered worse off by the enactment of a scheme such as one of the Attorney General's 1999 proposals. One interesting recommendation they made was that the government should fund test case litigation on how debts arising out of the marriage should be dealt with (an aspect of this is also discussed in the next case study). What reasons can you suggest for the fact that there is no case law (and therefore no binding precedent) to guide lawyers trying to assist clients to settle family law property proceedings that involve debts?[93]

4. In 1992, the Supreme Court of Canada, in a decision about spousal support (maintenance), commented that 'the feminisation of poverty is an entrenched social phenomenon'.[94] The court noted the empirical evidence about the decline in women's living standards after divorce and the increase in women's poverty in that country and considered the relationship between this and family law principles, especially the emphasis on the clean break principle:

> Women have tended to suffer economic disadvantages and hardships from marriage or its breakdown because of the traditional division of labour within that institution. Historically, or at least in recent history, the contributions made by women to the marital partnership were non-monetary and came in the form of work at home, such as taking care of the household, raising children, and so on. Today, though more and more women are working outside the home, such employment continues to play a secondary role and sacrifices continue to be made for the sake of domestic considerations. These sacrifices often impair the ability of the partner who makes them (usually the wife) to maximise her earning potential because she may tend to forgo educational and career advancement opportunities. These same sacrifices may also enhance the earning potential of the other spouse (usually the husband) who, because his wife is tending to such matters, is free to pursue economic goals.
>
> ... [O]nce the marriage dissolves, the kinds of non-monetary contributions made by the wife may result in significant market disabilities.

---

91 The Full Court increased Mrs Ferraro's share of the award to 37.5% of the total assets, an increase of only 7.5%. However, the Full Court also increased the pool of property available for distribution (from $10 million to $12 million) and this led to a more substantial increase in the wife's share in absolute terms.

92 Nicola Seaman, *Fair Shares? Barriers to Equitable Property Settlements for Women*, Women's Legal Services Network/National Association of Community Legal Centres, Canberra, 1999.

93 Compare Robert Mnookin and Lewis Kornhauser, 'Bargaining in the Shadow of the Law: The Case of Divorce' (1979) 88 *Yale Law Review* 950.

94 *Moge v Moge (Women's Legal Education and Action Fund, intervener)* [1992] 3 SCR 813 at 861-2. For the clean break principle in Australia, see *Family Law Act* 1975 (Cth) s 81, which provides that the court shall 'as far as practicable make such orders as will finally determine the financial relationships between the parties to the marriage and avoid further proceedings between them'.

> ... In effect, she is left with a diminished earning capacity and may have conferred upon her husband an embellished one.[95]

After referring to Canadian studies similar to the work carried out in Australia by the AIFS, the court held:

> [T]he general economic impact of divorce on women is a phenomenon, the existence of which cannot reasonably be questioned and should be amenable to judicial notice.[96]

This has been echoed by the Family Court of Australia in *In Marriage of Mitchell*.[97]

> We agree with these general propositions. Like Canada, Australia has a body of research indicating that mothers who are the primary carers of dependent children inevitably [*sic*] drop out of the paid work-force and consequently suffer financial deprivation which is exacerbated by marriage breakdown. ... In our view there are significant advantages to the court being able to take judicial notice of research concerning the economic consequences of marriage and its dissolution.
>
> We also agree with the caution contained in *Moge* against judicial notice being perceived as a substitute for evidence in the particular case.[98]

We return to the issue of 'judicial notice' in the third case study in this chapter on the assessment of personal injury damages.

5. In most jurisdictions, spousal maintenance ('alimony' in the United States or 'spousal support' in Canada) is available in financial adjustment proceedings after marriage breakdown. There are detailed provisions in the Family Law Act dealing with maintenance (see ss 72-75), but recent research arising from the Australian Divorce Transitions Project has shown that the payment of spousal maintenance is 'rare, minimal and brief'.[99] One possible reason for this is that the property provisions in the *Family Law Act* 1975 (Cth) allow for a 'future needs' component and, in the process of doing that, the court takes into account the factors that are used to determine spouse maintenance applications (see s 75(2)). Should there be an obligation to support a spouse after the breakdown of a relationship? What factors might affect that decision?[100]

6. The *Property (Relationships) Act* 1984 (NSW)[101] makes statutory provision for the alteration of property interests on the breakdown of relationships between unmarried cohabitants. Since 1999, this includes not only heterosexual couples, but same sex couples and others in certain interdependent caring relationships (see s 5). The Act permits a decision-maker to take into

---

95 *Ibid*, at 861-2.
96 *Ibid*, at 873. See also the Honourable Claire L'Heureux-Dubé, 'Recent Developments in Family Law' (1993) 6 *Canadian Journal of Women and the Law* 269 and Claire L'Heureux-Dubé, 'Making Equality Work in Family Law' (1997) 14 *Canadian Journal of Family Law* 103.
97 (1995) 19 Fam LR 44.
98 *Ibid*, at 62.
99 Juliet Behrens and Bruce Smyth, *Spousal Support in Australia* Working Paper No 16, Australian Institute of Family Studies, 1999, at 7.
100 See Katherine O'Donovan, 'Should all Maintenance of Spouses be Abolished?' (1982) 45 *Modern Law Review* 424; and Alison Diduck and Helena Orton, 'Equality and Support for Spouses' (1994) 57 *Modern Law Review* 681.
101 Previously the *De Facto Relationships Act* 1984 (renamed after the adoption of the *Property (Relationships) Legislation Amendment Act* 1999). For a detailed discussion of this legislation, see Reg Graycar and Jenni Millbank, 'The Bride Wore Pink ... to the *Property (Relationships) Legislation Amendment Act 1999*: Family Law Reform in NSW' (2000) 17 *Canadian Journal of Family Law* 227.

account only contributions (ie, not future needs). In States and Territories that do not make statutory provision for dealing with property issues arising out of the breakdown of de facto relationships or where such statutory schemes are limited to heterosexual couples, the only legal recourse available to those excluded from the legislation is to seek remedies under equitable principles such as the constructive trust.[102] Should different legal rules apply to dealing with property on relationship breakdown depending on the marital status or the sexuality of those involved? Are couple relationships inherently different from other types of close interpersonal relationships?

7. As the data earlier in this chapter shows, women's labour force participation and hours of work are overwhelmingly affected by the presence of children. A study published in 1988 showed that the average woman with secondary education forgoes an estimated $435,000 (in 1987 dollars) in lifetime earnings if she has a child (with the amount increasing as the number of children rises).[103] As the late Kate Funder pointed out:

> When a marriage ends, the costs of the depreciated earnings which were previously absorbed by the partnership are carried by the partner whose paid work has been interrupted and whose individual earnings are reduced.[104]

By 2001, this impact had reduced to around $160,000, according to research undertaken by Gray and Chapman.[105] They suggest that the changes are related to changes in the labour force participation of women, which has increased since the earlier study was undertaken. However, even though the amount has reduced, it is still a cost that will be borne by the woman in a heterosexual relationship unless there is some other way of dealing with it. How should the cost of raising children in relationships be factored into the division of matrimonial property?[106] Might the losses be less significant for women if they are bringing up children within lesbian relationships?[107]

8. A Working Paper published by the AIFS in 1999 points out that, in 68% of private property agreements concluded by divorcing couples, superannuation was not considered as part of the assets to be reallocated.[108] This is significant, since, apart from the family home, superannuation entitlements

---

102 See the discussion in Chapter 3 about the presumption of advancement and the extract from Lisa Sarmas' article on *Brown v Brown*.

103 See Matthew Gray and Bruce Chapman, 'Foregone Earnings from Child Rearing' (2001) 58 *Family Matters* 4. The earlier study they discuss is John Beggs and Bruce Chapman, *The Foregone Earnings from Child-Rearing in Australia*, ANU Centre for Economic Policy Research, Discussion Paper No 190, commissioned for the AIFS, June 1988, at 40-1. For an analysis of the manner in which the opportunity costs of women's withdrawal from the workforce may be calculated, see Kathleen Funder, 'Australia: A Proposal for Reform' in Lenore J Weitzman and Mavis McLean (eds), *Economic Consequences of Divorce: The International Perspective*, Clarendon Press, Oxford, 1992.

104 Funder, 'Australia: A Proposal for Reform', at 155.

105 Gray and Chapman, 'Foregone Earnings from Child Rearing', at 9.

106 For a proposal from the AIFS, see Margaret Harrison, Kathleen Funder and Peter McDonald 'Principles, Practice and Problems in Property and Income Transfers' in *Settling Down*.

107 See some of the data referred to earlier in this chapter.

108 John Dewar, Grania Sheehan and Jody Hughes, *Superannuation and Divorce in Australia*, Working Paper 18, AIFS, Melbourne, 1999, at 23.

constitute the most valuable asset of a marriage.[109] The Family Court has consistently held that superannuation entitlements cannot be divided as the Court can deal only with property owned by the parties at the time of the hearing and future superannuation entitlements are not 'property' (though they are 'financial resources').[110] This is of particular significance to women who are far less likely than men to have their own superannuation funds and, if they do so, are likely to have far smaller amounts in those funds.[111]

The Association of Superannuation Funds of Australia (ASFA) points out that:

- women live longer than men (life expectancy is 81 compared to 76 for men);
- women currently spend on average 20 years full time equivalent in the paid workforce, compared to 35 years for men;
- because women tend to be concentrated in occupations with low pay, their wages are lower and therefore superannuation contributions lower.[112]

The combination of the lower incidence of women's access to their own superannuation and the difficulties that have to date been experienced by the courts in giving proper effect to superannuation in family law has led the Federal Government to create a statutory scheme that will structure how superannuation is dealt with in divorce.[113] Kristie Dunn has criticised the government's plan (as set out in its 1998 discussion paper) for adopting a 'formal equality' approach.[114] How should superannuation be dealt with in family law? What considerations should a court, or a lawyer negotiating an agreement, have to take into account?[115]

The relevance of violence

Throughout the 1990s, there has been increasing attention to the relevance of violence to decision-making about property. In a key discussion in 1993, Juliet Behrens drew on some of the jurisprudence dealing with contributions and suggested that violence should be seen as a 'negative contribution' in property

---

109 *Ibid*, at 1. See also ABS, *Housing: Special Article: Value and equity in the family home*, Year Book Australia, 1999, which estimates that while the value of dwellings and residential land represents 50% of the total value of assets owned by the household sector, equity in superannuation funds accounted for 17% of household assets, ahead of any other form of property or asset: *ibid*, at 3.

110 For a discussion of the legal framework, see Dewar, Sheehan and Hughes, at 4-5; and see Attorney General's Department, *Superannuation and Family Law: A Position Paper*, 1998.

111 For some of the data about women's access to superannuation, see Kristie Dunn, 'Splitting the Difference: Superannuation, Equality and Family Law' (1998) 12 *Australian Journal of Family Law* 214; and see Ross Clare, *Equity in Retirement Income*, ASFA, 2001. We discuss the issue of occupational superannuation further in the next chapter, *Out to Work*.

112 Philippa Smith, *Superannuation – Sisters Start Doin' It for Themselves!*, ASFA Media Release, November 2000 (see <www.superannuation.asn.au>).

113 See Attorney General's Department, *Superannuation and Family Law: A Position Paper*, 1998. The *Family Law Legislation Amendment (Superannuation) Act* 2001 is due to come into effect no later than 28 December 2002. For a discussion, see Garry Watts, 'Family Law: Super Becomes Family Property' (2001) 39(9) *Law Society Journal* 54.

114 Kristie Dunn, 'Splitting the Difference'.

115 For some other discussions on superannuation, see Jenni Millbank, 'Hey Girls, Have We Got a Super Deal for You' (1993) 7 *Australian Journal of Family Law* 104; and Therese MacDermott, 'Linking Gender and Superannuation' (1997) 2 *International Journal of Discrimination and the Law* 271.

cases.[116] In 1994, the ALRC made a number of recommendations for how violence should be taken into account in family law decision-making, following its receipt of a large number of submissions on that topic as part of its reference on *Equality Before the Law*.[117] The Family Law Council has published a discussion paper[118] and, without any statutory change in relation to property, the Family Court has also given some attention to this issue.[119] In 1995, the *Family Law Act 1975* (Cth) was amended to include aspects of violence as a factor to consider in relation to children's cases,[120] but there has not been any statutory response to the issue thus far in relation to property. It was against this background that the Office of the Status of Women commissioned AIFS to undertake some empirical work on the relationship between violence and the economic outcome in property cases.

Grania Sheehan and Bruce Smyth, 'Spousal Violence and Post-separation Financial Outcomes'
(2000) 14 *Australian Journal of Family Law* 102

[102] Retrospective surveys suggest that couples whose marriages have ended are more likely than continuously married couples to have experienced spousal violence at some stage during the relationship. [*Sheehan and Smyth point out that notwithstanding research to this effect in other places*] there is a paucity of information [*in Australia*] about the prevalence and nature of spousal violence among couples whose marriages have ended despite the utility of this information for family law. ... The provision of information about the linkage between spousal violence and broader based economic consequences of marriage and divorce is also important to any consideration of whether the FLA should be reformed to make clear that violence is of relevance to the division of property on divorce at either the contributions stage (under s 79(4)) or the adjustment stage (as an amendment to s 75(2)(o)) or both.

[*The authors noted that there had been considerable discussion of these issues in the academic literature, and by the ALRC in its work on Equality Before the Law, yet these discussions were either anecdotal, or based on the reported cases which are not necessarily representative. Therefore, it was necessary to try to gather some empirical data about the relationship between spousal violence and property outcomes. After outlining the methodology of the study, and the various definitions of violence that were used, they set out their findings as follows:*]

---

116 Juliet Behrens, 'Domestic Violence and Property Adjustment: A Critique of 'no fault' discourse' (1993) 7 *Australian Journal of Family Law* 9; Behrens, 'Violence in the Home and Family Law: An Update' (1995) 9 *Australian Journal of Family Law* 58.
117 ALRC, *Equality Before the Law: Justice for Women?*, Report No 69 Part I, 1994, especially Chapter 9.
118 Family Law Council, *Violence and the Family Law Act: Financial Remedies*, 1998.
119 There are a number of cases involving children's issues in which the court considered this before the 1995 amendments which introduced issues of violence as relevant to the determination of a child's best interests: see *In Marriage of JG and BG* (1994) 18 Fam LR 255; *In Marriage of Patsalou* (1995) 18 Fam LR 426; *In Marriage of Jaeger* (1994) 18 Fam LR 126; *In Marriage of Irvine* (1995) 19 Fam LR 374; *In Marriage of Grant* (1994) FLC ¶92-506. Note also the discussion earlier about the use of the cross vested jurisdiction to award damages for assault in related proceedings in the Family Court and see generally the articles published in (1995) 9 *Australian Journal of Family Law*, issue No 1 (March 1995), a special issue on family violence.
120 See generally, *Family Law Act 1975* (Cth), Pt VII and s 43(ca); see also Helen Rhoades, Reg Graycar and Margaret Harrison, *The Family Law Reform Act: The First Three Years*, University of Sydney and Family Court of Australia, 2000.

[111] The findings for women are consistent with the hypothesis that a party's experience of spousal violence puts them at a disadvantage when dividing the matrimonial property. ... [112] Women who reported experiencing severe abuse were around three times as likely as women who reported no physical abuse to indicate receipt of less than a 40% share of the property (total and domestic [*or basic*] assets). These findings are striking given the circumstances of these women at separation. Almost half of the women who reported severe abuse were out of work at separation, more than half the women had spent one third of the time they were married out of the workforce, and almost all had primary responsibility for the care of dependent children after separation and divorce. Further, this group of women were the most likely to have left the family home soon after separation which, in turn, predicted receipt of a lower share of property [*referring here to findings in Settling Up*, 1986]. A similar level of disadvantage in receipt of property was apparent for women who reported physical violence without fear. These women were more than twice as likely as women who reported no physical abuse to have received a minority share of the property (total and domestic assets). [*Sheehan and Smyth point out that the domestic assets, or 'basic assets' are those most often used to compensate the resident parent (usually the mother) for costs associated with the marriage. As the earlier extract shows, women who are resident parents usually get more of the domestic or basic assets, while men are more likely to receive a greater share of non-domestic assets such as superannuation, businesses or investments. They concluded:*] [117] ... A commonality of violence among those who divorce is evident. When broadly defined, spousal violence is not an exceptional circumstance for divorced women and men but rather the norm – giving weight to concerns expressed that a broad consideration of spousal violence in property matters will 'open the floodgates'. At the other end of the spectrum, the findings also suggest that limiting the consideration of spousal violence to injurious violence may be overly restrictive as it fails to acknowledge the range of abusive behaviours and consequences of the abuse that characterise 'terroristic' violence. A working definition of spousal violence that acknowledges the varied nature of abusive behaviour as well as the emotional and/or physical consequences of such behaviour might reflect more fully women's and men's experiences of spousal violence and the financial hardship which often accompanies it. [118] ... [A] fear-based definition of violence, such as the definition of family violence in s 60D(1), may best fit these requirements. ...

[*The main finding of this research, that is, that women who report spousal violence are more likely than women who report no violence to receive a minority share of the property*] suggests that the financial provisions of the FLA have not always assisted these women and the children in their care. Rather, the share of property these women receive appears to reflect the practical difficulties they face in trying to negotiate a fair settlement with a violent former spouse – a situation where safety may be given precedence over the right to a fair share of the matrimonial property. Taken together these findings caution that any changes made to substantive law with regard to recognising the role of violence may be of limited effect in practice if impediments to these women accessing justice are not also addressed. Ensuring that the basic property rights of those who report experiencing spousal [*violence*] are met may thus be a matter of greater urgency than substantive law reform.

Notes

1. Section 60D, referred to in the extract, provides that family violence means:

    > conduct, whether actual or threatened, by a person towards or towards the property of, a member of the person's family that causes that or any other member of the person's family to fear for, or to be apprehensive about, his or her personal well being or safety.

    Is this an appropriate definition of violence to use in the context of family relationships? Are there other issues that should be addressed in any definition? The issue of violence (including questions of definition) is discussed further in Chapter 10.
2. What is the relevance of the researchers' pointing out that violence in the context of marriage breakdown is a common, rather than an aberrational, phenomenon? Do you think the lawyers and the courts that deal with disputes that flow from the end of such relationships all share this understanding?
3. In a portion of the article not extracted, Sheehan and Smyth note that a significant proportion of men also reported having experienced one of the forms of violence they asked about. However, there was no correlation between that experience and the share of property they received. What explanation(s) can you suggest for this? See also the discussion in Chapter 10 of the respective experiences of violence by women and men.
4. If violence throughout the relationship has had a deleterious effect upon a woman's earning capacity, how should a court deal with this? If violence can be seen as a 'negative contribution', should other forms of conduct, such as gambling, or substance abuse, also be considered? If violence or other negative contributions are taken into account, how does this relate to the notion of 'no-fault' divorce? Where does conduct such as adultery fit into this?[121]
5. Sheehan and Smyth suggest that law reform on its own will not necessarily address the disadvantages of women who have been targets of violence in their relationships. What other 'impediments to these women accessing justice' might they be referring to? See ALRC, *Equality Before the Law: Justice for Women*, especially Chapter 9.

The marriage 'contract': The move to private ordering

Political philosopher Carole Pateman has written extensively on marriage. In 'The Marriage Contract',[122] Pateman briefly describes the long history of feminist criticism of marriage which she dates back to at least 1700 and draws attention to commentators such as JS Mill who argued that the parties were not equally free to negotiate or alter the terms of the so-called 'marriage contract'. Despite the enactment of the Married Women's Property Acts, which purported to do away with many of the disadvantages experienced by married women solely based on their status (discussed earlier in this chapter), Pateman argues that there is still no

---

121 For further discussion of these issues, see Juliet Behrens, 'Domestic Violence and Property' (1993) 7 *Australian Journal of Family Law* 7; National Committee on Violence Against Women, *National Strategy on Violence Against Women*, October 1992; and see more generally the articles in (1995) 9 *Australian Journal of Family Law*.

122 In Norma Grieve and Ailsa Burns (eds), *Australian Women: New Feminist Perspectives*, Oxford University Press, Melbourne, 1986. See also Carole Pateman, *The Sexual Contract*, Polity Press, Cambridge, 1988; and 'The Shame of the Marriage Contract' in Judith Stiehm (ed), *Women's Views of the Political World of Men*, Transnational Publishers, New York, 1984; 'Women and Consent' (1980) 8 *Political Theory* 149.

free and equal contract in this context. Nor is there in fact any 'contract' which explicitly sets out the terms and conditions of the relationship, as there would be with regard to all other mutual arrangements, particularly business transactions. This is despite what Henry Maine described as the most significant feature of 19th century legal history, the movement 'from status to contract'.[123] Referring to some of the arguments that started to develop in the 1970s and 1980s in favour of allowing people to make their own agreements (these have been particularly popular in the US), Pateman commented: 'The popularity of what is called "contract marriage" in which the couple freely negotiate the terms of the written contract that will regulate their lives for the duration of the marriage is a good example of the contract ideal'.[124]

Since Pateman's discussion, there has been increasing attention, in Australia as elsewhere, to the notion of private arrangements (or 'contracts') in the areas of law governing financial arrangements after relationship breakdown. There have been several proposals in recent decades to legislate so as to give legal effect to pre-nuptial agreements, as well as to financial agreements made during the course of a marriage, and agreements made to finalise financial arrangements after relationships have broken down.[125] However, a number of concerns have been raised about the dangers for women in the increasing trend toward private ordering. For example, Marcia Neave has raised a number of concerns.[126] She notes that women's bargaining power is affected by men's violence against women, which is known to escalate at the time of separation.[127] Women with violent partners are considered particularly vulnerable to being pressured to make agreements to end the violence and protect their children. While in theory a woman pressured into an agreement can later seek to have it set aside, in practice a woman who is desperate to avoid contact with an ex spouse is unlikely to pursue the matter.

Another concern Neave expresses about private ordering flows from studies showing that women as well as men tend to undervalue non-financial contributions. Neave refers to research showing that people express their preferences in terms of what they perceive to be their entitlements. But their notion of those

---

123 Sir Henry Sumner Maine, *Ancient Law*, Oxford University Press, London, 1931.
124 Pateman, in Grieve and Burns (eds), at 181.
125 The detailed scheme has now been enacted and forms part of the *Family Law Act* 1975 (Cth). See *Family Law Amendment Act* 2000, which introduced these provisions into the act, and see also Senate Legal and Constitutional Legislation Committee, *Provisions of the Family Law Amendment Bill 1999* (December 1999).
126 Marcia Neave, 'Private Ordering in Family Law: Will Women Benefit?' in Margaret Thornton (ed), *Public and Private: Feminist Legal Debates*, Oxford University Press, Melbourne, 1995. In answer to the question 'Why do women do poorly when they negotiate family ... contracts?' she notes that women negotiate agreements against the background of pervasive gender inequality. Women earn less and own less; after marriage breakdown they may have difficulty meeting short-term living costs (let alone paying legal and accounting fees); and legal aid is probably not available: 'Thus they are more likely to be forced to make separation agreements (or to rely on alternative dispute resolution) because they can't afford to litigate'. They may lack accurate information about their partner's earning capacity or assets. The latter may be held in complex trust or company arrangements (on women's lack of control over business information see also: *Settling Up*, at 320). She suggests that more rigorous disclosure requirements would make some difference but not solve the problems. She also notes that the AIFS recommended that the Family Court use independent auditors which, she suggests, could improve the situation of women bargaining with their husbands.
127 See Hilary Astor, 'The Weight of Silence: Talking About Violence in Family Mediation' in Margaret Thornton (ed), *Public and Private: Feminist Legal Debates*, Oxford University Press, Melbourne, 1995.

entitlements is moulded by social context. So, for example, advantaged people see themselves as more entitled than disadvantaged people.[128] If, until recently, women's contributions to family welfare were not given economic recognition, it is not surprising that women do not see them as valuable. This is supported by the AIFS findings in *Settling Up*:

> Women generally acknowledged their husband's financial contributions, while men were more likely to overlook financial contributions made by their wives. Both men and women regarded financial contributions as more significant than non-financial ones.[129]

Despite these concerns and a significant lack of community support for the introduction of such agreements in Australia,[130] the *Family Law Act* was amended from December 2000 to give legal effect to agreements made either before, during or after marriage.[131]

Belinda Fehlberg and Bruce Smyth published a detailed critique in 2000 of the government's proposal as it was first presented (it was amended in a number of respects before enactment in late 2000).[132] In their article, they refer to overseas research questioning the 'equal bargaining power' of parties to such agreements. They continued by considering these studies:

> in the light of qualitative empirical research conducted by Belinda Fehlberg in the UK and Supriya Singh in Australia, regarding spousal guarantees and family businesses respectively. Their research is consistent with other research on domestic financial arrangements ... which suggests that women's power regarding domestic financial decisions decreases as the perceived importance of the decision increases. Fehlberg's and Singh's research also shows that women are less likely than men to think in the self-interested manner of commercial contracting parties, tending to merge relationship commitment with their individual self-interest, and also are inclined to blinker out questions about money that imply a lack of trust in their husband.[133]

Notes

1. One of the articles reviewed by Fehlberg and Smyth which analyses the use of premarital agreements in the US demonstrates that 'the purpose and effect of most premarital agreements is to protect the wealth and earnings of an economically superior spouse from being shared with an economically inferior spouse'.[134] That study concludes that premarital agreements exacerbate what is

---

128 Neave, 'Private Ordering', at 170.
129 *Settling Up*, at 240.
130 A Senate Committee reviewed the proposal to legislate in favour of legally binding agreements. Only one of the submissions made to that committee gave unqualified support to binding pre-nuptial agreements: see Senate Legal and Constitutional Legislation Committee, *Provisions of the Family Law Amendment Bill 1999* (December 1999), at para 1.78.
131 *Family Law Act* 1975 (Cth) Pt VIIIA.
132 Belinda Fehlberg and Bruce Smyth, 'Pre-Nuptial Agreements for Australia: Why Not?' (2000) 14 *Australian Journal of Family Law* 80.
133 *Ibid*, at 91. The references are to Belinda Fehlberg, *Sexually Transmitted Debt: Surety Experience and English Law*, Clarendon Press, Oxford, 1997, and Supriya Singh, *Women, Information and the Family Business*, Consumer Advocacy and Financial Counselling Association of Victoria, Melbourne, 1995.
134 Gail Frommer Brod, 'Premarital Agreements and Gender Justice' (1994) 6 *Yale Journal of Law and Feminism* 229.

already an inequality in the distribution of wealth along gender lines and 'have a disparate impact on women – and thereby discriminate against them'.[135]

2. In the Family Law Amendment Bill as first introduced in 1999, one of the formalities for the validity of an agreement was that the parties had received independent legal or financial advice. After considerable lobbying from the legal profession, the Senate Committee recommended that the Bill require all parties to obtain only independent legal advice and this has now been enacted. What are the respective purposes of legal advice and financial advice? If an agreement contains a certification that a party has received independent legal advice, how likely is it that an agreement would be set aside? We return to the discussion of the role of independent legal advice in the following case study.

3. The *Property (Relationships) Act* 1984 (NSW) has since 1984 made relationship agreements (previously cohabitation and separation agreements) legally binding (for heterosexual couples) if entered into in conformity with the Act. Since 1999, that Act now applies to same sex relationships. Are the concerns raised by Fehlberg, Neave and others equally applicable to lesbians or to gay men who make such agreements? Alternatively, are there particular advantages for gay men and lesbians in having relationship agreements legally enforceable?

4. Assume you have concerns about amending legislation that encourages all people entering into marriage to sign a prenuptial agreement. However, in response to expressing your concern that private ordering might disadvantage women, it is suggested that, by denying women the right to freely negotiate their own arrangements, you are presenting women in a demeaning way that presupposes that they cannot be trusted to look after their own interests. How would you respond to this?

In the following case study we move from 'family law' to the field of 'commercial law' and consider how what might be considered in one context arms length commercial decisions are complicated by the fact that they are made in the context of personal or familial relationships.

RELATIONSHIP DEBT OR 'SEXUALLY TRANSMITTED DEBT'

In the introduction to this part of the book, we discussed how women's unpaid work and other activities contribute substantially to the economy and to their households. The Australian Bureau of Statistics reported in *Unpaid Work and the Australian Economy*[136] that the bulk of unpaid work is housework, followed by voluntary and community work. Yet there is another area of (largely unpaid) work or economic participation that is perhaps less easy to capture and is difficult to quantify. This is the work that family members do in family businesses, or by assisting other family members in various ways to participate in such businesses. It may involve direct 'work' activities, such as the partner of the small businessperson who 'does the books'. But the participation may be more indirect than that. A particularly common way that women contribute to family businesses is by using their ownership of property, most frequently the family home, as security for borrowings that support a business undertaken by either their husband, children or some other person with

---

135 *Ibid*, at 294. See also Barbara Atwood, 'Ten Years Later: Lingering Concerns About the Uniform Premarital Agreements Act' (1993) 19 *Journal of Legislation* 127.
136 ABS, *Unpaid Work and the Australian Economy 1997*, Cat No 5240.0, 2000.

whom they have a relationship. This phenomenon, and the resulting consequences that can apply when the loan is not repaid or the relationship ends (or both), has come to be known in Australia as 'sexually transmitted debt'. While that term has gained considerable currency over recent years, the phenomenon is now more widely referred to as 'relationship' debt in recognition of the broader range of relationships in which these problems can arise.[137] In a 1999 report on *Relationship Debt*, the Australian Banking Industry Ombudsman described 'relationship debt' as 'a shorthand expression for the assumption by one person of responsibility for a debt owed by another person to whom they are related in some way'.[138] Belinda Fehlberg[139] has described the problem in the following way.

> Typically, such cases involve a wife who, under some emotional pressure caused by her husband, provides third party loan security (usually a second mortgage over the family home, but sometimes a personal guarantee) to secure a loan to a business which, although conducted by the husband, often provides the family's income. When the creditor later tries to enforce the security, the wife argues that it is invalid.[140]

There are a number of reasons for the increasing attention given to the issue of 'sexually transmitted', or 'relationship' debt'.[141] These include the effects of economic recession, the decline in long term employment (and the corresponding rise in self-employment and small businesses), as well as the work of women's and consumer credit legal services in drawing attention to the phenomenon.[142]

The following extract provides an illustration of a not uncommon fact situation that might give rise to an application by a woman for relief from a contract. In this case, the application was made under the NSW *Contracts Review Act* 1980, which empowers courts to vary contracts that are unjust. While that Act has no counterpart in other States, there are a variety of other common law and statutory avenues for seeking relief.[143]

---

137 See Australian Banking Industry Ombudsman Ltd, *Report on Relationship Debt*, Bulletin No 22, September 1999; Expert Group on Family Financial Vulnerability, *Good Relations, High Risks: Financial Transactions within Families and Between Friends*, Report, 1996.
138 Australian Banking Industry Ombudsman Ltd, *Report on Relationship Debt*, at 2.
139 See generally Belinda Fehlberg, *Sexually Transmitted Debt: Surety Experience And English Law*, Clarendon Press, Oxford, 1997.
140 Belinda Fehlberg, 'Surety Wives and Australian Law: *Akins v National Australia Bank*' (1997) 11 *Banking and Finance Law Review* 423 at 423.
141 Some commentators, notably Paula Baron, prefer the term 'emotionally transmitted debt': see Baron 'The Free Exercise of Her Will: Women and Emotionally Transmitted Debt' (1995) 13 *Law in Context* 23. There is an extensive literature on 'sexually transmitted debt': see, for some examples, Nicola Howell 'Sexually Transmitted Debt: A Feminist Analysis of Laws Regulating Guarantors and Co-Borrowers' (1995) 3 *Australian Feminist Law Journal* 93; Miranda Kaye; 'Equity's Treatment of Sexually Transmitted Debt' (1997) 5 *Feminist Legal Studies* 35; Julie Dodds Streeton, 'Feminist Perspectives on the Law of Insolvency' in Dodds Streeton & Langford, *Aspects of Real Property and Insolvency Law* (1994) Research Paper No 6, *Adelaide Law Review*, Adelaide. One of the most comprehensive treatments is by Kristie Dunn: see 'Yakking Giants: Equality Discourse in the High Court' (2000) 24 *Melbourne University Law Review* 427.
142 See, for example, Radmila Jukic, *Till Debt us do Part*, Melbourne, Consumer Credit Legal Service, 1994; Supriya Singh, *For Love Not Money: The Stories of Women in Family Business*, Consumer Advocacy and Financial Counselling Association of Victoria, Melbourne, 1995; and *Marriage Money: The Social Shaping of Money in Marriage and Banking*, Allen and Unwin, Sydney, 1997. See also NSWLRC, *Guaranteeing Someone Else's Debts*, Issues Paper No 17, 2000, especially Chapter 1.
143 See generally John Carter and David Harland, *Contract Law in Australia*, 3rd ed, Butterworths, Sydney, 1996, Chapter 15; Tyrone M Carlin, 'The Contracts Review Act 1980 (NSW)' (2001) 23 *Sydney Law Review* 125. See also NSWLRC, *Guaranteeing Someone Else's Debts*, Issues Paper No 17, 2000, especially Chapter 2, for a detailed account of the legal doctrines that might be relevant.

Gough v Commonwealth Bank of Australia
NSW Court of Appeal: Kirby P, Mahoney and Meagher JJA
(1994) ASC ¶56-270

Kirby P (dissenting) [58,834] Mrs Gough was born in 1945. Therefore, at the time of the subject mortgage to the bank, she was forty three years of age. ... She left school at the age of fifteen years. By the time she left school she had completed one and a half years of high school. After this relatively limited education, she worked as a fruit picker and a domestic employee until her marriage to her first husband in 1964 (at the age of nineteen years). Following that marriage, Mrs Gough worked at various intervals as a domestic, a kitchen hand and a seamstress. She deposed that she had "almost no understanding of matters of business" and that she did "not understand legal documents". ...

... [I]n 1966, her father paid the deposit on a house [*to assist Mrs Gough and her first husband to buy a house*]. Following her divorce from her first husband in 1972, the property was transferred to her name alone ... .

Mrs Gough married again in 1974. ... Mrs Gough and her second husband, Mr David Gough, lived in the house prior to the events giving rise to these proceedings. ...

Mr David Gough worked in his tyre wholesale retail business. ... The accountant [*who was incorporating the company*] informed Mrs Gough that "for legal reasons" her name would go onto the papers for the company. She [58,835] contended that she did not play any part in running the company and was "very rarely" on the premises. She asserted that the accountant prepared income tax returns and other papers for the business which she signed, allegedly, without carefully reading or understanding them. It is clear from the exhibited documents that Mrs Gough was a director of the company. In the income tax returns she was shown as working up to 35 hours a week. The company was clearly the source of Mr and Mrs Gough's family income. To that extent, Mrs Gough had a stake in its success. But the picture presented by the objective evidence is that Mrs Gough brought her unencumbered house ... into the marriage. Mr Gough had his tyre business. It does not take too much imagination to understand the reasons why Mrs Gough was shown as devoting many hours of work to the company. Her oral evidence was that she was a housewife:

"Q: How would you rate your own skills in reading? Would you describe yourself as a good reader or poor reader?
A: Not good.
Q: Do you for pleasure read books?
A: No.
Q: Do you buy and read a newspaper from time to time?
A: Very rare.
Q: Do you occasionally buy a women's magazine to read?
A: Yes, if there is something on the cover that looks interesting.
Q: What sort of magazines do you buy to read?
A: Woman's Day now and again or New Idea.
Q: Now are you able to read easily the whole of a magazine like the Woman's Day or New Idea?
A: No.
Q: Are there parts you can read and parts you can't read or what?
A: I read the parts where it has hints in it or knitting patterns or sewing or cooking.
Q: Do you read the short story parts of those magazines?
A: No.
Q: Why is that?
A: They take too long"

This is what Mrs Gough later said:

> Q: I suggest to you that before you signed [the tax returns] you checked that the contents were true, is that the case?
> A: They weren't filled in.
> Q: Do you say that you signed the tax returns before they were filled in?
> A: Well that's what the accountant got us to do. ...
> Q: You just signed blank tax returns, did you before you put them in, before you signed them?
> A: Yeah, he would bring them over, collect the work books. He would get us to sign a couple of them, take them all away and do them.
> Q: You don't seriously say that do you?
> A: Yeah, that's what he done."

A search of the title of the house ... disclosed a number of prior mortgages. Under cross-examination, Mrs Gough agreed that she had executed these. She said that her father had explained them to her at the time. ... Naturally enough, Mrs Gough was asked about these prior mortgages. She stated that they were in small amounts designed to help her to repay accumulated debts.

Sully J, who had the advantage of seeing Mrs Gough give evidence appears to have rejected the notion that an accountant would simply have asked Mrs Gough to sign the tax returns (disclosing her suggested hours of employment in blank). He said that he found it "incredible" that a professional accountant would do such a thing. Because Mrs Gough had not called the [58,836] accountant, he inferred that the accountant would not have given support to such evidence. It could scarcely be expected that the accountant would affirm such evidence, even if it were true. It would constitute serious misconduct and imperil the accountant's licence as a tax agent. For myself, I would be less inclined to reject Mrs Gough's testimony as "incredible". I would be more inclined than Sully J was to discount the failure of Mrs Gough to call the accountant. That failure does not necessarily prove that her evidence was false on this point. ...

According to Mrs Gough, in March 1988, Mr Gough told her that he was proposing to change his bank from the National Australia Bank Ltd to the Commonwealth Banking Corporation which, he hoped, could do more for him. Mrs Gough stated that an officer of the Commonwealth Bank, Mr Rule, called at her home one Sunday afternoon in early March 1988 with a relative who was a customer of the tyre business. Mrs Gough deposed that it: "... did not occur to me that it was unusual for business to be conducted on a Sunday as my husband and both my family and my husband's family had always worked seven days a week."

According to Mrs Gough, whilst her husband was getting drinks for their guests, Mr Rule produced a bundle of papers for her to sign. She says that the papers were in different shapes and sizes. She signed them. When her husband returned he also proceeded to sign them whilst Mr Rule was talking to him. She went on:

> "At no time did Mr Rule or anyone else talk directly to me about business. I did hear Mr Rule and my husband discussing 'business overdraft'. At no time did I hear anyone mention the word 'mortgage'. A few weeks later my husband rang me from work to say that there was another paper which the bank had forgotten to get us to sign. My husband said the bank needed the paper that day and so an employee of my husband ... brought it over to me at home. I signed it and [sent] it back to my husband. I did not read it. I cannot recall ever having signed any other papers from the Commonwealth Bank. At no time did I think any of the papers involved us in any personal liability, it being my understanding that the loan was to the business and therefore the business would be liable to pay it back. I did not think it unusual that I had to sign them because I understood that both my husband and I had to sign all papers for the business."

Mrs Gough claimed that, so far as she knew, the business was doing "fairly well" at this time. However, early in 1990, the premises in which the business was operated were to be sold. Mr Gough tried to find other premises but could not. In May 1990 the business closed. In October 1990 Mrs Gough received a letter from the Commonwealth Bank. She claimed that, until she received the demand of the bank, she did not even know that the bank had a mortgage over her home. ...

[Mr Rule's] evidence is important because Sully J accepted it. He did so upon the dual basis that he was impressed with Mr Rule's demeanour and he found what Mr Rule had to say "made sense". Where the versions of the facts given by Mrs Gough and Mr Rule differed, Sully J preferred the latter.

Sully J expressed some reservations about the appellant's credit or at least as to the reliability of her recollection. The doubts on credit appear to have been based upon the doubted testimony of unconfirmed income tax returns signed in blank (with which I have already dealt) ....

[58,837] Mr Rule did recollect a visit to the Goughs' home on one occasion. He had no precise recollection of his dealings with the Goughs. ... He was therefore forced back upon reconstruction of what had occurred. This reconstruction was based upon:

1. His recollection of his "invariable practice" or "standard procedure"; and
2. A bank file note which he had prepared at the relevant time and which he construed ....

Mr Gough acknowledged that he knew that the house which was offered for mortgage was Mrs Gough's house obtained as part of the divorce settlement with her first husband. He knew that it was her name alone that was on the title and not his. He understood that it had been her father who had put the deposit on the house for her and her children. He acknowledged that the income tax returns showed Mrs Gough spent "an average of 25 hours employed per week by the company". But he stated that this was "not true":

> "A: That is not true, that was only for a tax reason. I thought if she was the secretary, I thought why shouldn't she get something out of the company. We were putting enough hours in for it plus I never wanted her to work in the first place. ...

[58,838] Mr Gough also gave us an insight into the relationship that he had with his wife:

> Q: And you discussed [*the fact that if the company failed to meet its obligations the bank might take the house property and sell it*] with your wife, didn't you?
> A: No I didn't.
> Q: But that was a pretty important matter, wasn't it?
> A: It is an important matter but I said to myself that she should not worry about what is going on down at work when it was my own doing that got me into strife by giving too much credit in the first place.
> Q: But it was her home as well?
> A: Yes, that is right.
> Q: And indeed, it was her house, but that was a matter which you discussed with her?
> A: No it wasn't. ...

In the light of this evidence, which was not shaken, and which has a distinct appearance of truthfulness, Sully J's reservations about the credit of Mrs Gough seem surprising. With great respect to his Honour, the common sense conclusions which appear to emerge from the evidence were:

1. Mrs Gough was a person of limited education in humble avocations in a remote country town where she grew up. She had no real experience of business;

2. From the age of 19 she was a housewife looking after children, with extremely modest intellectual pursuits generally confined to simple magazines;
3. She was initially helped in respect of the purchase of a home for her first marriage by her father who also explained to her the obligations to pay the mortgage payments;
4. She brought her home into her second marriage to Mr Gough from her divorce settlement. It was her unencumbered asset. It was the product of her father's generosity. It was valuable to her as her separate property;
5. The income tax returns, however filled in, were not a truthful presentation of Mrs Gough's work for the company. Such "work" as she did was performed at home and was confined to a few hours. For the most part she was engaged in home duties with obligations to look after her children;
6. Whatever the precise details of the advice she received from Mr Rule for the bank (and his Honour accepted Mr Rule in this regard), Mrs Gough certainly did not receive separate and independent legal or financial advice … . Mrs Gough obtained no separate advice and was not advised to obtain any;
7. The bank was aware that Mr and Mrs Gough were living together. The bank may be taken to have been aware, from the [58,839] circumstances which would have been observed by Mr Rule and conversation which occurred in the acknowledged visit to the Gough home, that Mrs Gough stayed at home and had no real experience in business. This inference is supported by the statement in the bank file note: "David basically controls the total operations."

   The bank is also fixed with the knowledge that the title of the … home was exclusively in the name of Mrs Gough, that Mr and Mrs Gough were directors of the company and that Mr Gough, with whom most of the dealings with the bank were conducted, was the real principal of the company to which the loan was being extended. Yet Mr Gough did not have any legal interest in the property which was provided as security;
8. As the internal evidence of the bank, and the testimony of Mr Rule indicate, the bank was clearly aware that the extension to the company was improvident. …

[58,843] Banks have played an integral part in society for hundreds, perhaps thousands, of years. They are the cornerstones of economies. They provide the backbone to many people's lives. They obtain their funds from customers of all walks of life and backgrounds. As such, they have a special responsibility in relation to society. That responsibility is to act fairly: to not abuse their special position of power but to pay special attention when they are dealing with people who may be in an unequal bargaining position in relation to themselves. Some women are still treated by some financial institutions as appendages of their husbands. They are not provided with advice as separate legal entities in their own right. Where the woman is the sole legal owner of property which is the subject of a mortgage that will primarily benefit her husband's assets and imperil her own the protection of the law will often be afforded. …

[58,845] What are the policy considerations involved in this case? The Court should send a clear signal to financiers, such as the bank, that in circumstances like this case prudent practice, and the avoidance of a contractual arrangements [sic] that may later be impugned as unjust, will require the provision to a person such as Mrs Gough of independent legal and financial advice. With respect to those of a different view, I am of the opinion that the whole circumstances of the

case cried out for independent advice which neither Mr Rule nor any other officer of the bank could have given Mrs Gough. ...

[*Kirby P would have allowed the appeal and set aside the mortgage. However, the majority, Mahoney and Meagher JJA, denied relief in separate judgments. Mahoney JA held that the Act should be applied on a case-by-case basis, that the primary judge's findings of credibility ought to be upheld as a matter of law and that in any case the bank manager's account was most probably the correct one.*]

Meagher JA [58,856] ... The only point pursued by the appellant has been that she is entitled to relief under the Contracts Review Act, 1980. The particulars of this submission are:

    (1) That she was a person of limited education having no capacity to understand legal language; and

    (2) Gough's Tyre Service Pty Ltd was in reality her husband's business and she had little or nothing to do with it.

    (3) The mortgage was signed in "the most casual of circumstances" at Mrs Gough's home, with no explanation offered to her about what she was signing.

    (4) Mrs Gough had no independent advice before she signed the document.

These particulars may be readily refuted. As to (1), the plaintiff may not be extremely sophisticated or well lettered, but she is no gaping rustic. What is more to the point, whilst she may not have understood the finer points of the law of mortgages, his Honour accepted that she understood that failure to repay the loan when it was due would enable the Bank to sell her house. As to (2), she owned half the shares in the company and was one of its two directors. She was also in charge of dealing with the company's debtors, which was its most sensitive problem. As to (3), it was the subject of evidence from the then Manager of the Bank, directly contrary to Mrs Gough's; the Judge believed him and not her. As to (4), whilst it is true that she had no independent advice, that fact of itself does not entitle her to any relief in respect of the mortgage, any more than it would have in respect of the three or four previous mortgages she had executed.

The appeal should be dismissed with costs.

Notes

1. How helpful to your understanding of the case is the detailed information provided by Kirby P about Ms Gough's educational attainments and reading ability? Does that information present her as, to use Meagher JA's term, a 'gaping rustic'? If so, is there a way to avoid constructing the guarantor in such cases EITHER as a gaping rustic, OR as a fully independent 'masculine' individual?

2. Kirby P read the facts quite differently from how the trial judge viewed them and said he was using 'common sense'. Is it likely that the trial judge also relied on his notion of 'common sense' in determining both that Ms Gough's credibility was suspect because, in his view, no accountant would have asked her to sign a blank form, and that the bank officer's evidence of 'invariable practice' was more reliable than her recollection of the actual events about which she gave evidence? If so, what does that tell us about the use of 'common sense' as a judicial fact-finding method?

3. While the facts in Gough may be illustrative of some of the cases that involve issues of 'relationship debt', it should not be assumed that all those affected are women with little or no formal education. For example, Ms Garcia (see note 4 below) was a physiotherapist who ran her own practice; and in another

well-known case, Ms Akins,[144] while not employed during her marriage, had trained as a nurse.

4. In 1939, the High Court articulated a rule that relieved married women (but only married women) from liability in certain situations where they had given guarantees for their husband's loans. Dixon J (as he then was) developed this approach in the case of *Yerkey v Jones*[145] where a woman had given a guarantee in the form of a mortgage over her land in order for her husband to acquire a business. The principle in this case has two limbs. The first applies where the bank (or lender) leaves it to the husband to procure his wife's signature on a guarantee and the husband exerts undue influence in obtaining her signature. Unless the bank ensures that the woman receives independent advice, undue influence on the part of the husband in obtaining her signature may be attributed to the bank merely on the basis that the bank knew they were married. The second limb was summarised by Dixon J as follows:

> [I]f a married woman's consent to become a surety for her husband's debt is procured by the husband and without understanding its effect in essential respects she executes an instrument of suretyship which the creditor accepts without dealing directly with her personally, she has a prima facie right to have it set aside.[146]

Therefore, without the need to demonstrate any wrongdoing by the husband in obtaining the signature, lack of understanding on the part of the wife may itself provide the basis for relief.[147] The 'rule' in *Yerkey v Jones*, providing a 'special equity' for married women, has been expressly rejected by the House of Lords in England in *Barclay's Bank plc v O'Brien*.[148] It had also come to be doubted by the NSW Court of Appeal in a number of cases[149] until it came before the High Court in 1998 in *Garcia v National Australia Bank*.[150] The majority of the court in *Garcia* reaffirmed the *Yerkey v Jones* doctrine. It held that a lender need only be aware of the marriage relationship for the rule to be invoked, since the lender:

> is taken to have understood that, as a wife, the [guarantor] may repose trust and confidence in her husband in matters of business.[151]

Garcia involved a married couple and the issue of how far the principle extended, if at all, beyond applying to wives did not need to be decided in that case. However, the majority commented (though stressed that they did not need to decide the point):

> It may be that the principles applied in *Yerkey v Jones* will find application to other relationships more common now than was the case in 1939 – to long term and publicly declared relationships short of marriage between members of the same or of opposite sex.[152]

---

144 *Akins v National Australia Bank* (1994) 34 NSWLR 155.
145 *Yerkey v Jones* (1939) 63 CLR 649.
146 (1939) 63 CLR 649 at 683.
147 See Belinda Fehlberg, 'Surety Wives and Australian Law: *Akins v National Australia Bank*' (1997) 11 *Banking and Finance Law Review* 423 at 426.
148 [1994] 1 AC 180 (HL).
149 See, for example, *Akins v National Australia Bank* (1994) 34 NSWLR 155; *Teachers Health Investments P/L v Wynne* (1996) ASC ¶56-356 and *NAB Ltd v Garcia* (1996) 39 NSWLR 577.
150 (1998) 194 CLR 395.
151 *Ibid*, at [31].
152 *Ibid*, at [22].

While all members of the court agreed that Ms Garcia's appeal was to be allowed,[153] Kirby J would have gone further than the majority and extended the principle beyond the category of married couples only. In his view, the *Yerkey v Jones* principle was, as Dunn described it:

> [A]n 'historical anachronism' and an 'unprincipled discriminatory category'. He argued forcefully that it was inappropriate to treat married couples differently from unmarried couples, and inappropriate to treat women differently from men. He preferred the approach of the House of Lords in *O'Brien*, which is gender-neutral and applies to all debtor-guarantor relationships involving emotional dependence rather than being confined to marriage.[154]

Assume you have been briefed by a feminist litigation organisation and it has been granted leave to intervene in this case. What arguments would you make? What, if any, difference would it make to you if you were acting for Ms Garcia, rather than for the intervener?

5. In a number of cases in which the courts have refused to set aside transactions, the reason given has been that the wife benefited from the transaction and was therefore not a 'volunteer' as required by the *Yerkey v Jones* test.[155] Is it always possible to conclude so readily that a wife will benefit from something that provides an advantage to her husband's business? In recent decades, there has been extensive research that has cast doubt on the assumption that household income and assets are necessarily shared.[156] A considerable body of research undertaken in the 1980s and 1990s demonstrates that the fair distribution of income within a household cannot be assumed. How income is distributed depends upon a range of complex factors such as the level of income, level of education, type of work undertaken by either or both of the parties etc.[157] As Meredith Edwards has pointed out:

> There would appear to be two good equity reasons for abandoning policies resting on the assumption that husbands and wives pool income and share equally in its benefits.
>
> The first reason is that hardship and inequities occur when one person's standard of living is assumed to depend on another's. ...

---

153 Callinan J also delivered a separate concurring judgment.

154 Kristie Dunn, 'Yakking Giants', at 437. A preliminary study undertaken by the NSWLRC has shown that, by 2001, no court had yet extended the principle in *Garcia* beyond married couples. The relationships found to fall outside the principle include heterosexual de facto relationships, sibling relationships and close friendships: see Reg Graycar, Robyn Johansson, Jenny Lovric, 'Third Party Guarantees' (2001) 12 *Journal of Banking and Finance Law and Practice* 181 esp at 194-5.

155 See, for example, *Akins*: this was one of the reasons given by the court for refusing special leave: *Akins v NAB* S131/1994 (12 May 1995). Compare *Garcia* where the wife was a director and shareholder of the relevant company, yet the court held: 'Taken as a whole, those findings demonstrate that the appellant in fact obtained no real benefit from her entering the transaction; she was a volunteer. The fact that she was a director of the company is nothing to the point if, as the trial judge's findings show, she had no financial interest in the fortunes of the company' ((1998) 194 CLR 395 at [43]).

156 See, for example, Carolyn Vogler and Jan Pahl, 'Social and Economic Change and the Organisation of Money within Marriage' (1993) 7 *Work, Employment and Society* 71; Jan Pahl, 'Household Spending, Personal Spending and the Control of Money in Marriage' (1990) 24 *Sociology* 119.

157 See, Belinda Fehlberg, *Sexually Transmitted Debt: Surety Experience And English Law;* Supriya Singh, *Marriage Money: The Social Shaping of Money in Marriage and Banking*, Allen and Unwin, Sydney, 1997; Jan Pahl, *Money and Marriage*, St Martins Press, NY, 1989. See also Meredith Edwards, *The Income Unit in the Australian Tax and Social Security Systems*, AIFS, Melbourne, 1984; and Meredith Edwards, 'Individual Equity and Social Policy' in Jacqueline Goodnow and Carole Pateman (eds), *Women, Social Science and Public Policy*, Allen and Unwin, Sydney, 1985.

The second reason for abandoning policies that assume transfers of income between husband and wife is that the economic, social and demographic changes [*such as changes in women's workforce participation, and in family formation and structure*] make it less appropriate than even twenty years ago to assume either that a woman will be financially dependent once she marries, or that the marriage relationship will be long-lasting.[158]

Edwards was writing in 1985, yet the judgments show that little has changed in this respect. In more recent work, Supriya Singh studied the financial arrangements amongst a number of couples in Victoria. As part of that research, she looked at how the couples she interviewed handled their finances and concluded that it is increasingly common for couples to have joint bank accounts. Yet she questioned how appropriate it was to conclude that having a joint bank account necessarily showed that income and financial decision-making were shared.

Of the 83 married persons with joint accounts, 11 (12.8%) did not know their total household income and 14 (16.3%) did not have any information on their bank deposits. So anywhere between 13 and 16 per cent of persons with joint accounts could not exercise joint control, or even any control over their money.[159]

This led Singh to conclude that '[h]usbands continue to control money, but increasingly within the idiom of jointness'.[160]

The research data on the distribution and control of household income and assets has implications well beyond the test of 'who is a volunteer?' as Edwards' work, which focused on the social security and tax systems shows. For example, the assumption that household income is shared underpins the existence of a variety of household income and assets tests used in the *Social Security Act* 1991 (Cth) and it is also central to the dependent spouse rebate available under the *Income Tax Assessment Act* 1936 (Cth). How relevant is this assumption to Aboriginal households?[161] What are the arguments for and against using the individual as the unit of assessment in the tax and social security systems? Why do household or family income tests apply only to heterosexual couples? Indeed, why is the unit of assessment, or the unit often considered to be the central unit of 'family' for a variety of purposes, always a (hetero)sexual couple? Martha Fineman some years ago advocated a redefinition of the 'family unit' away from what she called the 'sexual family' to the mother-child dyad.[162] On what basis

---

158 Meredith Edwards, 'Individual Equity and Social Policy', at 100.
159 Singh, *Marriage Money*, at 108.
160 *Ibid*, at 87. See also Ken Dempsey, *Inequalities in Marriage: Australia and Beyond*, Oxford University Press, Melbourne, 1997, esp Chapter 6, 'Inequality in Decision Making'.
161 In a study on the relevance of the household unit, Diane Smith found that people in many Aboriginal households do not necessarily share their income. She concluded that extra-household economic networks, usually between linked clusters of households, were more significant determinants of expenditure capacity. See Diane Smith, 'Towards an Aboriginal Household Expenditure Survey: Conceptual, Methodological and Cultural Considerations', Discussion Paper No.10/1991, Centre for Aboriginal Economic Policy Research, Canberra.
162 Martha Fineman, *The Neutered Mother, the Sexual Family and Other Twentieth Century Tragedies*, New York, Routledge, 1995. Michael Freeman has also drawn on her notion (and critique) of the sexual family to argue that we omit elders from our sense of family, despite resort to notions of 'community care' (which is another word for looking after elders within families): Michael DA Freeman, 'Family Values and Family Justice' (1997) 50 *Current Legal Problems* 315 at 325.

should the existence of relationships (and of what kind) influence social and legal policy-making?[163]

6. Following the decision in *Barclays Bank v O'Brien*,[164] it has been held in a number of cases England that a guarantor who has received independent legal advice on the consequences of guaranteeing the relevant transaction cannot later have it set aside by claiming she did not understand its effect.[165] However, in 2001, the House of Lords reconsidered this issue and drew attention to some problems in assuming that legal advice is always effective.[166] In fact, Lord Nicholls noted:

> On behalf of the wives, it has been submitted that under the current practice the legal advice is often perfunctory in the extreme and, further, that everyone, including the banks. knows this. Independent legal advice is a fiction. The system is a charade. In practice it provides little or no protection for a wife who is under a misapprehension about the risks involved or who is being coerced into signing. She may not even know the present state of her husband's indebtedness.[167]

The High Court's majority judgment in *Garcia* also suggests that the fact that a wife has had legal advice will make the transaction difficult to set aside.[168] In the previous case study, we referred to the 2000 Commonwealth legislation making private family law agreements binding,[169] so long as, among other formalities, the signatories received independent legal advice. What might be some of the problems for women of making the receipt of independent legal advice the determinant of whether or not a transaction will be enforced?[170]

7. There are indications in some of the cases that the wife's signature was obtained by the husband through the use of some form of coercion. Some of the judgments explicitly refer to violence in the relationship as a background factor.[171] Given that it is quite rare for courts dealing with issues outside the criminal law to see violence as relevant to the context of a case, it seems fair to assume that there are many more such cases, both those that go to court, and those that do not, in which

---

163 For a detailed discussion of this issue, see Law Commission of Canada, 'Recognizing and Supporting Close Personal Relationships Between Adults', Discussion Paper, May 2000.
164 [1994] 1 AC 180.
165 See, for example, *Royal Bank of Scotland plc v Etridge (No 2)* [1998] 4 All ER 705.
166 *Royal Bank of Scotland v Etridge (No 2)* [2001] UKHL 44 (House of Lords).
167 *Ibid*, at para 52.
168 'If the creditor itself explains the transaction sufficiently, or knows that the surety has received "competent, independent and disinterested" advice from a third party, it would not be unconscionable for the creditor to enforce it against the surety even though the surety is a volunteer and it later emerges that the surety claims to have been mistaken': *Garcia v National Australia Bank Ltd* (1998) 194 CLR 395 at [40].
169 *Family Law Act* 1975 (Cth) Pt VIIIA.
170 See ALRC, *Equality Before the Law: Women's Equality*, Report No 69, Part II, 1994, particularly Chapter 13. See also NSWLRC, *Guaranteeing Someone Else's Debts*, Issues Paper 17, at 78-85.
171 See *Armstrong v Commonwealth Bank of Australia* [1999] NSWSC 588. For an English example see *BCCI v Aboody:* In that case, the bank had asked Mr Aboody to send a letter from his wife indicating that she was aware of the implications of the proposed charge. When the husband said he could not see any purpose in doing so, the bank insisted on arranging independent advice for her. While she was seeing the solicitor, away from the husband, and the solicitor was advising her not to sign, the husband burst into the room saying 'Why the hell don't you get on with what you're paid to do and witness her signature?' She was crying and, despite being advised not to sign, she eventually did, and did not accept the solicitor's suggested changes. The solicitor wrote on the certificate: 'Husband is a bully. Under pressure and she wants peace'. The Court held that she signed as a result of undue influence of her husband, but for other reasons did not set aside the transaction (*BCCI v Aboody* [1989] 1 QB 923 (CA)).

some form of violence or coercion was used to secure the guarantor's signature.[172] It is well known that, in relationships characterised by violence, the time of, and immediately after, separation/relationship breakdown is particularly dangerous.[173] And it is common to find in the factual background of so many cases involving marital partners and debt that the parties had separated since the agreement was signed.[174] The reported cases also show that the decision to enforce a guarantee is often precipitated by difficult family circumstances, either separation or divorce and consequential property settlement, or the failure of a business. These circumstances often occur around the same time,[175] something to which the Australian Banking Industry Ombudsman drew attention in its report on relationship debt.[176] It may be only after the relationship breaks down that the full picture emerges, both of the magnitude of the debt and of the circumstances in which the surety's signature was obtained.

Michael Trebilcock and Steven Elliott have suggested that some women sign guarantees that are not in their best interests out of fear of endangering a marriage.[177] They also show how this fear has a significant economic basis, as it is well established that, following divorce, women's standard of living declines, while men's increases.[178] In their discussion, one of the examples they use is a decision of the NSW Court of Appeal, *Teachers Health Investments Pty Ltd v Wynne*,[179] where there had been an explicit threat of this nature, that is, 'sign or I'll divorce you'. How can the law dealing with guarantees – quintessentially business/arms length legal relationships – factor in these contextual factors?

8. Cases involving guarantees for business loans that draw on family resources are not the only ones to raise the complicated question of how commercial doctrines should take account of the relationship between the parties in determining how to respond to disputes. In a related series of cases, particularly in the 1980s, a number of women who were directors of companies had actions brought against them under the *Corporations Law* for trading while insolvent (s 588G).[180] In

---

172 See Graycar, 'Telling Tales: Legal Stories about Violence Against Women' (1996) 7 *Australian Feminist Law Journal* 79.
173 See Astor, 'The Weight of Silence in Family Mediation' and see also Martha Mahoney, 'Legal Images of Battered Women: Redefining the Issue of Separation' (1991) 90 *Michigan Law Review* 1.
174 This is the factual situation in a number of the cases referred to here: see *Garcia, Akins, Wynne, Armstrong*.
175 Belinda Fehlberg, *Sexually Transmitted Debt: Surety Experience and English Law*, at 10. Examples from the well-known Australian cases include *Garcia v National Australia Bank Ltd* (1998) 194 CLR 395 and *Akins v National Australia Bank* (1994) 34 NSWLR 155.
176 Australian Banking Industry Ombudsman Ltd, *Report on Relationship Debt* (Bulletin No 22, 1999) at 16-17.
177 Michael Trebilcock and Stephen Elliott, 'The Scope and Limits of Legal Paternalism: Altruism and Coercion in Family Financial Arrangements' (Unpublished paper, February 1999, University of Toronto).
178 Australian data on this phenomenon is discussed in the previous case study in this chapter; see in particular Sheehan and Hughes, 2001.
179 (1996) ASC ¶56-356 (NSWCA).
180 For some of the case law on these issues, looking at the requirements placed upon directors and persons engaged in the management of companies, see *Metal Manufacturers Ltd v Lewis* (1988) 13 NSWLR 315; *Statewide Tobacco Services v Morley* (1990) 2 ACSR 405; *Group Four Industries v Brosnan* (1991) 9 ACLC 1181 (SASC); *Standard Chartered Bank v Antico* (1995) 13 ACLC 1381 (NSWSC). At the time of most of these cases, the *Corporations Law* required that proprietary companies have two directors; now, only one director is required: see *Corporations Act* 2001 (Cth) s 201A. See also Peta Spender, 'Corporations Law: Women as Directors of Companies' in Graycar and Morgan (eds), *Work and Violence Themes: Including Gender Issues in the Core Law Curriculum*, 1996, available at http://pandora.nla.gov.au/tep/10029.

Ferraro[181] (the 'Sissinghurst Gardens' case discussed in the previous case study), the Full Family Court noted:

> The issue of the wife's personal liability as a director of the companies ... is a matter of increasing relevance in recent times although of no actual relevance in this case. There is now a series of cases which underline the personal liability of company directors where the company continues to incur debts which it cannot meet as and when payment falls due or otherwise disregards the interests of creditors while the company is practically insolvent ... As it has been held that directors cannot absolve themselves from liability for insolvent trading by an assertion that they were merely a nominal director and took no part in the company's affairs, this development in the law is particularly relevant to a wife who is only nominally a director of a company which conducts a family business. As the judgment of the Full Court in [*Statewide Tobacco v*] *Morley* [(1990) 2 ACSR 405] notes, "the days of the sleeping, or passive, director are well and truly over".[182]

WOMEN'S WORK IN THE HOME: PERSONAL INJURY DAMAGES

In this part of the chapter, we look at two issues in the assessment of personal injury damages: first, the way courts deal with women's loss of capacity to work in the home; and, secondly, the way damages are assessed for the costs of care, in a context where generally, the carers of accident victims are women. A third issue, how damages for women's loss of earning capacity – that is, their loss of capacity to do paid work – are affected by gendered assumptions about women's lack of attachment to the paid labour market, is examined in Chapter 6 below, *Out to Work*.

The valuation of a woman's loss of capacity to work in the home

Because the law of torts values some losses of working capacity over others, injuries to women that affect their capacity to work in the home are frequently treated as non-economic loss, a characterisation that has significant consequences in damages assessment. This is closely related to the common law's historical treatment of a woman's loss of domestic working capacity as a loss not to herself but to her husband through his action for loss of 'consortium' and 'servitium' (loss of services).

As the following extract illustrates, at common law, a loss of capacity to provide household services was actionable *only* by the woman's husband in an action for loss of consortium (the action included damages not only for loss of services, but also for loss of society and companionship, including sexual services).

JK Kealley v Jones; PM Kealley v Jones
NSW Court of Appeal: Moffitt P, and Hutley and Samuels JJA
[1979] 1 NSWLR 723

[*Mr and Mrs Kealley were both injured in the same road accident for which the defendant Jones admitted liability. Mrs Kealley claimed damages for her injuries and her husband claimed damages for his own injuries and for his loss of*

---

181 (1992) 16 Fam LR 1.
182 (1992) 16 Fam LR 1 at [165].

consortium and diminution in the services of his wife. Hutley JA did not dispute that the husband was entitled to an award for loss of consortium, but he was "unable to find ... evidence which would justify the finding that the husband had suffered a very substantial financial loss under this head". He rejected as irrelevant the fact that the accident had placed strain on the marriage and caused considerable unhappiness, stating:]

[739] Hutley JA ... It is not lost happiness which is the subject of compensation, it is the loss of the wife's services. Whether she renders them with a smile or a scowl is immaterial.

[Hutley JA noted that the husband had paid for some domestic assistance; that an aunt of the wife had come to stay for some time and, though not paid, was provided with board; and that the husband himself had undertaken domestic tasks previously performed by the wife. The wife had returned to her employment, but was unable to do any additional work in the home. However, Hutley JA was not satisfied with the evidence led to prove the quantum of any actual losses incurred. He noted that the wife worked because of her financial commitments and "that she recognized that it would be preferable for the children if she did not". He continued:]

... [740] [The] fragility of marriage must be borne in mind in allowing a husband damages for loss of consortium in the future. The contingency that he may lose his wife's future services for reasons other than the accident is very real, and should be reflected in any award.

... The action for loss of consortium is based on a status which has long since passed away. As Holdsworth says in History of English Law, vol 8, pp 429, 430: "The same principles as were applied to the servant were applied to the wife. The husband's interest in his wife's consortium, unlike the parent's interest in the consortium of his children, was considered to be sufficiently proprietary to support an action of trespass". Just as a master had a quasi-proprietary interest in the services of his servant, a theory which, as Holdsworth, at p 429, points out "originated in the rules of law applicable to **villein** status", a husband had a proprietary interest in the services of his wife. The concept that a wife is more than just a servant has, however, affected the action, and has left the law with the difficult task of distinguishing between the temporal and spiritual benefits of having a wife whose health and strength are unimpaired. Damages are not recoverable for loss of spiritual benefit.

... [741] Though I appreciate that it is theoretically correct that a husband is entitled to monetary compensation for having to perform more services in the home than he did prior to the accident, where such services are not so onerous as to preclude him from working, with a consequent loss of actual money, I can see little justification for making anything more than a nominal award. In assessing damages in this situation, regard must be had to the public mores in Australia and, where a husband [*and*] wife are both working, unless they are in extremely well paid positions permitting the employment of full time domestic assistance, the sharing of domestic burdens with the wife is expected of the husband, even where his wife is perfectly healthy. To give monetary compensation to a husband just because there is some small variation of the amount of work in the home which he is required to perform in his leisure time would seem to me to disregard the realities of the Australian domestic scene.

Notes

1. As Hutley JA notes, the common law action for loss of consortium was available only to a husband whose wife's ability to provide services had been

impaired or destroyed by an injury caused by the negligence of the defendant. Since the House of Lords ruled in *Best v Fox*[183] that women had no corresponding right of action for loss of their husband's consortium, various suggestions have been made as to what to do with this anomalous action. Some States extended the action to wives,[184] while others have abolished it altogether.[185] In a compelling critique of the South Australian legislation, Ann Riseley demonstrated that, since the major element of a loss of consortium award is the services (as opposed to the 'spiritual') element, the 'reform' is a pyrrhic victory only; most women do not lose their husband's domestic services when the latter are injured since they never had them in the first place.[186] This means that a woman's award for loss of her husband's consortium would most likely be significantly lower than a man's corresponding award. What does this indicate about gender neutral or formal equality-based strategies as a means of resolving problems of women's status in law?

2. In *Kealley*, Hutley JA decided that 'public mores' required him to take account of the fact that 'the sharing of domestic burdens with the wife is expected of the husband, even where his wife is perfectly healthy'. This is not an unusual approach in the cases: see, for example, *Bagias v Smith*.[187] Such a finding is common despite the empirical evidence referred to earlier in this chapter that indicates that most women who work outside the home also do most of the housework. Consider the following (extra-curial) statement by Samuels JA when he was a member of the NSW Court of Appeal:

> Those, incidentally, who care to dabble in jurimetrics might care to consider what is to be made of this: of the seven wives of the seven judges of the Court of Appeal, three are in full-time professions or occupations, two are in part-time professions or occupations, one was in full-time employment before marriage, and the remaining one in part-time employment before marriage. I would think therefore that all of us have experience of what might be regarded as a more modern way of life, in which household tasks are shared.[188]

While in *Kealley*, this assumption – that housework is shared where two members of a couple work outside the home – was used to reduce the husband's damages in an action for loss of consortium, it can also be used with effectively the same impact in a primary action by the woman herself. For example, in a 1996 British Columbia case a trial judge noted:

> This is a family of two spouses both of whom work outside the home. The plaintiff plans to continue her career. In that type of family as opposed to a

---

183 [1952] AC 716.
184 See, for example, *Wrongs Act* 1936 (SA) s 33; *Compensation (Fatal Injuries) Act* 1974 (NT) s 10(2)(c); *Law Reform Act* 1995 (Qld) s 13.
185 *Law Reform (Marital Consortium) Act* 1984 (NSW); *Law Reform (Miscellaneous Provisions) Act* 1955 (ACT); *Common Law (Miscellaneous Actions) Act* 1986 (Tas). In the ACT, the *Law Reform (Miscellaneous Provisions) (Amendment) Act (No 2)* 1991 abolished the action for loss of consortium (s 32) and created in its place a cause of action for loss of capacity to do housework (s 33(1)).
186 AC Riseley, 'Sex, Housework and the Law' (1981) 7 *Adelaide Law Review* 421.
187 (1979) FLC ¶90-658.
188 *Assessment of Damages*, Committee for Postgraduate Studies in Law, University of Sydney, November 1982, at 311.

traditional family where one spouse remains at home, it is reasonable to expect both spouses to contribute fairly equally to the domestic work.[189]

What possible explanation is there for the fact that these judges have not considered it necessary to check their assumptions against the established evidence? Is the distribution of domestic work in the home a matter of which 'judicial notice' may be taken?[190]

3. The common law system of assessing damages requires courts to assess a 'once and for all' sum to compensate for all past, present and future losses. In *Kealley*, Hutley JA relied on the 'fragility of marriage' to reduce the husband's damages. By contrast, the next case extracted assumes that the composition of the household will remain static as it is expected that the adult daughter (aged 21 at the time of trial) would continue to be available to take over the mother's domestic duties, at least those which were characterised as being performed for the benefit of others.

Whose loss?

Burnicle v Cutelli
NSW Court of Appeal: Reynolds, Glass and Mahoney JJA
[1982] 2 NSWLR 26

[*The plaintiff suffered injuries in an accident which rendered her unable to perform household duties. This was an appeal from an assessment of damages. The trial judge had found that the plaintiff had suffered a partial loss of her capacity to do housework and that her daughter was now making up the deficit. The trial judge had decided that the daughter's work involved three hours assistance to the mother per day in personal attention and three hours to the rest of the family, a total of six hours per day. On appeal, Reynolds JA characterised the plaintiff's loss as follows:*]

[27] Reynolds JA. As I would analyze these findings, they involve a finding of a partial loss of capacity to carry out housework resulting in:
  (a) a loss to the family of part of her services quantified as $90 per week;
  (b) a loss to herself by inability to fully satisfy her personal needs in daily life which would require services valued at $90 per week; and
  (c) a personal loss of the capacity to perform services for others voluntarily.
... The problem in this case is how to treat the loss of capacity which was formerly exercised voluntarily for the benefit of her family and would have continued to be exercised for the benefit of those who from time to time comprised the family household. It is the loss of a capacity to render services to others with which we are concerned. ...

[28] There are two losses: one to the recipients of the services and the other to the plaintiff personally. It is easy to quantify the losses to the recipients as being

---

189 *Kroeker v Jansen* [1995] BCJ No 724, at para 20A. Therefore, it apparently followed that her damages for her loss of domestic working capacity were reduced.
190 Recall, as noted in the first case study, that the Supreme Court of Canada and the Full Court of the Family Court of Australia have both taken judicial notice of the fact that women are economically disadvantaged by divorce: see *Moge v Moge* [1992] 3 SCR 813; *In Marriage of Mitchell* (1995) 19 Fam LR 44. See more generally, Graycar, 'Hoovering as a Hobby and Other Stories: Gendered Assessments of Personal Injury Damages' (1997) *University of British Columbia Law Review* 17.

the value to them of the lost services. The difficulty lies in seeing how in principle the loss to her is to be measured in the same way as the loss to the recipients.

... I am of the opinion that an assessment must be made as a component of an award of general damages, just as must be done in respect of any other deprivation which does not produce financial loss. The injured plaintiff has in such a case as this lost part of a capacity, the exercise of which can give to her pride and satisfaction and the receipt of gratitude, and the loss of which can lead to frustration and feelings of inadequacy. ...

[29] To quantify the injured housewife's loss of capacity to perform the work voluntarily for the benefit of others by the measure of the value of those services if performed by a third party may be a convenient and simple way to do so, but it does not seem to accord with established principle or to be a satisfactory way of assessing what is reasonable.

[*The court awarded her general damages, but rejected the submission that the plaintiff's loss of capacity to render services to members of her family should be quantified by calculating the replacement cost of those services using as a guide the 15 hours a week being spent by her daughter.*]

The judgment in *Burnicle* makes explicit the artificial way in which a woman's injury can be compartmentalised into a loss to others (her husband and family) and a loss to herself. And of those others, only the husband could sue for loss of services (consortium) at common law until the action was abolished in 1984. Only the ACT has legislated to replace that action with a primary cause of action for loss of capacity to do housework.[191]

Housework as hobby: Economic or non-economic loss?

Even if the relevant loss were seen as the woman's, rather than some other person's, it cannot be assumed that it will be properly valued. In *Burnicle*, when Reynolds JA referred to the appropriate form of compensation as 'general damages', he was treating the loss as non-economic. This critical distinction in damages awards between economic and non-economic losses is explored in the next extract.

Regina Graycar, 'Hoovering as a Hobby: The Common Law's Approach to Work in the Home'
(1985) 28 *Refractory Girl* 22

[24] ... In *Burnicle v Cutelli* the judge described [*the plaintiff's*] lost capacity as one which had formerly been 'exercised **voluntarily** [*sic*] for the benefit of her family' (p 27) and went on to reject explicitly the notion that the value of 'voluntary' work of this nature should be measured by the cost of employing a third party to do the work.

Other courts have taken a similar approach, awarding damages for loss of amenity to a woman who previously 'derived significant satisfaction from her labours on [*her family's*] behalf' (*Maiward v Doyle* [1983] WAR 210, 239, per Kennedy J).

At common law, 'frustration, feelings of inadequacy and lost satisfaction' are compensated only under the rubric of 'loss of amenity, or loss of enjoyment of life': ie, non-economic losses. This depiction of the loss as non-economic in

---

191 See *Law Reform (Miscellaneous Provisions) Act* 1955 (ACT); and see now *Sullivan v Gordon* (1999) 47 NSWLR 319 (CA).

principle denies recognition to women's work in the home as economic in nature. In practice, it results in the undervaluation of the woman's loss of domestic working capacity.

To be fair, not all judges have taken this path. As early as 1976, Justice Lionel Murphy attempted to extend the notion of 'loss of earning capacity' to cover domestic work:

> The expression 'loss of earning capacity' does not precisely describe this element of loss in its modern application. *What is measured is the impairment or destruction of the capacity to engage in work that is economically valuable, whether it would be paid for in money or not. It is a loss of working capacity sometimes referred to as loss of economic capacity.* There is a discernible factor of economic loss in loss of ability to do non-earning work of economic value. ... A woman who loses her capacity to make the usual contributions of a wife and mother in a household suffers great economic deprivation. Actions for loss of services [consortium] correctly treat this as economic injury, but as a loss to the husband on the archaic view of the husband as master or owner of his wife. The economic loss is one of the wife or mother. It is her capacity to work, either in the household or outside, which is affected (*Sharman v Evans* (1977) 138 CLR 563, 598 (emphasis added)).

... The material effect of labelling domestic work as non-economic is to deprive women of substantial amounts of common law compensation. This is because awards for non-economic loss are relatively small compared to those made for economic losses, at least in cases of serious injury. It is still the exception, rather than the rule, for courts to compensate these losses in the same way as other economic losses, such as the cost of future care or loss of actual (demonstrated) earning capacity. ...

Perhaps more fundamentally, failure to recognise women's loss of domestic working capacity as economic loss has the effect of strengthening the presumption that women with domestic responsibilities are economically dependent upon men. This is exacerbated, in common law claims, by the lump sum once-and-for-all system of assessing damages. When damages are calculated and the loss treated as non-economic, courts reflect in that calculation an assumption that a woman will continue to be supported financially, indefinitely. But ... accidents and resulting injuries or illness are often the very thing that splits marriages apart. Thus an award assuming future financial dependence upon some other breadwinner may leave a subsequently divorced woman with neither a husband, nor compensation for her very real loss of working capacity, a capacity she can no longer exercise either in the paid workforce or in her home.

Notes

1. Responding to reports of the ALRC and the ACT Law Reform Commission,[192] the ACT government abolished the action for loss of consortium in 1991 and in its place created a new statutory right of action for loss of capacity to do housework.[193] A decade later, the ACT is still the only Australian jurisdiction to have established a statutory cause of action for loss

---

192 ALRC, Report Number 32 (Community Law Reform for the ACT), *Loss of Consortium: Compensation for Loss of Capacity to do Housework*, AGPS, 1986). This recommendation was echoed in the 1991 report of the Community Law Reform Committee of the Australian Capital Territory, *Loss of Consortium; Loss of Capacity to do Housework*, Report No 4, 1991 (ACTCLRC).
193 *Law Reform (Miscellaneous Provisions) Act* 1955 (ACT), Pt 10, 'Loss of Consortium and Loss of Capacity to do Household Work'.

of capacity to work in the home. Can you suggest why other jurisdictions have not followed this lead?

2. Since the early 1970s, increasing criticism of aspects of the tort system has led governments in Australia and elsewhere to supplement, and in some cases, replace, the common law with various statutory compensation schemes. Perhaps the most thorough (and best known) of these is the New Zealand Accident Compensation system, established in 1972 after the report by Sir Owen Woodhouse. Such statutory schemes do not necessarily solve the problems caused by common law assessment, as has been demonstrated by analysis of some of the disparate effects on women and men of the New Zealand *Accident Compensation Act* 1982 (discussed in Chapter 11 below). The NSWLRC undertook an extensive inquiry into accident compensation in the mid-1980s and the question of how to assess damages for losses of working capacity that were not exercised in the paid labour market was raised, though not resolved, in the course of the inquiry.[194] In light of concerns about increased insurance premiums and escalating common law damages awards, this trend away from the common law compensation system is likely to continue. How, if at all, might a statutory compensation system address the value of women's work that is not exercised in the paid labour force?

3. In the first edition of a widely used Australian torts text,[195] the authors, when discussing compensation for loss of earning capacity for accident victims who had not exercised that capacity, suggested:

> [I]t does not follow ... that a plaintiff who has not exercised an alleged earning capacity before the trial may never be awarded damages for loss of earning capacity. Most notably, plaintiffs who have not reached working age, or plaintiffs who are of working age but have never been able to find a job, or female plaintiffs who have spent most of their adult life as housewives but hope or plan to enter the workforce when circumstances allow, would not be disentitled from an award of damages representing the full value of their capacity by the fact that the capacity had never been exercised, or not, at any rate, for a very long time, even though by choice.[196]

What assumptions lie behind this selective use of adjectives in gendering the plaintiffs? Why is it not necessary to specify the sex of the other plaintiffs discussed? Is it accurate to assume that 'female plaintiffs' are necessarily planning to enter the paid workforce? Does the extracted passage deal with the valuation of the loss by 'female plaintiffs' of their capacity to work in the home?

---

194 NSWLRC, *Accident Compensation Working Paper 1: A Transport Accidents Scheme For New South Wales*, Working Paper 22, 1983, especially Chapter 7 'Compensation for Non-Earners', and the final report *Accident Compensation: A Transport Accidents Scheme for NSW*, Report 43, 1984; and for a critique of the final report, see Graycar, 'Non-Earners and Accident Compensation: Women Sold Out Again' (1985) 10 *Legal Service Bulletin* 86.

195 Francis Trindade and Peter Cane, *The Law of Torts in Australia*, Oxford University Press, Melbourne, 1985.

196 Ibid, at 390. The second edition (published 1993) does not contain this passage.

Damages for the costs of care

Assumptions about gender have a significant impact upon damages assessment where the accident victim needs considerable amounts of care, often provided by close family members most of whom (though of course not all) are women.[197] Care for children, the aged, people suffering from illness, people with disabilities, and those generally unable to look after themselves is considered quintessentially women's work – even where it is done by men – and valued (or perhaps more accurately, devalued) accordingly.[198]

In *Griffiths v Kerkemeyer*,[199] the High Court decided that an injured plaintiff can recover damages for the costs of care even where the care is provided 'gratuitously', thereby recognising that for an accident victim, there is often a person or group of people whose lives are significantly affected by taking on the onerous task of caring for the injured person. The *Griffiths v Kerkemeyer* doctrine, which recognises damages for the costs of care as an economic head of damages, is quite clearly distinct from the more usual characterisation of women's work in the home as non-economic in the context of women's claims for compensation for their own injuries. However, while Griffiths v Kerkemeyer damages relate to work done by carers (usually women), they are not paid to the care provider but instead are awarded to the accident victim in recognition of the injured person's need for the services.[200]

In a series of cases starting almost immediately after the High Court's 1977 judgment, State courts reduced the damages payable by reference to a quaint notion that, since caring work is part of the 'ordinary currency of family life and obligation', it is excessive to pay damages to injured accident victims for those services.[201]

The devaluation of caring work by the courts was reinforced by a number of statutory modifications (including in some cases abolition) of *Griffiths v Kerkemeyer* damages.[202] In *Van Gervan v Fenton*, the 1992 case in which the High Court agreed to reconsider aspects of this doctrine, the damages paid to the accident victim for the costs of his care had been calculated by reference, not to what the caring services would cost if they had to be purchased on the market, but by reference to the wages the accident victim's wife had forgone by leaving her work as a nurse's aide to look after him. It was this quantification that was the issue on appeal.[203]

Van Gervan v Fenton
High Court of Australia
(1992) 175 CLR 327

[330] Mason CJ, Toohey and McHugh JJ:
... [T]he appellant was involved in a motor vehicle accident which was caused by the respondent's negligence. As a result of the accident, the appellant is

---

197 'Care at home necessarily entails devoted care on someone else's part, often a wife or woman relative who may have to abandon her ordinary employment to nurse the plaintiff and who will in any event find the task a demanding one': *Griffiths v Kerkemeyer* (1977) 139 CLR 161 at 170-1 (per Stephen J).
198 See 'Caring in the Community' in Australian Bureau of Statistics, *Australian Social Trends 2001* Cat No 4102.0, at 46-50.
199 (1977) 139 CLR 161.
200 See Graycar, 'Women's Work: Who Cares?' (1992) 14 *Sydney Law Review* 86 at 104-5.
201 The key decision is *Kovac v Kovac* [1982] 1 NSWLR 656.
202 These are discussed in Graycar, 'Women's Work: Who Cares?'
203 *Van Gervan v Fenton* (1991) Aust Torts Reports ¶81-103 (TASSC, Full Court); *Van Gervan v Fenton* (1992) 175 CLR 327 (HCA).

in need of almost constant care which has been, and, on the findings of the trial judge, for some time will be, provided at home by his wife. The wife, who had been employed as a nurses' aide, gave up that work in 1985 to devote herself to caring for her husband on an essentially full-time basis. She was then earning about $15,000 net per year.

[The plaintiff had a poor short-term memory and could not be left at home alone and it was found that it was not practicable for his wife to continue paid employment. The trial judge had awarded damages by reference to what Mrs Van Gervan lost in wages by leaving her work and this assessment was upheld by the Full Court.]

[331] THE APPLICABLE PRINCIPLE

... As a general rule, the market cost or value of those services is the fair and reasonable value of such services.

... [335] [T]here are sound policy reasons why the law should reject the income lost by the provider as the criterion for measuring the plaintiff's loss. First, fairness to the provider as well as to the plaintiff requires that the plaintiff should have the ability to pay the provider a sum equivalent to what the provider would earn if he or she was supplying those services in the marketplace. It does not seem reasonable that the defendant's liability to pay damages should be reduced at the indirect expense of the provider by invoking notions of marital or family obligation to provide the services free of charge or at less than market rates. Yet post-*Griffiths* awards have been reduced on this or similar theories [See *Johnson v Kelemic* (1979) FLC ¶90-657; *Kovac v Kovac* [1982] 1 NSWLR 656; *Carrick v Commonwealth* [1983] 2 Qd R 365]. Moreover, a plaintiff should be entitled to arrange his or her affairs in the way in which that person pleases and should not be constrained by monetary considerations from dispensing with gratuitous services and obtaining outside services if they are desired. Indeed, the relationship between the provider and the plaintiff may continue to exist in some cases only because outside help is able to be obtained.

[336] Secondly, since there is no binding agreement with the provider to continue to provide the services, the Court would have to make a finding as to whether the care would continue to be provided and, if so, for how long. The task of reliably determining whether a person will continue to provide personal services on a voluntary basis is much more difficult than the task of determining the traditional types of hypotheticals which come before the courts in damages cases, such as whether a plaintiff is likely to obtain employment or whether a medical condition is likely to improve or worsen. The relationship between the parties may end for any of the myriad reasons which bring about the end of relationships. But the predictability of a relationship continuing in this class of case is made more difficult than usual by the effect that the plaintiff's condition and needs have or may have on the emotional needs of those involved in caring for him or her. There is also the prospect that the care provider will not reveal to the court his or her true feelings about continuing to provide the services even in cases where the provider is conscious of those feelings. ... The use of the market cost criterion enables the plaintiff to be properly compensated by the award of a reasonable sum whether or not the gratuitous care provider continues to provide that care. In the present case, the foundation of the judgment is the finding that the appellant's wife will continue to provide the services. If she should fail to do so for any reason, the basis of the assessment would be inoperative.

[337] ... While many of the services provided to the appellant may have been of the kind provided by a nurses' aide, the appellant's wife worked as a nurses' aide for only 40 hours per week. Her attendance on her husband is virtually constant. She has lost her freedom to work where she pleases and she is confined to the matrimonial home for long periods. She has also lost her freedom to engage

in social and other activities outside her home after ordinary working hours. With great respect to the learned judges in the Supreme Court of Tasmania, the nature and duration of the services provided by the appellant's wife to the appellant are not comparable with the nature and duration of the services for which she was paid as a nurses' aide. Consequently, the appellant's wife's earnings in this case provided no reasonable basis for the calculation of the appellant's damages. ...

[343] Deane and Dawson JJ (dissenting): ... The evidence established that some of the services which would be provided by the appellant's wife were provided by her before the accident and would have continued to have been provided by her if the accident had not occurred. Such services included, for example, most of the domestic cooking, washing and vacuuming. In addition, ... the very presence of the appellant's wife in the home attending to her own affairs would constitute a kind of "low level supervision" which made the engagement of outside services for such "supervision" unnecessary.

... It may be that, if the appellant had not been married, it would have been reasonable, for the purposes of assessing damages, for him to have continued to live at home and to have employed the services of a seven-day-a-week live-in housekeeper to attend to his accident-caused needs during the period of 7 years following the trial. The facts of the matter were, however, that the appellant was and was likely to remain a party to a stable marital relationship and that the ordinary incidents of that relationship and the give-and-take activities of the parties to it provided a significant part of the active services and passive attendance in and about the matrimonial home which were necessary to look after the appellant's accident-caused needs. In assessing compensatory damages in that context, the ordinary incidents of a particular continuing relationship, such as joint activities and companionship, cannot, in our view, legitimately be seen as transformed by the injury to one spouse into "services" rendered or to be rendered by the other spouse even if they obviate a need for such "services" which would otherwise exist. ...

[344] It is clear that, in the present case, the additional services which are being and will be provided by the wife to attend to the appellant's accident-caused needs during the relevant period are very extensive. They involve both active care and protective attention to an extent that represents an oppressive restraint upon the wife's freedom of activity. It was clearly reasonable that the appellant's damages for loss of capacity include a substantial amount calculated by reference to the value of those additional services and that, in ascertaining the extent of the wife's additional services, account be taken of the drastic curtailment of the appellant's ability to do things for his wife (and himself) in return. Nonetheless, it would be illegitimate to treat the burden of additional care which the wife has assumed in the context of a devoted marriage and in the environment of her own home as converting her into the equivalent of a full-time live-in housekeeper to be remunerated not only for the active services which she renders to her husband but on the basis that time spent with her husband in her own home is to be treated as if it were services rendered to a stranger in a strange environment.

We would dismiss the appeal.

[348] Gaudron J: ... The valuation of work is neither an exact science nor an exercise that proceeds by reference to objective and non-controversial criteria. Certainly, there is a degree of controversy as to the true value of work that is usually perceived as "women's work", whether that work is done in the home or in the paid work force. ...

It was not suggested that a full work value enquiry should be carried out whenever a question arises as to the value of care or services in respect of which compensation is claimed. Nor was it suggested that that question requires expert evidence. Obviously and like many other questions involved in the assessment of damages, it has to be answered by adopting a broad approach in which regard is had to general community standards. And, save where there is no true rate or no appropriate rate to which regard can be had, that will ordinarily involve the adoption of the commercial rate for generally comparable care or services although there may be cases where that rate should be adjusted up or down because of some difference which affects the value of the care or services provided.

[*Gaudron J referred to an argument that it was not appropriate to use the amount an agency would charge because regard should be had to "the specific person who is delivering the care", the fact that it is provided "in her own home", and that "she is not required to attend the house other than in the times when she would ordinarily be there in respect of some of the hours of the day"*].

The argument that it was proper to have regard to the fact that the services were being provided by Mrs Van Gervan in her own home was put on the basis that, to the extent that she was providing some domestic services before Mr Van Gervan became ill, the need for which he should be compensated was only for those services that were not previously provided by her. The assumption that a paid carer would take over the domestic services previously provided by Mrs Van Gervan can be put aside because the argument suffers from a more fundamental defect.

There are only two bases on which it can be argued that some reduction should be made by reason that Mrs Van Gervan provided domestic services before her husband became ill. The first is that, to the extent of the services previously provided, there was a pre-existing need and, thus, no need resulted from the accident. That assumes that the services were provided because they were needed and not as part of the give-and-take usually involved in domestic arrangements. There is no justification for an assumption of that kind, involving, as it does, incompetence and selfishness of a very high order. The second basis on which the argument can be put is that the accident would have given rise to a need for the services of a wife, but to the extent that Mr Van Gervan already had the services of a wife, no need actually resulted. At best, that equates a wife to an indentured domestic servant which she is certainly not. The argument must fail.

The only other basis on which it was put that the commercial rate was inappropriate was that, by reason of Mr Van Gervan's fear of strangers, no one but his wife could provide the care needed. This is not a matter that detracts from the value of the care provided. On the contrary, it suggests that, in some respects, Mrs Van Gervan provides care and attention over and above what might be expected from a person whose services were obtained commercially. This argument must also fail.

[*Gaudron J would have substituted an amount, while the other judges sent the matter back for re-trial.*]

Notes

1. Mason CJ, Toohey and McHugh JJ acknowledged (at 336) the strains that such situations can place on relationships, and the problem of this in the context of 'once and for all' assessment (that is, the calculation of damages is supposed to take into account all past, present and future losses and therefore must predict the future, including whether the relationship will continue). Accidents and injuries may themselves be catalysts for the relationship to break down.[204] Do you think this possibility played a part in the majority's

---

204 See 'Women's Work: Who Cares?', at 102.

decision that the damages should be awarded by reference to the market rate?[205]

2. The majority judgment also referred to the post-*Griffiths* development of the concept that the 'ordinary currency of family life and obligation' meant that damages were not to be awarded in such cases (see especially *Kovac v Kovac*).[206] Note also the description of this concept by Deane and Dawson JJ who referred to 'give and take activities' and the 'ordinary incidents of a particular continuing relationship, such as joint activities and companionship'. What conception of family life is understood here? Would it make any difference if the accident victim is a woman and the carer a man, as was the case in *Kovac v Kovac* and in *Veselinovic v Thorley*,[207] relied on by the Tasmanian Full Court in *Van Gervan*? In *Veselinovic*, the court described the husband carer as 'a grown man who deliberately takes himself outside the workforce to provide this type of service'.[208] What does this tell us about courts' views of women's and men's work, both in the home and in the paid work force?

3. While the judgment of the majority (at 339) made it clear that the care Mrs Van Gervan provided to her husband differs enormously from the work she did at the nursing home, not least because her 'attendance on her husband is virtually constant', the dissenting judges (Deane and Dawson JJ) described the same situation in the following way:

> [H]e could be left alone for periods of an hour or more; he could go out with his wife, for purposes such as shopping, for short periods; he walked to visit a nearby friend for a few hours each day; another person visited on Friday evening between 7.30 p.m. and 10.30 pm.[209]

How might we account for this different view of the circumstances?[210]

4. One issue that emerges from a reading of some of the cases on damages and caregiving work is the risk of violence by the accident victim to the carer. One reported decision from South Australia provides a clear illustration of this phenomenon. In *Bruno v Davies*,[211] the plaintiff had been injured in a motor vehicle accident in which he suffered brain damage, one consequence of which was that he became violent. His wife (the carer), for whom this was a constant threat, had developed a number of strategies for dealing with him, and the court described her day-to-day life with him as requiring 'quite heroic stamina and tolerance from her because his brain damage has rendered him most difficult to live with'.[212] Although by the time of trial incidents of the violence or threats of violence toward his wife were less frequent, the court noted that she may yet leave him because of his violence: 'the one thing she will not now tolerate is violence from the man whom she has cared for and

---

205 See, for some Family Court decisions where the court noted that there had been an injury and compensation awarded under the *Griffiths v Kerkemeyer* principle, *O'Brien v O'Brien* (1983) FLC ¶91-316 (especially at 78,148 on the wife's post-accident care of the husband) and *Williams v Williams* (1984) FLC ¶91-541 (Fam CA, Full Court); (1985) FLC ¶91-628 (HCA).
206 [1982] 1 NSWLR 656.
207 *Veselinovich v Thorley* [1988] 1 Qd R 191.
208 *Veselinovich v Thorley* [1988] 1 Qd R 191 per Connolly J at 195.
209 *Van Gervan v Fenton* (1992) 175 CLR 327 at 345.
210 See Graycar, 'Love's Labour's Cost: The High Court Decision in *Van Gervan v Fenton*' (1993) 1 *Torts Law Journal* 122.
211 *Bruno v Davies* (1988) 144 LSJS 226.
212 *Ibid*, at 227.

nursed so devotedly'.[213] Yet, despite this rare acknowledgement, the inference to be drawn from reading the judgment is that, however regrettable, this is a matter of only limited relevance for the court. Is there a more appropriate way for a court to take into account this kind of violence other than to do so *only* in relation to the possible future contingency that the wife may not at some time in the future be available to provide the care?[214]

5. Consider the following:

> Mothers are ten times more likely than fathers to be carers of a child with severe disabilities; daughters are three times more likely than sons to look after parents with severe disabilities; and most unpaid carers are poorer than the rest of the population and are women. More than 50% depend on social security compared to 27% of the total population. (*For Love Alone? Women's Unpaid Work*, NSW Women's Advisory Council, 1991, at 8).

Does this evidence about the gendered distribution of caring work affect your understanding of the case law about *Griffiths v Kerkemeyer* damages? The ABS has published data on caring work in the community that also looks at some of the costs, both financial and non-financial, to carers. They note:

> The physical, emotional and financial consequences of providing primary care can be beneficial or adverse. In 1998, while some primary carers felt satisfied as a result of their caring role, some felt weary, felt lacking in energy, or frequently felt worried, depressed, angry or resentful, and some have been diagnosed as having a stress-related illness as a result of their caring role. For some carers, time and energy spent caring limited participation in other activities or impacted on their personal relationships, sleep or financial wellbeing.

And their data on income support shows little change in 10 years from the figures referred to by the NSW Women's Advisory Committee.

> Primary carers are more likely to be reliant on government pensions and allowances than people who are not carers. In 1998, pensions and allowances were the principle [*sic*] source of cash income for 49% of primary carers aged 15-64 years and for 20% of 15-64 year olds not providing care.[215]

In the following chapter, we move on to consider women's involvement in paid work. It should be borne in mind when reading that chapter that the work done by women in the home, including caring work, has a significant impact on their capacity to engage in sustained and well remunerated paid workforce activities.

---

213 *Ibid*, at 236. See also Graycar, 'Women's Work: Who Cares?' at 101-3 and references cited there.
214 For further discussion of this issue, see Graycar, 'Telling Tales'.
215 'Caring in the Community' in Australian Bureau of Statistics, *Australian Social Trends 2001*, Cat No 4102.0, at 47-8.

Chapter Six

Out To Work

Introduction

In this chapter, we consider some aspects of how women experience their participation in paid work. We do this selectively in order to illustrate some themes that resonate with other issues raised in this book. The chapter is not intended to provide detailed information about gendered aspects of labour law: fortunately, this is now the subject of much academic and policy research and writing.[1] Our major focus is on the issue of women's wages – why do women still earn less than men? However, we commence our discussion of women's work in the paid workforce by considering a further aspect of the law on damages – the award of damages to women whose injuries have destroyed or reduced their earning capacity. We use the case of *Wynn*[2] to illustrate some of the ways in which gendered assumptions enter into damages assessment and how judicial comments in damages cases can reveal the ways in which women's paid work is constructed as aberrational. We then go on to consider some of the explanations for, and social policy responses to, the gender wage gap. We conclude by returning full circle to the issue of women's unpaid work, in order to explore the connections between paid and unpaid work.

Constructing women's work: Personal injury damages

NSW Insurance Ministerial Corporation v Wynn
NSW Court of Appeal: Clarke, Handley and Sheller JJA
[1994] Aust Torts Rep ¶81-304

[*Ms Wynn was injured in a motor vehicle accident when aged about 30. At the time she was employed by American Express and held a senior position, having worked with the company for a number of years and having been promoted several times. The job involved extensive computer work which aggravated her whiplash injury, leading her ultimately to resign, but before her resignation at age 32, she held a senior position, worked long hours (often working at home until 1 or 2 o'clock in the morning) and had a number of staff responsible to her. The work she undertook subsequently was only part-time and far less remunerative. By the time the matter came to trial, she had married her long-term partner (with whom she lived while*

---

1 See, for example, Rosemary Owens, 'Women, "Atypical" Work Relationships and the Law' (1993) 19 *Melbourne University Law Review* 399; Anne Edwards and Susan Magarey (eds), *Women in a Restructuring Australia: Work and Welfare*, Allen and Unwin, Sydney, 1995; Moira Gatens and Alison MacKinnon (eds), *Gender and Institutions: Welfare, Work and Citizenship*, Cambridge University Press, Melbourne, 1998; and Anne Morris and Therese O'Donnell (eds), *Feminist Perspectives on Employment Law*, Cavendish Press, London, 1999.
2 *NSW Insurance Ministerial Corporation v Wynn* (1994) Aust Torts Rep ¶81-304 (NSWCA); *Wynn v NSW Ministerial Corporation* (1995) 184 CLR 485 (HCA).

employed by American Express) and had given birth to a child. At trial, she was awarded damages of $168,005 for past loss of earning capacity and $705,980 for future loss of earning capacity. The defendant appealed.]

[61,740] Handley JA:

Future economic loss

The remaining challenge by the appellant was directed to the Judge's assessment of the plaintiff's future economic loss. The principal contention here was that his Honour failed to make proper allowance for vicissitudes. He held that it was not probable that but for injury, the plaintiff would simply have retired to the laudable but limited role of housewife and mother and abandon her business career. He thought that but for her injuries in the second accident she would have continued to work for American Express until sixty. ... He noted the possibility that following her marriage the plaintiff may have undertaken maternity leave on one or two occasions for several months or perhaps even for a year, but thought that she would then have returned to her executive position with American Express. He also found that it was quite probable in the light of her past career and given her promotion to Director of Customer Services at the age of thirty one that but for the second accident she would have been promoted at least once more to the position of Vice-President within American Express with the benefit of an enhanced salary package. He said that having weighed these and the other factors he referred to, he considered that there was no justification for applying a discount for the vicissitudes of life in the order of 15% when assessing her future economic loss and he allowed a deduction of only 5% for these matters.

The plaintiff married her childhood sweetheart in 1990 following her retirement from American Express. They have previously lived together in a stable de facto relationship for a number of years. Her husband said in evidence that he and the plaintiff had talked together about having two children. Initially she spoke of having "a child", but later said that she and her husband had discussed having [61,741] a second child but that no decision had been made. American Express were generous in allowing up to twelve months maternity leave to their female staff, and as his Honour held there was no reason for thinking that her wish to have one or two children would have required her to abandon her career with the company. However it seems that this maternity leave has not been allowed for in his Honour's assessment except to the extent that it may have been included in his 5% deduction for vicissitudes.

The plaintiff's working hours as Director of Customer Services following her promotion to that position in October 1987 were very long indeed. She was required to do paper work and to work on a computer. She got to work between 9 and 9.30 and would get home "any time 9, 10, 11 at night". She would then have something to eat and would then sit down at her desk at home and work on her computer until 1 or 2 o'clock in the morning. She said she worked "probably eighty per cent of my time in a whole week because not only would I work through the day, I still had work at home, so you virtually lived and breathed your job". Her job was stressful and carried a lot of responsibility. ... She said that if she had remained at American Express after having a child she would have arranged for her child to be cared for by a full time nanny with assistance from her mother-in-law until the child was old enough to attend a child minding centre. She said that she could assist her children with their homework and things of that nature at night.

If the plaintiff ... continued her demanding business career after marriage, and after the birth of her child or children, she and her husband would necessarily have been faced with the necessity of engaging a full time nanny for the children and substantial household help during the week. The Judge's assessments made no allowance for these costs which must have been substantial and under current tax law have to be paid out of taxed income.

The Judge considered that it was "quite probable" that she would have risen, but for her injuries, to the position of Vice-President of the company. The current Vice-President of Operations in Australia when she resigned was Pam Stephens. No evidence was given about her age, her likely retirement date, or her prospects of further promotion. The plaintiff acknowledged that her promotion to Vice-President would have involved her accepting an overseas posting. Prior to her accident she had been given a temporary position in Bangkok which she had enjoyed. ... Although, as the Judge found, the plaintiff's fiancé had been "extraordinarily supportive" the contingencies associated with any further promotion for the plaintiff to an overseas posting were very great indeed. It would have involved separation from her fiancé or husband, whose business interests would have kept him in Sydney, except during holidays, and likewise either separation from any children or a decision not to have any. The plaintiff was thirty two when she resigned and her childbearing years were already limited. There was no evidence as to the age or years of service of the other Vice-Presidents in the company. ...

In any event there has to be considerable doubt as to the plaintiff's ability and willingness to continue to devote eighty per cent of each week to her job involving, as she said, working until 1 or 2 in the morning. There was no suggestion that these long hours were only temporary.

In these circumstances I am satisfied that his Honour's allowance of only five per cent for contingencies was far too low. It presupposes that it was practically certain that the plaintiff, if uninjured, would have worked full time with the company in her last position and presumably at the same hectic pace until her retirement at sixty. The physical, mental and emotional strain of working indefinitely such long hours and in such a demanding job necessarily involved risks to the plaintiff's health and the possibility of loss of job satisfaction and "burn out". Moreover, in the light of the various contingencies involved, the Judge's finding that it was "quite probable" [61,742] that she would have been promoted to Vice-President cannot be supported.

... The allowance for vicissitudes in my opinion should include two years absence from work to have two children (8% of the 23.75 years) together with an allowance for the prospect that the plaintiff would be unable or unwilling to remain in her job which placed such heavy demands on her time, energy and health and the love and patience of her husband. The plaintiff, of course, could have worked until sixty or later in a less demanding job but would then have earned substantially reduced salary benefits. In my opinion the allowance for vicissitudes in respect of an award for future economic loss for this plaintiff over such a long period must reflect the chance that she would at some stage have chosen or been forced to accept a less demanding job. A fair allowance for such vicissitudes in my opinion would be 20% and this with the 8% allowance for having two children gives a total deduction for vicissitudes of 28% which I would adopt.

Notes

1. Ms Wynn's damages for future loss of earning capacity were reduced from over $700,000 to $411,350. She sought special leave to appeal to the High Court. When that application came on for hearing,[3] the respondent, who was

---

3 *Wynn v NSW Ministerial Corporation* (application for special leave to appeal, unreported, HCA, Mason CJ, Deane and McHugh JJ, 18 April 1995).

called on by the court (the applicant was not called on), noted that 'it was no more than a case where the applicant's award was based on a frenetic lifestyle which could not, in reality, be achieved without other offsetting costs and that the judgment of the Court of Appeal took those into account'.[4] McHugh J responded by asking: 'Well, supposing the applicant had been a male, could you imagine a judge making a finding like this?'[5] He also commented in response to the 28% deduction for vicissitudes: 'I cannot ever remember a case that got anywhere near that figure'.[6] Deane J further suggested that the amount of discount for her childcare responsibilities 'seems to assume retarded children' since 'the child minding seems to go on for a long time'.[7]

2. On appeal, the High Court decided that a more appropriate reduction for vicissitudes was 12.5% and refused to discount the award to allow for child care pointing out that such costs may be incurred by men or women whether or not the child's mother is in the paid workforce.[8] The court also said that there was 'nothing in the evidence to suggest that the appellant was any less able than any other career oriented person, whether male or female, to successfully combine a demanding career and family responsibilities'.[9]

There has been a steady rise in the use of formal child care for children under three: 14% of children under three in 1990 were in formal child care, with 22.3% in such care by 1999.[10] And '[i]n 1999, just over half of all children aged under 12 years of age received some type of formal and/or informal child care'.[11] The figure was 38% in 1984, but has been around 50% since 1990.[12] There has also been a large increase in government expenditure on child care:

> Over the last decade, the number of Commonwealth Government funded child care places increased from 122,600 in 1990, to 422,100 in 1999.

Commonwealth government spending increased in line with this from $292 million in 1990-91 to $1,011 million in 1997-98.[13]

However, it appears that this commitment is decreasing. It has been estimated that 'cuts to funding for the Australian Government's Family and Children's Services Program over the period 1996-97 to 2000-2001 reach $851m'.[14]

Despite substantial, albeit decreasing, government expenditure, there is also substantial expenditure on child care by individuals and families. In Chapter 2 we described the legal and policy debate around the tax deductibility of child-care expenses. As the Court of Appeal recognised in *Wynn*,

---

4 *Ibid*, at 2.
5 *Ibid*.
6 *Ibid*, at 3.
7 *Ibid*, at 2-3.
8 *Wynn* (1995) 184 CLR 485 at 495-6.
9 *Ibid*, at 494.
10 ABS, *Australian Social Trends*, Cat 4102.0, 2001, at 35. There was a slight decrease in the use of informal care (from 44.8% in 1990 to 43.0% in 1999 (*ibid*)).
11 *Ibid*, at 41.
12 *Ibid*.
13 *Ibid*, at 45.
14 Siobhan E Austen and Elisa R Birch, *Family Responsibilities and Women's Working Lives*, Women's Economic Policy Analysis Unit (WEPAU), Curtin University of Technology, Discussion Paper Series 00/9, August 2000, at 8, citing G McIntosh, 'Childcare in Australia: Current Provision and Recent Developments', *Background Paper 9*, Social Policy Research Group, Parliament of Australia, Parliament Library, Canberra, 1997/98.

such expenses are not deductible. Suppose the Women Lawyers' Association succeeded in persuading the Commonwealth Government to allow child-care expenses to be deducted as 'expenses necessarily incurred in earning an income'. If, like Ms Wynn, the child's mother is married or living with the child's father, which of them would most likely claim that expense as a deduction? Why? How relevant is this to assessing the value of a woman's loss of earning capacity?

3. In another case involving a *male* plaintiff, aged 29 at the time of the injury, who had an excellent work history (he had won an award as an outstanding apprentice carpenter), the Full Federal Court described the plaintiff as 'a young man with bright prospects, who has been deprived of the ability to choose to continue his career'.[15] The court also commented: 'It is also apparent that the appellant was destined for a supervisory role'.[16] What can we learn from these contrasting examples about the ways in which courts view women's and men's attachment to the paid workforce?

4. Wynn worked in a managerial position for a large multinational organisation. This makes her extremely unusual when we consider the data on the work Australian women do. Australia has one of the most sex-segregated labour forces of any OECD country: 'For example, in occupations such as health professionals, secretaries and personal assistants, and elementary sales workers over 70% of the workforce is female'.[17] And in relation to industrial segregation, 66% of workers in the education industry, and 80% of workers in the health and community services industries are women.[18] An International Labour Organisation report in 2001 revealed that although 35% of Australian employees were female, they only held 1.3% of the most senior executive positions in corporations.[19] Therefore, Australia not only has a poor record in relation to horizontal segregation across industries but, within industries, the upward mobility of female employees is also obviously very limited (vertical segregation).

5. Graycar has elsewhere commented that in many damages assessment cases:

> [There] is a tendency to treat women's paid work as marginal, as worthy of comment, as requiring an explanation, rather than as something that adult gender neutral people just do. The judgments often provide an explanation for why a woman works, coupled with an underlying assumption that should the particular reason given for her employment disappear she would no longer engage in paid work.[20]

---

15 *Tucker v Westfield Design and Construction Pty Ltd* (unreported, FCA, Full Court, 5 April 1993), at [22].
16 *Ibid*, at [12].
17 Jeff Borland, 'The Equal Pay Case – Thirty Years On' (1999) 32 *Australian Economic Review* 265 at 268, relying on ABS, *Labour Force Australia*, February 1999, Cat No 6203.0, Table 51. 'Elementary sales workers sell goods and services in retail and wholesale establishments and operate checkouts and perform routine financial transactions in retail, entertainment and office environments': ABS, *Australian Standard Classification of Occupations*, 2nd ed, Cat No 1220.0, 1997, at 541.
18 ABS, *Employee Earnings, Benefits and Trade Union Membership*, August 2000, Cat No 6310.0, Table 5.
19 Linda Wirth, *Breaking Through the Glass Ceiling: Women in Management*, International Labour Organisation, Geneva, 2001.
20 Graycar, 'Hoovering as a Hobby and Other Stories: Gendered Assessments of Personal Injury Damages' (1997) 31 *University of British Columbia Law Review* 17 at 23 and see also 'Damaged Awards: The Vicissitudes of Life as a Woman' (1995) 3 *Torts Law Journal* 160.

For example, in *Harper v Bangalow Motors Pty Ltd*, Kirby P stated: 'Especially as a single parent (a not uncommon status in today's society) every pressure would have been upon the appellant to return at least to part-time work'.[21] Or, in *Wallen v Hird*, Mackenzie J said: 'One has to take into account the statistical possibility that the relationship might end and that therefore there might be greater pressure on the plaintiff to return to the work force than there is while the relationship subsists'.[22]

These judgments seem to assume that women need some incentive – here the loss of their relationship with a man – to engage in the paid workforce. They also appear to assume that women who are sole parents are more likely to be in the paid workforce than those in continuing heterosexual relationships, an assumption that is not borne out by the data (see Chapter 5).

Alternatively, in *Stekovic*, it was suggested that the plaintiff worked in order to avoid her husband who had been violent.[23] Another worked because her husband was unemployed and therefore could not support her and the children,[24] another wanted to help her daughter to attend university.[25] One woman's religious beliefs were said by a judge to lie behind her view that 'her role was to provide financial support to her maximum capacity for her husband and children'.[26] Perhaps the best explanation comes from Lord Denning, then the English Master of the Rolls, in 1974:

> Many a married woman seeks work. She does so when the children grow up and leave the house. She does it, not solely to earn money, helpful as it is, but to fill her time with useful occupation, rather than sit idly at home waiting for her husband to return. The devil tempts those who have nothing to do.[27]

Paid work for women, particularly married women, is often seen to be in direct competition with other aspects of their lives – with other roles they fulfil or are expected to fulfil. In one Australian case, *Becin v GEL*, the court decided that a woman would not be successful running her own business because 'she may have succumbed to competing family demands'.[28] Women's capacity to bear children is also used, in a number of different (and often contrasting) ways, to construct the paid work they do, or might do, as peripheral. For young women, damages are discounted because they may in the future have time out of the workforce to have children (irrespective of whether they indicate that they did not want to do so, or planned to have no more children).[29] In 1996, the British Columbia Court of Appeal reduced a

---

21 *Harper v Bangalow Motors Pty Ltd* (unreported, NSWCA, Kirby P, Mahoney and Clarke JJA, 24 July 1990), per Kirby P at 20.
22 *Wallen v Hird* (unreported, QSC, 4 October 1993), per Mackenzie J.
23 *Stekovic v City Group Pty Ltd* (unreported, ACTSC, 2 November 1994), per Higgins J at [84].
24 *Angelopoulos v Rubenhold* (unreported, SASC, Full Court, 3 April 1991), per King CJ at 8.
25 *Randall v Dul* (1994) Aust Torts Reports ¶81-307.
26 *Kelson v Transport Accident Commission* (unreported, VSC, 5 May 1994).
27 *Langston v AEUW* [1974] 1 All ER 980 at 987.
28 *Becin v GEC Australia* (unreported, QSC, 13 May 1993), per Thomas J.
29 Cf *Bondin v Lamaro* (unreported, NSWCA, 14 October 1994), per Handley JA at 5: 'There was a chance that the plaintiff and her husband may have changed their minds and decided to have a third child anyway and they may also have had an unplanned pregnancy'. Or, compare *Partridge v GIO* (unreported, NSWSC, 5 May 1993), per Dunford J, discussing a 19-year-old plaintiff, with no evidence of any intention to have children in the foreseeable future: 'As to future loss of earning capacity ... [the plaintiff] would in all probability have taken time out of the work force to have a family and whilst the children were young' (at 8).

trial judge's award, deciding that the plaintiff would not have spent her working life at her pre-accident employment: 'She hopes to raise a family when her spouse is suitably employed'.[30] But an older woman might have her damages reduced when she no longer has children to care for[31] or because she is considered unemployable after a history of time out of the paid workforce for family responsibilities[32] or because, in the words of one judge, she 'may well have taken breaks from her employment, for example, when her children married and had families to visit and to assist them with their children'.[33]

Just like in *Wynn's* case, a court may consider that the workplace might prove too demanding for a woman who could not be expected to keep up such a pace[34] or that a woman's husband might not want her to undertake full-time paid work because, as she and he 'aged and became financially secure, her husband's attitude might have induced [her] to retire early or to reduce her working hours'.[35] And, while the NSW Court of Appeal treated difficulties that would confront Ms Wynn in travelling overseas to secure her promotion as almost insurmountable, another female plaintiff's award was reduced since she 'may well have taken breaks from her employment ... during any transfers in his work by her husband'.[36] For yet another woman, damages for future economic loss were reduced because of her husband's peripatetic employment since, according to the court, 'there must also be taken into account ... the consequences of being married to a serviceman'.[37] Echoing McHugh J in *Wynn*, how likely is it that a man's damages would be reduced if he were married to a 'servicewoman'?

Wages for women

Introduction

In the first edition of this book, we explored the invisibility of women in labour law texts by drawing attention to a commentary by Joanne Conaghan pointing out that 'labour law is a world made up of full-time male breadwinners and the legal rules reflect this conception of the worker'.[38] Or, as Carole Pateman put it:

> [T]he construction of the 'worker' presupposes that he is a man who has a woman, a (house)wife to take care of his daily needs. ... The sturdy figure of the 'worker',

---

30 *Lee v Swan* [1996] BCJ No 259 (BCCA) [1996] 19 BCR (3d) 21.
31 In a claim for non-economic loss under the *Motor Accidents Act* 1988 (NSW), the court commented: 'The difficulty with the ... assessment is to reconcile it with the assessment that might properly be made in the case of a much younger woman, say thirty, who before her injury had a similar range of interests and hobbies but had young children to help bring up': *Reece v Reece* (unreported, NSWCA, Clarke, Handley and Sheller JJA, 28 February 1994), per Handley JA at 5. There was no claim for economic loss in this case.
32 *NSW Insurance Ministerial Corporation v Rayner* (unreported, NSWCA, Kirby P, Mahoney and Cripps JJA, 19 March 1993), per Kirby P at 9.
33 *Tully v Cole* (unreported, QSC, 13 October 1993), per White J.
34 "The [trial] judge found that [Mrs Rasmus] had been a driving successful business woman, living at a considerable pace and very busy ... Even uninjured, the judge did not think she could have continued indefinitely at her pre-accident level of activity": *Rasmus v GIO* (unreported, NSWCA, Mahoney AP, Priestley JA and Samuels AJA, 22 December 1992), per Priestley JA at 5.
35 *Park v Hobart Public Hospitals* (unreported, TASSC, 12 December 1991), per Zeeman J at 12.
36 *Tully v Cole* (unreported, QSC, 13 October 1993), per White J.
37 *Smith v Smith* (unreported, ACTSC, 8 July 1991), per Master Hogan at [69].
38 Joanne Conaghan, 'The Invisibility of Women in Labour Law: Gender-Neutrality in Model-Building' (1986) 14 *International Journal of the Sociology of Law* 377 at 380. See also Rosemary Hunter, 'Representing Gender in Legal Analysis: A Case/Book Study in Labour Law' (1991) 18 *Melbourne University Law Review* 305.

the artisan, in clean overalls, with a bag of tools and lunchbox, is always accompanied by the ghostly figure of his wife.[39]

That is, the worker in labour law is constructed as masculine, just as in the law of damages, a special explanation of why women do paid work is often sought. The following section explores how the worker has been constructed by focusing on the key issue that has engaged feminist activist and academic work in labour law – the fact that women earn less than men.

In Australia, 'the ratio of average weekly ordinary time adult (AWOTE) female to male earnings has remained fairly firmly pegged just below the 84% mark, when the effects of part-time work, overtime, and juniors are excluded'.[40] When data on all work, including part-time work is included, women's average weekly earnings are 66% of those of men.[41] And '[s]ome 16% of females and 7% of males earned less than $200 per week in August 2000, whereas 2% of females and 7% of males earned $1400 or more per week'.[42]

Indigenous women were less likely than their non-indigenous counterparts to be in employment although there was growth in employment from 1971, when only 21.7% of indigenous women were in employment, to 1991, when 29.5% were in employment.[43] While the median income of indigenous men was only 45% that of non-indigenous men, for women the gap is much lower: indigenous women's income, despite their lower rates of employment, was 81% of that of non-indigenous women.[44] Anne Daly and Anne Hawke attribute the growth in indigenous women's income not so much to improvements in labour force status,[45] although this has occurred (as has an improvement in education levels), but, rather, they suggest the major reason is 'changes in access to welfare payments and the incorporation of indigenous people from remote areas into the welfare system'.[46]

And in relation to culturally and linguistically diverse women, 'while there was a substantial increase in the rate of female labour force participation in the 1980s and 1990s, this increase only occurred among Australia-born and ESB [*English speaking background*] women. NESB [*non-English speaking background*] women actually experienced a slight decline in labour force participation rates over that time period, leading to a marked widening of the gap in labour force participation rates between NESB immigrant women and other women'.[47]

The inequality in earnings between women and men continues to have an effect after retirement from the paid workforce. This is particularly clear with the increasing emphasis on the private provision of retirement income, through investment in superannuation. Employers are required to contribute an amount equal to

---

39 Carole Pateman, *The Sexual Contract*, Polity Press, Cambridge, 1988, at 131.
40 Barbara Pocock, 'Equal Pay Thirty Years On: The Policy and Practice' (1999) 32 *Australian Economic Review* 279 at 279.
41 ABS, *Employee Earnings, Benefits and Trade Union Membership*, Cat 6310.0, August 2000, at 3.
42 *Ibid*.
43 Anne Daly and Anne Hawke, 'The Impact of the Welfare State on the Economic Status of Indigenous Australian Women' (1995) 28 *Australian Economic Review* 29 at 31. In 1971, some 36% of non-indigenous women were in paid employment; in 1991, that figure was some 47% (*ibid*). The same period saw an overall decline in indigenous male employment, with 60.4% of indigenous men in employment in 1971, 40.4% in 1986 and 45% in 1991 (*ibid*).
44 *Ibid*.
45 Indeed, for those in employment, there was a fall in indigenous women's proportion of non-indigenous women's income from 86% in 1976 to 83 % in 1991 (*ibid*).
46 *Ibid*, at 36.
47 Audrey VandenHeuvel and Mark Wooden, *Non-English-Speaking Background Immigrant Women and Part-Time Work,* AGPS, Canberra, 1996, at 25-6.

8% of an employee's wages to compulsory superannuation, if the employee earns more than $450 a month.[48] While superannuation funds do not directly discriminate on the basis of gender (except where it is actuarially justifiable), they do discriminate against same sex partners.[49] However, there could well be indirect discrimination against women:

> Differences in labour force participation mean that more men than women have superannuation. As at December 1996 there were 9.4 million superannuation accounts held by males, compared to 6.6 million for females. ... As at June 1994 Treasury has estimated that the average superannuation entitlement for women was around $17,000 compared to $42,000 for men. The proportion of all superannuation assets held by women was 23 per cent. ...
>
> Treasury ... estimates show catching up in the future, with a projected real average balance for women of $77,000 in the year 2019, and $121,000 for men. The proportion of super assets held by women is projected to rise to 32 per cent in that year.[50]

This inequality is not just a function of participation rates: women's lower wages more generally mean a lower level of superannuation entitlement in retirement.

Barbara Pocock commences her article on equal pay with the following statement:

> Justice Mary Gaudron was the source of one of the most frequently repeated quotations at the ... NSW Pay Equity Inquiry: "We got equal pay once, then we got it again, and then we got it again, and now we still don't have it".[51]

What is the nature of such a 'victory' that it needs to be 'won' over and over again? The gendered wage gap has persisted despite three 'equal pay' judgments, the introduction of affirmative action and sex discrimination legislation, and pay equity campaigns by the union movement. In the rest of this chapter, we briefly explore a series of explanations for, and responses to, this issue.

The 'family wage'

In 1907, in its first opportunity to set a 'fair and reasonable wage' the Conciliation and Arbitration Court (as it then was) laid the seeds for what became known as the 'family wage'.[52] In *Harvester*, the court decided that a fair and reasonable wage was the amount a man needed to support himself, his wife and three children. To ascertain this figure, the court heard evidence from 'nine housekeeping women':

> The lists of expenditure submitted to me vary not only in amounts, but in bases of computation. But I have confined the figures to rent, groceries, bread, meat, milk, fuel, vegetables, and fruit; and the average of the list is £1 12s 5d. This expenditure does not cover light (some of the lists omitted light), clothes, boots, furniture, utensils (being casual, not weekly expenditure), rates, life insurance,

---

48 *Superannuation Guarantee (Administration) Act* 1992 (Cth).
49 Ross Clare, *Equity and Retirement Income Provision in Australia*, The Association of Superannuation Funds of Australia, February 2001, at 24. Discrimination against lesbians and gay men when their partner dies, is, according to Clare, required by taxation and superannuation industry regulations (*ibid*).
50 *Ibid*, at 24-5.
51 Pocock, 'Equal Pay Thirty Years On', at 279, citing NSW Pay Equity Inquiry, 1998, Vol 1, at 5. Cf Mary Gaudron and Michal Bosworth, 'Equal Pay?' in Judy Mackinolty and Heather Radi (eds), *In Pursuit of Justice: Australian Women and the Law 1788-1979*, Hale and Iremonger, Sydney, 1979, at 161.
52 *Ex parte HV McKay* (1907) 2 CAR 1 (the *Harvester* judgment).

savings, accident or benefit societies, loss of employment, union pay, books and newspapers, tram and train fares, sewing machine, mangle, school requisites, amusements and holidays, intoxicating liquors, tobacco, sickness and death, domestic help, or any expenditure for unusual contingencies, religion or charity. ... One witness, the wife of one who was formerly a vatman in candle works, says that in the days when her husband was working at the vat at 36s a week, she was unable to provide meat for him on about three days in the week. This inability to provide sustaining food – whatever kind may be selected – is certainly not conducive to the maintenance of the worker in industrial efficiency. ... Under the circumstances, I cannot declare that the applicant's conditions of remuneration are fair and reasonable as to his labourers.[53]

In the 1912 *Fruitpickers* case, the court had to deal for the first time with 'the problem of female labour':[54] both men and women worked in that industry. The union had argued that there should be 'equal pay for equal work' which Higgins J described as an ambiguous phrase, despite having an 'attractive sound'. Higgins J referred back to his decision in *Harvester,* noting that, in that case, he had fixed as a 'fair and reasonable wage' 'an amount which would meet the normal needs of an average employee, one of his normal needs being the need for domestic life'.

> If he has a wife and children, he is under an obligation – even a legal obligation – to maintain them. How is such a minimum applicable to the case of a woman picker? She is not, unless perhaps in very exceptional circumstances, under any such obligation. The minimum cannot be based on exceptional cases. ... There has been observed for a long time a tendency to substitute women for men in industries, even in occupations which are more suited for men; and in such occupations it is often the result of women being paid lower wages than men. Fortunately for society, however, the greater number of bread winners still are men. The women are not all dragged from the homes to work while the men loaf at home; and in this case the majority even of the fruitpickers are men.[55]

The court decided that while both men and women were engaged in fruitpicking, the reasonable wage could be the same for both of them (at 1s per hour) and an employer would then be free to hire either men or women. But the court went on to note that since, in its view, packing work was inherently more suited to women, it could therefore be paid at a lesser rate – 9d per hour.[56]

Notes

1. Higgins J in *Fruitpickers* suggests that men have a legal obligation to support their wives. How accurate a statement is this? Is there any enforceable obligation on a man to support his wife during a subsisting marriage? After the marriage has broken down? See *Family Law Act* 1975 (Cth) s 72.
2. Does the reliance by the Commission on the evidence of 'nine housekeeping women' – wives – reinforce an assumption that income is always shared within a household? The extent of sharing of income within a household is explored in the previous chapter.

---

53 *Ibid*, at 6-7.
54 *Rural Workers' Union v Mildura Branch of Australian Dried Fruits Association* (1912) 6 CAR 62 at 70.
55 *Ibid*, at 71-2.
56 Cf *Federated Clothing Trade v JA Archer* (1919) 13 CAR 647 where wages for women were set at 54% of men's on the assumption that women did not have dependants.

3. Despite Higgins J's romanticised concern that women not be 'dragged' from their homes into the paid workforce, Bettina Cass's historical research shows that at the time he was writing, women were frequently in paid work, and often the sole supporters of their families. Cass has demonstrated that the empirical evidence of the time simply did not support this 'breadwinner/ dependant' ideal so clearly reflected in the wage-fixing judgments. In fact, in the first Australian household expenditure survey undertaken in 1911, it emerged that in only one-third of heterosexual households was the husband the sole breadwinner.[57]
4. Rosemary Hunter points out that the *Harvester* decision is included in most labour law casebooks.[58] However, it is rarely described as central or even important to the issue of wages for women. Rather, its influence is described – and lauded – in terms of entrenching a needs-based method of setting wages (rather than one which was driven solely by the employer's capacity to pay).
5. Barbara Pocock emphasises that the entrenchment of a lower 'female wage' in areas where men did not work 'provided a vigorous wage-based incentive for occupational sex-segregation. It is no surprise that the Australian labour market remains one of the most sex-segregated in the industrial world'.[59] As she has put it elsewhere, writing at the end of 1998:[60]

> [T]he index of occupational segregation suggests that rather than improving over the past decade, segregation has remained obstinately fixed. There are some signs of a slow shift in segregation in some occupations, as women lessen their concentration in female dominated occupations. However, there are few signs of a systematic shift the other way, and long-term male domination of skilled trade work remains unmoved (which is not surprising, in view of its sluggish employment growth and the collapse of apprenticeship training). Secondly, women's entry to male dominated work has been strongest in the upper levels of the occupational hierarchy, presumably where formal tertiary education has provided a gateway. This entry has been particularly strong in public sector areas (for example, the proportion of female legislators and government officials among managers and government officials rose from 3.4 per cent in 1986 to 21.7 per cent in 1996). Thirdly, while it seems that women's concentration in feminised occupations is declining overall, the shift of men into a number of female dominated occupations has been slow (despite strong growth in many of them), whether at the professional, para-professional or operative level; indeed, female domination is increasing in traditionally feminised occupations like teaching, nursing, numerical clerking, sales, filing sorting and copying, material recording and despatching, and in receptionist and telephonist jobs.

How would you explain this pattern of change? Why might men be reluctant to move into traditional female areas, while women at the higher occupational levels are moving into traditional male areas?

---

57 Bettina Cass, 'Rewards for Women's Work' in Carole Pateman and Jacqueline Goodnow (eds), *Women, Social Science and Public Policy*, Allen and Unwin, Sydney, 1985, at 70-1.
58 Rosemary Hunter, 'Representing Gender in Legal Analysis: A Case/Book Study in Labour Law' (1991) 18 *Melbourne University Law Review* 305 especially at 307-8 and 320.
59 Pocock, 'Equal Pay Thirty Years On', at 280. Some of the data are quoted above in note 4 under the discussion of *Wynn*.
60 Barbara Pocock, 'All Change, Still Gendered: The Australian Labour Market in the 1990s' (1998) 40 *Journal of Industrial Relations* 580 at 593.

The 'equal pay' cases

Pocock has described the various equal pay decisions in the following way:

Barbara Pocock, 'Equal Pay Thirty Years On: The Policy and the Practice'
(1999) 32 *Australian Economic Review* 279

[279] **2. A Long, Slow Road: The Legacy of the Family Wage** ...

[280] When it came to its consideration of equal pay in 1969, the AIRC [*Australian Industrial Relations Commission*] found a confusion of rates with some women receiving equal pay alongside men and some not, and it stated that 'a relic of the concept of the family wage' was present in most wage levels. Its 1969 decision to award 'equal pay for equal work' affected only about 18 per cent of women and did not address the sex-segregation of work. As one commentator put it at the time:

> it will be a very limited victory for females to be awarded equal pay for work of equal value if social prejudices continue to prevent women from occupying anything but a small proportion of responsible and well paying positions. [PA Riach, 'Equal Pay and Equal Opportunity' (1969) *11 Journal of Industrial Relations* 99 at 107.]

And so it has proved.

Pay equity activists were well aware that, having achieved in theory at least, the formal elimination of award-based direct discrimination, the systematic undervaluation of the jobs in which women were concentrated, remained. This task was taken up in the 1972 case when – to a limited extent – claims for equal pay for work of equal value became possible, enabling some revaluation based on work value assessments. The 1974 case went on to establish a non-discriminatory minimum wage. The existence of a national award system setting the wages and conditions of most workers provided an effective transmission belt for the national application of both the 1969 and 1974 decisions, and provided the means for a significant narrowing of the gap in the 1970's, putting us to the front of the international pack in terms of gender pay equity.

3. What Caused the Narrowing of the Pay Differential

The gradual edging up of women's earnings relative to men's over the century, through two world wars and the postwar years, largely reflected changing economic and social conditions and the need to protect men's work from women's 'unfair competition', rather more than any principle of fairness. The 1969, 1972 and 1974 decisions were not far from the actual market rates paid to many women. Key federal decisions such as these tended to reflect market and social realities (and sometimes follow changes in state jurisdictions), rather more than moving in advance of them. ...

The forces of labour market supply and demand can be clearly seen underlying these decisions. Alongside these are the effects of social change in part caused by the political activism of women, both within and outside parliaments in Australia and internationally.

Very often, at the institutional level, women affected by these inequities have been the silenced observers of mostly male actors. For example, D'Aprano observed of the 1969 case:

> The evidence given by Bob Hawke, the ACTU advocate of the time, was irrefutable. The women sat there day after day as if we were mute, while the men presented evidence for and against our worth. It was humiliating to have to sit there and not say anything about our own worth. I found the need to sit

there silent almost beyond my control and was incensed with the entire set up. [Zelda D'Aprano, *The Becoming of a Woman*, Widescope International Publishers, Melbourne, 1978, at 16.]

On other occasions, D'Aprano and the many women who campaigned for equal pay were far from silent, and their organisation, activism [281] and research has underpinned every significant Australian advance on women's relative pay throughout this century ... . While the logical arguments in relation to pay inequity have been well established for many decades ..., progress at each turn has awaited the confluence of market forces, social change, women's activism and supportive governments. In other cases, change awaited the alignment of men's interests with women's, for example, in the partial support offered by pragmatic men and their unions for equal pay when lower rates for women threatened their employment.[61]

Anti-discrimination laws

Pocock goes on to describe the enactment of the *Sex Discrimination Act* 1984 (Cth)[62] (SDA) and the *Affirmative Action (Equal Opportunity for Women) Act* 1986 (Cth) (see now *Equal Opportunity for Women Act* 1999), both 'designed to reduce sex-segregation and the structural barriers that mean that women are disproportionately found in lower paying jobs'.[63] The former Act provides a remedial framework for individuals (or groups of individuals) to make a complaint of discrimination against an employer (or service provider, provider of accommodation etc). The discrimination outlawed can be direct – the less favourable treatment of a woman than a man because of her sex, or indirect, where a neutral rule or practice has a disparate impact on women. Although, as Pocock suggests, the SDA has had a limited impact on the gender wage gap,[64] some of the early litigation suggested both that it could be a weapon, albeit a blunt one, in reducing sex segregation, and that its use would be vigorously resisted. For example, in *Australian Iron and Steel v Banovic*,[65] a group of 34 women alleged that Australian Iron and Steel (AIS) had discriminated against them. Donka Najdovska had first applied for employment in August 1977 but was not hired until February 1981. She and a number of other women had complained to the NSW Anti-Discrimination Board (ADB) in April 1980 about the company's refusal to hire them, arguing that AIS had discriminated against them on the ground of sex by treating women applicants less favourably than men.

These complaints were conciliated by the ADB and, in late 1980 and early 1981, a number of women were hired by AIS. However, shortly afterwards, there was a downturn in the industry and AIS began retrenching workers on a 'last on, first off' basis, ultimately retrenching all those who had commenced after 6 January 1981. This meant that most of the women who had originally complained to the ADB were retrenched. They argued that the last on, first off rule, or reverse gate seniority, was both directly and indirectly discriminatory. The

---

61 Pocock, 'Equal Pay Thirty Years On', at 280-1.
62 And see also equivalent State legislation and the discussion in Chapter 3 (equality).
63 Pocock, 'Equal Pay', at 281.
64 *Ibid.*
65 *Australian Iron and Steel Pty Ltd v Banovic* (1989) 168 CLR 165. Earlier proceedings were reported under the name *Najdovska v AIS* in the NSW Equal Opportunity Tribunal (1985) EOC ¶92-140 and as *AIS v Najdovska* in the NSW Court of Appeal (1988) EOC ¶92-223. The case was in fact pursued under the *Anti-Discrimination Act* 1977 (NSW) rather than the federal SDA, which was not in force at the time. The first complaint by the women to the ADB had been lodged in 1980.

company denied the allegations and argued that they were not allowed to hire women because of restrictions on the weights they could lift contained in the *Factories, Shops and Industries Act* 1962 (NSW).

It was clear that very few women had been hired by AIS before the initial complaint to the ADB: between June 1977 and April 1980, 4289 ironworkers had been hired of which only 58 or 1.35% were women.[66] Between 1 July 1980 and 22 August 1980, 428 employees were hired, 15.2% of whom were women.

> Notwithstanding the sudden increase the waiting time for women as compared with men was still vastly disproportionate being measured in years rather than a few days or weeks. All the statistical material points to the fact that for the period in question there was an exceptionally low employment rate for women and a long waiting list which no doubt helped to discourage some women from applying at all, a point further emphasised from the evidence ... that the CES office refused to even refer female applicants to AIS.[67]

The Tribunal discussed the company's argument that many positions in the steelworks were 'weight-barred' – that is, women could not be employed in them because there were restrictions on lifting weights greater than 16 kilograms. However, the Tribunal found that, when this limit was applied, 31% of production jobs were available to women, yet there were women in only 12% of these classifications.[68] Further, there were women in seven classifications which were weight-barred to them, and '[n]early one-quarter of job classifications treated as weight-barred required lifting masses over the 16 kilogram limit only 5% of the time according to company sources'.[69] The Tribunal thus rejected the argument that the company had a defence because of weight-lifting restrictions under the *Factories, Shops and Industries Act*. It found that the company had directly discriminated against the women in determining who should be offered employment. It also found that the 'last on first off' rule, a common policy in unionised workplaces, was indirectly discriminatory:

> It appears to us to be undeniable that the selection of "gate" seniority as the criterion, while facially neutral, operated to the disadvantage of women who had to wait years to get jobs as compared with men who were employed immediately or without significant delay. All the complainants were in the position that because of the continuing effect of past discrimination at the point of hiring they had very much less "gate" seniority than men who applied for jobs at or about the same time.[70]

The Tribunal also found that the rule was directly discriminatory. The complainants were awarded some $1 million damages. The decision was challenged and the NSW Court of Appeal overturned the finding that the 'last on first off' rule amounted to direct discrimination[71] but confirmed both the finding of indirect discrimination and the award of damages. The High Court dismissed AIS's appeal.[72]

---

66 *Najdovska v AIS* (1985) EOC ¶92-140 at 76,387.
67 *Ibid.*
68 *Ibid*, at 76,388.
69 *Ibid.*
70 *Ibid*, at 76,393.
71 Street CJ found it could not be direct discrimination because there were no men who were in the same or similar circumstances as the women as there were no men whose appointment had been delayed by discrimination: *AIS Pty Ltd v Najdovska* (1988) EOC ¶92-223 at 77,103. See also the discussion of sex discrimination in Chapter 3.
72 (1989) 168 CLR 165.

Notes

1. Michael Kidd and Xin Meng have examined the effect of the *Sex Discrimination Act* 1984 (Cth) (SDA) and affirmative action legislation on the gender wage gap. They note that while there were rapid gains by women in the 1970s in response to the various equal pay decisions, in the 1980s, the era of the 'equality' legislation, change was much slower.[73] And they attribute what change there was to women's greater investment in 'human capital', viz education and level of labour market experience, rather than any effect of the legislation.[74] Rosemary Hunter is even more sceptical about the relevance of the SDA in addressing women's economic position in an era of globalisation, economic restructuring and conservative neo-liberal governments:

    > The last five years have seen an average of only five or six sex discrimination cases reported per year, at either federal or state level. Only a handful of these have sought remedies for women caught in some of the new economic traps.[75]

    And, as Hunter points out, most of these have not been successful.[76]

2. American lawyer Frances Olsen's critique is more focused on the discourse generated by such legislation:

    > Anti-discrimination law does not end the actual subordination of women in the market but instead mainly benefits a small percentage of women who adopt "male" roles. Meanwhile, it legitimates the continued oppression of most women: the reforms maintain the status quo by particularizing and privatizing inequality and encouraging women to blame themselves for failures in the market.
    > ... It obscures for women the actual causes of their oppression and treats discrimination against women as an irrational and capricious departure from the normal objective operation of the market, instead of recognizing such discrimination as a pervasive aspect of our dichotomized system.[77]

    Would it be possible to draft sex discrimination legislation that addressed Olsen's concerns?

3. One of the most controversial US cases endeavouring to challenge sex segregation in the largest private employer in that country is the *Sears* case.[78] There the Equal Employment Opportunity Commission (EEOC) argued that Sears had discriminated against women in that they were significantly under-represented in the company's higher paying commission sales positions (that is, selling the 'big ticket items' – these included car accessories, large appliances, home entertainment and sporting goods). Sears agreed women were

---

73 Michael P Kidd and Xin Meng, 'Trends in the Australian Gender Wage Differential over the 1980's: Some Evidence on the Effectiveness of Legislative Reform' (1997) 30 *Australian Economic Review* 31.
74 *Ibid*, at 40-1.
75 Rosemary Hunter, 'The Mirage of Justice: Women and the Shrinking State', Paper presented Feminist Legal Academics Workshop (FLAW), Brisbane, February 2001.
76 The cases she discusses include *Finance Sector Union v Commonwealth Bank* (1997) EOC ¶92-889 (HREOC) and *Commonwealth Bank v HREOC* (1998) EOC ¶92-908 (FCA, Full Court); *Gibbs v Commonwealth Bank* (1997) EOC ¶92-877; *McCrostie v Boral Resources* (1999) EOC ¶92-994; *Van Druten v Sheraton Pacific Hotels* (1996) EOC ¶92-855.
77 Frances Olsen, 'The Family and the Market: A Study of Ideology and Legal Reform' (1983) 96 *Harvard Law Review* 1497 at 1552.
78 *EEOC v Sears, Roebuck and Co* 628 F Supp 1264 (1986). The EEOC unsuccessfully appealed against the decision: 839 F 2d 302 (7th Circuit, 1988).

under-represented in these higher paying positions but argued that it was not because they had discriminated against women. Rather, they argued, using the evidence of historian Rosalind Rosenberg, that '[h]istorically, men and women have had different interests, goals and aspirations regarding work',[79] which, while 'diminishing, have persisted into the present'.[80] By contrast, Alice Kessler-Harris, the historian engaged by the EEOC, argued:

> Sears' experts have argued that women's occupations in the labor force are the product of women's choice, that women do not want better-paying jobs, and cannot handle stress, competition, or risk. History does not support these contentions, and instead places Sears' witnesses' statements squarely within a long tradition of employer excuses for, and manipulations of, women's work force experience.[81]

In effect, the litigation came to revolve around different understandings of women's choices, which in turn depended heavily on arguments about women's nature and women's 'difference', relying, if implicitly, on contested accounts of issues such as women's socialisation into domesticity.

In a 200-page judgment, the trial court held that Sears had not discriminated against women.[82] As Judge Nordberg stated, echoing Rosenberg's evidence:

> Sears has proven, with many forms of evidence, that men and women tend to have different interests and aspirations regarding work, and that these differences explain in large part the lower percentage of women in commission sales jobs in general at Sears, especially in the particular divisions with the lowest proportion of women selling on commission.[83]

One of the most controversial aspects of this case, at least amongst feminist scholars, was the fact that two self-described feminist historians appeared on opposing sides in the case.[84] The EEOC case was constructed around a mass of statistical evidence, rather than on the testimony of individual complainants and ultimately this worked against them. The court stated:

> [D]espite its allegations of nationwide discrimination in more than 900 stores over 8 years, EEOC was unable to produce one Sears employee to

---

79 Offer of Proof Concerning Testimony of Dr Rosalind Rosenberg, reproduced in (1986) 11 *Signs* 757.
80 *Ibid*.
81 Written Testimony of Alice Kessler-Harris, reproduced in (1986) 11 *Signs* 757 at 765 et seq.
82 *EEOC v Sears, Roebuck and Co* 628 F Supp 1264 (1986).
83 *Ibid*, at 1305. Judge Cudahy, in dissent in the 7th Circuit Court of Appeals, criticised the acceptance of this lack of interest argument. Such a conclusion was 'of a piece with the proposition that women are by nature happier cooking, doing the laundry and chauffeuring the children to softball games than arguing appeals or selling stocks. The stereotype of women as less greedy and daring than men is one that the sex discrimination laws were designed to address. ... Perhaps ... [*the courts*] have forgotten that women have been hugely successful in such fields as residential real estate, door-to-door sales and other direct outside merchandising. There are abundant indications that women lack neither the desire to compete strenuously for financial gain nor the capacity to take risks' (839 F 2d 302 at 361 (1988)).
84 See Carol Sternhell, 'Life in the Mainstream: What Happens when Feminists Turn up on Both Sides of the Court Room?' *Ms Magazine*, July, 1986; Ruth Milkman, 'Women's History and the *Sears* Case' (1986) 12 *Feminist Studies* 108; Eileen Boris, 'Looking at Women Historians Looking at "Difference"' (1987) *Wisconsin Women's Law Journal* 213. See also Alice Kessler-Harris, '*EEOC v Sears Roebuck and Company*: A Personal Account' (1987) 25 *Feminist Review* 46. And for a strident defence of Rosenberg's role, see Thomas Haskell and Sanford Levinson, 'Academic Freedom and Expert Witnessing and the *Sears* Case' (1987) 66 *Texas Law Review* 1629. See also the response by Kessler-Harris (1988) 67 *Texas Law Review* 429 and their response to her at (1989) 67 *Texas Law Review* 1591.

testify that Sears discriminated against her by refusing to promote her to commission sales. This total lack of any testimony to "bring the statistics to life" is but further confirmation of the failures of EEOC's statistical evidence.[85]

Rosenberg has been quoted as saying that she would not have agreed to give evidence for Sears if the EEOC had produced a single complainant against Sears.[86] What reasons might the EEOC have had for relying solely on statistical evidence? Recall the material discussed in Chapter 4 on legal storytelling. Do both Rosenberg's and the court's response to the case suggest that a storytelling methodology might have particular purchase?

Joan Scott has criticised the way in which the opposing arguments in the case have been crudely characterised as representing equality (or sameness) (EEOC) versus difference (Sears). She suggests that the Sears case itself set up the EEOC position as one of 'equality' by attributing to it 'an assumption that no-one had made in those terms – that women and men had identical interests'.[87] She points out that the detailed arguments made by Kessler-Harris were not accepted by the court because of the artificial demands of the courtroom context. Referring to the cross-examination, Scott suggests: 'Each of her carefully nuanced explanations of women's work history was forced into a reductive assertion by the Sears lawyers' insistence that she answer questions only by saying yes or no'.[88] Scott concludes by suggesting that this case illustrates the need to avoid the discursive framework of 'equality versus difference'.

> Placing equality and difference in antithetical relationship has, then, a double effect. It denies the way in which difference has long figured in political notions of equality and it suggests that sameness is the only ground on which equality can be claimed. It thus puts feminists in an impossible position, for as long as we argue within the terms of a discourse set up by this opposition we grant the current conservative premise that because women cannot be identical to men in all respects, we cannot expect to be equal to them. The only alternative, it seems to me, is to refuse to oppose equality to difference and insist continually on differences – differences as the condition of individual and collective identities, differences as the constant challenge to the fixing of those identities, history as the repeated illustration of the play of differences, differences as the very meaning of equality itself.[89]

If, as Scott appears to be suggesting, Kessler-Harris had more strongly emphasised the diversity amongst women and in that way challenged Sears' categorisation of women's preferences, what effect would that have had on the EEOC's legal claim of discrimination against women?

---

85   *EEOC v Sears, Roebuck and Co* 628 F Supp 1264 (1986) at 1327.
86   Carol Sternhell, 'Life in the Mainstream', at 86. Ruth Milkman quotes Rosenberg as saying: 'I said in the beginning, if there's ever a complainant in this case, I'm not going to testify … . [F]or me, symbolically, the absence of complainants was critical': Milkman, 'Women's History and the *Sears* Case', at 392.
87   Joan Scott, 'Deconstructing Equality-versus-Difference: or the Uses of Poststructuralist Theory for Feminism' (1988) 14 *Feminist Studies* 33 at 40. For an example of this, see the first line of Rosenberg's proof of testimony, extracted above, referring to the 'EEOC assumption'. Cf MacKinnon, *Toward a Feminist Theory of the State*, Harvard University Press, Cambridge, MA, 1989, at 223.
88   Scott, at 41.
89   *Ibid*, at 46.

Scott accepts that, in the face of current discourses which accept fixed categories, merely to assert difference is inadequate:

> What is required in addition is an analysis of fixed gender categories as normative statements that organize cultural understandings of sexual difference. This means that we must open to scrutiny the terms women and men as they are used to define one another in particular contexts. ...
>
> If in our histories we relativize the categories woman and man, it means, of course, that we must also recognise the contingent and specific nature of our political claims. Political strategies then will rest on analyses of the utility of certain arguments in certain discursive contexts, without, however, invoking absolute qualities for women or men. ...
>
> In histories of feminism and in feminist political strategies there needs to be at once attention to the operations of difference and an insistence on differences, but not a simple substitution of multiple for binary differences for it is not a happy pluralism we ought to invoke. The resolution of the "difference dilemma" comes neither from ignoring nor embracing difference as it is normally constituted. Instead, it seems to me that the critical feminist position must always involve two moves. The first is the systematic criticism of the operations of categorical difference, the exposure of the kinds of exclusions and inclusions – the hierarchies – it constructs, and a refusal of their ultimate "truth". A refusal, however, not in the name of an equality that implies sameness or identity but rather (and this is the second move) in the name of an equality that rests upon differences – differences that confound, disrupt, and render ambiguous the meaning of any fixed binary opposition. To do anything else is to buy into the political argument that sameness is a requirement for equality, an untenable position for feminists (and historians) who know that power is constructed and so must be challenged from the ground of difference.[90]

Could this analysis have been introduced into the Sears litigation?

Affirmative action laws

It was noted above that in 1986 the federal government enacted affirmative action legislation, the *Affirmative Action (Equal Opportunity for Women) Act* 1986 (Cth) (now known as the *Equal Opportunity for Women Act* 1999 (Cth)). Chris Ronalds argued:

> In contrast to anti-discrimination legislation, affirmative action legislation does not place the emphasis on individual solutions but on analysis of and remedies for, structural discrimination which is reflected in an individual employer's patterns of employment. An overall review of employment policies and practices addresses the underlying policies that are being pursued by an employer and promotes their reform insofar as they have the effect of unjustifiably disadvantaging women. The intervention is proactive in nature and does not rely on an individual complaint from an aggrieved person. ...
>
> Affirmative action legislation places the onus on employers, rather than on a disadvantaged employee or prospective employee, to examine and if necessary change organisational and institutional practices. It tackles the same issues as sex discrimination legislation but in a different way. Sex discrimination legislation is of value to the aggrieved individual and has a ripple effect which may cause a broader change to employment policy to ensure similar complaints do not arise.

---

90   *Ibid*, at 46-8.

This is an indirect and ad hoc method of achieving the necessary structural changes required for equal employment opportunity. Affirmative action extends sex discrimination legislation by requiring employers to confront their practices directly and systematically.[91]

The Act sets out an eight step plan for the implementation of an affirmative action program, ranging from the issuing of a policy statement committing the organisation to affirmative action, to data collection to assess the current position of women in the workforce, through to the setting of objectives for the future and monitoring achievements. However, the Australian affirmative action legislation is quite soft, refusing to impose quotas on the employment of women and providing that the only sanction for a failure to comply with the Act is naming in Parliament. Pocock argues:

> Australia's affirmative action law has created a vehicle that some companies, and energetic individuals within them, have used to improve gender equity in individual workplaces. But real change in these companies has been very dependent upon internal activism and many companies have seen little real change. What is more the law does not reach the large number of smaller companies, and is now being reduced by the conservative federal government to a much weaker exhortative device.[92]

Notes

1. The legislation has been renamed, removing the introductory words in the title 'Affirmative Action'. Why might the government have done that?
2. Throughout the debate on the introduction of affirmative action legislation, employers were frequently assured that the legislation was not going to interfere with appointment on the basis of merit.[93] Margaret Thornton suggested that the term 'merit' was used throughout the debates, and indeed in the legislation, without being defined. It is 'persistently used as if it were an objective, value-free absolute, whether by supporters or detractors of affirmative action'.[94] In the late 1980s, the Affirmative Action Agency, the agency charged with the administration of the Act, published a monograph scrutinising the concept of 'merit'.[95] In it the author, the late Clare Burton, argued that one of the underlying problems of reliance on 'merit' is the perception that men have more natural ability than women, a form of stereotyping that she attributes to:

---

91 Chris Ronalds, *Affirmative Action and Sex Discrimination*, 2nd edition, Pluto Press, Leichhardt, 1991, at 12-13.
92 Pocock, 'Equal Pay', at 281.
93 See, for example, 'Affirmative action is compatible with appointment and promotion on the basis of merit, skills and qualifications. It does not mean women will be given preference over better qualified men. It does mean men may expect to face stiffer competition for jobs. This is not discrimination': Policy Discussion Paper (Green Paper), *Affirmative Action for Women*, Vol 1 at 3 and Robert J Hawke, Prime Minister, 2nd Reading Speech, 19 February 1986. Section 3(4) of the *Equal Opportunity for Women Act* 1999 provides that 'Nothing in this Act shall be taken to require a relevant employer to take any action incompatible with the principle that employment matters should be dealt with on the basis of merit'.
94 Margaret Thornton, 'Affirmative Action, Merit and the Liberal State' (1985) 2(2) *Australian Journal of Law and Society* 28 at 36.
95 Clare Burton, *Redefining Merit,* Monograph No 2, Affirmative Action Agency, AGPS, Canberra, 1988.

> [A]ttitudes and practices which are based on the idea that women are better at emotional work such as that involved in looking after children, and men in hard physical work or hard mental work, such as that involved in particular jobs in the paid work force. The end result is that when women and men perform identically on tasks, their performances are perceived differently.[96]

She illustrates this with a summary of a well-known research finding:

> The most frequently cited experimental situation is one where an identical piece of work – article, essay, art object – is attributed to John McKay with one group of subjects and Joan McKay with the other. Each group is asked to evaluate the work on a number of dimensions. The standard result is that any work done by a man is evaluated more favourably than the identical work done by a woman. This result changes only when the woman's work has been independently highly rated, as when it has won an award.[97]

After listing a variety of factors that lead to women being disadvantaged in the workforce (for example, streaming into 'women's work' within one occupational level, different measures of encouragement from superiors, failure to understand women's prior experience, lack of access to formal and informal training and development processes etc), Burton concludes:

> These processes, among others, affect women's capacity to demonstrate their ability, their capacity to advance. People's experiences at work – the opportunities provided, the expectations of others, people's attitudes towards them – have a significant effect on people's aspirations and their competencies. Merit, then, is in part an outcome of organisational processes, of access to opportunities which develop it and which allow for its demonstration.[98]

The *Equal Opportunity for Women Act* 1999 contains an objects clause, which was not included in the *Affirmative Action (Equal Opportunity for Women Act)* 1986. Section 2A commences: 'The principal objects of this Act are:

(a) to promote the principle that employment for women should be dealt with on the basis of merit. ...

3. In the context of her exploration of the meaning of 'merit', Margaret Thornton discusses the processes of appointment within universities, a process we also touched on in Chapter 4 while examining the techniques of legal storytelling. Thornton argues that hiring practices in universities are dependent on an 'evaluative element which is subject to the vagaries of individual perception and bias' and accordingly 'bound to perpetuate homogeneity in the workplace'.[99]

> [T]his means that the appointing personnel, usually male professors untrained in selection techniques, are going to favour the appointment of young men as much like themselves as possible. This homosocial reproduction or cloning is facilitated by the adduction of a number of other factors of a much less formal nature which operate to maintain the

---

96 *Ibid*, at 2.
97 *Ibid*, at 2-3. The study Burton cites for this is Sharon Toffey Shepela and Ann T Viviano, 'Some Psychological Factors Affecting Job Segregation and Wages' in Helen Remick (ed), *Comparable Worth and Wage Discrimination: Technical Possibilities and Political Realities*, Temple University Press, Philadelphia, 1986. See also Clare Burton et al, *Woman's Worth: Pay Equity and Job Evaluation in Australia*, AGPS, Canberra, 1987.
98 *Ibid*, at 8-9.
99 Thornton, 'Affirmative Action', at 31.

hegemony of a group of middle-aged, Anglo-Saxon men who have had all the advantages of education and encouragement emanating from their middle class background.[100]

If, as both Thornton and Burton suggest, the process of '"homosocial reproduction" – the appointment and promotion of men by men'[101] is so entrenched, what effect are government affirmative action measures, premised on 'merit', likely to have?[102]

4. Carol Bacchi explores how the category of 'woman' is constructed and deployed in affirmative action policies in Australia and elsewhere.[103] She draws attention to the work of Aileen Moreton-Robinson in the early 1990s, analysing the differential impact of Commonwealth employment policies on indigenous men and indigenous women.[104] Moreton-Robinson concluded that 'Equal Employment Opportunity seems to favour indigenous men over indigenous women and over some non-indigenous women'.[105] However, Moreton-Robertson also observed that the federal Affirmative Action Agency, the agency charged with the implementation of affirmative action for women, did not even collect data on the employment of indigenous women.[106] Is the neglect of the specific needs and interests of indigenous women inevitable in legislation addressed to the category 'woman'? How would you ensure that distinct groups of women are included in the work of such generic agencies?

5. Affirmative action initiatives are often referred to as 'positive' or 'reverse' discrimination. What are the implications of the use of such language?[107]

Comparable worth and job evaluation

In the context of disparities of income between women and men, it could be said that sex discrimination and affirmative action legislation was largely addressed to barriers hindering women's entry into the complete range of occupational and industrial categories. (In relation at least to sex discrimination legislation, it is clear that its focus is also very much on the treatment of women while they are employed, not least in relation to sexual harassment, discussed in detail in Chapter 12). One other strategy designed to reduce the gender wage gap has been the

---

100 Ibid.
101 Burton, *Redefining Merit*, at 5 (citing Jean Lipman-Blumen, 'Toward a Homosocial Theory of Sex Roles: An Explanation of the Sex Segregation of Social Institutions' in Martha Blaxall and Barbara Reagan (eds), *Women and the Workplace*, University of Chicago Press, Chicago, 1976).
102 See also Margaret Thornton, 'Discord in the Legal Academy. The Case of the Feminist Scholar' (1994) 3 *Australian Feminist Law Journal* 53, where Thornton explores the subject positions available to women in the legal academy – 'the Body Beautiful, the Adoring Acolyte, the Mother Confessor, the Dutiful Daughter and the Queen Bee' (at 58). Cf Richard Collier, '"Nutty Professors", "Men in Suits" and "New Entrepreneurs": Corporeality, Subjectivity and Change in the Law School and Legal Practice' (1998) 7 *Social and Legal Studies* 27, which explores subject positions available to men in the legal academy – these include the 'Sexual Predator/History Man', the 'Nutty Professor', the 'Administrator', the 'New Entrepreneur', the 'Young Man in a Hurry' and the 'Pro-Feminist' (at 36-9).
103 Carol Lee Bacchi, *The Politics of Affirmative Action: 'Women', Equality and Category Politics*, Sage, London, 1996.
104 Aileen Moreton-Robinson, 'Masking Gender and Exalting Race: Indigenous Women and Commonwealth Employment Policies' (1992) 15 *Australian Feminist Studies* 5.
105 *Ibid*, at 9.
106 *Ibid*.
107 See, for example, Joan Eveline, 'The Politics of Advantage' (1994) 19 *Australian Feminist Studies* 129.

pursuit of 'comparable worth' – efforts to revalue more accurately the sort of paid work women traditionally do. Or as described by Jane Innes:

> Comparable worth is the phrase used to refer to the idea that jobs which are of equal value based on effort, skill, responsibility and working conditions should receive equal wages, irrespective of the sex of an employee. The concept of comparable worth is directed towards establishing procedures for the review of inequalities in wage structures. This is generally achieved by the use of work value inquiries by which male and female occupations are compared, using an agreed set of objective criteria.[108]

This was often attempted under the various equal pay decisions and Innes goes on to describe the unsuccessful attempt by the ACTU in 1985 to get nursing revalued in this way.[109]

> The substance of the ACTU's argument was that nursing is an occupation which has been undervalued because it is a traditionally female occupation. Comparable worth increases were justified, it was argued, to rectify this undervaluation in accordance with the principle of equal pay for work of equal value. ... The ACTU ... argued:
> - that the 1972 Equal Pay case embraced the concept of comparable worth through the acceptance of the principle of equal pay for work of equal value, and
> - that in implementing the 1972 decision the Commission should not be constrained by the [*then*] current wage-fixing principles set down by the 1983 National Wage case.
>
> Both these arguments were rejected. The Commission expressly discarded the concept of comparable worth as being incompatible with, and potentially threatening to the centralised wage-fixing system.[110]

At the federal level, while awards do still exist, the principle of enterprise bargaining, where wages are negotiated within an enterprise rather than across an occupational grouping,[111] has become more common. The *Workplace Relations Act* 1996 (Cth) does still allow equal pay claims (see s 170BC) but these will be, as Pocock describes it, on a 'firm by firm' basis.

> These cases ... have essentially been in pursuit of revaluation of feminised jobs, non-discriminatory access to allowances, and multi-level classification structures. ... In practice the AIRC has proved persistently allergic to the notion of comparable worth, so that the revaluation road has been long, slow, complicated, legalistic and the slipperiest of all.[112]

Pocock goes on to describe the most recent large inquiry into pay equity, the NSW Pay Equity Inquiry.[113] This is also analysed by Rosemary Hunter, in the first Clare

---

108 Jane Innes, 'Equal Pay and the *Sex Discrimination Act* 1984' (1986) 11 *Legal Service Bulletin* 254.
109 *Private Hospitals' and Doctors' Nurses (ACT) Award* (1986) 13 IR 108.
110 Innes, 'Equal Pay', at 254.
111 But note that women are more likely to be employed in industries governed by awards than enterprise bargains.
112 Pocock, 'Equal Pay Thirty Years On', at 262.
113 See NSW Pay Equity Inquiry, *Report to the Minister, Volume I,* 14 December 1998, Matter No IRC6320 of 1997, Industrial Relations Commission of NSW, Sydney; NSW Pay Equity Inquiry, *Report to the Minister, Volume II,* 14 December 1998, Matter No IRC6320 of 1997, Industrial Relations Commission of NSW, Sydney; and NSW Pay Equity Inquiry, *Appendices to the Report to the Minister,* 14 December 1998, Matter No IRC6320 of 1997, Industrial Relations Commission of NSW, Sydney.

Burton Memorial Lecture[114] under the title *The Beauty Therapist, the Mechanic, the Geoscientist and the Librarian: Addressing the Undervaluation of Women's Work*.[115] The beauty therapist, the mechanic etc of her title refer to the case studies the Pay Equity Taskforce (which preceded the Inquiry) undertook 'to examine the differential valuation of men's and women's work in particular areas'.[116]

> The case studies chosen included child care workers in private sector long day care centres, who were compared with engineering associates in the metal industry, and hairdressers and beauty therapists, who were compared with motor mechanics. These case studies sought to identify the particular skills exercised by women workers that needed to be valued, and to put the theory of comparable worth into practice. ...
>
> Additional case studies considered by the Inquiry included librarians and geoscientists in the NSW public sector, female trimmers and male butchers in a major seafood processing enterprise in southern NSW, and clothing industry outworkers. The outworkers were compared with metal industry machinists (a male-dominated occupation), and also with female clothing machinists working in factories as opposed to their own homes. ...
>
> ... [T]he Inquiry ... did not find the comparisons between male- and female-dominated work conclusive or determinative. In some instances, it did not find the comparisons particularly persuasive. But this did not mean that it rejected the existence of pay inequity in the case studies. Instead of relying on comparisons, it shifted the focus to the issue of undervaluation of women's work *per se*.
>
> This move to the simple question of undervaluation ... was strategically very important. It allowed the Inquiry to sidestep a host of difficult issues that have arisen in attempting to apply the doctrine of comparable worth in other jurisdictions. It avoided the problem of potential gender bias in job evaluation systems, given the evidence of Clare Burton, and especially her point that job evaluation systems are not good at evaluating jobs considered semi-skilled or unskilled, which are the types of jobs that women tend to occupy. It avoided the problem of determining how comparisons should appropriately be made other than by means of job evaluation, given that job evaluation is not well accepted in the Australian industrial relations system. ... It avoided the need for extensive argument over whether the chosen comparators were appropriate. It avoided the difficulty of finding that the work chosen for comparison was not of equal value (whether the female-dominated work turned out to be of lesser or greater value than the male dominated work). Instead it enabled the Inquiry to concentrate on the real issue.
>
> In considering whether the work of the women in the case studies was undervalued, the Inquiry looked at a wide range of matters such as the nature and economics of the industry, the history of work in the particular jobs and the history of the award, current work and remuneration structures, qualification requirements and training provisions, and unionisation rates. Looking at male comparators (or other female comparators) could be instructive *in this context*, to determine the nature and extent of the undervaluation. Undervaluation may be attributed to different factors or combinations of factors in each case.

---

114 Clare Burton died in 1998. She was one of Australia's leading experts on pay equity and comparable worth: see Clare Burton with Raven Hag and Gay Thompson, *Women's Worth: Pay Equity and Job Evaluation*, AGPS, Canberra, 1987; Clare Burton, *Gender Bias in Job Evaluation*, Affirmative Action Agency, Monograph No 3, Sydney, 1988; and *The Promise and the Price: The Struggle for Equal Opportunity in Women's Employment*, Allen and Unwin, Sydney, 1991.

115 Rosemary Hunter, *The Beauty Therapist, the Mechanic, the Geoscientist and the Librarian: Addressing the Undervaluation of Women's Work,* ATN, Wexdev, University of Technology, Sydney, 2000.

116 *Ibid*, at 15.

Thus, for example, child care workers in long day care centres had a low unionisation rate, and worked in isolated workplaces in close proximity to employers and parents, on whom any wage increase would have a direct impact. Rates had also been historically depressed by the female and charitable characterisation of the industry, and nothing had occurred more recently to correct this position. There had been no examination of work value by the NSW Industrial Relations Commission for the last 12 years ... Some of the skills, responsibilities and qualifications of child care workers remained unrecognised in the award, especially the quasi-professional aspects of their work. On the basis of qualifications and work performed, the Inquiry considered that a qualified child care worker should properly be aligned with ... [*a higher*] level of the Metal Industry Award .... However, this would not fully remedy the undervaluation of child care work, since child care workers enjoyed few overaward payments, and worked considerable amounts of unpaid overtime. Engineering associates in the metal industry, by comparison, had an award with clearly established gradations based on qualifications and experience, and also enjoyed many additional allowances, overaward and regular overtime payments.

[*Hunter then discusses the case studies involving hairdressers and beauty therapists, public sector librarians, butchers and trimmers in a seafood plant.*]

Finally, the position of outworkers in the clothing industry was analysed within the context of reduced tariff protection for the Australian clothing industry, introduced under the Hawke and Keating governments. As a result, men's fashion production had moved almost entirely offshore, while the production of ladies' fashions had largely shifted from factory workers to outworkers. Outworkers bore the brunt of demands from consumers, retailers, fashion houses and middlemen to keep prices down while maintaining profits. In addition, isolation of outworkers and their frequent dependence on the middleman or maker who delivered work to them, left them in no bargaining position at all. They undertook often difficult, complex, highly skilled work for extremely low piece rates, resulting in hourly rates well below the award. They worked long and unpredictable hours with no benefits or leave entitlements, sometimes relying on unpaid assistance from other family members, and compelled to carry their own overheads. This was a clear case of undervaluation *per se* without any need for comparators.

The Inquiry found that payment at award rates would "radically" increase outworkers' remuneration. Even so, their work would remain undervalued, since they had never been subject to any formal appraisal of work value, and there was no classification in the award that adequately comprehended many of the skills and tasks undertaken by outworkers. By contrast, award-paid factory employees undertook less complex work and more limited tasks, and also enjoyed overaward payments, paid overtime and bonuses, along with better physical conditions and a high level of unionisation. Although the Inquiry also considered a comparison between the work of female outworkers and male metal industry machinists, the comparison with other female clothing workers demonstrated more starkly and compellingly the undervaluation of outworkers.

What the Inquiry made clear is that the question of undervaluation requires case by case study. ... [T]here is no reason why employers cannot initiate this kind of exercise as part of their affirmative action program or in the course of enterprise bargaining negotiations. To make things somewhat easier, the Inquiry identified a set of profile indicators of undervaluation. These include: female-dominated employment and female characterisation of work; a new industry or occupation, a service industry or a home-based occupation; a history of consent awards or agreements, and the absence of any work value exercise conducted by an industrial tribunal; inadequate application of previous equal pay principles; a weak union or few union members; small workplaces; a large component of casual workers; lack of or inadequate recognition of qualifications; and lack of access to training or career paths. Where these indicators are present, the work in question will almost inevitably be undervalued.[117]

Note

1. In Chapter 3 we discussed various approaches to equality. Is an approach that endeavours to undertake job evaluation of work in which women are concentrated without comparison with jobs where men predominate more consistent with a subordination approach to equality? In that chapter we also discussed the ALRC's proposals for an Equality Act. The majority of the Commission recommended that any such Act should guarantee gender equality to both women and men (while, it will be recalled, the minority recommended that it apply to women only). One of the reasons the majority gave for its view was that equality 'is applicable to all and cannot logically be confined to any one group'.[118] Hunter commends the Pay Equity Inquiry for moving away from a comparative model of job evaluation and addressing the issue of the undervaluation of women's work *per se*. What are the implications of putting such an approach into practice? Is comparison inherent in any job evaluation system?[119]

Labour market institutions

Despite the persistent sex segmentation of the Australian labour force, the differential in earnings between women and men is less than for many other OECD countries. This comparative wage equity is often attributed to the high level of unionisation in Australia and our centralised wage-fixing system.[120] Both of these have changed in recent years, with a steady decline in union membership and an increasing emphasis on enterprise-based wages and individual contracts of employment negotiated without union involvement. It was, of course, predicted that women's wages would start to move backwards in Australia with these moves.[121] Mark Wooden has summarised some of the reasons for this prediction:

> The basic argument is that women are in a weaker bargaining position than men because of: (i) the concentration of women in lower status jobs and occupations; (ii) women's relative concentration in part-time, and frequently casual, employment and (iii) lower levels of both union membership (which is itself a

---

117   *Ibid*, at 15-21.
118   ALRC, *Equality Before the Law: Women's Equality*, Report No 69, Part II, at para 4.26.
119   Pocock, 'Equal Pay', at 284, note 1, states: 'The report rejects the use of comparable worth, but it is not clear how a 'non gender-biased work value' approach will be significantly different from a version of comparable worth. The difficult task of devising such non-biased work principles and practices remains ahead of NSW reformers'.
120   See, for example, Bob Gregory, 'Labour Market Institutions and the Gender Pay Ratio' (1999) 32 *Australian Economic Review* 273: 'Countries with centralised wage-fixing systems and strong unions, such as Australia, were able to increase the relative pay of all women quite quickly during the 1970s. Other countries, such as the United States, found it more difficult to change the gender pay ratio, even though they responded with the institutional structures they possessed. Equal pay provisions and civil rights legislation were relatively ineffective' (at 277).
121   See, for example, Meredith Burgmann, 'Women and Enterprise Bargaining in Australia' in Suzanne Hammond (ed), *Equity Under Enterprise Bargaining*, ACIRRT Working Paper No 33, Australian Centre for Industrial Relations Research and Teaching, University of Sydney, 1994; and Laura Bennett, 'Women and Enterprise Bargaining: The Legal and Institutional Framework' (1994) 36 *Journal of Industrial Relations* 191.

function of the distinct patterns of employment among women) and involvement in union affairs among women as compared with men. Further ..., women may be disadvantaged by social conditioning which leads them to avoid behaviour that might be interpreted as aggressive, and thus be more likely to accept less satisfactory arrangements .... It thus follows that if wage outcomes are the result of direct bargaining between employers and employees ... rather than the result of arbitrated settlements determined at an industry or national level, women's wages should, on average, fall behind that of men.[122]

The evidence on the effect of enterprise bargaining on the gender gap in wages is mixed, with little or no apparent change in the overall wage gap. However, some authors report differences amongst the States, with a greater gap in the States who have gone furthest down the individualist path (Victoria and West Australia) and least in NSW which retains some collectivist elements.[123] Hence, making national estimates can be misleading. Bob Gregory suggests that, at least in relation to the influence of labour market institutions, it is also difficult to make generalisations:

> [L]abour market institutions are impacting differentially on different subsets of women. Wages of low paid women will probably be adversely affected by recent changes in labour market institutions, such as the weakening of unions and moves towards decentralised pay setting, but wages of high paid women now seem largely independent of labour market institutions ... .[124]

Notes

1. What implications do Gregory's observations have for campaigns around equal pay?
2. Level of earnings is, of course, not the only measure of gender equity. Paul Boreham et al undertook a survey in the mid-1990s of enterprise agreements made in Queensland to examine the incidence of 'equity enhancing measures'.[125] As part of their study, they reviewed other empirical evidence then available:

> [C]ontent analysis of agreements consistently identifies trends in working hours that are explicitly not family friendly, such as increased spread of hours and variability of shifts; and comparisons of male and female dominated agreements suggests that the degree of consultation over changes to workplace agreements is greater in male dominated areas ... . Furthermore, a study of the twenty largest federal agreements showed that male dominated agreements tended to involve more limited introduction, and more regulation, of irregular working time, while in female dominated

---

122 Mark Wooden, 'Enterprise Bargaining and the Gender Earnings Gap' (1997) 23 *Australian Bulletin of Labour* 214 at 214. See also Richard Hall, *Gender Equity and Enterprise Bargaining*, Australian Centre for Industrial Relations Research and Training (ACIRRT), Working Paper No 57, June 1999, Sydney, at 3-4.
123 See Alison C Preston and Geoffrey V Crockett, *Effects of Labour Market Regulation on the Gender Pay Gap*, Women's Economic Policy Analysis Unit (WEPAU), Curtin University of Technology, Discussion Paper Series 99/5, October 1999; see also Alison C Preston, *Deregulation and Relative Wages: Stability and Change in Australia*, Women's Economic Policy Analysis Unit (WEPAU), Curtin University of Technology, Discussion Paper Series 00/04, August 2000: see <http://www/cbs.curtin.edu.au/Workingpapers/WEPAU/00-4.pdf>.
124 Gregory, 'Labour Market Institutions', at 277.
125 Paul Boreham, Richard Hall, Bill Harley and Gillian Whitehouse, 'What Does Enterprise Bargaining Mean for Gender Equity? Some Empirical Evidence' (1996) 7 *Labour and Industry* 51.

areas the trend has been towards higher levels of management control of working time ....

With respect to other equal employment opportunity measures such as parental leave and childcare arrangements the evidence is no more encouraging. ADAM [*Agreements Database and Monitor*] data indicate that only 0.3 per cent of agreements had provisions relating to childcare.[126]

Their own survey covered 77 organisations in Queensland which had registered an enterprise agreement, 86% of which were in the private sector.[127] They found generally a relatively low incidence of gender equity enhancing measures (2.6% had childcare facilities, 33.8% paid maternity leave, 19.5% paid paternity leave) and state:

> Much more striking than the relatively low incidence of most of the measures is the failure of respondents to use enterprise bargaining as a means of further developing gender equity arrangements. In just three of the 27 cases which reported the existence of employment arrangements designed to advance women's careers was enterprise bargaining used to establish the arrangements. Similarly, in neither of the two organisations that offered childcare support was this the subject of the enterprise bargain and in none of the three cases that had employment targets for women was this part of the enterprise agreement. Parental leave was included in the enterprise bargain in only two cases.[128]
>
> Large workplaces, non-manufacturing workplaces and public sector workplaces are more likely than others to have a range of gender equity measures in place. This led us to consider the possibility that the level of female employment was an important explanatory variable, since these sorts of workplaces tend to have relatively high levels of feminisation. However, in terms of the introduction of equity measures, highly feminised workplaces fared no better, and in some instances worse, than other workplaces.
>
> This finding suggested the possibility that, even where women are present in large numbers, their interests are systematically marginalised and remain unrepresented.[129]

Conclusion

In the previous chapter we examined unpaid work in the home through a variety of legal doctrines or legal areas and in this chapter we have concentrated on paid work. The separation of these aspects of the work women do is not meant to imply that paid and unpaid work are separate and independent spheres; rather, they are intimately connected and our separate treatment of these issues is merely for ease of exposition.

---

126 *Ibid*, at 56.
127 They in fact sent questionnaires to all 131 organisations with operational enterprise agreements as at December 1993, and received 77 replies, a response rate of 59%.
128 *Ibid*, at 59.
129 *Ibid*, at 65. See also Hall, *Gender Equity and Enterprise Bargaining*, who argues that when increases in pay under workplace agreements are examined there is an enterprise bargaining gender wage gap; he suggests that the failure to see this manifest in overall earnings figures is related to the comparatively better performance of women at the lowest end of the earnings scale compared to men at that level: 'men are becoming more like women in the bottom part of the earnings distribution' (at 10).

However, the interconnections between the two spheres of work are by no means straightforward.[130] Early in Chapter 5, we cited data on women's participation in the paid workforce. What is of equal interest is the change in that level of participation over the past three decades:

> In May 2000, approximately 56% of married women participated in the labour force. Thirty years earlier, in May 1970, this participation rate was only 33.5 per cent. In addition, there has been a substantial increase in the number of mothers seeking employment over the past 25 years. For example, in 1979 44.4 per cent of all married females with children were participating in the labour force. By June 1999, this figure had increased over 40 per cent to 62.9 per cent.[131]

Perhaps it was this very dramatic change in participation in the paid workforce that led Mason and Wilson JJ to observe in 1979:

> [T]here has come a radical change in the division of responsibilities between parents and in the ability of the mother to devote the whole of her time and attention to the household and to the family. As frequently as not, the mother works, thereby reducing the time which she can devote to her children. A corresponding development has been that the father gives more of his time to the household and to the family.[132]

Yet, as we know from the data presented in Chapter 5, this rather rosy view of domestic life, where housework and childcare are shared, does not correspond to reality. As we pointed out there, while women in 1997 were spending slightly less time caring for children than they did in 1992, there was little change in the amount of time men spent doing childcare.

Janeen Baxter has explored the lack of change in the division of household labour and explanations for the persistent gendered differences.[133] She argues that 'sex role theory' – the notion that women and men are socialised into different household roles – has proved inadequate as an explanatory paradigm – it assumes that roles never change, 'ignor[ing] evidence of struggle, contradiction and resistance';[134] it is often assumed to be an explanation when it is really just a description;[135] sex roles are often presented as if they had no connection with other aspects of the social structure, so that 'role theory slides inexorably into a biologically based theory of sex differences';[136] finally, Baxter argues, 'role theory is unable to theorise power and differing social interests'.[137] Baxter instead turns to feminist work that sees housework as 'a means of producing gender':[138]

---

130 See, for example, Miriam A Glucksman, 'Why "Work"? Gender and the "Total Social Organization of Labour"' (1995) 2 *Gender, Work and Organization* 63 who suggests that a useful way to examine work both paid and unpaid is to see them as encompassed within a 'total social organisation of labour'. This would allow the examination of links between the domestic and market economy: 'Inequalities in the market and domestic economies are incommensurable in the sense that one cannot be translated into or added on to the other; they are not reducible to each other but nevertheless they compound each other and are structurally connected. ... [I]nequalities are not generated solely within each sphere but are rather an effect of the connection between the two' (at 68).
131 Siobhan E Austin and Elisa R Birch, *Family Responsibilities and Women's Working Lives*, Women's Economic Policy Analysis Unit, Curtin University of Technology, Discussion Paper Series 00/3, 2000, at 2 (citing ABS Cat No 6204.0, May 1970 and 6203.0, May 2000).
132 *Gronow v Gronow* (1979) 144 CLR 513 at 528.
133 Janeen Baxter, 'Moving Towards Equality? Questions of change and equality in household work patterns' in Gatens and MacKinnon (eds), *Gender and Institutions*, at 55.
134 *Ibid*, at 64.
135 *Ibid*.
136 *Ibid*.
137 *Ibid*.
138 *Ibid*, at 65.

This perhaps goes some way toward explaining the enduring nature of women's responsibility for housework. The domestic division of labour is not a rational allocation of labour based on attitudinal variations, time availability or economic power. It is a much more fundamental system of producing and reproducing differences between men and women. ... Establishing new patterns of domestic labour therefore requires a fundamental reorganisation of gender itself, not just of the allocation of tasks. Perhaps more fundamentally, this understanding of gender undermines the causal relationships inherent in many studies of the domestic division of labour. Rather than gender being causally prior to the domestic division of labour, the relationship is dialectical; gender produces the domestic division of labour; but at the same time, the domestic division of labour produces gender.[139]

Notes

1. What are the implications of Baxter's analysis for feminist unionists' work around equal pay? On Baxter's analysis, why doesn't a change in the allocation of household tasks also change 'gender'? If it were possible to change the allocation of household tasks in heterosexual households by, say, the introduction of new laws requiring equal sharing of domestic tasks and proper enforcement of that equal sharing of domestic work, why would that not change 'gender'? Leslie Cannold recently argued that 'in the same way feminists insist it is men's moral and social responsibility – not prerogative – to share domestic work, so must we insist women have an obligation to share the work of bringing home the bacon. The best and most equitable way for this to be done is for both partners to work part-time'.[140] How realistic is Cannold's suggestion?
2. Baxter goes on to compare the situation on the sharing of household work in a number of different countries. She points out that '[t]he assumption is that social democratic regimes, such as the Nordic countries, will exhibit more egalitarian gender relations compared to liberal regimes, such as Australia and the United States, and conservative-corporatist regimes, such as France, and the Netherlands'.[141] She continues:

    [I]t may be argued that Sweden has made the most progress in moving away from a male breadwinner welfare state model to an individual welfare state model. As a result, Sweden is usually identified as the key example of a country which has done the most to assist women in combining paid and unpaid work .... A combination of parental leave policies, flex-time, and extensive child care facilities, all of which may be understood as elements of institutional design, have raised expectations about moves towards equality in the private sphere. In contrast, it is assumed that in countries such as the United States and Australia, where comparatively little effort has been directed at redesigning institutions to accommodate work and family demands, there will be little evidence of change in gender relations within the home. ...

    [H]owever, ... at least in the five countries considered here – the United States, Sweden, Norway, Canada and Australia – there is little evidence of

---

139 *Ibid*, at 65-6.
140 Leslie Cannold, 'Staying Mum's a Cop-out', *The Age*, 6 June 2001, at 19. Note that some studies show that this type of arrangement is more common in households where lesbian co-parents are raising children: see Chapter 5.
141 Baxter, 'Moving Towards Equality?', at 69.

significant variations in men's participation in housework. In all countries, men report doing about 25 per cent of total housework activities with the exception of Sweden, where they report a slightly higher level of involvement – 27.9 per cent. These results are remarkably consistent across all five countries and tend to undermine the view that institutional variations in political, cultural and economic settings will lead to variations in men's involvement in domestic labour.

More broadly, these results suggest that policies aimed at integrating work and family demands, such as the provision of extensive child care facilities, parental leave rights and a progressive taxation system, have little impact on the gender division of labour in the home.[142]

Baxter goes on to argue that '[s]ocial democratic policies may have made it easier for women to combine paid and unpaid work, but they have done little to reshape gender relations in the home. It may well be easier to develop strategies that enable women to carry out both kinds of work, rather than strategies which will encourage men to do more domestic labour'.[143] Why might this be the case?

3. Currently a lot of 'lip-service' is paid by organisations claiming to have 'family friendly' work policies. How adequate are these policies in practice? In Australia, employers are legally required to provide only one year of unpaid maternity leave. Only three industrialised countries – Australia, the United States and New Zealand – do not require employers to give women paid maternity leave (and New Zealand plans to introduce paid maternity leave legislation in 2002).[144] Would paid maternity leave benefit all women? How could the legislature ensure that such legislation would not deter employers from hiring women? Cathy Sherry has suggested that 'a right to unpaid leave until one's youngest child is of school age would benefit far more women than paid maternity leave'.[145] Does this assume income from an outside source? How many women could survive without some form of income? What other kinds of strategies would enable women to carry out 'both kinds of work'?

4. Just as we suggested above that women's inequality in earnings was reflected in the recent trend toward the private provision of superannuation as the focus of retirement income provision, so too the more traditional welfare state provision has very much influenced the discourse of women's (in)dependence. Bettina Cass argues that the Australian social security system (a means-tested, non-contributory, flat rate social assistance scheme) 'was predicated on contradictory assumptions about the position of women'.[146]

> On the one hand, women were and continue to be treated as independent of male partners in terms of their eligibility for payment, and entitlement is not derived from formal workforce participation of the woman or her husband as in most social insurance systems of income support. On the other hand, women's market related dependence has been reinforced in the constitution

---

142 *Ibid.*
143 *Ibid*, at 71.
144 Tom Allard and Lee Glendinning, 'For Now, Aussie Mums are Still a World Apart' *Sydney Morning Herald*, 16 August 2001, at 1.
145 Cathy Sherry, 'Paid Maternity Leave Will Benefit the Privileged Few' *Sydney Morning Herald*, 16 August 2001, at 12.
146 Bettina Cass, 'Gender in Australia's restructuring labour market and welfare state' in Anne Edwards and Susan Magarey (eds), *Women in a Restructuring Australia: Work and Welfare*, Allen and Unwin, Sydney, 1995, at 42.

of the married couple – whether *de jure* or *de facto* – as the unit of income testing ... and as the unit of payment in the case of some benefits ... .

Paradoxically, the Australian system of welfare payments, while based on individual entitlement, reinforced the prevailing social assumptions of women's dependency by providing, for example, widow's pension for older divorced and widowed women but not widower's pension, wife's pension for the wives of male age and invalid pensioners but not husband's pension for men in similar circumstances. Such assumptions of women's 'difference' in the social and market divisions of labour have been overturned in some social security arrangements since 1987 – in particular the abolition of widow's pension – and replaced by the principle of 'equality', well in advance of women's actual achievement of labour market and income equality. Nevertheless, this system of social security payments ... has provided an extremely important source of income support for women, reducing to some extent the inequalities derived from the distribution of market incomes throughout the life course.[147]

Deborah Mitchell in turn suggests that Australia is in a process of transition from a social welfare system based on a breadwinner model – where women's entitlement to state-provided benefits is based on their attachment to a breadwinner – to that of an individual model.[148] However, she argues that something other than this dichotomised approach is required.

5. Mitchell argues that part of the answer to Baxter's question 'Why don't men do more housework?'[149] is 'tied up in two features of the design of our welfare state institutions'.

> First, it is much more difficult for men to exit from the labour force to become full-time carers. Despite legislative changes to the social security system which theoretically make it possible for men to draw a limited range of benefits and become involved with child-rearing and domestic work, the reality is that the administration of benefits in relation to the *work test* presumes a primary breadwinner role. This may reinforce existing psychological and social barriers, for instance, being labelled as a dole bludger. Second, the reality is that most husbands earn around 15 to 20 per cent more than their wives (on an hourly basis) which, again, makes it difficult for couples to decide to share child care at home. Thus the removal of these sorts of penalties on care participation may provide one avenue for rethinking the institutional design of our welfare state.[150]

How easy is it to 'remove these sorts of penalties'?

Mitchell argues that we should not be pursuing the whole-hearted adoption of the individual model of welfare state provision adverted to above but rather we should:

> premise welfare state structures on a flexible division of labour which will allow both partners to engage in alternating patterns of market work and care work across the life course. This model would imply a number of changes, for example:
> - allowing men greater access to social security benefits during time spent out of the labour force. Rather than having to claim on the basis of being

---

147 *Ibid*, at 42-3.
148 Deborah Mitchell, 'Life-course and Labour Market Transitions: Alternatives to the breadwinner welfare state' in Gatens and MacKinnon (eds), *Gender and Institutions*, at 19-37.
149 See Janeen Baxter, 'Why Don't Men Do More Housework?' (1994) 4(9) *Eureka Street* 37.
150 Deborah Mitchell, 'Life-course and Labour Market Transitions', at 34.

unemployed, men could opt for a care-based payment and not be required to submit to work tests.
- during those periods spent out of the labour market – for both men and women – the government should contribute to the superannuation accounts of those who undertake care work.
- in other parts of the economy, current moves to make employment conditions more responsive to care participation should be encouraged.
- state responsibility for care should be guaranteed, especially where both partners are in the labour force.[151]

Mitchell concludes on an optimistic note:

> While current trends in the labour market seem to be leading us into a period of transience in employment patterns, I argue that rather than being a source of yet more gloom for the welfare state, there is now room for a feminist agenda which focusses on the increasing availability of men to undertake care work.[152]

What might be the elements of that feminist agenda? Are they those identified earlier by Mitchell? If a care-based payment was to be made available to men, as she suggests, should it also be available to women?

---

151 *Ibid*, at 36-7.
152 *Ibid*, at 37.

PART THREE

WOMEN AND CONNECTION

This part of the book examines ways in which women have been, and continue to be, dealt with in legal discourses in terms of their relationships with others, for example, as wives, as mothers, and as women with reproductive capacities. As Carol Smart has argued:

> [W]here women resort to law, their status is always already imbued with specific meaning arising out of their gender. They go to law as mothers, wives, sexual objects, pregnant women, deserted mothers, single mothers and so on. They are not simply women (in distinction to men) and they are most definitely not ungendered persons.[1]

For a variety of historical reasons,[2] women as independent actors in the legal process rarely appear as characters on the major stages of legal theatre: in the law reports and in the treatises and casebooks that (re)present legal doctrine. A well known article by the late Mary Joe Frug closely examines a contracts casebook, looking at the extent to which women are represented as litigants, judges or in hypothetical case examples.[3] To the minimal extent to which women appear in that book, Frug suggests that, with few exceptions, '[t]heir disputes involve contract problems arising from some experience in a family relationship – as wife, as mother-in-law, sister-in-law, or niece'.[4]

If, as Smart suggests, women encounter law as gendered persons or, in Frug's account, as relatives of others, what consequences follow for women when they have dealings with the legal system? In contrast with a contracts casebook, women appear frequently in the doctrinal examples used in Part 3 of this book. Aspects of law that connect women to their children or their childbearing capacities are the areas that are most readily identified with women, whereas areas of doctrine seen as 'gender-neutral', such as tort and contract, are rarely perceived as being relevant to women. For example, in chapter 9 we examine aspects of child custody law, one of the few areas of doctrine where it can readily be assumed that a woman will be a party to any dispute. If these assumptions can be made only in areas that involve women's relationships with children, what does this mean for the treatment (and perception) of women in other areas of law?

---

1   Carol Smart, 'Law's Truth: Women's Experience' in Graycar (ed), *Dissenting Opinions: Feminist Explorations in Law and Society*, Allen and Unwin, Sydney, 1990, at 7.
2   Most notably, before the enactment of the Married Women's Property Acts, the law's refusal to treat married women as full independent persons with legal capacity (see Holcombe, *Wives and Property*, 1983, extracted in Chapter 5); and, before the guardianship of infants legislation, the absolute right of fathers to custody of legitimate children (discussed below in Chapter 9).
3   Mary Joe Frug, 'Rereading Contracts: A Feminist Analysis of a Contracts Casebook' (1985) 34 *American University Law Review* 1065.
4   *Ibid*, at 1078.

This part of the book comprises three chapters. First, Chapter 7 introduces the theme of women as constructed by reference to their relationships with others. This theme is illustrated through doctrinal examples mainly from tort law (with some reference to other areas) and refers to various theoretical explanations, including Robin West's 'connection thesis'. Chapter 8 is principally concerned with having children and the choices involved in reproduction. It considers the issues of abortion, 'foetal rights' and access to motherhood for lesbians and single heterosexual women. Finally, in Chapter 9, we look at ways in which women who are mothers might lose their children through the legal system. While the principal example of this, at least for non-indigenous women, is child custody and access disputes (now referred to in Australia as 'residence' and 'contact' disputes), we also examine some of the other ways in which women who do not meet the law's standard of 'white able-bodied heterosexual motherhood' may have their relationships with their children interfered with. For example, for many years in Australia, indigenous mothers were not considered fit parents and their children were taken from them under policies described by the Human Rights and Equal Opportunity Commission in *Bringing Them Home*,[5] as genocidal. Chapter 9 (and Part 3) conclude with some brief illustrations of criminal law and tort law responses to the death of children. In that chapter, we also discuss the media's treatment of Lindy Chamberlain, perhaps Australia's best known mother, whose tragic encounter with the legal system after the death of her baby at Ayers Rock in 1980 is examined critically in an extract from an article by Adrian Howe.

The areas of doctrine discussed in this part of the book illustrate legal responses to women's participation in families and their broader relationships with others (some of the financial aspects of these relationships are dealt with in Chapter 5 above). While the majority of examples used here, such as child custody and reproduction, are centrally concerned with 'motherhood', it will become apparent in this chapter that the legal treatment of motherhood, and the construction of women as mothers or as defined by their relationships with others, transcends these isolated 'women-centred' areas of doctrine. This is why we have chosen to begin and end this part with illustrations from tort law.

---

5   HREOC, *Bringing Them Home*, Report of the National Inquiry into the Separation of Aboriginal and Torres Strait Islander Children From their Families, Commonwealth of Australia, Sydney, 1997.

Chapter Seven

Constructing Relationships

This chapter commences with a brief discussion of two tort law issues: 'nervous shock' and 'wrongful birth' cases arising mainly out of failed sterilisations. We then move to the field of administrative law and consider a challenge to a woman's participation in legal decision-making based on the fact that 'the tribunal was pregnant'. After briefly describing a theoretical account of the centrality of women's connection to others by American Robin West,[1] we conclude this introductory chapter by contrasting this theme of women's connection with some doctrinal instances involving men that arise out of their relationships.

A doctrinal introduction from tort law

Nervous shock

In addition to allowing those directly injured through negligence to seek compensation against the person whose negligence caused the injury, tort law also permits people who have suffered 'nervous shock' to make claims in limited circumstances. The action for nervous shock is available to people who witness, or in some cases have heard about, injuries caused by the negligence of a third party to someone with whom they have a relationship. The rule has evolved in a number of phases from the 19th century when psychiatric injuries simply were not recognised by law[2] to the current position where the High Court of Australia[3] upheld a claim by a wife for damages suffered upon hearing of injuries to her husband, even though she did not see the effects or aftermath of the accident until some time after it occurred.[4]

One of the important stages through which this rule evolved concerned the issue of whether it was necessary for the plaintiff to fear injury to herself in order to recover damages,[5] or was it sufficient that she feared for someone else? The issue arose squarely in <u>Hambrook v Stokes</u>.[6] There a pregnant mother saw a lorry disappearing down a hill in the direction of her child. Hearing shortly thereafter that a young girl had been injured she searched for her child unsuccessfully until she ultimately found her in a hospital. The mother suffered severe nervous shock at her terror over what might have happened to the child, haemorrhaged and died shortly thereafter. Her survivors sued the lorry driver and the issue in the *Fatal Accidents Act* action[7] was whether she would have recovered damages had she

---

1 Robin West, 'Jurisprudence and Gender' (1988) 55 *University of Chicago Law Review* 1.
2 *Victorian Railways Commissioner v Coultas* (1888) 13 App Cas 222.
3 *Jaensch v Coffey* (1984) 155 CLR 549.
4 The situation is similar in England: see the decision of the House of Lords in *McLoughlin v O'Brian* [1983] 1 AC 410 (but compare *Alcock v Chief Constable of South Yorkshire Police* [1992] 1 AC 310).
5 In *Dulieu v White* [1901] 2 KB 669, the plaintiff recovered for nervous shock where, although she was not herself physically injured by the defendant's negligence, she suffered nervous shock resulting from her fear that she would be injured.
6 [1925] 1 KB 141.
7 This is a tort law action for wrongful death, available to the dependants of an accident victim.

survived the experience. Extending the legal principle so as to allow recovery for nervous shock in this broader category of cases, Bankes LJ failed to see any relevant distinction between this case and a case of a woman whose fear was not for her child but for herself.

> Assume two mothers crossing this street at the same time when this lorry comes thundering down, each holding a small child by the hand. One mother is courageous and devoted to her child. She is terrified, but thinks only of the damage to the child, and not at all about herself. The other woman is timid and lacking in the motherly instinct. She also is terrified but thinks only of the damage to herself and not at all about her child. The health of both mothers is seriously affected by the mental shock occasioned by the fright. Can any real distinction be drawn between the two cases? Will the law recognise a cause of action in the case of the less deserving mother, and none in the case of the more deserving one? Does the law say that the defendant ought reasonably to have anticipated the non-natural feeling of the timid mother, and not the natural feeling of the courageous mother? I think not.[8]

Notwithstanding this British court's recognition that a mother's fear of injury to her child is a real fear, experienced by her in a material, harmful and ultimately compensable way, Australia's High Court dismissed a claim for nervous shock by a woman whose child was drowned as a result of the negligence of the defendant local council in an infamous decision in 1939.[9] The council was undertaking work in the street, and had dug a trench which was left exposed and became filled with water. Mrs Chester went to look for her child after he had been missing for a time, became distressed upon failing to find him and suffered severe nervous shock when, some time later, the child's body was removed from the ditch. The High Court dismissed her claim, though there was a compelling dissenting judgment by Evatt J. Extracts from the majority judgments and Evatt J's dissent are reproduced below.

Chester v Waverley Corporation
High Court of Australia
(1939) 62 CLR 1

[7] Latham CJ: But in this case the plaintiff must establish a duty owed by the defendant to herself and a breach of that duty. The duty which it is suggested the defendant owed to the plaintiff was a duty not to injure her child so as to cause her a nervous shock when she saw, not the happening of the injury, but the result of the injury, namely, the dead body of the child. It is rather difficult to state the limit of the alleged duty. If a duty of the character suggested exists at all, it is not really said that it should be confined to mothers of children who are injured. It must extend to some wider class – but to what class? There appears to be no reason why it should not extend to other relatives or to all other persons, whether they are relatives or not. ...

[9] [T]he question to be determined is a question as to the definition, the scope and extent, of any relevant duty. ... Thus in the present case the circumstance that the plaintiff in fact suffered a shock does not establish the existence of any duty in the defendant [10] or any breach of duty by the defendant. The question which must be asked in order to determine whether the defendant was negligent or not is whether the defendant should have foreseen that a mother would suffer from nervous shock amounting to illness if she saw the

---

8   [1925] 1 KB 141 at 151 (Bankes LJ and Atkin LJ allowed recovery, while Sargent LJ dissented).
9   *Chester v Waverley Corporation* (1939) 62 CLR 1.

dead body of her child where the death of the child had been brought about by the negligence of the defendant towards the child. This mode of formulating the question is very favourable to the plaintiff. For reasons which I have indicated, the question should probably be put in a form which substituted the words "person" and "another person" for "mother" and "child"....

In my opinion it cannot be said that such damage (that is, nervous shock) resulting from a mother seeing the dead body of her child should be regarded as "within the reasonable anticipation of the defendant". "A reasonable person would not foresee" that the negligence of the defendant towards the child would "so affect" a mother. A reasonable person would not antecedently expect that such a result would ensue. ... Death is not an infrequent event, and even violent and distressing deaths are not uncommon. It is, however, not a common experience of mankind that the spectacle, even of the sudden and distressing death of a child, produces any consequence of more than a temporary nature in the case of bystanders or even of close relatives who see the body after death has taken place.

In my opinion there was no evidence to establish the existence of the duty of the defendant to the plaintiff which was a necessary part of the plaintiff's case and the learned trial judge acted rightly in directing a verdict for the defendant.

The appeal should be dismissed.

[*In his judgment, Starke J described the 'shock to the appellant [as] not within the ordinary range of human experience': at 13. Evatt J dissented. After considering at length the danger of the trench to small children, and the evidence of the fact that the defendant did not adequately guard against the risk, he continued:*]

[16] Evatt J: There was evidence that from the moment when the plaintiff discovered that her child was missing, she searched for him without intermission, that in the course of her search she came to the trench for the purpose of finding or aiding her child, and that while the water in the trench was being explored for the same purpose and until the body was recovered, she suffered severe nervous shock as a result of her own unaided sense impressions.

According to the mother's evidence, the child left his home after lunch at about 2 pm. The family lived at Allen's Parade, Waverley, in the street where the trench was being excavated. At about 3 pm. his mother became concerned and commenced to look for her child. Upon her husband's returning from work, both parents called in the aid of nearby relatives, who all helped in the search. The plaintiff had resided in Allen's Parade for only 14 days, and [17] at first was unaware of the special menace of the deep trench. As a result it did not occur to her or her fellow searchers for some time that the child might have fallen into the trench. Late in the afternoon, however, it was suggested by someone, perhaps by the mother of the little boy who was called as a witness, that Maxie, the plaintiff's child, might have fallen in the water. Coming with her husband to the side of the trench the plaintiff was at once beset with fear at the sinister significance of the trench, especially when one of the searchers was unable to plumb the depth of its water.

The plaintiff was a woman of Polish extraction, and found special difficulty in narrating the precise nature of her feelings, her fears, her hopes and her sufferings. But it is quite easy, I think, to perceive the order of events. It is abundantly clear that until the recovery of the body she did not know that her child had been drowned in the trench. Like most mothers placed in a similar situation, she was tortured between the fear that he had been drowned and the hope that either he was not in the trench at all, or that, if he was, a quick recovery of his body and the immediate application of artificial respiration might still save him from death. In this agonized and distracted state of mind and body she remained for about half an hour, when the police arrived and the child's body was discovered and removed.

During this crucial period the plaintiff's condition of mind and nerve can be completely understood only by parents who have been placed in a similar agony of hope and fear with hope gradually decreasing. In the present case the half hour of waiting was the culmination of a long and almost frantic searching which had already reduced her to a state of nerve exhaustion. Even after the finding of the body, an attempt at artificial respiration was made and abandoned only after expert lifesavers had worked on the child's body for some time.

William Blake's imaginative genius has well portrayed suffering and anxiety of this kind:-

"Tired and woe-begone
Hoarse with making moan ...
Rising from unrest
The trembling woman prest
With feet of weary woe;
She could no further go."

[*Evatt J at this point also included a quote from Australian novelist, Tom Collins, in Such is Life, which deals with 'the agony of fearfulness caused by the search for a lost child' ... He continued:*]

[18] Not only its poets and novelists, but, at any rate in recent years, those engaged in the administration of the common law of England have recognized that shock of the most grievous character can be sustained in circumstances analogous to those of the present case.

V. In the circumstances, it is not remarkable that there was evidence of some permanent injury to the plaintiff's nervous system. According to the doctor who attended upon her:

"Time will heal it to a certain extent, but in her case the scar will be always there to a more extent than in the ordinary case of the ordinary death of a child, owing to the fact of her having seen the body as the boy was taken from the water and the fact that it was a tragic end, also the fact that this boy was a particularly brilliant boy and seemed to be the hope of her family, as she told me."

I have dealt with the facts of the case at some length not only because an understanding of them is important from the point of view of liability, but because, in my opinion, they are summarily but insufficiently set out in the Full Court's statement that "the discovery that her son had been drowned caused her a severe shock." This statement takes no account of (a) the plaintiff's long agony of [19] waiting when she feared that her son had been drowned but certainly did not "know" it, or of (b) the effect upon the plaintiff of the actual removal from the water of her child, especially as the circumstances suggested at least to her and her husband that even at that moment life was not quite extinguished.

[*Evatt J went on to discuss what he considered to be the inadequacy of the facts put to the jury, in particular the impossibility of abstracting 'from the totality of events any factor' which, in particular, 'contributed to her distress and shock'. He was also critical of the NSW Supreme Court's judgment: see (1938) 38 SR (NSW) at 607-8*].

[22] The present case presents legal difficulties of a special kind, but nothing is to be gained by giving a special interpretation or colour to the facts. That is one reason why I have stated them so fully. It seems indisputable that the jury could have found that the onset of the plaintiff's nervous shock took place at a point of time when the plaintiff, although at the side of the trench, did not know or even believe that her child had been drowned. Equally she was not "looking for the body of a child." She was looking for her child. She was terrified lest he should have been drowned, was taking notice of little except what her own senses were

telling her, was hoping against hope that her very worst fear would not be realized. It is true that from the point of legal liability these differences in fact may not be decisive, but such differences may make the issue of liability easier to determine. Not only the facts, but all reasonable inferences to be drawn from the facts were for the jury; ...

The Full Court considered that the plaintiff's case as to the existence of a duty towards her is prejudicially affected by the fact that at the scene of the fatality she was not present "in the character of a wayfarer startled by a distressing sight." A priori it would [23] be surprising if, in relation to the question of breach of duty towards a mother, a defendant is in a stronger position in cases where, by reason of the consequences of his primary negligence towards her child, the mother is trying desperately to find and rescue him than in cases where, knowing nothing of any danger or accident she merely stumbles across the child's body after the accident has occurred. In the distinction made by the Full Court there seems to lurk the fallacy that the principle of *Hambrook v Stokes Brothers* ([1925] 1 KB 141) applies only for the benefit of "wayfarers" or "passers-by". I think that the law is at once more civilized and more humane. ...

Let us apply this criterion to a reasonable person in the situation of the defendant council. Such a person would foresee that, by leaving the trench inadequately guarded, it would probably become, especially when filled with water and provided with sand, a very attractive place to children in the neighbourhood of the trench. He would also foresee that, having regard to the unfortunate but notorious fact that children of workpeople are frequently compelled to play in the streets and also to the fact that the water was in the trench, the special menace of the place would be that small children might fall in and be drowned. He would also foresee when "directing his mind" to the dangers that, if a child got into the zone of the special danger, his parents (and others) would resort to the spot either to seek for the child or, upon hearing his cries, to rescue him from danger; and that, in so doing, they might themselves sustain physical injury or illness caused by nervous shock and distress. ...

[24] But it is necessary to deal at once with an argument which seems to have been accepted by the Full Court. It may be put as follows: A few people – "susceptible and emotional mothers" let us say – would have suffered nervous shock and injury after undergoing an experience similar to that of Mrs Chester. This fact a reasonable person would or might have foreseen. But only persons in such exceptional category would have suffered. Therefore the defendant's [25] secondary duty existed only towards those who did not belong to the exceptional category, ie, only towards the "ordinary normal human being." The non sequitur is easily discernible. So far as the argument rests upon the contention that no other parents would have suffered shock and illness from the ordeal undergone by Mrs Chester, I think this is a mere assertion and is contradicted by all human experience. I think that only "the most indurate heart" could have gone through the experience without serious physical consequences.

So far as the argument rests upon law, it may, perhaps, claim some support from Professor *Winfield's* suggestion that the plaintiff's right to recover for physical illness caused by nervous shock is dependent upon the fact that the plaintiff was a "normally firm and reasonable person" (*Winfield* on the *Law of Tort* (1937), p 58). That learned author says:- "Thus, if a nervous old lady sees B, a stranger, hurt in a trivial accident due to A's negligence in a crowded London street and suffers shock in consequence, she has no cause of action against A, not because the consequence is too remote, but because A owes no legal duty to take care towards unreasonably nervous people and if he owes no such duty he cannot commit a breach of it" (*Winfield* on the *Law of Tort* (1937), p 87). ...

[*Evatt J here quoted from Lord Atkin's judgment in Hambrook v Stokes which had been relied on by Winfield for his proposition about the 'nervous old lady' and continued:*]

Atkin LJ was pointing out that, inasmuch as liability in ordinary street-accident cases comes into existence only where the accident is due to the negligence of the defendant, the decision in *Hambrook v Stokes Brothers* as to nervous shock casts no additional duty [26] upon careful drivers of vehicles. Providing they drive carefully, the "old lady at Charing Cross" who becomes frightened on witnessing an accident can have no cause of action against them. It is not that there is no duty owed to the "frightened old lady," but – the duty being to take reasonable care – that there has been no breach of it. ...

[*Evatt J then discusses some of the case law before turning to Goodhart for the proposition:*] "A man who strikes another ought to foresee that his victim may be suffering from some weakness. We all know that the average man in the street is not necessarily the average man" (*Essays in Jurisprudence and the Common Law* (1931), pp 126, 127).

This general principle seems reasonably applicable to cases like the present. The defendant could not have been assured in advance that if it negligently failed to guard the trench, the mother of any child injured thereat would conform to one category rather than to another. Therefore the duty was to all members of all categories. ...

[30] There is not the slightest ground for supposing that in *Hambrook v Stokes Brothers* the Court of Appeal stopped to inquire whether Mrs Hambrook was "a normal person of ordinary firmness and mental stability" or gave any support to the curious theory that no duty to take care existed except with respect to such persons. *Atkin* LJ was clearly of opinion that a reasonable person should have anticipated nervous shock at least to persons like Mrs Hambrook, not finding it necessary for the decision to determine finally whether the same anticipation should have been made in respect of all "bystanders". It seems to be curious to argue that unless a reasonable person should have anticipated nervous shock to all and sundry, including the casual passer-by, he would not, and could not, have anticipated damage to the parents of the child. Here, as in *Hambrook v Stokes Brothers*, the duty cannot in principle be limited to parents or relatives. But here, as in *Hambrook v Stokes*, the duty certainly extended to the particular plaintiff, the mother of the injured child.

Notes

1. The dissenting judgment of Evatt J has been almost universally preferred by courts and commentators since the decision in the 1939 case. *Chester v Waverley* is no longer considered good law; the High Court decision in *Jaensch v Coffey*[10] is now the principal authority in Australia.
2. Is there a consistent understanding in *Hambrook* and *Chester* of the way women experience the pain of injury to, or the death of, their children? How important to the outcome of *Hambrook v Stokes* is the court's assessment of the plaintiff as a 'good mother'? What does the court mean when it talks of the hypothetical mother who is 'lacking in the motherly instinct'?
3. How helpful do you find the detailed discussion of the facts in Evatt J's judgment in *Chester v Waverley*? Do you think that his attention to those facts was a significant factor in his reaching a different conclusion to the majority? Would you characterise Latham CJ's reformulation of the duty question

---

10 (1984) 155 CLR 549.

(changing the words 'mother' and 'child' to 'person' and 'another person') as an example of judicial gender-neutrality? Are the differences in formulation significant?

4. *Woods v Lowns*[11] concerned the duty of a doctor to attend an emergency. Patrick Woods suffered an epileptic seizure resulting in severe brain damage. A nearby GP who had refused to attend when requested to do so was found to have breached his duty of care to the boy and this finding was upheld by majority on appeal.[12] The reported version of the trial judge's decision ends with the comment: 'His Honour then considered matters not calling for report'.[13] What was omitted from the reported version were the separate actions of the child's mother and father for nervous shock. Extracts from the trial judge's discussion of the nervous shock claims are set out below:

Woods by his next friend Harry Woods v Lowns; Light v Lowns; Woods v Lowns,

NSW Supreme Court, Badgery-Parker J, 9 February 1995, unreported

... The crucial questions of fact are therefore as to the nature and diagnosis of the symptoms of which each plaintiff complains and as to the way in which those symptoms arose following Patrick's illness – specifically whether as the result of shock in the sense of a sudden perception (sudden acquisition of knowledge) of the seriousness of his plight.

There is no doubt at all that each of the adult plaintiffs has experienced a great deal of emotional torment, commencing, in the case of Lesley Light, at the moment when she became aware that Patrick was fitting in her bedroom at the home unit at The Entrance, and in the case of Harry Woods, when his former wife telephoned him from Gosford Hospital to inform him of what had occurred. That emotional torment fluctuated as the plaintiff first appeared likely to die then showed signs of recovery which could perhaps have been complete, only then to relapse into his present condition. That emotional torment has continued to the present day. The defendants do not dispute those propositions. I accept the evidence, which appears to be common to all of the psychiatrists in the case, that each of the adult plaintiffs is afflicted, at the least, by a reaction to Patrick's plight which is akin to a grief reaction following upon bereavement and which, in the case of each of them, has been prolonged because their loved one is not dead and gone but continues to live as a daily reminder of what they have lost. Such grief reaction and the associated emotional torment attract the utmost sympathy; but they do not attract an award of damages unless the evidence shows in respect of either plaintiff that what he or she suffers or has suffered constitutes or did constitute an actual psychological injury or illness.

(i) LESLEY MARIA LIGHT Mrs Light has been seen on three occasions, at the behest of her solicitor, by a psychiatrist, Dr James P Maguire. ... Dr Maguire has not given her any treatment, having seen her only for medico-legal purposes. ... He concluded that the history was consistent with her having suffered a chronic reactive depression which had tended to fluctuate

---

11 *Woods by his next friend Harry Woods v Lowns; Light v Lowns; Woods v Lowns*, NSW Supreme Court, Badgery-Parker J, 9 February 1995.
12 (1996) Aust Torts R ¶81-376.
13 (1995) 36 NSWLR 344 at 360.

over the years. He thought that at the date of that report she was not currently suffering from a psychiatric disorder but that he could not rule out the possibility of a subsequent depressive episode at some point in the future should there be any marked deterioration in her son's condition. ... Dr Maguire gave oral evidence in which he confirmed the opinions expressed in his reports. He regarded her grief as abnormal and pathological by reason of the duration over which it had continued. Mrs Light herself gave evidence confirming the existence of the symptoms referred to in Dr Maguire's reports.

I am satisfied on the balance of probabilities that by the time when Mrs Light first saw Dr Maguire ... a little over 18 months after Patrick's fit, she was suffering from a grief reaction and reactive depression of such intensity as appropriately to be regarded as a psychiatric illness capable of being held to be an injury in respect of which, subject to its aetiology, damages might be awarded. Equally, I am satisfied that with the further passage of time, ... that psychiatric illness had resolved by the time when Dr Maguire last saw the plaintiff, on 8 October 1993. No doubt as Dr Maguire suggests in that latest report, she has received a significant boost by reason of the birth of a child to her second husband.

What appears to be lacking, however, in her case is evidence of some identifiable occasion upon which she was made suddenly aware of the gravity of Patrick's plight and by reason thereof received a shock to which her subsequent psychiatric illness can be attributed. The sad fact seems to be that she has continuously experienced emotional stress from the time of the original discovery of Patrick's fit and throughout the period of his treatment and partial rehabilitation. It is not suggested anywhere in Dr Maguire's evidence that her condition can be attributed to any sudden perception or acquisition of awareness of Patrick's plight. Throughout, he attributes her reactive depression to the stress of watching her son's progress not knowing exactly what his degree of disability would ultimately be. In her own evidence, she refers to particular stressful episodes in the course of the long period of Patrick's unconsciousness – for example when she became aware of the possibility of serious liver damage such as might require a transplant, when she became aware of the possibility that he might die, when she became aware that he had some brain damage ... but it was not until after Patrick had left the children's hospital and had been transferred to Coorabell Rehabilitation Hospital that the realisation came to her that he was never going to be anything like what he was before. That was no doubt, among all of the events of his progress, the most devastating, but it is abundantly clear that long before that time, she was experiencing the emotional disorder which I have characterised as a psychological illness. I find that it has not been established that any psychological illness incurred by the plaintiff Lesley Light amounts to an injury by way of mental or nervous shock such as to entitle her to damages. Her action, therefore, must fail.

(ii) HARRY FRANCIS WOODS Mr Harry Woods was also seen on three occasions by Dr Maguire who records in his case also symptoms of severe emotional disturbance which led Dr Maguire to a diagnosis of a depressive illness of some severity which he described as "a direct result of the effect this whole tragic episode has had on him". [*Mr Woods had separated from Patrick's mother in 1982 and was remarried. At the time of the incident, he lived on the NSW North Coast and was part owner and manager of a hotel at Yamba. In 1990, he had been elected to Federal Parliament as the ALP member for Page and Dr Maguire attributed his recovery to this change of career. Another doctor who examined him considered that his response was a typical grief reaction of a father whose son has suffered brain damage. However, another doctor who examined him at the behest of his solicitor diagnosed him as suffering from a serious depressive illness and believed that he was in need of urgent treatment particularly because of the risk of suicide and he was referred for treatment to another doctor (Dr Lianos) who reported 'a diagnosis of a major depressive illness which may have initially started off as a grief reaction'. He was treated with anti depressant medication and psychotherapy. Dr Lianos concluded:]* "It is more than likely that he will be left with a chronic depressive condition and that this will continue to limit his social and occupational functioning." ...

I am satisfied that Mr Woods developed a severe depressive illness which was substantially in remission for a period during 1992 and early 1993 but has since recurred and is currently a matter of some seriousness. I accept that it will respond to continuing treatment but that there is significant risk that his recovery will not be complete. [*The trial judge rejected an argument that Mr Woods' failure to seek treatment earlier was a factor to take account in mitigation of damages*]. Mr Woods' condition clearly meets the description of a psychiatric illness capable of attracting an award of damages, subject only to the question of its aetiology. It appears to me that in this regard there is a significant difference between his case and that of Mrs Light. The evidence of Mr Woods, which I accept, shows that although he was obviously upset and concerned about Patrick's condition during the time when Patrick was in Gosford Hospital and thereafter when he appeared to be gravely ill after his transfer to the children's hospital, Mr Woods was optimistic of a satisfactory outcome. Indeed, it may be that that optimism, apparently encouraged by the doctors in good faith but ultimately misplaced, may have set him up for a greater fall when he became aware of the truth. His evidence identifies a particular occasion four or five weeks after Patrick was transferred from the intensive care unit to the normal ward and about the same period before his transfer to Coorabell, when he had a meeting with Dr Procopis. On that occasion, Dr Procopis told him that Patrick had massive brain damage, and that was the first time that Mr Woods had been made aware of that fact. I accept his description that: "I felt like I had been hit by a sledge hammer. I was distraught. I was in despair. I broke down crying." He said, and I accept, that subsequently he was unable to talk about that meeting to anybody and felt utterly helpless and inadequate. His hope of a successful outcome was destroyed. I am satisfied on a perusal of the whole of the evidence that it really is from that time that Mr Woods commenced to develop the symptoms which have attracted a diagnosis to which I have referred. I am satisfied that in his case the evidence does establish that he has suffered injury by way of nervous shock for which he is entitled to damages.

It is unnecessary to set out in detail his symptoms which are adequately recorded in the medical reports beyond noting that they include sleep disturbance, loss of appetite, sustained depression of mood, feelings of hopelessness, difficulties with attention and concentration and organisation. I accept his evidence that his parliamentary performance is less good than it was initially and that he finds difficulty in coping. I accept his evidence that he is forced to depend more than he should on his staff to perform duties which he should have carried out himself. I accept that there is a real possibility that unless his response to treatment is substantial he may not continue in the Parliament for very much longer.

He has suffered no economic loss other than to incur treatment expenses which were agreed at $2,800 to the date of trial, nor will he incur economic loss in the future other than the cost of continuing treatment at the rate of about $80 per week, so long as such treatment continues to be necessary. I propose to allow the sum of $5,000 for the cost of ongoing and future treatment. Otherwise, his claim is one only for general damages and having regard to the intensity of his symptoms, the fact that they have continued now for about eight years, albeit with a period of a year or 18 months when they were of much less severity, and anticipating that they will in all probability continue at a significant level for at least another year and at a reduced level for an indefinite period thereafter, I assess general damages at $50,000.

5. Consider the following fact situation: Claire had suffered from meningitis and one of the consequences of this was that she was blind. Her mother, Patricia, had invested considerable time and effort in successfully encouraging and assisting her to accommodate to her disability. Claire had been married, but had separated from her husband. She was working in Townsville when she suffered serious injuries in a motor vehicle accident, which left her permanently comatose. Her mother, Patricia, was at the time living in Brisbane where she received the news of Claire's injury (and likely death) from police officers in the middle of the night. She went to Townsville the following morning where she saw her daughter in a coma with a tracheal insertion. At first Patricia thought Claire was dead until she was later advised otherwise. She fell to the floor in a faint, followed by vomiting and dry retching.

For the next three years, she never gave up hope for Claire's recovery. During that period, Claire suffered several fits in her mother's presence and, on occasions, Patricia received phone calls, some in the middle of the night, informing her of Claire's need for emergency surgery and the expectation that she would not survive. When Claire did die, suddenly and unexpectedly, Patricia was very distraught at the news. She had been planning to bring her home to live. Soon after the death, she was confined to bed for 10 days and developed suicidal thoughts. She had difficulty with concentration and was referred to a psychiatrist for the first time. She eventually ceased paid work, on the advice of a psychiatrist, and moved to an area where her opportunities for paid work were limited. She sued the defendant driver for nervous shock and her claim was dismissed. What reasons might the court have had for dismissing her claim? See *Spence v Percy* [1992] 2 Qd R 299.

6. How important to the outcomes of these two cases are traditional understandings of fatherhood and motherhood? Do they affect the courts' findings in respect of nervous shock, which in turn is premised upon a particular construction of mental illness? Were these understandings more important than any 'sudden awareness' of the plight of the children concerned? Note the contrasting language in *Woods v Lowns*, the description of the father feeling 'helpless and inadequate' and the impact upon his career as a parliamentarian. Why are apparently similar symptoms described as a 'grief reaction' for a mother who is the primary carer of her child, but as 'severe' and 'chronic' for a father who does not live with his (severely incapacitated) son? If nervous shock is a legal concept built upon relationship (or connection), is there a tension between the expectations

where the relationship is closest and those where the re[...] tained at some (physical) distance? How does the ou[...] father compare with the outcome of Claire's mothe[...] Percy)?[14]

[handwritten: Why does Woods win of Spera ease(?)]

Wrongful birth/wrongful conception[15]

In recent years, a number of negligence actions have been brought against doctors and/or hospitals in situations where children have been born as a result of unplanned pregnancies. The most frequent context in which this occurs is where a sterilisation procedure has been unsuccessful,[16] or a doctor has failed to warn of the possibility that such a procedure might not prevent pregnancy.[17] However, not all the cases involved failed sterilisations. Some have involved failed procedures for terminating pregnancies[18] while others, including *CES v Superclinics*,[19] flowed from medical negligence in failing to diagnose a pregnancy until it was too late to consider any safe alternative to carrying the pregnancy to term. In each of these situations, the plaintiff has sued for wrongful birth or wrongful conception and as part of that claim, has asked for damages for the costs of upkeep of a child. In this section, we consider *CES v Superclinics,* a decision of the NSW Court of Appeal, which led to a re-examination of this doctrine.

Reg Graycar and Jenny Morgan, ' "Unnatural Rejection of Womanhood and Motherhood":[20] Pregnancy, Damages and the Law. A Note on *CES v Superclinics (Aust) Pty Ltd*'
(1996) 18 *Sydney Law Review* 323

[*A 21-year-old woman, concerned that she might be pregnant, made several visits to a medical centre. She claims that she advised the doctors she saw that she did not want to have a child and would terminate the pregnancy if it transpired that she was pregnant. Through a series of errors, including some false negative test results, her pregnancy was not finally diagnosed until she saw her family doctor at which time she was 19.5 weeks pregnant and it was decided that it would not be safe to terminate the pregnancy at that late stage. All the medical evidence adduced at the trial was to the effect that the doctors were negligent and the medical treatment she received was inadequate. The trial was heard before Newman J who, without making any formal findings on the facts, and having*

---

14 For a discussion of the historical development of nervous shock doctrine in the United States, see Martha Chammalas and Linda K Kerber, 'Women, Mothers and the Law of Fright: A History' (1990) 88 *Michigan Law Review* 814. For some more recent discussions, see Elizabeth Handsley, 'Mental Injury Occasioned by Harm to Another: A Feminist Critique' (1996) 14 *Journal of Law and Inequality* 391; Carolyn Goodzeit, 'Rethinking Emotional Distress Law: Prenatal Malpractice and Feminist Theory' (1994) 63 *Fordham Law Review* 175; Barbara Ann Hocking and Alison Smith, 'From *Coultas* to *Alcock* and Beyond: Will Tort Law Fail Women'? (1995) 11 *Queensland University of Technology Law Journal* 120.
15 Wrongful conception is the term preferred by Lord Clyde in the House of Lords decision in *MacFarlane v Tayside Health Board* [2000] 2 AC 59 at 99 (discussed below), who in turn was citing it with approval from the Ontario judgment in *Kealey v Bereszowski* (1996) 136 DLR (4th) 708.
16 For example, in *Udale v Bloomsbury Area Health Authority* [1983] 2 All ER 522.
17 *Thake v Maurice* [1984] 2 All ER 513.
18 See, for example, *Sciuriaga v Powell* (1979) 123 Sol J 406; *Cherry (Guardian ad Litem of) v Borsman* (1990) 75 DLR (4th) 668.
19 (1995) 38 NSWLR 47; and see also *Gardiner v Mounfield* (1989) 5 BMLR 1 (QBD).
20 The phrase is from *Udale v Bloomsbury Area Health Authority* [1983] 2 All ER 522 at 531.

expressly taken the woman's case at its highest for the purpose of his legal analysis, said that if these were the only issues, he would have to agree that there had been a breach of duty. He referred particularly to the evidence of the late Dr Shearman, Professor of Obstetrics and Gynaecology at the University of Sydney, who, in his report of 2 December 1987 (quoted by Kirby A-CJ in Superclinics, at 52), had commented: "[T]here is quite an extraordinary statement in the card dated 27th January 1987. This states "LMP [last menstrual period] 19th October. Nil symptoms of pregnancy". This is really quite remarkable. *The symptom of early pregnancy is amenorrhoea [absence or suppression of menstrual discharge]. In a young sexually active woman with previously regular periods ... responsible medical practice indicates that the onset of amenorrhoea is due to pregnancy until proved otherwise"*].

[324] However, Newman J decided that the plaintiff was not entitled to damages since her case depended upon a claim that she had lost an opportunity to do something he determined was illegal (viz, have her pregnancy terminated) and therefore the law did not permit her to claim damages. The Court of Appeal [(1995) 38 NSWLR 47] by majority (Kirby A-CJ, Priestley JA; Meagher JA dissenting), reversed this decision, but the majority could not agree on the appropriate approach to the assessment of damages. ...

[*We examine this aspect of the decision in this chapter, while the issue raised as to the relevance of the 'legal status' of abortion is dealt with in the following chapter. In relation to damages, the defendants argued, both in the Court of Appeal and in their special leave application to the High Court, that as a matter of public policy, "the birth of a healthy child can never sound in damages"*].

[333] There is a significant body of case law on that issue in England, and a smaller number of cases in Australia. With one exception, *Udale v Bloomsbury Area Health Authority,* the courts in England, Scotland and Australia [334] have not seen fit to impose a blanket bar on recovery of damages for the costs of upkeep of a child in such cases.

The main legal context in which such cases have arisen is failed sterilisations. ... As the first of the reported English cases, and the one relied on by Meagher JA and the appellants in their application for special leave, *Udale* warrants some discussion, before the contrasting decisions are referred to.

In *Udale,* the plaintiff was the mother of four daughters. She and her husband decided not to have any more children and in October 1977, she underwent a laparoscopic sterilisation. However, in November 1978 she gave birth to a baby boy. There was no dispute about the negligence of the doctor in performing the operation: the only issue was the question of damages.

After the operation, Mrs Udale had complained of pain, particularly after intercourse, and intermenstrual bleeding. She was referred to a psychiatrist and was also prescribed antibiotics and medication for blood pressure. Finally, in July 1978 she discovered she was 16 weeks' pregnant. Mrs Udale stated that she was shattered by the news and was angry at having been deprived of the choice of bearing a child or having an abortion, since it was too late for the latter option. She was also worried about the possible effects on her baby of the medication which she would not have taken had she known that she was pregnant.

In his judgment, Jupp J described Mrs Udale as "a motherly sort of woman, nice looking but rather overweight .... Psychologically, she gave the appearance of being healthy" ([1983] 2 All ER 522 at 526). He continued:

> It did take ... some time for Mrs Udale to settle down to the idea of having a baby. But then things began to change. She is not only an experienced mother but, so far as I am able to judge, a good mother, who has all the proper maternal instincts which make her work long and hard to look after her

offspring. ... Moreover, as she said in evidence, her husband had always wanted a boy and I think she must have wished one of her four children had been a boy (*ibid*).

Jupp J said:
> Mrs Udale was grateful [David] was a boy, she felt it was her reward at the end of it all. Another girl, she said, would not have been welcome. Of [335] course, the housework was (to use her expression) 'colossal', but she went back to her job, as before, when David was not quite a year old. Mrs Udale, to her credit, made no attempt to play down the fact that here was a son, David, who was happy, healthy and, as it turned out, much loved. One is inevitably reminded of the Gospel (John 16:21): 'A woman when she is in travail hath sorrow, because her hour is come: but as soon as she is delivered of the child, she remembereth no more the anguish, for joy that a man is born into the world' (*Id*, at 527).

The defendants did not dispute that damages were payable for her loss of earnings, for the original operation, the shock and anxiety of an unwanted pregnancy, the symptoms of pregnancy which she thought attributable to illness or disease and which led to her taking unnecessary medication; "the very real fear, after the pregnancy was diagnosed, that the drugs may have harmed, even deformed, the child; she must have feared a mongol might be born," and the two further operations. However, Mrs Udale had also claimed damages for the extra costs involved in raising the child to age 16. On those matters, Jupp J concluded as follows:

> The considerations that particularly impress me are the following. (1) It is highly undesirable that any child should learn that a court has publicly declared his life or birth to be a mistake, a disaster even, and that he or she is unwanted or rejected. Such pronouncements would disrupt families and weaken the structure of society. (2) A plaintiff such as Mrs Udale would get little or no damages because her love and care for her child and her joy, ultimately, at his birth would be set off against and might cancel out the inconvenience and financial disadvantages which naturally accompany parenthood. By contrast, a plaintiff who nurtures bitterness in her heart and refuses to let her maternal instincts take over would be entitled to large damages. In short virtue would go unrewarded; unnatural rejection of womanhood and motherhood would be generously compensated. This, in my judgment, cannot be just. (3) Medical men would be under subconscious pressure to encourage abortions in order to avoid claims for medical negligence which would arise if the child were allowed to be born. (4) It has been the assumption of our culture from time immemorial that a child coming into the world, even if, as some say, 'the world is a vale of tears', is a blessing and an occasion for rejoicing.
>
>   I am reinforced in the second of these considerations by the fact that, if I had to award damages to Mrs Udale under the disputed heads, I would have to regard the financial disadvantages as offset by her gratitude for the gift of a boy after four girls. Accordingly ... the last three heads of damage are irrecoverable (at 531).

Jupp J concluded that it was legitimate, "without detracting from the above principles of public policy, to have some regard to the disturbance to the family finances which an unexpected pregnancy causes" (ibid). In fact, he decided that increasing the award for "pain, suffering, inconvenience, anxiety and the like" could take some account of those factors "without regarding the child as unwanted" and awarded £8,000 under that head.

... [T]he English Court of Appeal has twice declined to follow Jupp J's approach. In *Thake v Maurice* [[1984] 2 All ER 513] a case involving a failed vasectomy, Peter Pain J in the English High Court upheld a claim for breach of contract and negligence in failure to warn of the possibility that the vasectomy would not be completely successful. He awarded damages, including for the costs of upkeep, and explicitly rejected the policy arguments put by Jupp J in that case.

> I do not accept that it is part of our culture that the birth of a healthy child is always a blessing. It may have been the assumption in the past. I feel quite satisfied that it is not the assumption today (*id*, at 527).
>
> ... I have to have regard to the policy of the state as it expresses itself in legislation and in social provision. I must consider this in light of modern developments. By 1975 family planning was generally practised. Abortion had been legalised over a wide field. Vasectomy was one of the methods of family planning which was not only legal but was available under the national health service. It seems to me to follow from this that it was generally recognised that the birth of a healthy baby is not always a blessing. It is a blessing when the baby is to be born to the happy family life which we would all like a baby to have. Many people hold that that end can be best achieved by restricting natural fertility.
>
> The policy of the state, as I see it, is to provide the widest freedom of choice. It makes available to the public the means of planning their families or planning to have no family. If plans go awry, it provides for the possibility of abortion (*id*, at 526).

He also dismissed the suggestion that an award of damages would lead the child to feel rejection.*(ibid)* The Court of Appeal rejected the claim based on breach of contract, but upheld the negligence finding and allowed a cross appeal increasing the damages by £1,500. [[1986] QB 644].

In *Emeh v Kensington Area Health Authority* [[1985] 1 QB 1012], a child was born with a congenital abnormality (thereby needing extra care) to a plaintiff who had undergone a negligently performed sterilisation operation, and did not discover that she was pregnant until she was 20 weeks pregnant. The Court of Appeal allowed an appeal by the plaintiff, awarding her damages for loss of future earnings, maintenance of the child to trial and in the future, the plaintiff's pain and suffering up to the time of the trial and future loss of amenity and pain and suffering, including the extra care that the child would require. After considering the decisions in *Udale* and *Thake*, all three members of the Court of Appeal expressed their preference for the approach in Thake [For another English decision following this approach, see *Allen v Bloomsbury* [1993] 1 All ER 651].

A smaller number of analogous cases have come before Australian courts. In *F v R* [(1983) 33 SASR 189], the Full Court in South Australia overturned a finding of negligence in [337] a wrongful birth case [per Mohr J (1982) 29 SASR 437]... More recently, two courts in Queensland have awarded damages for the costs of upkeep of a child. In *Dahl v Purnell* [(1992) 15 Qld Lawyer Reports 31] the male plaintiff had had a vasectomy after which his sperm count did not reduce sufficiently to render him sterile. Unfortunately, a staff member of the surgeon told the female plaintiff (the wife) over the telephone that the sperm count was "okay" which led them to cease using other contraception. She became pregnant and sued, inter alia, for the costs of upkeep of the child. ... Pratt DCJ stated:

> ... I feel that in Queensland 1992, where family planning is officially encouraged, where vasectomy expenses may be claimed on Medicare, and where, although abortion on demand is still illegal, anyone interested is aware that an abortion can be had on demand, at worst, after an hour or two's ride in a motor car or aeroplane to a neighbouring Australian state, the approach of Jupp J in *Udale* ... is positively anachronistic. (*id*, at 35)

Pratt DCJ ... rejected [*the policy considerations outlined in Udale*]. On the fourth, ie, that a child coming into the world is always a blessing, he stated:

[W]hatever the assumptions may have been from time immemorial as to the blessing of children, despite the view from time to time that the world is a vale of tears, the reality for modern Queenslanders is that their children will have to be educated well into their 20s if they are to take a comfortable place in the society of the 21st century. (*id*, at 36).

... [E]very baby, however lovely, has a belly to be filled and a body to be clothed. ... The law relating to damages is concerned with reparation in money terms, and this is what is needed for the maintenance of a baby". (*ibid*)

However, he did take into account the factor of offsetting for the benefits of the child and reduced the award for the costs of "services, physical care and upbringing, past and future" by $1,000 leaving an award of $3,000 under that head, making a total award of $64,561.05.

[338] And, in *Veivers v Connolly* [[1995] 2 Qd R 326], damages were also awarded for the cost of the child's upbringing though ..., they were reduced by 5% to take account of the possibility that the plaintiff may not have been able to terminate her pregnancy. ... [*We discuss this aspect of the decision in a section of the article not extracted here, at 328-30.*]

In *CES v Superclinics,* only Kirby A-CJ addressed these issues in any detail. Meagher JA simply restated some of the *Udale* considerations with approval: the tenor of his judgment suggests, however, that he would not agree that **any** damages could be awarded: to do so would in his view provide "a significant bonus for unnatural motherhood".[21] Priestley JA would have allowed damages to the time of the birth, but treated the claim for the costs of upkeep as not causally connected to any damage flowing from the negligence of the defendants: the plaintiff 'chose' to keep her child rather than give her up for adoption, and this 'choice' constituted a novus actus interveniens, thereby severing the chain of causation. On the issue of adoption, Meagher JA agreed with Priestley JA, though he treated it not as an issue of novus actus, but of mitigation: in his view, since the law requires a plaintiff to mitigate her loss, "why does that not require the mother to put the child of which she vociferously complains out to adoption?"[22]

Notes

1. In his judgment, Meagher JA made clear his disapproval of the plaintiff as follows:

   > The case is not about the morality of abortion; nor is it really about whether the plaintiff would or would not be legally entitled to have an abortion. It is about the question whether a woman may in our courts sue a defendant because he allegedly deprived her of the opportunity of having an operation, with the result that she involuntarily gave birth to a child. Having given birth to a healthy child in August 1987, the plaintiff claimed at a Court hearing in December 1993 that the child, then over six years old, was unwelcome, a misfortune, perhaps a disaster, certainly a head of damages. For all I know the child was in court to witness her mother's rejection of her. Perhaps, on the other hand, the plaintiff had the taste to keep her child out of court. Even if that be so, it does not mean that unfortunate infant will never know that her mother has publicly declared her to be unwanted. When she is at school some *ame charitable* – perhaps the mother of one of her "friends" – can be trusted to direct her attention to the point. That a court of law should sanction such an action seems to me improper to the point of obscenity.

---

21 (1995) 38 NSWLR 47 at 87.
22 *Ibid*.

[*After referring to what he saw as the difficulties of assessment, and the need to discount for the joy a child brings, he continued:*] ... If the mother says of the child "I adore it; it gives me constant and enormous pleasure" presumably a heavy discount should be allowed; if she says "I am indifferent to the brute" only a small discount would be appropriate but if she says "I hate and loathe the child, and have done so ever since she was born" no discount at all would be justified. Thus there would be a significant bonus for unnatural motherhood. Does that not indicate that the law has strayed into an area in which it has no business?

Even that is not the end of the problem. The law ordains that a plaintiff must mitigate her damages. In the present context, why does that not require the mother to put the child of which she so vociferously complains out to adoption? Why should the law treat seriously her claim for the recovery of expenses which she does not need to incur? On this point the judgment of Priestley JA is distinctly to be preferred to that of Kirby P.[23]

How realistic is the suggestion, by both Meagher and Priestley JJA, that the plaintiff could have 'put the child ... out to adoption'? How widespread a practice is giving up a child for adoption in Australia in the late 20th century?[24] Why might the incidence of adoption have declined so dramatically over the past two or three decades?

2. Kirby A-CJ made considerable reference in his judgment to so-called 'policy' arguments. In a discussion of wrongful birth cases in England and Germany, Josephine Shaw has noted that 'policy' is usually used as a rationale for denying recovery.[25] She points out, however, that a number of policy arguments favour recovery. Consider the policy arguments for and against recovery for the costs of bearing and raising an unplanned child.

3. Since the decision in *CES v Superclinics*, there have been other notable overseas cases involving claims for damages for the cost of upkeep of a child born after the child's parents had sought, through medical intervention, to prevent further pregnancies. In a Canadian decision, *Kealey v Berezowski*,[26] the trial judge, Lax J, having found the doctor negligent, awarded damages for the pregnancy, the labour and delivery, and the resterilisation, and also to cover the parents' loss of income during the periods of maternity and parental leave taken after the child's birth. However, she declined to award damages for the costs of upkeep. Lax J noted that 'the underlying rationale for the award of child-rearing costs ... is to ensure that the plaintiffs can meet their financial responsibilities to the child' and concluded that 'this is not a case of economic necessity, imposing unreasonable financial burdens on an impoverished family'.[27] Does this suggest that damages will be available or not depending on the financial circumstances of the child's parents? Is this an appropriate way to decide cases of this nature?

---

23   *Ibid*, at 86-7.
24   Rates of adoption in Australia have declined dramatically from a high of 9798 adoptions in 1971-72 to 543 adoptions in 1998-99. Of those 543, only 127 were local (cf inter-country) adoptions by non-relatives of children under one year old. The other main category is 'known' child adoptions, mostly step-parent adoptions: see Australian Institute of Health and Welfare, *Adoptions in Australia, 1998-1999*, <http://www.aihw.gov.au/publications/welfare/aa98-9/index.html>.
25   Josephine Shaw, 'Wrongful Birth and the Politics of Reproduction: West German and English Law Considered' (1990) 4 *International Journal of Law and the Family* 52.
26   (1996) 136 DLR (4th) 708.
27   *Ibid*, at 741.

4. In 1999, the House of Lords had its first opportunity to consider a wrongful birth case. In *MacFarlane v Tayside*,[28] a couple who had decided not to have any more children made a claim against the local authority for the costs of upkeep of their fifth child who was born after the husband's vasectomy had not been effective. In addition to the claim for the cost of upkeep, they also sought to recover the mother's costs during pregnancy and childbirth. The Lords were unanimous in rejecting the claim for the upkeep of the child, while four of the five judges did allow the mother's claim for costs directly associated with the birth (Lord Millett dissented).

In the course of the judgment, the House of Lords reviewed all the previous UK case law referred to in the extract from the article on *CES*, as well as cases from South Africa, the USA, Canada (*Kealey*), Australia (*CES*) and New Zealand. Significantly, while no member of the Court would have upheld the claim for the child's upkeep, a majority of the Lords rejected the *Udale* public policy approach (which, it will be recalled, was expressly relied upon by Meagher JA in *CES*). They also rejected the argument used by Priestley JA in *CES*, that is, that the failure to have the child adopted (or indeed, the pregnancy terminated)[29] constituted a 'novus actus interveniens' and therefore broke the chain of causation. Lord Slynn preferred to rely upon general negligence principles in characterising the claim as one for pure economic loss and holding that, while reasonable foreseeability was necessary for liability, it was not sufficient. He concluded, emphasising that his decision was not based on 'public policy': 'The doctor undertakes a duty of care in regard to the prevention of pregnancy: it does not follow that the duty includes also avoiding the costs of rearing the child if born and accepted into the family. ... If a client wants to be able to recover such losses he or she must do so by an appropriate contract'.[30] Similarly, Lord Steyn started his judgment by pointing out that the Court of Appeal's decision in *Emeh* (discussed in the extract above), which had for so long been considered authoritative, predated the House of Lords' reconsideration of the test for the existence of a duty of care in *Murphy v Brentwood District Council*.[31] He also noted that a much fuller argument had been put in the House of Lords than was available to the Court of Appeal in *Emeh*. Lord Steyn rejected each of the policy arguments that had been raised, including the view that the joy of the child could be set off against the costs of her maintenance.

> [T]o explain decisions denying a remedy for the cost of bringing up an unwanted child by saying that there is no loss, no foreseeable loss, no causative link or no ground for reasonable restitution is to resort to unrealistic and formalistic propositions which mask the real reasons for the decisions. And judges ought to strive to give the real reasons for their decision. It is my firm conviction that where courts of law have denied a remedy for the cost of bringing up an unwanted child the real reasons have been grounds of distributive justice. That is of course, a moral theory. It may be objected that the House must act like a court of law and not like a court of morals. That would only be partly right. The Court must apply positive law. But judges'

---

28 [2000] 2 AC 59.
29 The suggestion that a failure to terminate the pregnancy breaks the chain of causation was also put, and rejected, in *Emeh v Kensington Area Health Authority* [1985] 1 QB 1012.
30 [2000] 2 AC 59 at 76.
31 [1991] 1 AC 398.

sense of the moral answer to a question, or the justice of the case, has been one of the great shaping forces of the common law.[32]

Lord Steyn concluded:

> In my view it is legitimate in the present case to take into account considerations of distributive justice. That does not mean that I would decide the case on grounds of public policy. On the contrary, I would avoid those quicksands. Relying on principles of distributive justice I am persuaded that our tort law does not permit parents of a healthy unwanted child to claim the costs of bringing up the child from a health authority or a doctor.[33]

He distinguished this approach from one that relies on grounds of public policy, and also noted that it had the benefit of coherence since, as there is no recovery for an action by a child for 'wrongful life',[34] it would be inconsistent to allow the parents to claim for 'wrongful birth or wrongful conception in a case such as this.[35]

Lord Hope noted:

> The question for the court is ultimately one of law, not of social policy. If the law is unsatisfactory, the remedy lies in the hands of the legislature. ... [I]t has not been suggested that the costs of rearing the child are too remote, in the sense that they were not a reasonably foreseeable consequence of the defender's negligence. ... But in the field of economic loss foreseeability is not the only criterion that must be satisfied. There must be a relationship of proximity between the negligence and the loss which is said to have been caused by it and the attachment of liability for the harm must be fair, just and reasonable.[36]

He held that the parents' costs of maintaining the child were not recoverable as damages, as it could not be established that the costs would exceed the value of the benefits the child brought to them. Lord Clyde also expressed his dissatisfaction with relying on principles of public policy in such cases and saw the issue instead as one of reasonable restitution. However, he found it difficult to assess what, if anything, would put the plaintiffs back into the position they would have been in but for the negligence and concluded that, while they had accepted the child into their family, it was not reasonable that they should be relieved of the burden of financial care.[37] Finally, Lord Millett alone of the judges not only rejected the claim for the cost of the child, but agreed with the trial judge that the claim for the costs of childbirth and pregnancy ought also to be dismissed, as 'the advantages and disadvantages of parenthood are inextricably bound together'.[38]

What is the principle of 'distributive justice'? How does it differ from taking into account public policy considerations? Why is the House of Lords so keen to avoid being seen to decide the case on public policy grounds? Lord Slynn also directly referred to the law making moral judgments, while Lord Hope suggested that this was an issue of 'law, not social policy'. How do we distinguish questions of morals, law and social policy?

---

32 *MacFarlane v Tayside* [2000] 2 AC 59 at 82.
33 *Ibid*, at 83.
34 See *McKay v Essex Area Health Authority* [1982] QB 1166.
35 *MacFarlane v Tayside* [2000] 2 AC 59 at 83.
36 *Ibid*, at 95.
37 *Ibid*, at 104-5.
38 *Ibid*, at 114.

5. In 2001, the Queensland Court of Appeal faced a similar issue in *Melchior v Cattanach*.[39] That case involved a negligence action brought by the parents of a child born after the defendant doctor failed to inform Mrs Melchior of the possibility that she might still become pregnant following a sterilisation procedure.[40] Not only did the majority of the court approve the award of damages for the costs of rearing the child, they also expressly disapproved the House of Lords decision in *MacFarlane v Tayside*.

McMurdo P confronted traditional policy arguments directly:

> Whilst recognising that only the crustiest of curmudgeons is not warmed by the miracle of new life, I am far from persuaded that the blessing of parenthood should prohibit or even limit a claim for the modest reasonable costs of rearing to majority the baby conceived as a result of medical negligence following a failed sterilisation performed for socio-economic reasons. ... The benefit argument appeals to some for religious or moral reasons. It has its origins in a past society where children, especially males, were regarded as an economic asset; the larger the family the more likely that enough children would survive to care for the parents in poverty, old age or illness.[41]

In discussing the benefit argument, McMurdo P also quoted Bickenbach's comment that '[n]o court would be moved by the argument coming from a putative father that he should not be required to provide financial support for the child he has fathered on the grounds that he has bestowed on the mother a priceless blessing'.[42]

McMurdo P and Davies JA both strongly rejected offsetting the financial costs against the benefits of having a child. Davies JA stated that weighing the likely prospective good and bad qualities of a child is 'morally offensive', while McMurdo P noted that it was 'not measuring like with like'. Her Honour continued:

> It is only the financial and social burden arising from the negligence that was unwanted, not the child that is consequently born ... [I]n Australian society, we have become accustomed to claimants pursuing tortious claims against insured friends and relatives; we are no longer shocked when a husband sues his wife in a motor vehicle accident case for damages for personal injuries, children sue parents for whom they work when injured in the work place or students sue their school for damages arising from negligence. What then is wrong with a parent or parents claiming damages for raising a child conceived because of medical negligence; this is no criticism of the blameless child but is a recognition of the parent's entitlement to economic loss suffered through the appellants' negligence'.[43]

---

39 [2001] QCA 246.
40 The facts were somewhat unusual, since, while most of the cases simply involve a claim that the doctor failed to warn of the slight possibility of the procedure proving ineffectual, in this case the doctor's negligence was due to a failure to take into consideration an earlier operation when informing the patient of the risks of the sterilisation procedure he performed. He failed to inform the patient that he could not confirm the absence of the right Fallopian tube, that there was a procedure by which it could be confirmed and that, if the tube was present, there was an increased risk of pregnancy (at [72]).
41 *Ibid*, at [49].
42 Bickenback, JE, 'Damages for Wrongful Conception: *Doiron v Orr*' (1980) 18 *University of Western Ontario Law Review* 493, cited by McMurdo P in *Melchior v Cattanach* at [55].
43 *Melchior v Cattanach* at [60].

In the context of discussing whether damages extended to cover private school fees and holiday expenses, McMurdo P commended a modest approach to damages for the reasonable costs of child raising, an approach with which Davies JA concurred. What types of expenditure should be included in such a claim? What, if anything, should be excluded?

Thomas JA dissented and proposed a bar on recovery of the costs of rearing 'a normal and healthy child' born as the result of medical malpractice. His Honour held that while 'the identification of a child as 'a healthy normal child' may present difficulties ... [t]he difficulty of identifying such a child is certainly less than that of assessing and setting-off perceived benefits against perceived burdens'.[44] His Honour noted that the obligations of natural parents to contribute to the maintenance of their children are the 'cornerstone of society' and to transfer that burden to the defendant would be 'unfair and inappropriate' in the circumstances. Thomas JA's limitation seems to apply only to 'healthy' children. Should a distinction apply when the child is born with a disability that requires extra care or support? Who is to decide what is a 'healthy' child and what is a relevant disability for these purposes?

6. Another concern often raised about assessing damages for the costs of raising a child is that the damages are 'too hard to calculate'. This resonates with the federal government's response to the HREOC report on the 'stolen children'.[45] In its submission to the inquiry, the Commonwealth Government gave as a reason for not supporting the payment of compensation the difficulty in estimating the monetary value of losses, on the grounds that '[t]here is no comparable area of awards of compensation and no basis for arguing a quantum of damages from first principles'.[46] What criteria, if any, could be used for assessing those damages? What is done in other areas of law where value must be placed on interests that have no obvious market value? See Shaw's discussion of this issue (refer note 2 above), and note that the Australian Institute of Family Studies has for many years published data on the costs of raising children.[47]

Pregnant tribunals: Biology as destiny?

Early in 1989, a remarkable court action (which did not ultimately proceed) received considerable media attention in Australia. The subject was an application for judicial review lodged by a Melbourne solicitor on the ground that 'the tribunal was pregnant'. The incident is discussed in the following extract.

Bronwyn Naylor, 'Pregnant Tribunals'
(1989) 14 *Legal Service Bulletin* 41-2

[41] Towards the end of 1988 a planning decision of the Victorian Administrative Appeals Tribunal was challenged in the Supreme Court on the novel ground that a member of the tribunal was five months pregnant when making the decision (*GTB Nominees Pty Ltd v Uniting Church Property Trust in Australia and City of Kew*,

---

44 *Ibid*, at [204].
45 *Bringing Them Home*, 1997.
46 *Bringing Them Home*, at 306.
47 See Gregg Snider, 'Measuring the Cost of Children' (1995) 40 *Family Matters* 44. See also Graycar, 'Compensation for the Stolen Children: Political Judgments and Community Values' (1998) 21 *University of New South Wales Law Journal* 253.

Supreme Court of Victoria, 25 January 1989). The grounds of appeal (under the *Administrative Appeals Tribunal Act* [Victoria]) included the allegation that, when the presiding member heard the case and gave her decision, she 'suffered from the well-known medical condition ('placidity') which detracts significantly from the intellectual competence of all mothers-to-be'. The applicant claimed that he had therefore been denied natural justice, on the ground of bias.

The applicant was Garry Bigmore, a Melbourne solicitor who had been one of the objectors at the AAT hearing into plans to rebuild part of a nursing home in a quiet affluent street in prestigious Kew. Mr Bigmore had been acting for himself. He obtained legal advice as the matter was about to proceed and the appeal was then abandoned. Nonetheless he later repeated his criticisms of the tribunal to the waiting journalists outside the court, and to George Negus on the 'Today' television program.

Mr Bigmore, apparently unembarrassed by the implications of his action, said in an affidavit, 'Had I become aware of Ms Smith's pregnancy during the course of the hearing, I would have immediately suspected a likelihood of bias or incompetence on the part of the tribunal'. He is also quoted in the *Age* (26.1.89) as stating, 'the proposition seemed absurd that a tribunal would purport to exercise wide discretions while pregnant'.

... [W]hat would the legal position have been if the case had run? It is clear that, to establish bias in a tribunal such as the AAT, there must be at least a 'reasonable apprehension' of bias (*Livesey v NSW Bar Association* (1983) 151 CLR 288). This commonly means a pecuniary interest, for instance, or a known prejudice which could reasonably be seen as creating an interest in the success of one party. It is not easily shown. There is no expectation that decision makers have no views of their own, or that they will be 'devoid of any sense of moral or social direction'; the issue is 'whether persuasion is a genuine possibility' (Aronson and Franklin, *Review of Administrative Action*, 1987, p 196).

And what was the bias complained of? Mr Bigmore in his affidavit stated his belief that because of her pregnancy, Ms Smith 'might well be unduly biased in favour of a non-profit organisation looking after very old people'. One letter writer commented on this assertion, 'why would Ms Smith be likely to favour a nursing home? A maternity wing, maybe ...' (*Age* 4.2.89). Why indeed might she not favour the interests of nearby homeowners? And what of Ms Smith's (male) colleague on the AAT, who also found in favour of the nursing home?

There was no suggestion that Mr Bigmore or his fellow objectors made any objection on the ground of bias during the AAT hearing (although Ms Smith was visibly pregnant). Nor was there any objection made at the hearing about the manner in which it was conducted by Ms Smith and her colleague, over a period of three days. Further, it was not suggested that there was any evidence that Ms Smith personally suffered from a peculiar condition known to have affected her mental competence at that time.

The argument was, simply, that all pregnant women are intellectually incompetent! This is unsupportable. But even if it could be argued, it would not provide an argument as to bias.

Mr Bigmore cited in support of his assertion of incompetence a passage from Derek Llewellyn-Jones' book *Everywoman*, which says that the [42] pregnant woman 'notes an increasing placidity and drowsiness as pregnancy advances'. She 'no longer has the clarity of mind and precision of thought she had before pregnancy ... she will have to look inwards into the warmth of her womb, rather than attempting to equal Einstein'! This was the basis of his claim that the AAT member's intellectual competence had been reduced.

Few other gynaecologists agree that such a condition exists. And recent doctoral research by Zevia Schneider, a midwife educator, gives a different picture. The women studied, most of whom worked through their pregnancy, if anything showed *improved* performance in a series of regular cognitive tests during pregnancy. Although they all complained that they suffered lapses of concentration or memory, the tests showed the opposite (*Age* 27.1.89). Ms Schneider observed, however, that many Melbourne midwives accepted the myth that women are less competent during pregnancy, and that women themselves sometimes contributed to the myth, by suggesting they were not functioning as well during pregnancy, and occasionally lagging in mood and motivation.

Pregnant women, particularly in the late stages, sometimes say they are distracted by the thought of the imminent changes, lifestyle changes and so on. Just as people going through relationship breakup, dealing with death in the family, moving house or renovating are likely to feel distracted. This is not to say they become less competent, or lose their skills. It is not a question of competence, or bias. GTB Nominees was an attempted remake of an old movie, 'Biology as Destiny'. In this case even the backers withdrew before it had the chance to flop.

Note

1. While the tort cases discussed earlier in this chapter involve women as parties in legal actions, this case provides a rare example of a woman playing a key role in the legal process and having her ability to do so questioned because of her pregnancy – her potential motherhood. It will be recalled that the use of bias challenges against women decision-makers (a constant reminder that women are 'outsiders' or 'fringe dwellers of the jurisprudential community', as Margaret Thornton has described it)[48] is discussed by way of a more detailed case study in Chapter 4. The challenge to the 'pregnant tribunal' resonates with another use of the bias rule to challenge a decision-maker directly on the basis of her marital relationship. In *Kaycliff Pty Ltd v Australian Broadcasting Tribunal*, it was suggested that the chair of a federal tribunal might have breached the rules of procedural fairness by discussing a matter that came before her with her husband, also a legal practitioner.[49]

   In addition to the rules of procedural fairness (the bias rule and the hearing rule), a further ground of judicial review in administrative law is that the decision was 'so unreasonable that no reasonable decision maker could possibly have' made that decision.[50] Might this ground have had a better chance of success in the case of the 'pregnant tribunal'? How many 'reasonable decision-makers' are pregnant? To what extent do these (failed) challenges question the legitimacy of women as judges or tribunal members? Is it conceivable that a male decision-maker would be challenged for bias on the grounds that he might have discussed a matter with his wife?

A connection thesis?

In the 1980s, educational psychologist Carol Gilligan's work on moral reasoning was highly influential in early feminist critiques of law. In her book, *In a Different Voice,* Gilligan developed a thesis based on the argument that women speak in a 'different voice' – instead of reasoning by reference to a hierarchy of rights,

---

48 Margaret Thornton, *Dissonance and Distrust: Women in the Legal Profession*, Oxford University Press, Melbourne, 1996, at 3.
49 *Kaycliff Pty Ltd v Australian Broadcasting Tribunal* (1989) 90 ALR 310.
50 See, for example, *Administrative Decisions (Judicial Review) Act* 1977 (Cth), s 5(2)(g); and *Associated Provincial Picture Houses Ltd v Wednesbury Corporation* [1948] 1 KB 223; *Chan v Minister for Immigration and Ethnic Affairs* (1986) 169 CLR 379.

women resort to a 'web of connection'.[51] Many legal scholars have attempted to incorporate Gilligan's insights about a different voice into legal scholarship.[52] But Gilligan's insights have not been uncritically adopted, either within the legal community or, for that matter, elsewhere. For example, MacKinnon has suggested that Gilligan's work on moral reasoning achieves 'what the special protection rule achieves in law: the affirmative rather than the negative valuation of that which has accurately distinguished women from men, by making it seem as though those attributes, with their consequences, really are somehow ours, rather than what male supremacy has attributed to us for its own use'.[53] MacKinnon has described that voice as 'morality in a higher register, in the feminine voice';[54] it is the voice of the victim, who might speak differently if permitted to do so. 'Let what we say matter, then we will discourse on questions of morality. Take your foot off our necks, then we will hear in what tongue women speak'.[55] Despite these misgivings about the causal basis of this 'voice', it seems fairly widely agreed that Gilligan has correctly observed and described a real phenomenon: viz, 'the ethic of care and connection' and that this ethic is more strongly identified with women than with men.[56]

In an article called 'Jurisprudence and Gender', Robin West refers to the Gilligan position and those identified with it as 'cultural feminism'.[57] She contrasts this with 'radical feminism', as represented by MacKinnon and others like Andrea Dworkin.[58] West argues that, despite the differences in position between radical and cultural feminism, their commonality is the connection thesis, briefly described in the following extract. She begins her discussion by arguing that modern non-feminist legal theory, both critical and liberal, is irretrievably masculine because of its embrace of the 'separation thesis', emanating from such writers as Nozick and Sandel: 'We are distinct individuals first, and *then* we form relationships and engage in co-operative arrangements with others'.[59]

West suggests that:

[T]he cluster of claims that jointly constitute the "separation thesis" – the claim that human beings are, definitionally, distinct from one another, the claim that the referent of "I" is singular and unambiguous, the claim that the word "individual" has an uncontested biological meaning, namely that we are each physically individuated from every other, the claim that we are individuals "first", and the claim that what separates us is epistemologically and morally prior to what connects us – while "trivially true" of men, are patently untrue of women. Women are not essentially, necessarily, inevitably, invariably, always, and forever separate from other human beings: women, distinctively, are quite clearly "connected" to

---

51 Carol Gilligan, *In a Different Voice*, Harvard University Press, Cambridge, 1982.
52 See, for a few examples, Carrie Menkel-Meadow, 'Portia in a Different Voice: Speculations on a Woman's Lawyering Process' (1985) 1 *Berkeley Women's Law Journal* 39; Kenneth Karst, 'Woman's Constitution' [1984] *Duke Law Journal* 447; Suzanna Sherry, 'Civic Virtue and the Feminine Voice in Constitutional Adjudication' (1986) 72 *Virginia Law Review* 543; Paul J Spiegelman, 'Integrating Theory and Practice in the Law School Curriculum: The Logic of Jake's Ladder in the Context of Amy's Web' (1988) 38 *Journal of Legal Education* 243.
53 *Feminism Unmodified*, at 38-9.
54 *Ibid*, at 39.
55 *Ibid*, at 45.
56 The work of Carol Gilligan, and some of the controversy it has generated, are discussed at some length in Chapter 3 of the first edition of this book.
57 (1988) 55 *University of Chicago Law Review* 1 at 2.
58 Relying here on Dworkin's book, *Intercourse*, Arrow Books, London, 1987. We discuss Dworkin and MacKinnon's work against pornography in Chapter 12.
59 Michael J Sandel, *Liberalism and the Limits of Justice* (1982), cited by West, at 2.

another human life when pregnant. In fact, women are in some sense "connected" to life and to other human beings during at least four recurrent and critical material experiences: the experience of pregnancy itself; the invasive and "connecting" experience of heterosexual penetration, which may lead to pregnancy; the monthly experience of menstruation, which represents the potential for pregnancy; and the post-pregnancy experience of breast feeding. Indeed, perhaps the central insight of feminist theory of the last decade has been that woman [sic] are "essentially connected", not "essentially separate", from the rest of human life, both materially, through pregnancy, intercourse and breast-feeding, and existentially, through the moral and practical life. If by "human beings" legal theorists mean women as well as men, then the "separation thesis" is clearly false. If, alternatively, by "human beings" they mean those for whom the separation thesis is true, then women are not human beings. It's not hard to guess which is meant.[60]

... The "connection thesis" is simply this: Women are actually or potentially materially connected to other human life. Men aren't. This material fact has existential consequences. While it may be true *for men* that the individual is "epistemologically and morally prior to the collectivity," it is not true for women. The potential for material connection with the other defines women's subjective, phenomenological and existential state, just as surely as the inevitability of material separation from the other defines men's existential state. Our potential for material connection engenders pleasures and pains, values and dangers, and attractions and fears, which are entirely different from those which follow, for men, from the necessity of separation.[61]

Notes

1. If one accepts West's account, both 'cultural feminism', as she describes it, and 'radical feminism', which she associates with the work of writers such as Catharine MacKinnon and Andrea Dworkin, share a perception of women as intimately connected to others. As will be clear from the extract above, this notion of 'connection' is experienced very differently depending upon whether one adopts a cultural or radical feminist position. West's connection thesis has also come in for considerable criticism, not least because of the argument's basis in biology: see, for example, Joan Williams, 'Deconstructing Gender' (1989) 87 *Michigan Law Review* 801 at 802-3 and Sheila Noonan, 'Theorizing Connection' (1992) 30 *Alberta Law Review* 719. Several theorists have also commented on the failure of the 'connection thesis' to take into account issues of intersectionality: see Angela Harris, 'Race and Essentialism in Feminist Legal Theory' (1990) 42 *Stanford Law Review* 581 at 603; Mary Eaton, 'At the Intersection of Gender and Sexual Orientation: Toward Lesbian Jurisprudence' (1994) 3 *Southern California Review of Law and Women's Studies* 183 at 197; and Patricia Cain, 'Feminist Jurisprudence: Grounding the Theories' (1989-1990) 4 *Berkeley Women's Law Journal* 191. Nonetheless, there are certain resonances between West's connection thesis, and the ways in which women's participation in legal disputes tends to be characterised; that is, as we noted above, women generally are presented in judgments by reference to their relationships; only rarely are they presented in legal discourses as separate independent individuals.

---

60 (1988) 55 *University of Chicago Law Review* 1 at 2-3.
61 Robin West, 'Jurisprudence and Gender' (1988) 55 *University of Chicago Law Review* 1 at 14.

2. By contrast with women's connection being foregrounded – often to their disadvantage – in legal contexts, men most often appear in legal discourses as separate and independent; only rarely is their marital status or role within a family or community mentioned.[62] Yet, perhaps paradoxically, there are a number of cases where men have successfully brought legal actions that arise out of their relationships. For example, in Chapter 4, we discussed the case of the 'lovestruck' solicitor, *Louth v Diprose*,[63] where the plaintiff succeeded in having set aside the transfer of a house to a woman in circumstances where the court accepted his argument that it was unconscionable for her to keep the property as she was found to have taken advantage of his infatuation with her.[64] And, in *Kais v Turvey*, a West Australian court found in favour of a man who claimed that a woman to whom he had given a gift had breached her promise to marry him, thereby invalidating the gift.[65] In that case, the man had moved into the woman's apartment (which she had bought in her own name, before she met him) and offered to pay out her mortgage. The court accepted that at no stage did she intend to transfer any interest in the property to him and therefore, it was held that there was no common intention to do so. However, the court found the fact that she had agreed to marry him critical to finding that the money he gave her entitled him to a share of her flat. Her evidence on this point was that he repeatedly asked her to marry him and eventually she agreed. As she put it in her evidence, 'I had only got engaged mainly to stop him from pressurising me, saying "Let's get married; let's get married", so I thought, "Well if I get engaged he'll shut up about getting married".'[66]

   In a case referred to by the court in *Kais v Turvey*, another man's promise to marry a woman from a neighbouring property who worked extensively on his property was not considered sufficient to give her an interest in his property after he died, even though he had deceived her about his marital status (he had not told her that he had divorced and therefore was in fact free to marry).[67] In that case, despite the disproportionate amount of time Ms Kukula spent working on the man's property compared to the lesser time the man spent working on her property, the court was not prepared to find that a constructive trust was warranted since the work he did on her property, while lesser in time, involved his contributing 'heavy farming machinery'.[68]

3. Another instance of a legal doctrine where men's connection is foregrounded is the (partial) defence of provocation, which can be used to reduce a charge of murder to manslaughter. A high proportion of cases where provocation is raised as a defence involve men who killed their wives or partners after the woman had left, or after she has told him she had decided to leave.[69] *Moffa v R*,[70] discussed

---

62   There is an analogy here with the issues discussed in the beginning of Chapter 6, where we note that in cases involving damages for loss of earning capacity, courts often provide an explanation for why a woman works, while men are simply presumed to engage in paid work as a natural phenomenon. So also men's place in the world is generally (re)presented in judgments as independent of their relationships with others. However, as the cases discussed here show, there are exceptions.
63   *Louth v Diprose* (1992) 175 CLR 621.
64   See the detailed discussion by Lisa Sarmas, 'Storytelling and the Law: A Case Study of *Louth v Diprose*' (1994) 19 *Melbourne University Law Review* 701.
65   *Kais v Turvey* (1994) 17 Fam LR 498.
66   *Ibid*, at 507 per Ipp J.
67   *Public Trustee v Kukula* (1990) 14 Fam LR 97.
68   *Ibid*, at 103.
69   See Jenny Morgan, 'Provocation Law and Facts: Dead Women Tell No Tales, Tales are Told about them' (1997) 21 *Melbourne University Law Review* 237.
70   (1977) 138 CLR 601.

in Chapter 4, is a typical example: there the killing occurred after Ms Moffa had told her husband that she was planning to leave him. Yet the court focused on a range of other factors, and we discuss the varying views of the background facts in our analysis in Chapter 4. Think of the facts surrounding the cases you studied in criminal law that raised the issue of provocation: how many involved killings in those circumstances? See also the data in Chapter 10 that suggests that the most dangerous time for a woman is immediately upon and after separation and see also the stories told in *Blood on Whose Hands?: The killing of women and children in domestic homicides.*[71] There is clear data showing that women overwhelmingly are the ones who end marriages, with many men reporting that the separation was unexpected and came as a 'bolt out of the blue'.[72] Yet the data also show that the repartnering rate for men is far higher than it is for women.[73] How does all this square with the law's tendency to describe women by reference to their relationships, but men as independent individuals?

4. Another important form of connection that is much less focused on individuals is indigenous people's connection to their communities and cultures. In Chapter 9, we discuss a complex family law dispute over a child from the Tiwi Islands between an individual (non-related) caregiver, and the community from which the child came.[74] We also look at a personal injury case involving an indigenous woman whose negligently caused injuries left her unable to have children.[75] The court considered the impact of that loss within the context of the community in which she lived, building upon some well established case law in which courts have awarded damages for non-economic loss to indigenous men whose injuries deprived them of the opportunity to be initiated and therefore become full members of their cultural communities.[76]

In the remainder of this part of the book, we expand on the theme of connection by looking first at issues that affect women via their unique capacity to bear children and, secondly, we explore various ways in which the law can come between the relationship between a women and her child(ren). In the next chapter, we examine the legal aspects of abortion and explore how discourses of 'foetal rights' may be used as a form of control over women. We also discuss an issue that has become extremely contentious in Australia: the right of single heterosexual women and lesbians to choose to mother outside heterosexual relationships. Finally, in the last chapter of this part, we look at the ways in which family law can be used to control, regulate and sometimes destroy women's relationships with their children. We also discuss other ways in which women 'lose' their children and conclude the chapter by looking at some criminal and tort law responses to women losing children.

---

71 Women's Coalition Against Family Violence, Melbourne, 1994.
72 Ilene Wolcott and Jody Hughes, *Towards Understanding the Reasons for Divorce,* AIFS, Working Paper no 20, June 1999 (relying on data from the Australian Divorce Transitions Project); see, for some earlier discussions, Helen Gluckstern and Pauline Presland, *Divorce for Mature Age Women: Why Now?* Family Court Research Report No 11, June 1993, especially at 14; and see Peter Jordan, *The Effects of Marital Separation on Men: 'Men Hurt'* Family Court Research Report No 6, 1985.
73 See Jody Hughes, 'Repartnering After Divorce: Marginal Mates and Unwedded Women' (2000) 55 *Family Matters* 16; this confirms earlier findings by AIFS in 1986 (this is discussed in more detail in Chapter 9).
74 *In re CP* (1997) 21 Fam LR 486.
75 *Namala v Northern Territory* (1996) 131 FLR 468.
76 See *Napaluma v Baker* (1982) 29 SASR 192 and *Dixon v Davies* (1982) 17 NTR 31.

Chapter Eight

Controlling Reproductive Bodies

Introduction

This chapter looks at three important issues in women's reproductive choices: abortion, 'foetal rights' and 'assisted pregnancy'. We have chosen to focus on these three areas for a number of reasons. While all three illustrate the 'connection' theme of this part of the book, each of them highlights a very different aspect of 'connection'. A woman who is seeking an abortion presumably wishes to break the connection between herself and the foetus. Despite this, she may not see the relationship between herself and the foetus as involving an inherent tension (as the law often does); at the same time, she does not necessarily discount the foetus as nothing more than a worthless group of cells. Most feminists would oppose the elevation of the status of the foetus over that of the woman carrying it. The discussion of 'foetal rights' raises the latter point clearly and acutely: if 'foetal rights' become more important than the woman's control over her own body, that is, if we oppose the interests of women and foetuses, are we really recognising the connection between a woman and the foetus she is carrying? Finally, we discuss the heteronormativity of the regulation of assisted pregnancy, illustrating this through discussion of some recent cases and controversies.

These three doctrinal areas also illustrate recurrent themes raised in Part One. Is abortion a private decision? Do understandings of equality help us to resolve who should decide when a woman can have an abortion or whether she should have an operation for the sake of the foetus she is carrying? How has the issue of access to assisted reproduction been seen as 'about equality'? Obviously the three areas we have chosen do not exhaust the field of women's reproductive choices; we do not deal, for example, with all aspects of involuntary infertility and the new reproductive technologies. However, all three areas deal with some crucial questions for women: questions about the relationship between the manufacture of autonomy on the one hand and the construction of 'connectedness' on the other.

ABORTION

Access to safe, publicly funded abortion has been a central demand of feminists. The demand has been variously formulated: for example, as 'the right to choose', as 'every child a wanted child' or 'free abortion on demand'.[1] These demands have been necessitated by criminal prohibitions on abortion.

---

1   Abortion as an equality issue is discussed further below. For descriptions of feminist activity around the abortion issue, see, for example, Karen Coleman, 'The Politics of Abortion in Australia: Freedom, Church and the State' (1988) 29 *Feminist Review* 75 at 89-91; Kristin Luker, *Abortion and the Politics of Motherhood*, University of California Press, Berkeley, 1984; Barbara Brookes, *Abortion in England 1900-1967*, Croom Helm, London, 1988; Rebecca M Albury, *The Politics of Reproduction: Beyond the Slogans*, Allen and Unwin, Sydney, 1999.

A brief legal survey[2]

In the following section, we have chosen to organise the materials we consider under traditional legal categories – criminal law, constitutional law, etc. This is not because we believe that the traditional doctrinal divisions give us any clear understanding of the appropriate legal regimes under which abortion law could be understood or applied. Rather, we want to illustrate the way an issue of central importance to women has played itself out across a very broad range of legal doctrines. However, the categories themselves are obviously permeable. For example, criminal prohibitions on abortion have led to the use of constitutional arguments to defend access to abortion, or to attempts to influence the parliamentary arena, and cases in the civil arena have threatened long-standing interpretations of criminal statutes, interpretations that have allowed Australian women fairly free access to abortion.

Criminal law

There is some doubt as to whether abortion was an offence at common law in England. It seems likely that it was only a common law offence if it occurred after 'quickening' (when the first movements of the foetus are felt by the mother, usually between the 16th and 18th weeks).[3] In 1803, an abortion offence was placed in statutory form, though this did not criminalise women who induced an abortion on themselves, and abortions performed before quickening carried a lesser penalty.[4] A substantial amendment to these provisions in 1861 criminalised a woman's self-induced abortion.[5] This amendment was effectively enacted in all Australian States and essentially continues to be the statutory form of the law in most States in 2002.

By way of example, the Victorian *Crimes Act* 1958 provides:

65. Whosoever being a woman with child with intent to procure her own miscarriage unlawfully administers to herself any poison or other noxious thing or

---

2   For information on some of the countries not covered here, see, for example, Mary Ann Glendon, *Abortion and Divorce in Western Law*, Harvard University Press, Cambridge, MA, 1987; Joyce Outshoorn, 'Abortion Law Reform: A Woman's Right to Choose?' in Mary Buckley and Malcolm Anderson (eds), *Women, Equality and Europe*, MacMillan Press, Hampshire, 1988; Rebecca J Cook and Bernard M Dickens, *Issues in Reproductive Health Law in the Commonwealth*, Commonwealth Secretariat, London, 1986; Kerry Petersen, *Abortion Regimes*, Dartmouth, Aldershot, 1993.

3   See Brookes, *Abortion in England*, at 22 and at 42, note 2; Shelley Gavigan, 'The Criminal Sanction as it Relates to Human Reproduction: The Genesis of the Statutory Prohibition of Abortion' (1983) 3 *Journal of Legal History* 20; and per McGuire J in *R v Bayliss and Cullen* (1986) 9 Qld Lawyer Reps 8 at 11. The common law is also reviewed by Blackmun J in *Roe v Wade* 410 US 113 (1973) at 134-6 where he doubts that abortion was ever a common law offence, even post-quickening.

4   Brookes, *Abortion in England*, at 24; and *R v Bayliss and Cullen* (1986) 9 Qld Lawyer Reps 8 at 11. Brookes notes that the medical profession did not find the 1803 Act 'entirely satisfactory', particularly the quickening distinction as it was 'reliant on women's subjective experience of pregnancy' rather than a medical understanding (at 25). Cf Reva Siegel, 'Reasoning from the Body: A Historical Perspective on Abortion Regulation and Questions of Equal Protection' (1992) 44 *Stanford Law Review* 261 at 287: 'the doctors employed a scientific account of conception to attack the idea of quickening; they sought to discredit the common law's understanding of gestational life, which deferred to the testimony of pregnant woman, and to replace it with a definition of life that deferred to the authority and perspective of medical science'. Cf Barbara Duden, *Disembodying Women: Perspectives on Pregnancy and the Unborn*, Harvard University Press, Cambridge, MA, 1993.

5   See Brookes, *Abortion in England*, at 25-6; and *R v Bayliss and Cullen*.

unlawfully uses any instrument or other means, and whosoever with intent to procure the miscarriage of any woman whether she is or is not with child unlawfully administers to her or causes to be taken by her any poison or other noxious thing, or unlawfully uses any instrument or other means with the like intent, shall be guilty of an indictable offence, and shall be liable to imprisonment for a term of not more than fifteen years.

66. Whosoever unlawfully supplies or procures any poison or other noxious thing or any instrument or thing whatsoever, knowing that the same is intended to be unlawfully used or employed with intent to procure the miscarriage of any woman, whether with child or not, shall be guilty of an indictable offence, and shall be liable to imprisonment for a term of not more than three years.[6]

There seems little doubt that, despite the existence of such laws, women have always sought and obtained abortions. Brookes, writing about England in the early part of the 20th century, documents the trade in 'women's pills' and various remedies for procuring a miscarriage that were passed amongst women; likewise, women traded information on where an abortion could be obtained.[7] Brookes suggests that, for many working class women, abortion, at least before quickening, was not perceived as a crime and the practice of abortion was not usually intensively policed. Similarly, Judith Allen argues that, amongst working class women in NSW in the late 19th and early 20th centuries, abortion was a very common form of 'birth control' and largely tacitly tolerated by various state agencies.[8]

The lawfulness of abortion in Victoria currently rests on the statement of the law to a jury in a 1969 prosecution of a Charles Davidson for four counts of unlawfully using an instrument to procure the miscarriage of a woman and one count of conspiring to unlawfully procure the miscarriage of a woman. Menhennit J focused on the inclusion of the word 'unlawful' in the statutory provisions and directed the jury that the defence of necessity could apply in the following circumstances:

> For the use of an instrument with intent to procure a miscarriage to be lawful the accused must have honestly believed on reasonable grounds that the act done by him was (a) necessary to preserve the woman from a serious danger to her life or her physical or mental health (not being merely the normal dangers of pregnancy and childbirth) which the continuance of the pregnancy would entail; and (b) in the circumstances not out of proportion to the danger to be averted.[9]

The clarification achieved in this direction is that it allows an abortion to be performed not only where there is a danger to life, but where there is a danger to a woman's physical or mental health. It was followed in NSW in *R v Wald*,[10] although the District Court Judge there, Levine DCJ, made it clear that a doctor could also take account of economic and social grounds in assessing danger to a woman's physical or mental health. These factors can presumably also be considered in Victoria. It should be noted that, unlike the equivalent English case

---

6   See also, *Crimes Act* 1900 (NSW), ss 82-83; *Criminal Code* (Qld), ss 224-226; *Criminal Code Act* 1924 (Tas), ss 134-135; *Criminal Law Consolidation Act* 1935 (SA), ss 81-82.
7   Brookes, *Abortion in England*, at 2-7.
8   Judith Allen, 'Octavius Beale Re-considered: Infanticide and Abortion in NSW 1880-1939' in Sydney Labour History Group, *What Rough Beast? The State and Social Order in Australian History*, George Allen and Unwin, Sydney, 1982, at 111; see also Judith A Allen, *Sex & Secrets: Crimes Involving Australian Women Since 1880*, Oxford University Press, Melbourne, 1990.
9   *R v Davidson* [1969] VR 667 at 672.
10 (1971) 3 DCR (NSW) 25.

of *R v Bourne*,[11] the ruling in *Davidson* is not restricted to medical practitioners. In practice, almost all abortions in these two States would be carried out by medical practitioners or, at least, under their supervision.[12]

These two rather flimsy precedents, known as the Menhennit and Levine rulings respectively, are the legal foundation of women's access to abortion in these two States. We use the term flimsy because neither of these judgments has been subjected to direct appellate scrutiny. However, the judgments seem well established and have been effectively approved in other Australian decisions. For example, Helsham CJ in Equity in *K v Minister for Youth and Community Services*[13] accepted the Levine ruling as a correct statement of the law in NSW. In *R v Bayliss and Cullen*,[14] McGuire J held that the analysis accepted in *R v Davidson* also represented the law in Queensland. More recently, the NSW Court of Appeal considered the meaning of the NSW equivalent to s 65 of the Victorian *Crimes Act* in *CES v Superclinics*[15] (discussed in the context of 'wrongful birth' birth cases in Chapter 7). It will be recalled that Newman J at trial had decided that CES's claim for negligence against the doctors who had failed to diagnose her pregnancy could not be sustained as, in his view, abortion was 'illegal'. A majority of the Court of Appeal effectively adopted the Levine ruling and confirmed the legality of abortion in certain circumstances. Kirby ACJ (as he then was) clarified the circumstances in which abortion was not unlawful. He found that the relevant economic and social grounds for assessing the danger to a woman's health included an assessment, not just of her situation at the time of seeking the termination, but also of the effect the birth of a child would have on the woman.[16]

Using constitutional law

Where countries have bills or charters of rights in their constitutions, women have been able to challenge criminal restrictions on access to abortion through constitutional litigation. In the United States, abortion was widely available following the Supreme Court decision in *Roe v Wade*.[17] This was hailed by pro-choice activists in 1973 as the landmark culmination of a long-running political

---

11 [1939] 1 KB 687.
12 Waller and Williams suggests that 'those who operate without possessing proper qualifications, ... are in serious danger of conviction, for they will find it hard to satisfy the requirement of proportion': L Waller and CR Williams, *Criminal Law: Text and Cases*, 9th ed, Butterworths, Sydney, 2001, at 141.
13 [1982] 1 NSWLR 311 at 318.
14 (1986) 9 Qld Lawyer Reps 8. See also the discussion in this case about the effect of s 282 of the Queensland *Criminal Code* (a defence to the child destruction provisions).
15 (1995) 38 NSWLR 47.
16 *Ibid*, at 60 where Kirby ACJ said, in reference to the *Wald* test: 'There seems to be no logical basis for limiting the honest and reasonable expectation of such a danger to the mother's psychological health to the period of the currency of the pregnancy alone. Having acknowledged the relevance of other economic and social grounds which may give rise to such a belief, it is illogical to exclude from consideration, as a relevant factor, the possibility that the patient's psychological state might be threatened *after* the birth of the child, for example, due to the very economic and social circumstances in which she will then probably find herself. Such considerations, when combined with an unexpected and unwanted pregnancy, would, in fact, be most likely to result in a threat to a mother's psychological health *after* the child was born when those circumstances might be expected to take their toll'.
17 410 US 113 (1973). See also the companion case of *Doe v Bolton* 410 US 179 (1973).

battle.[18] In that case, the US Supreme Court struck down as unconstitutional a Texas statute which made it a crime to procure or attempt to procure an abortion unless it was 'an abortion procured or attempted by medical advice for the purpose of saving the life of the mother'. Similar statutes were then in force in a majority of the States.[19]

The constitutional basis articulated by the judges for striking down the Texas abortion law in *Roe v Wade* was the right to privacy, even though such a right is nowhere explicitly mentioned in the US Constitution or the amendments to it. Justice Blackmun, writing for seven members of a nine-member bench, found the right to privacy in 'the Fourteenth Amendment's concept of personal liberty' which was broad enough to encompass a woman's decision whether or not to terminate her pregnancy.[20] Justice Douglas, concurring, presented an even more expansive reading of the 14th Amendment, suggesting that numerous rights came within its concept of liberty, including 'freedom of choice in the basic decisions of one's life respecting marriage, divorce, procreation, contraception, and the education and upbringing of children'.[21] He concluded 'that a woman is free to make the basic decision whether to bear an unwanted child'.[22] It should be noted that the Supreme Court found explicitly that the foetus was not a person and thus not protected by the 14th amendment.[23]

However, the right to privacy did not give a woman an unfettered discretion. As is well known, the court varied the degree of permissible state regulation depending on the stage of foetal development. During the first trimester, a woman, in consultation with her physician, had to be free to decide on an abortion without state intervention. This period of (relative) freedom was allowed because, during this period, mortality rates from abortion were lower than those for childbirth. The state begins to have a compelling interest in maternal health at the beginning of the second trimester, when abortion becomes more medically dangerous than childbirth, and can impose regulations as to the qualifications of the abortionist, the site where the abortion should be performed, etc. At 'viability', the state begins to have a compelling interest in the 'potential life' of the foetus, and could proscribe abortion in this period 'except when it is necessary to preserve the life or health of the mother'.[24]

In early 1988, the Supreme Court of Canada struck down the federal criminal prohibition on abortion,[25] finding that it violated s 7 of the *Canadian Charter of Rights and Freedoms* in that it interfered with 'the right to life, liberty and security

---

18   Janice Goodman, Rhonda Copelon Schoenbrod and Nancy Stearns, 'Doe and Roe: Where Do We Go From Here?' (1971-1973) 1 *Women's Rights Law Reporter* 20 at 20 and 23. Kristin Booth Glen describes this attitude in 'Abortion in the Courts: A Laywoman's Guide to the New Disaster Area' (1978) 4 *Feminist Studies* 1 at 2-3. For descriptions of that political battle, see Lawrence Lader, *Abortion II: Making the Revolution*, Beacon Press, Boston, 1973; Rosalind Pollack Petchesky, *Abortion and Women's Choice: The State, Sexuality and Reproductive Freedom*, Northeastern University Press, Boston, 1985, particularly at 125-32; Linda Gordon, *Woman's Body, Woman's Right: A Social History of Birth Control in America*, Grossman, NY, 1976.
19   410 US 113 (1973) at 118.
20   *Ibid*, at 153. The 14th Amendment states in part that no State shall 'deprive any person of life, liberty or property, without due process of law'.
21   *Ibid*, at 211.
22   *Ibid*, at 214.
23   *Ibid*, at 156-62.
24   *Ibid*.
25   *Morgentaler v The Queen* [1988] 1 SCR 30.

of the person'.[26] Abortion was available under s 251 of the *Criminal Code* of Canada, but only in very limited circumstances: a hospital therapeutic abortion committee (which had to have at least three members) had to approve the abortion and could do so only if the carrying through of the pregnancy would endanger the life or health of the woman. Further, an abortion could only be carried out in a hospital. Four out of five judges in the majority found that the prohibitions interfered with the security of the person, emphasising the procedural restriction on the s 7 right, in particular the delay caused by the need for committee approval. In a more expansive reading of the s 7 right, Wilson J found that not only did the criminal law interfere with the security of the person, it also interfered with the right to liberty:

> [T]he right to liberty contained in s 7 guarantees to every individual a degree of personal autonomy over important decisions intimately affecting their private lives. ...
> The fact that the decision whether a woman will be allowed to terminate her pregnancy is in the hands of a committee is just as great a violation of the woman's right to personal autonomy in decisions of an intimate and private nature as it would be if a committee were established to decide whether a woman should be allowed to continue her pregnancy. Both these arrangements violate the woman's right to liberty by deciding for her something she has the right to decide for herself.[27]

Wilson J also stated:

> [T]he decision of a woman to terminate her pregnancy ... is one that will have profound psychological, economic and social consequences for the pregnant woman. The circumstances giving rise to it can be complex and varied and there may be, and usually are, powerful considerations militating in opposite directions. It is a decision that deeply reflects the way the woman thinks about herself and her relationship to others and to society at large. It is not just a medical decision; it is a profound social and ethical one as well. Her response to it will be the response of the whole person.
> It is probably impossible for a man to respond, even imaginatively, to such a dilemma, not just because it is outside the realm of his personal experience (although this is, of course, the case) but because he can relate to it only by objectifying it, thereby eliminating the subjective elements of the female psyche which are at the heart of the dilemma.[28]

No new federal criminal laws have been enacted (the criminal law is a federal rather than a provincial (State) matter in Canada) and there is therefore no criminal prohibition on abortion in Canada. However, there are other means of denying access to abortion and we discuss some of these below.

Legislative amendment

In 1969, South Australia legislated to reform the law on abortion. The *Criminal Law Consolidation Act* 1935 has provisions concerning abortion similar to the Victorian sections reproduced above, which continue in force.[29] The amendments

---

26 Section 7 provides that 'everyone has the right to life, liberty and security of the person and the right not to be deprived thereof except in accordance with the principles of fundamental justice'.
27 *Morgentaler v The Queen* [1988] 1 SCR 30 at 171-2 per Wilson J.
28 *Ibid*, at 171.
29 *Criminal Law Consolidation Act* 1935 (SA), ss 81 and 82.

in 1969 additionally provide that no offence is committed under these sections if two medical practitioners form the opinion, in good faith,

> that the continuance of the pregnancy would involve greater risk to the life of the pregnant woman or greater risk of injury to the physical or mental health of the pregnant woman than if the pregnancy was terminated.[30]

The termination must be carried out in a hospital or prescribed hospital, except in an emergency, and in these circumstances the opinion of one doctor is enough.[31] This legislation, then, effectively restricts abortion operations to hospitals (no other clinics have been prescribed by regulation as prescribed hospitals) and also requires the certification of two doctors.

The legislative changes achieved in South Australia were, in part, the product of feminist lobbying. The late Jill Blewett has documented the activities of the South Australian Abortion Law Reform Association leading up to the enactment of the 1969 legislation.[32] This group was constantly faced with the dilemma of whether to push for abortion on request or to accept and promote more limited reform: the latter course was adopted, bringing the legislation broadly into line with the earlier UK legislation which 'legalised' abortion in 1967.[33]

An apparently more progressive piece of legislation was passed in Western Australia in 1998.[34] Early in 1998 the West Australian DPP charged two doctors with performing an unlawful termination. The termination had come to the attention of the authorities as the woman concerned had asked to have the foetus in order to bury it in accordance with her religious and cultural beliefs. She had kept it in her fridge and her child described this at his school. The Western Australian Criminal Code,[35] while it had some similarities to the Victorian and NSW legislation referred to above, was not the same and there was some doubt whether the Levine and Menhennit rulings applied in that jurisdiction. The charging of the doctors led to the introduction of legislation by the Hon Cheryl Davenport which would have removed abortion from the Criminal Code altogether. After a lengthy debate, the original criminal offences were abolished and replaced by a new s 199 which provides that:

> It is unlawful to perform an abortion unless
> (a) the abortion is performed by a medical practitioner in good faith and with reasonable care and skill; and
> (b) the performance of the abortion is justified under section 334 of the *Health Act* 1911.

---

30 *Criminal Law Consolidation Act* 1935 (SA), s 82a(1)(a)(i). In determining whether such a risk is involved, 'account may be taken of the pregnant woman's actual or reasonably foreseeable environment': s 82a(3). A further defence is provided where the child, if born, is likely to be seriously handicapped: s 82a(1)(a)(ii).
31 *Criminal Law Consolidation Act* 1935 (SA), s 82a(1)(b).
32 Jill Blewett, 'The Abortion Law Reform Association of South Australia: 1968-1973' in Jan Mercer (ed), *The Other Half: Women in Australian Society*, Penguin, Melbourne, 1975, 377 at 385-6.
33 *Abortion Act* 1967 (UK). For a discussion of UK abortion law, see Sally Sheldon, *Beyond Control: Medical Power and Abortion Law*, Pluto Press, London, 1997. For a comprehensive examination of statutory 'abortion' laws in a number of jurisdictions, see Kerry Petersen, *Abortion Regimes*.
34 *Acts Amendment (Abortion) Act* 1998 (WA).
35 Established by the *Criminal Code Act* 1913 (WA).

Section 334 of the *Health Act* provides that an abortion is lawful if the woman concerned has given 'informed consent'.[36] Informed consent is consent freely given after a doctor has informed her of the medical risks of both termination and carrying a pregnancy to term, and has *offered* referral to 'appropriate and adequate counselling about matters relating to termination of pregnancy and carrying a pregnancy to term',[37] and informed her that counselling will be available if she wants it after the termination or birth. The doctor who imparts this information must be different to the practitioner who performs the termination.[38] So, although two doctors must be involved and counselling must be offered, it is not mandatory to undergo it, there is no restriction on where abortions can be performed and the decision is expressed to be one for the woman rather than for a medical practitioner.[39]

Notes

1. In Victoria and NSW, despite, or perhaps because of, the absence of 'permissive' legislation, only one doctor need be involved and there are many free-standing clinics offering abortion in a non-hospital environment. What criteria would one use to evaluate the success of those statutes that 'legalise' abortion?
2. Although the Supreme Court denied standing to the doctor who attempted to intervene in *Roe v Wade*,[40] it by no means rejected a medical model for the abortion decision. The decision to have an abortion was seen very much as

---

36 If it is not practicable for her to give informed consent, an abortion can be performed if the pregnancy is causing serious danger to her physical or mental health, or serious danger will result if the abortion is not performed (see Health Act 1911 (WA), s 334(3)(c), (d) and (4)). This section was inserted into the *Health Act* by the *Acts Amendment (Abortion) Act* 1998.

37 *Health Act* 1911, s 334(5).

38 Section 334(6). The Act also provides that an abortion cannot be performed after 20 weeks gestation unless 2 doctors from a panel appointed by the Minister agree that the mother has a severe medical condition which justifies the procedure (s 334(7)). It also provides that a dependant (sic) minor (a woman under the age of 16 and supported by a custodial parent) cannot give informed consent until a custodial parent has been informed that an abortion is being considered and has been given the opportunity to participate in consultations with the doctor and counselling (s 334(8)), unless the Children's Court orders that the custodial parent should not be given that information (s 334(9) and (11)). (There is nothing in the legislation which suggests criteria that the court should apply in making such an order; for a general discussion of the common law in relation to minors and consent to medical treatment, especially contraception and abortion, see Morgan, 'Controlling Minors' Fertility' (1986) 12 *Monash University Law Review* 161.)

39 Compare this with the 1998 ACT amendments when the ACT parliament enacted the *Health Regulation (Maternal Health Information) Act* 1998. The Act provides that where an abortion is proposed, a medical practitioner should provide a woman with information about the medical risks of termination of pregnancy and carrying a pregnancy to term, any risks specific to her, any particular medical risks associated with the type of abortion procedure proposed *and* 'the probable gestational age of the foetus at the time the abortion will be performed' and offer referral to appropriate counselling (s 8). The Act contemplates that some of the information which may be provided could include 'materials which present pictures or drawings and descriptions of the anatomical and physiological characteristics of a foetus at regular intervals' (s 14(4)). These are to be approved by a panel made up of five specialists (in neonatal medicine, obstetrics and psychiatry) and two nurses, one of whom is to be a specialist in women's health. Failure to provide information in accordance with s 8 carries a penalty of 50 penalty units (s 7), as does performing an abortion without consent (s 10), which can only be obtained at least 72 hours after the information and referrals have been provided (s 10). However, non-compliance (or, indeed, compliance) with these provisions does not affect the lawfulness of the abortion performed for the purposes of the *Crimes Act* 1900 (s 4 of the *Health Regulation (Maternal Health Information) Act* 1998).

40 410 US 113 (1973), at 125-7.

one to be made in consultation with a doctor.[41] Similarly, the South Australian legislation requires the certification of two doctors, as does the UK *Abortion Act*.[42] The influence of the medical profession can be seen in most countries' abortion laws and Western Australia is one of the few jurisdictions that has at least moved to de-emphasise that involvement. How do you explain this medical involvement?[43]

3. The fact that abortion is recognised as a constitutional right by no means renders access to abortion any less subject to challenge than under purely statutory regimes. Individual US States have enacted a variety of laws attempting to restrict the *Roe v Wade* decision and several of these have been challenged as unconstitutional.[44] For example, in *Webster v Reproductive Health Services*,[45] the US Supreme Court upheld the State ban on the use of public facilities for performing abortions. It decided it was unnecessary to rule on the constitutionality of a preamble to the statute, which provided that 'the life of each human being begins at conception' and that 'unborn children have protectable interests in life, health and well being'. However, it ruled that it was constitutional to provide that, where a doctor reasonably believed a woman seeking an abortion was 20 or more weeks pregnant, the physician was required to determine whether the foetus was viable. It was this aspect of the decision that was seen to be most controversial, as it could have been read as contradicting *Roe v Wade*, which the court in *Webster* refused to explicitly overrule. Scalia J, who was in favour of overruling *Roe v Wade*, berated the court for not explicitly doing so:

> Alone sufficient to justify a broad holding is the fact that our retaining control, through *Roe*, of what I believe to be, and many of our citizens recognize to be, a political issue, continuously distorts the public perception of the role of this Court. We can now look forward to at least another Term with carts full of mail from the public, and streets full of demonstrators, urging us – their unelected and life-tenured judges who have been awarded those extraordinary, undemocratic characteristics precisely in order that we might follow the law despite the popular will – to follow the popular will. Indeed, I expect we can look forward to even more of that than before, given our indecisive decision today.[46]

Is Scalia J correct in suggesting that the court should have 'let go' of the issue of abortion and returned it to the political arena?

---

41 See Kristin Booth Glen, 'Abortion in the Courts: A Laywoman's Guide to the New Disaster Area' (1978) 4 *Feminist Studies* 1. Cf Reva Siegel, 'Reasoning from the Body: A Historical Perspective on Abortion Regulation and Questions of Equal Protection' (1992) 44 *Stanford Law Review* 261 where she discusses the 19th century agitation by doctors in the United States to make abortion unlawful.

42 Indeed, the *Abortion Act* 1967 (UK), s 1, requires the certification of two doctors other than the treating physician.

43 For a detailed exploration of the medical involvement in abortion decision-making in Britain, see Sally Sheldon, *Beyond Control: Medical Power and Abortion Law*, Pluto Press, London, 1997.

44 And for analyses of attempts in various Australian States to restrict access to abortion in the 1980s, see Rebecca Albury, 'Abortion: But I Thought That Was Settled Years Ago' (1989) 31-32 *Refractory Girl* 12; Rebecca M Albury, *The Politics of Reproduction: Beyond the Slogans*, Allen and Unwin, Sydney, 1999.

45 492 US 490 (1989).

46 *Ibid*, at 535.

The language of claims

Privacy

Where access to abortion has been subject to constitutional litigation it has, as we have seen, been justified as an aspect of a 'right to privacy'. We have drawn attention to the problematic nature of 'the private' and the public/private dichotomy in Chapter 2. Catharine MacKinnon has analysed the particular problems of formulating women's demand for access to abortion in terms of a right to privacy. She suggests that:

> To fail to recognize the meaning of the private in the ideology and reality of women's subordination by seeking protection behind a right *to* that privacy is to cut women off from collective verification and state support in the same act.[47]

Elizabeth Kingdom has developed a similar analysis in relation to the use of the slogan 'a right to choose' in the UK. She argues that the demand 'appeal[s] to the values of freedom and privacy' and continues:

> In terms of political philosophy, this means that the concept of free choice is more easily situated in the ideology of liberal individualism, and the right to control one's own body is more easily placed within the ideology of the private citizen resisting the morally illegitimate encroachment of the bourgeois state into private matters, than with the ideology of solidarity and collective decision-making characteristic of much socialist and feminist thinking.[48]

Kingdom is particularly critical of the articulation of an *absolute* right to choose. She argues that it disengages us from social and legal debates to realise access to abortion for all women:

> [I]f it is accepted that an absolute right can have no expression in actual or foreseeable social and legal conditions, then it is a natural, if not a logical, inference that the only social conditions compatible with that absolute right are ones in which there is no relevant legislation at all. In the case of abortion, this would mean not merely the decriminalisation of abortion but also its deregulation. There would be no regulations governing the organisation and distribution of abortion services, no controls over the technical competence of persons performing abortions, and no regulations on safety standards.[49]

---

47 Catharine A MacKinnon, 'Privacy v. Equality: Beyond Roe v Wade' in Catharine A MacKinnon, *Feminism Unmodified*, Harvard University Press, Cambridge, MA, 1987, at 101-2; see also Catharine A MacKinnon, 'The Male Ideology of Privacy: A Feminist Perspective on the Right to Abortion' (1983) 17 *Radical America* 23; Laurence Tribe, *Constitutional Choices*, Harvard University Press, Cambridge, MA, 1985, at 243; Zillah R Eisenstein, *The Female Body and the Law*, University of California Press, Berkeley, 1988, at 187-8. Wendy Brown, 'Reproductive Freedom and the Right to Privacy: A Paradox for Feminists' in Irene Diamond (ed), *Families, Politics and Public Policy: A Feminist Dialogue on Women and the State*, Longman, New York, 1983, at 322, has a similar analysis to MacKinnon's, including an historical perspective on the development of 'reproductive privacy'.
48 Elizabeth Kingdom, 'Legal Recognition of a Woman's Right to Choose' in Julia Brophy and Carol Smart, *Women in Law*, Routledge, London, 1985, at 152-3. See also Brenda Cossman, 'The Precarious Unity of Feminist Theory and Practice: The Praxis of Abortion' (1986) 44 *University of Toronto Faculty Law Review* 85. See also the discussion below on access to abortion after decriminalisation in Canada.
49 *Ibid*, at 158-9. See also Susan Himmelweit, 'More Than "A Woman's Right to Choose"' (1988) 29 *Feminist Review* 38.

Note

1. Jennifer Nedelsky has also argued that 'privacy fosters debate in the pernicious terms of the rights of the foetus versus the rights of the woman'.[50] Do you agree?

Equality

Quite clearly, many women active in the campaign to remove restrictive abortion laws are motivated by an ideal of women's equality. And, as a corollary, some have argued that the opposition to women's abortion demands in America had more to do with fear of the removal of gender subordination than abortion per se.[51]

As Laurence Tribe stated, in a critique of *Roe v Wade*:

> [A]bortion was not perceived as involving the intensely public question of the subordination of women to men through the exploitation of pregnancy, or the equally public question of the subordination of the poor to the rich. ... [A] right to end pregnancy might be seen more plausibly as a matter of resisting sexual and economic domination than as a matter of shielding from public control "private" transactions between physicians and patients.[52]

At first glance, it may appear that women's capacity to reproduce has nothing to do with equality between women and men. For the US Supreme Court, for example, a policy that excluded pregnant women from access to a disability insurance program otherwise available in a workplace was a distinction between pregnant and non-pregnant persons[53] or, as it has been described more pithily by Ann Scales, 'no discrimination exists if pregnant women and pregnant men are treated the same'.[54] As Reva Siegal has pointed out, the court's analysis rests on a notion of 'physiological naturalism' – that physiology determines all.[55] While it remains true that it is women who become pregnant and bear children, the implications of this, the meaning of this biological process, extend far beyond the physiological:

> When abortion-restrictive regulation is analyzed in physiological paradigms, ... the inquiry focuses on questions concerning gestation. By contrast, if restrictions on abortion are analyzed in a social framework, they present questions concerning the regulation of motherhood, and, thus, value judgments concerning women's role.[56]

---

50 Jennifer Nedelsky, 'The Practical Possibilities of Feminist Theory' (1993) 87 *Northwestern University Law Review* 1286 at 1288.
51 See Rosalind Pollack Petchesky, *Abortion and Woman's Choice: The State, Sexuality, and Reproductive Freedom*, Northeastern University Press, Boston, 1984, at 246-7, 252, 262-3; and generally Kristin Luker, *Abortion and the Politics of Motherhood*, University of California Press, Berkeley, 1984, at 159-63 and 199-206; Linda Gordon, *Women's Body, Women's Right: A Social History of Birth Control in America*, Penguin, New York, 1977, at 415; and Donald Granberg, 'The Abortion Activists' (1981) 13 *Family Planning Perspectives* 157 where he notes that most members of the National Right to Life Committee opposed enactment of the Equal Rights Amendment.
52 Laurence Tribe, *Constitutional Choices*, Harvard University Press, Cambridge, MA, 1985, at 243. This view is shared by Sylvia Law, 'Rethinking Sex and the Constitution' (1984) 132 *University of Pennsylvania Law Review* 935. Cf Guido Calabrese, *Ideals, Beliefs, Attitudes and the Law*, Syracuse University Press, Syracuse, 1985, at 97-100.
53 See *Geduldig v Aiello* 417 US 484 (1974).
54 Ann Scales, 'The Emergence of Feminist Jurisprudence: An Essay' (1986) 95 *Yale Law Journal* 1373 at 1399.
55 Reva Siegel, 'Reasoning from the Body: A Historical Perspective on Abortion Regulation and Questions of Equal Protection' (1992) 44 *Stanford Law Review* 261.
56 Siegel, 'Reasoning from the Body', at 265.

There is now a great deal of evidence that public attitudes about whether abortion should be freely available to women are influenced by attitudes about women's role in the paid workforce;[57] that is, that public attitudes reveal a connection between women's claims to equality and reproductive decision-making.[58] Decisions about reproduction involve questions of equality and inequality not just because it is women who bear children, but because of the social circumstances in which women become pregnant and raise children. The Women's Legal Education and Action Fund (LEAF), the Canadian feminist litigation organisation, has endeavoured to present this equality-based understanding of reproductive decision-making in court.[59] They point out that women often do not control the circumstances under which they become pregnant: they may be subject to sexual assault and contraception is often inadequate or expensive. Social and economic support for women during pregnancy is often inadequate and decisions made about pregnancy are often not truly autonomous.[60] Women are overwhelmingly allocated the responsibility of caring for children after birth and 'often do not control the circumstances in which they rear children, because of poverty, inadequate housing, lack of day care, and the structuring of the world of paid work on the assumption that everyone in it – women included – has a life-cycle like the male's and the same freedom from child care responsibilities that has long characterized male workers'.[61] That is, the social as well as the biological implications of pregnancy and child-birth have overwhelmingly different impacts on women and men.[62]

Furthermore, some controls on reproduction have specific effects on particular groups of women, or, in other words, raise issues of class and racial inequality. For example, the cost of contraception particularly impacts on those with lower incomes; women of colour and immigrant women are disproportionately subject to court-

---

57 See, for example, Jonathan Kelley and MDR Evans, 'Should abortion be legal?: Australians' opinions and their sources in ideology and social structure' in Jonathan Kelley and Clive Bean, *Australian Attitudes: Social and political analysis from the National Social Sciences Survey*, Allen and Unwin, Sydney, 1988, at 10 and 16.

58 And see also Reva Siegel's analysis of the historical regulation of contraception and abortion: 'the argument for protecting unborn life that stood at the heart of the campaign cannot be understood apart from the social concerns that motivated the campaign. Men interested in establishing their professional authority over women's role in reproduction encouraged other men to assert their political authority over women's role in reproduction by criminalising the means of controlling birth, each acting to preserve the social order as they knew it. There is no reason to doubt that advocates of criminalising sought to protect unborn life; but it is equally clear that they perceived the unborn as threatened by rebellious middle-class women and teeming immigrant populations, and it is in this context that their judgments about the morality of abortion and contraception must be understood. Those who valued the unborn as worthy of protection valued women as worthy of respect only insofar as they adhered to their social role in the reproduction of life': 'Reasoning from the Body' at 318.

59 See, for example, the factum of LEAF in *Daigle v Tremblay* in LEAF, *Equality and the Charter: 1985-1995*, Emond Montgomery, Toronto, 1996; and the LEAF factum in *R v Sullivan and Lemay* [1991] 1 SCR 489, reproduced in Lynn Smith, 'An Equality Approach to Reproductive Choice' (1991) 4 *Yale Journal of Law and Feminism* 93; and in LEAF, *Equality and the Charter 1985-1995*.

60 Paras XVIII-XX of the LEAF factum and reproduced in Smith, 'An Equality Approach' (1991) 4 *Yale Journal of Law and Feminism* 93 at 115-16.

61 Para XXI of the LEAF factum, reproduced in Smith, 'An Equality Approach', at 116.

62 See also Laurence H Tribe, *Abortion: The Clash of Absolutes*, WW Norton and Co, New York, 1990, esp at 105; Ruth Colker, *Abortion and Dialogue: Pro-Choice, Pro-Life, and American Law*, Indiana University Press, Bloomington and Indianapolis, 1992, Chapter 5. Cf Drucilla Cornell, *The Imaginary Domain: Abortion, Pornography and Sexual Harassment*, Routledge, New York, 1995, esp Chapter 2. For a suggestion that the US Supreme Court is showing signs of adopting an equality approach to abortion, see Christine Bell, 'Case Note: *Planned Parenthood of Southeastern Pennsylvania, et al v Robert P Casey, et al*' (1993) 1 *Feminist Legal Studies* 91.

ordered caesareans;[63] Aboriginal women in Australia have been subject to the forcible use of contraceptives such as depo provera;[64] in the US, pregnant women of colour who use drugs are much more likely to be prosecuted than white women;[65] and women with disabilities have been sterilised, often for eugenic purposes.[66]

It has also been suggested that an equality approach may encourage a move away from a medical model toward the development of abortion services that are controlled by women.[67] This demand could be encompassed either as part of ensuring equal access for all women or as a practice that ends gender hierarchy.

Notes

1. In Australia, because of the absence of a constitutional right to 'equality', it is not easy and probably not even possible to present an equality argument to a court in the context of, say, a criminal prosecution of a doctor for performing an abortion. But the way in which the demand for access to safe, free abortion is conceptualised is clearly important. Would the language of equality allow us more easily to articulate a feminist vision of reproductive freedom and encompass, for example, concerns about sterilisation abuse of minority women,[68] in a way that the more liberal value of privacy does not? How would each framework deal with the decision to abort a female foetus solely on the grounds of its sex?[69] Is the fact that it is extremely difficult to present an argument about abortion in an Australian judicial forum using the language of equality, a reason for pursuing legislative change? Is the political arena likely to be more amenable to equality arguments? For a discussion of the

---

63 See Veronika EB Kolder, Janet Gallagher and Michael T Parsons, 'Court-Ordered Obstetrical Interventions' (1987) 316 *New England Journal of Medicine* 1192, discussed further below.

64 Phyllida Bunkle, 'Calling the Shots: The International Politics of Depo Provera' in *Second Opinion: The Politics of Women's Health in New Zealand*, Oxford University Press, Auckland, 1988, at note 13; see also the report that Inuit women in Canada may be disproportionately offered depo provera as a form of contraception: *Globe and Mail*, 23 October 1991, at A5.

65 See Dorothy Roberts , 'Punishing Drug Addicts who have Babies: Women of Colour, Equality and the Right of Privacy' (1991) 104 *Harvard Law Review* 1419.

66 See the discussion by Brennan J (as he then was) in *Marion's Case* (1992) 175 CLR 218 at 275. This is discussed further in Chapter 11.

67 Petchesky, *Abortion and Woman's Choice: The State, Sexuality, and Reproductive Freedom*, at 129 and 131; Luker, *Abortion and the Politics of Motherhood*, at 98-99, 110.

68 See Kristin Booth Glen, 'Understanding the Abortion Debate: A Legal, Constitutional and Political Framework' [1986] *Socialist Review* 51 at 68; and Susan Himmelweit, 'More than "A Woman's Right to Choose"' (1988) 29 *Feminist Review* 38.

69 There has been a great deal written on selective abortion of female foetuses. See, for example, Betty B Hoskins and Helen Bequaert Holmes, 'Technology and Prenatal Femicide', Kumkum Sangari, 'If you would be the mother of a son', Viola Roggencamp, 'Abortion of a special kind: Male sex selection in India' all in Rita Arditti, Renate Duelli Klein and Shelley Minden (eds), *Test-Tube Women: What Future for Motherhood*, Pandora Press, London, 1984; and Helen B Holmes and Betty B Hoskins, 'Prenatal and Preconception Sex Choice Technologies: A Path to Femicide?', Madhu Kishwar, 'The Continuing Deficit of Women in India and the Impact of Amniocentesis', Roberta Steinbacher and Helen B Holmes, 'Sex choice: Survival and Sisterhood', Robyn Rowland, 'Motherhood, Patriarchal Power, Alienation and the Issue of 'Choice' in Sex Preselection' all in Gena Corea et al, *Man-Made Woman: How New Reproductive Technologies Affect Women*, Hutchinson, London, 1985. For an argument that the selective abortion of female foetuses is legal under the *Abortion Act* 1967 (UK) and can be helpful for an individual woman in the 'here and now', see Derek Morgan, 'Foetal Sex Identification, Abortion and the Law' (1988) 18 *Family Law* 355. See also Cornell, *The Imaginary Domain*, at 77-8, 83-7; and Nivedita Menon, 'Abortion and the Law: Questions for Feminism' (1993) 6 *Canadian Journal of Women and the Law* 103.

language used by politicians in debating legislative change in Western Australian law, see Lisa Teasdale, 'Confronting the Fear of Being "Caught": Discourses on Abortion in Western Australia' (1999) 22 *University of New South Wales Law Journal* 60.

2. Lise Gotell has argued that LEAF's analysis of the right to abortion as an issue of equality is flawed, not because it uses the language of equality, but because it uses the language of victimisation:

> The theme of 'being controlled' and 'lacking control' weaves through this discourse, thereby denying the degree of control which women have always exercised over their reproductive lives. Not only does this representation erase the existence of women's authority, however marginal, over their fertility, it also denies the impact of long-standing feminist struggles to enhance reproductive control. In this process, women's political agency is obscured and a traditional view of women, as passive and in need of protection, is reified in legal discourse for eager consumption by the courts.[70]

We have noted above that women have always sought, and found, ways to control reproduction, even when abortion was completely illegal. However, such access was often dangerous, both physically – women often died from 'backyard' abortions – and legally – there was the risk of prosecution and extortion because of it. While Gotell does describe women's control over fertility as 'marginal', there is a question of whether her critique denies the very limited nature of the agency women have exercised. Is there a way to make equality arguments about abortion while recognising what Kathryn Abrams has described (and we discuss further in Chapter 10) as 'partial agency'?[71]

Morality

Abortion has, unsurprisingly, generated a vast amount of philosophical literature struggling with the morality of the abortion decision. Much of the traditional debate has centred around 'when life begins', with those of an anti-choice or 'right-to-life' perspective taking the view that life begins at conception. Some 'pro-choice' feminists have argued in response that the foetus is merely a 'lump of tissue'.[72] Susan Himmelweit, amongst others, has suggested that this is an inadequate response to the 'right-to-life' position, in part because it does not recognise (some) women's own experience of abortion.[73]

---

70 Lise Gotell, 'Litigating Feminist "Truth": An Antifoundational Critique' (1995) 4 *Social and Legal Studies* 99 at 109.
71 See Kathryn Abrams, 'Sex Wars Redux: Agency and Coercion in Feminist Legal Theory' (1995) 95 *Columbia Law Review* 304.
72 Such a position is described in Susan Himmelweit, 'More than "A Woman's Right to Choose"' (1988) 29 *Feminist Review* 38 at 49-50.
73 *Ibid.* See also Kathleen McDonnell, *Not an Easy Choice: A Feminist Re-Examines Abortion*, South End Press, Boston, 1984, esp Chapter 2; Carol Gilligan, *In a Different Voice*, Harvard University Press, Cambridge, MA, 1982, at 70 et seq; and in 'Feminist Discourse, Moral Values and the Law' (1985) 34 *Buffalo Law Review* 11 at 38: 'The way in which women were talking about the moral problem in abortion did not fit the public discussion of abortion in this country. In other words, it was *not* constructed as an adversary fight between the mother and the fetus. In fact, the whole dilemma arose from the very connection between them'.

Catriona MacKenzie suggests that feminist analyses that justify 'the demand for abortion in terms of a right to an evacuated uterus, rather than a right to autonomy with respect to one's own life' are inadequate.[74] She argues that:

> To think that the question of autonomy in abortion is just a question about preserving the integrity of one's body boundaries, and to see the fetus merely as an occupant of the woman's uterus, is thus to divorce women's bodies from their subjectivities. Ironically, it comes close to regarding women's bodies as simply fetal containers – the very charge that many feminists have leveled against the fetal rights movement. ... It is because of ... [the] psychic and bodily connectedness between the woman and the fetus that in pregnancy questions about the fate of the fetus cannot be separated from the issue of a woman's right to self-determination.
>
> ... What the abortion decision involves is a decision that this part of herself should not *become* a being in relation to whom ... questions of parental responsibility and emotional attachment arise.[75]

Notes

1. If a foetus could be kept alive if removed from a woman's uterus at, say, eight weeks, do you think she should have the right to decide on the fate of that foetus, including deciding that it should not be kept alive?[76]
2. Catharine MacKinnon addresses both the 'lump of tissue' argument and the question of who is to decide:

   > My stance is that the abortion choice must be legally available and must be *women's*, but not because the fetus is not a form of life. In the usual argument, the abortion decision is made contingent on whether the fetus is a form of life. I cannot follow that. Why should women not make life or death decisions?[77]

Abortion in practice

There is often a disjunction between the apparent availability of abortion according to the 'law in the books' as compared to its actual availability. That is, the law can apparently restrict the availability of abortion, yet, in practice, it is relatively easily obtainable; alternatively, restrictions in legislation may be minimal and, yet, practically, abortion is not easily accessible because it is, say, not publicly funded.

Public funding

One of the most obvious prerequisites to the actual accessibility of abortion is adequate government funding. Catharine MacKinnon has pointed out that the rhetoric of the right to privacy used in *Roe v Wade* also provided the appropriate constitutional framework for a judicial upholding of the 'Hyde Amendment' in

---

74 Catriona MacKenzie, 'Abortion and Embodiment' (1992) 70 *Australian Journal of Philosophy* 136 at 150.
75 *Ibid*, at 151-2.
76 See Peter Singer and Deane Wells, *Making Babies: The New Science and Ethics of Conception*, Scribners Sons, NY, 1985, at 135; and Leslie Cannold's response, in Leslie Cannold, *The Abortion Myth: Feminism, Morality, and the Hard Choices Women Make*, Allen and Unwin, Sydney, 1998, esp at xxi-xxiv.
77 *Feminism Unmodified*, at 94.

Harris v McRae,[78] which effectively blocked federal funding for abortion in the USA.[79] As she argues:

> To guarantee abortions as an aspect of the private, rather than of the public, sector is to guarantee women a right to abortion subject to women's ability to provide it for ourselves. This is to guarantee access to abortion only to some women on the basis of class, not to women *as women*.[80]

Accepting the rhetoric of abortion as a private decision relieves the state of its social responsibility to make that right real and accessible for all women. In MacKinnon's words again: 'It is apparently a very short step from that which the government had a duty *not* to intervene in to that which it has *no* duty to intervene in'.[81]

Similarly, Elizabeth Kingdom argues that demand for abortion without restrictions is fundamentally incompatible with demands by English feminists for 'mandatory provision of abortion facilities under the National Health Service'.[82]

In Australia, abortion is a claimable item under the Federal Government's Medicare system and some 77,000 terminations are performed each year and paid for through the Medicare system.[83] In 1979, the federal parliament debated the so-called 'Lusher Amendment', a private member's bill introduced by Stephen Lusher, MP, which would have amended the *Health Insurance Act* 1973 (Cth) to remove government funding for all abortions (except those performed in public hospitals).[84] After a lengthy debate, the amendment was defeated and the parliament in fact passed the 'Simon Amendment' which stated:

> That this House is of the opinion that the Commonwealth Government should not pay any medical benefits for or in relation to the termination of a pregnancy unless the procedure is performed in accordance with the law of a State or Territory.[85]

Why do you think the 'Hyde Amendment' passed and was upheld by the Supreme Court in the United States, but the 'Lusher Amendment' failed in Australia?[86]

---

78 448 US 297 (1980).
79 Under the Medicaid program, the US provides financial assistance to States to provided health care for the poor. The 'Hyde Amendment' restricted federal funding to abortions where the life of the mother would be endangered if the fetus was carried to term and to victims of reported rape or incest. (In fact there were various 'Hyde Amendments', some more, some less restrictive than the one under challenge in *Harris v McRae*.)
80 'The Male Ideology of Privacy: A Feminist Perspective on the Right to Abortion' (1983) 17 *Radical America* 23 at 24.
81 Catharine A MacKinnon, 'Privacy v Equality: Beyond Roe v Wade', at 96.
82 Kingdom, 'Legal Recognition of a Woman's Right to Choose', at 159.
83 In the year 1994-95, there were 77,231 payments under the Medicare scheme for 'evacuation of gravid uterus by curettage' (figures supplied by the Health Insurance Commission). Cf Pamela Adelson, Michael Frommer and Edith Weisberg, 'Termination of Pregnancy in New South Wales, 1990' (1996) 20 *ANZ Journal of Public Health* 64.
84 Abortion would also have been a claimable item if it was performed to 'protect the life of the mother from a pathological condition and that the life could be protected in no other way' and a doctor so certified. See Parliamentary Debates, House of Representatives, 21 March 1979, at 963.
85 Parliamentary Debates, House of Representatives, 21 March 1979, at 967. Some of the political agitation surrounding the Lusher motion is described in Karen Coleman, 'The Politics of Abortion in Australia' (1988) 29 *Feminist Review* 75 at 89-91; and see also Judith Allen, *Sex & Secrets*, at 211, 214.
86 On the general issue of abortion funding, see Kerry Petersen, 'The Public Funding of Abortion Services: Comparative Developments in the United States and Australia' (1984) 33 *International and Comparative Law Quarterly* 158. In 1988, the NSW Legislative Council voted in favour, in a very close vote, of a motion put by Upper House Festival of Light member Marie Bignold which

'Hospital autonomy' and 'free speech'

We have noted above that the Supreme Court of Canada held in *Morgentaler* that the previous restrictions on access to abortion in Canada were unconstitutional and that no further criminal provisions have been enacted. However, Hester Lessard has demonstrated that this apparent constitutional success may have been somewhat of a pyrrhic victory in terms of practical access to abortion services.[87] The Supreme Court has decided that the Charter is designed to protect against the actions of the state or government – the state or government action doctrine – and not against the actions of non-state or private actors.[88] Furthermore, it decided in *Vancouver General Hospital* that, despite the fact that that hospital was largely government funded and that the government appointed the vast majority of its board members, it was a private entity. This meant that hospitals that chose to respond to an 'anti-abortion constituency' by restricting access to abortion could not be challenged.[89]

Abortion clinics in many countries have been subject to persistent demonstrations by anti-choice protesters.[90] In 1995, British Columbia enacted legislation which 'creates access zones, colloquially called "bubble zones", around the homes and offices of doctors who provide abortion services' and around the homes of other employees.[91] In these zones, no protest activity is permitted. Such zones were created around two free-standing clinics in Vancouver where protest activity in previous years had included blockades interrupting access to the clinic, wiring of the clinic doors shut, graffiti on clinic walls including 'unwanted children murdered here' and 'Auschwitz again' and the carrying of signs saying things like 'only one of the people that enter this

---

(cont)
      condemned abortion and its public funding. This has no legal effect. See Rebecca Albury, 'Abortion: But I Thought That Was Settled Years Ago' (1989) 31-32 *Refractory Girl* 12. For some general discussion of the differences in the debate about abortion in the US and Australia, see Rebecca M Albury, *Beyond the Slogans: The Politics of Reproduction*, Allen and Unwin, Sydney, 1999, at 59-60.

87 Hester Lessard, 'Health Care in Canadian Constitutional Law' (1993) 2 *Annals of Health Law* 121. This is discussed at more length in Chapter 2.

88 See Lessard, 'Health Care', at 138-44, discussing *McKinney v University of Guelph* (1990) 76 DLR (4th) 545, *Douglas/Kwantlen Faculty Association v Douglas College* (1990) 77 DLR (4th) 94 and *Vancouver General Hospital* (1990) 76 DLR (4th) 700; cf Hester Lessard, 'The Idea of the "Private": A Discussion of State Action Doctrine and Separate Spheres Ideology' (1986) 28 *Dalhousie Law Journal* 107.

89 Lessard, 'Health Care', at 141. But see now *Eldridge v Attorney General of British Columbia and Medical Services Commission* [1997] 3 SCR 624 where the Supreme Court found that the Charter did apply to a hospital and its failure to provide interpreters for deaf patients stating that it 'applies to private entities in so far as they act in furtherance of a specific government policy or program': at para 42. See Margot Young, 'Change at the Margins: *Eldridge v British Columbia (AG)* and *Vriend v Alberta*' (1998) 10 *Canadian Journal of Women and the Law* 244.

90 For the UK, see *Morrow v DPP* [1994] Crim LR 58. In the US and in Canada, abortion providers have been violently attacked and on occasion killed; for the US, see Marlene Gerber Fried (ed), *From Abortion to Reproductive Freedom: Transforming a Movement*, South End Press, Boston, MA, 1990, at 195; and for Canada, *R v Lewis* (1996) 139 DLR (4th) 480 esp at para 46, describing the shooting of an abortion provider at his home in Vancouver in 1994.

91 *Lewis*, at para 1. See the *Access to Abortion Services Act*, SBC, 1995, c 35. The preamble to the Act states: 'WHEREAS all people in British Columbia are entitled to access to health care, including abortion services; AND WHEREAS all people who use the British Columbia health care system, and who provide services for it, should be treated with courtesy and with respect for their dignity and privacy' (cited in *Lewis*, at para 36).

[building] will come out alive'.[92] Protesters had also engaged in 'sidewalk counselling', approaching those likely to enter the building and accusing them of being murderers[93] and handing them pamphlets 'which purport to describe abortion',[94] and had recorded licence plate numbers of those visiting the clinic.[95] The Supreme Court of British Columbia stated:

> Although much of the protest activity has been described as peaceful, in my view that is a mischaracterization. Peace connotes harmony. There is, on the evidence tendered at trial, no harmony here between protesters and those entering the clinic. At its most benign the protest activity could be described as non-violent.[96]

The case arose out of the prosecution of an anti-choice protester, Lewis, who had breached the 'bubble zone' (an area some 25 metres around the clinic), 'wearing a sandwich board bearing an image centred on the board. Above the image were the words: "Our Lady of Guadalupe, Patron of the Unborn"[.] Below the image were the words: "Please help us stop abortion"[.] The words "stop abortion" were in large print'.[97] Was the Act valid? The BC Supreme Court confirmed that the Act 'infringe[d] Mr Lewis' freedom of conscience and religion [*contrary to s 2(a) of the Charter*] by limiting his ability to manifest his conscientiously held, religiously-based views at the place he considers most effective for their communication'.[98] However, the *Canadian Charter of Rights and Freedoms* contains a further provision, in s 1, which allows a parliament to enact legislation that, even though it infringes a right in the Charter, is 'a reasonable limit prescribed by law as can be demonstrably justified in a free and democratic society'. The court concluded that the government had discharged its burden under this section and the Act should be upheld. Although it was difficult for the government or the clinics to provide evidence from women who had used the service (or tried to), of their distress for privacy reasons, 'the evidence … [was] sufficient to identify a concern for those persons' well-being, in addition to concerns for their privacy and dignity'.[99] It was also reasonable for the government to take account of the shootings of abortion service providers in Canada and the US, and threats to the clinics, so that some measure of protection should be provided to ensure continuing provision of abortion services in the province.[100] Further, the government could legitimately consider the invasion of privacy of the women using the clinic, given that the protesters photographed them and recorded their car licence plate numbers.[101] The court stated:

> While non-violent, even passive, expression of disapproval is captured by this Act, the evidence establishes that such activity, in the context of the well-known history of vigorous protest and the vulnerable nature of many of those who enter the clinic, is contrary to the well-being, privacy and dignity of those using the clinics' services. …

---

92 *Lewis*, paras 20-23.
93 *Ibid*, at para 27.
94 *Ibid*, at para 29.
95 *Ibid*, at para 25.
96 *Ibid*, at para 32. Note also that '[i]n response to the protest activity, the clinic has a high security level. It does not have windows. Entrance is through one door only, a double "persontrap" arrangement with bars on the exterior door' (*ibid*, at para 34).
97 *Ibid*, at para 54.
98 *Ibid*, at para 65.
99 *Ibid*, at para 95.
100 *Ibid*, at paras 96-97.
101 *Ibid*, at para 98.

The objective of reducing the tension and negative environment created by this protest, for those persons employed by the clinic also has significant value.

Health care has fundamental value in our society. A woman's right to access health care without unnecessary loss of privacy and dignity is no more than the right of every Canadian to access health care.[102]

Note

1. Although considerations of women's equality may have influenced the court's decision in *Lewis* – for example, one factor mentioned was the basic necessity to ensure continued access to abortion clinics – the court appears to emphasise the privacy rights of women who seek access to abortion clinics as justifying the legislation. Do you think the decision would have been stronger if it was articulated in terms of equality and reproductive choice? How could this have been done? Is it likely that interpretations of the state or government action doctrine, which construct various health providers as 'private', would be influenced by decisions in totally different legal doctrinal areas that construct reproductive decisions as private?

Public opinion and abortion

Whilst so-called 'pro-life' lobby groups attract a great deal of media attention, survey data indicate that they do not represent the views of a majority of Australians. Two major surveys of attitudes to abortion have been undertaken in Australia, in 1984-85 and 1996-97.[103] In both surveys there was a strong consensus that abortion should be legally available where, for example, 'there is a strong chance of a *serious defect* in the baby', 'if the family has a very low income and cannot afford any more children' and 'if she is not married and does not want to marry the man'.[104] In terms of changes over time:

> [T]here has been a sharp movement away from both extremes towards the middle. First, if the baby would be seriously defective [*sic*], the proportion taking an extreme position pro or con – saying either definitely yes or definitely not – shrank from 80% to 60% over the period. That is a dramatic change. Moreover it is echoed in opinion shifts on abortions in milder situations. For abortion in the case of poverty, the proportion taking an extreme position pro or con shrinks from 65% to 41%. And on allowing abortion for an unmarried woman, the extremes pro or con also drop from 65% to just 41%.
>
> This dramatic moderation of opinion makes abortion a more tractable political issue than it was in the 1980s. Instead of an intractable conflict between entrenched positions pro and con, we see a full spectrum of opinion with the majority near the center. For most Australians, abortion is no longer a black and white issue, but much less of a clear issue, perhaps because more people see both

---

102 *Ibid*, at paras 130 and 147-148.
103 See Jonathan Kelley and MDR Evans, 'Should abortion be legal?', at 3, for the 1984-85 survey and Jonathan Kelley and MDR Evans, 'Attitudes toward abortion: Australia in comparative perspective' (1999) 2 *Australian Social Monitor* 83 for the later survey and comparisons between the two and with overseas data.
104 For example, in the 1996-97 survey, 89% of respondents said that a legal abortion should definitely or probably be allowed if there is a strong chance of a serious defect in the baby, 69% said the same if poverty was the reason and 68% approved if she is not married and does not want to marry the man.

good and harm resulting. This is ... in contrast to the pattern of polarisation which some observers have claimed for the US ....[105]

The strongest predictor of opposition to abortion was Christian churchgoing, with Catholics more opposed than those of other denominations.[106] Disapproval of premarital sex is also a strong predictor of opposition to abortion: 'people strongly opposed to premarital sex oppose abortion because they see fear of an unwanted pregnancy as a useful deterrent to premarital sex'.[107] Further:

> Although less important than any of these other cultural influences, endorsement of traditional women's roles increases opposition to abortion .... This is less than half as important as church-going, religious belief or opposition to premarital sex. It seems reasonable to follow previous research in interpreting this effect as reflecting a relatively rare, but not absent, desire to limit women's freedom to engage in non-traditional roles by increasing their childbearing – to 'keep them in the kitchen' by keeping them pregnant.[108]

Note

1. Do you have any views on why attitudes to abortion appear to have become less polarised in Australia over the past 10 to 15 years? Kelley and Evans argue that their regression analysis of intercountry data show that the reasons for opposition to abortion – for example religious belief – are the same in all the countries surveyed. Hence: 'While Americans are more opposed to abortion than Australians, ... the reason for that is that they are more religious. ... Australians as religiously devout and sexually conservative as the average American would be just as opposed to abortion as the average American'.[109] If religious differences between Australia and the US explain the difference between attitudes to abortion in the two countries, what relevance does a decision like *Roe v Wade* have in shaping attitudes?

Who decides whether a woman can have an abortion?

We have drawn attention above to the issue of medical control of the abortion decision. In Australia, England and North America, there has also been litigation by putative fathers who wish to participate in the decision to have an abortion. In the US after *Roe v Wade*, many States enacted legislation which they hoped would avoid the impact of the Supreme Court's decision. Before *Webster*, many of these

---

105 Kelley and Evans, 'Attitudes', 1999, at 86. Interestingly, Australians are more liberal towards abortion than most other countries included in the International Social Survey Program (though results from Japan, where abortion is widely practised as a form of birth control, are not included). Great Britain, New Zealand and Australia report similar levels of acceptance, with Hungary showing even less opposition (see Table 1, at 87).
106 Kelley and Evans, 'Attitudes', 1999, at 86-7. In the earlier article, Kelley and Evans make the point that the majority of Catholics have more favourable views than traditional Catholic doctrine would enjoin. See Jonathan Kelley and MDR Evans, 'Should abortion be legal?', at 3.
107 Kelley and Evans, 'Attitudes', 1999, at 87. Cf Jonathan Kelly, MDR Evans and Bruce Headey, 'Moral Reasoning and Political Conflict: The Abortion Controversy' (1993) 44 *British Journal of Sociology* 589.
108 Kelley and Evans, 'Attitudes', 1999, at 87.
109 *Ibid*, at 89. They also argue that when religion and other social factors are controlled for, 'Ireland, West Germany, Northern Ireland, East Germany, the Netherlands and Norway remain more opposed to abortion than Australians – something in their culture and history, quite apart from religion and sexual attitudes, predisposes them against abortion' (*ibid*).

provisions had been declared unconstitutional. For example, Missouri enacted a law which required spousal consent before an abortion could be performed. In *Planned Parenthood of Central Missouri v Danforth, Attorney-General of Missouri*,[110] the US Supreme Court declared the Missouri statute unconstitutional saying:

> [S]ince the State cannot regulate or proscribe abortion during the first stage when the physician and his patient make that decision, the State cannot delegate authority to any particular person, even the spouse, to prevent abortion during that same period.[111]

Similarly, the US Supreme Court has rejected mandatory parental consent laws for minors' abortions.[112]

In the English case, *Paton v Trustees of BPAS*,[113] Sir George Baker P rejected an application for an injunction by a husband to restrain his wife from having an abortion. The court decided that the foetus had 'no right of its own, at least until it is born and has a separate existence from the mother'[114] and concluded, in relation to the father's rights, that '[p]ersonal family relationships in marriage cannot be enforced by the order of a court'.[115]

A similar view was taken by Gibbs CJ in *Attorney-General (Qld) (ex rel Kerr) v T*.[116] Mr Kerr and Ms T had sexual intercourse on one occasion and she became pregnant. After Ms T rejected Kerr's offer to live with her, to maintain her through the pregnancy and then have the child adopted, Kerr applied for an injunction to restrain her from having an abortion. In the High Court, Gibbs CJ discussed the hesitation courts have in using the civil law to prevent breaches of the criminal law. He concluded:

> It would seem to me quite unjustifiable, in the circumstances of the present case, to assume that the respondent would be convicted by a jury of an offence against s 225 of the Code if she proceeded to have an abortion, and on that assumption to interfere in the most serious way with her liberty of action.[117]

And Gibbs CJ agreed with the court's decision in *Paton* that 'a foetus has no right of its own until it is born and has a separate existence from its mother'.[118] The court concluded:

> There are limits to the extent to which the law should intrude upon personal liberty and personal privacy in the pursuit of moral and religious aims. These limits would be overstepped if an injunction were to be granted in the present case.[119]

---

110   428 US 52 (1976).
111   *Ibid*, at 69. Cf *Planned Parenthood v Casey* 505 US 833 (1992).
112   *Planned Parenthood v Casey* 505 US 833 (1992): it is constitutional for a state to provide that an unemancipated minor under 18 can only get an abortion if either one of her parents consents, or a judge determines that she is mature and capable of consenting. Cf *Planned Parenthood v Danforth* 428 US 52 (1976); cf *Bellotti v Baird* 443 US 622 (1979); *HL v Matheson* 450 US 398 (1981); *Akron v Akron Center for Reproductive Health, Inc* 462 US 416 (1983); *Planned Parenthood v Ashcroft* 462 US 476 (1983). And see also *K v Minister for YACS* [1982] 1 NSWLR 311 concerning a minor in the care of a Minister and, for the UK, *Re P (A minor)* (1982) 80 LGR 301.
113   [1978] 2 All ER 987.
114   *Ibid*, at 989.
115   *Ibid*, at 990.
116   (1983) 57 ALJR 285; see also *C v S* [1987] 1 All ER 1230.
117   (1983) 57 ALJR 285 at 286.
118   *Ibid*.
119   *Ibid*.

In another Australian case, *In Marriage of F*,[120] Lindenmayer J found that the Family Court did have jurisdiction to grant an injunction to prevent a woman who was estranged from her husband from having an abortion, although he declined to exercise the jurisdiction in the particular case.

> At the time of the hearing Ms F was 15 weeks pregnant. She had been married for some 5 years and she and her husband had one child, then almost four. Mr and Ms F, according to the court, had made a deliberate decision to have another child in March 1989. On 28 June, Ms F left the former matrimonial home. ... She stated that part of the reason she decided to try to get pregnant was she thought it 'would bring the parties closer together'.[121]

According to the court:

> The wife says that she decided to terminate the pregnancy because, contrary to her expectations, it was not enough to bring her and the husband together and because she had fallen pregnant for the wrong reasons.[122]

Ms F told the court she had formed a relationship with another man and that her marriage was finished. The court continued:

> The husband's reasons for seeking to restrain the wife's intended termination of the pregnancy ... are:
> (1) that he does not believe in "killing a child"; and
> (2) that because he and the wife both planned the child, he feels it was a joint decision and he "wanted to have another child".
>
> The first of these reasons is, of course, an emotive one and it is a matter of violent public debate whether an abortion amounts to the killing of a child. That is really a moral or ethical question and it is not a question which this court, or any court, for that matter, is required to answer. This court, like any other, is concerned with legal rights and obligations, not moral or ethical ones. My task is to interpret and apply the law, not any particular moral or ethical precepts.
>
> The husband went on to say that he does not have a clear-cut moral objection to abortion in all circumstances, but that he believes that when two people have planned to have a baby, as he and his wife have done in this case, the child should not be denied life. He said further that the fact of the parties' separation has not changed his mind about that.
>
> He has offered to accept the wife's decision as to custody of the child when it is born and to support her through her pregnancy and afterwards, as may be required, and he has expressed the opinion that he is capable of doing so from the income of his business. He denied that his present application is motivated by a desire to force the wife to return to him.
>
> The wife says that she accepts the sincerity of the husband's offer to support her through her pregnancy and beyond, but she is concerned about whether that support will be there in reality.

The Family Court held that it had jurisdiction to entertain the action arising out of the general injunction power in s 114 of the *Family Law Act* 1975 (Cth). This gives the court power to grant injunctions in respect of 'matrimonial causes' including (s 4(1)(e)) 'proceedings between the parties to a marriage for an order or injunction in circumstances arising out of the marital relationship ...'. Lindenmayer J said:

---

120 (1989) 13 Fam LR 189.
121 *Ibid*, at 191.
122 *Ibid*, at 191-2.

> It seems to me that there is perhaps no more fundamental personal relationship between spouses than the relationship involved in the procreation of children, and the question whether a pregnancy which the wife has undergone as a result of an agreement between the parties to have a child should be terminated or should continue.[123]

Having decided that the Family Court had jurisdiction, the court then considered whether this particular application should be granted. It rejected the husband's application stating:

> First, the marriage does appear to have broken down. The wife has formed a relationship with another man which she desires and intends to pursue. Thus the underlying and fundamental basis upon which the parties embarked upon the procreation of their intended offspring, namely the continuation of the marriage and the nurturing of that child within that relationship, has now disappeared.
>
> Secondly, to grant the injunction would force the wife, under threat of proceedings for contempt of court, to carry to the end a foetus which she clearly does not want and, barring unforeseen events, to give birth to a child which she clearly does not want and which she may very well resent in those circumstances. One can only speculate as to how well, in those circumstances, she would perform her important functions as a mother of a newly born child, but her will and her capacity to do so well, must at least be in question.
>
> Thirdly, the fact that the foetus must grow within the wife's body, not the husband's cannot, in my opinion, be overlooked. To grant the injunction would be to compel the wife to do something in relation to her own body which she does not wish to do. That would be an interference with her freedom to decide her own destiny. Whilst it may be said that to refuse the injunction will permit the wife to interfere with the destiny of the intended child, I have already held that the unborn child has no legal right to be born which this court can protect.
>
> It would be wrong for any person to interpret this decision, however, as in any way condoning, encouraging or permitting the wife to undergo an abortion. That is not the issue in these proceedings. ... Whether the wife goes ahead with her planned abortion is a matter for her conscience, and if she elects to do so she must take the consequences, so far as her health is concerned, and so far as the application of the criminal law is concerned. My decision in this case can have no bearing on the question of criminality of any subsequent conduct of the wife or any other person.
>
> It may also be said that to fail to grant the injunction will allow the wife to override the husband's proper interest in having his intended offspring born. That is undoubtedly true, but I have concluded, on balance, that the legitimate interest of the husband is, in the circumstances of this case, subordinate to the legitimate interest of the wife in being left free to decide a matter which affects her far more directly than it does the husband.[124]

And, in *Tremblay v Daigle*, in a unanimous decision, the Supreme Court of Canada discharged an injunction preventing a woman having an abortion (granted at the instigation of man who had lived with the woman for a few months). It held that the foetus does not have a right to life under the *Quebec Charter of Rights and*

---

123 (1989) 13 Fam LR 189 at 195-6. The husband had argued a number of alternative bases of jurisdiction, all of which were rejected by the court. These included the power to make orders with respect to children, rejected because the court held that the word 'child' did not include an unborn child; an argument that Mr F had a 'common law right to procreate'; and an argument that the foetus had a right to be born. This latter argument was also rejected following *Paton* and *Kerr*.

124 *Ibid*, at 197-8.

Freedoms and that a father has no legal right based on his interests in a foetus to support an injunction to restrain an abortion.[125]

Notes

1. Was Zoe Rathus correct when she suggested that the effect of *In Marriage of F* was 'that if a married couple cannot agree as to whether or not an abortion should be performed, the Family Court and not the woman has the right to the final say'?[126] Given the broad approach taken to jurisdiction in *F* based on the reference in s 114 to matters 'arising out of the matrimonial relationship', what other issues might the Family Court find itself dealing with in disputes between parties to a marriage?[127] Could the Family Court make an order as to how work in the home was to be shared between husband and wife?
2. Carol Gilligan has argued that there is a form of moral reasoning that emphasises connection, which is either more often used by women or, at least, more readily identified with women.[128] This stands in contrast to an individualised rights-based form of reasoning, more commonly identified with men, and, it has been suggested, more familiar to a common law legal tradition. If connectedness is an important value for feminists, how does this sort of analysis contribute to the question of men's participation in a woman's decision to have an abortion?
3. Are the decisions in *Paton* and *Kerr* manifestations of the doctrine of privacy protecting abortion decisions? Is the judge's reasoning in *F v F*, 'that there is perhaps no more fundamental personal relationship between spouses than the relationship involved in the procreation of children', another example of 'privacy' doctrine? Is this an appropriate basis on which to reach these decisions? Can you think of other ways to argue and determine these cases?
4. Lindenmayer J in *F v F* says the court is not concerned with 'moral or ethical' obligations but only with 'legal rights and obligations'. Is the distinction he draws there a relevant or tenable distinction?

'FOETAL RIGHTS'

We have described in the previous section attempts by men to prevent their pregnant 'partners' from having an abortion. In some cases, state agencies have also pursued legal claims to protect the 'life' of a foetus against the will of the woman who is carrying it. Such actions have taken a variety of legal forms, including criminal law, invoking the wardship jurisdiction and attempts to have a court order medical treatment. No such actions have yet been reported in Australia, but they have been common enough to provoke considerable feminist

---

125 [1989] 2 SCR 530. In fact, Ms Daigle had had an abortion before the Supreme Court made its decision. This was revealed to the court during the hearing, but the court decided (after her counsel indicated that 'because of the continued importance of a decision ... for his client and for other women in Canada he wished to continue') that the appeal should be heard and determined' (at 539).
126 Zoe Rathus, 'Inroads into the Rights of Married Women' (1989) 14 *Legal Service Bulletin* 184 at 184.
127 In fact, the Family Court has not received any other applications from a husband concerning his wife's decision-making about abortion, nor has it been asked to consider other types of decisions that arise out of the marital relationship.
128 Carol Gilligan, *In a Different Voice: Psychological Theory and Women's Development*, Harvard University Press, Cambridge, MA, 1982.

analysis in North America under the terminology of 'foetal rights' (or, in the US, 'fetal' rights), and there have been similar developments in the UK. These cases resonate with those discussed in the previous section, particularly those brought by spouses or putative fathers either explicitly or implicitly in the name of 'foetal rights'. The actions by state agencies are dealt with separately here for they raise different questions and arguably present an even more frightening scenario.

In the following material, we outline some of the reported cases and some responses to this litigation tendency.

Policing women

In California, in 1986, a woman was charged with 'child abuse' of the foetus she was carrying. The charge alleged that she had failed to provide necessary medical treatment. She was accused of failing to follow her doctor's advice to cease using amphetamines, not to engage in sexual intercourse and to seek medical attention if she began to haemorrhage.[129] The particular statute she was charged under criminalised a parent's failure to provide necessary clothing, food, shelter or medical treatment to a minor child. The Act also provided that a 'child not yet born' was a person for the purposes of the Act. The Californian court dismissed the charge, finding that the obligation to a 'child not yet born' had been introduced into the legislation in order to ensure that men who had impregnated women provided financial support, rather than to criminalise the conduct of pregnant women.[130]

Laura Gomez notes that this 'prosecution of Pamela Rae Stewart in 1987 ignited national interest in the issue of pregnant women's drug use'.[131] Perhaps the greatest prosecutorial (and legislative) activity in relation to the use of drugs by pregnant women in the US occurred in the 1980s in response to the use of 'crack cocaine'. 'Crack cocaine is a hardened, smokeable form of cocaine made by heating a combination of high-quality powder cocaine, baking soda, and water' which became widely available on the street in 1985 in Los Angeles, New York, San Diego and Miami.[132] This was closely followed by the appearance of 'crack babies', babies born prematurely with serious health problems. Gomez documents the appearance of this phenomenon in the media and in medical research. It is the latter which is the focus of the following extract, describing 'the cadre of medical researchers who, quite literally, discovered prenatal cocaine exposure in the 1980's'.[133] She argues that the interest in 'identifying an additional group of at-risk newborns'[134] followed closely on the then-recent development of intensive care units for newborns and continues:

---

129 The description of the facts is taken from Note, 'Maternal Rights and Fetal Wrongs: the Case Against the Criminalization of Fetal Abuse' (1988) 101 *Harvard Law Review* 994.
130 *Ibid*.
131 Laura E Gomez, *Misconceiving Mothers: Legislators, Prosecutors and the Politics of Prenatal Drug Exposure*, Temple University Press, Philadelphia, 1997, at 42.
132 *Ibid*, at 11. Gomez notes that, although 'crack cocaine' was the drug that received the media exposure and was represented as much more addictive than powder cocaine, 'it now seems unlikely that crack cocaine has different pharmacological effects from powder cocaine' (*ibid* and see references cited therein).
133 *Ibid*, at 19.
134 *Ibid*.

The material incentive to develop a new sub-field of research related to fetal and newborn drug exposure was intensified by increasing competition between paediatricians and obstetricians as the birthrate declined during the 1960's and 1970's....

[*Gomez here describes the efforts by researchers to establish that the problem was a serious one; this commenced with efforts to establish the 'number of newborn infants exposed to drugs in their mothers' wombs' (at 20). Early studies found that* 'between 5 and 31 percent of newborn infants are exposed to *some* amount of *some* illegal drug, and that between 7 and 73 percent are exposed to alcohol in utero' (*at 22*)].

Documenting the number of infants affected by cocaine was a necessary but not sufficient condition for successful claims-making about a new social problem. The remaining step in getting the problem on the public agenda was documenting that maternal cocaine use causes genuine harm. The harm research divides into two generations, studies published in the 1985-1990 period and those published later. The two differ in scientific reliability, and later researchers self-consciously responded to the alarmist tone of much of the early medical literature. ...

[*Gomez describes the results of the three earliest articles in 1985 and 1986, which were quite speculative in nature but reported finding that* 'prenatal cocaine exposure was associated with premature birth, lower birth weight, and smaller size' (at 23) *and mental and emotional disturbance*].

Within five years of ...[the] first study, American medical journals had published 80 articles concerning prenatal exposure to cocaine. Early researchers in this area had many incentives to find "positive results," that is to find that prenatal cocaine exposure had some effect on the newborn (as opposed to finding that cocaine had no effect). For one reason, medical journals were more likely to publish articles showing a positive effect, even when negative-effect studies were more scientifically rigorous in using control groups, larger samples and the like. Given their preliminary nature, these early studies raised as many questions as they answered: How did the extent of maternal drug use affect newborn outcomes? Was the timing of drug use (first versus third trimester, for instance) relevant? Why were some exposed babies seemingly unaffected? What were the long-term effects of prenatal cocaine exposure?

A second generation of studies has sought to answer many of these questions. Chasnoff's research team has followed three categories of children for three years; those prenatally exposed to cocaine as well as other drugs; those prenatally exposed to multiple illicit drugs, but not cocaine; and those not exposed to drugs (the control group). ... At three years of age, there were no statistically significant differences in physical development among the three groups of children, but researchers reported small cognitive ability differences between the control group and children exposed to any type of drug or alcohol, although they did not find a difference between the cocaine-exposed children and those exposed to other drugs or alcohol.[135]

However, it was the first wave of medical research which influenced the media, legislators and prosecutors. One of those high profile prosecutions is described by Gomez in the following way:

In April 1989, [*Jennifer*] Johnson was indicted on two counts of "delivery of a controlled substance [cocaine]" to her son Carl and her daughter Jessica at the time of their births. The prosecution's theory of the case was that Johnson had

---

135 *Ibid*, at 19-24.

delivered drugs, via the uncut umbilical cords, to her children immediately following their birth. Johnson, an African American mother of four who was twenty-five at the time of the trial, told hospital personnel, at both deliveries, that she had used cocaine within 24 hours of each child's birth. Both Carl and Jessica were born healthy, but each tested positive at birth for the cocaine metabolite.

... After a two day trial before a judge, Johnson was convicted and sentenced to one year of community supervision, two hundred hours community service and fourteen years probation. In 1992, the Florida Supreme Court reversed Johnson's convictions on the grounds that the prosecution had contravened legislative intent [*the legislature had specifically rejected a statutory provision which would have allowed prosecution of mothers for delivering drugs to their foetuses – Johnson v State* 602 So 2d 1288 at 1294] and that the state's medical testimony had been insufficient to support the verdict.[136]

Notes

1. John Robertson has argued that prosecution could be pursued 'for culpable prenatal conduct that causes severe impairment to offspring. ... The speculative danger of abuse is no reason to exempt children from legal protection against pregnant women who are not able to meet reasonable community standards about safe conduct during pregnancy'. In reply, Lynn Paltrow suggests '[r]ecognizing "fetal abuse" moves us toward criminalizing pregnancy itself because no woman can provide the perfect womb'.[137] Both authors suggest voluntary compliance is the most desirable policy, but Paltrow argues there is no role for the criminal law. What arguments can you suggest for exempting pregnant women from the criminalisation of their conduct towards their foetuses during pregnancy?
2. Dorothy Roberts has pointed out that the majority of women who have been charged with crimes after their babies test positive for drugs are poor and African-American.[138]

> Poor Black women bear the brunt of prosecutors' punitive approach. These women are the primary targets of prosecutors, not because they are more likely to be guilty of fetal abuse, but because they are Black and poor. Poor women, who are disproportionately Black, are in closer contact with government agencies, and their drug use is therefore more likely to be detected. Black women are also more likely to be reported to government authorities, in part because of the racist attitudes of health care professionals. Finally, their failure to meet society's image of the ideal mother makes their prosecution more acceptable. ...
>
> Focusing on Black crack addicts rather than on other perpetrators of fetal harms serves two broader social purposes. First, prosecution of these

---

136 *Ibid*, at 78-9. Gomez describes in more detail the sentence conditions: 'Johnson would have been required to submit to physical or chemical examinations (such as drug tests), remain gainfully employed, refrain from consuming alcohol, refrain from entering a bar without permission from her probation officer, and notify officials should she become pregnant for the entire fourteen years of her sentence': note 22, at 146. See also *Johnson v State* 602 So 2d 1288 (Fla Sup Ct 1992).
137 John Robertson, Lynn Paltrow, '"Fetal Abuse": Should We Recognize it as a Crime?' (1989) 75 *ABA Journal* 38-9 (August). See also John Robertson, 'Reconciling Offspring and Maternal Interests during Pregnancy' in Sherrill Cohen and Nadine Taub (eds), *Reproductive Laws for the 1990's*, Humana Press, Clifton, NJ, 1989.
138 Dorothy Roberts, 'Punishing Drug Addicts Who Have Babies: Women of Colour, Equality, and the Right to Privacy' (1991) 104 *Harvard Law Review* 1419 at 1421.

pregnant women serves to degrade women whom society views as undeserving to be mothers and to discourage them from having children. If prosecutors had instead chosen to prosecute affluent women addicted to alcohol or prescription medication, the policy of criminalizing prenatal conduct would very likely have suffered a hasty demise. Society is much more willing to condone the punishment of poor women of color who fail to meet the middle-class ideal of motherhood.

In addition to legitimizing fetal rights enforcement, the prosecution of crack-addicted mothers diverts public attention from social ills such as poverty, racism, and a misguided national health policy and implies instead that shamefully high Black infant death rates are caused by the bad acts of individual mothers. Poor Black mothers thus become the scapegoats for the causes of the Black community's ill health.[139]

3. Part of Gomez's study included an examination of legislative activity in California in response to the 'crack baby crisis'. She notes that despite the introduction of 57 Bills in that State addressing the use of drugs by pregnant women:

> None of the punitive bills won passage or even made it through a major policy committee. The bills that won passage addressed the social problems by providing funding for public education, health care (especially prenatal care), and a range of social services for mothers and children at risk for prenatal drug exposure. ...
>
> At first glance, this outcome seems to be at great odds with the social problem's initial momentum, both in the discovery stage and in terms of the legislature's early interest in the issue. The sensationalistic news media coverage and alarmist scientific studies that characterized the initial awareness of the social problem in the late 1980s could have been expected to fuel punitive responses to the social problem. Indeed, the early legislative responses took a harder line (either in proposing a punitive response or couching the provision of services in inflammatory rhetoric about the social problem) consistent with the media and medical research representations of the issue. ... A coalition composed of professional organizations (employing professional lobbyists), practitioners in the public health and drug treatment spheres, and women's rights activists opposed the punitive approach. Working with legislators and their staffs, this coalition succeeded in killing the punitive bills and ultimately enacted laws that provided a range of treatment services to pregnant women.[140]

In her conclusion, Gomez points to two explanations of the apparent paradox between the initial media frenzy and the way the issue came to be dealt with subsequently. She suggests that:

> Since the process [*of institutionalisation of a social problem*] is inherently dynamic, a problem's portrayal, at the discovery-stage, is important but not determinative of its later constitution. Competition for ownership of the

---

139 *Ibid*, at 1435-6. One of the studies Roberts refers to in her article is that by Ira J Chasnoff, Harvey J Landress and Mark E Barrett, 'The Prevalence of Illicit Drug or Alcohol Use During Pregnancy and Discrepancies in Mandatory Reporting in Pinellas County, Florida' (1990) 322 *New England Journal of Medicine* 1202. In this study, the researchers tested pregnant women for alcohol and other drugs in both private and public clinics in an area of Florida. (Florida had introduced a policy requiring the reporting to the local health department of births to mothers who it was suspected had used alcohol or drugs while pregnant). The study found 'that a significantly higher proportion of black women than white women were reported, even though ... the rates of substance abuse were similar' (at 1205).
140 Gomez, *Misconceiving Mothers*, at 41-2.

social problem characterizes the later stage, drawing forth additional parties who support or contest early portrayals, who seek to control tangible state resources, and who seek to tell a particular kind of story about the causes and solution of the problem that is consistent with other interests with which they are concerned.[141]

She notes, in particular, that even though doctors had been active in the first phase of creating crack babies as a social problem, when this generated calls for a punitive response, they later 'advocat[ed] their ownership of the problem, as one better suited to treatment than punishment'.[142]

The second explanation involves an examination of how feminists organised around this issue. After observing that problems that are identified as happening to women more than men are more likely to be medicalised than criminalised, Gomez continued:

> But women's problems are not universally medicalized, and problems linked to white, middle-class women are substantially more likely to be so categorized than those associated with poor or racial-minority women. Part of the strategy to medicalize rather than criminalize prenatal drug exposure, then, depended on recasting it as a more generic women's problem rather than as one limited to a subset of women presumably more apt to be viewed as having criminal propensities. Feminist claims-makers (with allies in the medical profession) chose to downplay racial and class specificity and, alternatively, to emphasize threats to all women's reproductive autonomy. Unlike African American legislators who had initially opposed punitive legislation by seeking to earmark funds or programs for racial minority communities or poor women specifically, the feminist coalition succeeded in shifting the discourse from one about bad women who need to be punished to one about sick women who needed help by focusing on drug-using women in general.[143]

Can you think of other political situations where this sort of strategy either by the medical profession or feminist activists has worked or might work? Are there any negative implications of such a feminist strategy? Would your assessment of any such feminist strategy be affected by knowing which groups were part of the relevant coalition?

4. Another strategy used in the United States to police the behaviour of drug-using women is to require, as a condition of probation, that they use the contraceptive Norplant.[144] 'Norplant consists of six matchstick-size silicone capsules implanted under the skin of a woman's upper arm. These capsules suppress ovulation and inhibit fertilization through the release of hormones. Implanting the contraceptive requires a local anaesthetic and takes approximately fifteen minutes. Norplant is extremely effective, with a failure rate lower than that of oral contraceptives. It remains effective for five years after implantation or until the capsules are removed'.[145] Its use cannot 'be discontinued without the advice and assistance of a

---

141 *Ibid*, at 119-20.
142 *Ibid*, at 121-2.
143 *Ibid*, at 122-3.
144 Many of these cases are discussed in Stacey L Arthur, 'The Norplant Prescription: Birth Control, Woman Control, or Crime Control?' (1992) 40 *UCLA Law Review* 1.
145 Catherine Albiston, 'The Social Meaning of the Norplant Condition: Constitutional Considerations of Race, Class, and Gender' (1994) 9 *Berkeley Women's Law Journal* 9 at 10.

physician'.[146] And, as the extract from Roberts in note 2 above illustrates, poor women of colour are more likely to be prosecuted for drug-taking than white women and thus disproportionately exposed to such probation conditions.[147]

> States have shown little interest ... in promoting programs such as in-home care, economic assistance, prenatal care, drug treatment for pregnant addicts, or counselling that are more directly rehabilitative than contraception. Norplant as a remedy focuses on one risk factor, pregnancy, to the exclusion of many others that also put stress on the family. Because Norplant is so loosely related to rehabilitation, it appears that the state's real interest is the prevention of children being born to "unacceptable" mothers – that is, to drug addicts and child abusers.[148]

5. However, Stacey Arthur has argued:

> [T]he financial crisis plaguing local governments across the country could mean that probationary schemes requiring great commitments of social service resources are simply not feasible. It is hard to make an honorable argument that civil liberties should be curtailed because it costs too much to solve social problems in a less oppressive manner. But neither is there value in concocting alternatives that are theoretically attractive but practically destined to fall short of their objectives.[149]

Are financial viability arguments relevant in this area?[150] If a government had provided appropriate treatment and financial support and other forms of care, and yet a woman continued to engage in child abuse, could the imposition of a long-term contraceptive like Norplant be justified?

Civil actions

Wardship

Civil actions have also been used to try to control women's drug-using behaviour. In England, in *In re F (In Utero)*,[151] a local authority sought to make an unborn child a ward of court. The authority also sought orders to direct a court officer to find the mother and take her to a particular hospital. The matter was heard in the mother's absence. The woman was 36 and had a 10-year-old child who had been the subject of wardship proceedings and was then living with foster parents. The mother had been denied access to him. According to medical reports before the court, she had 'suffered from severe mental disturbance, accompanied by drug abuse from time to time – drugs which included Hallucinogens – and she had suffered from delusions and hallucination'[152] since her early 20s. She had also lived what was described as a 'nomadic lifestyle', with frequent trips to Europe.

---

146 *Ibid*, at 11. Note also that '[t]he medical side effects of Norplant include headaches, depression, nervousness, enlargement of the ovarian and/or fallopian tubes, inflammation of the skin, weight gain, inflammation of the cervix, nausea, dizziness, acne, abnormal hair growth, tenderness of the breasts, and prolonged or irregular bleeding. Norplant is contraindicated for women who suffer from heart disease, kidney disease, liver disease, diabetes, or high blood pressure' (*ibid*, at 10).
147 Cf Albiston, 'The Social Meaning of the Norplant Condition'.
148 *Ibid*, at 46.
149 Stacey L Arthur, 'The Norplant Prescription', at 73-4.
150 See Albiston, 'The Social Meaning of the Norplant Condition', at 49-50.
151 [1988] 2 WLR 1288. For a note on this case, see Jane ES Fortin, 'Can You Ward a Foetus?' (1988) 51 *Modern Law Review* 768.
152 [1988] 2 WLR 1288 at 1290.

Hollings J refused the orders sought and, after noting that the *Guardianship of Minors Act* 1971 (UK) required courts to regard the welfare of the minor as the paramount consideration, concluded that it could not apply to a 'child still within the body of the child's mother'.[153]

An appeal was dismissed by the Court of Appeal the following day. In the course of the appeal decision, May LJ stated:

> Even though this is a case in which, on its facts, I would exercise the jurisdiction if I had it, in the absence of authority I am driven to the conclusion that the court does not have the jurisdiction contended for. ...
>
> Secondly, I respectfully agree with Hollings J in this case that to accept such jurisdiction and yet to apply the principle that it is the interest of the child which is to be predominant is bound to create conflict between the existing legal interests of the mother and those of the unborn child and that it is most undesirable that this should occur.
>
> Next, I think that there would be insuperable difficulties if one sought to enforce any order in respect of an unborn child against its mother, if that mother failed to comply with the order. I cannot contemplate the court ordering that this should be done by force, nor indeed is it possible to consider with any equanimity that the court should seek to enforce an order by committal.
>
> ... If the courts are to have this jurisdiction in a sensitive situation such as the present, I think that this is a matter for Parliament and not for the courts themselves. I do not think that even if the courts were minded to extend the jurisdiction in this type of case, they could in law or practice limit this, as Mr Jubb suggested, to children having a gestation period of not less that 28 weeks.[154]

Staughton LJ concluded:

> The court cannot care for a child, or order that others should do so, until the child is born; only the mother can. The orders sought by the local authority are not by their nature such as the court can make in caring for the child; they are orders which seek directly to control the life of both mother and child. As was said by the European Commission of Human Rights in *Paton v UK* (1980) 3 EHRR 408 at 415 (para 19): 'The "life" of the foetus is intimately connected with, and cannot be regarded in isolation from, the life of the pregnant woman.'
>
> We were urged by counsel to extend the wardship jurisdiction; but, in my judgment, we are being asked to create a new, perhaps similar, jurisdiction to care for mother and foetus together. I can see that there may be arguments that the court should have such powers. One would hope that they would be needed very rarely, but a need may well exist. I do not think that it is for this court to create that jurisdiction. The exercise of it would, in this case, directly impinge on the liberty of the mother.[155]

A similar case arose in the Canadian province of Manitoba.[156] In *Winnipeg Child and Family Services (Northwest Area) v G(DF)*, the Supreme Court of Canada upheld a decision of the Manitoba Court of Appeal overturning a trial judge's decision ordering that DFG could be kept at the Health Sciences Centre until the birth of her child. DFG was addicted to glue sniffing and two of her children had

---

153 *Ibid*, at 1296.
154 [1988] 2 All ER 193 at 196-7.
155 *Ibid*, at 201.
156 *Winnipeg Child and Family Services (Northwest Area) v G(DF)* [1997] 3 SCR 925. Cf *Re Baby F* (1987) 9 RFL 415 and (1988) 15 RFL 225.

been injured by this addiction and were in the permanent care of the state.[157] The court considered two possible bases for jurisdiction: tort law and the inherent parens patriae jurisdiction. A majority of the court found that neither could give jurisdiction. In relation to parens patriae, the Supreme Court of Canada followed the reasoning of the English Court of Appeal in *Re F* and stated:

> The law sees birth as the necessary condition of legal personhood. The pregnant woman and her unborn child are one. ... [T]o make orders protecting fetuses would radically impinge on the fundamental liberties of the pregnant woman, both as to lifestyle choices and how and as to where she chooses to live and be.[158]

In similarly rejecting tort law as a basis for jurisdiction, the court said:

> [U]nder the law as it presently stands, the fetus on whose behalf the agency purported to act in seeking the order for the respondent's detention was not a legal person and possessed no legal rights. If it was not a legal person and possessed no legal rights at the time of the application, then there was no legal person in whose interests the agency could act or in whose interests a court order could be made.
>
> Putting the matter in terms of tort, there was no right to sue, whether for an injunction or damages, until the child was born alive and viable. The law of tort as it presently stands might permit an action for injury to the foetus to be brought in the child's name after its birth. But there is no power in the courts to entertain such an action before the child's birth. The action at issue was commenced and the injunctive relief sought before the child's birth. It follows that under the law as it presently stands, it must fail.[159]

Notes

1. Major J dissented.[160] One primary ground for his dissent was his view that the requirement that the foetus be born alive before a tort action could be pursued was outmoded:

   > Historically, it was thought that damage suffered by a foetus could only be assigned if the child was born alive. It was reasoned that it was only at that time that damages to the live child could be identified. The logic for that rule has disappeared with modern medical progress. Today by the use of ultrasound and other advanced techniques, the sex and health of a foetus can be determined and monitored from a short time after conception. The sophisticated surgical procedures performed on the foetus before birth further belies the need for the "born alive" principle.[161]

---

157 Major J, who dissented in the case, described the medical evidence as to the effect of substantial glue sniffing: 'a multitude of acute effects such as nausea, vomiting, tremors, blurred vision, joint pain, chest pain, decreased level of consciousness, and seizures. The most severe effects are a progression to coma and respiratory or cardiac arrest, leading to death. Kidney, liver and bone marrow failure can also result from chronic use. ... [It] could cause a decrease in her intellectual capacity. ... [T]here is considerable evidence that solvent abuse causes damage to the cerebellum, the part of the brain which controls motor co-ordination. The abuse could also cause peripheral neuropathy' ([1997] 3 SCR 925 at para 82).
158 At para 55.
159 At paras 16-17.
160 Sopinka J agreed with Major J. Major J's judgment is critically analysed in T Brettel Dawson, 'First Person Familiar: Judicial Intervention in Pregnancy, Again: *G(DF)*' (1998) 10 *Canadian Journal of Women and the Law* 213; and Laura Shanner, 'Pregnancy Intervention and Models of Maternal-Fetal Relationship: Philosophical Reflections on the *Winnipeg CFS* Dissent' (1998) 36 *Alberta Law Review* 751
161 [1997] 3 SCR 925 at para 67.

Does Major J's analysis carry the implication that not only are the foetus and the mother separate, but that they are also in an adversarial relationship?[162] What is the connection between 'modern medical progress' and legal responses? To what extent do you think (lack of) medical knowledge influenced the requirement of live birth as a prerequisite for legal action?

2. One of the reasons the majority gave for deciding that there was no jurisdiction to impose treatment on the woman in this case was that, if there were, a foetus could sue its mother for any prenatal injury. The majority noted that the only cases where this had occurred were those involving prenatal injuries caused in a motor vehicle accident.[163] The court here referred to the Australian case of *Lynch v Lynch*,[164] where the NSW Court of Appeal had stressed that third party compulsory insurance was available and explicitly recognised that different policy considerations would arise if a child was suing its mother in respect of other types of negligent conduct during pregnancy:

> There are, however, different policy considerations which arise in the context of a claim based on negligent driving and those which may arise, for instance, in a claim based on the mother's taking of unjustified risks of physical injury.
> ... [N]o consideration of justice operate in favour of singling out children whose injuries were inflicted prior to birth as the one class of individuals who are to be denied access to the [*third party compulsory insurance*] fund.[165]

McLachlin J, for the majority in *Winnipeg*, stated that:

> Behind the refusal of the courts and at least one legislature to permit a child to sue its mother for prenatal injuries related to her lifestyle, lies the fear that such suits would take the courts into the difficult policy issue of the extent to which a mother's lifestyle is actionable. Leaving the special relationship between mother and unborn child aside for the moment, there is little precedent for suing any defendant in tort for damages one has suffered as a consequence of his or her lifestyle. While it is not inconceivable that the courts, proceeding properly in their incremental law-making capacity, may one day recognize such claims, the appellant agency faces the difficulty that on this point too it is asking this Court to break new ground in a controversial area. Once again, the consequences for the law of

---

162 See, per McLachlin J: 'To permit a child to sue its pregnant mother-to-be would introduce a radically new conception into the law; the unborn child and its mother as separate juristic persons in a mutually separable and antagonistic relation' (at para 29). See also Janice Raymond, *Women as Wombs: Reproductive Technologies and the Battle Over Women's Freedom*, Harper, San Francisco, 1993, at 65: 'In the panoply of many new reproductive technologies – in vitro fertilization, embryo experimentation, transfer and freezing, and fetal tissue transplantation – we see the *separability* and *severability* of the embryo/fetus from the woman. As the new reproductive technologies increasingly separate and sever the fetus/embryo from the woman, the medical progenitors create an adversarial relationship between woman and fetus. ... If the fetus becomes the primary "patient" while still in the womb, how much more so when it is detached from the woman's body in which fetuses can be grown, frozen, and thawed technologically. Modern obstetrical practice has confirmed the pregnant woman as mere maternal environment for the fetus. Surrogacy has confirmed the pregnant woman as incubator for someone else's child-to-be-born. And other new reproductive technologies such as IVF and embryo transfer confirm the woman as egg producer or baby machine'.
163 *Winnipeg*, at paras 28-31. The Canadian Supreme Court (at para 32) also referred to UK legislation which restricts the right of infants to sue their mothers for prenatal injuries to those incurred in motor vehicle accidents: see *Congenital Disabilities (Civil Liability) Act* 1976 (UK).
164 (1991) 25 NSWLR 411.
165 (1991) 25 NSWLR 411 at 415-16 per Clarke JA, for the court.

tort generally might be great. Are children to be permitted to sue their parents for second-hand smoke inhaled around the family dinner table? Could any cohabitant bring such an action? Are children to be permitted to sue their parents for spanking causing psychological trauma or poor grades due to alcoholism or a parent's undue fondness for the office or the golf course? If we permit lifestyle actions, where do we draw the line?[166]

Major J responded to this 'slippery slope' argument:

> Once the mother decides to bear the child the state has an interest in trying to ensure the child's health. What circumstances permit state intervention? The "slippery slope" argument was raised that permitting state intervention here would impose a standard of behaviour on all pregnant women. Questions were raised about women who smoked, who lived with a smoker, who ate unhealthy diets, etc. In response to the query of where a reasonable line should be drawn it was submitted that the pen should not even be lifted. This approach would entail the state to stand idly by while a reckless and/or addicted mother inflicts serious and permanent harm on to a child she had decided to bring into the world.[167]

One limitation Major J proposes on the state's right to intervene is that the woman's 'abusive activity *will* cause serious and irreparable harm to the foetus'.[168] Does this standard provide a brake on court intervention? What evidence would a court need to make such a finding? Recall the earlier discussion of the comparison between the preliminary research on the effect of crack-cocaine on neoneates and that undertaken in subsequent years. Can published research provide a reliable standard to guide state authorities?

3. In 1999, the Supreme Court of Canada dealt directly with the situation of a child injured in utero by its mother's negligent driving.[169] A majority of the Supreme Court rejected the distinction that had been prominent in the New Brunswick Court of Appeal's decision (and had formed part of the NSW Court of Appeal's decision in *Lynch*), between the ability of a child injured in utero by a mother's lifestyle choices during pregnancy (for example, smoking, drinking etc) and injury caused by the mother's negligent driving. The New Brunswick Court of Appeal had decided that a child injured in utero should not be able to sue for its mother's lifestyle choices that were 'peculiar to parenthood', but could if she breached 'her general duty of care' or, at least, if she drove negligently.[170] The majority of the Supreme Court of Canada rejected this distinction. Cory J stated:

> I am of the view that this distinction is unworkable. It fails to consider the scope of the role of a parent. Driving is an integral part of parenting in a great many families. ... Indeed, I doubt whether any court can articulate a sound legal test, which is both theoretically coherent and workable in practice, that could effectively limit maternal prenatal liability to cases of motor vehicle negligence. Ultimately, only the legislature can create such a narrow and specific basis of tort liability. ...

---

166 *Winnipeg,* at para 33.
167 *Ibid,* at para 95.
168 *Ibid,* at para 96, emphasis in original; and this must be established on the civil standard, that is, the balance of probabilities.
169 *Dobson (Litigation Guardian of) v Dobson* [1999] 2 SCR 753.
170 See *Dobson (Litigation Guardian of) v Dobson* (1997) 148 DLR (4th) 332 (NBCA) and described in *Dobson (Litigation Guardian of) v Dobson* [1999] 2 SCR 753 esp at para 49.

> Moreover, it is clear that the duty of care imposed by the Court of Appeal is by no means narrow. It would impose tort liability on mothers for prenatal negligence *in all situations* in which a "general duty of care" is owed to third parties. The distinction between lifestyle choices and a so-called "general duty of care" involves a standard which can be readily applied to many areas of a pregnant women's behaviour, most of which are not protected by insurance. ...
>
> In essence, a rule of tort law attempting to distinguish between acts of a mother-to-be involving privacy interests and those constituting common torts would of necessity result in arbitrary line-drawing and inconsistent verdicts. Simply to state that a "general duty of care" will not apply to "lifestyle choices" is to leave open the possibility that many actions taken by pregnant women will not be considered lifestyle choices for the purposes of litigation. Is drug use, if prescribed by a physician, a lifestyle choice? Is a hazardous work environment a lifestyle choice? Indeed, is it not arguable that driving while pregnant, for the benefit and welfare of the family, constitutes a lifestyle choice?[171]

The majority drew attention to the fact that the New Brunswick Court of Appeal had relied on the model of legislation in the United Kingdom – the *Congenital Disabilities (Civil Liabilities) Act* 1976. This Act bars all tort actions by children injured while in utero, except those incurred in motor vehicle accidents. Cory J stated that it could not be used, as the Court of Appeal had done, to support their decision because it was a response developed by the legislature and to use it 'presumes it is appropriate for courts to resolve an extremely sensitive and complex issue of public policy and insurance law'.[172] Cory J noted that, if a court in Canada imposed tortious liability for motor vehicle accidents, it would not place Canadian women in the same legal position as their UK counterparts. To allow recovery here would be to 'recognize a duty and articulate a standard of care for the pregnant woman. As a matter of tort law, this carries the risk that the duty would be applied in other contexts where it would impose unreasonable obligations upon pregnant women'.[173] Some of these were articulated in the following way:

> [T]he ingestion of prohibited drugs, the consumption of alcohol, and the smoking of cigarettes – all could be found to breach a duty of care owed by a pregnant woman to her foetus or subsequently born child. Perhaps the decision to avoid eating fruits and vegetables could also be found to constitute tortious conduct. The same conclusion might be reached with regard to unprotected sexual intercourse, rigorous exercise or no exercise. Every aspect of the life of a pregnant woman would be subjected to external scrutiny if liability for tortious conduct to her foetus were imposed.[174]

The majority also specifically rejected the insurance-based rationale (which was relied on by the NSW Court of Appeal in *Lynch*):

> An insurance-driven judicial solution to the issue raised in this appeal imposes liability on the mother on the basis of her ability to satisfy a

---

171 *Dobson* [1999] 2 SCR 753 at paras 57-61 (Lamer CJ, L'Heureux-Dubé, Gonthier, Iacobucci, and Binnie JJ agreed with Cory J's judgment; McLachlin J wrote a separate concurring opinion, in which L'Heureux-Dubé J joined; Major J dissented, joined by Bastarache J).
172 *Dobson*, at para 64.
173 *Ibid*, at para 65.
174 *Ibid*, at para 66.

> judgment by means of her insurance coverage. However, tort law is not and should not be, result-oriented in this manner. ...
>
> Quite simply, the existence of insurance is not an appropriate basis for the determination of tort liability between litigating parties. ...
>
> Moreover, problems of application are bound to arise with a judicial exception to maternal tort immunity based on motor vehicle insurance. For instance, should liability be confined to the limits of the mother's insurance policy? Contributory negligence as a vehicle passenger may not be covered by insurance. In addition, the mother's action may be barred by a wide range of coverage defences available to her insurer.[175]

The majority of the court refused to decide the case on Charter grounds, noting that the Charter had not been raised by any of the parties and only mentioned by one intervener.[176] However, McLachlin J, joined by L'Heureux-Dubé J, did comment on the Charter:

> Liability for foetal injury by pregnant women would run contrary to two of the most fundamental of these [*Charter*] values – liberty and equality.
>
> I turn first to liberty. Virtually every action of a pregnant woman – down to how much sleep she gets, what she eats and drinks, how much she works and where she works – is capable of affecting the health and well-being of her unborn child, and hence carries the potential for legal action against the pregnant woman. Such legal action in turn carries the potential to bring the whole of the pregnant woman's conduct under the scrutiny of the law. This in turn has the potential to jeopardize the pregnant woman's fundamental right to control her body and make decisions in her own interest ....
>
> The intrusion upon the pregnant woman's autonomy worked by the proposed common law rule would also violate her right to equal treatment. Canadians generally enjoy the full right to decide what they will eat or drink, where they will work and other personal matters. Pregnant women, however, would not enjoy that right. In addition to the usual duties of prudent conduct imposed on all who engage in life's various activities, pregnant women would be subject to a host of additional restrictions. Any other individual can avoid being a tortfeasor by isolating himself or herself from other members of society. The pregnant woman has no such choice. She carries her foetus 24 hours a day, seven days a week.
>
> To say women choose pregnancy is no answer. Pregnancy is essentially related to womanhood. It is an inexorable and essential fact of human history that women and only women become pregnant. Women should not be penalized because it is their sex that bears children .... To say that broad legal constraints on the conduct of pregnant women do not constitute unequal treatment because women choose to become pregnant is to reinforce inequality by the fiction of deemed consent and the denial of what it is to be a woman. ...
>
> The goal of the Court of Appeal and those who advocate liability in this case is modest. They simply want children who are born with injuries sustained before birth due to their mother's negligence in operating a motor vehicle to be able to recover under the mother's liability insurance policy. That may be a laudable goal. The difficulty is that in order to achieve this modest goal judicially, they cast themselves on the horns of a dilemma: either they shape the common law in a way that has the potential to render

---

175 *Ibid*, at paras 73-75.
176 *Ibid*, at para 20.

pregnant women liable for a broad range of conduct and unjustifiably trammel liberty and rights to equal treatment; or they accept category-based restrictions antithetical to the common law method. Legislative action, the route chosen in England, can accomplish the limited goal of permitting children like the respondent to access motor vehicle liability insurance without these negative consequences. In these circumstances, the courts should not intervene.[177]

Does the majority of the Supreme Court of Canada too easily reject the pragmatic approach of the NSW Court of Appeal in *Lynch*? How important is the judgment of McLachlin and L'Heureux-Dubé JJ in its insistence on discussing women's equality and liberty interests? The Supreme Court of Canada in *Winnipeg* refers to the fact that it is up to parliament to decide whether child welfare legislation should be expanded to protect foetuses; and in *Dobson* it also emphasises that it is a matter for the legislature to decide whether children injured whilst in utero by the negligent driving of their mothers should be able to sue them. If the equality interests of women remain unarticulated by the court,[178] what guidance is available for the legislature?[179]

4. Major J in *Winnipeg* suggested that a woman's liberty interests must 'bend when faced with a situation where devastating harm and a life of suffering can so easily be prevented'.[180] He went on to say 'this interference is always subject to the mother's right to end it by deciding to have an abortion'.[181] How realistic is the abortion option in these circumstances?

5. Major J also asserted in his *Winnipeg* judgment that 'the tragedy of FAS [Fetal Alcohol Syndrome] and FAE [Fetal Alcohol Effects] is particularly felt in aboriginal communities'.[182] He stated:

> The interveners Southeast Child and Family Services and West Region Child and Family Services are aboriginal child and family service agencies responsible for delivering services to 18 First Nation communities in Manitoba. These parties intervened, in part, to urge upon this Court the creation of a legal remedy to use in their fight against FAS/FAE. These interveners submitted that such a remedy would be consistent with the aboriginal world view, and that the common law should be expanded to help alleviate what is particularly an aboriginal problem.[183]

Other interveners included the Metis Women of Manitoba Inc and the Native Women's Transition Centre Inc. These two groups had representation which was separate to that of the two Child and Family Services organisations, and we do not know from the judgments what position they put to the court.[184]

---

177 *Ibid*, at paras 84-90.
178 In relation to *Winnipeg*, see Sanda Rodgers, '*Winnipeg Child and Family Services v DFG*: Juridical Interference with Pregnant Women in the Alleged Interest of the Fetus' (1998) 36 *Alberta Law Review* 711 at 720. There is one mention of equality in the decision: the court cited with approval the Royal Commission on New Reproductive Technologies report, *Proceed with Care* (1993): 'Judicial intervention ... ignores the basic components of women's fundamental human rights – the right to bodily integrity, and the right to equality, privacy, and dignity' (at para 36). And, at another point, the court refers to 'the rights of women' (at para 56).
179 See Morgan, 'Foetal Imaginings: Searching for a Vocabulary in the Law and Politics of Reproduction' (2000) 12 *Canadian Journal of Women and the Law* 371.
180 *Winnipeg* [1997] 3 SCR 925 at para 93.
181 *Ibid*.
182 *Ibid*, at para 88.
183 *Ibid*.
184 They were represented by the solicitor who also represented two other interveners, the Manitoba Association of Rights and Liberties Inc and the Women's Health Clinic.

Assume they put arguments similar to those ascribed by Major J to the (Aboriginal) Child and Family Service Organisation. Does this affect your own view of an appropriate resolution to this case?
6. It will be noted that the UK court in *Re F* used the language of 'unborn child' in its decision, while the Supreme Court of Canada, some nine years later referred throughout its decision to a 'foetus'. What are the implications of the use of the term 'unborn child' rather than 'foetus'?[185]

Court-ordered treatment

Hospitals in the US, Canada and the UK have sought to obtain court orders requiring pregnant women to undergo particular forms of treatment, usually, but not always, caesarean sections.

Perhaps the most widely publicised example of state action in this area is the case of *In re AC*.[186] Angela C was 26 weeks pregnant, hospitalised and dying of cancer. She had been admitted to hospital when a large tumour had been discovered in her lung: she had struggled with cancer for many years but at the time she became pregnant her cancer had been in remission for three years. Some four days after her admission she had been told she might die within a few days. By the time the hospital authorities sought a court order to perform a caesarean section, AC was heavily sedated to allow her to breathe. Before the sedation, she had indicated that once the foetus reached 28 weeks she would relinquish her life so that the foetus could survive. However, her doctors had not discussed what her choice would be prior to the foetus reaching 28 weeks. At the time of the court application, medical evidence suggested that there was a 50-60% chance the foetus was viable and a less than 20% risk of severe disability.[187] The doctors' evidence on what they believed AC would have wanted to do was contradictory, but the court noted that AC had taken medication throughout the pregnancy knowing that it might harm the foetus, expressing 'a desire to be kept as comfortable as possible throughout her pregnancy and to maintain the quality of her life'.

The trial court decided that the foetus was viable and, relying on *In re Madyun*,[188] concluded that the caesarean should be performed. The following extract is from the District of Columbia Court of Appeals decision, written after they had

---

185 As Diana Majury notes: 'Where the issue to be decided is whether or not a fetus can be considered a child in need of protection, it would seem preferable to avoid the word "child" when referring to the fetus. ... Whereas the term "fetus" is neutral on the question of whether it might be included in the definition of "child" for the purposes of child welfare legislation, the term "unborn child" seems to favour such a finding': 'Annotation' to *Re Baby R* (1988) 15 RFL 225.
186 533 A 2d 611 (1987). For a discussion of another related case, see Robert H Sturgess, '*In Re AC*: A Court-Ordered Cesarean Becomes Precedent for Nonconsensual Organ Harvesting' (1989) 13 *Nova Law Review* 649 at 667-8. There he discusses the case of a 27-year-old pregnant woman who became brain dead when she was 22 weeks pregnant. His description of the case comes from Field et al, 'Maternal Brain Death During Pregnancy: Medical and Ethical Issues' (1988) 260 *Journal American Medical Association* 816.
 'Referred to as a "beating heart cadaver", she was kept alive artificially for nine weeks until a successful cesarean could be performed. The mother was disconnected from her life support after the cesarean, and she died almost immediately. With surprising bravado, the physicians announced, [e]*ven a maternal refusal expressed before death does not, itself, carry weight against the possibility of fetal survival*. The mother is not harmed; no right of hers is violated, and great good can be done for another. Thus, this case seems to present a straightforward instance of the medical rescue of the fetus from death' (at 667-8).
187 Mary Mahowald, 'Beyond Abortion: Refusal of Caesarean Section' (1989) 3 *Bioethics* 106.
188 114 Daily Wash L Rptr 2233 (DC Super Ct, 26 July 1986).

refused to grant a stay on the court order permitting a Caesarean section to be performed. The baby died immediately and Angela C two days after the operation.[189]

In re AC, Appellant
533 A 2d 611 (DC App 1987)

[613] Shortly after the trial judge made his decision, AC was informed of it. She stated, during a period of lucidity, that she would agree to the surgery although she might not survive it. When another physician went to AC to verify her decision, she apparently changed her mind, mouthing the words, "I don't want it done." There was no explanation for either decision. ...

The court based its decision to deny a stay on the medical judgment that AC would not survive for a significant time after the surgery and that the fetus had a better, though slim, chance if taken before AC's imminent death. If AC died before delivery, the fetus would die as well. Though AC might have lived twenty-four to forty-eight hours, the surgery might have hastened her death. The ordinary question of likelihood of ultimate success on the merits was deemed subsumed in the immediate necessity to balance the delicate interests of fetus survival with the mother's condition and options on her behalf. ...

[*The court here considered American precedent on the right to abortion, the right to bodily integrity, including the right to refuse medical treatment, cases ordering medical treatment of minors over their parents' refusal, and other 'foetal rights' cases and concluded:*]

[616] There is a significant difference, however, between a court authorizing medical treatment for a child already born and a child who is yet unborn, although the state [617] has compelling interests in protecting the life and health of both children, and viable unborn children. ... Where birth has occurred, the medical treatment does not infringe on the mother's right to bodily integrity. With an unborn child, the state's interest in preserving the health of the child may run squarely against the mother's interest in her bodily integrity.

It can be argued that the state may not infringe upon the mother's right to bodily integrity to protect the life or health of her unborn child unless to do so will not significantly affect the health of the mother and unless the child has a significant chance of being born alive. Performing Caesarean sections will, in most instances, have an effect on the condition of the mother. That effect may be temporary in otherwise normal patients. The surgery presents a number of common complications, including infection, hemorrage, gastric aspiration of the stomach contents, and postoperative embolism. ... It also produces considerable discomfort. In some cases, the surgery will result in the mother's death.

Even though we recognize these considerations, we think they should not have been dispositive here. The Caesarean section would not significantly affect AC's condition because she had, at best, two days left of sedated life; the complications arising from the surgery would not significantly alter that prognosis. The child, on the other hand, had a chance of surviving delivery, despite the possibility that it would be born handicapped. Accordingly, we concluded that the trial judge did not err in subordinating AC's right against bodily intrusion to the interests of the unborn child and the state, and hence we denied the motion for stay.

---

189 See Joan Mahoney, 'Death With Dignity: Is There An Exception for Pregnant Women?' (1989) *University of Missouri-Kansas City Law Review* 221 at 226.

Notes

1. The judgment in *AC* was set aside and a rehearing granted.[190] The DC Court of Appeals in their later judgment, delivered in 1990, some years after AC died, concluded:

   > We hold that in virtually all cases the question of what is to be done is to be decided by the patient – the pregnant woman – on behalf of herself and the fetus. If the patient is incompetent or otherwise unavailable to give an informed consent to a proposed course of medical treatment, then her decision must be ascertained through the procedure known as substituted judgment.[191]

   After reviewing a series of cases, the DC Court of Appeals found that:

   > [E]very person has the right, under the common law ... to accept or refuse medical treatment. This right of bodily integrity belongs equally to persons who are competent and persons who are not. Further, it matters not what the quality of the patient's life may be; the right of bodily integrity is not extinguished simply because someone is ill, or even at death's door. To protect that right against intrusion by others ... we hold that a court must determine the patient's wishes by any means available and must abide by those wishes unless there are truly extraordinary or compelling reasons to override them'.[192]

   And later in the judgment, the court expressed its opinion even more forcefully:

   > We do not quite foreclose the possibility that a conflicting state interest may be so compelling that the patient's wishes may yield, but we anticipate that such cases will be extremely rare and truly exceptional. This is not such a case. ...
   > Indeed, some may doubt that that there could ever be a situation extraordinary or compelling enough to justify a massive intrusion into a person's body, such as a caesarean section, against that person's will.[193]

   Aside from reliance on the right to bodily integrity, the court also endorsed a submission from the American Public Health Association. The APHA had argued that court-ordered caesareans '[r]ather than protecting the health of women and children ... erode the element of trust that permits a pregnant woman to communicate to her physician – without fear of reprisal – all information relevant to her diagnosis and treatment'.[194] They also pointed out that such a practice would actually drive women with high-risk pregnancies away from the health system.

2. That women pregnant with a full-term foetus are able to make autonomous decisions has also been resoundingly endorsed in the UK Court of Appeal's decision in *St George's Healthcare NHS Trust*.[195] There a young woman had made contact with a doctor for the first time during her pregnancy when she

---

190 *In Matter of AC, Appellant* 539 A 2d 203 (1988).
191 *In re AC, Appellant* 573 A2d 1235 at 1237 (DC App 1990). Substituted judgment requires the court or other decision-maker to 'as nearly as possible, ... ascertain what the patient would do if competent' (at 1249).
192 *Ibid*, at 1247.
193 *Ibid*, at 1252. This passage was cited with approval in the UK Court of Appeal decision, *Re MB (Medical Treatment)* [1997] 2 FLR 426 at 443-4.
194 *In re AC, Appellant* 573 A2d 1235 at 1248.
195 *St George's Healthcare NHS Trust v S; R v Collins; Ex parte S* [1998] 3 All ER 673.

was 36 weeks pregnant. She was diagnosed as suffering from pre-eclampsia, a condition which can have life-threatening effects on both the foetus and the mother. Her doctor recommended inducing the birth but S refused. She was involuntarily admitted to a psychiatric hospital under the *Mental Health Act 1983* for 'assessment' and later transferred to an obstetrics hospital. At all times, she refused treatment, stating in writing her '"extreme objection to *any* medical or surgical intervention" and made it "absolutely clear that it is against my wishes and I shall consider it an assault on my person"'.[196] She also consulted her lawyer who confirmed her right to refuse medical treatment. The hospital ultimately decided to seek a court order authorising treatment. It did not notify S's lawyers that it was doing so and there was very little discussion of her capacity to consent in the hearing and the judge 'knew no more than that S had been admitted for assessment as a *Mental Health Act* patient'.[197] A declaration was granted authorising, amongst other things, a caesarean section under general anaesthetic. A caesarean was performed, with S refusing to sign the appropriate consent form and 'acquiescing' in the treatment having 'decided that to struggle physically and be overcome would be undignified' or, as the Court of Appeal later put it, in words reminiscent of that of the Court of Appeal in *Olugboja*,[198] a rape case, '[u]nder the pressures of an exhausting and emotionally charged situation, and faced with the court order, S ceased to offer any resistance. This was not consent but submission'.[199] The declaration was overturned by the Court of Appeal:

> [E]ach woman is entitled to refuse treatment for herself. It does not follow *without any further analysis* that this entitles her to put at risk the healthy viable foetus which she is carrying. ...
> Whatever else it may be, a 36-week foetus is not nothing; if viable, it is not lifeless and it is certainly human. ...
> When human life is at stake the pressure to provide an affirmative answer authorising unwanted medical intervention is very powerful. Nevertheless, the autonomy of each individual required continuing protection even, perhaps particularly, when the motive for interfering with it is readily understandable, and indeed to many would appear commendable; .... If it has not already done so, medical science will no doubt one day advance to the stage when a very minor procedure undergone by an adult would save the life of his or her child, or perhaps the life of a complete stranger. The refusal would rightly be described as unreasonable, the benefits to another human life would be beyond value, and the motives of the doctors admirable. If however the adult were compelled to agree, or rendered helpless to resist, the principle of autonomy would be extinguished. ...
> In our judgment while pregnancy increases the personal responsibilities of a woman it does not diminish her entitlement to decide whether or not to undergo medical treatment. Although human, and protected by law in a number of different ways set out in the judgment in *Re MB* [[1997] 2 FLR 426; *see note 4 below*], an unborn child is not a separate person from its mother. Its need for medical assistance does not prevail over her rights. She is entitled not to be forced to submit to an invasion of her body against her

---

196 [1998] 3 All ER 673 at 680. Cf her later written statement quoted at 681.
197 *Ibid*, at 682.
198 [1982] QB 320 at 332: '[E]very consent involves a submission, but it by no means follows that a mere submission involves consent'.
199 [1998] 3 All ER 673 at 684.

will, whether her own life or that of her unborn child depends on it. Her right is not reduced or diminished merely because her decision to exercise it may appear morally repugnant.[200]

What significance, if any, can be given to the fact that the UK Court of Appeal, in contrast to the DC Court of Appeals, explicitly referred to the foetus as human?[201] Are there risks in doing so?

3. The Court of Appeals in *AC* had drawn attention to some of the practical difficulties in these cases, which it saw as further support for its view that AC's objections to a caesarean should not have been overridden:

> [A]ny judicial proceeding in a case such as this will ordinarily take place ... under time constraints so pressing that it is difficult or impossible for the mother to communicate adequately with counsel, or for counsel to organize an effective factual and legal presentation in defense of her liberty and privacy interests and bodily integrity. Any intrusion implicating such basic values ought not to be lightly undertaken when the mother not only is precluded from conducting pre-trial discovery ... but also is in no position to prepare meaningfully for trial.[202]

Celia Wells, in commenting on analogous UK critiques,[203] has argued that these cases *are* emergencies and must be treated as such: 'They cannot be de-emergencied by the magic means of suspension of reality (or suspension of labour)'.[204] If you agree with Wells that understanding these cases as emergencies is necessary to understand the issues they raise, how does this realisation assist in reaching a resolution of them?

And medical diagnoses are not always infallible. In Georgia, the Supreme Court ordered a pregnant woman who had refused surgery or a blood transfusion on religious grounds to undergo a caesarean section.[205] Jessie May Jefferson was 39 weeks pregnant and the court had evidence before it that there was a 99% chance that the baby could not survive vaginal birth and a 50% chance of Jefferson dying during a vaginal delivery.[206] On the other hand, the doctor who had examined Jefferson stated that, if a caesarean occurred prior to labour commencing, there was a close to 100% chance of preserving the life of both the child and the mother. The trial court, in making the order sought, stated:

> Because the life of defendant and of the unborn child are, at the moment, inseparable, the Court deems it appropriate to infringe upon the wishes of the mother to the extent it is necessary to give the child an opportunity to live.[207]

---

200 *Ibid*, at 686-8; emphasis added.
201 See Morgan, 'Foetal Imaginings', at 392-4.
202 *In re AC* 573 A 2d 1235 at 1248, citing Janet Gallagher, 'Prenatal Invasions and Interventions: What's Wrong with Fetal Rights?' (1987) 10 *Harvard Women's Law Journal* 9 at 49. Cf the procedural guidelines laid out in the UK Court of Appeal decision in *Re MB (Medical Treatment)* [1997] 2 FLR 426 at 445.
203 See, for example, Michael Thomson, 'After *Re S*' [1994] *Medical Law Review* 127.
204 Celia Wells, 'On the Outside Looking in: Perspectives on Enforced Caesareans' in Sally Sheldon and Michael Thomson (eds), *Feminist Perspectives on Health Care Law*, Cavendish, London, 1998, at 246.
205 *Jefferson v Griffin Spalding County Hospital* 274 SE 2d 457 (1981) Supreme Court, Ga.
206 Jefferson had placenta previa (the afterbirth was between the foetus and the birth canal).
207 Quoted in *Jefferson v Griffin Spalding County Hospital* 274 SE 2d 457 at 458 (1981).

In fact, the defendant did not return to the hospital to submit to the order of the court. She uneventfully delivered a healthy baby vaginally and without surgical intervention.[208]

4. In *Re MB (Medical Treatment)*,[209] a decision which preceded *St George's NHS Health Care Trust*, the English Court of Appeal considered a request by a hospital that wanted to perform a caesarean on a woman who consented to the caesarean, but who had a severe needle phobia and who withdrew consent when the time for the caesarean approached. Her foetus was in a footling breach presentation, 'an obstetric complication with potentially serious consequences for the unborn child'.[210] The English Court of Appeal stated:

> The law is, in our judgment, clear that a competent woman who has the capacity to decide may, for religious reasons, other reasons, or for no reasons at all, choose not to have medical intervention, even though ... the consequence may be the death or serious handicap of the child she bears or her own death. She may refuse to consent to the anaesthesia injection in the full knowledge that her decision may significantly reduce the chances of her unborn child being born alive. The foetus up to the moment of birth does not have any separate interest capable of being taken into account when a court has to consider an application for a declaration in respect of a caesarian [sic] section operation.[211]

However, the court dismissed an appeal against the decision ordering a caesarean and held that MB lacked the capacity to make the decision for herself due to a severe needle phobia. They found that:

> A fear of needles ... has got in the way of proceeding with the operation .... At the moment of panic, ... her fear dominated all ... at the actual point she was not capable of making a decision at all ... at that moment the needle or mask dominated her thinking and made her quite unable to consider anything else.[212]

Is it possible to reconcile the strong statement of principle in this case with the result? The court appears to set up two dichotomous categories. The first involves a woman who is not incapacitated to consent to medical treatment but may be refusing an apparently necessary caesarean perhaps 'for no reason at all': she is entitled to refuse treatment. The second woman is suffering from some sort of relevant phobia and may be, so it is argued, apparently incapable of consenting to some aspect of the treatment. Her refusal to consent can be overridden because of this incapacity. Can a court, or a medical practitioner, practically differentiate between these two women?

---

208 Sanda Rodgers, 'Fetal Rights and Maternal Rights: Is There a Conflict?' (1986) 1 *Canadian Journal of Women and the Law* 456; and cf the Georgia Medical Associations headline: 'Georgia Supreme Court Orders Caesarean Section – Mother Nature Reverses on Appeal' quoted in Janet Gallagher, 'Fetus as Patient' in Sherrill Cohen and Nadine Taub (eds), *Reproductive Laws for the 1990's*, Humana Press, Clifton, NJ, 1989, at 205. Cf *In re Baby Doe* 632 NE 2d 326 (Ill App 1 Dist 1994) where the court refused to order a caesarean over the objections, for religious reasons, of the woman. The doctors had diagnosed that the foetus was not receiving enough oxygen and the chances of the child surviving natural labour were 'close to zero' and if he did he 'would be retarded' (at 328). The woman 'vaginally delivered an apparently normal and healthy, although somewhat underweight, baby boy' (at 329).
209 [1997] 2 FLR 426.
210 *Ibid*, at 428.
211 *Ibid*.
212 *Ibid*, at 437-8.

5. The trial judge in *Re AC* relied on the earlier decision in *Madyun*.[213] There, a Muslim woman had been in labour for some 60-70 hours and there was a substantial risk of foetal sepsis. The woman refused a caesarean and argued that her religion allowed her to make a decision whether she would risk damage to her own health for the sake of the foetus. Her husband also claimed that the hospital had not allowed his wife to, for example, stand or walk around, which would have assisted a vaginal delivery. The court ordered a caesarean stating: 'All that stood between the Madyun fetus and its independent existence ... was, put simply, a doctor's scalpel'.[214] The Court of Appeals in *AC* expressly stated that its decision was not to be taken as either approving or overruling *Madyun*.[215] The *Madyun* decision is also referred to in *MB*. There the court also cites a decision of the Illinois Court of Appeal, *Re Baby Boy Doe*.[216] The court in *Doe* decided that neither *Madyun* nor *Jefferson* represented the law in Illinois and unequivocally rejected an approach that required a balancing of the mother's and the foetus' interests.
6. In the mid-1980s, Veronika Kolder, Janet Gallagher and Michael Parsons surveyed medical personnel in the United States about their knowledge of attempts in the previous five years to use the courts to override a pregnant women's refusal to accept medical treatment. They received reports of 21 cases – 15 cases seeking a court-ordered caesarean section, three seeking hospital detention and three seeking court-ordered intrauterine transfusions. Court orders were successfully obtained in 86% of these 21 cases and in 81% of all cases the woman concerned was black, Asian or Hispanic.[217]
7. Many of those opposed to allowing courts to order caesarean operations against the will of the woman concerned have pointed out that Anglo-American law has never enforced a 'duty to rescue'. For example, George Annas has argued that a mother would never be required to have a particular surgical operation to save the life of her three-year-old child.[218] And, in *McFall v Shimp*,[219] a court refused to order a man to undergo a bone marrow transplant for the sake of his cousin, even though the cousin was dying of cancer and there was no other compatible donor. John Robertson, a proponent of 'foetal rights' has argued in favour of a 'duty to rescue' in these

---

213 114 Daily Washington Reporter 2233 (1986). One of the judges in *In re AC*, who dissented in part, attached that decision to the court's reason as an appendix: *In re AC, Appellant* 573 A2d 1235 at 1259-64.
214 114 Daily Washington Reporter 2233 at 2240.
215 *In re AC, Appellant* 573 A2d 1235 at 1252, note 23: 'There are substantial factual differences between *Madyun* and the present case. In this case, for instance, the medical interests of the mother and the fetus were in sharp conflict; what was good for one would have been harmful to the other. In *Madyun*, however, there was no real conflict between the mother and the fetus; on the contrary, there was strong evidence that the proposed operation would be beneficial to both. Moreover, in *Madyun* the pregnancy was at full term, and Mrs Madyun had been in labour for two and a half days; in this case, however, AC was barely two-thirds of the way through her pregnancy and there were no signs of labour'.
216 632 NE 2d 326 (1994).
217 Veronika EB Kolder, Janet Gallagher and Michael T Parsons, 'Court-Ordered Obstetrical Interventions' (1987) 316 *New England Journal of Medicine* 1192. See also Lisa C Ikemoto, 'Furthering the Inquiry: Race, Class, Culture in the Forced Medical Treatment of Pregnant Women' in Adrien Katherine Wing (ed), *Critical Race Feminism: A Reader*, New York University Press, New York, 1997.
218 George Annas, 'Forced Cesareans: The Most Unkindest Cut of All' (1982) 12 *Hastings Center Report* 16 at 17.
219 127 Pitts Leg J 14 (1978).

circumstances. He has argued that, where a caesarean is 'essential' to save the foetus' life or prevent injury to it, a court-ordered caesarean may be 'distasteful' but is the 'proper outcome': 'To impose on the mother a duty to undergo surgical delivery where it is necessary to save the child's life or prevent it from being injured is not unreasonable where she has chosen to lend her body to bring the child into the world'.[220] Interestingly, Robertson does comment that his analysis would lead to the conclusion that a court could order tissue donation (not a major organ) by a parent to a child.[221] A similar analysis was put by one of the dissenting judges in *AC*, Belson AJ:

> A woman carrying a viable unborn child is not in the same category as a relative, friend or stranger, called upon to donate bone marrow or an organ for transplant. Rather, the expectant mother has placed herself in a special class of persons who are bringing another person into existence, and upon whom that other person's life is totally dependent. Also, uniquely, the viable unborn child is literally captive within the mother's body. No other potential beneficiary of a surgical procedure on another is in that position.[222]

Could the 'literal captivity' of the foetus within the body of a woman lead to precisely the opposite conclusion? That is, could it not be argued that the foetus should not be envisaged separately from the woman who is carrying it and therefore *her* wishes must prevail? (This issue is returned to in the case study at the end of this section.) Does Belson J clarify the responsibilities of a father who has agreed to bring another being into existence?

Morris and Nott argue 'it is impossible to escape the conclusion that a parent is under a heavy moral responsibility to take steps to preserve the life of a foetus, but the presence of an ethical imperative is by no means a *sufficient* justification for the imposition of a legal responsibility'.[223] They support, therefore, the traditional understanding of a general lack of a 'duty to rescue'. Is it possible to separate out ethical or moral responsibilities from legal responsibilities? Is it desirable?

Revisioning the relationship between a woman and the foetus she is carrying

Marie Ashe has tried to introduce women's experiences of pregnancy into legal discourse.[224] She argues that the medical model of pregnancy, which 'informs legal discourse as well as medical theory and practice', emphasises 'the separability of the pregnant woman and the fetus and ... defin[es] the female reproductive process in terms of discontinuity rather than continuity'.[225] She suggests that while this model, particularly the emphasis on separability, may be an adequate description of some women's experience of pregnancy, particularly an

---

220 John A Robertson, 'Procreative Liberty and the Control of Conception, Pregnancy, and Childbirth' (1983) 69 *Virginia Law Review* 405 at 456.
221 *Ibid*, at note 166.
222 *In re AC, Appellant* 573 A2d 1235 (1990) at 1256 per Belson AJ.
223 Anne Morris and Susan Nott, 'The Law's Engagement With Pregnancy' in Jo Bridgeman and Susan Millns (eds), *Law and Body Politics: Regulating the Female Body*, Dartmouth, Aldershot, 1995, at 60.
224 Marie Ashe, 'Law-Language of Maternity: Discourse Holding Nature in Contempt' (1988) 22 *New England Law Review* 521.
225 *Ibid*, at 539.

unwanted one, it is by no means true of all.[226] While the decisions in *AC, MB* and *St George's NHS Health Care Trust* appear to recognise, at least to some extent, women's claims to autonomy, with the exception of the latter case, the relationship between a woman and the foetus she is carrying is not clearly articulated in the judgments. It is arguable that the cases on forced medical treatment have become the 'easy' cases. The difficulties courts have in understanding that relationship are revealed when women's claims to autonomy are not so directly raised. In this section we discuss two criminal cases, both of which raise the question of how the criminal law should articulate the harm done to a foetus when the women carrying that foetus is the target of the harm.

A UK example

In *Attorney-General's Ref No 3 of 1994*,[227] a man had stabbed his girlfriend, knowing that she was five months pregnant, in the abdomen. He was convicted of wounding her with intent to commit grievous bodily harm (and sentenced to four years imprisonment). Some three weeks after the assault, the woman suddenly went into premature labour and gave birth to a daughter, after some 22-26 weeks gestation. It became apparent that the knife wound had injured the foetus. The child survived 120 days. The man was then charged with murder of the child. There is a well-established common law principle that if a foetus is injured before birth, *and is subsequently born alive*, it is quite possible to find liability for murder.[228] However, in this case, the trial judge directed an acquittal, deciding that no conviction for murder or manslaughter could lie. The Crown pursued the matter to the Court of Appeal as a question of law and ultimately to the House of Lords.

The Court of Appeal concluded that a conviction for murder or manslaughter could be sustained in these circumstances. The House of Lords was, by contrast, not convinced that the requisite intention for murder could be found; however, it found that the actus reus, or 'unlawful act' part of a homicide offence, could be established and concluded that a person could, in these circumstances, be found guilty of manslaughter. The difference in the legal analyses of the two courts arises largely from the way in which they each envisaged the relationship between a woman and the foetus she is carrying. The Court of Appeal decided:

> In the eyes of the law the foetus is taken to be a part of the mother until it has an existence independent of the mother. Thus an intention to cause serious bodily injury to the foetus is an intention to cause serious bodily injury to a part of the mother just as an intention to injure her arm or her leg would be so viewed.[229]

The Court of Appeal's analysis was subject to severe criticism by the House of Lords. Lord Mustill objected strongly to the notion that the foetus and the mother were 'the same':

> [T]he relationship was one of bond, not of identity. The foetus and the mother were two distinct organisms living symbiotically, not a single organism with two aspects. The mother's leg was part of the mother; the foetus was not.

---

226 Ashe mentions technology as having contributed to the envisioning of mother and foetus as separate. On this see also Rosalind Pollack Petchesky, 'Foetal Images: The Power of Visual Culture in the Politics of Reproduction' in Michelle Stanworth (ed), *Reproductive Technologies: Gender, Motherhood and Medicine*, Polity Press, Cambridge, 1987; and Barbara Katz Rothman, *The Tentative Pregnancy*, Viking, New York, 1986.
227 [1996] QB 581 (Court of Appeal) and [1998] AC 245 (House of Lords).
228 *R v West* (1848) 2 Cox CC 500. See also *R v F* (1996) 89 A Crim R 250.
229 [1996] QB 581 at 593.

> ... The reason for the uniqueness of S was that the development of her own special characteristics had been enabled and bounded by the collection of genes handed down not only by M but also by her natural father. This collection was different from the genes which enabled and bounded the development of M, for these had been handed down by her own mother and natural father. S and her mother were closely related but, even apart from differing environmental influences, they were not, had not been, and in the future never would be "the same".[230]

Lord Hope of Craighead relies most explicitly on the possibilities of the modern technology of reproduction, emphasising even more strongly the separateness of the foetus from the woman who is carrying it:

> The creation of an embryo from which a foetus is developed requires the bringing together of genetic material from the father as well as the mother. The science of human fertilisation and embryology has now been developed to the point where the embryo may be created outside the mother and then placed inside her as a live embryo. ... It serves to remind us that an embryo is in reality a separate organism from the mother from the moment of its conception.[231]

Note

1. Do you think that the relationship between a woman and the foetus she is carrying is adequately captured by either describing the foetus as part of the women like a leg or as one of symbiosis? Are these the only possibilities? How is the different genetic character of the foetus relevant to the description of the relationship? Some authors have described the foetus as parasitic on the woman.[232] Is this a more accurate characterisation?

A Canadian example

Lynn Smith has also argued that there is very little analysis of the relationship between a woman and the foetus she is carrying 'and none to be found in legal discourse'.[233] Indeed, LEAF made the point that:

> Had women not been excluded from participation in the legal system, the unique relationship between the woman and her foetus and the experience of pregnancy in the life of a woman – hardly new facts – might have engendered their own fundamental legal concepts and doctrines, as elaborate as, for example, the doctrines dealing with the legal relationship between partners in a commercial venture or between employer and employee.[234]

---

230 [1998] AC 245 at 255. Lord Mustill does concede that: 'There was, of course, an intimate bond between the foetus and the mother, created by the total dependence of the foetus on the protective physical environment furnished by the mother, and on the supply by the mother through the physical linkage between them of the nutrients, oxygen and other substances essential to foetal life and development. The emotional bond between the mother and her unborn child was also of a very special kind' (*ibid*).
231 *Ibid*, at 267.
232 See, for example, Catharine MacKinnon's description: 'Physically, no body part takes so much and contributes so little. ... [O]n a biological level, the fetus is more like a parasite than a part. ... She is whole with it or without it': 'Reflections on Sex Equality Under Law' (1991) 100 *Yale Law Journal* 1281 at 1314.
233 Lynn Smith, 'An Equality Approach to Reproductive Choice: *R v Sullivan*' (1991) 4 *Yale Journal of Law and Feminism* 92 at 105.
234 Para XXIX of LEAF's factum, reproduced in Smith, 'Equality Approach', at 118.

LEAF endeavoured to develop such an analysis when they intervened in the case of *R v Sullivan and Lemay*.[235] The case concerned clear negligence in the assistance provided by two midwives[236] to a woman during the birth process. Her foetus died and the legal issue was whether 'they should have been convicted of criminal negligence causing death to a person [the foetus], criminal negligence causing bodily harm to the woman, or neither charge'.[237]

What happened during the birth is described by the Supreme Court of Canada:

> After five hours of second-stage labour, the child's head emerged and no further contractions occurred. Sullivan and Lemay attempted to stimulate further contractions but were unsuccessful. Direct pressure was applied to the uterus, causing soreness to the mother's stomach and back and some bruising. Approximately 20 minutes later, emergency services were called and the mother was transported to the hospital. Within two minutes of arrival, an intern delivered the baby using what the trial judge characterized as "a basic delivery technique". The child showed no signs of life and resuscitation attempts were unsuccessful.[238]

Smith describes the positions of other participants in the litigation:

> LEAF was aware ... that the appellants [*the midwives*] would be arguing that the foetus is neither a person (so there could be no conviction of criminal negligence causing death) nor part of the pregnant woman's body (so there could be no conviction of criminal negligence causing bodily harm). REAL Women [*Realistic, Effective and Active for Life Women, a right-wing, anti-choice group*] would be arguing that the foetus is a person with a right to life from the moment of conception.[239]

Smith discussed some of the difficulties LEAF faced in developing a position in this case. They did not want to be seen as opposing midwifery given that this 'is consistent with women's empowerment and with access to high-quality health care; yet so is support for a legal system that imposes criminal sanctions upon *negligent* assistance with childbirth, whether by midwives, medical practitioners or anyone else'.[240] The tragic circumstances of the case also made arguing a pro-choice position difficult. Thirdly,

> There has been a tendency for the pro-choice position to be subsumed in a privacy-autonomy analysis that refuses to talk about the foetus .... The foetus in this analysis is sometimes characterized as no more than a part of the woman's body, no matter what its stage of development. On the other hand, many women's experiences of pregnancy and childbirth indicate the "part-of-the-body" characterization is inaccurate and incomplete.[241]

Fourthly,

> The appellants' position that the foetus is neither a person nor part of the woman's body but instead an "independent entity" seemed creative, yet it was highly dangerous to the pro-choice position on abortion and reproductive health care. The interest of the state or others in protecting the foetus-as-independent-entity could

---

235 [1991] 1 SCR 489.
236 Note that independent midwifery was unlawful in British Columbia: Smith, 'Equality Approach', at 100.
237 *Ibid*, at 94.
238 *Sullivan* [1991] 1 SCR 489 at 494.
239 Smith, 'Equality Approach', at 104.
240 *Ibid*.
241 *Ibid*, at 105.

be used against the pregnant woman in the same way as the state's or others' interest in protecting the foetus-as-person.[242]

The following extract, from the factum presented by LEAF to the Supreme Court of Canada, indicates the position they came to in order to reinvisage the relationship between a pregnant woman and her foetus:

(b) *The Foetus Is In and Of the Pregnant Women ...*

XLIII. Not only is a foetus in the woman but it is also "of" her in that it is interconnected with her in many intricate and intimate ways.

XLIV. While in and of the pregnant woman, the foetus is not just another body part, ... It is not analogous to an appendix, which is the Appellants' suggested comparison. The foetus and the pregnancy are not even analogous to those parts of the woman's body, like her breasts and vagina, which have specific gender connotations. A sex equality perspective lets us see that what is a foetus to others is lived by the pregnant woman through her pregnancy. Pregnancy is not, in fact or in social meaning, like a "body part", even a female body part. Pregnancy has many cultural meanings which have significant consequences for women. It can be an emblem of female inferiority or adulation, of elevation or denigration, of heightened or lowered social status. It can bring pain or joy, fear or hope, dreams or dread of the future, and closeness or estrangement between women and between women and men. It can give a new sense of the meaning of life and new depth to the experience of family. It can attract violence against the woman, sentimentality towards her, and attempts to control her, and it can give rise to financial cost and disadvantage and the need for difficult decisions. Women have lost jobs and have been stigmatized and excluded from public life because they are pregnant, jobs and access they had in spite of being females. No body part, not even one evidently emblematic of gender (like a breast), has the profound and distinct effect on women's social destiny that pregnancy and the possibility of pregnancy can have.

XLV. The intimate and complex connections between the pregnant woman and her foetus are unique, and feature many ways in which the foetus is quite unlike a body part. The foetus is ordinarily created through intercourse, a social relation which has impregnation as a consequence. During pregnancy, a woman experiences wide-ranging physiological changes that only the pregnancy initiates; without the foetus, they will not occur. From its outset, the connection between the pregnant woman and her foetus is expected to end and it inevitably does end, whether through spontaneous or planned abortion or through birth. Further, the foetus carried to term involves the commitment of almost one year of a woman's life to the creation of a child.

XLVI. Yet the foetus is deep within the body of a pregnant woman, connected to many of her body's systems. The two are jointly nourished. There is no access to the foetus except through the pregnant woman; whatever happens to the foetus happens to the pregnant woman but not always in the same way, and whatever happens to the pregnant woman happens to the foetus but not always in the same way. Through her body, the pregnant woman perceives and experiences the foetus in ways that no one else can duplicate; she alone can witness the foetus and its development through her own senses without the intermediation of technology.

XLVII. Viewing the foetus, either as a person or as a person-like separate entity, or alternatively as just another body part of the pregnant woman, does not capture the unique reality of pregnancy. These views illustrate the limitations of

---

242 *Ibid.*

attempting to conceptualize the foetus from an outside perspective, which abstracts the foetus from its context, namely the woman.[243]

LEAF argued that the midwives should not be convicted of criminal negligence causing death to a person, as the foetus was not a person. To suggest otherwise would, they argued, breach women's equality claims. And, in relation to the charge of criminal negligence causing bodily harm to the woman, they argued that the midwives should be found guilty; bodily harm had been caused to her '(a) through the death of her full term foetus; and (b) through the physical consequences of unduly prolonged labour and the Appellants' failed attempts to complete the birth'.[244]

In the event, the Supreme Court of Canada did not have to rule on most of these issues.[245] They did confirm that a foetus was not a person, but the equality argument was not addressed; rather, the court relied on traditional legal understandings that a foetus was not a person.

Notes

1. Are there inadequacies in an understanding of the foetus as part of the woman who is carrying it?[246] Does the LEAF argument slide into presenting the foetus as an independent entity or does their description of the 'embeddedness' of the foetus maintain the connection between a woman and the foetus she is carrying?
2. Isabel Karpin has also developed a language to express the relationship between a woman and the foetus she is carrying.[247] She describes the foetus and the woman as 'Not-One-But-Not-Two'.[248] John Seymour has argued that the implications of a full appreciation of the 'Not-One-But-Not-Two' model is that it is 'only the mother who should be empowered to articulate the rights of

---

243 *Ibid*, at 123-4.
244 Para X of LEAF's factum, reproduced in Smith, 'Equality Approach', at 112.
245 At trial, the judge found that Ms Voth did not suffer bodily harm, and therefore there was no criminal negligence causing bodily harm to her, but the midwives were guilty of criminal negligence causing death to the foetus. The BC Court of Appeal had quashed this conviction, but set aside the acquittal on the charge of criminal negligence causing bodily harm to the woman and a conviction was substituted. The Supreme Court of Canada held that the Court of Appeal had no power to substitute a conviction for the acquittal.
246 See Morgan, 'Foetal Imaginings' and John Seymour, *Childbirth and the Law*, Oxford University Press, Oxford, 2000, esp Chapter 9.
247 Isabel Karpin, 'Legislating the Female Body: Reproductive Technology and the Reconstructed Woman' (1992) 3 *Columbia Journal of Gender and Law* 325.
248 *Ibid*, at 329. See also Laura Shanner, 'Pregnancy Intervention and Models of Maternal-Fetal Relationship: Philosophical Reflections on the *Winnipeg CFS* Dissent' (1998) 36 *Alberta Law Review* 751. Shanner, reflects on Judith Jarvis Thomson's famous analogy comparing a woman and the foetus she is carrying to a person who is kidnapped and unconsentingly attached to a famous dying violinist who will die if detached from his 'host' (see 'A Defence of Abortion' (1971) 1 *Philosophy and Public Affairs* 47). Shanner argues the analogy is inadequate: '[T]he conflict-of-individual-rights model fails to explain the nature and significance of a non-conflicted pregnancy. ... The fully developed violinist is not an embryonic or fetal violinist, and thus cannot account for the coming-into-being that is the hallmark of pregnancy. The model also fails to account for the perception by many pregnant women that they have become an embodied *self-and-other* in a uniquely transcendent way that is quite unlike any non-pregnant relationship, including self-connected-to-other as in the violinist example. ... [We need] a more complex logic of both/and: pregnancy is both unity and duality, both woman and fetus, entities not identical and yet inseparable' (at 759-60, emphasis added).

the fetus'.[249] Otherwise, he argues, if in some circumstances a third party is authorised to intervene, it re-introduces a notion of the foetus and mother as separate and 'does not reflect an appreciation of the special relationship between mother and fetus'.[250] Is it likely that this argument would be accepted in a judicial forum without some exploration of the equality implications of reproduction?[251] Is the 'Not-One-But-Not-Two' model the same as the analysis developed by LEAF describing the foetus as 'in and of the woman'? How important is it to develop an appropriate language to describe this relationship?

ASSISTED REPRODUCTION

As well as seeking control over fertility via access to safe and inexpensive terminations, some women also seek assistance in achieving a pregnancy, including the right to use safe sperm for artificial insemination by donor (AID) or in vitro fertilisation (IVF). In some States in Australia, access to such services has been heavily regulated and is often highly restrictive. For example, the (now repealed) *Infertility Medical Procedures Act* 1984 (Vic)[252] restricted the availability of IVF to married persons (and heterosexual de facto spouses who were participants in the program before the legislation was enacted). When this Act was replaced in 1995 by the *Infertility Treatment Act*, this exclusion continued.[253] However, three unmarried heterosexual couples successfully challenged their exclusion, claiming discrimination on the ground of marital status.[254] The Act was amended to allow access to assisted reproduction for heterosexuals in de facto relationships,[255] but it continues to exclude single heterosexual women and lesbians. The challenge to this latter exclusion, and its aftermath, is discussed in the following extract.[256]

---

249 John Seymour, 'A Pregnant Woman's Decision to Decline Treatment: How Should the Law Respond?' (1994) 2 *Journal of Law and Medicine* 27 at 34. See also the report prepared by John Seymour for the Australian Medical Association, *Fetal Welfare and the Law*, nd; and John Seymour, *Childbirth and the Law*.
250 Seymour, 'A Pregnant Woman's Decision', at 34.
251 See Morgan, 'Foetal Imaginings'.
252 This was enacted in the same year as the (now repealed) *Equal Opportunity Act* 1984 (Vic). See also *Human Reproductive Technology Act* 1991 (WA): s 23 provides that access to IVF is only available to those who are married or have been in a heterosexual de facto relationship for five years or more (and says nothing about access to AID); and *Reproductive Technology Act* 1988 (SA): s 13 restricts access to assisted reproductive technology to those who are married or have been in a heterosexual de facto relationship for five years or more. However, see now *Pearce v South Australian Health Commission* (1996) 66 SASR 486 where a woman separated from her husband successfully challenged her exclusion from an IVF program. The South Australian Council on Reproductive Technology states that, since *Pearce*, 'single women who meet the criteria have been granted access to [*assisted reproductive technology*] ART': South Australian Council on Reproductive Technology, *Quarterly Bulletin*, No 10, March 2000, at 4. The Northern Territory *Anti-Discrimination Act* 1992 exempts assisted reproductive technologies, including AID, from its scope (s 4(8)).
253 See Kristen L Walker, 'Equal Access to Assisted Reproductive Services: The Effect of *McBain v Victoria*' (2000) 25 *Alternative Law Journal* 288; and '1950s Family Values vs Human Rights: In Vitro Fertilisation, Donor Insemination and Sexuality in Victoria' (2000) 11 *Public Law Review* 292.
254 *MW, DD, TA and AB v Royal Women's Hospital* [1997] HREOCA 6 (5 March).
255 See *Infertility Treatment (Amendment) Act* 1997 (Vic).
256 See also *W v D and Royal Women's Hospital* (unreported, HREOC, 24 December 1999), where a single Victorian woman was awarded $8551 after being denied access to assisted reproduction services, which was held to be discrimination on the ground of marital status. HREOC did not have the power to determine whether the exclusion was constitutionally invalid.

Kris Walker, 'Equal Access to Assisted Reproductive Services: The Effect of *McBain v Victoria*'
(2000) 25 *Alternative Law Journal* 288

[288] Dr John McBain, a prominent Melbourne infertility practitioner, challenged the validity of this exclusion in a recent Federal Court case, *McBain v Victoria*. [[2000] FCA 1009 (28 July)].

Section 8(1) of the Victorian Act, as amended in 1997, provided that a "treatment procedure" could only be provided to a woman who was married or in a de facto relationship. A "treatment procedure" was defined to include both in vitro fertilization ("IVF") and donor insemination ("DI"). Dr McBain wished to provide IVF services to Leesa Meldrum, a single woman. ... Dr McBain was prohibited by the Victorian legislation from treating Ms Meldrum. Yet he was also potentially exposed to a discrimination claim by Ms Meldrum under the Commonwealth *Sex Discrimination Act* (1984) (SDA), which prohibited discrimination on the basis of marital status. He thus took action in the Federal Court seeking a declaration that section 8(1) of the Victorian Act was invalid because it was inconsistent with the SDA. He succeeded and on 28 July 2000, Justice Sundberg declared that s 8(1) of the Victorian Act was invalid, as were various other sections of the Act to the extent that they were dependent on what he termed the "marriage requirement" in section 8(1). That is, in so far as the Victorian Act required a woman to be married or in a de facto relationship to receive assisted reproductive services, the Act was invalid under s 109 of the Constitution and inoperative so long as the inconsistency remained in place.

[*Walker goes on to describe the response of the Victorian authorities to this decision. Although section 8(1) was declared invalid, it was not entirely clear what the impact was on other parts of the Act. The Infertility Treatment Authority sought a legal opinion from Gavan Griffith QC, who concluded that s 8(3), which provided that a woman who was to undergo treatment had to be 'unlikely to become pregnant ... other than by a treatment procedure' required*] [289] that a woman seeking either IVF or DI [*donor insemination*] be "clinically" infertile.

[*Walker argued that this*] simply continues, or reimposes, the discrimination on the basis of marital status that Sundberg J has ruled invalid. ...

Griffith essentially draws a distinction between single women or lesbians who are "clinically" infertile and those who are "socially" infertile, though he does not use the latter term. This is a distinction that is difficult to draw in many cases. Is a woman who has chosen to have a tubal ligation medically infertile or socially infertile? In addition, we might note that a "clinically" fertile married woman seeking assisted reproductive services because of her husband's infertility is in fact socially infertile. She is able to become pregnant if she finds an alternative, fertile sexual partner. We do not, as a society, expect her to take this step; rather, she will be provided with the appropriate medical assistance. To this extent, the Victorian legislation never intended to deny assisted reproductive services to women who are "socially" infertile. Yet a single woman or lesbian who is not "clinically" infertile is expected to find a male sexual partner if she wishes to become pregnant.

[*Walker argues that a plain reading of the legislative phrase 'unlikely to become pregnant ... other than by a treatment procedure'*] can be applied to a married woman, a single woman or a woman in a lesbian relationship. A married woman is 'unlikely to become pregnant' if her husband is infertile and she is not engaging in unprotected sexual intercourse with any other men. A single woman is 'unlikely to become pregnant' without a treatment procedure if she is abstaining from sexual intercourse or if she is engaging in only safe sexual practices. A woman in a lesbian relationship is 'unlikely to become pregnant' if she is only having sexual relations with her female partner. ...

It should be noted that, so far as IVF is concerned, the requirement of infertility is not a major issue. IVF is an invasive procedure that involves significant hardship for the woman involved; it is thus exceedingly unlikely that a "clinically" fertile single or lesbian woman would in fact seek IVF. The real issue for most single heterosexual women and lesbians (whether in a relationship or not) is access to medically assisted DI. Medically assisted DI permits access to sperm from men who have been tested for a variety of diseases, including the various hepatitis strains, HIV and possibly genetic diseases. It also allows women access to assistance in the insemination process, which may improve the chances of conception. For women who do not have a known donor available to provide sperm, DI is the only way to become pregnant apart from a potentially unsafe casual sexual encounter. The Victorian Act as presently interpreted denies these women access to safe sperm, requiring them to travel interstate or engage in potentially risky conduct that may place them or their future child at risk. ...

There are also lesbian couples who wish to use a known donor to become pregnant who intend that the donor will be known to the child and be involved in the child's life. Such women are denied the opportunity for medical assistance in becoming pregnant and are potentially committing a criminal offence, punishable with up to 4 years in prison, if they engage in self-insemination (under s 7 of the Victorian Act, only a licensed medical practitioner may carry out a treatment procedure).

Notes

1. The Australian Catholic Bishops Conference and the Australian Episcopal Conference of the Roman Catholic Church applied to be heard as an amicus curiae in the *McBain* case, an application that was accepted.[257] One of the arguments put before Sundberg J by the Catholic Church was that assisted reproduction services were services that could only be provided to women and were therefore exempt from the relevant provisions in the SDA under s 32 of the Act.[258] Sundberg J rejected this argument saying:

    > [T]he nature of these treatments is such that they are capable of being provided to both sexes. ... The reason for undertaking these procedures may be because of some physical feature of a man or a woman. ... Whether the primary beneficiary of the treatment is a man or a woman, in the typical case the service is directed to achieving the desire of the couple to have a child. The fact that for biological reasons the embryo is placed into the body of the woman is but the ultimate aspect of the procedure.[259]

    None of the parties to the *McBain* case sought to appeal against it. However, the Australian Catholic Bishops Conference, granted only amicus status (not party status) in the Federal Court, sought review of Sundberg J's decision in the High Court. There would have been real doubts as to whether the Catholic

---

257 As Sundberg J noted, the State of Victoria and the Minister for Health were 'neutral' on the question of whether there was an inconsistency between the *Equal Opportunity Act* and the *Infertility Treatment Act* and, given that neutrality, he allowed the Catholic intervention (*McBain*, at [3]).
258 Section 32 of the SDA provides that 'Nothing in Division 1 or 2 applies to or in relation to the provision of services the nature of which is such that they can only be provided to members of one sex'. Section 22, the basic provision outlawing discrimination in the provision of services on the ground of sex, marital status etc, is in Division 2.
259 *McBain*, at [15].

Church had the requisite standing to appeal the decision. Hence the Church sought, and was granted, the Attorney-General's fiat – that is, the Attorney-General effectively agreed to confer standing on the Church. This does not conclude the matter: the High Court, in the course of argument, expressed grave doubt whether they would grant a remedy to a non-party.[260]

In the High Court, the Catholic Church sought to reagitate their argument that assisted reproduction could only be provided to women. The Human Rights and Equal Opportunity Commission (HREOC), granted intervener status by the High Court,[261] argued that Sundberg J's decision was correct.[262] They also pointed out that s 32 was introduced in order to prevent women arguing that it was sex discrimination if the state refused to provide abortion services. Is this an early recognition in Australia that access to abortion is, indeed, an issue of equality for women, as we suggested in the first part of this chapter? What model of equality does such an argument draw on?

2. The Catholic Church in *McBain* in the High Court also argued that the Convention on the Elimination of All Forms of Discrimination Against Women (CEDAW) did not support the enactment of legislation outlawing discrimination on the ground of marital status – it was concerned only with discrimination against women on the ground of their sex. Can you encompass discrimination on the ground of marital status within the CEDAW proscriptions of sex discrimination?[263] HREOC argued:

> Marital status discrimination has resulted in distinctions, exclusions or restrictions being applied to women of a particular marital status in, inter alia, their employment, their education and their financial arrangements and welfare entitlements. Those distinctions, exclusions or restrictions have operated between women of differing marital statuses. Such treatment is ... a form of discrimination 'made on the basis of sex' (as that phrase is used in article 1 of CEDAW). It involves the application of distinctions, exclusions or restrictions to women or certain groups of women by reference to negative stereotypes associated with their sex, particularly stereotypical perceptions regarding the dependency of women upon men.[264]

---

260 See transcript of argument, *Ex parte Australian Catholic Bishops Conference; Re Sundberg* (C 22/2000, 4, 5 and 6 September 2001). At the time of writing, the High Court had reserved its decision.
261 See order made by Gummow J on 17 August 2001.
262 'Outline of submission of the Human Rights and Equal Opportunity Commission intervening before the High Court in the IVF Case'. In 2001, their submissions in the case could be found at the HREOC web site at <www.hreoc.gov.au/about_the_commission/guidelines/hcaivf>.
263 Note that the federal Attorney-General's Department, in arguing for the validity of the federal legislation that would allow the States to (continue to) discriminate against single heterosexual women and lesbians (discussed in more detail in note 3) said it was a 'side-issue' whether CEDAW supported marital status discrimination legislation as such legislation could be supported via other international obligations, for example, the International Covenant of Civil and Political Rights (ICCPR): see Senate Legal and Constitutional Legislation Committee, *Inquiry into the Provisions of the Sex Discrimination Amendment Bill (No 1) 2000*, Canberra, February 2001, at para 4.8.
264 'Outline of submission of HREOC', at para 60. See also Senate Legal and Constitutional Legislation Committee, at paras 4.12-4.14. The Committee expressed the view that 'the CEDAW text could be read as directed to eliminating discrimination against women in relation to men and as supporting the human rights of women, including a general right not to be discriminated against in relation to other women. ... [T]he Bill will amend the Commonwealth Act so as to conflict with the very treaty (CEDAW) that it was intended to implement' (at paras 5.7-5.8).

Is HREOC's argument a recognition of the fact that women not only have a sex but also a marital status? Recall the discussion in Chapters 3 and 4 where we raised questions about who is included within (feminist) claims on behalf of women. If single heterosexual women and lesbians are discriminated against by restrictions on access to assisted reproduction, why is that not discrimination on the ground of sex (as well as discrimination on the ground of marital status)? If this argument is accepted, why would there be any need for anti-discrimination legislation to cover discrimination on the ground of marital status as well as sex?

3. The federal government, as well as procedurally assisting the Catholic Church in its High Court case, introduced legislation to amend the SDA to allow the States (to continue) to discriminate against single heterosexual women and lesbians. When originally introduced, the Sex Discrimination Amendment Bill 2000 would have allowed States and Territories to discriminate against heterosexual women in de facto relationships; when this was pointed out, the government, in October 2000, introduced further modifications which 'specifically exclude married and de facto couples from groups to whom State and Territory governments might refuse or restrict ART [*assisted reproductive technology*] services'.[265] The legislation was referred to the Senate Legal and Constitutional Legislation Committee, who agreed that the legislation would have discriminated against women.[266] One of the bases of its conclusion concerned the government's major justification for the legislation:

> [The] issue raised by the amendments is said by the Attorney-General to primarily involve 'the rights of a child within our society to have the reasonable expectation, other things being equal, of the care and affection of both a mother and a father'.
>
> Irrespective of whether it agreed that the best interests of a child were served by having the reasonable expectation of the care and affection of a mother and a father, the Committee concluded that the proposed amendments did nothing of themselves to ensure such an outcome because they were so remote from it.[267]

In its report the Committee noted the estimates of the incidence of the use of assisted reproduction services by single heterosexual women and lesbians: they cited Dr David Molloy from the Fertility Society of Australia, who estimated that 'only 1% of the 14,000 ART treatments provided annually in Australia would be for lesbian or single women, affecting a total of about 150 women'.[268] Given this very low rate of utilisation of assisted reproduction services by single heterosexual women and lesbians, why do you think the *McBain* decision was greeted with such an outcry? Note also that the federal government apparently quickly accepted that women in heterosexual de facto relationships should not be discriminated against by state providers of assisted reproduction services.[269] Do you agree with Millbank who suggests that there

---

265 Senate Legal and Constitutional Legislation Committee, *Inquiry into the Provisions of the Sex Discrimination Amendment Bill (No 1) 2000*, at para 2.9.
266 *Ibid*, Chapter 5.
267 *Ibid*, at paras 5.5-5.6.
268 *Ibid*, at Appendix 4, para 1.3.
269 And this despite the fact that the States of South Australian and Western Australia, in 2000, did discriminate against heterosexual de facto women, requiring them to have been in a de facto relationship for five years before they could use the services, while a married couple could access the services with no waiting period: Senate Legal and Constitutional Legislation Committee, *Inquiry into the Provisions of the Sex Discrimination Amendment Bill (No 1) 2000*, Appendix 3.

is an exaggerated 'fear of female-centred families, particularly when they are seen to conceal lesbians or lesbian possibilities'?[270]

4. In Chapter 2 we remarked that, while there was much emphasis at the rhetorical level (and sometimes also in the policies and practices of state agencies, including the courts) on the notion of the privacy of the family, law also indirectly intervenes in the family. How useful is it to see legislation such as the *Infertility Medical Procedures Act* as indirect intervention in the private sphere?

5. The fact that some States and Territories (for example, NSW and Queensland), do not have legislative restrictions on access to assisted reproductive services does not necessarily mean that such services are freely accessible to lesbian couples and single women.[271] JM, a lesbian living in a stable relationship, challenged her exclusion from access to AID by a clinic in Queensland,[272] arguing that she had been discriminated against on the ground of 'lawful sexual activity'.[273] She was successful at first instance, with the President of the Anti-Discrimination Tribunal concluding:

> The discrimination against JM is both direct and indirect. It is direct in that Dr GK has refused JM service because of her lawful sexual activity of being engaged in an exclusive lesbian relationship. It is indirect discrimination ... because of the term that she would not receive treatment unless she returned the form stating the name of her male partner and signed by her husband.[274]

On appeal, Ambrose J found that the reason JM was refused AID was not because of her lawful sexual activity, but rather her (lawful) (hetero)sexual inactivity. In his view, there was thus no direct discrimination. In relation to indirect discrimination, Ambrose J decided that the Tribunal had not properly considered whether the doctor's refusal to make assisted reproduction services available was reasonable and should reconsider that matter. The Queensland

---

270 Jenni Millbank, 'Every Sperm is Sacred?' (1997) 22 *Alternative Law Journal* 126 at 128.
271 Jenni Millbank has described the indirect regulation by the National Health and Medical Research Council (NHMRC) which licenses service providers and issues guidelines. Millbank notes that, between 1982 and 1996, the NHMRC guidelines recommended restricting access to those in 'accepted family relationships', a phrase which was not further defined. After 1996, the guidelines have a child-centred focus, but Millbank argues they are not really less restrictive since, rather than focusing on compliance with the federal *Sex Discrimination Act* 1984, they recommend that service providers seek exemption from the Act ('Every Sperm is Sacred', at 126-7).
272 It would appear that the Clinic was operating in accordance with guidelines from the Queensland Department of Health: see *QFG and GK v JM* [1997] QSC 206; (1997) EOC ¶82-202; and *Morgan v GK* [2001] QADT 10 (22 May). The Clinic confined treatment to those who met a criterion of what was called medical infertility defined as an inability to become pregnant after 12 months of heterosexual intercourse (see *Morgan*, at page 13) The inexactitude of the notion of infertility has been referred to above and is discussed in an analysis of the *JM* case by Bronwyn Statham, '(Re)producing Lesbian Infertility: Discrimination in Access to Assisted Reproductive Technology' (2000) 9 *Griffith Law Review* 112.
273 See *Anti-Discrimination Act* 1991, s 7(1).
274 *JM v QFG, GK and Queensland* (Anti-Discrimination Tribunal, Decision of RG Atkinson, 31 January 1996) quoted in *QFG and GK v JM* [1997] QSC 206, at page 4. Direct discrimination is defined in s 10 of the *Anti-Discrimination Act* 1991. This provides that direct discrimination on the basis of an attribute (for example, sex, race lawful sexual activity) occurs if a person treats someone with an attribute less favourably than a person without that attribute where they are both in the same or similar circumstances. Section 11(1) of the Act provides that there is indirect discrimination if a person imposes a term and a person with an attribute is not able to comply, and a higher proportion of those without the attribute can or do comply with the term, and to impose that term is not reasonable.

Court of Appeal upheld Ambrose J's decision.[275] Thomas JA states: 'Minds may differ on the question, but common sense suggests that many lesbians are also prepared to engage in heterosexual activity'.[276] In Chapter 4 we noted that judges often bolster their fact-finding by reference to common sense. Where does this particular piece of 'common sense' come from?

When the matter was returned to the tribunal to assess 'reasonableness', the tribunal took into account that the doctor:

* desired to practice in his chosen field of treating infertility, and to treat what he believed to be medical conditions;
* made no conscious determination to discriminate against lesbians, and applied his policies to all prospective patients;
* did not act out of malice, or exclude lesbians from treatment because of any philosophical or religious grounds or because of any prejudices he held;
* acted in good faith in complying with accepted medical and ethical guidelines when limiting his treatment to infertile heterosexual couples;
* complied with the requirements of the Queensland Department of Health in accepting and maintaining a licence to operate as a day theatre for the purposes of infertility ... which included requirements to adhere to ethical standards which recommended restricting infertility treatment to heterosexual couples who had been unable to achieve pregnancy naturally;
* did not have the benefit of any clear legislative enactment nor definitive and binding guidelines when accepting the ethical and medical recommendations to which he adhered;
* would, *prima facie*, have lost his licence to operate ... a day theatre had he not complied with the restrictive (discriminatory) guidelines required by the licensing authority; and
* considered that the complainant was not infertile and therefore not eligible for treatment, not because she was a lesbian, but because she did not fulfil the definition of infertility required by the guidelines.

The Tribunal also took into account that the complainant:

* was well aware that she would be likely to be refused treatment at the respondent's clinic, but proceeded to request treatment to "test" the issue;
* was able to access a different clinic for the same treatment, and did so;
* did not establish that she was financially disadvantaged by accepting treatment at an alternative clinic;
* conceded that her emotional distress at being refused treatment arose not only from that fact, but partly from her lifestyle, and partly from her efforts to fight for a cause;
* has not been subjected to any allegations that she is not a fit and proper parent, by reason of her sexuality or otherwise;
* has not been refused treatment by the respondent for the reason of her sexuality.[277]

---

275 *JM v QFG* [2000] 1 Qd R 373.
276 [2000] 1 Qd R 373 at 396.
277 *Morgan v GK* [2001] QADT 10, at pages 15-16 typescript.

Do you agree that these factors are relevant to an assessment of 'reasonableness'?[278] Are there other factors you think are relevant? Do you think it is accurate to say that JM was not subject to an allegation that she was not a fit and proper parent?

6. Should there be any restrictions at all on who has access to assisted reproduction services? In South Australia, the *Reproductive Technology Code of Ethical Clinical Practice* 1995 provides that a couple seeking access to assisted reproduction must supply a referral letter from a medical practitioner asserting that, to his or her knowledge, neither spouse is suffering from a disease, illness or disability that would 'interfere with the ability and capacity of the couple to care for a child throughout childhood'.[279] Further, the couple must sign a statutory declaration that, amongst other things, neither has been found guilty of an offence involving violence or a sexual offence involving a child.[280] If the declaration cannot be signed, treatment services cannot be made available.[281] Are these sorts of restrictions appropriate? Kris Walker considers the exclusion of someone with a conviction for child abuse or a sexual offence. She asks:

> Even the person with a conviction for child abuse, a seemingly straightforward category of exclusion may raise thorny issues. Do we exclude the 40 year old man who, when aged 19, had a sexual relationship with a 15 year old girl, and who has no other convictions? What of the 15 year old who was convicted of molesting an eight year old, but 20 years on has no further convictions? Or should we only be concerned with convictions in the last 5 years? Or 10 years? Do we exclude the young gay man who was convicted of an offence under discriminatory age of consent laws? Or the mother who, during a period of post-natal depression, harmed her child? And, of course, merely acting on convictions could allow those who have been charged and acquitted, or never charged, to slip through. Does the fact that our system of regulation will be imperfect mean that we should have no system at all? Further, the number of persons seeking access to assisted reproductive services who fall into this category will no doubt be incredibly small – so do we need regulation to deal with such rare problems?[282]

How would you answer the questions she poses? Does the test in the South Australian code requiring a doctor to report on whether the capacity to care for a child is affected by an illness or disability smack of eugenics?

---

278 Section 11 (2) of the *Anti-Discrimination Act* provides that the assessment of whether the imposition of a term is reasonable requires assessment of all the relevant circumstances including 'for example – (a) the consequences of failure to comply with the term; and (b) the cost of alternative terms; and (c) the financial circumstance of the person who imposes ... the term'.
279 See *Reproductive Technology Code of Ethical Clinical Practice* 1995 (SA), cl 11(1)(b)(ii) (contained in the schedule to the *Reproductive Technology (Code of Ethical Clinical Practice) Regulations* 1995 (SA)).
280 *Ibid*, cl 11(1)(c)(ii).
281 Services may also be refused if either of the members of the couple has had a child permanently removed from their guardianship under a law other than an adoption law. There is now an appeal mechanism available where the reason for the inability to sign the form is due to the conviction of either of them for a crime of violence. The appeal body is to regard the welfare of any child which may be born as the paramount consideration in reconsidering access to assisted reproduction services: see cl 14E. The Regulations are reproduced in the South Australian Council on Reproductive Technology, *Quarterly Bulletin*, No 10, March 2000; see also Belinda Bennett, 'Reproductive Technology, Public Policy and Single Motherhood' (2000) 22 *Sydney Law Review* 586.
282 Kristen Walker, 'Should there be Limits on Who May Access Infertility Services? A Legal Perspective', 2002 (forthcoming).

7. Carol Smart has pointed out that there was much feminist agitation in the 1980s and 1990s seeking regulation, and on occasion, prohibition of aspects of medical intervention in reproduction, especially IVF and surrogacy.[283] She suggests that:

> [T]here is a clear political desire for a simple legal solution to the problems that are seen to follow in the wake of the new technologies. The desire to use law to ban or restrict the development of infertility services is as much a part of radical feminists' demands as the moral right's. It is interesting that both look to law for the solution to their concerns, as if law were a neutral tool which can be applied to resolve satisfactorily any set of political problems. ... [W]e can see a 'chain of reasoning' which posits law as the ultimate and most powerful authority which can and should be invoked to transform concerns (which may or may not be well-founded) into unambiguous state control. The problem is first that, although law exercises power, it is rarely simple or unambiguous, and second it is impossible to ensure that legislation, once in force, will be used progressively in the future.[284]

Smart argues that this emphasis on regulation may have led to the situation of restriction of access to AID for women 'who do not conform to the patriarchal ideal'.[285] How plausible is Smart's suggestion?

Conclusion

This chapter has explored three issues that concern, as the chapter title implies, legal control of women's reproductive bodies. In the first two cases – abortion and foetal rights – we are discussing the legal regulation of pregnant women's bodies and, in the third, the regulation of women who require assistance in becoming pregnant. The next chapter turns its attention to the regulation of women who have become mothers, focusing on the loss of children through custody disputes either with the state or with their partner, and, towards the end of the chapter, considers aspects of the legal system's response to women whose child has died.

---

283 See Carol Smart, 'Law, Power and Women's Bodies' in *Feminism and the Power of Law*, Routledge, London, 1989, at 106. Some of the feminist debate about surrogacy is discussed in the first edition of this book. On IVF, see Janice G Raymond, *Women as Wombs: Reproductive Technologies and the Battle Over Women's Freedom*, Harper, San Francisco, 1993; Rita Arditti, Renate Duelli Klein and Shelley Minden (eds), *Test-Tube Women: What Future for Motherhood?*, Pandora Press, London, 1984.
284 Smart, *Feminism and the Power of Law*, at 106.
285 *Ibid*.

Chapter Nine

Losing Children

Introduction

In the two previous chapters, we addressed the theme linking this part of the book: women and their relationships with others. Women often encounter the legal system in disputes about those relationships, particularly those involving children. In Chapter 7, we illustrated by way of some doctrinal examples (in particular, aspects of tort law) how law often constructs women as connected to others. In Chapter 8, we explored women's choices in having children, looking at the ways in which reproduction issues have been characterised in legal discourses. Here we consider a different aspect of women's relationships to children: circumstances in which that relationship may be disrupted or destroyed through legal action, most notably through 'family law' actions such as residence and contact disputes (previously known as child custody, guardianship and access). We then briefly consider some other ways in which women encounter law through loss of their children, for example the crime of infanticide, and legal responses to tortious harms that cause the death of children or prevent women from having children.

Australian child custody law

A brief history

Historically, Australian fathers (like their British counterparts) had absolute rights to the guardianship of their legitimate infant children, even to the extent that, on their death, they could will away guardianship of the child, irrespective of the mother's wishes.[1] Once the equity courts were given power in the 19th century to consider applications for custody from mothers according to principles under which the welfare of the child came to be considered as paramount,[2] the courts began to elevate the status of motherhood into a sacred virtue. This led to the development of the 'tender years' doctrine, under which young children, particularly girls, were considered best looked after by their mothers in the event of separation or divorce. As one judge in NSW put it in 1976:

> I am directed by authority to apply the common knowledge possessed by all citizens of the ordinary human nature of mothers. ... That knowledge includes an understanding of the strong natural bond which exists between mother and child. It includes an awareness that young children are best off with both parents, but if the parents have separated, they are better off with their mother. The bond between a child and a good mother ... expresses itself in an unrelenting and self-sacrificing fondness which is greatly to the child's advantage. Fathers and

---

1 See Heather Radi, 'Whose Child?' in Judy Mackinolty and Heather Radi (eds), *In Pursuit of Justice: Australian Women and the Law 1788-1979*, Hale and Iremonger, Sydney, 1979.
2 See the discussion of the English legislation and its adoption in Australia by the *Testators Family Maintenance and Guardianship of Infants Act* 1916 (NSW) in Radi, 'Whose Child?', at 120-3.

stepmothers may seek to emulate it and on occasions do so with tolerable success. But the mother's attachment is biologically determined by deep genetic forces which can never apply to them.[3]

Feminists and others soon came to challenge the notion that women were innately suited to motherhood, since it followed, in some renditions of this view, that they were suited to little else. This biologically determinist account also presumes that men are neither capable of being, nor willing to be, primary caregivers. Their fatherhood role, so the conventional wisdom went, was best served by removing themselves from the home for many hours a day to earn the money to support their women and children. Men are the breadwinners and women the dependants and child carers in this simple construction of domestic life. But at a time when women were starting to enter the paid work force in greater numbers, yet were still constrained by primary responsibility for child care, women wanted men to take more responsibility for the care of their children. The recognition that an increasing number of women were working outside the home (even if much of that work was, and still is, part-time, badly paid 'women's work' (see Part Two above)) led to campaigns about the provision of childcare, which remains inadequate in Australia. These developments led to a rejection of biological notions of mothers' innate capacity and suitability for the care of children.

The Family Law Act 1975 (Cth)

In 1976, Australian family law underwent something of a revolution when the *Family Law Act* came into force. The Act, which in the majority of Australian states deals with custody of *all* children, including ex-nuptial children,[4] provided (until the *Family Law Reform Act* 1995 came into effect) that, in the absence of a contrary order, each of the parents was a guardian of the child and they both had custody. 'Custody' involved the practical right to make day to day decisions relating to the care of a child and the former s 63E of the *Family Law Act* provided that a person who was 'granted custody of a child' had 'the right to have the daily care and control of the child' and 'the right and responsibility to make decisions concerning the daily care and control of the child'. However, since 1996, the concept of 'custody' is no longer used under the *Family Law Act* (nor is guardianship or access). Instead, in the absence of a contrary order, parents share 'parental responsibility'. A residence order simply describes where the child lives and, to that extent, is quite different from what was a 'custody' order. By contrast, 'contact' as it is now called, is much the same as what used to be called 'access'. Parents are expected to exercise parental responsibility jointly, though it is not clear what 'shared parenting' actually requires by way of consultation. If there is a dispute between the parents, the court can make a 'specific issues' order that spells out what the allocation of responsibilities is.[5] When making decisions about parenting issues

---

3   *Epperson v Dampney* (1976) 10 ALR 227 at 241 per Glass JA.
4   For constitutional reasons, the *Family Law Act* 1975 (Cth), a federal law, originally applied only to 'children of a marriage' (see Owen Jessep and Richard Chisholm, 'Children, The Constitution and the Family Court' (1985) 8 *University of New South Wales Law Journal* 152). However, this changed from 1988 after all the States bar WA referred their legislative powers over children to the Commonwealth (see Constitution, s 51(xxxvii)).
5   See *Family Law Act*, s 64B(6).

(residence, contact or specific issues orders), the Family Court is directed to regard the 'best interests of the child' as the 'paramount consideration' (s 65E).[6]

In 1979, the High Court of Australia expressly rejected the 'tender years' doctrine, or the mother principle, stating in *Gronow v Gronow* that this had never been a rule of law, but was rather a 'canon of common sense founded on human experience'.[7] The court said that '[i]n earlier days, when there was no role for a father in the upbringing of children and in the running of a household',[8] these matters were left entirely to mothers. But the court went on to state, without citing any evidence for this, that:

> [T]here has come a radical change in the division of responsibilities between parents and in the ability of the mother to devote the whole of her time and attention to the household and to the family. As frequently as not, the mother works, thereby reducing the time which she can devote to her children. A corresponding development has been that the father gives more of his time to the household and to the family.[9]

This rather rosy view of domestic life, where housework and childcare are shared, does not correspond with reality.[10] But courts and judges sometimes appear to eschew hard data when discussing the practices of domestic life and these assumptions about 'recent changes in the practices of domestic life' are as widespread as they are ill-founded.

These assumptions also fit well within the increasing use of discourses of gender neutrality in the area of family law, discourses that serve to obscure the highly gendered nature of caregiving and childrearing. The following section illustrates some of the ways in which gender neutrality has worked against women in disputes about their children, with some examples from case law. The first extract is from a now relatively old Californian case, which we include in this edition because it provides a succinct introduction to some of the disparate ways in which mothers have been, and continue to be, challenged in child custody litigation.

Gender neutrality in custody law

Burchard v Garay
229 Cal Rptr 800 (California Supreme Court, 1986)

> [*This case concerned a dispute about the custody of William Garay Junior, who was aged two and one half at the time of the trial. His mother, Ana Burchard, appealed from a decision awarding custody to his father, William Garay. The parents had had a brief liaison as a result of which Ms Burchard became pregnant. The father, when informed of this, refused to believe that he was the father. The child was looked after solely by the mother (with some family assistance) and she worked at two jobs as well as continuing her nursing training. The father did not visit or provide any financial support for him.*

---

6   For an outline of the differences between the *pre-Reform Act* and *post-Reform Act* law, see Margaret Harrison and Regina Graycar, 'The Family Law Reform Act: Metamorphosis or More of the Same?' (1997) 11 *Australian Journal of Family Law* 327 at 329-30. Some of the changes are discussed in more detail by Helen Rhoades, in the extract later in this chapter.
7   *Gronow v Gronow* (1979) 144 CLR 513 at 528 per Mason and Wilson JJ.
8   *Ibid.*
9   *Ibid.*
10 The data is reviewed in detail in Chapter 5 and see more broadly, Graycar, 'The Gender of Judgments: Some Reflections on "Bias"' (1998) 32 *University of British Columbia Law Review* 1.

In 1980, Ana brought a paternity and support action. After court-ordered blood tests established William's paternity, he was ordered to pay support. In December 1980 (William Jnr was born in September 1979), he visited his child for the first time. The next month, he moved in with Ana and the child, but after six weeks he moved out again.

William sought visitation rights (access/contact) and Ana refused and filed a petition for exclusive custody. William's response was to seek exclusive custody himself. Applying the 'best interests' test, the trial court awarded William custody, on the basis of three considerations. Two of these are discussed in the extract below. The third, per Broussard J (at 802), related to what is known as the 'friendly parent' rule: ie, the court considered the father more likely to provide the mother with access, whereas she had opposed his having contact with the child.]

BIRD, CJ ... [807] The trial court's primary reason for awarding custody to William was that Ana worked and had to place her child in day care, while William could afford to have his new wife quit her job and stay home. The court's other reason was William's larger income. No other facts appear in the record to justify the court's ruling. Today's decision ought to make it crystal clear that neither of these reasons is a proper basis for an award of custody.

In an era where over 50 per cent of mothers work and almost 80 per cent of divorced mothers work, this stereotypical thinking cannot be sanctioned. When it is no longer the norm for children to have a mother at home all day, courts cannot indulge the notion that a working parent is ipso facto a less satisfactory parent. Such reasoning distracts attention from the real issues in a custody dispute and leads to arbitrary results.

The court's reliance on the father's greater income was equally inappropriate. The child's best interests – especially when the child is very young – cannot be assessed in such materialistic terms. "[T]here is no basis for assuming a correlation between wealth and good parenting or wealth and happiness." (Klaff, *The Tender Years Doctrine: A Defense* (1982) 70 Cal L Rev 335, 350). ... [808] In fact, common experience suggests that there is no such correlation.

Stability, continuity and a loving relationship are the most important criteria for determining the best interests of the child. ... Implicit in this premise is the recognition that existing emotional bonds between parent and child are the first consideration in any best-interests determination. ...

[*A decision as to the best interests of the child*] cannot be based on a presumption that a working mother does not or cannot provide such care.

When the record contains no evidence as to which parent does provide this care, clearly the "working mother" factor operates as a negative presumption. Even more clearly, this factor operates unfairly when the record indicates that the mother has in fact been the primary caregiver. The use of such a presumption as a basis for a custody award is of dubious constitutionality.

Furthermore, the presumption is inappropriate because the relationship between maternal employment and the "presumed facts" about the child's best interests is not supported by reason or experience. Typically, it is the mother who provides most day-to-day care, whether or not she works outside the home. ... A presumption which ignores this fact is likely to lead to erroneous and unfair decisions.

Moreover, there is no accepted body of expert opinion that maternal employment per se has a detrimental effect on a child. ... Thus, the trial court's presumption lacks any expert support.

The burden of the trial court's reasoning would certainly fall most heavily on women. In those cases where the father contests custody, he is the parent likely to [809] have superior economic resources. ... This alone would give him an advantage under the trial court's reasoning. Further, such resources may well include the ability to support a nonworking spouse. Conversely, the mother is likely to have no choice about working, particularly if she does not remarry. ... In the 25 to 45 age range, the remarriage rate of divorced men is almost double that of divorced women. ...

Yet, under the trial court's rationale, it is the mother – not the father – who would be penalized for working out of the home. She and she alone would be placed in this Catch-22 situation. If she did not work, she could not possibly hope to compete with the father in providing material advantages for the child. She would risk losing custody to a father who could provide a larger home, a better neighbourhood, or other material goods and benefits.

If she did work, she would face the prejudicial view that a working mother is by definition inadequate, dissatisfied with her role, or more concerned with her own needs than with those of her child. This view rests on outmoded notions of a woman's role in our society. Again, this presumption is seldom, if ever, applied even-handedly to fathers. The result – no one [810] would take an unbiased look at the amount and quality of parental attention which the child was receiving from each parent.

The double standard appears again when, as here, the father is permitted to rely on the care which someone else will give to the child. It is not uncommon for courts to award custody to a father when care will actually be provided by a relative, second wife, or even a babysitter. ... However, the implicit assumption that such care is the equivalent of that which a nonworking mother would provide "comes dangerously close to implying that mothers are fungible – that one woman will do just as well as another in rearing any particular children." [Polikoff, 'Why are Mothers Losing: A Brief Analysis of Criteria Used in Child Custody Determinations' (1982) 7 *Women's Rights L Rptr* 235, 241] ... This is scarcely consistent with any enlightened ideas of childrearing.

The reasons on which this trial court relied are discriminatory. They fall unequally on women and men. They penalize women for failing to conform to a 19th century role which is no longer possible or desirable for many. They imply that a woman who leaves her "proper sphere" to participate fully in modern life cannot be an adequate mother. Such a view denies full humanity to women. It cannot be tolerated in our courts.

To force women into the marketplace and then to penalize them for working would be cruel. It is time this outmoded practice was banished from our jurisprudence.

Notes

1. Of the trial judge's reasons for decision, the third, concerning the parties' relative views about contact (formerly called 'access' in Australia and usually referred to as 'visitation' in North America), is not dealt with in the extract from Bird CJ's judgment. Essentially, this is known as the 'friendly parent rule' under which some courts have held that, if one of the parents is reluctant to allow the other contact with the child, the parent more willing to allow the non-custodial parent contact should be given residence or custody. The rationale for this is that it is in the best interests of the child to have continuing contact with both parents and therefore the one who is most likely to facilitate this is preferred as the custodial parent. The friendly parent rule has a statutory basis in some jurisdictions, for example, in Canada.[11] It has been the subject of

---

11   See s 16(10) of the *Divorce Act* 1985 (Canada), discussed by Susan Boyd, 'Ideologies in Canadian Child Custody Law' in Carol Smart and Selma Sevenhuijsen (eds), *Child Custody and the Politics of Gender*, Routledge, London, 1989, at 143.

some criticism because it may have the effect of placing a parent who fears for the safety of her child, such as where she believes the child to have been subject to abuse, in the position of either facilitating access or losing residence/custody altogether to the person she believes may be responsible for abusing the child.[12] While the friendly parent rule has no formal basis in Australia, the fact that it is widely considered to be in the best interests of a child to have an ongoing relationship with both parents, even though there is no evidence that this is in fact the case, may well lead to its de facto adoption.[13] If there were a clear exception for situations of abuse or suspected abuse, would it be appropriate to add 'willingness to facilitate contact with the other parent' to the list of factors that an Australian court must consider in deciding what is in a child's best interests?[14] Why or why not?

2. It is not uncommon for concerns to be raised about the suitability as custodial parents of mothers who work outside the home. In Australia, a 1987 decision of the Family Court received considerable public notoriety when questions were asked about the case in the Senate.[15] Two professional parents (both medical practitioners) went to court in Adelaide in a dispute over custody of their children.[16] The judge initially awarded the wife custody on a conditional basis: on August 6 she agreed to the wife having custody *if, but only if*, she resigned her job and was pregnant by 7 October. In her judgment on 6 August, Murray J had stated: 'The major question mark hanging over the wife ... is whether she would be prepared to sacrifice her career for the sake of the children'.[17] The wife had told the court that she wished to complete her examinations and continue to work part-time. She had also given evidence that she planned to have another child with her new husband. The judge decided that the wife would not give up her job – 'she wants her cake and eat it too [sic] – unremarkable in these days of equality of opportunity'.[18] When they came back to the court on 7 October, and the wife had not become pregnant, the judge awarded custody to the father, despite the fact that she had earlier commented that the father, at 57, was more like a grandfather to them. There

---

12 See Boyd, cited above, and Anne Marie Delorey, 'Joint Legal Custody: A Reversion to Patriarchal Power' (1989) 3 *Canadian Journal of Women and the Law* 33. The High Court has held that in a disputed case of custody or access where allegations of abuse are in issue, custody or access will not be granted to a parent if to do so would expose the child to an unacceptable risk of sexual abuse: see *M and M* (1988) 166 CLR 69.

13 A recent analysis of all the research studies on children's wellbeing and adjustment after parental separation confirmed that, in situations of conflict, a good relationship with one parent is better for them than a conflict-laden relationship with two parents: see Bryan Rodgers and Jan Pryor, *Divorce and Separation: The Outcomes for Children*, Joseph Rowntree Foundation, York, 1998. This is also discussed by Helen Rhoades in 'Posing as Reform: The Case of the Family Law Reform Act' (2000) 14 *Australian Journal of Family Law* 142.

14 See *Family Law Act* 1975 (Cth), s 68F(2), for the list of factors that a court must consider in determining what is in a child's best interests. Those factors include such matters as the wishes of a child, the nature of the relationship between the child, the parents and others, the practical difficulties of contact and the effect that may have on a child, the capacity of each parent to meet the child's needs, the need to protect the child from harm (this includes being exposed to abuse of another person), any family violence and achieving finality. Another provision refers to 'any need to maintain a connection with the lifestyle, culture and traditions of Aboriginal peoples or Torres Strait Islanders': this factor is discussed in more detail later in this chapter.

15 See Parliamentary Debates, Australian Senate, 20 October 1987, at 959 *et seq*.

16 *Ward and Ward* (unreported, No AD 1039 of 1985, Fam CA, Adelaide, 6 August, 7 October, 1987).

17 *Ibid*, at 19.

18 *Ibid*.

was no suggestion that he give up his job in order to qualify as a suitable full-time parent, and it was made clear in the judgment that his new wife would undertake the day-to-day care of the children, both of whom were school-aged girls. This judgment was reversed on appeal by the Full Family Court which held that the exercise of the trial judge's discretion had miscarried by requiring the mother to demonstrate that she was pregnant before she would be granted custody.[19] The Full Court noted that the trial judge had made the condition that the wife become pregnant the 'prime prerequisite' and concluded:

> It was unreasonable, in our view, and against public policy, in any event, to require a party to become pregnant, a circumstance over which that party lacked complete control.[20]

By contrast, in *Macmillan and Jackson*,[21] Rourke J had made an order awarding custody of a young boy to his maternal grandparents, rather than to the applicant father. The judge had been critical of the father's plan to refrain from seeking paid work outside the home until the child reached school age because, in the trial judge's view, such a period away from paid employment would lead to 'entrenched welfare dependency' and represented a 'poor role model' for the child. The Full Court set aside the decision. Given the high proportion of women who are sole carers for their children and whose main source of income is social security payments,[22] how likely is it that a court would express this view of a mother who chose to forgo paid work and be a full-time carer?

3. In her judgment in *Burchard v Garay*, Bird CJ referred to the disparate rates of repartnering for women and men after separation and divorce. The Australian Institute of Family Studies (AIFS) has also published data showing that the situation is similar in Australia. In its mid-1980s study of the economic consequences of divorce, AIFS found that divorced Australian men were considerably more likely than women to repartner.[23] The starkest contrast was between the repartnering rates for the older persons[24] interviewed in the survey: while 44% of the men had repartnered by the time of interview (1984), only 15% of the women had done so. For the younger group, while the difference was not so dramatic, the proportions of men that repartnered were consistently substantially higher than those for women.[25] This disparity in repartnering rates also emerged from the Australian Divorce Transitions Project data, published in 2000.[26] That research showed:

---

19   *Swaney v Ward* (1988) FLC ¶91-928.
20   *Ibid*, at 76,717.
21   (1995) FLC ¶92-610.
22   See Ruth Weston and Bruce Smyth, 'Financial Living Standards After Divorce' (2000) 55 *Family Matters* 10.
23   Peter J McDonald (ed) and the Australian Institute of Family Studies, *Settling up: Property and Income Distribution on Divorce in Australia*, Prentice Hall, Melbourne, 1986.
24   These were people divorced in 1981 who had been married for at least 15 years, with the wife aged between 45 and 59 at the time of separation: McDonald (ed), at 17. They were therefore all women over 50 with some considerably older.
25   Of the younger couples divorced in 1981, 59% of men, but only 43% of women had repartnered and, of those divorced in 1983, 45% of men and 35% of women were repartnered.
26   Jody Hughes, 'Repartnering After Divorce: Marginal Mates and Unwedded Women' (2000) 55 *Family Matters* 16. See also Ruth Weston and Bruce Smyth, 'Financial Living Standards After Divorce'. Weston and Smyth found that of post-divorce households (including the categories of alone, sole parent, repartnered, and partnered with child) the most advantaged group were those living with a partner and no children. In the study, this group was almost solely constituted by men (because it was women who were the primary caregivers of the children after separation and sole parent mothers are much poorer than sole parent fathers).

Women who had responsibility for children all or most of the time (resident mothers) were less likely to repartner than women whose parenting responsibilities were less onerous. In contrast, having primary responsibility for children did not appear to influence men's propensity to repartner.[27]

What factors might lead to this disparity in repartnering rates? What is the relationship between repartnering and post-separation financial circumstances?

4. It is common for men and the groups that advocate on their behalf to claim that they are discriminated against in the Family Court, particularly when it comes to parenting decisions.[28] The fathers' groups persistently claim that the court is 'biased' against them.[29] But their claims have no empirical support: the literature and the available studies show that, when cases go to the Family Court for a decision in a contested residence case, the court makes orders (in disputed cases) in favour of fathers at twice the rate of those made by consent.[30] In fact, most disputes about children are dealt with by consent agreements, that is, by the parents coming to a private arrangement[31] and, in a very high proportion of those cases, the research data shows that mothers continue to be the primary caregiver.[32]

Commenting on one of the first Family Court studies on the outcome of divorce cases, former Family Court Justice Peter Nygh suggested in 1985 that:

> [T]he mother preference is still alive and well in the general community, the fathers generally not contesting custody. The fact that fathers do appreciably better in contested cases does not mean, of course, that if only more fathers were encouraged to stand up for their rights, more would gain custody. The figures do not suggest how many successful fathers will personally undertake the caring responsibility and how many delegate that responsibility to relatives, de factos, new spouses or hired help.[33]

The study he was referring to was undertaken in part to respond to claims by fathers' rights groups and, in particular, the 'Army of Men' that the court

---

27 Hughes, 'Repartnering After Divorce' at 21.
28 See Miranda Kaye and Julia Tolmie, 'Fathers' Rights Groups in Australia' (1998) 12 *Australian Journal of Family Law* 19; Kaye and Tolmie, 'Discoursing Dads: The Rhetorical Devices of Fathers' Rights Groups' (1998) 22 *Melbourne University Law Review* 162.
29 See Kaye and Tolmie, 'Fathers' Rights Groups in Australia', at 33; Kaye and Tolmie, 'Discoursing Dads'; Graycar, 'Equal Rights Versus Fathers' Rights: The Child Custody Debate in Australia' in Smart and Sevenhuijsen (eds), *Child Custody and the Politics of Gender*.
30 Sophy Bordow, 'Defended Custody Cases in the Family Court of Australia: Factors Influencing the Outcome' (1994) 8 *Australian Journal of Family Law* 252; Frank Horwill and Sophy Bordow, *The Outcome of Defended Custody Cases in the Family Court of Australia*, Research Report No 4, Family Court of Australia, 1983; Margaret Harrison, 'Family Law, Recent Issues and Initiatives' (1999) 52 *Family Matters* 61; and see also Janet Fife-Yeomans, 'Court to investigate custody 'bias'' *The Australian*, 1 October 1998. Note that it has been suggested that most of the cases that actually proceed to a hearing involve some form of violence or abuse; that is, they are the most intractable of all disputes: see Thea Brown et al, *Violence in Families – Report No 1: The Management of Child Abuse Allegations in Custody and Access Disputes before the Family Court of Australia*, Monash University, Melbourne, 1998.
31 See Rosemary Hunter, *Family Law Case Profiles*, Justice Research Centre, Sydney, June 1999, at xiii.
32 For a discussion of the significance of the fact that most of the cases are settled by consent, see Helen Rhoades, 'The No-Contact Mother: Reconstructions of Motherhood in the Era of the "New Father"' (2002) 16 *International Journal of Law, Policy and the Family* (forthcoming).
33 Justice Peter Nygh, 'Sexual Discrimination in the Family Court' (1985) 8 *University of New South Wales Law Journal* 62 at 67-8.

discriminated against men and in favour of women and that men had a less than 2% chance of being awarded custody.[34] In fact, the study, which looked at all orders made in 1980 in the Melbourne registry of the Family Court, demonstrated that 79% of orders, including consent orders, vested sole custody ('care and control') in the mother. Defended cases accounted for only 10% of the total: of these, fathers obtained sole custody in 31% of cases. Added to this were 'split' decisions involving either separating children, or awarding joint custody: after these were taken into account, care and control (as it then was) of at least one child of the family was awarded to the father in 44% of contested cases.[35]

Even though the research evidence does not support these persistent claims of bias, such claims appear to have influenced the 1995 changes to the *Family Law Act* 1975 (Cth) that introduced a regime of shared parenting. One of the stated aims of these reforms was to create a new normative standard of shared parenting for separated couples.[36] Apparently, it was believed that this change in the law might change the long-standing practice of one parent assuming day-to-day responsibility for the children after parents separate.[37] The fathers' rights groups' success in capturing the attention of the politicians is apparent from the government's Second Reading speech and the Parliamentary Debates where there are numerous references to the hope that a shared parenting law would alleviate the distress of non-custodial parents, the majority of whom are fathers.[38] A particularly interesting feature of the fathers' lobbying that has been so effective with Australian politicians is their reliance on the discourses of 'victimhood' and 'formal equality'[39] in much the same way as happened in the lead up to the *Children Act* 1989 reforms in the UK.[40] Given that the empirical data do not support these claims of discrimination and bias, how do you explain the success of these groups' advocacy?

---

34 Frank Horwill and Sophy Bordow, *The Outcome of Defended Custody Cases in the Family Court of Australia*, Research Report No 4, Family Court of Australia, Sydney, 1983, at 1.
35 Horwill and Bordow, *The Outcome of Defended Custody Cases*.
36 See Helen Rhoades, 'Posing as Reform: The Case of the Family Law Reform Act' (2000) 14 *Australian Journal of Family Law* 142; Richard Chisholm, 'Assessing the Impact of the *Family Law Reform Act 1995*' (1996) 10 *Australian Journal of Family Law* 177; Harrison and Graycar, 'The Family Law Reform Act: Metamorphosis or More of the Same?'; Helen Rhoades, 'Child Law Reforms in Australia – A Shifting Landscape' (2000) 12 *Child and Family Law Quarterly* 117; Graycar, 'Law Reform by Frozen Chook: Family Law Reform for the New Millennium?' (2000) 24 *Melbourne University Law Review* 737.
37 The pre-Reform Act law had provided that, in the absence of a contrary order, both parties had joint custody and each had guardianship. Nevertheless, the more common practice was (and remains) for the children to live with their mothers, but have contact with their (non-resident) fathers. For results of research into the operation of the new legislation, see Rhoades, Graycar and Harrison, *The Family Law Reform Act 1995: The First Three Years*, University of Sydney Faculty of Law and Family Court of Australia, 2000.
38 See, for some examples, House of Representatives, Family Law Reform Bill 1994, *Hansard*, 21 November 1995 at, 3303; Senate, Family Law Reform Bill, *Explanatory Memorandum*, November 1994, at para 5.
39 Miranda Kaye and Julia Tolmie, 'Discoursing Dads: The Rhetorical Devices of Fathers' Rights Groups' (1998) 22 *Melbourne University Law Review* 162.
40 Jeremy Roche, 'The Children Act 1989: Once a Parent Always a Parent?' (1991) 5 *Journal of Social Welfare and Family Law* 345; Richard Collier, *Masculinity, Law and the Family,* London, Routledge, 1995; Arthur Baker, 'Post-divorce parenting – Rethinking Shared Residence' (1996) 8 *Child and Family Law Quarterly* 217; Carol Smart and Bren Neale, *Family Fragments?*, Polity Press, Cambridge, 1999, at 31-2.

5. The other factor mentioned by Bird CJ in the extracted case is the relative economic position of the parties. Again, while this has not been an overt factor in Australian decision-making, all indicators show that as a group women who are sole parents (and their children) experience significant economic disadvantage.[41] Catharine MacKinnon has commented on this factor, and on the fact that men repartner more than women:

> Under the rule of gender neutrality, the law of custody and divorce has been transformed, giving men an equal chance at custody of children and at alimony. Men often look like better "parents" under gender-neutral rules like level of income and presence of nuclear family, because men make more money and (as they say) initiate the building of family units. In effect, they get preferred because society advantages them before they get into court, and law is prohibited from taking that preference into account because that would mean taking gender into account. The group realities that make women more in need of alimony are not permitted to matter, because only individual factors, gender-neutrally considered, may matter. So the fact that women will live their lives, as individuals, as members of the group women, with women's chances in a sex-discriminatory society, may not count, or else it is sex discrimination.[42]

The primary caregiver: A feminist alternative?

Some feminists (particularly in North America) have campaigned for the adoption of a primary caregiver presumption to guide decision-making in post-separation disputes about children. Proponents suggest that, in a disputed parenting case, the best interests of the child are secured by ensuring that the parent who has primarily been responsible for past care is recognised for having performed that role. The primary caregiver presumption looks to past practices during the relationship to determine what is in the future best interests of the child once a relationship has broken down. As a gender neutral principle, it is able to recognise the situations in which men have been primary carers, while responding to the reality that the primary caregiving role still is predominantly performed by women.[43]

Canadian Professor Susan Boyd has been an advocate of the primary caregiver presumption, though in recent writing her support has become somewhat more qualified. Boyd and two Australian researchers, Helen Rhoades and Kate Burns, published a 'conversation' about the principle in 1999. Extracts are included below.

Susan B Boyd, Helen Rhoades and Kate Burns, 'The Politics of the Primary Caregiver Presumption: A Conversation'

(1999) 13 *Australian Journal of Family Law* 233

[Susan B Boyd] ... [*After describing the historical development of the presumption Boyd then turns to some concerns about it:*]

---

41 See Weston and Smyth, 'Financial Living Standards After Divorce' (2000) 55 *Family Matters* 10 at 15. They conclude: '[B]eing female, older, and a sole parent provided the greatest likelihood of economic disadvantage'.
42 MacKinnon, *Feminism Unmodified*, at 35.
43 See Richard Neely, 'The Primary Caretaker Parent Rule: Child Custody and the Dynamics of Greed' (1984) 3 *Yale Law and Policy Review* 168. Neely is a former US Family Court judge.

[239] These concerns relate to whether the presumption, if put in place, would benefit women and their children regardless of their race, class, sexual orientation, (dis)ability, or culture. For example, Judith Mosoff ... has argued that such a presumption, far from assisting mothers with disabilities, would disadvantage them in their custody claims. ['"A Jury Dressed in Medical White and Judicial Black": Mothers with Mental Health Histories in Child Welfare and Custody' in SB Boyd, (ed), *Challenging the Public/Private Divide: Feminism, Law, and Public Policy*, University of Toronto Press, Toronto, 1997 at p 227]. Women with disabilities are often assumed to be unfit as mothers from the outset. Once they become mothers, women with physical disabilities may arrange for physical caregiving tasks to be done by others, and act in [240] more of a supervisory role. It may therefore be very difficult for them to establish that they were the primary caregiver, as the term is typically defined. Women with mental disabilities may be encouraged by the psy-professions to focus on themselves in order to deal with their mental health issues, yet this self-absorbed and introspective behaviour is completely contradictory to the selfless behaviour that is typically expected of mothers.

Marlee Kline ... has shown that assumptions that there will be one primary caregiver of a child may work against (Canadian) Aboriginal mothers in their disputes with the child protection system ['Complicating the Ideology of Motherhood: Child Welfare Law and First Nation Women' (1993) 18 *Queen's LJ* 306]. It may exacerbate difficulties that they experience in showing that they are "good mothers", as their parenting patterns may not resemble primary caregiving due to reliance on an extended family and/or community network to share parenting responsibilities. [*Some of these concerns are discussed by Kate Burns in another extract from this conversation, reproduced later in this chapter*].

Another general concern is that in a society that is sexist, that undervalues women and mothers generally, and in which there is a powerful fathers' rights lobby ... it may be difficult in many cases to establish that an emphasis on primary caregiving is applied without engaging problematic ideological assumptions. In some United States jurisdictions, where judges purport to take primary caregiving into account, this trend has been subverted in a manner that defeats its original purpose. Laura Sack has shown that excessive attention may be paid, in a negative manner, to the sexual conduct of mothers, their survival of domestic abuse, or the paucity of their economic resources. ['Women and Children First: A Feminist Analysis of the Primary Caretaker Standard in Child Custody Cases' (1992) 4 *Yale Journal of Law & Feminism* 291]. In Canada, just at the point when primary caregiving language began to be used in Canadian courts in the 1980s, other trends have operated to obscure women's primary responsibility for caregiving. Fathers have been constructed as having a vital role to play in the raising of children. Mothers who are viewed as "depriving" fathers of this opportunity – for example, by limiting access to children by moving away or by breaking up a relationship "unnecessarily" – are viewed increasingly negatively in society and in law. Given the huge focus on contact between the child and their non-residential parent that has emerged over the past decade, the work that primary caregiver mothers do in relation to their children, and also in relation to the other parent, has acquired a new invisibility. Mothers may well now receive an order that the child live primarily with them, but they are required to facilitate contact with the other parent, prepare the children for such contact, and ensure that it occurs. Not only is such work not generally recognised, if at any point it is withdrawn, a mother may be punished.

In addition, as mothers have entered the labour force in increasing numbers, it has become difficult for judges and other legal actors to "see" that caring for children remains a privatised, gendered phenomenon, with women continuing to take more responsibility on the whole. The very gender neutrality of the primary caregiver presumption may preclude its application in a gender-sensitive manner. Judges find it much easier to determine that a mother has been a primary caregiver when she has been a full-time homemaker than in more complex circumstances, even though some of the first courts to articulate the presumption were careful to note that a parent who works outside the home might well be the primary caregiver parent. ...

[242] ... Finally, I am not sure that anyone knows how a primary caregiver presumption should operate in relation to lesbian co-mothers. Questions include whether there is more equal sharing of childcare responsibilities in lesbian relationships. Would this be the assumption by judges simply because there are two women involved in parenting, even if not actually true? What impact will the fact that one mother will probably have the biological link to the child have? ...

[*While Boyd is very wary about the primary caregiver presumption, she still cautiously supports its use, in a context where, she argues,*] we must recognise that at present, women are still primarily responsible for child care, and the legal system should be required to take this social fact into account. This recognition may be especially important in the current climate of backlash against mothers' claims. In my view, laws are poor tools for creating progressive social change; however they are arguably somewhat better at recognizing current social facts such as women's primary caregiving. Lending more certainty to child custody law through a primary caregiver presumption could be a benefit, and could allow some important public debate concerning the unequal division of labour around children that still exists. Overall then, despite its many flaws, the presumption may be our best (if a poor) hope of recognising continuing gendered patterns in the division of labour in heterosexual households at least, while also empowering women, predominantly the primary caregivers in our society, after family breakdown. To be sure, the presumption does not carry us forward to social transformation of familial relations, and may not enhance recognition of new and dynamic familial forms outside the nuclear family. It will also be subject to interpretation by judges and other legal actors who may or may not use their discretion in a manner that is attentive to sexism, racism, and other biases within the legal system and society. But the extreme gender neutrality within which custody law debates are currently framed makes me feel that we need to continue emphasising that in current families, gender is still not a neutral factor. Emphasising primary caregiving patterns may provide a way to do so.

[Helen Rhoades] ... [244] Far from acknowledging the continuing social reality that women are most often the primary caregivers of children, the new statutory regime [under the *Family Law Reform Act* 1995 (Cth)] is based on the premise that mothers and fathers shared their caregiving responsibilities while their family was "intact". The Reform Act was designed to encourage parents to continue co-parenting their children after separation, in the way that they are assumed to have done prior to separating. To promote this "shared parenting" aim, the new law severs the previous legislation's nexus between caregiving work and parental authority. Both parents are now constructed as having equal "powers, responsibilities and authority" for their children, regardless of which parent the children live with. Even if one parent obtains a "residence order", this will not by itself diminish the non-resident parent's powers in the way a custody order did. As a result, the concept of the "custodial parent" with primary decision-making authority to support their caregiving work, no longer exists in Australia. The prospects of successfully inserting a primary caregiver presumption into such a framework seem remote. ...

[246] The unreported decisions show that the fact of the woman's primary caregiver role is rarely seriously challenged by men who seek a residence order. It is the quality of the woman's caregiving that is attacked. What takes place in a residence trial is a critical assessment of the mother's parental performance. However, the totality of the woman's labour is not drawn on for this appraisal; what is scrutinised is a decontextualised selection of "incidents" by which the father seeks to show her failure to meet the standard of the "good mother". As against that, his suitability as a resident parent is generally judged according to the much lower standard of caregiving expected of fathers, or in some cases, by his mother's capacity to care for the children. Furthermore, ... the "approved" version of motherhood rests on assumptions that privilege white, middle class, able-bodied women. Women who have come into contact with a child protection authority (and these are disproportionately poor and Indigenous women), mothers suffering from medical conditions such as depression or bi-polar disorder, and women in relationships with violent men, are particularly vulnerable to assaults on their parental worthiness.

The case of *In the Marriage of D* [unreported, 1996] provides an example. Each parent sought an order for residence in relation to their seven year old son, "Peter". Mrs D was the undisputed primary caregiver and had been since the time of Peter's birth. However Mr D argued that she was not capable of properly caring for Peter because she suffered from depression. His affidavit material detailed a number of incidents of "bad" parenting which were used to demonstrate the mother's unfitness to continue as the resident parent. These included several occasions on which Mrs D had "lost her temper" with the father in front of the child, as well as allegations that she regularly "shared her matrimonial troubles" (for example discussing financial matters) with Peter. Evidence of the father's caregiving capacity focused on his "frequent" visits to Peter's school to help with his reading and to discuss his academic performance with the teacher, his regular attendance at school functions, and evidence that he often collected the child from school. Mr D also pointed to the flexibility of his work-hours, although in cross-examination it became clear that he often worked on weekends and would need to arrange for other people to care for Peter at those times.

[247] ... The ... counsellor who prepared the [family] report ... praised the father for his "extraordinary patience in the circumstances of the wife's depressive condition" and for contributing "generously and constantly in parent/school activities". On the other hand, the counsellor was critical of the mother for sharing her problems with her child, and the report noted that Mrs D had complained about having to have her interactions with her child assessed for the hearing.

There are no details in the judgment of Mrs D's daily caregiving work, presumably because the father had conceded her role as primary caregiver. There is also very little that provides any context for the incidents of "bad" parenting, although the mother's counsel would no doubt have attempted to "explain" them to the court. We are told only that Mrs D was seeing a psychiatrist because of "loss of confidence and anxiety and panic and difficulty sleeping", and that she was taking anti-depressant medication. Her psychiatrist gave evidence that her condition had "improved considerably" as a result. Nevertheless, the judgment lists a number of findings about the quality of Mrs D's caregiving. The trial judge found that she had "managed to cope well" as the primary caregiver despite her depression, but that regardless of her efforts, she had failed to control her temper. He expressed "a great deal of sympathy" for her situation. Decisively, he found that her parenting had been "erratic", and that the father would be able to provide the child with "a much better model of coping with stress". Mr D was successful in obtaining a residence order as well as an order giving him sole responsibility for making the long-term parenting decisions.

The way in which the father's case was conducted, which is typical of residence cases, shows that a primary caregiver presumption already operates as the starting point for adducing evidence, albeit in an unacknowledged way. The outcome does not turn on proving who did the bulk of the caregiving work before separation; it involves demonstrating that the (usually conceded) primary caregiver is "unfit" for the job. This is pursued by maximising the mother's "parental failures", and highlighting the father's exemplary achievements. In addition to that already skewed scrutiny, the qualitative assessment of each parent's caregiving work is measured against the very different social expectations of mothers and fathers. Carol Smart has argued that family law "has been typically more impressed by statements on caring about (when expressed by fathers) than the activities of caring for (when described by mothers)". ['Losing the Struggle for Another Voice: The Case of Family Law' (1995) 18 *Dalhousie LJ* 173 at 177.] She describes how a mother's "sacrifices" go unacknowledged because they are "seen as being as normal as breathing", while fathers' "utterances [of care] seemed to reverberate around the courts with a deafening significance". Thus Mr D is praised for attending parent/teacher meetings and occasionally collecting his child from school, while the extent of Mrs D's daily caregiving work remains invisible. A similar silencing effect occurs when the parents' attachments to the children are [248] assessed. Judicial statements that "the father clearly loves his children" are common, while mothers rarely receive the same credit.

Women's caregiving labour is also marginalised when they contest residence against a violent partner. In Australia, the Family Court has shown itself to be sensitive to the issue of domestic violence in recent years, particularly in children's matters. For example, the Full Court has ruled that evidence of violence may justify a refusal of contact to a father where it is likely to impact adversely on the mother's capacity to care for the children. [*In Marriage of JG and BG* (1994) 18 Fam LR 255; *In Marriage of Patsalou* (1995) 18 Fam LR 426; *In Marriage of Jaeger* (1994) 122 FLR 209; 18 Fam LR 126; *In Marriage of Irvine* (1995) 19 Fam LR 374; *In Marriage of Grant* (1994) FLC ¶92-506.] The Reform Act too includes a number of provisions designed to ensure the safety of children and their caregivers when parenting orders are made. [*Family Law Act* 1975 (Cth) ss 68F(2)(i), 68K and 68T.] Yet women who raise the issue of domestic violence are still especially vulnerable to negative evaluations of their parenting when they seek a residence order. First, they may be subjected to assessments by judges and counsellors that are based on misleading stereotypes of 'battered women' and the nature of domestic violence. An example is the case of *In the Marriage of R* [unreported, 1996] where the judge gave the following reason for rejecting the mother's allegations:

> She had, for instance, been able to on her own initiative to (sic) find employment out in the community in [a shop]. That is not the sort of self-confident behaviour that one would expect from someone who was the victim of a domineering domestic situation and I am not able to be comfortably satisfied that the wife in fact has laboured under the difficulties that she claims in her application should be held against the husband. ...

... Secondly, even when a woman's evidence of abuse is accepted, the court may fail to acknowledge the effects of that abuse on the mother's caregiving. In *T v C* [unreported, 1997] the trial judge found that the mother's "housekeeping had deteriorated", but said, "whether this was due to the father's violence, or to fault on her part, or to both, I am unable to say". Thus the mother whose parenting capacity has been adversely affected risks losing her children to her abuser.

Thirdly, a woman may find herself being blamed for the violence she has lived with. ... Although judges generally tend to dismiss the suggestion of "equal violence", they may find the parties' relationship was one [249] of "high conflict" or "co-dependence", rather than abuse, that the woman was in some way responsible for being in a violent relationship in the first place. The findings in *T v C* were of this kind:

> I find that the relationship between the mother and father was at times violent, and that the mother was not blameless in this. Each abused the other. The father appears a powerfully built man, the mother a slender somewhat worn (at least in the ... period of the trial) woman. I find that she came off by far the worse in any combat between them, and I find that he did not hesitate to beat her.

... [T]he current system for determining residence orders, with its fixation on parental conduct, tends to pathologise the "victim" of domestic violence. The point is demonstrated most clearly in *K v D* [unreported, 1996]. The counsellor who prepared the family report in *K v D* recommended that the father, who she accepted had assaulted the mother on numerous occasions, be given "custody" of the three children. Until then, two of the children had always been cared for by the mother, and the third child was being cared for by the paternal grandmother. In the words of the trial judge, the counsellor's reason for preferring the father was "not so much [that she was] impressed by the father's good relationship with those children, ... but by the irresponsibility of the mother in becoming pregnant again". At the time of the hearing the mother was two months pregnant with the father's child.

K v D also provides an example of the ways in which the focus on the caregiver's "parental faults" camouflages the issue of the man's violence. Counsel for the mother adduced a considerable amount of evidence of the father's abusive conduct. The judge accepted that the father was a violent man, that he had breached domestic violence orders on numerous occasions by assaulting the mother and damaging her home, and that he had abused and threatened her in relation to the outcome of the residence hearing. In addition, the mother was the undisputed primary caregiver for two of the children. The father's case was therefore a difficult one. However, he was able to show the court that the mother bore little resemblance to the ideal parent. She had [250] convictions of her own (for dishonesty), her parenting had been the subject of several notifications to the child protection authorities (although most had been made by the paternal grandmother), she had a history of withdrawing her complaints to the police about the father's assaults, and, in the words of the judge, "[s]he does not even own a refrigerator". In the end, the issue of the father's violence was effectively dismissed, with the trial judge deciding that the parties' relationship was characterised by co-dependency.

... It is difficult to see how a primary caregiver presumption would lead to any lessening of these uneven evaluations of men's and women's parenting. The decisions I have discussed suggest that even assuming its enactment was not a dim prospect in Australia, such a principle is unlikely to lead to women's empowerment. Rather, I suspect it would further entrench the present system that encourages scrutiny of women's lives. The primary caregiver presumption sets up a dichotomy that is inherently gendered, and the "secondary" caregiver will usually be the father. Despite its gender neutral appearance, I think "primary caregiver" is already widely understood as a code for "mother", and the presumption would inevitably be perceived by fathers as evidence of discrimination against them. In this era of the dominance of equality discourses in family law, such a presumption is bound to fail.

[*Rhoades suggests that one way to avoid the ' "gender war" problem of the primary caregiver presumption' is to draw upon the 'existing arrangements' principle that is currently used in making interim residence decisions.*] The central concern of the principle is to promote children's stability, which is assumed to be met by continuing the existing caregiving arrangements unless there are "strong or overriding indications to the contrary", such as evidence that the children would be harmed unless the arrangements are varied. The advantage of this principle over the primary caregiver presumption is that it is child-focused rather than adult-focused. The court's gaze would be directed at the children's lives – their daily activities and weekly routine – instead of evaluating the performances of their parents.

In addition, the qualification to this principle requires a high standard of proof of negative effects before the existing situation would be disturbed. The issue is not "who is the better parent", but "what are the present caregiving arrangements and are they likely to endanger the children". Thus the scope for the kind of "lifestyle" attacks that currently occur in residence cases may be reduced. To use the example of Mr and Mrs D, under the "existing arrangements" principle, it would not have been sufficient to disturb the long-standing caregiving arrangements for the father to show that Mrs D suffered from depression and that he coped better with stress. Instead of illuminating a parent's points of departure from the "good mother" standard, evidence would focus on the details of the caregiving arrangements that are already in place. In the process, the extent of the woman's involvement in that caregiving would be exposed. ...

... [252] No doubt the "best interests" principle would also remain, although my own feeling about that is that it has no independent content but simply acts as "an umbrella for a number of presumptions", so that its meaning is constantly shifting. The best interests of the child with a violent father in 1976 was to have unsupervised contact with him, while in 1994 it meant supervised or no contact, and in 1999 it probably means unsupervised contact with a "neutral hand-over" arrangement to keep the parents apart.

... [T]he "existing arrangements" guideline I have in mind differs from the "old" English case law "status quo" principle. That principle, which was primarily predicated on the idea propounded by John Bowlby in the 1950's, and by Goldstein, Freud and Solnit in the 1970's, was that discontinuity of the relationship between a child and their "primary attachment figure" was damaging to the child. Another version of the status quo principle focused on providing children with continuity of their physical environment. The principle I have suggested is broader in its focus than these psychological bonding and residence aspects, ... and ... it can be rebutted by evidence of harm. With that qualification, the principle provides decision-makers with sufficient flexibility to deal with those situations where the caregiver has left the children in the family home with a violent partner (as, for example, where a woman leaves for a refuge under the pretence of going to the shops).

Of course, even with such a principle to guide judicial decision-making and lawyers' and counsellors' advice to clients, it would do nothing to alter the unequal expectations we continue to have of mothers and fathers as parents. It will do nothing to alter the effects of the Reform Act mentioned earlier, [253] unless it is to be used as a basis for determining orders about parental responsibility, and not simply residence. Given the ingrained practices of lawyers in "running" residence cases, it is easy to believe that an exploration of existing caregiving arrangements could end up in the same critical appraisal of the mother's performance as happens now. Nevertheless, a principle which focuses on the caregiving arrangements for the children rather than the caregiver herself, may help to avoid the present attacks on women's lives as well as the gendered battle lines that the cases suggest would be endemic if a primary caregiver presumption were enacted.

Notes

1. As noted above in the discussion about the claims by fathers' rights groups of 'bias' against them, in fact women remain overwhelmingly the primary caregivers of children in Australia. This is clearly demonstrated by Australian Bureau of Statistics data, which shows that father-headed families constitute just 2.3% of families with a child under fifteen, while mother-headed families comprise 18.6% of those.[44]

2. The pre-1995 *Family Law Act* 1975 (Cth), s 63E, provided that a person who was 'granted custody of a child' had 'the right to have the daily care and control of the child' and 'the right and responsibility to make decisions concerning the daily care and control of the child'. Now, however, as Rhoades noted, a residence order carries with it none of the previous 'bundle of rights': instead, it describes simply where the child lives. Parents are expected to exercise parental responsibility jointly, though there is no statutory definition of 'shared parenting' and it is not clear what, if any, consultation a parent must have with the other parent. In a report on how the new legislation was operating, a majority of counsellors (generally the 'front line' workers of the Family Court, given how few cases go to a hearing) observed that the reforms had increased the expectations of fathers and correspondingly affected the expectations of mothers. Some of their comments included:

   > 'A lot of men think the reforms mean they have more rights eg. the right to have the children half the time. A lot of women think the changes mean they can never move, or they have to let the father have shared (50/50) residence'.

   > 'Men frequently take it to mean that shared parenting is automatic'.

   > 'I often find myself explaining that the concept of shared parental responsibility does not mean that children live half the time with each parent'.[45]

   And the parents interviewed also had different perceptions:

   > The responses to the client questionnaires issued in 1999 disclosed a divergence between the views of mothers and fathers. The concepts of 'equality', 'fairness' and 'justice' were central to many fathers' understanding of the reforms. Comments linking shared residence to child support were also prevalent among the responses by male clients. ... Women's responses to the client questionnaires tended to reflect a different emphasis, one that focussed on the caregiving and domestic labour consequences of the residence arrangements, and upon the impact on the children.[46]

   > ... The majority of the clients who responded to the questionnaires had an arrangement in which the children's primary residence was with the mother and there was periodic contact with the father. The children were living with the father in 4 cases, and one of those was a consequence of the

---

44   ABS, *Australian Social Trends 2001*, Cat No 4102.0, at 34.
45   Rhoades, Graycar and Harrison, *The Family Law Reform Act 1995: The First Three Years*, 2000, Faculty of Law, University of Sydney, and the Family Court of Australia, at para 4.10; available at: <http://www.law.usyd.edu.au/teaching/2001/famlawref95_report/index.htm> and <http://www.familycourt.gov.au/papers/html/fla.html> (2000).
46   *Ibid*, at para 4.11.

mother having fled the home to a refuge because of violence and she was trying to obtain a residence order. Only 4 of the parents had a shared residence arrangement.[47]

Solicitors interviewed were also concerned about unrealistic expectations:

'There is a public perception that contact parents, usually fathers, have more control over residence parents. There is also a perception that grandparents now have rights that they did not have before the amendments. I don't think the amendments have affected "reasonable" people very much at all. I think they have aggravated the aggressive and antisocial behaviour of others – perhaps as a result of disappointment of unrealistic expectations.'

'Fathers are fighting harder than ever for more involvement in children's lives and for an EQUAL rights approach to children. A lot of litigation about children seems to have been encouraged. It to some extent has been seen as a charter for non-resident parents' rights. Best interests of children perhaps diluted somewhat'.[48]

3. The *Family Law Reform Act* was introduced at a time when the issue of violence, and its incidence in the population of those involved in family law disputes, had become a matter of increasing public discussion. For example, in 1994 the Australian Law Reform Commission had published its first report on its reference, *Equality Before the Law: Justice for Women.*[49] In the chapter on Family Law, the Commission had noted the large number of submissions from women who had claimed that the violence they had experienced in the context of family law disputes had not been taken into account as a factor when their cases had been decided. A high proportion of those who made submissions to the ALRC inquiry did so in relation to family law and specifically on the issue of violence, and the Commission made a number of recommendations including amendments to the child-related provisions of the *Family Law Act*. Around the same time, the National Committee on Violence Against Women published reports also containing recommendations about dealing with violence in the context of family law and a number of articles were published drawing attention to the body of research involving the impact of violence on children.[50] Significantly, that research demonstrated that it is not just violence directed at a child that causes harm: violence against a child's caregiver can also have a significant impact on a child's well being.[51] It was pointed out that the issue of violence was of particular relevance to a jurisdiction that dealt with family law disputes as the separating population was especially likely to contain a high proportion of people who had been targets of violence. Moreover, research has demonstrated that the period immediately after

---

47   *Ibid*, at para 4.15.
48   *Ibid*, at para 4.20.
49   ALRC, *Equality Before the Law: Justice for Women,* Report No 69, Part I, Chapter 9.
50   National Committee on Violence Against Women, *National Strategy on Violence Against Women*, October 1992; see also articles published in (1995) 9 *Australian Journal of Family Law*, issue No 1 (March 1995), a special issue on family violence.
51   Some of the research is discussed by Patrick Parkinson, 'Custody, Access and Domestic Violence' (1995) 9 *Australian Journal of Family Law* 41. See also *In Marriage of Patsalou* (1995) 18 Fam LR 426.

separation is the most dangerous for women who have been the targets of violence.[52]

In the early 1990s, the Family Court made a number of decisions that dealt specifically with the impact of violence on children in the context of disputes over what was then 'custody'. In several cases decided in 1994 and 1995, the court held that an unacceptable risk of harm to a child might be established by evidence of domestic violence even though the child him or herself was in no danger of being physically assaulted and had not witnessed the violence.[53] This case law represented a departure from the approach taken by the Family Court to evidence of domestic violence in the earlier days of the court's history when the court had relied upon its no-fault philosophy to suggest that violence against a spouse was not necessarily a relevant consideration in determining a child's best interests.[54]

The *Family Law Reform Act* introduced into the children's provisions of the Act a number of changes that were designed to ensure that the need to protect children and their parents from family violence is taken into account when parenting orders are made.[55] They include a reference to 'the need to ensure safety from family violence' among the general objectives of the *Family Law Act*,[56] and new references to 'family violence' and to 'family violence orders' as relevant considerations when determining the best interests of the child.[57] A further provision requires judges to ensure that parenting orders do not expose a person to an 'unacceptable risk' of family violence.[58] In addition, a new Division 11 in Part VII cautions judges against making orders for contact that are inconsistent with existing family violence orders.[59]

However, this recognition of the broad impact of domestic violence upon children's welfare appears to be in conflict with the 'right to contact' provision introduced in the *Reform Act*.[60] Research on the impact of the new children's provisions has demonstrated that the right to contact is seen as

---

52 Martha Mahoney, 'Legal Images of Battered Women: Redefining the Issue of Separation' (1991) 90 *Michigan Law Review* 1; Alison Wallace, *Homicide: The Social Reality*, Research Study No 5, Bureau of Crime Statistics and Research, Attorney General's Department, Sydney, 1986; and Hilary Astor, 'The Weight of Silence: Talking About Violence in Family Mediation' in Margaret Thornton (ed), *Public and Private: Feminist Legal Debates*, Oxford University Press, Melbourne, 1995. See also Elizabeth Hore, Janne Gibson and Sophy Bordow, *Domestic Homicide*, Family Court of Australia, Research Report No 13, March 1996.
53 This jurisprudence is discussed by Helen Rhoades in the extract above.
54 For a discussion of this, see *In Marriage of JG and BG* (1994) 18 Fam LR 255. See also Graycar, 'The Relevance of Violence in Family Court Decision Making' (1995) 9 *Australian Journal of Family Law* 58.
55 Senate, *Family Law Reform Bill 1994, Explanatory Memorandum*, November 1994, at paras 6 and 7.
56 *Family Law Act* 1975 (Cth), s 43(ca).
57 *Family Law Act* 1975 (Cth), s 68F(2)(i) and (j).
58 *Family Law Act* 1975 (Cth), s 68K.
59 When a judge or magistrate intends to make an inconsistent contact order, she or he must now comply with a number of requirements, including an obligation to explain the reasons for the order to the parties (s 68R) and magistrates are empowered to vary or suspend a contact order when making a family violence order (s 68T).
60 Section 60B(2)(b) provides that one of the principles underlying the children's part of the Act is that 'children have a right of contact, on a regular basis, with both their parents and with other people significant to their care, welfare and development'. All the provisions of s 60B(2) are expressed to apply 'except when it is or would be contrary to a child's best interests'.

'trumping' the violence provisions:[61] one solicitor commented: 'Domestic violence is now down-played like 10 years ago. Unless it affects the children, he'll still get contact'.[62]

How does the 'no fault' philosophy of the legislation square with the provisions that indicate that violence is to be taken into account in making decisions about children? Is it possible for the 'right to contact' to be effective without undermining the statutory attempts to protect children from violence?

4. In her discussion, Rhoades indicated a preference for what she describes as a modified status quo principle. The 'status quo' principle is given statutory recognition in the 'best interests' factors by s 68F(2)(c) which requires a court to consider 'the likely effect of any changes in the child's circumstances, including the likely effect on the child of any separation from (i) either of his or her parents; or (ii) any other child or other person with whom he or she has been living'. Do you agree with Rhoades that the status quo principle differs from the primary caregiver principle by focusing on the child's needs and interests, rather than on the caregiver herself? How would a 'status quo' preference take account of those women who, because of violence, have been forced to leave their children when they end their relationships?

Child custody: A narrow white heterosexual perspective?

Indigenous families and family law

In the extract from Susan Boyd's part of the primary caregiver conversation, she drew attention to the difficulties that could be experienced by women who for various reasons did not undertake primary caregiving of their child(ren). Two groups she singled out for discussion were women with disabilities and indigenous women. In Australia, there has been a long and complicated history of indigenous families' interaction with the legal system. In the following section, we start by outlining some of that history via extracts from *Bringing Them Home*, the 1997 HREOC report into the 'Stolen Generations'. We then return to the 'conversation' via Kate Burns' engagement with some of these issues.

While there is a plethora of feminist literature on custody, most of it tends to ignore the particular problems experienced by minority women (in Australia, especially indigenous women). Disputes concerning children from minority communities are likely to be qualitatively different from those experienced by Anglo-Australian women. Canadian scholar Marlee Kline has suggested that traditional feminist analyses of custody law are limited: first, because they have tended to overlook the racial identity of the participants and, secondly, because they have tended to focus on intra-family child custody issues rather than undertaking a broader analysis of the many ways in which women lose custody of their children.[63] As she notes, for indigenous women, the disputes are far more likely to have been with 'the state' than against a partner. And as is now notorious,

---

61 John Dewar, Stephen Parker et al, *Parenting, Planning and Partnership: The impact of the new Part VII of the Family Law Act 1975 (Cth)*, Family Law Research Unit Working Paper No 3, Griffith University, 1999; John Dewar and Stephen Parker, 'The Impact of the New Part VII' (1999) 13 *Australian Journal of Family Law* 96; Rhoades et al, *The Family Law Reform Act: The First Three Years*, 2000, esp Chapter 5.

62 Rhoades et al, *The First Three Years*, at para 5.39.

63 Marlee Kline, 'Race, Racism and Feminist Legal Theory' (1989) 12 *Harvard Women's Law Journal* 115; Marlee Kline, 'Complicating the Ideology of Motherhood: Child Welfare Law and First Nations Women' (1993) 18 *Queen's Law Journal* 306.

Australian 'child welfare policies' were extremely destructive of Aboriginal families and communities: the principal tool of oppression was the removal of Aboriginal children from their families under the authority of bodies like the Aboriginal Protection Board which operated from 1909 to 1969.[64] This history is exhaustively documented in the HREOC report, *Bringing Them Home*.

HREOC, *Bringing Them Home*: *National Inquiry into the Separation of Aboriginal and Torres Strait Islander Children from Their Families*
Commonwealth of Australia, Sydney, 1997

Chapter 2 National Overview

[27] Colonisation

Indigenous children have been forcibly separated from their families and communities since the very first days of the European occupation of Australia.

Violent battles over rights to land, food and water sources characterised race relations in the nineteenth century. Throughout this conflict Indigenous children were kidnapped and exploited for their labour. ...

Governments and missionaries also targeted Indigenous children for removal from their families. Their motives were to 'inculcate European values and work habits in children, who would then be employed in service to the colonial settlers'

... In 1814 Governor Macquarie funded the first school for Aboriginal children. Its novelty was an initial attraction for [28] Indigenous families but within a few years it evoked a hostile response when it became apparent that its purpose was to distance the children from their families and communities.

Although colonial governments in the nineteenth century professed abhorrence at the brutality of expansionist European settlers, they were unwilling or unable to stop their activities. When news of the massacres and atrocities reached the British Government it appointed a Select Committee to inquire into the condition of Aboriginal people.

Protection and segregation of Indigenous people in the nineteenth century

The Select Committee Inquiry proposed the establishment of a protectorate system, ... based on the notion that Indigenous people would willingly establish self-sufficient agricultural communities on reserved areas modelled on an English village and would not interfere with the land claims of the colonists.

By the middle of the nineteenth century the protectorate experiment had failed and the very survival of Indigenous people was being questioned. Forced off their land to the edges of non-Indigenous settlement, dependent upon government rations if they could not find work, suffering from malnutrition and disease, their presence was unsettling and embarrassing to non-Indigenous people. Governments typically viewed Indigenous people as a nuisance.

The violence and disease associated with colonisation was characterised, in the language of social Darwinism, as a natural process of 'survival of the fittest'. According to this analysis, the future of Aboriginal people was inevitably doomed; what was needed from governments and missionaries was to 'smooth the dying pillow'.

The government response was to reserve land for the exclusive use of Indigenous people and assign responsibility for their welfare to a Chief Protector or Protection Board. By 1911 the Northern Territory and every State except

---

64 See Peter Read, *The Stolen Generations: the Removal of Aboriginal Children in New South Wales 1883 to 1969*, NSW Ministry of Aboriginal Affairs, Occasional Paper No 1, and; see also Jennifer Lock, *The Aboriginal Child Placement Principle*, NSWLRC, Research Report No 7, 1997.

Tasmania had 'protectionist legislation' giving the Chief Protector or Protection Board extensive power to control Indigenous people. In some States and in the Northern Territory the Chief Protector was made the legal guardian of all Aboriginal children, displacing the rights of parents. The management of the reserves was delegated to government appointed managers or missionaries in receipt of government subsidies. Enforcement of the protectionist legislation at the local level was the responsibility of 'protectors' who were usually police officers.

[29] In the name of protection Indigenous people were subject to near-total control. Their entry to and exit from reserves was regulated as was their everyday life on the reserves, their right to marry and their employment. With a view to encouraging the conversion of the children to Christianity and distancing them from their Indigenous lifestyle, children were housed in dormitories and contact with their families strictly limited.

Tasmania was the exception to this protectionist trend. By the turn of the century most Indigenous families had been removed to Cape Barren Island off the north coast of the Tasmanian mainland where they were effectively segregated from non-Indigenous people. Until the late 1960s Tasmanian governments resolutely insisted that Tasmania did not have an Aboriginal population, just some 'half-caste' people. ...

Merging and absorption

By the late nineteenth century it had become apparent that although the full descent Indigenous population was declining, the mixed descent population was increasing. .... In social Darwinist terms they were not regarded as near extinction. The fact that they had some European 'blood' meant that there was a place for them in non-Indigenous society, albeit a very lowly one.

Furthermore, the prospect that this mixed descent population was growing made it imperative to governments that mixed descent people be forced to join the workforce instead of relying on government rations. In that way the mixed descent population would be both self-supporting and satisfy the needs of the developing Australian economy for cheap labour.

The reality that Indigenous people did not identify as Europeans, however much European 'blood' they had, was not taken into account. Nevertheless, the difficulties of permanently distancing mixed descent children from their Indigenous families was a matter of constant concern to government officials. Clearly they recognised the strength of the family bonds they were trying to break.

Unlike white children who came into the state's control, far greater care was taken to ensure that [Aboriginal children] never saw their parents or families again. They were often given new names, and the greater distances involved in rural areas made it easier to prevent parents and children on separate missions from tracing each other (van Krieken, *Children and the State: Social Control and the Formation of Australian Child Welfare*, 1991 page 108).

Government officials theorised that by forcibly removing Indigenous children from their families and sending them away from their communities to work for non-Indigenous people, this mixed descent population would, over time, 'merge' with the non-Indigenous population. ...

[30] In Neville's [*the Chief Protector of WA*] view, skin colour was the key to absorption. Children with lighter skin colour would automatically be accepted into non-Indigenous society and lose their Aboriginal identity.

Assuming the theory to be correct, argument in government circles centred around the optimum age for forced removal. At a Royal Commission in South Australia in 1913 'experts' disagreed whether children should be removed at birth or about two years old.

The 'protectionist' legislation was generally used in preference to the general child welfare legislation to remove Indigenous children. That way government officials acting under the authority of the Chief Protector or the Board could simply order the removal of an Indigenous child without having to establish to a court's satisfaction that the child was neglected.

In Queensland and Western Australia the Chief Protector used his removal and guardianship powers to force all Indigenous people onto large, highly regulated government settlements and missions, to remove children from their mothers at about the age of four years and place them in dormitories away from their families and to send them off the missions and settlements at about 14 to work. Indigenous girls who became pregnant were sent back to the mission or dormitory to have their child. The removal process then repeated itself.

Another method of forcing people of mixed descent away from their families and communities and into non-Indigenous society was to change the definition of 'Aboriginality' in the protection legislation to fit the government's current policy in relation to Aboriginal affairs. People with more than a stipulated proportion of European 'blood' were disqualified from living on reserves with their families or receiving rations. This tactic of 'dispersing' Aboriginal camps was used in Victoria and New South Wales. ... However the notion that people forced off the reserves would merge with the non-Indigenous population took no account of the discrimination they faced. [31] Unable to find work and denied the social security benefits that non-Indigenous people were granted as of right, they lived in 'shanty' towns near the reserves or on the edges of non-Indigenous settlement.

In New South Wales, Western Australia and the Northern Territory many children of mixed descent were totally separated from their families when young and placed in segregated 'training' institutions before being sent out to work. ...

As the ultimate purpose of removal was to control the reproduction of Indigenous people with a view to 'merging' or 'absorbing' them into the non-Indigenous population, Indigenous girls were targeted for removal and sent to work as domestics. Apart from satisfying a demand for cheap servants, work increasingly eschewed by non-Indigenous females, it was thought that the long hours and exhausting work would curb the sexual promiscuity attributed to them by non-Indigenous people. ...

[32] **Merging becomes assimilation**
In 1937 the first Commonwealth-State Native Welfare Conference was held, attended by representatives of all the States (except Tasmania) and the Northern Territory. ...

The conference was sufficiently impressed by Neville's idea of 'absorption' to agree that,

> ... this conference believes that the destiny of the natives of aboriginal origin, but not of the full blood, lies in their ultimate absorption by the people of the Commonwealth, and it therefore recommends that all efforts be directed to that end.

In relation to Indigenous children, the conference resolved that,

> ... efforts of all State authorities should be directed towards the education of children of mixed aboriginal blood at white standards, and their subsequent employment under the same conditions as whites with a view to their taking their place in the white community on an equal footing with the whites.

From this time on, States began adopting policies designed to 'assimilate' Indigenous people of mixed descent. Whereas 'merging' was essentially a passive process of pushing Indigenous people into the non-Indigenous community and denying them assistance, assimilation was a highly intensive process necessitating constant surveillance of people's lives, judged according to non-Indigenous standards. Although Neville's model of absorption had been a biological one, assimilation was a socio-cultural model.

Implicit in the assimilation policy was the idea current among non-Indigenous people that there was nothing of value in Indigenous culture. ...

[33] Removal of Indigenous children under child welfare legislation

New South Wales was the first jurisdiction to reshape its Indigenous child welfare system according to the assimilationist welfare model. After 1940 the removal of Indigenous children was governed by the general child welfare law, although once removed Indigenous children were treated differently from non-Indigenous children. ...

Under the general child welfare law, Indigenous children had to be found to be 'neglected', 'destitute' or 'uncontrollable'. These terms were applied by courts much more readily to Indigenous children than non-Indigenous children as the definitions and interpretations of those terms assumed a non-Indigenous model of child-rearing and regarded poverty as synonymous with neglect. It was not until 1966 that all eligibility restrictions on Indigenous people's receipt of social security benefits were fully lifted. Before that time Indigenous families in need could not rely on the financial support of government which was designed to hold non-Indigenous families together in times of need. Moreover, ongoing surveillance of their lives meant that any deviation from the acceptable non-Indigenous 'norm' came to the notice of the authorities immediately.

From the late 1940s the other jurisdictions followed New South Wales in applying the general child welfare law to Indigenous children while still treating removed Indigenous children differently. State government child welfare practice was marked more by continuity than change. The same welfare staff and the same police who had previously removed children from their families simply because they were Aboriginal now utilised the neglect procedures to remove just as many Aboriginal children from their families. ...

At the third Native Welfare Conference held in 1951 the newly appointed federal Minister for Territories, Paul Hasluck, vigorously propounded the benefits to [34] Aboriginal people of assimilation and urged greater consistency in practice between all the States and the Northern Territory. Hasluck pointed out that Australia's treatment of its Indigenous people made a mockery of its promotion of human rights at the international level (Hasluck 1953 page 9).

The conference agreed that assimilation was the aim of 'native welfare measures'.

> Assimilation means, in practical terms, that, in the course of time, it is expected that all persons of aboriginal blood or mixed blood in Australia will live like other white Australians do (Hasluck 1953 page 16).

During the 1950s and 1960s even greater numbers of Indigenous children were removed from their families to advance the cause of assimilation. Not only were they removed for alleged neglect, they were removed to attend school in distant places, to receive medical treatment and to be adopted out at birth.

As institutions could no longer cope with the increasing numbers and welfare practice discouraged the use of institutions, Indigenous children were placed with non-Indigenous foster families where their identity was denied or disparaged. ...

While Indigenous children were being removed from their families at a young age, child welfare practice in relation to non-Indigenous children was being influenced by the work on maternal deprivation conducted by John Bowlby for the World Health Organisation and by a 1951 United Nations report which stressed that child welfare services should be focussed on assisting families to keep their children with them ... .

By the early 1960s it was clear that despite the mandatory way in which the assimilation policy had been expressed, Indigenous people were not being assimilated. Discrimination by non-Indigenous people and the refusal of Indigenous people to surrender their lifestyle and culture were standing in the way. Consequently the definition of assimilation was amended at the 1965 Native Welfare Conference to include an element of choice.

> The policy of assimilation seeks that all persons of Aboriginal descent will choose to attain a similar manner of living to that of other Australians and live as members of a single community ... .

Following the successful 1967 constitutional referendum the Commonwealth obtained concurrent legislative power on Aboriginal affairs with the States [*and as a result, the Commonwealth began to play an increased role in Aboriginal Affairs*]. [35] A federal Office of Aboriginal Affairs was established and made grants to the States for Aboriginal welfare programs.

> 'Assimilation' was discarded as the key term of Aboriginal policy in favour of 'integration', though precisely what this signified was somewhat unclear ... (Altman and Sanders 1995 ['From exclusion to dependence: Aborigines and the welfare state in Australia' in John Dixon and Robert P Schevrell (eds), *Social Welfare with Indigenous Peoples*, Routledge, London] page 211).

Self-management and self-determination

The election of the Whitlam Labor Government in 1972 on a policy platform of Aboriginal self-determination provided the means for Indigenous groups to receive funding to challenge the very high rates of removal of Indigenous children. Aboriginal legal services began representing Indigenous children and families in removal applications, which led to an immediate decline in the number of Indigenous children being removed. In Victoria the first Aboriginal and Islander Child Care Agency (AICCA) was started offering alternatives to the removal of Indigenous children.

In 1976 a paper delivered at the First Australian Conference on Adoption directed the attention of social workers to the large numbers of Indigenous children who were being placed by non-Indigenous welfare workers with non-Indigenous families. The paper drew on the experience of Indigenous services with children who had been removed and placed away from the Indigenous community. This practice was inconsistent with the policy of self-determination and harmful to the Indigenous children concerned.

> For the Aboriginal child growing up in a racist society, what is most needed is a supportive environment where a child can identify as an Aboriginal and get emotional support from other blacks. The supportive environment that blacks provide cannot be assessed by whites and is not quantifiable or laid down in terms of neat identifiable criteria.
>
> Aboriginal people maintain that they are uniquely qualified to provide assistance in the care of children. They have experienced racism, conflicts in identity between black and white and have an understanding of Aboriginal life-styles [Elizabeth Sommerlad, 'Homes for Blacks: Aboriginal Community and Adoption' in C Picton (ed), *Proceedings of First Australian Conference on Adoption*, 1976, at 163-164].

[36] The activism of Indigenous organisations and the growing awareness of welfare workers of the ways in which government social welfare practice discriminated against Indigenous people forced a reappraisal of removal and placement practice during the 1980s. In 1980 the family tracing and reunion agency Link-Up (NSW) Aboriginal Corporation was established. Similar services now exist in all States and the Northern Territory. In 1981 the Secretariat of National Aboriginal and Islander Child Care (SNAICC) was formed and there are now approximately 100 Aboriginal community-run children's services under its umbrella ... .

These Indigenous services formulated the Aboriginal Child Placement Principle ... and lobbied for it to be adopted by State and Territory welfare departments as a mandatory requirement. It has now been incorporated into the child welfare legislation and/or the adoption legislation in the Northern Territory, the ACT and all States other than Tasmania and Western Australia where it takes the form of administrative guidelines.

Estimating the numbers removed

It is not possible to state with any precision how many children were forcibly removed, even if that enquiry is confined to those removed officially. Many records have not survived. Others fail to record the children's Aboriginality.

[37] ... Nationally we can conclude with confidence that between one in three and one in ten Indigenous children were forcibly removed from their families and communities in the period from approximately 1910 until 1970. In certain regions and in certain periods the figure was undoubtedly much greater than one in ten. In that time not one Indigenous family has escaped the effects of forcible removal (confirmed by representatives of the Queensland and WA Governments in evidence to the Inquiry). Most families have been affected, in one or more generations, by the forcible removal of one or more children.

Consider this context when you read the following extract from Kate Burns' part of the 'conversation' with Boyd and Rhoades, the other parts of which have been extracted earlier in this chapter.

'The Politics of the Primary Caregiver Assumption: A Conversation'
(1999) 13 *Australian Journal of Family Law* 233

[Kate Burns] ...[256] ... The Family Court has taken positive steps to sensitise itself to the kinship obligations operating in particular cases and more generally, through the creation of an Aboriginal and Torres Strait Islander Awareness Committee. Initiatives of that committee have included the appointment of Aboriginal Family Consultants to work with court counsellors in the Northern Territory and North Queensland and judicial education programs. One of the tasks of the family consultants is to identify extended family members who should be consulted before any parenting arrangements are discussed in the counselling context.

However, in hearing matters the court is constrained by the limits imposed by the Family Law Act. In *In re CP* [(1997) 21 Fam LR 486] the Full Court expressed its frustration that the assumptions underlying the Act operated as a hindrance to the recognition of Indigenous caregiving arrangements. The Act failed to "contemplate circumstances where the child will live and be cared for within a kin network" (at 505). It also presupposed that orders will be made in favour of identified persons rather than recognising "the fluidity of indigenous care arrangements [which do] not lend themselves to such a priori specificity and may give rise, as was evident in this case, to criticisms about the uncertainty of arrangements for a child" (at 505).

Given the nature of Indigenous parenting, the imposition of a primary caregiver presumption upon Indigenous mothers is likely to prove problematic. Where Indigenous mothers have left one or more of their [257] children with another family member on the understanding that when circumstances allowed they would resume the care of that child, the presumption may operate to effectively permanently deprive them of the child.

But even assuming that Indigenous mothers are able to surmount this first hurdle of primary caregiving, the unfitness proviso to the primary caregiving presumption may prove insuperable. As Carol Smart has written, law discursively constructs "good" and "bad" mothers. Indigenous mothers have a long history in Australian law of being defined as unfit simply for being Aboriginal, as evidenced by the "protectionist" legislation which applied to Indigenous people throughout Australia, as late as 1971 in Queensland.

A study by Merridy Malin, Katho Campbell and Laura Agius comparing the ways in which Indigenous and white mothers care for their children found very noticeable differences in parenting styles. ["Raising Children in the Nunga Aboriginal Way" (1996) 43 *Family Matters* 43]. Careful analysis of the competencies of independence and affiliation, and the practices fostering them, revealed that while Aboriginal children were encouraged by their mother to be independent, self-regulating and self-reliant, a white perception of their parenting was that the children were not being adequately supervised, were non-compliant and were teased in a cruel way. The study also noted how [258] the children's mother used the techniques of teasing and scaring to toughen the children emotionally, so as to equip them to deal with adversity outside the home.

If, as Helen [*Rhoades, above*] narrates currently occurs in contested residence cases, unfitness is assessed by reference to the assumptions to be drawn from a series of de-contextualised incidents, the intricate ways in which Indigenous mothers transmit values, assist their children to take pride in their racial heritage in a racist world, and share the care of their children with others, may be interpreted simply as instances of neglect. This is particularly so if the opposing party can demonstrate greater conformity with white parenting style. At the moment, these attacks on a mother's fitness at least take place within the context of an assessment of her "parenting capacity" rather than her character per se. To focus solely on the mother, without reference to the benefits of her particular parenting style to her children, risks judging Indigenous mothers by irrelevant standards. Even if the presumption specifically provided that parenting within an extended family context was not, of itself, a marker of unfitness, I doubt this would address a court's concerns about the mother herself, her parenting style and the environment in which she proposes to live with her children.

[*Burns goes on to consider what might be an appropriate model for determining disputes involving indigenous children. She notes that Rhoades preferred a focus on 'status quo' or existing arrangements, rather than 'primary caregiver'. Burns suggests that this has 'the dual advantages for Indigenous mothers of avoiding the need to prove primary caregiving, and lessening the attention on a mother's fitness as opposed to the child's well-being'. However, she also notes that a status quo or existing arrangements emphasis could have a negative impact on those women who leave their children with others to be cared for, or in situations where 'simultaneous or multiple caregiving takes place'. She then considered a proposal flagged by Susan Boyd, that is*] [262] to adopt a different model for Indigenous children. But what? What balance should be struck between gender and race, particularly bearing in mind that some cases involving Indigenous children concern white primary caregiving mothers and Indigenous fathers? And besides, separate consideration of the special position of Indigenous peoples is likely to be politically unpalatable in the current climate.

In the face of these difficulties I find myself returning to the best interests test with a number of modifications. First, that the status quo, as Helen argues, be given greater, but not overwhelming, status. And secondly, that the family law recommendations of the *National Inquiry into the Separation of* [263] *Aboriginal and Torres Strait Islander Children from their Families* [*Bringing Them Home*] be implemented. ... These changes, together with continuing judicial education about Indigenous family life, including the particular needs of Indigenous children as articulated in *B v R* [(1995) 19 Fam LR 594], and measures to allow Indigenous women effective access to the processes of family law would go some way to strengthening the position of Indigenous women in family law.

Notes

1. Recommendation 54 of *Bringing Them Home* provides as follows:

    That the Family Law Act 1975 (Cth) be amended by:

    1. Including in [*the objects clause*] a new paragraph (ba) 'children of Indigenous origins have a right, in community with the other members of their group, to enjoy their own culture, profess and practice their own religion and use their own language' and

    2. [*Rephrasing the current s* 68F(2)(f) *which sets out the criteria to be considered to determine a child's best interests so that it reads*] 'the need of every Aboriginal and Torres Strait Islander child' to maintain a connection with the lifestyle, culture and traditions of Aboriginal peoples or Torres Strait Islanders.

    The relevant part of s 68F(2)(f), inserted as part of the 1995 amendments, currently provides (as one of a list of factors to which a court considering the best interests of a child must have regard): 'the child's maturity, sex and background (including any need to maintain a connection with the lifestyle, culture and traditions of Aboriginal peoples or Torres Strait Islanders) and any other characteristics of the child that the court thinks are relevant'.[65]

2. In her discussion, Burns refers to two significant decisions of the Full Family Court, *In B and R and Separate Representative*[66] and *In re CP*.[67] In *B and R*, the Full Court reviewed some of the earlier cases that involved disputes between indigenous and non-indigenous parents and held that evidence concerning the history and effects of removal of indigenous children to non-indigenous environments was relevant to placement decisions under the *Family Law Act*. In the course of its judgment, the Full Court commented: 'Racism still remains a marked aspect of Australian society. Daily references in the media demonstrate this. Aboriginal people are often treated as inferior members of the Australian society and regularly face discriminatory behaviour and conduct as part of their daily life'.[68]

    In re CP involved a dispute about a four-year-old boy whose parents were from the Tiwi Islands. He had been living in Darwin with F, an indigenous woman from the Torres Strait, who had taken him to Darwin after she had been to the Tiwi Islands. She made an application to the Family Court for custody and guardianship of C, and C's mother responded by asking the Court to make an order that C be 'in the custody of his extended maternal and paternal family at Bathurst and Melville [*the Tiwi*] islands'.[69] In a comment on this case, John Dewar points out that this is not an order available to the court under the *Family Law Act* since residence (custody as it then was) has to be vested in an 'individual'.[70] The court considered evidence of the child-rearing practices of the Tiwi people and heard from an anthropologist about differences between mainland and island communities. The trial judge had made an order in favour of F but the Full Court set aside the decision, holding that the judge had not given

---

65 The Court Counselling Service has published *Guidelines for Family Consultants in Assisting Aboriginal and Torres Strait Islander Clients of the Court Counselling Service:* See Stephen Ralph, 'Working with Aboriginal Families' (1997) 46 *Family Matters* 46.
66 (1995) 19 Fam LR 594.
67 (1997) 21 Fam LR 486.
68 (1995) 19 Fam LR 594 at 605.
69 (1997) 21 Fam LR 486 at 491.
70 John Dewar, 'Indigenous Children and Family Law' (1997) 19 *Adelaide Law Review* 217 at 223.

sufficient weight to the particular indigenous culture to which the child belonged. The Full Court considered that the trial judge erred 'by not approaching the case with an eye to the significance of differences between Aboriginal groups and, by his implicit emphasis on shared attributes [*he demonstrated*] an incorrect view of homogeneity of Aboriginal cultures'.[71]

The Full Court also disagreed with the trial judge's finding that a factor weighing in F's favour was the failure of C's mother to present a clear picture of who would be caring for the child, instead commenting that the judge had failed to have regard to the importance of the group or community to his care.

> Aboriginal experience of adoption is largely that of having had children taken away by non-Aboriginal people in positions of power, who thus alienate them from their own children, what many may refer to as a form of cultural genocide because it both denies the child the right to be socialised within its own cultural context as well as denies the right of both parents and the whole kinship network to their relations with this child. Fostering too, as a temporary transfer of rights is equally inapplicable in indigenous terms. The sharing of the caregiving role is a more fluid system .... The child is understood to be moving within the one family unit, even if it involves a number of kin and different communities.[72]

Most significantly, the Full Court commented that 'for formal legal purposes, the many non-biological mothers of a Tiwi child are invisible to the law'.[73]

> [T]his case has highlighted difficulties in the applicability of the *Family Law Act* to cultural systems of family care which, like the Tiwi way, contemplate circumstances where the child will live and be cared for within a kin network. ... [T]he Act proceeds on the basis that orders will be made in favour of identified persons.[74]

Is it possible for courts such as the Family Court to give effect to child-caring arrangements that do not resemble the nuclear 'norm'? Does the legislation need to be amended or could the Act be interpreted more fluidly to take account of indigenous caregiving practices? If questions of indigenous culture are quintessentially group issues, rather than matters that arise on a case-by-case basis, is it possible for the existing family law dispute resolution structure to take account of those issues?[75]

3. In the first edition of this book, we drew attention to a number of cases that involved disputes between an indigenous and a non-indigenous parent (see *Marriage of Goudge*,[76] *Sanders v Sanders*[77]). Commentators on those cases, such as Richard Chisholm,[78] have argued that the Family Court should adopt

---

71 (1997) 21 Fam LR 486 at 501.
72 *Ibid*, at 503 (referring to the report of an expert witness).
73 *Ibid*, at 506.
74 *Ibid*, at 505.
75 For some discussions of this case and some of these issues, see Robyn Davis and Judith Dikstein, 'It Just Doesn't Fit', (1997) 22 *Alternative Law Journal* 64; John Dewar, 'Indigenous Children and Family Law' (1997) 19 *Adelaide Law Review* 217; Ailsa Burns, Kate Burns and Karen Menzies, 'Strong State Intervention: The Stolen Generations' in JM Bowes and A Hayes (eds), *Children, Families and Communities*, Oxford University Press, Melbourne, 1999.
76 (1984) FLC ¶91-534.
77 (1976) FLC ¶90-078.
78 Richard Chisholm, 'Case Note: *Marriage of Goudge*' (1985) 13 *Aboriginal Law Bulletin* 9; Chisholm lists in a footnote a number of other custody and adoption cases involving Aboriginal children, suggesting that *Goudge* is not an isolated case. (Richard Chisholm has since become a judge of the Family Court of Australia.)

an Aboriginal child placement principle, something that the extract from *Bringing Them Home* shows is now relatively well accepted by State and Territory child welfare authorities.[79] Such a principle requires a child in need of care (under State and Territory child welfare laws) to be placed either within their extended family or kinship group or, where that is not possible, within another family in their community. In a comment on *Re CP,* Robyn Davis and Judith Dikstein make the point that while, under the *Family Law Act*, a non-Tiwi person can obtain residence/custody of a Tiwi child, 'it is near impossible for a non-Tiwi person to be nominated as a carer of a Tiwi child' under the NT *Community Welfare Act* 1993.[80]

How does the Aboriginal child placement principle measure against other proposed ways of determining custody/residence disputes, such as giving priority to status quo (which in this case, would have been to leave the child with F) or focusing on who had been the primary caregiver (also F)? How would you respond if the child had an indigenous father, who he had rarely or never met, and a non-indigenous mother, who he had lived with since birth? In what ways are common sense understandings of what is in 'the best interests of children' subject to race, class and sexuality stereotypes?

Lesbians as mothers in the family law system

In the first edition of this book, we drew attention to some of the difficulties faced by lesbians in the context of family law disputes. As the discussion in the previous chapter reinforces, lesbians have been disadvantaged by views that their sexuality detracts from their capacity to be effective and loving parents. While by 1983, it was well established that lesbianism *per se* would not disentitle a woman to custody, some of the cases, including those where conditions have been placed by the court on the mothers' awards, do not manifest a clear understanding of the fact that a person's sexuality is no more or less likely to make them a good parent.[81]

Jenni Millbank, 'Same Sex Couples and Family Law'
(1998) Paper presented at Family Court conference, October 1998, available at <http://www.familycourt.gov.au/papers/html/millbank.html>

[L]esbian and gay families face the very real possibility of discriminatory treatment within the legal system if and when they have been successful in squeezing themselves into its relatively narrow confines.

In the area of disputes over the **residence and care of children**, however, Australian law is far less formally exclusive. There are three main areas that mark

---

79 For a national review, see Jennifer Lock, *The Aboriginal Child Placement Principle,* NSWLRC, Research Report No 7, 1997. For an earlier discussion, see ALRC reference on Aboriginal Customary Law, Research Paper No 4, *Child Custody, Fostering and Adoption; The Recognition of Aboriginal Customary Laws,* Report No 31, AGPS, Canberra, 1986.
80 They refer here to a protocol between the Northern Territory Government and KARU, the Aboriginal Child Care Agency: 'It Just Doesn't Fit' (1997) 22 *Alternative Law Journal* 64 at 66.
81 For some early decisions, see *L and L* (1983) FLC ¶91-353 and see also the judgment of Wootten J in a State court decision of *Jarman v Lloyd* (1982) 8 Fam LR 878 at 889-91. For discussions of some of the case law, see Jenni Millbank, 'Lesbian Mothers, Gay Fathers: Sameness and Difference' (1992) 2 *Australian Gay and Lesbian Law Journal* 21 and 'Lesbians, Child Custody and the Long, Lingering Gaze of the Law' in Susan Boyd (ed), *Challenging the Public/Private Divide: Feminism, Law and Public Policy,* University of Toronto Press, Toronto, 1997; Margaret Bateman, 'Lesbians, Gays and Child Custody: An Australian Legal History' (1992) 1 *Australian Gay and Lesbian Law Journal* 47.

out the *Family Law Act* and the Family Court as among the most progressive and inclusive family law regimes in the world in terms of their approach to same sex families. These are that:

1. There has never been a presumption against lesbians and gay men as parents in disputes

It is notable that the Family Court has never in 20 years held that being a lesbian or a gay man is in itself evidence of inability to parent – as courts in England, the USA and Canada have all done at one time or another in the past, and as some states in the USA continue to do to this day. On the basis of available case law it seems that in Australia a lesbian mother has about a 50-50 chance of winning a contested custody case – which is a fair chance, and certainly far better than many other countries, notably the USA.

2. There is no statutory barrier to non biological parents bringing or being party to an action

Australian family law is far more accessible to lesbian families than most other jurisdictions, because a person need not in fact be a biological parent to seek residence or contact with a child. This means that lesbian or gay couples who jointly parent a child may use the court to resolve a dispute between themselves. In other jurisdictions, lesbian co-parents in particular, who have raised children jointly with a partner from birth, are facing tremendous difficulties arguing for standing in courts which limit their jurisdiction to biological parents.

3. The court has the ability to give parenting orders by consent to non-disputing parties

When a lesbian couple has a child together, only the biological parent has a legal relationship with that child. The Family Court has the power to make parenting orders in favour of parents and 'any other person concerned with the care, welfare or development of the child.' The breadth of the Act means that a mother and co-mother may apply jointly to the Family Court for joint parenting orders, establishing a legal relationship between the co-mother and her child. Such orders have been applied for and granted to lesbian couples … .

The court's actions and decisions have not, however been all plain sailing. Before I touch on some of the particular examples of discrimination which have arisen in recent years, I want to place the discussion in the context of what I think is an overarching legal and cultural hostility to lesbian and gay families. While the Court has truly been a leader in many areas of family law, and has been at the vanguard of changing attitudes … courts and judges, like counsellors, like legislators, reflect the society around them. That social context is still one which views lesbians and gay men as a threat to children's well being, and posits that threat, covertly or overtly, as including: sexual abuse, conversion to homosexuality, confusion of gender role, and exposure to community abuse or just general brain washing.

Hostility to lesbian and gay men having children of their own, or raising those of other people, is extraordinarily strong and examples from various jurisdictions are almost too easy to point to – in brief, adoption and donor insemination have been flash points in recent years. The *JM* case in Qld, [*discussed in Chapter 8*] where a lesbian who was refused access to a fertility service brought a complaint of sexuality discrimination, has now been through three levels of adjudication and has been a focus of overwhelming hostility directed at lesbians and lesbian parents – notably from the press, the judiciary, and politicians.

… Overall, there remains deeply entrenched suspicion that lesbian or gay sexual orientation in a parent will be either generally or specifically harmful to a child's welfare – when specified it tends to focus on the idea that children will grow up to be gay and/or to be confused about their gender identity. This presumption of danger is heightened when the parent has a same sex partner.

[*Millbank then outlined available research, including longitudinal studies on the adjustment of children brought up in lesbian households, which show that family processes rather than family structures are the main indicia of children's well being; that is, parenting stress and conflict are the determining factors for adjustment problems and these are completely unrelated to family structure. She then applied some of these research findings to discussions in the case law, such as L and L, a 1983 decision where the court listed eight matters to take into account when faced with a lesbian mother or gay father (1983) FLC ¶91-353. These were:*

1. Whether children raised by their homosexual parent may themselves become homosexual, or whether such an event is likely
2. Whether the child of a homosexual parent could be stigmatised by peer groups, particularly if the parent is known in the community as a homosexual
3. Whether a homosexual parent would show the same love and responsibility as a heterosexual parent
4. Whether homosexual parents will give a balanced sex education to their children and take a balanced approach to sexual matters
5. Whether or not children should be made aware of their parents' sexual preferences
6. Whether children need a parent of the same sex to model upon
7. Whether children need both a male and a female parent figure
8. The attitude of the homosexual parent to religion, particularly if the doctrines, tenets and beliefs of the parties' church are opposed to homosexuality.

Millbank goes on to discuss a 1995 decision of the Full Court: A and J (1995) 19 Fam LR 260.] ... *A and J* is a very disturbing illustration of the role that such unspoken, unproven, and unprovable, assumptions have in lesbian and gay custody cases to this day. In that instance, although the court expressly stated that being a lesbian [is] not a negative factor and also that the mother's new partner had a good relationship with the child, the result was to hold the mother's relationship as a factor that directly increased the merit of the father's claim. This was because the court held that it was of overriding importance for the child to have a close male influence to "balance" the effects of the mother's lesbian relationship and granted custody to the husband apparently on those grounds. The Full Court upheld this decision ... adding that "it must be borne in mind" ... that the first instance court had made a primary finding of fact that "it was important that the child maintain regular and close contact with the husband for reasons which included [that] the wife's proposals entailed her continuing homosexual relationship" (270). ...

Any past or current same sex relationship is often the subject of extreme scrutiny by the Court (compared to the scrutiny applied to the heterosexual parent's relationship/s), and in the past, the Court has subjected lesbian parents to invasive restrictions upon their behaviour, such as banning a partner from the house permanently or when the children are present, or prohibiting the parent and partner from sharing a room overnight. Although to my knowledge the court itself has not imposed such an order since 1987, there is anecdotal evidence that consent orders along these lines are still being sought by lawyers and confirmed by the court. ...

The view that partners pose a threat to children also continues to operate in the court's current decisions in that mothers' relationships with their female partners are seen as something which must be "discreet", even if no bar on living in is imposed. Love and affection are still viewed as something harmful for children to witness: ... in 1995 in *A and J* the trial judge stated ... that it was inappropriate for the mother and her partner to show affection towards each other in front of the child. ... [S]ame sex partners are rarely given credit for any positive contributions to children's welfare. For instance, same sex partners are never seen to contribute to the reformulation of a stable family unit in the way that new opposite sex partners do. In many Australian cases where the mother has re-partnered, the new partner has been living with the mother and the children for a year or even two years before the case comes to trial. In that time she may have built up a relationship with the children and probably provided them with a significant amount of care. Yet in all of the dozens of custody cases I have read from Australia and elsewhere I have *never* once seen the lesbian step-mother represented as anything other than a potential threat to the health and well being of the children. In contrast, and it is so unsurprising that perhaps I don't even need to say it – the father's new female partner in such cases are extolled for their altruism in caring for children which aren't even 'theirs', and for providing stability and security.

Notes

1. Millbank mentions the 'dangers' of children witnessing affection between their mother and her lover, a theme that also emerged in a moving 1980 account by a woman, writing anonymously, about her own experience of losing custody of her son after a Family Court dispute based on the fact that she had left her marriage for a lesbian relationship.[82] 'Anon' also made the point that courts tend to see lesbians and gay men as sexually irresponsible.

   > Unlike heterosexual women, lesbians cannot be trusted to keep their sexual urges under control in front of children. This seems to be the implication of questions asked about my behaviour in front of my child. How, I was asked, did I kiss my lover? In the normal fashion of people in an ordinary relationship? Was it passionate or not? Similarly my friend was asked by the judge how we behaved at parties, whether as two heterosexual lovers would who were newly in love or in some other way? What did the judge expect? 'Unnatural practices' beside the wine cask?[83]

   How do you respond to this in light of the ambivalence that has been shown to the issue of the harm to children caused by witnessing violence against their carer, discussed earlier in this chapter?

2. In her discussion, 'Anon' also pointed out that she was prejudiced not only by her lesbianism (and the resulting expectations of what she so eloquently described as the judge's concern that she and her partner would engage in 'unnatural practices beside the wine cask' at parties), but also by the stereotypical views of working women that affect both lesbian and non-lesbian mothers. For example, she was asked on the one hand why she had continued postgraduate study for so long, rather than work as a teacher so as to contribute to the family finances. Yet she also noted the assumptions that her husband's earnings were seen as the 'really significant input' to household finances and that for her opting out of any of the child care and housework was seen as a minus, while for men '*any* share of domestic duties is a definite plus in the custody stakes'. Do you think this focus, not only on

---

82 See Anon, 'Lesbian Custody – A Personal Account' (1980) 20 *Refractory Girl* 2. This was extracted in our first edition.
83 *Ibid*, at 4.

her lesbianism but also on her attachment to career, is explicable by the fact that her case was heard over 20 years ago? Are lesbians more likely to have other aspects of their lives, such as paid work, more closely scrutinised than heterosexual women?

3. In another 1980 article, Kate Harrison suggested:

> It is important ... that we do not see the homosexual custody cases as a collection of infrequent, odd cases which have no relevance for family law as a whole. Seen in terms of a broader social perspective they are part of a trend away from the traditional nuclear family, and should be viewed in that context. Homosexual relationships are merely one of the non-nuclear living situations in which children are currently being raised. Perhaps the real problem is the family itself, and not the homosexual parent. Given the rising divorce rate, the court's perception of the homosexual parent in a negative light, and the heterosexual couple as the ideal environment is at least arguably outmoded. There is no doubt that family law will have to develop and diversify and become more flexible in order to adequately cope with the changing structure of the family in modern society.[84]

Harrison raised a number of other questions about these cases, for example, whether these decisions are most appropriately made by courts in an adversary context; whether the judges are suitably qualified to make decisions as to the best interests of the child(ren), including who might be the more suitable parent; judges' capacity to evaluate psychological research on homosexuality and homosexual parents and whether judges are capable of assessing the relative benefits of children being raised in a nuclear, as opposed to a non-nuclear, family unit.[85] How would you respond to these questions and doubts? For some more recent discussions of how lesbian mothering has challenged notions of 'the family', see Paula Ettelbrick, 'Who is a Parent? The Need to Develop a Lesbian Conscious Family Law' (1993) 10 *New York Law School Journal of Human Rights* 513; Nancy Polikoff, 'Recognizing Partners But Not Parents/Recognizing Parents But Not Partners: Gay And Lesbian Family Law In Europe And The United States' (2000) 17 *New York Law School Journal of Human Rights* 711.

4. In NSW, Victoria and the ACT, there are comprehensive laws that recognise same sex relationships for a variety of State and Territory purposes (such as property transfer, inheritance, consent to medical treatment, etc)[86] and there are movements in that direction in the other States and Territories. How then do we account for the fact that there is still widespread discrimination against lesbian mothers and they still appear to be seen by courts to be a problematic category? Some of the (mostly North American and European) studies of lesbian households in which children are being raised are reviewed by Jenni Millbank in a briefing paper prepared for the NSW Gay and Lesbian Rights Lobby.[87]

---

84 Kate Harrison, 'Child Custody and Parental Sexuality: Just Another Factor?' (1980) 20-21 *Refractory Girl* 7 at 14.
85 *Ibid.*
86 See *Domestic Relationships Act* 1994 (ACT); *Property (Relationships) Act* 1984 (NSW) and see also *Property (Relationships) Legislation Amendment Act* 1999 (NSW) which lists other legislation amended by the principal Act; *Statute Law Amendment (Relationships) Act* 2001 (Vic).
87 Jenni Millbank, 'Meet the Parents: A Review of the Research on Lesbian and Gay Parenting', Gay and Lesbian Rights Lobby, Sydney, 2002.

5. One of the issues that Millbank mentions as having been extremely contentious in Australia is the resistance to gay and lesbian couples being able to adopt children as couples. In NSW, the State's Law Reform Commission recommended in its review of the law of adoption that the barriers on adoption based solely on sexuality should be lifted, a recommendation immediately rejected by the Government.[88] And in Victoria, adoption was not included in 2001 legislation that amends over 40 different Acts to recognise gay and lesbian relationships for various purposes.[89] Yet what is puzzling is how much heat this debate generates in proportion to how few children are actually available for adoption.[90] In the United States, by contrast, a number of states have allowed lesbian and gay couples to adopt children, though there are still states in which either legislatures or courts have refused to permit such adoptions.[91] What possible explanations are there for this difference in approach? Adoption may also be an issue where the gay or lesbian partner of a biological parent wants to adopt the child of their partner, a situation also excluded from our current adoption laws.[92] What are the advantages and disadvantages of second parent adoption?

Losing children: Criminal and tort law perspectives

In the concluding part of this chapter we briefly consider some of the ways in which other legal doctrines impact on women in relation to their children, in particular, the law of infanticide as well as aspects of tort law and its role in compensating for injuries suffered by mothers resulting from negligently caused death of their child(ren). However, we start by extracting a discussion of Australia's most infamous trial of a mother wrongly charged with the murder of her nine-week-old baby.

---

88 NSWLRC, *Review of the Adoption of Children Act 1965 (NSW)*, Report No 81, (March 1997); recommendation 58; see *Adoption Act* 2000 (NSW), which implements many of the recommendations, but not the one in question.
89 *Statute Law Amendment (Relationships) Act* 2001 (Vic). Instead, the government proposes to refer the matter to the State's Law Reform Commission, though had not done so by the time of writing (late 2001).
90 Australian rates of adoption have declined dramatically from a high of 9798 adoptions nationally in 1971-72 to 543 adoptions in 1998-99. Of those 543, only 127 were local (cf inter-country) adoptions by non-relatives of children under one year old. The other main category is 'known' child adoptions, mostly step-parent adoptions. The relevant analogy in lesbian or gay families would be second parent adoptions: see Australian Institute of Health and Welfare, *Adoptions in Australia, 1998-1999*, <http://www.aihw.gov.au/publications/welfare/aa98-9/index.html>.
91 For some discussions of second parent adoption in the United States, see Nancy Polikoff, 'The Deliberate Construction of Families Without Fathers: Is it an Option for Lesbian and Heterosexual Mothers?' [1996] *Santa Clara Law Review* 375; Julie Shapiro, 'A Lesbian Centred Critique of Second Parent Adoptions' (1999) 14 *Berkeley Women's Law Journal* 17; Ruthann Robson, 'Making Mothers: Lesbian Legal Theory and The Judicial Construction Of Lesbian Mothers' (2000) 22 *Women's Rights Law Reporter* 15. In Canada, a number of provinces also permit such adoptions: for discussion of one of the earliest cases, see Danny Sandor, 'Same-Sex Couples Can Adopt in Ontario: The Canadian Case of *Re K* and its significance to Australian Family Law' (1997) 11 *Australian Journal of Family Law* 23.
92 See, for example, *Adoption Act* 2000 (NSW), s 26, which provides that only a 'couple' can adopt. The Act defines 'couple' as a man and a woman who are married or in a de facto relationship.

An Australian cause celebre: The story of Lindy Chamberlain

The Lindy Chamberlain case needs no introduction to Australian readers.[93] Ms Chamberlain was convicted of the murder of her baby Azaria after the baby disappeared near Ayers Rock in 1980. She and her then husband (Michael Chamberlain, who was convicted of having been an accessory after the fact) have since had their convictions set aside.

Adrian Howe, 'Chamberlain Revisited: The Case Against The Media'
(1989) 31-32 *Refractory Girl* 2

[2] ... I propose to put the media on trial for murder. My case is this: the Australian media, aided and abetted by a large cross-section of the Australian people, murdered, killed in cold blood, the possibility of a fair trial for Lindy Chamberlain.

... My concern here is not with legal technicalities but rather with examining the media's construction of the criminality of that ultra 'deviant' woman who is accused of murdering her own child. ... [*Howe points out here that her main source has been the Sydney newspapers which she considers to be representative of the national reporting of the case.*]

The Witch hunt

[*Howe suggests a motive for the media's case:*] The motive was the perception of Lindy Chamberlain as a dangerous woman: a dangerous, provoking counter-stereotypical woman who refused to play her assigned gender role; who spoke out on her behalf and on behalf of all women, demanding her right to tell her story, her dreadful story of the death of her child, in her own [3] way, her own defiant, nonpassive way, a right which was denied her by a male-dominated media which was angered and terrified by her refusal to play the role of a properly gendered woman.

Lindy herself felt their fear when she asked: "Why were they so desperate to get hold of me? Why would they be so anxious to spend millions to get me? If Jack the Ripper was running amok, you could understand it. But why me? Somebody is scared of something."

Yes, Lindy, they were afraid of you.

Chamberlain's perceived dangerousness, then, supplies the motive in this case against the media. Next, the murder weapon. Unlike the Chamberlain trial, in which the prosecution was unable to supply a motive, an identifiable weapon, let alone a body, we do have a murder weapon. It was a witch-hunt, a media-orchestrated witch-hunt in which the question of Lindy's criminality and guilt was predetermined by the Australian media and many Australian people.

Finally, we have a body in this case, the sexualised body of Lindy Chamberlain, the body which, if we can believe the media, solicited crimi-nalisation.

The media's preoccupation with Lindy's body was the first step in the creation of Lindy the Witch. The witch, a figure embodying the power and threat of female sexuality, a wild, uncontrollable sexuality which must be tamed, tamed, in this case by the objectifying gaze of the media. Lindy's sexuality became a major point of discussion among the male journalists. Hear them incriminate themselves. She was "the pert brunette" wearing a different outfit to court each

---

93 See John Bryson, *Evil Angels*, Viking, Melbourne, 1985. The award winning movie, 'Evil Angels', starring Meryl Streep as Lindy Chamberlain, was released in other countries under the title 'A Cry in the Dark'.

day, but always looking "striking"; her "filmy apricot dress with thin straps over the shoulders" led many to ogle and tip that "she was braless beneath". The "soft roundness of her tanned shoulders" attracted their attention, and helped them formulate their opinion that "it's easy to see why Michael is a pastor and not a priest". Such views were easily formed because she looked "ravishing", her "lithe body faultlessly sun-tanned as far as could be seen". In short, she "dressed in a fairly sexy sort of way" and during the second inquest she "wore a different dress almost everyday". For these male journalists, Lindy, with her "petite frame", her "constantly changing dresses" and her "eye-catching figure", was "beautiful".

Lindy's appearance became a media obsession. It was as if her photo could tell us about her guilt, as if the media was seeking evidence which could not be used in court – evidence about her femaleness. Their photos became the evidence by which we prejudged her criminality. ...

The mainstream media's obsession with Lindy Chamberlain's body continued unabated through the two inquests and the trial. Innumerable male journalists became obsessed with her body, especially with its witch-like ability to change shape. Dianne Johnson has noted how Lindy's ability to change her image caused concern: "On one day, said a journalist, she would look 'like a schoolgirl ...' and on the next she would look 'like a filmstar with a black dress, red lips, shoes and handbag'".

Johnson notes too how by the time of her trial, Lindy's pregnancy had changed her shape again, "as if Lindy's herself was pushing the contradictions of her situation to the limits".

... The pregnancy fuelled more rumours, media-instigated rumours. Was her pregnancy a play for sympathy? Who would convict a pregnant woman? More crucially, however, her pregnancy [4] raised the vital issue of motherhood. Media attention now focussed on her as a mother, and the assessment began of her mothering skills. In the process Lindy Chamberlain lost her status as a woman. The headlines tell the story: she became "the Guilty Mother", "Azaria's Mother", the "Young Mother with Far Away Eyes", "the Dingo Baby Mother". By the time of her trial in September 1982, she had been found guilty, in the media, of more than child murder: she stood condemned for violating the stereotypes and sanctity of motherhood, of transgressing the boundaries of normal, passive motherhood. Moreover, by raising the possibility of having killed her child, she became transformed into an unnatural mother and a witch.

The evidence put forward to support the witch theory took two forms. First, there was her changing body shape. Diane Johnson has observed that in the Middle Ages witches were thought to change shape and assume the shape of a beast. She traces the journalist musings: "Did Lindy purposefully change her form? None of her children were accidental, Lindy had asserted at the first inquest. Could she really have killed her dearly beloved baby? Could she have invented the dingo story? Could she indeed have been the 'two-legged dingo'?"

What were we to make of this weird 'Dingo Baby Mother'? A second body of evidence focussed on her weird, 'unnatural' non-stereotypical behaviour. Her 'unnatural' impassiveness – most crucially, she didn't cry – caught the media's attention. Moreover, it was not only the male journalists who were alert to her: women journalists shared their masculinist concerns. According to one woman: "As a mother, and a young, good-looking, eloquent woman, Lindy Chamberlain is easy for most people to identify with and difficult to picture as a murderer, especially of her own child. Yet her reaction to the loss of her child has not fitted the stereotype of the distraught mother: her composure at most times is confusing."

Furthermore, as Kerryn Goldsworthy accurately observed, hundreds of Australian women were convinced of Chamberlain's guilt largely on the basis of "what they saw as her flaunting, during the trial of her tanned shoulders, and her large wardrobe. Their 'logic' was that a woman interested in looking attractive at such a time must be a bad woman, and everyone knows that a bad woman cannot be a good mother." ...

The unnatural mother

... The role of ideas about motherhood in the conviction of Lindy Chamberlain has been most fully developed by Kerryn Goldsworthy. She argues that Lindy was condemned, "rightly or wrongly not for murder as such, but because of a public belief that she had violated the sanctity of motherhood". She continues: "In almost all of the millions of words spoken or written about her ... the representation of Lindy Chamberlain has been focused for good or ill on aspects of her femaleness: on her qualities as a mother, and on her sexuality". In Goldworthy's view, ... it was "public attitudes to motherhood and to female sexuality which informed and to a great degree shaped the course of Lindy Chamberlain's trial – a trial by jury, media, and by the collective unconscious of an entire nation". ...

[5] Goldsworthy concludes ... "[t]here is a good chance that had she not been pregnant and prettily dressed when she stood trial she never would have been in Berrima Jail".

[Howe next deals with the critical role played by 'expert' scientific evidence in this case: in particular the evidence of Professor Cameron, who had also worked on the Turin Shroud and was brought to Australia from England by the prosecution. At the 1986 inquiry, Justice Morling had said of the Crown's evidence that blood had been found in the car that he 'wouldn't hang a dog on it'. Howe makes the point that the scientific evidence completely displaced the eyewitness accounts and in particular, the evidence of an Aboriginal tracker Barbara Tjikadu who had identified tracks of a dingo carrying a baby and the places where it put the child down on the sand. It was only at the time of the 1986 inquiry that this evidence came out. Howe suggests that the media's failure to report the evidence of Black trackers was also 'profoundly racist'.

She goes on to accuse the Australian public of aiding and abetting the media's denial of a fair trial to Lindy, discussing some of the rumours which were circulated in the media (for example, that Azaria means 'sacrifice in the wilderness') many of which were found to have originated with the police. She continues:]

[7] Lindy reclaimed

In February 1986 Lindy Chamberlain was released from prison, ostensibly (reportedly) because of the discovery of the matinee jacket which, all along, she had said Azaria had been wearing. The unofficial unreported reason for her release was fear the Northern Territory government had repressed evidence pertaining to the crown's scientific evidence against her.

At least while she was in prison, she was protected from the intense media gaze. Now she was to be once more thrust into the limelight. With the tide of public opinion turning in her favour, largely due to the groundswell of public support and the publication of John Bryson's *Evil Angels*, it was time for the media to start decriminalising her by reclaiming her as a normal, natural woman and deconstructing the witch image. It helped that she went on national television and cried throughout the interview (although some said she cried crocodile tears). It helped undo some of the damage done by the media. ...

Throughout the reclamation process, the media remained obsessed with Lindy's body. According to one report, she "looked trim and taut after her months in prison" (read three years and emaciated: she had lost five stone). Two female journalists, debriefing her when she arrived home, discovered, or rather, re-discovered that "she had a lot of sex appeal". She might be a woman who "feels that everybody was against her", and she had "this sense of terrible injustice", but it was now time to "admire the way she has reacted to it". ...

[*Howe here gives several more examples of media reports of the Morling Inquiry focused on Lindy Chamberlain's body.*] ...

[8] Lindy Chamberlain was pardoned by the Northern Territory Government in June 1987 following the findings of the Morling Inquiry which had established the new 'truth' about her, namely, that she was a "normal, healthy caring mother" who loved her normal healthy baby girl right until the time she disappeared. The inquiry had also determined that if the evidence now available had been given at the trial, the trial judge would have been obliged to direct the jury to acquit the Chamberlains on the ground that the evidence could not justify their convictions. Lindy Chamberlain, however, was not interested in a pardon for something she didn't do. "There was steel in her voice as she said this." But the "main impression" she gave was one of "determination and self-mastery". Had she ever felt crushed by the battle? "You always feel crushed by it", she said. "But whether you are crushed or flattened are two different things." Had she ever been flattened? "No way", came the answer. And, finally, what about nightmares? "I don't have nightmares", she said. "I have day-mares. It is reality that hurts."

Notes

1. The articles referred to in the extract are Kerryn Goldsworthy, 'Martyr to her sex', *The Age Saturday Extra*, 15 February 1986 and Dianne Johnson, 'From Fairy to Witch: imagery and myth in the Chamberlain case' (1984) 2 *Australian Journal of Cultural Studies* 90. For some more recent discussions, see Adrian Howe, 'Imagining Evidence, Fictioning Truth – Revisiting (Courtesy of OJ Simpson) Expert Evidence in the Chamberlain Case' (1997) 3 *Law Text Culture* 82; Phillipa Sawyer, '"Naming Whiteness": An Inquiry into Lindy Chamberlain's *Through My Eyes* and Australian Nationalist Discourses' (1997) 3 *Law Text Culture* 107; Briar Wood, 'The Trials of Motherhood: the case of Azaria and Lindy Chamberlain' in Helen Birch (ed), *Moving Targets; Women, Murder and Representation*, Virago, London, 1993; Gary Edmond, 'Azaria's Accessories' (1998) 22 *Melbourne University Law Review* 396. The High Court dismissed an appeal against the conviction in *Chamberlain v The Queen (No 2)* (1984) 153 CLR 521. See especially the dissenting judgment of Murphy J.
2. During the period that the Lindy Chamberlain trial fascinated Australia, there was considerable speculation (at least those amongst those convinced that she had killed her daughter) as to why Ms Chamberlain had not been charged with infanticide. Some jurisdictions (but not the Northern Territory) have a statutory offence of infanticide with which women who have killed their babies may be charged instead of being charged with murder, or relying on one of the other defences, such as diminished

responsibility.[94] For example, s 22A of the *Crimes Act* 1900 (NSW) provides:

> (1) Where a woman by any wilful act or omission causes the death of her child, being a child under the age of twelve months, but at the time of the act or omission the balance of her mind was disturbed by reason of her not having fully recovered from the effect of giving birth to the child or by reason of the effect of lactation consequent upon the birth of the child, then, notwithstanding that the circumstances were such that but for this section the offence would have amounted to murder, she shall be guilty of infanticide, and may for such offence be dealt with and punished as if she had been guilty of the offence of manslaughter of such child.

Similar provisions are in force in Victoria[95] and Tasmania.[96] As is clear from the NSW provision, only women can be charged with infanticide. What are the arguments for and against the existence of a gender-specific offence of infanticide?

3. Toni Morrison's book *Beloved*[97] is the story of a slave woman in the United States in the 19th century who killed her child rather than have her taken back into slavery. It is a moving account of a situation where the unimaginable, killing a loved child, is presented as at least as viable a choice as the other options available to her. In a moving description, the woman's mother-in-law (the mother of her missing husband Halle) muses:

> What was left to hurt her now? News of Halle's death? No. She had been prepared for that better than she had for his life. The last of her children, whom she barely glanced at when he was born because it wasn't worth the trouble to try to learn features you would never see change into adulthood anyway. Seven times she had done that: held a little foot; examined the fat fingertips with her own – fingers she never saw become the male or female hands a mother would recognize anywhere. She didn't know to this day what their permanent teeth looked like; or how they held their heads when they walked. Did Patty lose her lisp? What color did Famous' skin finally take? Was that a cleft in Johnny's chin or just a dimple that would disappear soon's his jawbone changed? Four girls, and the last time she saw them there was no hair under their arms. Does Ardelia still love the burned bottom of bread? All seven were gone or dead. What would be the point of looking too hard at that youngest one?[98]

In her article, 'On Being the Object of Property', US law professor Patricia Williams also provides some insight into the different cultural contexts in

---

94 For some discussions of infanticide, see Judith Allen, *Sex & Secrets: Crimes Involving Australian Women since 1880*, Oxford University Press, Melbourne, 1990; Constance Backhouse, 'Desperate Women and Compassionate Courts: Infanticide in Nineteenth Century Canada' (1984) 34 *University of Toronto Law Review* 447; Kathy Laster, 'Infanticide: A Litmus Test for Feminist Criminological Theory' (1989) 22 *ANZ Journal of Criminology* 151; Shurlee Swain and Renate Howe, 'Death: a very army of murderesses within our midst' in Shurlee Swain and Renate Howe, *Single Mothers and their Children: Disposal, Punishment and Survival in Australia*, Cambridge University Press, Cambridge, 1995; Ania Wilczynski, 'Child-Killing by Parents: Social, Legal and Gender Issues' in R Emerson Dobash et al (eds), *Gender and Crime*, University of Wales, Cardiff, 1995, 167-80; Lucy Sussex, 'Portrait of a Murderer in Mixed Media: Cultural Attitudes, Infanticide and the Representation of Frances Knorr' (1995) 4 *Australian Feminist Law Journal* 39.
95 *Crimes Act* 1958 (Vic), s 6.
96 *Criminal Code* (Tas), s 165A.
97 Picador, London, 1988.
98 *Ibid*, at 139.

which to consider the meaning of the death of a child.[99] She describes the different ways in which African American women experience 'a right to choose'. In the midst of the debate about women's control of their own bodies, the fact that black women are often sterilised against their will sits uneasily with some of these campaigns. For further discussion of 'rights' discourses in relation to reproduction issues, see Chapter 8.

Tortious death to children: The law's response

Leslie Bender, in her 'A Lawyer's Primer on Feminist Theory and Tort',[100] asks: 'Why ... do tort damages recognize financial loss and yet remain reluctant to recognize relational loss, such as loss of the companionship of a child ...?' The answer lies in the law's general reluctance to recognise anything other than pecuniary losses. At common law, 'the death of a human being could not be complained of as an injury' in a civil action.[101] This meant that, if a person died as a result of a wrongful injury, the right to sue for compensation died with her or him. It was not until the passage of legislation in England in the 19th century (Lord Campbell's Act), which was adopted in the Australian States and Territories, that the right to claim compensation for the death of another person was available to surviving dependants. The basis of these compensation to relatives, or fatal accidents' actions,[102] is to compensate for pecuniary losses only since the cause of action is based on the loss of financial support. Accordingly, they exclude non-pecuniary damages.[103]

However, some jurisdictions (in Australia, only South Australia and the Northern Territory) provide a statutory right of action by way of *solatium* for the emotional losses following the death of a child or spouse.[104] 'Solatium' is a sum of money intended to provide consolation both for the loss of the society of the deceased and for the suffering endured by the plaintiff contemporaneously with, and after, the death.[105] In South Australia, the maximum award is $3000 for the death of a child[106] and $4200 for the death of a spouse.[107] In the Northern Territory, anyone entitled to claim under Lord Campbell's Act, including an infant child who has lost one or both parents, may recover damages by way of solatium.[108] Despite the suggestion in 1951 by Sir Owen Dixon[109] that the law should provide close relatives with 'fair and just compensation' for the destruction of their intangible interest in the life of the deceased, no damages are recoverable for solatium in New South Wales, Victoria or the other States and the ACT.

In a Northern Territory damages case, an indigenous woman who lost her capacity to have children was awarded compensation for that loss by the Supreme

---

99   (1988) 14 *Signs* 5.
100 (1988) 38 *Journal of Legal Education* 3 at 37.
101 *Baker v Bolton* (1808) 1 Camp 493 per Lord Ellenborough.
102 See, for example, *Compensation to Relatives Act* 1897 (NSW).
103 For a detailed discussion of these forms of action, see Harold Luntz, *Assessment of Damages for Personal Injury and Death*, 3rd ed, Butterworths, Sydney, 1990, Chapter 9. For a discussion of the basis of compensation in such actions, see *Nguyen v Nguyen* (1990) 169 CLR 245.
104 See Luntz, *Assessment of Damages*, at 442-5.
105 *Ibid*, at 443.
106 See *Wrongs Act* 1936 (SA), s 23a.
107 *Wrongs Act* 1936 (SA), s 23b.
108 See *Compensation (Fatal Injuries) Act* 1974 (NT), s 10.
109 Owen Dixon, 'The Survival of Causes of Action' (1951) 1 *University of Queensland Law Journal* 1 at 4-5.

Court.[110] The plaintiff had suffered injuries as a result of medical negligence in the course of having her first child. The woman's husband left her after she told him, upon returning from the hospital with her son, that as a result of those injuries, she was unable to bear any more children. The court noted:

> [The plaintiff] gave evidence as to the importance of children in Aboriginal families in that vicinity. ... [S]he also testified that it was important for Aboriginal women in that community to have daughters, so that they are able to fully participate in ceremonial women's business.[111]

An anthropologist who gave evidence also emphasised the importance of children in that community, both as an aspect of personal protection and because – as there was such a paucity of employment opportunities – 'women's economic empowerment is only through the receipt of child endowment [family allowance] funds'.[112] By the time of trial, the plaintiff had remarried, but the anthropologist also stated that her relationship with her second husband could be in jeopardy. The trial judge awarded her $15,000 for loss of cultural fulfilment.

Notes

1. How appropriate is it to treat the loss of a child as an economic loss? For a historical perspective on the economic value of children, see Viviana A Zelizer, *Pricing the Priceless Child: the changing social value of children*, Basic Books, New York, 1985. What rationale lies behind the law's preference for compensating pecuniary over non-pecuniary losses? What arguments might be mounted for taking up Bender's (and Sir Owen Dixon's) suggestion that tort law should pay more regard to relational losses?
2. What dangers for women might flow from reconstructing heads of damages in order to recognise the harms caused by relational losses? How does this debate fit within the equal treatment/special treatment dichotomy discussed in Chapter 3? Would any of the other theories of equality discussed there provide a better basis for revaluing the losses that women experience through these forms of injury and death to loved ones? We revisit the issue of how to value the loss of capacity to bear children in our discussion of a range of injuries to women in Chapter 11.

---

110 *Namala v Northern Territory* (1996) 131 FLR 468.
111 *Ibid*, at 470.
112 *Ibid*.

PART FOUR

GENDERED HARMS

This part of the book concerns violence against women or gendered harms. That is, it considers an array of injuries which have in common that they happen overwhelmingly to women, because they are women, and therefore may usefully be characterised as gendered harms. In the late 1980s Adrian Howe built on the concept of 'social injury' first used by Edwin Sutherland to bring white collar crime within the scope of criminology.[1] Howe uses the social injury notion to explore and develop an understanding of the harm caused by injuries which happen to women *as women*. In 1994,[2] she summarised her earlier work[3] in the following way:

> The [*social injury*] strategy is premised on what I have described as a distinctive aspect of women's experience – namely, 'our' injuries. I meant the hidden injuries of all gender-ordered societies, the injuries associated with lower gender status, the once privatised injuries we have begun to name over the last twenty years, such as domestic violence (now criminal assault in the home), incest (now father-daughter rape) and sexual harassment which is now, at least in the workplace, sex discrimination. I have argued that while these injuries have become public issues they are still trivialised in the wider culture because we missed a crucial step in our argument. Insisting that our private injuries become public issues has not been enough: to ensure that our distinctive mode of alienation as women is not lost in its translation into a legal claim, we need to demonstrate that the injuries we feel at a private, intimate level are socially created, indeed, social injuries, before we demand that they become public issues ... .[4]

Howe proceeds to engage in criticism of the position she had espoused:

> [P]ostmodern aficionados must be in a state of apoplexy. A distinctive aspect of *women's experience*? *Our* injuries? *Our* private injuries? *All* gender-ordered societies? And '*our distinctive mode of alienation as women*'? Haven't such foundational universalising myths withered before the postmodern onslaught? ... This will not do, it will not do at all, as a response to the problem of dealing with - women's class-differentiated and race-differentiated socially injurious experi-

---

1   Edwin Sutherland, *White Collar Crime*, Holt, Rinehart and Winston, New York, 1949.
2   Adrian Howe, *Punish and Critique: Towards a Feminist Critique of Penality*, Routledge, London, 1994.
3   See Adrian Howe, '"Social Injury Revisited": Towards a Feminist Theory of Social Justice' (1987) 15 *International Journal of the Sociology of Law* 423; 'The Problem of Privatised Injuries: Feminist Strategies for Litigation' in Martha Fineman (ed), *At the Boundaries of Law: Feminism and Legal Theory*, Routledge, New York, 1990; and 'Sweet Dreams: Deinstitutionalising Young Women' in Graycar (ed), *Dissenting Opinions: Feminist Explorations in Law and Society*, Allen and Unwin, Sydney, 1990.
4   Howe, *Punish and Critique*, at 171.

ences. Furthermore, some women may not recognise, or may not wish to recognise, their life experience as injured ones, however socially based these may be represented to be. More critically, the social injury strategy ignored the problems raised by the postmodern pressure on the category of 'woman' to act as the foundation of a feminist politics. ...

Can anything be salvaged from this kind of strategy ...? ... Two possibilities currently present themselves. On the one hand, we could take the path of those feminists who question whether a postmodern politics is seriously conceivable and insist that theorising needs some closures or 'stopping points', and that gender is one of them. ... [*Howe here quotes Nancy Hartsock, whom we have cited in Chapter 4, who asks why it is that, when women are finally claiming the right to act as subjects rather than objects, 'the concept of subjecthood becomes problematic'. Howe argues that such a critique*] is a caricature of postmodern feminist interrogations of the foundational categories of feminist politics, interrogations which do not lead to a refusal of representational politics on behalf of oppressed groups of women.

Howe then turns to the work of Judith Butler.[5] Butler argues:

> To take the construction of the subject as a political problematic is not the same as doing away with the subject; to deconstruct the subject is not to negate or throw away the concept; on the contrary, deconstruction implies only that we suspend all commitments to that which the term, "the subject", refers, and that we consider the linguistic functions it serves in the consolidation and concealment of authority. To deconstruct is not to negate or dismiss, but to call into question and, perhaps most importantly, to open up a term, like the subject, to a reusage or redeployment that previously has not been authorized.
>
> Within feminism, it seems as if there is some political necessity to speak as and for *women*, and I would not contest that necessity. Surely, that is the way in which representational politics operates, and in this country [*the USA*], lobbying efforts are virtually impossible without recourse to identity politics. So we agree that demonstrations and legislative efforts and radical movements need to make claims in the name of women.[6]

Howe concludes that she is prepared to defend her social injury strategy:

> First, it need not rest on a universal, essentialising notion of 'women'. The whole point of the strategy is that it be utilised by groups who recognise a socially-based injury to themselves – that is, an injury to them as members of a particular social group. ... [I]nasmuch as a specificity of application is built into the strategy, it is therefore open to any group who perceive a socially-based injury to themselves. Second, ... the strategy is not dependent on gender identity: any member of a marginalised group who recognises a harm or discrimination as an injury to themselves as members of that group could deploy that strategy.[7]

One other advantage we see in the use of the concept of 'social injury' is that it encourages a focus beyond that traditionally understood as encompassed within

---

5 Howe especially draws on Judith Butler, 'Contingent Foundations: Feminism and the Question of "Postmodernism"' in Judith Butler and Joan Scott (eds), *Feminists Theorize the Political*, Routledge, New York, 1992. See also Butler, *Gender Trouble: Feminism and the Subversion of Identity*, Routledge, New York, 1990.

6 Butler, 'Contingent Foundations', at 15. These themes have been explored more fully in Chapter 4.

7 Howe, *Punish and Critique*, at 176.

the epithet 'violence against women'.[8] Within a legal context the notion of 'violence against women' immediately focuses attention on the criminal law, the harms to women which have been criminalised, such as rape or sexual assault. While what is criminalised and how the criminal law deals with violence against women is important – and indeed is the focus of the next two chapters – not all gendered harms are criminalised. Furthermore, one more recent project of feminist scholars in law has been to ensure that the physical and sexual violence to which women are subjected in a domestic context is visible in legal doctrines beyond the criminal law. The concept of social injury or gendered harms might assist in both these projects. Hence, in this part of the book we examine not only rape (in Chapter 11), but also in that chapter we consider medical abuses of women's bodies looking at the sterilisation of women, particularly of women identified as having an intellectual disability, the use of dangerous drugs to control women's fertility and the cervical cancer 'experiments' in New Zealand. In Chapter 12 we move again beyond the criminal law, to discuss both sexual harassment and pornography. The examination of these two areas allows us to focus on the role of law in redressing harm, and in relation to pornography, on how harm might be defined. However, it is the case that we have not discussed in this part of the book other examples of what Howe and MacKinnon might have defined as gendered harms – women's unequal pay, the injury of fathers' rights discourses etc. This is in part because they have been canvassed in other parts of the book. There is also the question, addressed at the end of this chapter, of whether the relentless depiction of women as victims – the very language of injury – may carry its own risks, risks which may be exacerbated if all gendered difference, or even subordination, was (re)presented as injury.

Apart from discussing the so-called 'victim-agency' debate, the remainder of this next chapter provides some basic data on the incidence of violence, particularly the level of domestic violence or violence in the home. We examine the language we might want to use to discuss this sort of violence, and the representation of violence as a non-gendered phenomenon. And before our discussion of the victim-agency debate, we examine the creation of 'special laws' to respond to domestic violence. It is important to bear in mind the extent to which we have been successful in making claims about women's injuries which recognise the diversity of women.

---

8   As noted, the concept of social injury came from Sutherland's attempt to include white collar crime as crime. Howe also relates its use to the concept of 'aggregate social harm' developed by the NSW Prisoner Action Group in the early 1980s in an abolitionist political campaign.

Chapter Ten

Violence: An introduction

The incidence of violence against women

The most comprehensive survey of violence against women in Australia was undertaken by the Australian Bureau of Statistics in 1996.[1] They interviewed some 6300 women, in private.[2] 7.1% of those women had experienced physical or sexual violence in the previous 12 months.[3] 'Younger women were more at risk of violence than older women: 19% of women aged 18-24 had experienced an incident of violence in the previous 12 month period, compared to 6.8% of women aged 35-44 and 1.2% of women aged 55 and over'.[4] 36.4% of women had experienced some violence since the age of 15.[5] In other words, more than one in three women reported experiencing violence at some point in their lives. Women are most likely to be targetted by people they know. Some 45% of sexual violence and some 55% of physical violence was committed by a current partner, a previous partner or a boyfriend/girlfriend or date.[6]

While this is the most comprehensive survey undertaken in Australia, it may still underestimate the level of violence against women.[7] Some women, for

---

1   ABS, *Women's Safety Australia*, Cat No 4128.0, Commonwealth of Australia, 1996. However, the survey underrepresents women in rural and remote areas, and therefore underrepresents indigenous women. It also does not accurately represent the experiences of women born in particular countries, though data relating to women born in English-speaking and non-English speaking countries overall is more reliable (at 2-3).
2   *Ibid*, at 2. This represented a response rate of 78%.
3   *Ibid*, at 4. Physical violence is defined as 'the use of physical force with the intent to harm or frighten a woman' and includes attempts to inflict physical harm 'if a woman believes it is able and likely to be carried out' (at 4) and '[s]exual assault includes acts of a sexual nature carried out against a woman's will through the use of physical force, intimidation or coercion, or any attempts to do this' (*ibid*). Unwanted sexual touching is excluded, but indecent assault is mentioned as included (at 82); sexual threat that 'involves the threat of a sexual nature which the woman believes is able and likely to be carried out' is included (*ibid* and definitions at 82).
4   *Ibid*, at 5 and Table 3.11 at 17. Note that only adult women were surveyed, so the figures for violence experienced in the last 12 months exclude violence against children, and in particular young women between 15 and 18. As Russo notes, women between 15 and 19 are the most likely to be subject to sexual violence (Laura Russo, *Date Rape: A Hidden Crime*, Australian Institute of Criminology, Trends and Issues Paper No 90, Canberra, 2000, at 2).
5   30.1% physical and 17.6% sexual violence, though to calculate the overall figure, women who had experienced both are only counted once: *Women's Safety Australia*, at 14, Table 3.7.
6   Calculated from Table 3.18. The figures we have cited are somewhat higher than the totals reported by the ABS: the ABS, when reporting total levels of violence, only counts a woman once if she experienced violence from more than one perpetrator; we have counted *incidents* of violence, giving higher figures.
7   Even so, the authors of the survey suggest that their figures are expected to provide more reliable data than the general Crime and Safety surveys carried out regularly by the ABS: 'The women's safety survey found that 5.9% of women had experienced physical violence in the last 12 month period and 1.5% had been sexually assaulted. Corresponding figures from the 1993 Crime and Safety Survey are 1.8% and 0.6%' (*ibid*, at 3). They suggest that this increased reliability arises from the specific focus of the Women's Safety Survey (*ibid*).

example, may be reluctant to discuss their experience of violence with a stranger.[8] Other data indicating the extent of 'domestic' violence against women come from hospital, police and other state and non-government sources. Of course this kind of data relies on women being able to make contact with some formal organisation, and/or to reveal the cause of their injury. Therefore, such data will always be incomplete.[9] However, the NSW Ombudsman opened its report on policing and domestic violence with the following observation:

> In 1998-99, more resources were utilised by police in responding to domestic violence incidents than any other reported crime. Police responded to 77,000 reported incidents of domestic violence during that period.[10]

Homicide data is probably the most reliable of all non-survey data we have though, on its face, it clearly concerns only the most serious violence. Alison Wallace drew attention to the gendered nature of homicidal violence in a 1986 NSW study.[11] She found that men committed 85% of all homicides reported to the police in NSW between 1968 and 1981[12] and 42.5% of all homicides occurred within the family.[13] Spouse killings, of which 73% were committed by men on their wives or de facto wives, accounted for nearly one quarter of all killings in the State.[14] These figures are echoed in later studies. In another study examining all homicides in Australia which came to the attention of police between 1989 and 1996, again one quarter of the killings were of spouses (or former spouses),[15] and 77% of these were committed by men on their then current or former female partners.[16] Jenny Mouzos examined all homicides reported to police in Australia between 1989 and 1998.[17] She found that only 14.6% of women victims were killed by strangers, and 'almost 60% were killed by an intimate partner'.[18] By contrast 'only 11% of men were killed by an intimate partner'.[19] Aboriginal or Torres Strait Islander (TSI) women were even more likely to be killed by an

---

8   The survey also excluded women resident in 'non-private dwellings, such as hospitals, retirement villages, refuges etc' (at 72). Obviously, women in refuges are almost invariably survivors of violence.
9   Anna Ferrante, Frank Morgan, David Indermaur and Richard Harding, *Measuring the Extent of Domestic Violence*, Hawkins Press, Sydney, 1996, discusses the strengths and weaknesses of a variety of data sources, including police and hospital records, and victimisation surveys, in Chapter 1 (1-23); they also summarise much of the existing Australian data collected from these sources.
10 NSW Ombudsman, *Policing Domestic Violence in NSW: A Special Report to Parliament under s.31*, December 1999, at 1.
11 Alison Wallace, *Homicide: The Social Reality*, Research Study No 5, Bureau of Crime Statistics and Research, NSW Attorney General's Department, 1986.
12 *Ibid*, at 31.
13 *Ibid*, at 72.
14 *Ibid*, at 83.
15 Carlos Carcach and Marianne James, *Homicide Between Intimate Partners in Australia*, Australian Institute of Criminology, Trends and Issues Paper No 90, Canberra, 1998.
16 *Ibid*, at 3. A woman killed a man in 21% of cases, and 2% involved same-sex relationships (with only two cases involving a woman killing a woman and 10 involving a man killing a man).
17 Jenny Mouzos, *Femicide: An Overview of Major Findings*, Australian Institute of Criminology, Trends and Issues Paper No 124, Canberra, 1999. See also Jenny Mouzos, *Femicide: The Killing of Women in Australia 1989-1998*, Research and Public Policy Series, No 18, Australian Institute of Criminology, Canberra, 1999 and Jenny Mouzos, *Homicidal Encounters: A Study of Homicide in Australia 1989-1999*, Research and Public Policy Series, No 28, Canberra, 2000.
18 *Femicide: An Overview*, at 2.
19 *Ibid*.

intimate partner – 75.4% (compared to 54.2% of Caucasian victims).[20] 'Overall, Aboriginal/TSI women accounted for approximately 15 per cent of the femicide victims, although comprising only about 2 percent of the total female population'.[21]

We have some information on what has led to killings in an intimate context:

> [A]pproximately 90% of femicide victims were killed as a result of "altercations of a domestic nature", referring to general domestic arguments, desertion, or termination of an intimate relationship, jealousy, and/or rivalry.[22]

Mouzos concludes:

> When women are killed intentionally by another, they are more likely than not to die at the hand of an intimate partner. It follows that factors that are associated with a woman spending more time at home – that is, not working – are also associated with an increased likelihood of victimisation. Not surprisingly, when a woman is killed, she is most likely to be killed in the privacy of her own home.[23]

The homicide data routinely collected by the Australian Institute of Criminology (AIC), while an extremely valuable resource, is not comprehensive. While it has been very important in allowing us to identify 'domestic', and in particular, 'intimate killings' and the very high proportion of killings that are perpetrated by men on their current or former female partners, the details of the context in which those killings occur are much harder to identify. So while the data can indicate whether partners were killed in 'an altercation of a domestic nature' as defined above, what it cannot tell us is the extent to which these intimate homicides were preceded by other 'domestic violence'.[24] However, Wallace's more detailed study of NSW homicides between 1968 and 1981 showed that:

> [S]pouse killings were found to occur almost exclusively against a background of severe marital discord. Escalating conflict and tension between a husband and wife often preceded one or more violent confrontations. A history of violent confrontation was highly prevalent. Rarely was marital murder an isolated act activated by mental illness, jealousy or "passion"; typically it followed a series of violent exchanges and threats that culminated in a lethal attack. ... The most striking feature of cases in which men killed their wives were the large number who killed wives from whom they were separated ...; the high incidence of often severe physical abuse by the husband against his wife prior to the actual killing; and finally, the very large number of cases in which the men

---

20 Ibid, at 3; 51% of 'Asian' femicide victims were killed by an intimate partner (ibid). Note that classification of racial background is tripartite – Asian, Caucasian or indigenous, and is made by police and in many circumstances it will be based on external appearance alone; the Institute suggests this will under-represent the rates of indigenous homicide: see Jenny Mouzos, *Indigenous and Non-Indigenous Homicides in Australia: A Comparative Analysis*, Trends and Issues Paper No 210, Australian Institute of Criminology, 2001, at 2. Aboriginal men were also more likely to be killed by an intimate partner – 21.7% versus 10.2% for Caucasian men (*Femicide: An Overview*, at 4).

21 *Femicide: An Overview*, at 4.

22 Ibid, at 2.

23 Ibid, at 6.

24 Carcach and James state in the conclusion of their analysis: 'With increased resources, one possibility would be to expand the coverage of the National Homicide Monitoring Program (NHMP) to collect data from Coroners' Reports and Court transcripts regarding the nature of the day-to-day relationship between victims and offenders and the circumstances surrounding the incident. These data could be used ... as a diagnostic tool for the prevention and treatment of domestic violence in general' (at 6). However, since 1996 the NHMP has collected data on prior violence: from 1996 to 1999 in 30% of the 193 intimate partner homicides over that period violence was known to be present (Mouzos, *Homicidal Encounters*, at 119).

subsequently attempted or succeeded in taking their lives following the killing, particularly following separation. Women, in contrast, rarely killed husbands from whom they were separated and almost never killed over sexual jealousy or termination of a relationship. **Most notable was the very high prevalence and degree of prior domestic violence suffered by these women at the hands of their husbands.** The immediate precipitating events in husband-killings reflected this history of maltreatment: the majority of women killed in response to violence or threat of violence perpetrated on them by the victim, their husband. ...

A clear relationship emerged between the women who became victims of marital murder and the women who killed their husbands. In terms of the issues over which conflict occurred, and the form of mistreatment, physical and mental, that women as both victims and offenders had endured, their experiences were very similar. The difference between the two appeared to be that whereas in husband-killings the women took action into their own hands and retaliated, in the wife-killings, the women did not.[25]

In other words, the women who kill and the women who are killed share the same history, a history of violence against them.[26]

Attitudes to violence against women

In 1987, the federal Office of the Status of Women commissioned a nationwide survey on opinions and attitudes to violence against women.[27] One in five of those interviewed (22% of men and 17% of women) considered that there were circumstances in which the use of physical force by a man against his wife was justifiable. This survey was repeated (and expanded) in 1995 and indicates some very interesting changes in attitudes.[28] While 18% of people in 1995 indicated that there were circumstances in which they though it was justified for men to use physical force against their female partners, there was a marked reduction in those seeing so-called provocation by the woman as justifying violence:

> The 1995 ANOP survey monitored a question from the 1987 Public Policy Research Centre survey about whether physical force is justified in any circumstances. First of all, survey respondents were asked generally whether there were any circumstances in which it would be acceptable for a man to use physical force against his wife (Section A of the question). All were then asked whether physical force would be acceptable in seven specific circumstances (Section B of the question). ...

---

25 Wallace, *Homicide*, at 102-3 (emphasis added).
26 See, *ibid*, at 97. Cf Ken Polk and David Ranson, 'Patterns of Homicide in Victoria' in Duncan Chappell, Peter Grabosky and Heather Strang (eds), *Australian Violence: Contemporary Perspectives*, Australian Institute of Criminology, Canberra, 1991. Polk and Ranson examined all homicides in Victoria in 1985 and 1986 using coroners' files: homicides involving sexual intimates accounted for 31% of all the homicides, and where sexual intimacy was involved, 76% of the offenders were men and 78% of the victims were women. And, in five of the six cases where women killed men, there was a history of violence against the woman. See also Ken Polk, *When Men Kill: Scenarios of Masculine Violence*, Cambridge University Press, Melbourne, 1994.
27 Public Policy Research Centre, *Community Attitudes Towards Domestic Violence in Australia*, 1988.
28 Office of the Status of Women, *Community Attitudes to Violence Against Women: Detailed Report*, AGPS, Canberra, 1995.

Less than one in ten (8%) **feels that physical force is justifiable when the man is "provoked"** by his wife in seven given circumstances (that is, 8% said "yes" to any part of Section B). The number who see provocation as an excuse has **almost halved since 1987** (14%). The specific circumstances given include "if the wife ...":

- "argues or refuses to obey him" (1% in 1995, compared to 2% in 1987);
- "wastes money" (1% in 1995, compared to 2% in 1997)
- "doesn't keep the house clean" (1% in 1995, compared to 2% in 1987);
- "doesn't have the meals ready on time" (1% in 1995 and 1% in 1987);
- "keeps nagging him" (2% in 1995, compared to 4% in 1987);
- "refuses to sleep with him" (1% in 1995, compared to 3% in 1987) and
- "admits to sleeping with another man" (6% in 1995, compared to 11% in 1987)

In response to the general question, **less than two in ten (18%) can perceive circumstances in which physical force is acceptable. However, most of these (15%) do not see "provocation" as a valid excuse** (that is, they said "no" to all parts of Section B, but "yes" to Section A). This pattern of responses in 1995 is very different to 1987, when more saw provocation as an excuse (14%) than initially perceived physical force to be justifiable (8%).

In 1995, those (15%) who perceive physical force can be acceptable but do not see provocation as an excuse were asked, in a new open-ended question, for their reasons ... . **Self-defence** (10%) **emerges as the main circumstance in which physical force is perceived as acceptable** among this group. There are also minor mentions of physical force to restrain the wife (3%); and to protect the family (2%).[29]

Notes

1. While attitudes to violence appear to have become more progressive, the data we refer to above show that the rate of domestic homicide has not changed over the past seven years. (This can be contrasted with US data, which show domestic homicides declining.)[30] How relevant are attitudes about violence to violent behaviour? What might have changed attitudes to violence?
2. Some attitudinal data remains extremely disturbing. Daws et al undertook a survey of young people.[31] They interviewed some 250 15-18 year olds in southern Queensland and northern New South Wales and administered some 218 questionnaires (a response rate of 54.9%). The questionnaire included questions on whether 'it's okay for a man to pressure a woman to have sex' in a series of different circumstances, which showed the following disturbing results:

---

29 *Ibid*, at 36-7 (emphases in original). See also Partnerships Against Domestic Violence, *Attitudes to Domestic and Family Violence in the Diverse Australian Community*, Commonwealth of Australia, June 2000.

30 See Carcach and James, *Homicide Between Intimate Partners in Australia*, at 2. They note that in the US over the previous 20 years, there has been a one-third drop in the number of intimate partner homicides. They state that this 'declining trend ... has been linked inter alia to factors such as shifts in patterns of family formation associated with declining domesticity, the improved economic status of women, and increases in the availability of domestic violence services' (*ibid*).

31 Leonie Daws, Jillian Brannock, Ross Brooker, Wendy Patton, Georgia Smeal and Shane Warren, *Young People's Perceptions of and Attitudes to Sexual Violence*, National Youth Affairs Research Scheme, National Clearinghouse for Youth Studies, Hobart, 1995.

Its okay for a man to pressure a woman to have sex if	Females N=137	Males N=91
He spends a lot of money on her	1.5%	12.1%
He is so turned on he can't stop	2.9%	13.2%
She has had sex with other boys	2.9%	11%
She is stoned or drunk	1.5%	14.3%
She lets him touch her	7.3%	20.9%
She says she's going to have sex with him and then changes her mind	4.4%	20.9%
They have dated a long time	3.6%	23.1%
She's led him on	8.6%	29.7%
She gets him sexually excited	6.6%	29.7%

Adapted from Table 5.9.

These data show a remarkable difference between young women and young men. Can you suggest strategies that might help to address and overcome these differences?

Gender neutrality and the language of domestic violence

From time to time, it is suggested that men are as likely to be the victims of domestic violence as women. In Australia, this suggestion was made most recently by Bruce Headey, Dorothy Scott and David de Vaus.[32] They argue that, on the basis of their survey of both men and women:

1) Men were just as likely to report being physically assaulted by their partners as women. Further, women and men were about equally likely to admit being violent themselves.
2) Men and women report experiencing about the same levels of pain and need for medical attention resulting from domestic violence.
3) Violence runs in couples. In over 50% of partnerships in which violence occurred both partners struck each other.[33]

They explicitly recognise that their findings 'run counter to conventional wisdom' and thus say '[i]t is fair to ask researchers how much confidence they have in their own findings'.[34] They go on to state:

> We are reasonably confident about the first and third results; that female and male partners assault each other about equally often and that violence runs in couples. ... We have much less confidence in the second result, finding it hard to credit that women injure men as seriously as men injure women. ... [I]n future work it will be important to compare subjective assessments of severity to more reliable and objective measures.[35]

This report has been subject to a compelling critique by Dale Bagshaw and Donna Chung.

---

32 Bruce Headey, Dorothy Scott and David de Vaus, 'Domestic Violence in Australia: Are women and men equally violent?' (1999) 2 *Australian Social Monitor* 57.
33 *Ibid*, at 61.
34 *Ibid*.
35 *Ibid*.

Dale Bagshaw and Donna Chung, 'Gender Politics and Research: Male and Female Violence in Intimate Relationships'
(2000) 8 *Women Against Violence: An Australian Feminist Journal* 4

[6] Headey et al (1999) cite studies conducted in North America in support of their claim that men and women are equally violent. The proposition in these studies ... is predominantly based on the use of strictly quantitative methodologies, the most common being the Conflict Tactics Scale (CTS) – developed by Murray Straus in the 1970s ['Measuring Intra Family Conflict and Violence: The Conflict Tactics Scale' (1979) 41 *Journal of Marriage and the Family* 75] – and some hospital admission data.

The CTS has been used by many North American researchers, including Straus and Gelles ['Societal Change and Change in Family Violence from 1975-1985 as revealed by two National Surveys' (1986) 48 *Journal of Marriage and the Family* 465] in the often cited *Behind Closed Doors* telephone survey. The CTS is an incidence-recording tool.

One partner (not both) is telephoned and asked about their experience of violence in their relationship. Acts of violence are recorded according to a violence incidence scale ranging from minor violence (including 'discussing calmly', 'crying', 'shouting') to severe violence (including 'threw something at him/her', 'beat him/her up'). In 1986, Gelles and Straus found rates of domestic violence to be 122:1000 male to female violence and 124:1000 female to male violence.

The extent to which these reported rates of violence accurately reflect the nature of domestic violence has been seriously questioned by many researchers. Moreover, Gelles and Straus themselves [*Physical Violence in American Families: Risk Factors and Adaptations to Violence in 8145 Families*, Transaction Press, New Brunswick, 1990] later argued that two important factors should not be overlooked, namely: that the greater size and strength of the male affects the impact of the violence; and that nearly three-quarters of women's violence is self-defence. ...

Many researchers have highlighted a range of problems with the use of quantitative surveys alone to measure the incidence and prevalence of domestic violence. For example, the limitations that have been identified with versions of the CTS are:

- the complex nature of the experience of domestic violence is reduced to single quantitative acts;
- no distinction is made between offensive and defensive acts;
- there is no consideration of the situational contexts in which the violence occurred that allows for adequate interpretation of measurements;
- there is no consideration of the meaning or intent behind the acts;
- there is no discrimination between the intent and the effects of the violent acts;
- the CTS assumes, incorrectly, that partners are equal in negotiations;
- [7] the types of violence are rank-ordered and poorly differentiated (for example 'having kicked, bit, hit or tried to hit with an object', 'beat up' or 'choked', or 'threatened with a knife' or 'fired a gun' are all naively grouped as 'severe violence');
- many violent acts are *not* included in the CTS including burning, suffocating, squeezing, spanking, scratching, sexual assault and many forms of psychological, social and economic abuse;
- violence is only looked at in one year and so the history of the violence in the relationship is not considered (a single slap can be equated with many years of terrorism);

- violence is understood as differences or conflicts and does not take into account attempts by one partner to control the other for no identifiable reason; and
- the crudity of the CTS does not enable complex understandings of domestic violence to be used in the interpretation of the data.

Similarly, hospital admissions data record single incidents of violence and fail to record the context in which the violence occurred. In addition, many violent acts are not picked up by hospitals because of the lack of adequate screening protocols and victims' choices not to disclose the violence .... .

Concern has been expressed by many people ... about the reported findings of the International Social Science Survey Australia (IsssA) 1996/1997 Family Interaction module that included questions about domestic violence to determine its prevalence. [*This is the survey reported on by Headey et al, noted above.*] As with the North American prevalence research using the Conflict Tactics Scale in surveys, women and men reported approximately equal rates of being assaulted by their partner for the three types of assault asked about.

The IsssA survey asked only one of each couple whether they or their partner had (1) slapped, shaken, scratched the other (2) hit the other with the fist or with something held in the hand, thrown, or (3) kicked the other. There was no reference in the IsssA survey to a wide range of physically violent acts (including smashing objects, torturing pets and sexual violence) or to the various forms of psychological, emotional, social and economic abuse which are commonly used by perpetrators in situations of domestic violence .... .

Most of the criticisms of the Conflict Tactic Scale are also applicable to the IsssA survey, including that the survey does not discriminate between intent or effect and does not record the history of violence or the context in which the violent behaviour took place. The IsssA researchers, like Straus, interviewed only one partner but other studies that have independently interviewed both partners found that their accounts of violence did not match. The researchers relied on self-reports of violence by one member of each household, however other studies have suggested than men who are violent in intimate relationships typically under-report their violence by as much as 50%.

The IsssA survey did ask about 'threats' and 'feelings of intimidation' which give a clue to the different experiences of men and women. Similar percentages revealed that their partner had threatened to 'slap, hit or attack' but significantly more women (7.6%) than men (4.0%) said they felt 'frightened and intimidated' .... The researchers also footnoted other significant information, namely that, 'some victims of domestic violence are in refuges and so not available in surveys' and 'perpetrators and victims of severe violence may also be less willing to admit what is going on than are people in milder situations' ... .They also found that men were as likely as women to be victims of domestic assaults that led to injury and pain which is contrary to the findings of the SA Health Goals and Targets Survey (1998) where a much greater rate of women reported being injured compared to men. The researchers, however, did note that this evidence 'needs treating with caution because it runs counter, not just to conventional belief, but also to medical and police records. The issues needed further research'.[36]

---

36 See also Anna Ferrante, Frank Morgan, David Indermaur and Richard Harding, *Measuring the Extent of Domestic Violence*, Hawkins Press, Sydney, 1996; and Michael Flood, 'Claims about Husband Battering', <http://www.anu.edu.au/~a112465/XY/husbandbattering.htm>.

Notes

1. This critique of the research methods used in the International Social Science Survey Australia (IsssA) returns us to the homicide data cited above.[37] This tells us that men are overwhelmingly responsible for homicidal violence and, when partner violence is considered, men are much more likely to kill their women partners than women their men partners. While clearly not all domestic violence ends in death, this data must influence the understanding of self-report data on violence in intimate heterosexual relationships.

    The understanding of domestic violence as gender neutral, as likely to be committed by women as men, appears to have influenced the Law Reform Commission of Victoria's analysis of data on the provocation defence.[38] On the basis of an empirical study of all homicide prosecutions in the State between 1981 and 1987, the Commission concluded that the provocation defence (which is a partial defence reducing murder to manslaughter) was not gender biased.[39] They reached this conclusion on the basis of the data which showed that men were more likely to raise the defence when they kill a man not a woman, and it was more likely to be rejected where a man killed a woman (36%) than if a man killed a man (12%). And, when women raised provocation, they were more likely to be successful. But, as Adrian Howe has pointed out, 30 men (but only eight women) did raise provocation in a domestic context and, more importantly, the study failed to address the circumstances that were alleged to amount to provocation in each category.[40] Howe's criticism was echoed by the NSW Law Reform Commission in its discussion paper on provocation:

    > [I]t is ... important to be aware of what lies behind these figures. The general pattern that emerges from the cases is that men use the provocation defence when they kill their partners or ex-partners in a jealous rage and that women use it ... when they have been the victims of long term domestic abuse. The data treat these situations as commensurate – something which should itself be examined for gender bias.[41]

    This analysis, and that of Bagshaw and Chung, highlight the necessity of gathering information on the context in which violence occurred in any purported measurement of domestic violence.

---

37 Cf Ferrante et al, *Measuring the Extent of Domestic Violence*, at 11.
38 Law Reform Commission of Victoria, *Homicide Prosecutions Study*, Report No 40, nd, especially Appendix 6, published separately, 1991.
39 *Homicide Prosecutions Study*, at para 154. Cf Hugh Donnelly, Stephen Cumines and Ania Wilczynski, *Sentenced Homicides in NSW 1990-1993: A Legal and Sociological Study*, Judicial Commission of NSW, Sydney, 1995.
40 Adrian Howe, 'Provoking Comment: The Question of Gender Bias in the Provocation Defence – A Victorian Case Study' in Norma Grieve and Ailsa Burns (eds), *Australian Women: Contemporary Feminist Thought*, Oxford University Press, Melbourne, 1994, at 228-9.
41 New South Wales Law Reform Commission, *Provocation, Diminished Responsibility and Infanticide*, Discussion Paper No 31, 1993, at para 3.98. For an analysis in the English context, indicating similar patterns of murder and the use of the provocation defence, see Jeremy Horder, *Provocation and Responsibility*, Clarendon Press, Oxford, 1992. Horder states: 'Superficial reflection on these bare statistics might lead one to suppose that it is easier for women than for men to "get off" with manslaughter on the grounds of provocation when charged with murder. If one bears in mind, though, the very large percentage of women facing a murder charge in domestic homicide cases who have themselves been battered, something rarely true of men facing such a charge, it might be thought rather surprising that the proportion of women who are convicted only of manslaughter is not much higher, compared to their male counterparts' (at 187).

2. Ferrante et al attempted to present a picture of the level of domestic violence in Western Australia. They recognised the limits of relying on any one particular data source, so they tried to bring together a wide array of such sources, including victimisation surveys, hospital data, data from non-government agencies like refuges, and court and police statistics on domestic violence. They state: 'In a surprisingly consistent result, females constituted between 88% and 92% of the victims of domestic violence in most of the data sources'.[42]

3. Mary Eaton argues that intra-lesbian violence cannot be explained by traditional (feminist) understandings of heterosexual domestic violence.[43] She argues that the invisibility and silence surrounding intra-lesbian abuse are central to understanding it:

> The argument that erasure from the cultural imagination distinguishes lesbian oppression from other forms of systematic inequality is by no means novel: the observation that, unlike heterosexual women and gay men, lesbians labour under the unique burden of being invisible has long been made by lesbian critics. To the extent, then, that battering is connected with this notion of erasure, neither gender nor gay theories of intimate abuse, which do not factor enforced invisibility into their analyses, can speak fully to the experience of lesbians with domestic violence. ... If erasure is understood to exist on a continuum, from closetry at one pole to physical annihilation at the other, the phenomenon of intralesbian violence can be seen to span its entire spectrum. Battering complicates the difficult process of coming out, and contributes to the already widespread reticence to do so. Battered or battering lesbians have ample reason ... not to come out as lesbians. The shame of individuals involved in such relationships, and the silence or ignorance with which their appeals for assistance are met, all foster closetry. ...
>
> At the other extreme, battering fosters and sometimes accomplishes erasure in its most graphic and literal sense: dead lesbians are neither seen nor heard. Although one could say that it is internalized self-hatred, a belief that a lesbian really ought not to inhabit the earth, that feeds a battering lesbian's motivation to abuse and a battered lesbian's decision to withstand her own violation, my point does not stop with such psychoanalytic insights. Whether or not it is self loathing that drives the battering dynamic, the further question remains as to how to conceive of the response of the

---

42 Ferrante et al, *Measuring the Extent of Domestic Violence*, at 104.
43 Mary Eaton, 'Abuse by Any Other Name: Feminism, Difference and Intralesbian violence' in Martha Albertson Fineman and Roxanne Mykitiuk (eds), *The Public Nature of Private Violence: The Discovery of Domestic Abuse*, Routledge, New York, 1994, at 195. Eaton examines theorists who see intra-lesbian violence as gendered and those who argue it is not gendered: she suggests that the former see gender as socially constructed – the battering lesbian is taking on a socially male role, while the latter see gender as 'synonymous with biological sex' (at 200). Eaton argues that both theories assume that intra-lesbian abuse is the same as, or very similar to, heterosexual domestic violence (*ibid*). Eaton argues that in fact very little is known about intra-lesbian violence and while there may well be many similarities with heterosexual domestic violence, there are also differences. For example, she suggests that intra-lesbian violence is less likely to be sexualised than heterosexual domestic violence (at 205-6) and that some lesbians use the threat of 'outing' in their abuse (at 206). Eaton also comments on more radical feminist theories of domestic violence which focus on the systematic power inequalities between women and men, and in particular the legal entrenchment of (physical) inequality of wives. When this is applied to lesbian battering 'the particular sociopolitical inequalities undergirding the marriage relationship, which constitute the core of the critique, simply do not apply homologously to the phenomenon of lesbian battery' (at 212). Cf Ruthann Robson, 'Lavender Bruises: Intra-Lesbian Violence, Law and Lesbian Legal Theory' (1990) 20 *Golden Gate University Law Review* 567.

social problem apparatus, a response most often characterised by a seeming indifference. Societal willingness to allow lesbians to wreak destruction on one another unchecked and unabated begins to appear very much like a kind of genocidal practice. Sisters, as the song goes, are doin' it for themselves.[44]

While Eaton suggests that what is required for analyses of lesbian and heterosexual domestic violence is quite different, she also urges that 'commonality of experience' is *not* required for 'viable political unity':[45]

> [H]eterosexual and lesbian feminists can join cause against domestic tyranny in a way that both attends to the specificity of male-on-female and female-on-female violence and respects what is common to both. Lesbians need our own conceptual paradigms for making sense of the particularities of intralesbian violence, and the notion of invisibility may serve us particularly well in that regard. So, too, heterosexual women should not be required to forfeit too readily theoretical models which speak meaningfully to the violence of their intimate relations with men.[46]

4. Eaton's analysis suggests that there may not be a conceptual paradigm that will invariably deal adequately with the experience of both heterosexual women and lesbians, but that this is not a necessary sign of inadequacy of a theoretical approach. Do you think Eaton's thesis would apply beyond the area of domestic violence? How often do feminist analyses recognise that their claims are only likely to apply to heterosexual women? Should male homosexual domestic violence be explained and understood in a different way than male on male violence between comparative strangers in a hotel?

5. We might also question the terms in which feminists have analysed violence against women in the family context, that is, the use of the term 'domestic violence'. Does the language of 'domestic violence' itself neutralise the harm that is done? Does it correctly or usefully label the harm done? Is there a more appropriate language? Isabel Marcus argues:

> [W]e must acknowledge the fact that retention of the modifying term "domestic" handicaps and narrows further inquiry.
>
> When we talk about violence, we do not utilize the terms "stranger violence" and "domestic violence" as parallel terms. We separate out from "violence" abuse which occurs between partners or in a family by modifying it and characterizing it with a term connoting a status relationship – "domestic". The unmodified term "violence" which is applied to situations not involving intimates is "real" and, therefore, clearly punishable. By its linguistic location, the category "domestic", which modifies and specifically locates violence, is residual and, perhaps, less clearly subject to disapproval or punishment. While we recognise the unmodified term "violence" as a strategy for asserting control and domination, and creating terror, we may fail to make the same connection for the modified term, even though violence during a partnering relationship or at the time of separation is a strategy designed to achieve the same results.[47]

---

44 Eaton, 'Abuse by Any Other Name', at 219-20.
45 *Ibid*, at 220.
46 *Ibid*.
47 Isabel Marcus, 'Reframing "Domestic Violence": Terrorism in the Home' in Fineman and Mykitiuk (eds), *The Public Nature of Private Violence*, at 26.

Do Marcus' comments neglect the historical revolution required in connecting 'violence' with 'the domestic'? Even if it is accepted that the connection of violence and the intimate sphere with the term 'domestic violence' was both useful and radical when first introduced, has the term been used, in more recent times, to trivialise violence women experience from male batterers in the home?

6. Harry Blagg suggests that indigenous peoples in Australia, Canada, New Zealand and the USA prefer the language of family violence to that of domestic violence:

> The story of indigenous family violence is inextricably linked to the violence of colonialism and its legacy. The traumatic impact of this original 'founding violence' continues to send shock waves through indigenous communities.
>
> This concept embodies an historical narrative about the collective suffering of a people, rather than being simply a term defining a discrete social problem or a specific set of power relationships. The story of family violence and colonialism is the way by which indigenous people have been able to wrest control of an historical narrative. It allows a re-telling of the story of 'settlement' in ways which foreground its devastating impact on their culture, and challenges non-indigenous definitions of violence between intimates.
>
> While there are some clear points of overlap with the literature developed within the domestic violence paradigm, the family violence approach differs in a number of crucial respects including:
> - rejection of 'criminalisation' as the main strategy to deal with family violence;
> - less reliance on an explicitly feminist analysis and explanation of violence within intimate relationships;
> - greater stress on the impact of colonialism, trauma, family dysfunction and alcoholism as primary causes;
> - a view which sees male violence less as an expression of patriarchal power than as a compensation for lack of status, esteem and value;
> - greater stress on the impact of family violence on the family as a whole, rather than just women and children; and
> - emphasis on a range of potential perpetrators, including husbands, sons, grandsons and other male kin.[48]

Violence against women and legal categories

While there has been an enormous amount of work by feminist activists over the past 20 or 30 years to try to ensure an adequate response from the legal system to violence against women, the success of these endeavours is far from clear. And most of that work has gone into legal issues that directly address violence against women, usually criminal or quasi-criminal laws, for example, the laws on sexual assault addressed later in the next chapter. While these efforts may have had limited impact, there has been even less impact in areas of law not identified by the legal system as 'about violence against women'. That is, violence can be present in legal disputes that do not directly involve violence – the violence is not the reason for the litigation – but is an underlying factor in the case. In these

---

48   Harry Blagg, *Crisis Intervention in Aboriginal Family Violence*, Summary Report, Commonwealth of Australia, 2000, at 2-3.

circumstances, the violence is often ignored, even though it should be central to the resolution of the case.[49] Here we briefly address one example of a legal doctrine, outside the criminal arena, which deals with violence – the forfeiture rule in the law of succession.

The forfeiture rule

One of the best known legal aphorisms is 'no man [sic] shall profit from his own wrong'. A common example of this is the rule that a person cannot benefit under the will of someone that person has killed, known as the forfeiture rule.[50] However, the circumstances of some homicide cases, in which women have killed their husbands after a long history of abuse, have confronted some courts with the dilemma of how – or whether – to apply this principle. For example, in *Re Keitley*, the Supreme Court of Victoria was confronted with an application for probate by a woman named in her husband's will as his executor who had pleaded guilty to his manslaughter.[51] The judge noted that he had before him materials from the criminal proceeding, which demonstrated that the relationship involved violence or threats of violence directed by the deceased to his wife.

> The cumulative effect of the deceased's behaviour was to engender in his wife a very real and understandable fear of him.[52]

After reviewing a number of authorities concerned with the principle, the court decided, in view of its finding that her level of moral culpability was markedly diminished, that this was not a case in which the rule should operate to prevent the granting of probate.[53] Similarly, in the NSW case of *Public Trustee v Evans*,[54] the court decided that the forfeiture rule should not apply where the applicant had been subjected to a prolonged history of violence before the killing.

Notes

1. In the course of his decision in *Evans*, Young J stated:

    > I have to decide whether in 1985 in NSW there is a rule of public policy which makes it anti-social to permit a wife who has been threatened by her husband that he will kill her and her children, and who has shot him to prevent mayhem, to be debarred from recovery.[55]

    And later:

    > My view of the ethos prevailing in this State at this time is that it is commonly recognised that unfortunate situations may occur in family groups whereby a death regrettably occurs because of a situation of domestic violence.[56]

---

49 See Graycar, 'Telling Tales: Legal Stories About Violence Against Women' (1996) 7 *Australian Feminist Law Journal* 79.
50 See *Cleaver v Mutual Reserve Fund Life Association* [1892] 1 QB 147. For the US equivalent, see *Riggs v Palmer* 115 NY 506; 22 NE 188 (1889).
51 [1992] 1 VR 583. Mrs Keitley was released after entering into a three-year community based order.
52 *Ibid*, at 584.
53 *Ibid*, at 588.
54 (1985) 2 NSWLR 188.
55 *Ibid*, at 191.
56 *Ibid*, at 192.

Does this latter statement detract from the impact of the first statement? Is the latter statement denying the context of violence between sexual intimates noted above?

Some legislatures have responded to the perceived strictures of the forfeiture rule. For example, s 3 of the *Forfeiture Act* 1991 (ACT) provides that 'the Supreme Court may make an order modifying the effect of the forfeiture rule where it is satisfied that, having regard to the conduct of the offender and of the deceased and to such other circumstances as appear to the court to be material, the justice of the case requires the rule to be modified'. The language used in the *Forfeiture Act* 1991 is gender neutral. It does not suggest that it is designed to address the particular situation of women who have been abused in their homes by their partners. Should it? Are there other situations where similar questions reducing the level of moral culpability of a felonious killing might arise?

2. In Chapter 5 we discussed *Griffiths v Kerkemeyer* damages – damages paid to an injured party to pay for the costs of care, care often provided by a family member.[57] We noted the case of *Bruno v Davies*[58] where the plaintiff was injured in a motor vehicle accident and became violent toward his carer, his wife, as a result of the injuries. The court there noted the violence but only in order to take account of the possible contingency that the wife might leave because of the violence. Would it be more useful to include a component of damages to compensate others, such as the wife/carer, for the consequences of the violence. Is this possible? Are there other ways a court assessing personal injury damages could take account of the violence a carer is exposed to?[59]

3. In traditional legal education, violence against women is not typically a subject in the law course in its own right nor, perhaps more importantly, is it a topic in a general compulsory course such as property law, contract, equity or administrative law. Violence against women is an essential part of criminal law courses in Australian law schools but how visible is it in fact? How would you make violence against women more visible, not only in criminal law, but also in other compulsory law subjects?[60]

Traditional legal responses to violence against women

There are a variety of legal doctrines that can be utilised to respond to violence against women. These include the enforcement of existing criminal laws, such as the law of assault; the use of administrative law remedies, such as a writ of mandamus to compel police to exercise their powers under the criminal law in appropriate cases; injunctions under the *Family Law Act* 1975 (Cth) or under laws such as the *Property (Relationships) Act* 1984 (NSW) (formerly the *De Facto Relationships Act* 1984); tort law; criminal injuries compensation legislation; and the equitable doctrine of breach of fiduciary duty, which focuses on the abuse of power inherent in some instances of violence.[61]

---

57 *Griffiths v Kerkemeyer* (1977) 139 CLR 161.
58 (1988) 144 LSJS 226.
59 See Graycar, 'Telling Tales', at 86-7.
60 See Graycar and Morgan, 'Legal Categories, Women's Lives and the Law Curriculum OR: Making Gender Examinable' (1996) 18 *Sydney Law Review* 431.
61 Most of these were explored in the first edition of this book: see Chapter 11. The doctrine of breach of fiduciary duty was not examined as it had not then been used to respond to violence against women. It is explored in Chapter 12 of this edition.

Of the traditional legal remedies, tort law, or the law of civil wrongs, has been increasingly used to respond to violence against women. Actions for negligence have been brought in cases where the defendants have breached their duty to protect women at foreseeable risk of violence. Examples include an action against the police for failing to protect women against a serial rapist[62] and actions against landlords for failing to protect tenants from rape and other forms of assault.[63] Negligence actions are potentially available against any body or person with responsibility to protect the community or provide a safe environment, for example, a school,[64] or university, an occupier of a public building, or perhaps a local government authority with responsibility for street lighting. The tort of trespass to the person, which includes assault and battery, has also been used directly against perpetrators.[65]

'Special laws' to respond to violence against women

Perhaps the most visible feminist legal response to violence in the 1970s was the development of special laws that provide for what are variously known as restraining orders, apprehended violence orders, intervention or protection orders. These are civil remedies, though because they have some hybrid characteristics, they are often also described as quasi-criminal remedies. Broadly, these orders are addressed to the future behaviour of the perpetrator, although whether they are restricted to those living in domestic relationships or are available to all targets of violence varies from jurisdiction to jurisdiction. They are designed to restrain the behaviour of the perpetrator in some way by, for example, prohibiting him being within a certain distance of the target. The orders are not concerned with the past assaults of the perpetrator – these can and should be dealt with by traditional criminal law remedies. Hence, in contrast to criminal offences that must be proved beyond reasonable doubt, as a civil action, the fact that a target is likely to be subject to violence need only be proved on the balance of probabilities. However, any breach of the order is a criminal offence. These laws have been subject to feminist criticism. Jocelynne Scutt was one of their major critics. Her views are summarised by Egger and Stubbs:

> Among her concerns were that the reforms legitimated police claims that they lacked powers to deal with domestic violence ...; that the first assault, that which provided the basis for the complainant seeking an order, would go unpenalised and that it was the breach of the subsequent court order, rather than the assault on the woman, which would invoke police action; that the civil orders reinforced the notion that domestic violence is a civil matter and not a criminal offence; and that

---

62 See *Jane Doe v Metropolitan Toronto (Municipality) Commissioners of Police* (1998) 160 DLR (4th) 697, discussed in Chapter 12.
63 See, for example, *Q v Minto Management* (1985) 49 OR (2d) 531; and *Allison v Rank City Wall Canada Ltd* (1984) 45 OR (2d) 141.
64 See, for example, the report of litigation in Queensland where two victim/survivors of sexual abuse by a teacher (and former politician) sued him, the government and the education minister for negligence: *The Age*, 19 April 2001, at 6. But see now *R and S v Queensland* (2001) Aust Tort Reports ¶81-626 (Qld Court of Appeal).
65 One of the most innovative uses of intentional tort actions has been in the Family Court, using the cross-vesting provisions that allowed actions such as assault and battery to be heard with Family Court proceedings, usually dealing with property. In some cases, for example *Marsh v Marsh* (1994) 17 Fam Law R 289, and *W v W; R and G (by their next friend P), intervener* (1994) FLC ¶92-475, courts have made orders for damages and used the pool of property as the equivalent of 'insurance'. However, since the demise of the cross-vesting scheme, this is no longer possible. This issue is discussed further in Chapter 5.

the reforms gave policy-makers and others the chance to argue that they had taken some decisive action against the problem whatever the reality for the women suffering abuse.[66]

Egger and Stubbs in response suggest:

> The argument that domestic violence has been decriminalised is overstated, and is at odds with the explicit dual focus of policy development in most jurisdictions where both criminal sanctions and protection orders are promoted as complementary responses to domestic violence. The argument also denies the extent to which changes in police policies and enforcement practices have been achieved by means other than law reform.[67]

Notes

1. Early evaluations of the protection order regime indicated that police were not substituting protection orders for prosecution of domestic violence offences.[68] However, such data are not always available.[69] A detailed study of the effectiveness of protection orders was undertaken in NSW in 1997.[70] This study was not directed to the question of the substitution of civil for criminal remedies, but rather to an assessment of how effective protection orders are in stopping violence. Trimboli and Bonney interviewed a sample of 250 people after they had sought an apprehended violence order (AVO); smaller sub-samples were followed up at one month, three months and six months after the AVO was served. At the time of the study, such orders were available against both those with whom one is in a domestic relationship (for example, spouses) known as domestic violence orders – DVOs – and against those with whom one is in some other kind of personal relationship (for example, colleague or neighbour) known as personal violence orders (PVOs). Women were 86.8% of the subjects in the study (93.5% of the DVO applications).[71] In

---

66   Julie Stubbs and Sandra Egger, *The Effectiveness of Protection Orders in Australian Jurisdictions*, AGPS, Canberra, 1993, at 5, discussing Scutt, 'Going Backwards: Law Reform and Women Bashing' (1986) 9 *Women's Studies International Forum* 49 and 'The Incredible Woman: A Recurring Character in Criminal Law' in Patricia Easteal and Sandra MacKillop (eds), *Women and the Law*, Conference Proceedings No 16, Australian Institute of Criminology, 1993. See also the exchange between interviewers Meredith Carter, Ariel Couchman and Kim Windsor, and Jocelynne Scutt, 'Women, Reform and the Law', *Australian Society*, April 1986, at 24-7, which was extracted in the first edition of this book.
67   Stubbs and Egger, *The Effectiveness of Protection Orders*, at 6.
68   Julie Stubbs, 'Domestic Violence Reforms in NSW: Policy and Practice' in Suzanne Hatty (ed), *National Conference on Domestic Violence, Vol 2*, Australian Institute of Criminology, Canberra, 1986.
69   See Stubbs and Egger, *The Effectiveness of Protection Orders*, who summarise the research available from each State and Territory as at 1993, and comment that apart from Stubbs' work noted above and some work by Ngaire Naffine (*Domestic Violence and the Law: A Study of s.99 of the Justices Act (SA)*, Women's Adviser's Office, Department of Premier and Cabinet, Adelaide, 1985, showing variations in police practice), 'none of the data reviewed for this report allowed an analysis of this issue' (at 51).
70   Lily Trimboli and Roseanne Bonney, *An Evaluation of the NSW Apprehended Violence Order Scheme*, NSW Bureau of Crime Statistics and Research, Sydney, 1997. Note that this study summarised then available overseas research. See also Margrette Young, Julie Byles and Annette Dobson, *The Effectiveness of Legal Protection in the Prevention of Domestic Violence in the Lives of Young Australian Women*, Trends and Issues Paper No 148, Australian Institute of Criminology, Canberra, 2000.
71   Trimboli and Bonney, at 24. Subjects were selected by an interviewer attending at a local court and approaching applicants who were not accompanied by the defendant to take part in the study.

relation to DVOs, 58% of orders were sought against former partners and 17% against current partners.[72] Interestingly, subjects were asked what triggered the violence from the defendant: 26% identified the defendant's jealousy and possessiveness and 25% identified the defendant being drunk.[73] In terms of whether a protection order led to a change in the behaviour of the defendant, the authors concluded:

> With one exception, there was a *reduction* in the prevalence of each behaviour prohibited by the AVO legislation – stalking, physical assault, threats of physical assault, verbal abuse, nuisance telephone calls, being sent inappropriate letter or flowers or gifts, and 'other' forms of intimidation or harassment. These effects were sustained even among subjects who maintained contact with the defendant. ...
>
> The one behaviour which was an exception to this general pattern involved the defendant's approach to the subject's family, social and work networks to obtain information regarding the subject. Before applying for the AVO, the networks of about two in five subjects were approached by the defendants. During the month after the AVO was served, the situation improved for a majority of these subjects; the defendant did not approach her/his networks. However, as time passed, the networks of *all* subjects were approached by the defendant in an attempt to obtain information about the subject.[74]

The authors raise – and reject – the possibility that this improvement could have occurred by chance, independently of the AVO, pointing out that some 85% of subjects had experienced sustained violence before seeking an AVO.[75] More than 90% of subjects stated that they perceived positive effects from the AVO being issued, the most commonly reported being reduced contact with the defendant.[76] However, some 30% of orders were breached during each of the follow-up phases of the study.[77] Some 36% of these breaches were reported to the police, and in 73% of these cases the police took no action.[78] How important are empirical studies of the implementation of protection order schemes? Do studies like this address Scutt's criticisms of civil protection order schemes?

2. Assume the police conclude, on the basis of studies such as that by Trimboli and Bonney, that seeking an AVO or equivalent order is an appropriate response to violence and they will seek such an order on behalf of a victim, or that immediate arrest of an offender committing domestic violence should occur. What account should they take of a victim's attitude to such an approach? If the victim does not want the offender arrested, or if she does not want a protection order, should the police desist?

3. It is noted above that NSW special domestic violence laws apply to relationships where parties do not live together and indeed have no domestic component.[79] A Commonwealth, State and Territory Working Group in 1999

---

72   *Ibid*, at 28.
73   *Ibid*, at 31.
74   *Ibid*, at 64 and see detailed results reported at 38-55.
75   *Ibid*, at 65.
76   *Ibid*, at 61.
77   *Ibid*, at 56.
78   *Ibid*, at 58-9.
79   Though the provisions in relation to each type of order are slightly different since amendments in 1999: in relation to domestic violence matters, an authorised justice must issue a summons or an arrest warrant (see *Crimes Act* 1900 (NSW), s 562AF) but in relation to non-domestic relationships, an authorised justice can refuse to take any action unless the order is sought by a police officer (see s 562AK).

recommended that proposed national domestic violence laws should focus only on domestic relationships:

> [T]he Working Group is keen to ensure that the scope of this model is limited to domestic situations and is not extended to situations of a casual or purely temporary nature, such as dating relationships. The Working Group considers that these relationships lie beyond the scope of 'domestic' interaction and that other protective legislation, such as laws proscribing stalking, are better suited to deal with those situations.[80]

Do you agree with the Working Group?[81]

4. In a submission to the Australian Law Reform Commission's reference on Equality for Women, the Victorian Lesbian Legal Rights Group argued:

> Lesbian women may be subject to violence or abuse from people they know, and this bears similarity to the experiences of heterosexual women. But this does not epitomise the major experiences of anti-lesbian violence, as lesbians are still more likely than heterosexual women to experience stranger violence.
>
> In other words the unique status occupied by lesbian women in a heterosexist culture suggests that anti-lesbian violence is not simply the result of anti-homosexual sentiment. Violence against lesbians can be understood as a form of social control and retribution for women who refuse to conform to a conventional 'feminine' gender role, a role which presupposes heterosexuality and reproduction. For many lesbians the existence of racist and ageist attitudes are equally important in understanding experiences of hostility and aggression.
>
> A strong belief in the sexual entitlements of heterosexual men and the subordinate status of women in our society appears to motivate some men to attack lesbian women on the basis of the woman's apparent rejection of her 'appropriate' role; thus, anti-lesbian violence can be seen to be punishment for sexual autonomy.[82]

How does this information affect your approach to the question in note 3 above?[83]

5. In a 2001 report on violence in indigenous communities, Memmott et al[84] note Judy Atkinson's observations 'that Indigenous women, in increasing numbers, are questioning the benefit to them of mainstream domestic violence legislation, and its capacity to effect long-term change on indigenous men and

---

80 Working Group, *Model Domestic Violence Laws: Report*, Partnerships Against Domestic Violence, Canberra, 1999, at 27.
81 For a critique of the report, see Rosemary Hunter and Julie Stubbs, 'Model Laws or Missed Opportunity?' (1999) 24 *Alternative Law Journal* 12.
82 Lesbian Legal Rights Group (Victoria), Submission 251, at 18, cited in ALRC, *Equality Before the Law: Women's Equality*, Report No 69, Part II, Commonwealth of Australia, Sydney, 1994, at 339.
83 Note that in NSW when deciding whether to exercise the discretion against issuing an arrest warrant or order to appear, a justice is ordered to take account of whether the harassment relates to a person's homosexuality (or race, religion, transgender status, HIV/AIDS or other disability): see *Crimes Act* 1900 (NSW), s 562AK(4).
84 Paul Memmott, Rachael Stacy, Catherine Chambers and Catherine Keys, *Violence in Indigenous Communities: Full Report*, Report to Crime Prevention Branch of the Attorney-General's Department, Commonwealth of Australia, January 2001, available at <www.ncp.gov.au/Publications/PDF/violenceindigenous>. See also Aboriginal and Torres Strait Islander Women's Task Force on Violence, *Aboriginal and Torres Strait Islander Women's Task Force on Violence Report*, Queensland Department of Aboriginal and Torres Strait Islander Policy and Development, Brisbane, 2000 (the 'Robinson report').

the causes underlying the extent of their behaviour'.[85] However, Atkinson goes on to observe:

> I am seeing and hearing a rising anger at our men, a sense of frustration and impatience at what seems to be increasing levels of violence. On the other hand I constantly sit with men who are also concerned about male (sometimes their own) behaviours and who voice a rising frustration and concern, asking for support to establish programs for Aboriginal men who are violent. They are beginning to see that they must also be about the business of decolonisation.[86]

Memmott et al observe:

> The impact of personal, family and community disintegration in many Aboriginal societies, enacted by missions, statutes and regulation, and State and Commonwealth policies, is still being realised today and should not be underestimated if genuine and workable solutions to prevent violence in Indigenous communities are to be developed. What is required is treatment and 'healing' on a massive scale, including the healing of individuals, families and whole communities.
>
> The ability of Aboriginal people to be self-determining must be addressed if Indigenous communities are to implement programs that come some way to resolving the issues of violence ... .
>
> ... The holistic approach to tackling the violence problem involves providing land, housing, health services, education, employment, substance abuse services etc as well as violence programs.[87]

What might 'healing on a massive scale' look like? What would it require?

6. In 2000, the Northern Rivers Legal Service, based in Lismore NSW, released its report of research conducted in the Northern Rivers region investigating police responses to breaches of AVOs.[88] The research, which involved a number of indigenous researchers who worked with women in Aboriginal communities,[89] revealed some of the difficulties that are distinctively faced by women in country towns and more remote areas in obtaining prompt and effective police responses to their calls. One significant finding was that police appeared 'reluctant to take action when breaches occurred in the context of contact handovers',[90] and these were generally dismissed as 'family matters'. Katzen notes that, in most such cases, 'officers not only took no action, but also did not record the reported breach. ... In the matters where no action was taken, the reasons given in the police records included that contact rights were being exercised, the conduct did not amount to a breach, a witness refuted the allegations and the protected person merely wanted the matter recorded'.[91] What other kinds of difficulties might be experienced differentially for women who have been targets of violence in remote, rural or regional parts of Australia?

---

85 Memmott et al, at 38, citing Judy Atkinson, 'A Nation is Not Conquered' (1996) 3 (80) *Aboriginal Law Bulletin* 4.
86 *Ibid*, at 7, cited in Memmott et al, *Violence in Indigenous Communities*, at 38-9.
87 Memmott et al, at 17-18.
88 Hayley Katzen, *How do I prove I saw his shadow? Responses to breaches of Apprehended Violence Orders: A Consultation with Women and Police in the Richmond Local Area Command of NSW*, 2000. See also Hayley Katzen, 'It's a Family Matter, Not a Police Matter: The Enforcement of Protection Orders' (2000) 14 *Australian Journal of Family Law* 119.
89 The research design drew heavily upon the methodology described in Stephanie Milroy, 'Maori Women and Domestic Violence: The Methodology of Research and the Maori Perspective' (1996) 4 *Waikato Law Review* 58.
90 Katzen, 'It's a Family Matter', at 121.
91 *Ibid*, at 132-3.

The victim-agency debate

In Part One we canvassed the argument that MacKinnon's approach to analysing gender inequality homogenises the experiences of women or discounts the experiences of women who are not white, middle-class, heterosexual and able-bodied. This is not the only criticism that has been made of her work.[92] Another major criticism of MacKinnon's approach is that it relentlessly depicts women as always already victims. It is suggested that this unremitting description of women's victimisation distracts attention from situations and circumstances where women do in fact exercise agency and strength, and may indeed 'fix' women in that victim position: '[I]ts emphasis on sexual victimization obscure[s] the extent to which women made choices, resisted coercion, and exercised agency in their own lives'.[93] Kathryn Abrams analyses a variety of critiques of what she calls dominance feminism. She commences by describing the more popular works of authors like Camille Paglia,[94] Katie Roiphe,[95] and Naomi Wolf.[96]

> They allege that the dominance theorists' focus on a pervasive male sexual aggression has obscured the satisfaction and self-direction in many women's sex lives. It has also enlivened a neo-Victorian regulatory urge that has produced a spate of restrictive campus rules and homogenizing education programs on date rape and sexual harassment. ... [T]hese writers claim ... that this feminism has "betrayed" women by presenting them as wholly victimized and by encouraging a whiny introspection. Instead of acquiescing in these images of powerlessness – images these writers reject not only as partial or damaging, but as substantially untrue – women should respond in ways that highlight and utilize their present agency.[97]

MacKinnon directly addressed this concern in *Feminism Unmodified*:

> [T]he parade of horrors demonstrating the systematic victimization of women often produces the criticism that for me to say women are victimized reinforces the stereotype that women "are" victims, which in turn contributes to their victimization. If this stereotype is a stereotype, it has already been accomplished, and I come after. To those who think "it isn't good for women to think of themselves as victims," and thus seek to deny the reality of their victimization, how can it be good for women to deny what is happening to them? Since when is politics therapy?[98]

Abrams suggests that MacKinnon's argument was designed to discourage 'individual women from exempting themselves from her analysis. Yet her reluctance to confront the unintended consequences of her depictions led some feminists to believe that she viewed women's agency under oppression as insufficiently important to defend'.[99]

Abrams goes on to describe an academic critique of dominance feminism which she suggests is 'less antagonistic towards the basic message of dominance

---

92 MacKinnon's approach to claims to truth and criticisms of that approach are also discussed in Part One.
93 Kathryn Abrams, 'Sex Wars Redux: Agency and Coercion in Feminist Legal Theory' (1995) 95 *Columbia Law Review* 304 at 325-6.
94 *Sex, Art and American Culture*, Vintage Books, New York, 1992.
95 *The Morning After: Sex, Fear, and Feminism on Campus*, Little, Brown and Co, Boston, 1993
96 *Fire with Fire: The New Female Power and How it Will Change the 21st Century*, Random House, New York, 1993.
97 Abrams, 'Sex Wars Redux', at 330.
98 MacKinnon, *Feminism Unmodified*, at 220, cited in Abrams, 'Sex Wars Redux', at 329.
99 Abrams, 'Sex Wars Redux', at 329.

feminism. ... [*It has*] sought to describe a subject whose agency emerges against the backdrop of, and co-exists in tension with, systematic gender-based oppression'.[100] One strand of this critique is from Black feminists who

> argue that the victimized depictions of dominance feminism fail to square with the agency manifested by women of many racial groups. Some ... point to the way women of color have forged their own self-conceptions and have mobilized within their own communities to oppose oppression on the basis of race and sex. Others have noted that a portrait of women as victims obscures the very real agency white women exercise in constructing race in society and perpetuating race based thinking within the feminist movement.[101]

Another strand 'endorse[s] the critical insight of dominance feminism but fear[s] that its muted approach to agency might be manipulated and misunderstood'.[102]

> This concern has been underscored by two recent developments: the first is a conservative critique of the feminist resort to law. This critique, mounted by social and political conservatives but fueled by the pointed accounts of writers such as Paglia and Roiphe, [*and in the Australian context see the discussion of Helen Garner's The First Stone, later in this part*] questions the growing number of women seeking legal remedies in response to sexual harassment or acquaintance rape. In a familiar yet highly effective move, it seeks to turn the spotlight from the wrongs of the offenders to the attributes of their victims. The critique describes victims of the most severe violations as wholly compromised beings; it labels others as overly sensitive souls who find offense in the most innocuous of circumstances or lack the savvy to steer themselves clear of trouble. The critique claims that those who seek legal recourse have expanded the scope of an already-intrusive state through their inability to fight their own fights. ...
>
> Many feminists view this critique as a cynical effort by anti-feminists to make the role of the victim or the legal complainant unpalatable. But the conservatives' warning – that dominance theory might shape the victim as well as expose the perpetrator – has been echoed by a less conclusively hostile source. [*Abrams here adverts to judicial decisions that have led to losses of custody for women on the grounds that they were too passive in the face of battering partners; see also the discussion by Helen Rhoades in the 'conversation' on custody in Chapter 9.*] ...
>
> These influences have led some feminists to fear that the critical contributions of dominance feminism will be overwhelmed by the negative political and personal consequences of failing to recognize agency among oppressed women. Their response is to highlight, in the course of describing women's oppression, those incidents of self-direction that emerge in the lives of systematically oppressed women. This approach seeks to acknowledge the limited but salient instances of resistance and responsibility that occur in that context, and to prevent the emergence of legal doctrines that add stigmatizing representations to the oppressions women already endure.[103]

Abrams considers the work of Martha Mahoney,[104] who has argued that some of the feminist work on male violence, particularly in relation to women exercising fatal violence against their assailants, has presented women as 'pathologically

---

100 *Ibid*, at 333.
101 *Ibid*, at 335.
102 *Ibid*, at 343.
103 *Ibid*, at 343-4.
104 Martha Mahoney, 'Legal Images of Battered Women: Redefining the Issue of Separation' (1991) 90 *Michigan Law Review* 1. See also Mahoney, 'Victimization or Oppression? Women's Lives, Violence, and Agency' in Fineman and Mykitiuk (eds), *The Public Nature of Private Violence*, at 59.

passive. This view has led to denial and confusion among battered women who do not recognize themselves in the unitary images of victimization and to legal detriment when they seek custody of their children'.[105]

> Mahoney proposes that the unitary images of dominance theory be supplemented by accounts that incorporate the daily acts of self-preservation, familial protection, and outright resistance that she sees in the narratives of battered women. These narratives suggest, for example, that a battered woman is not simply in thrall to her spouse. She sees someone who was once a loving partner or perhaps an attentive parent; she also sees a menace whose violence threatens her well-being and her life. And she is not simply passive in the face of physical onslaughts. She may endeavour to control the location or timing of the violence, to secure her children from its force, to escape it entirely if she is not impeded by financial dependency or her partner's violent pursuit. ... Mahoney believes that law can play a crucial role in fostering the recognition and serving the needs of such a subject.[106]

One of the strategies Mahoney has developed to make women's acts of agency more obvious, and to draw attention to the high level of often fatal violence women are subject to after they leave, is to identify 'separation assault' as a distinct phenomenon:

> Separation assault is the attack on the woman's body and volition in which the partner seeks to prevent her from leaving, retaliate for the separation, or force her to return. It aims at overbearing her will as to where and with whom she will live, coercing her in order to enforce connection in a relationship. It is an attempt to gain, retain, or regain power in a relationship, or to punish the woman for ending the relationship. It often takes place over time.[107]

And as Mahoney has argued elsewhere:

> Identifying separation assault helps reveal both the woman's action (separation) and the batterer's retaliation, demonstrating both oppression and resistance in battered women. Once attacks on separation are cognizable, it becomes obvious that not all domestic violence happens in the home. Domestic violence does not only happen to women who fit the stereotype of a battered woman as dependent, helpless, or homebound. Repeated separation assaults characterize many of the published cases in which battered women killed their abusers. In custody determinations, separation assault can help reveal the batterer's quest for control as part of the dynamics among the parties.[108]

Notes

1. How would highlighting women's resistance to violence affect the self-defence claims of women who kill battering spouses? (For further discussion of this issue, see Chapter 13.)
2. Abrams argues that the critique she describes as one of partial agency 'challenges the dominant legal accounts of human subjectivity':[109]

   > [L]aw tends most frequently to assume a simplified version of the liberal subject: a subject capable of uncompromised agentic self-determination, to whom legal authorities ascribe full responsibility for actions taken, and on

---

105 Abrams, 'Sex Wars Redux', at 345.
106 *Ibid.*
107 Mahoney, 'Legal Images of Battered Women', at 65.
108 Mahoney, 'Victimization or Oppression?', at 79-80.
109 Abrams, 'Sex Wars Redux', at 351 (emphasis in original).

whose behalf they are generally reluctant to intervene. The strength of these assumptions has often required lawyers seeking to depart from them to describe a sharply contrasting legal subject. In justifying legal intervention or a mitigation of legal sanction, lawyers have described, and judges have acknowledged, a female subject wholly incapable of self-direction, whom the law must rescue from her plight or relieve of responsibility for her actions. The pragmatic interest of feminist lawyers in securing positive outcomes for their clients has often made them complicit in this dichotomizing tendency. They have stressed the extent of their clients' subordination and constraint in ways that have muted any capacity for self-direction or agency.[110]

In challenging the ways anti-discrimination law has operated, Nitya Duclos/Iyer has also examined aspects of 'victim' discourses:

> From the perspective of the privileged, no one but another member of the dominant group would have the power to discriminate against another. In the world envisaged by antidiscrimination doctrine, you are either a victim or a member of the dominant group. There are no degrees within each category and no possibility of membership in both.[111]

Abrams argues for a middle ground: 'a subject who is neither as unencumbered as the law's traditional subject nor as immobilized as the exceptional subject of the law's protection'.[112] What risks and advantages can you see in using and promoting such a vision in different areas of law?

3. Marilyn Lake comments on the construction of women as endless victims,[113] by drawing on the work of Joan Scott. Scott argued:

> In the age of democratic revolutions, 'women' came into being as political outsiders through the discourse of sexual difference. Feminism was a protest against women's political exclusion; its goal was to eliminate 'sexual difference' in politics, but it had to make its claim on behalf of 'women' (who were discursively produced through 'sexual difference'). To the extent that it acted for 'women', feminism produced the 'sexual difference' it sought to eliminate. This paradox – the need both to accept and to refuse 'sexual difference' – was the constitutive condition of feminism as a political movement through its long history.[114]

And Lake argues:

> The sexual difference produced by Australian feminism 100 years ago represented women as violable and men as violators, women as powerless and men as powerful. In making claims on behalf of such women, it is arguable that feminists helped produce the vulnerable bodies they then sought to protect and govern.[115]

She concludes her article in the following way:

---

110 *Ibid*, at 351-2. See also the critique of the use of battered women syndrome, and its tendency to relentlessly depict women as victims in Elizabeth A Sheehy, Julie Stubbs and Julia Tolmie, 'Defending Battered Women on Trial: The Battered Woman Syndrome and its Limitations' (1992) 16 *Criminal Law Journal* 369 (extracted in Chapter 13).
111 Nitya Duclos, 'Disappearing Women: Racial Minority Women in Human Rights Cases' (1993) 6 *Canadian Journal of Women and the Law* 25 at 43.
112 *Ibid*, at 352.
113 Marilyn Lake, 'Dealing with Sexual Difference' (1999) 24 *Alternative Law Journal* 265.
114 Joan Wallach Scott, *Only Paradoxes to Offer: French Feminists and the Rights of Man*, Harvard University Press, Cambridge, 1996, at 3-4.
115 Lake, 'Dealing with Sexual Difference', at 265.

> The challenge for activists and law makers interested in advancing the rights of women remains a philosophical as well as a political challenge. It is a challenge posed by paradox, that is, the necessity of refusing sexist discrimination, while demanding acknowledgment of sexual difference, but in such a way as to prevent sexual difference becoming the ground for the political subordination that defines relations of protection.[116]

Is Lake's argument similar to that made by Abrams? Or is Abrams' argument for the recognition of partial agency better seen as a specific example of the broad approach Lake advocates?

Conclusion

Most of the data we have presented in this chapter, and most of the case examples we have raised, have concentrated on violence in the home. The remainder of this part both pursues this theme and expands the focus to violence outside the home. We commence the next chapter by discussing what might best be described as medical or institutional abuses, canvassing injuries caused by medical treatment and experimentation. We then move to discuss sexual assault where, although women are more likely to be assaulted by someone they know, they are also victimised by strangers. In the following chapter, we commence by discussing sexual harassment where women are targetted both in the workplace, and on the street, by people they know and by strangers. We then examine the harm that might be caused by pornography and interrogate the role of law in responding to it.

---

116 *Ibid*, at 278.

Chapter Eleven

Invading Women's Bodies

As we explained in the Introduction to the Part, we have used the concept of social injury to construct this part of the book. The structure of Chapters 11 and 12, dealing with specific injuries to women, can perhaps best be understood by also bearing in mind the concept of a continuum.

All the injuries that we discuss here happen to women because they are women. For that reason, they are best understood as group or social injuries. The order in which we deal with them reflects a continuum from harms that are most individually invasive to women's bodies, through to more pervasive and more common injuries that generally target all women. The injuries we deal with in this chapter have, in the main, a specific individual woman as their focus and involve direct, usually physical, injury to women's bodies and/or their bodily integrity. We discuss harm done to women's bodies by pharmaceutical products and medical treatment including a form of (unconsented-to) experimentation on women's bodies (the 'unfortunate experiment' in New Zealand). We then discuss rape, looking both at criminal and civil law responses, and examine changes to our understanding of sexual violence to women that flow from feminist activism. Chapter 12 commences with a discussion of sexual harassment before briefly considering another pervasive form of injury to women – pornography.

Our notion of continuum, though focusing on the gradation of types of harm to women, has much in common with the notion of the continuum of sexual violence developed by Liz Kelly.[1] She uses this concept to make sense of data she gathered from women about their experiences of sexual violence.

> The Oxford English Dictionary provides two meanings [*of continuum*] ... : 'a basic common character that underlies many different events' and 'a continuous series of elements or events that pass into one another and cannot readily be distinguished'. The first meaning enables discussion of sexual violence in a general sense: the basic common character underlying the many different events is that men use a variety of forms of abuse, coercion and force in order to control women. The second meaning enables documenting and naming the range of abuse, coercion and force that women experience. ... This meaning also allows for the fact that there are no clearly defined and discrete analytic categories into which women's experience can be placed. The experiences women have and how they are subjectively defined shade into and out of a given category such as sexual harassment, which includes looks, gestures and remarks as well as acts which may be defined as assault or rape.
>
> In both senses the concept is intended to highlight the fact that sexual violence exists in most women's lives, whilst the form it takes, how women define events and its impact on them at the time and over time varies. The meaning of continuum, as used ... [*here*], does not refer to the meaning common in social science which involves the application of statistical measurement to clearly

---

1   Liz Kelly, 'The Continuum of Sexual Violence' in Jalna Hanmer and Mary Maynard (eds), *Women, Violence and Social Control,* Macmillan Press, London, 1987. See also Liz Kelly, *Surviving Sexual Violence,* Polity Press, Cambridge, 1989.

defined, discrete categories. The concept should not be seen, therefore, as a linear straight line connecting the different events or experiences. There are a number of dimensions which affect the meaning for, and impact on, women of experiences of sexual violence at the time they happened and later in time. Amongst these are the particular nature of the assault, the relationship between the man and the woman or girl, whether the assault was a single incident or part of ongoing abuse, the extent of threat perceived by the woman at the time and the context of the assault for the woman, including how she defined the man's behaviour and whether it connected to previous experiences.

Nor should the term continuum be interpreted as a statement about seriousness either at the time or over time. ... [T]he impact of sexual violence on women is a complex matter. With the important exception of incidents of sexual violence which result in death, the effects on women cannot be read off simplistically from the form of sexual violence women experience. How women react to and define their experiences at the time and how they cope with them over time differs and a complex range of factors affect the impact of particular experiences.[2]

Whilst Kelly was concerned with sexual violence, we have not confined ourselves to what is commonly understood as sexual violence, having included in this chapter a section on medical abuses of women. Similarly, although her discussion of sexual violence does encompass sexual harassment, she did not include in her discussion pornography and other more general abuses of women. However, the comments she makes about the continuum concept are apposite to our understanding of these broader social injuries. In particular, the order in which we present the material is not meant to reflect a view on our part that some injuries are necessarily more serious than others. While reading the material that follows, consider whether Kelly's continuum could also have a further dimension added to it, that of race.

INVADING WOMEN'S BODIES: MEDICAL AND OTHER INJURIES TO WOMEN

In this part of the chapter, we look at a range of injuries to women's bodies, focusing in particular on injuries caused by drugs or products specifically designed to affect aspects of women's sexual or reproductive health. We also examine 'the unfortunate experiment' that came to public light in the mid 1980s in New Zealand, as well as some related subsequent events. These raise fundamental questions about the impact on women of changes in the tort compensation system. We start, however, by looking at one of the most invasive of all kinds of injury to women: sterilisation.

Eugenic sterilisation of women

In Chapter 8, we discussed the importance to women of their right to control their own fertility. One important aspect of that is the right *not* to be forced to have unwanted and unplanned-for children, that is, the right to choose to bear children. Here we look at some other ways in which women's fertility has been controlled, often without the woman actively choosing a particular form of intervention. One way women's fertility has been limited is by the use of arguably unsafe drugs or products such as intrauterine devices (IUDs); but the most conclusive and intrusive

---

2   *Ibid*, at 48-9.

form of intervention has been surgical sterilisation, a method that has been widely used to limit the fertility of women who are not considered to be appropriate mothers.[3] The most common use of sterilisation (at least, in Australia) has been for young women with intellectual disabilities,[4] but there is also evidence that in many countries women of colour, many of whom are also poor, are disproportionately subjected to sterilisation procedures.[5] This modern use of sterilisation is reminiscent of the widespread practice of eugenics in the latter 19th and early 20th centuries. This practice received the imprimatur of the US Supreme Court in the notorious case of *Buck v Bell*.[6] Upholding the constitutionality of a Virginia statute, which permitted involuntary sterilisation of the 'feeble-minded', Justice Oliver Wendell Holmes stated:

> It is better for all the world, if instead of waiting to execute degenerate offspring for crime, or let them starve for their imbecility, society can prevent those who are manifestly unfit from continuing their kind. ... Three generations of imbeciles are enough.[7]

In 1991, Jeff Goldhar exhaustively reviewed the history of eugenic sterilisation practices in Australia.[8] He was writing at a time when the issue was receiving considerable publicity as the Family Court had been faced with a number of applications from parents seeking approval from the court for the surgical sterilisation of their daughters with intellectual disabilities. While some judges took the view that this was a private matter for the family to decide, others had held that only the Family Court could authorise such a procedure.[9]

---

3   A slightly less extreme version is the use of drugs such as Depo Provera, a long-acting contraceptive that, it has been suggested, has been disproportionately used on young women in institutional care: see the discussion of this by S Lazarus, J Trucano and K McCarthy, 'Young Women and the Penal System in Victoria', paper delivered to Australian Law and Society conference, 6 December 1987. It has also been suggested that Depo has been used in indigenous Australian communities: see the references cited by Phillida Bunkle, 'Calling the Shots: the International Politics of Depo Provera' in *Second Opinion: the Politics of Women's Health in New Zealand*, Oxford University Press, Auckland, 1988, at note 13.
4   Cf Helen Rhoades, 'Intellectual Disability and Sterilisation – An Inevitable Connection?' (1995) 9 *Australian Journal of Family Law* 234.
5   See Laurie Nsiah-Jefferson, 'Reproductive Laws, Women of Color, and Low-Income Women' in Sherrill Cohen and Nadine Taub (eds), *Reproductive Laws for the 1990s*, Humana Press, Clifton, NJ, 1989; Adele Clarke, 'Subtle Forms of Sterilization Abuse: A Reproductive Rights Analysis' in Rita Arditti, Renate Duelli-Klein and Shelley Minden (eds), *Test Tube Women: What Future for Motherhood?*, Pandora, London, 1984. It has also been suggested that some women undergo voluntary sterilisation procedures as the price of obtaining employment in industries that work with lead in various countries: see Sally J Kenney, 'Reproductive Hazards in the Workplace: The Law and Sexual Difference' (1986) 14 *International Journal of the Sociology of Law* 393; and compare *HREOC v Mt Isa Mines* (1992) EOC ¶92-420 and, in the US, *International Union UAW v Johnson Controls* 499 US 187 (1991).
6   274 US 200 (1927).
7   *Ibid*, at 207. Note however, that in a 1942 case, *Skinner v Oklahoma* 316 US 535 (1942), the court struck down a statute providing for the compulsory sterilisation of 'habitual criminals', stating '[w]e are dealing here with legislation which involves one of the basic civil rights of man. Marriage and procreation are fundamental to the very existence and survival of the race' (316 US 535 at 541). For a detailed discussion of some of these issues, see Susan Stefan, 'Whose Egg is it Anyway? Reproductive Rights of Incarcerated, Institutionalized and Incompetent Women' (1989) 13 *Nova Law Review* 405 at 413-27; and see, in particular, her discussion of Carrie Bell (of *Buck v Bell* 'fame') at note 35.
8   Jeff Goldhar, 'The Sterilisation of Women with an Intellectual Disability' (1991) 10 *University of Tasmania Law Review* 157.
9   In *In re a Teenager* (1988) 13 Fam LR 85 and *In re S* (1989) 13 Fam LR 660, the court held that parents could consent while, in *Re Jane* (1988) 12 Fam LR 662 and *Re Elizabeth* (1989) 13 Fam LR 47, it was held that a court's consent was required. This issue is discussed further in Chapter 2.

In 1992, the High Court decided in *Marion's Case*[10] that the common law does not generally allow parents or guardians to give a valid and effective consent to certain medical procedures where the child lacks the capacity to do so.[11] Only a court or an appropriate statutorily authorised body may make such a decision.[12] A majority of the judges adopted the '*Gillick*' principle,[13] under which children who are sufficiently mature may make decisions concerning their own medical treatment.

Following the decision of the High Court in *Marion's Case*, the Family Law Council recommended in 1994 that federal legislation be enacted clearly spelling out a set of specific criteria to govern such decisions. This is in contrast with the *Family Law Act* 1975 (Cth), under which decisions are governed only by the requirement that 'the best interests of the child [is] the paramount consideration'.[14] The Council proposed that there should be a three-stage decision-making process. First, the legislation would have specified four situations in which sterilisation could never be authorised. These were sterilisation for eugenic reasons; sterilisation purely for contraceptive purposes; sterilisation as a means of masking or avoiding the consequences of sexual abuse;[15] and sterilisations performed on young women before the onset of menstruation, based on predictions about future problems that might be encountered with menstruation.[16] Before an application could be approved, it had to be shown that the surgery was necessary to save life or to prevent serious damage to the person's physical or psychological health.[17] In making a decision, the decision-maker would be required to have regard to whether the availability of less permanent means of contraception has been explored and menstrual management strategies trialled. If a decision maker was

---

10   *Secretary, Department of Health and Community Services v JWB and SMB ('Marion's Case')* (1992) 175 CLR 218.
11   The majority was constituted by Mason CJ, Dawson, Toohey and Gaudron JJ. Brennan, Deane and McHugh JJ (on different grounds and in separate judgments) held that, in certain circumstances, parents could consent to sterilisation procedures.
12   The Family Court has jurisdiction over 'children of a marriage' but, in some States and Territories, Guardianship Boards or tribunals deal with adults (16 and over) who cannot make decisions about such issues for themselves. For some discussion of the interaction of these bodies and the Family Court, see the later decision of the High Court in *P v P* (1994) 181 CLR 583. See also Family Law Council, *Sterilisation and Other Medical Procedures on Children*, AGPS, Canberra, 1994; Terry Carney and David Tait, *The Adult Guardianship Experiment: Tribunals and Popular Justice*, Federation Press, Sydney, 1997.
13   See the decision of House of Lords in *Gillick v West Norfolk and Wisbech Area Health Authority* [1986] AC 112. For a discussion, see Morgan, 'Controlling Minors' Fertility' (1986) 12 *Monash University Law Review* 161.
14   *Family Law Act* 1975 (Cth), s 65E.
15   This factor was addressed directly in *L and GM and MM and the Director General, Department of Family Services and Aboriginal and Islander Affairs (Re Sarah)* (1994) FLC ¶92-449. In response to a submission that sterilisation might well increase the risk of sexual abuse if it were known that Sarah had been sterilised, the trial judge said (at 80,675): 'Speculation as to the workings of an abuser's mind may be an especially hazardous business, but it does seem reasonable to observe that there is certainly no correlation between sterilisation and removal of the *risk* of abuse, as distinct from *one potential consequence*' (emphasis in the original).
16   Several of the earlier Family Court decisions approved the performance of sterilisations before the onset of menstruation. In *In re a Teenager*, Cook J relied on evidence as to the young woman's phobic reaction to blood and stated: 'It is obviously a matter of concern that a woman, whether young or old, may well suffer distinct embarrassment and emotional trauma if, unable to manage menstruation, sudden bleeding takes place in a public, or even private situation. Our society is full of taboos, and attitudes and perceptions about menstruation are not the least of such taboos': *In re a Teenager* (1988) 13 Fam LR 85 at 128.
17   Compare *Guardianship Act* 1987 (NSW), s 45.

inclined to approve the application, s/he should not do so unless performance of the procedure would be in the child's 'best interests'.[18]

The Council's report has never been implemented and, despite the clear requirement laid down by the High Court in *Marion's Case* (and confirmed in the decision in *P v P*),[19] it has been suggested in a report published by the Human Rights and Equal Opportunity Commission in 2001 that such procedures continue to be carried out on children, frequently without court approval having been sought.[20]

Australia is certainly not the only country to have a history of eugenic sterilisations, as reference earlier in this chapter to the decision of the US Supreme Court in *Buck v Bell* indicates. In Canada, the issue has received considerable attention in recent years following a successful action brought by Leilani Muir against the provincial government of Alberta.[21] Ms Muir was admitted to the province's training school for 'mental defectives' in 1955 and remained there for 10 years. After only the most cursory medical tests, she had been labelled a 'mentally defective moron' and was surgically sterilised, under the province's *Sexual Sterilisation Act* RSA 1955, c 311.

In the course of its judgment, reviewing the history of the practice in the province, the court noted:

> [T]he Board not only authorized sexual sterilizations, and tolerated routine but medically unnecessary appendectomies, but also routinely authorized non-medically necessary processes such as biopsies of testicular tissue. In some cases, the Board directed a vasectomy only, but partial castration by unilateral orchidectomy was carried out. In some cases, the Board authorized the hysterectomy or oophorectomy (removal of the ovaries) in order to eliminate menstruation in females; according to the language of one typical case, the female trainees were "difficult to handle and to keep clean during menstrual periods". These operations were also ordered where female trainees masturbated or had lesbian tendencies.[22]

The court held that the sterilisation and the detention of Ms Muir were unlawful and she was awarded damages of over $700,000, which included an amount of aggravated damages. Ms Muir had also sought punitive damages, but the court said:

> The defendant's actions were unlawful, offensive and outrageous. Punitive damages in the amount of $250,000 suggested by Ms Muir would certainly have been ordered had it not been for the fact that the government allowed Ms Muir to bring this action. It could have put an end to her claim; her claim was made too late, and the government could have used this delay as a complete answer to all of Ms Muir's claims. This deliberate abandonment of a complete defence is in the nature of an apology. Indeed, it is more than an apology: it is an amendment – a

---

18   See Family Law Council, *Sterilisation and Other Medical Procedures on Children*, AGPS, Canberra, 1994; Graycar, 'Sterilisation of Young Women with Disabilities: Towards a New Regulatory Framework' (1994) 1 *Australian Journal of Human Rights* 380.
19   *P v P* (1994) 181 CLR 583.
20   See Susan Brady, John Briton and Sonia Grover, *The Sterilisation of Girls and Young Women: Issues and Progress*, 2001 (available at <www.humanrights.gov.au//disability_rights/sterilisation/index.html>). This report follows an earlier one commissioned by the then Disability Discrimination Commissioner: see Susan M Brady and Sonia Grover, *The Sterilisation of Girls and Young Women in Australia: A legal, medical and social context*, commissioned by the Disability Discrimination Commissioner, HREOC, Sydney, 1997.
21   *Muir v Alberta* (1996) 132 DLR (4th) 695.
22   *Ibid*, at 734-5.

real effort to make things right. As a matter of public policy, this and other governments should be encouraged to recognize historical wrongs and to make fair amends for them. They should not be punished for doing so.[23]

Notes

1. The extract from *Muir* refers to vasectomies and orchidectomies, indicating that sterilisations were also performed on young men. However, the vast majority of those subjected to such procedures have been women. As former Supreme Court of Canada judge Bertha Wilson commented, in relation to *Re Eve*, a sterilisation decision of that court:

    > Particularly when one has regard to the fact that it has been mentally disabled women who have been the victims of involuntary obstetrical intervention, the gender dimensions of *Re Eve* ([1986] 2 SCR 388) become painfully evident. ... Since it is primarily women who carry the burden in our society of child rearing, it would likely be a woman and not a man who would be responsible for rearing the child of a woman such as Eve.[24]

    What explanations can you suggest for the higher incidence of sterilisations being performed on young women than young men? Why might parents still choose to avoid obtaining court authorisation for the sterilisation of their daughters? What weight, if any, should be given to the carer's views in such cases?

2. It has been estimated that, during the period the Alberta *Sexual Sterilisation Act* was in operation, the Board approved 4725 applications and 2822 sterilisation procedures were carried out.[25] After the decision in *Muir v Alberta*, hundreds of claims were filed against the provincial government and, in June 1998, the government announced the creation of a settlement package.[26] Between June 1996 and November 1999, 635 claims were settled for a total of $60 million. In November 1999, the government announced that it had negotiated a settlement with the remaining claimants and, at the time it made this announcement, the Government of Alberta 'expressed its profound regret to those who suffered as a result of being sterilised'.[27]

3. In the United States, considerable attention has been paid to the disproportionate incidence of sterilisation on women of colour. Adele Clarke has documented what she terms 'blatant sterilization abuse' which, she suggests, 'continued quite actively under the authority of state eugenics ... until about 1960, focused on the unconsenting and/or coerced sterilizations of the (usually incarcerated) mentally retarded, physically disabled and mentally ill, often immigrants'.[28] This practice, common in the US South, came to be known as 'Genocide in Mississippi' and, alternatively, by the euphemism, 'Mississippi appendectomies'.[29] And Nsiah-Jefferson has suggested:

---

23   *Ibid*, at 735.
24   The Hon Bertha Wilson, 'Women, the Family and the Constitutional Protection of Privacy' (1992) 17 *Queen's Law Journal* 5 at 17-18.
25   Goldie M Shea, *Redress Programs relating to Institutional Child Abuse in Canada*, background paper for the Law Commission of Canada, October 1999, available at <http://www.lcc.gc.ca/en/themes/mr/ica/shea/redress/index.html>; citing Timothy Caulfield and Gerald Robertson, 'Eugenic Policies in Alberta: From the Systematic to the Systemic' (1996) 35 *Alberta Law Review* 59 at 60.
26   The details of the package are outlined by Shea, in *Redress Programs*, at 4-5.
27   *Ibid*.
28   Adele Clarke, 'Subtle Forms of Sterilization Abuse'.
29   *Ibid*.

Blatant sterilisation abuse was exposed in the 1970s. Public assistance officials tricked illiterate black welfare recipients into consenting to the sterilization of their teenage daughters. Native American women under 21 years of age were subjected to radical hysterectomies, and informed consent procedures were ignored. Doctors agreed to deliver the babies of black Medicaid patients on the condition that the women be sterilized. Doctors have also conditioned the performance of abortions on 'consent' to sterilisation.[30]

Both authors also suggest that less blatant forms of sterilisation abuse continued, at least into the 1980s, via such factors as the lack of abortion options,[31] the incidence of unnecessary hysterectomies,[32] economic constraints upon reproductive choice,[33] lack of knowledge of the permanence of sterilisation,[34] lack of knowledge or access to other means of contraception, simultaneous sterilisation and childbirth or abortion, and iatrogenic (medically caused) sterility or infertility. More recently, as we noted in Chapter 8, the drug 'Norplant', a long acting contraceptive, has been relatively widely used in the US, particularly for women convicted of child abuse or for 'welfare mothers'.[35] Women of colour have been disproportionately affected and, since the drug was approved by the US Food and Drug Administration in 1990, several States have proposed and/or passed legislation which seeks to encourage (or in some cases) require women receiving welfare benefits to be implanted with Norplant.[36] This type of legislation may profoundly influence a targeted woman's reproductive decision-making. Why are women such as sole parents who are dependent on welfare payments more likely to be subject to such controls? Is there a connection between the use of sterilisation for women with disabilities, and the attempt to control the fertility of 'welfare mothers'?

In the 1990s, a number of women who suffered negative reactions to Norplant brought class actions against the manufacturer in various States.[37] Despite the extensive evidence of the dangers of the product, most of the cases were settled or failed on the basis that the manufacturer did not have a duty to warn the women of those dangers.[38] Considering the limited influence and resources of many of the women who have been implanted with Norplant, what redress, if any, might be available to them?

---

30   Laurie Nsiah-Jefferson, 'Reproductive Laws, Women of Color, and Low-Income Women' in Sherrill Cohen and Nadine Taub (eds), *Reproductive Laws for the 1990s*, Humana Press, Clifton, NJ, 1989 at 46. Clarke also discusses the disproportionate sterilisation of women on welfare in 'Subtle Forms of Sterilization Abuse', at 200-1.
31   Note here, as pointed out in Chapter 8, that in the US, public funds are not available for abortion as a result of legislation upheld by the US Supreme Court in *Harris v McRae* 448 US 297 (1980).
32   Clarke points out that, if the then current rate of hysterectomy continued, 50% of all women in the US would have had this surgery by the time they are 65 (Clarke, 'Subtle Forms of Sterilization Abuse', at 193).
33   For example, workplace requirements that women be sterile or sterilised in order to gain employment, and the simple economic imperative of not being able to 'afford' a child: *Ibid*, at 194-5.
34   See also Nsiah-Jefferson, at 46.
35   See Chapter 8 for a description of how Norplant works and its potential side-effects. See also Janet Ginzberg, 'Compulsory Contraception as a Condition of Probation: The Use and Abuse of Norplant' (1992) 58 *Brooklyn Law Review* 979.
36   *Ibid*.
37   One such action is described by Charles Orstein, 'Norplant company agrees to settle suits', *Dallas Morning News*, 6 August 1999.
38   *Ibid.* Each plaintiff received around $1500 less attorney's fees.

4. In July 2001, the Wisconsin Supreme Court upheld an order that bars a man convicted of failure to pay child support from having more children unless he can support all his children. The 34-year-old man had nine children by four women and owed $25,000. The court split four to three along gender lines, with the four male justices joining in the ruling and the three women opposing it as 'an unconstitutional intrusion on a basic right to procreate'.[39] Do you agree with the majority or the minority view? What arguments might you put for the view you support?

Dangerous products and dangerous drugs

A number of researchers have noted that there is a plethora of pharmaceutical and other products that have been designed for women, often in relation to issues to do with their sexuality or reproductive capacity, and which have led to large numbers of women being harmed.

> **Lucinda Finley, 'The Pharmaceutical Industry and Women's Reproductive Health: The Perils of Ignoring Risk and Blaming Women'**
> in Elizabeth Szockyj and James G Fox (eds), *Corporate Victimisation of Women*, Northeastern University Press, Boston, 1996
>
> [59] Too many of the most tragic and preventable instances of unsafe drugs and medical devices have been products used in women's bodies, often in connection with sexuality and reproduction. The litany includes thalidomide; DES (diethylstilbestrol); the early unduly high-hormone birth control pills, which increased risks of strokes and cancer; intrauterine contraceptive devices (IUDs), with their huge toll of pelvic inflammatory disease and sterility; super-absorbent tampons, with their attendant risk of toxic shock syndrome; Parlodel, a drug to suppress lactation that has caused at least nineteen maternal deaths from stroke or heart attack; and silicone breast implants, which leak or rupture and have been connected to debilitating autoimmune system diseases.
>
> These drugs and devices were developed not in response to disease but for use in healthy women to enhance what nature had provided or to control the natural processes of reproduction. Medical science has long sought to control women's reproductive capacity and to surgically manipulate or technologically "improve on" women's bodies. Normal female attributes, such as small breasts or menopause, have been classified as disease conditions requiring treatment. It is women exclusively who have faced the risks of iatrogenic injuries and disease from drugs and devices designed to alter the natural processes or shape of their healthy bodies. Drugs that have injured men are "gender-neutral"; developed to treat disease rather than healthy conditions, they can be used equally by men and women. As Professor Joan Steinman has noted, there has not yet been an instance of a "mass tort in which men were injured by a product made for men to use or take, ostensibly to enhance their well being. It appears that women, far more than men, take it on the chin from products made ostensibly for our own good". [Joan Steinman, 'Women, Medical Care and Mass Tort Litigation' (1992) 68 *Chicago-Kent Law Review* 409 at 412.]
>
> [60] Is the disproportionate number of drugs and medical devices that have wreaked havoc on women's previously healthy bodies coincidental? I think not. The desire to control or "improve" women's bodies reflects a devaluation of

---

39 Tamar Lewin, 'Father Owing Child Support Loses a Right to Procreate', *New York Times* on the web, 12 July 2001, <http://www.nytimes.com/2001/07/12/national/12DAD.html>.

women and their health. One manifestation is that pharmaceutical manufacturers have been lax about testing for or heeding signs of danger to women. Drug companies have often blamed women themselves for any reported problems, and doctors and manufacturers have ignored complaints or attributed women's descriptions of adverse effects to emotional reactions by stereotypically "hysterical" women. Marketing and profit considerations have proved more important to the pharmaceutical industry than women's health and safety concerns, and the corporate framework too readily allows for the evasion of individual legal or social accountability.

The mass product liability actions for injuries to women's reproductive health caused by such corporate behaviour lead one to wonder whether drug companies would have responded so callously to mounting evidence that a drug was harming men's reproductive or sexual well-being. The federal judge who presided over many of the legal proceedings against AH Robins Company, the manufacturer of the Dalkon Shield, came to the same conclusion. In February 1984, Judge Miles Lord called several AH Robins executives before him and castigated them with remarks that aptly summarize the corporate victimization of women: ...

[*Finley goes on to quote part of what he said when he called three of the executives into his court*:]

> Today, as you sit here, attempting once more to extricate yourselves from the legal consequences of your acts, none of you has faced up to the fact that more than 9,000 women have made claims that they gave a part of their womanhood so that your company might prosper. It is alleged that others gave their lives so you might prosper. And there stand behind legions more who have been injured but who have not sought relief in the courts of this land. I dread to think what would have been the consequences if your victims had been men rather than women, women who seem through some strange quirk of our society's mores to be expected to suffer pain, suffering and humiliation.
>
> If one poor young man were by some act of his, without authority or consent, to inflict such damage upon one woman, he would be jailed for a good portion of the rest of his life. And yet your company, without warning to women, invaded their bodies by the millions and caused them injuries by the thousands. And when the time came for these women to make their claims against your company, you attacked their characters, you inquired into their sexual practices and into the identity of their sex partners. You exposed these women and ruined families and reputations and careers in order to intimidate those who would raise their voices against you. You introduced issues that had no relationship whatsoever to the fact that you planted in the bodies of these women instruments of death, mutilation, and of disease.[40]

In the remaining part of her chapter, Finley focuses particular attention on the Dalkon Shield and DES disasters. The Dalkon Shield was one of a number of intrauterine devices developed in the late 1960s and 1970s: aspects of its design led to a high rate of infection amongst women who used it, sometimes coupled with infertility.[41] It emerged that the company knew for some time that it was

---

40 The full text of this address to the three company executives is available at 'The Dalkon Shield Litigation: Revised Annotated Reprimand by Chief Judge Miles W Lord' (1986) 9 *Hamline Law Review* 7.

41 See Morton Minsk, *At Any Cost: Corporate Greed, Women and the Dalkon Shield*, Pantheon, NY, 1985; and, for an Australian discussion, see Peter Cashman, 'The Dalkon Shield' in Peter Grabosky and Adam Sutton (eds), *Stains on a White Collar*, Federation Press, Sydney, 1989.

unsafe and, even though it had ceased marketing the product, it did not warn women to have it removed. Following a number of successful legal actions against the company, the company went into bankruptcy.

DES (diethylstilbestrol) was a drug marketed to pregnant women in the 1950s. It subsequently emerged that it caused forms of cancer in the daughters of women who took the drug while pregnant and Finley discusses some of the complicated legal issues that flowed from attempts to seek redress for that kind of harm (such as limitation periods, problems of attributing responsibility to a particular manufacturer etc).

Notes

1. Perhaps the best known drug developed for use by pregnant women was Thalidomide, a drug that caused significant birth defects to women who took it in the 1950s and 1960s. In Australia and the UK, while the consequences of Thalidomide use were widely known, no English or Australian court ever made a finding of liability against the manufacturer, Distillers.[42]
2. In addition to his reprimand to the AH Robins executives, Judge Miles Lord also placed a notation on the agreement in the Dalkon Shield litigation. The company appealed, and also sought to bring disciplinary proceedings against him. The Eighth Circuit Court of Appeals declared that Judge Lord's entry of the notation on the parties' agreement was improper: the AH Robins company personnel's due process rights had been violated as they had 'received no adequate notice of the nature of the informal and personal charges'.[43] The Court of Appeals struck the reprimand from the record of the District Court. The Judicial Council of the Eighth Circuit followed the recommendations of a five-judge investigative panel and dismissed the misconduct complaints that had been filed by the company and the three officers against Judge Lord.[44]
3. In his statement extracted above Judge Lord referred to some of the questions to which plaintiffs were subjected in the course of the Dalkon Shield litigation.[45] These included women being asked about the number of sexual partners they had had, the forms of sex they engaged in (for example, oral sex) and whether they wiped from front to back, or back to front. One woman, asked whether the pantyhose she wore had a cotton or nylon crotch, after she had already been asked a series of questions about her sexual practices, is reported to have replied: 'I'll answer that, but this sounds more like an obscene phone call than anything else'.[46] AH Robins expert witnesses and company executives were unable to relate any particular question to relevant issues of causation.[47]
4. In another part of the chapter extracted above, dealing with breast implant litigation, Finley points out how the 'good girl/bad girl' dichotomy is used by defendants who, she claims, distinguish between women who have breast

---

42 See Sunday Times Insight Team, *Suffer the Children: The Story of Thalidomide*, Andre Deutsch, London, 1979. Note that the *Sunday Times* was prosecuted for contempt of court for writing about the issue: see *Sunday Times v United Kingdom* (1979) 2 EHRR 245.
43 *Gardiner v AH Robins Co* 747 F 2d 1180 at 1191 (8th Cir 1984).
44 This account of the events is taken from the editor's note of the revised annotated reprimand: see (1986) 9 *Hamline Law Review* 7.
45 Some detailed accounts are contained in notes 14, 15 and 16 ((1986) 9 *Hamline Law Review* 7 at 28-30).
46 *Ibid*, at 29.
47 *Ibid*, at 29-30.

implants following surgery (such as mastectomies performed as a response to breast cancer), and those who do so for cosmetic reasons. She quotes data indicating that, while 80% of the former category have succeeded in their negligence actions when their implants caused them injury, only 50% of the latter category have done so.[48] Can you think of any comparable or analogous way that male plaintiffs could be discredited by defendant lawyers in litigation?

The 'unfortunate experiment'

In her chapter extracted above, Lucinda Finley suggests that, when DES was first used in the 1950s, many women were given it as part of a trial, though without their knowledge. She comments that at that time notions of informed consent were not well established and clear ethical guidelines were yet to be imposed on those who undertake medical trials. Consider this as you read the following extract which deals with a much more recent incident in New Zealand. The 'unfortunate experiment' first came to public attention after two women, Sandra Coney and Phillida Bunkle, published an article in the monthly magazine, *Metro*, in 1987. Dr Herbert Green, a gynaecologist at National Women's Hospital in Auckland, had apparently for some years been withholding what was then considered conventional treatment for cancer of the cervix (hysterectomies) when a patient was diagnosed with carcinoma in situ (CIS), a condition that generally leads to invasive cancer, on the grounds that he did not believe the conditions were connected. According to Coney:

> Green was concerned at any reduction in a woman's fertility. He was an opponent of abortion, and could see virtually no grounds for sterilisation, medical or social. Once sterilised, he said, a woman had 'thrown away a unique possession'. It was her 'heritage' to keep her uterus, Green told one woman.
>
> Green became a man with a mission. He wanted to avoid sterilising surgery and to save women's fertility. To do so he had to prove what at first he had suspected, but then he came to believe: that CIS was a harmless disease which hardly, if ever, progressed to invasive cancer.[49]

The article extracted here was written by one of the medical experts to the inquiry that was established to investigate these claims.

Charlotte Paul, 'The New Zealand cervical cancer study: Could it happen again?'
(1988) 297 *British Medical Journal* 533

[533] ... [A] magazine article, entitled "An 'unfortunate experiment' at National Women's", alleged that an experimental research programme had been undertaken at the hospital entailing the study of the natural course of carcinoma in situ of the cervix by withholding conventional treatment from some patients. The authors of the article further alleged that an internal inquiry, set up after criticisms of the programme by two hospital doctors, had been a "white wash" and that there was no evidence that the research and the withholding of conventional treatment had ever formally ceased.

---

48 Finley, at 93, citing Thomas Koenig and Michael Rustad, 'His and Her Tort Reform: Gender Injustice in Disguise' (1995) 70 *Washington Law Review* 1 at 44.
49 Sandra Coney, *The Unfortunate Experiment*, Penguin, Auckland, 1988, at 50-1.

These allegations resulted in the setting up of a committee of inquiry led by one woman, Judge Silvia Cartwright. At the public hearings further claims were made. Among these were that vaginal smears had been taken from over 2000 newborn babies, as part of the same research, apparently without the knowledge or consent of their mothers; that a randomised controlled trial of treatment for invasive cervical cancer had been undertaken without the consent of patients; that groups of students had carried out vaginal examinations of anaesthetised women without their consent; and that postgraduate students had inserted and removed intrauterine devices on anaesthetised women before hysterectomy.

... **The allegations**

The investigations leading to the magazine publication were made by two feminists: one a journalist (Coney), the other an academic in the area of women's studies (Bunkle). The starting point for their investigation was the paper "The invasive potential of carcinoma in situ of the cervix," recording the apparent outcome of the study, written by McIndoe *et al* and published in 1984. Two of the authors, McIndoe and McLean, were the doctors who had criticised the programme in 1973. The authors reported on 948 patients with carcinoma in situ of the cervix diagnosed histologically between 1955 and 1976 who were followed for five to 28 years. One group of patients continued to produce abnormal cytological results consistent with cervical neoplasia after initial diagnosis or treatment. Among this group of 131 women, 29 (22%) subsequently developed invasive cancer of the cervix or vaginal vault. Among the other 817 women who had normal cytological results on follow up 12 (1.5%) developed invasive cancer.

Coney and Bunkle alleged in their article that these results were part of the findings in a study initiated by associate professor Herbert Green in the mid-1960s, which entailed following women with abnormal cytological findings after a diagnosis of carcinoma in situ. Some cases were diagnosed by colposcopically directed punch biopsy and the women were then offered no further treatment. Other women who had abnormal smears after cone biopsy or hysterectomy were alleged to have also received no further treatment. Coney and Bunkle claimed that there was no intention to cure these patients. The story of one woman, who had been a patient at the National Women's Hospital from 1964 to 1979, was outlined. This woman had a histological diagnosis of carcinoma in situ in 1964. "By the date of her discharge in 1979, "Ruth" had visited National Women's Hospital 34 times, she had had 28 cervical smears, five biopsies, four operations under GA, and 10 colposcopic examinations. But as the final histology clearly showed she still had cancer [carcinoma in situ]." In 1985 "Ruth" had returned to the National Women's Hospital with invasive cervical cancer.

... Coney and Bunkle claimed that no one could give them an assurance that the study had ever ended. They quoted Professor Bonham, the professor of obstetrics and gynaecology, head of the postgraduate school, and chairman of the hospital ethics committee, as saying that the study "merged into general treatment. It stopped being a study and became general treatment." They also suggested that the views held at the National Women's Hospital had resulted in an attitude of neglect for cervical screening in New Zealand, and consequently a rise in the incidence of and mortality from cervical cancer in young women.

The judicial inquiry

[534] ... The Minister of Health directed Judge Cartwright to inquire into ... the research programme and treatment of women with carcinoma in situ and also more generally into the procedures observed currently at the hospital for the approval and surveillance of research and treatment; into the information made available to patients; and into teaching about the treatment of carcinoma in situ and the value of cervical screening.

FINDINGS

Judge Cartwright found that a research programme into the natural course of carcinoma in situ of the genital tract had been approved in 1966 and that it had resulted in the failure to treat adequately several women with carcinoma in situ. For a minority of women their management had resulted in persisting disease, the development of invasive cancer, and in some cases death. She found that additional reasons for the failure to treat adequately were the failure to stop the trial as soon as cogent evidence of risk began to emerge and the failure of some colleagues and administrators to impinge on clinical freedom and act decisively in the interests of the safety of patients.

The research programme had included the 1966 trial and the studies of vaginal cytology in the newborn and of the histology of fetal cervices. The great majority of patients did not know that they were participants in the 1966 trial. The trial had been reviewed by the hospital medical committee in 1975, following expressions of concern, but had never formally been ended.

A review was undertaken for Judge Cartwright of the case notes of patients with carcinoma in situ treated at the hospital. Several women were recommended for further advice or treatment. The National Women's Hospital ethical committee procedures were found to be inadequate and to lack impartiality. The judge recommended that the ethical committee should be disbanded.

[*Other recommendations included the appointment of a patient advocate and a health commissioner, more education for hospital staff on the value of cervical screening and the implementation of an organised screening program for the whole country.*

Paul goes on to discuss the ethical issues involved, specifically questioning whether a study of this nature, which entailed withholding generally accepted treatment from patients, should have been approved by the hospital committee in 1966, given the known risk of CIS progressing to invasive cancer. She then questions whether consent should have been sought from the patients to be part of such a study and discusses the inadequate monitoring of the study, suggesting that the trial should have been stopped as soon as it became apparent that some of the women had developed invasive cancer. She notes that, despite concerns expressed by two of the doctors involved, McIndoe and McLean, both authors of the key 1984 article, an internal inquiry had failed to stop the trial. Paul goes on to look at questions of accountability, before focusing on the sex specific nature of the episode:]

… [537] Complaints about the treatment of patients in hospital usually come from the patients themselves. In this case, however, it seems there were no such complaints. Undoubtedly this is partly accounted for by the symptomless nature of the initial condition, which had in most cases been detected by routine screening. The women could not gauge the effectiveness of treatment by monitoring their own symptoms in the usual way. Some women had complained to their general practitioners that they were going back repeatedly to the hospital and nothing seemed to be being done. … The general practitioners had been helpful … but no woman or general practitioner had apparently made a formal complaint to the hospital.

Could men have been in exactly the same position? It seems to me likely that women were more vulnerable at that time to being included in a trial of treatment without their knowledge and consent and more likely to endure such a trial without making a formal complaint. Women have been familiar with being patients in many aspects of reproductive function.

The 1960s probably saw the height of the medicalisation of childbirth. The extraordinary patience of women such as "Ruth," who returned to the hospital for an endless series of examinations and biopsies, was possibly conditioned by earlier years of antenatal clinic attendance. I suggest that women were vulnerable because they were used to submitting to medical checks without being told the exact purpose. ... [T]hey were also vulnerable because they were exposed to examination of the genital area by male doctors; in this situation the asymmetry of power between the doctor and the patient is exaggerated. Finally the sense of trust and good faith that most women had in the hospital and its staff also in my view [538] made women vulnerable. Those less trusting women were the ones who went back to their general practitioners and asked for treatment. The most trusting continued to attend. ... The trust that existed has been shown not only to have been misplaced but to have been dangerous to the women concerned.

I have emphasised the special characteristics of women that might have made them vulnerable to worse treatment than men would have received. Others will point to the behaviour of doctors towards women patients. I suspect that some doctors have treated women with less regard for their autonomy than they have shown to men. But in this women may have shared the experience of men in other less powerful groups: the poor, the old, and the mentally ill. ...

Notes

1. In her report, Judge Cartwright (now Dame Silvia Cartwright, appointed New Zealand's Governor General in 2001) stated:

    > In the absence of a Bill of Rights, and in a jurisdiction where the financial accountability of the medical profession has been distorted by no-fault Accident Compensation legislation, there needs to be a procedure which patients or their relations can follow if they want more information about their health problems; if they need someone to negotiate or mediate on their behalf; or they want some form of sanction to be considered.
    >
    > I believe that most patients would not want a return to the days when doctors could be sued for negligence. Not one patient told me she wanted financial redress.[50]

    However, Sandra Coney argued in *The Unfortunate Experiment*:

    > The ACC [*Accident Compensation Commission*] system had effectively made doctors immune from actions for negligence; it is thus a system favoured by the profession, for it protects them from the financial burden of paying for their mistakes. The insurance premiums paid by New Zealand doctors are among the lowest in the world. ... The ACC system renders consumers in New Zealand especially vulnerable.[51]

    In New Zealand, actions for negligence for 'personal injury by accident', which occurred after 1 April 1974, were abolished by the *Accident Compensation Act* 1972.[52] However, it has been held that the Act (and its various

---

50 Silvia Cartwright, *The Report of the Committee of Inquiry into Allegations Concerning the treatment of Cervical Cancer at National Women's Hospital and into Other Related Matters*, July 1988, at 172.
51 Coney, *The Unfortunate Experiment*, at 161.
52 For discussion of the scheme generally, its history, and its effects on compensation for injuries, see Geoffrey Palmer, *Compensation for Incapacity*, Oxford University Press, Wellington, 1979; John Miller, 'The Accident Compensation Act and damages claims' [1987] *New Zealand Law Journal* 159; on medical injuries, or medical misadventure, see Margaret AM Vennell, 'Medical injury compensation under the New Zealand Accident Compensation Scheme: an assessment compared with the Swedish Medical Compensation Scheme' (1989) *Professional Negligence* 141 (September/October 1989); Vennell, 'Medical misadventure in a no fault society' in Ronald D Mann and John Havard (eds), *No Fault Compensation in Medicine*, Royal Society of Medicine Services Ltd, London/New York, 1989; Vennell, 'Informed Consent or Reasonable Disclosure of Risks: The Relevance of an Informed Patient in the Light of the New Zealand Accident Compensation Scheme' [1987] *Recent Law* 160 (June, 1987).

subsequent incarnations)⁵³ does not preclude actions for exemplary damages.⁵⁴ This is because exemplary damages are not compensatory – they are designed to punish the defendant rather than to compensate the plaintiff.⁵⁵ Therefore, they are not seen as inconsistent with abolishing all forms of common law compensation and replacing them with a statutory compensation scheme (the ACC).

2. The 'Ruth' mentioned in the extracts above is a woman called Clare Matheson. She has published her own account of these events in a book, *Fate Cries Enough*.⁵⁶ In her submission to the inquiry, she recounted the following exchange with Dr Green:

> An incident which occurred then and which in hindsight had more significance than I could ever have imagined at the time, was Professor Green's complete over-reaction to a comment I made to him. The comment was in the nature of a request for information concerning the reasons why I was being required to undertake continual visits to the clinic. I cannot recall exactly what I said, but I remember implying that I wondered whether I was being used as a "guinea pig".
>
> I was stunned by his reaction and clearly recall the look of extreme anger which came over his face. He changed colour and his manner altered abruptly. The incident has remained so vivid that I am quite sure his reply was, "You'll do as you're told". I was so shocked at the time at being spoken to in this manner that I could make no reply.⁵⁷

Ms Matheson unsuccessfully sued Dr Green. In *Green v Matheson*,⁵⁸ the New Zealand Court of Appeal held that her claims for trespass to the person, breach of fiduciary duty and negligence were all barred by s 27 of the Act (which provided that where any person suffers personal injury by accident, 'no proceedings for damages arising directly or indirectly out of the injury ... shall be brought in any court in New Zealand independently of the [1982] Act).⁵⁹ Nonetheless, as noted above, this did not preclude any claim for exemplary damages.⁶⁰

3. Over the years, the benefits available via the statutory scheme have been significantly reduced. By the end of the 20th century, the accident compensation scheme effectively supported only people who had experienced a loss of earning capacity, as virtually all lump sum payments (generally for

---

53 See now *Accident Insurance Act* 1998 (NZ), s 394. For a detailed account of the scheme and its history over the past 30 years, see Stephen Todd, 'Privatisation of Accident Compensation: Policy and Politics in New Zealand' (2000) 39 *Washburn Law Journal* 404.

54 See *Donselaar v Donselaar* [1982] 1 NZLR 97; and, more recently, *A v Bottrill* (unreported, NZ CA 75/00, 13 June 2001) (discussed below).

55 These damages are awarded where the conduct of the defendant is considered to 'disclose fraud, malice, violence, cruelty, insolence or the like' (per McTiernan J) or to show 'contumelious disregard' of the rights of the plaintiff (per Menzies J): see *Uren v John Fairfax and Sons* (1966) 117 CLR 118.

56 Clare Matheson, *Fate Cries Enough*, Spectre, Auckland, 1989.

57 *Ibid*, at 157. Matheson also appeared extensively in an ABC *Four Corners* documentary, 'The Unfortunate Experiment', screened on 8 August 1988.

58 [1990] NZAR 49.

59 This case is discussed extensively in a note by John Hughes, 'Case and Comment: The National Women's Case in the Court of Appeal' [1990] *New Zealand Law Journal* 114 (April 1990).

60 *Green v Matheson* [1990] NZAR 49 at 57.

non-economic losses) had by then been excluded.[61] This obviously has a significant impact on women who were not in paid employment outside the home at the time of their injury, a situation that applied to many of the women who were the subject of the 'unfortunate experiment' (a disproportionate number of the women were poor women, many of Maori or Samoan background).[62]

4. One of the outcomes of the Cartwright inquiry was the establishment of a national cervical cancer screening program. Yet, in 1999, another 'unfortunate' incident to do with screening for cervical cancer came to light.[63] A had developed cancer of the cervix, despite having had smears wrongly reported over a period of years as 'low grade or normal' by Dr Bottrill, a pathologist. It subsequently emerged that Dr Bottrill's error rate in reading the smears was so high that 'statistically speaking, a blind person could have achieved the same rate of correct readings of cervical slides in the category of "high grade abnormality" as did Dr Bottrill'.[64] Ms A brought a civil action for exemplary damages in 1999 and, while the court found that Dr Bottrill had been negligent, it was held that he had not been so 'grossly incompetent as to warrant an award of exemplary damages'.[65] However, shortly after this decision, a re-reading of all Dr Bottrill's results was commissioned which showed extensive under-reporting and, as a result, a national inquiry was established.[66] The inquiry found that the level of under-reporting was 'unacceptable'; 16 women who had had smear tests read as 'normal' by Dr Bottrill developed cervical cancer. The inquiry also found that Dr Bottrill had no awareness of the risk his negligence (and, it transpired, lack of accreditation) caused the women. The Committee of Inquiry did not recommend any compensation for the women affected, noting that they would receive little if anything under the Act as what they had experienced was 'medical misadventure'.[67] After it reported, Ms A sought to reopen her claim for exemplary damages, on the ground that there was fresh evidence. While the original trial judge agreed, a majority of the Court of Appeal dismissed her application, finding that exemplary damages were available only when the defendant is subjectively aware of the risk to which his or her conduct exposes the plaintiff and acts deliberately or recklessly taking that risk.[68] Given the finding that Dr Bottrill was so negligent or incompetent that he did not even realise the risk he created, no damages were awarded under this approach to exemplary damages.[69]

---

61 See Joanna Manning, 'Exemplary Damages in Negligence: The Story of A Screening Programme' (2001) 9 *Torts Law Journal* 229 at 230; Stephen Todd, 'Privatisation of Accident Compensation: Policy and Politics in New Zealand' (2000) 39 *Washburn Law Journal* 404.
62 See Silvia Cartwright, *The Report of the Committee of Inquiry into Allegations Concerning the Treatment of Cervical Cancer at National Women's Hospital and into Other Related Matters*, July 1988 at 115-16 for a discussion of the different cultural implications of this type of injury for Maori, Pakeha and Samoan women.
63 For a detailed account of this case and the litigation that surrounded it, see Manning, 'The Story of A Screening Programme'.
64 Manning, at 243-4.
65 *A v B* (unreported, NZ HC Auckland, Young J, 19 March 1999).
66 Ailsa Duffy, Druiscilla Barrett and Maire Duggan, *Report of the Ministerial Inquiry into the Under-Reporting of Cervical Smear Abnormalities in the Gisborne Region* (April 2001) (available at <http://www.csi.org.nz>).
67 *Ibid*, at para 1.13.
68 *A v Bottrill* (unreported, NZ CA 75/00, 13 June 2001), especially at paras 41, 53 and 62.
69 In his dissenting judgment, Thomas J referred to this approach under the heading 'An exemption for those who are obtuse!' (at para 149).

What do these examples tell us about the effects of a no-fault compensation system? In particular, is it the case that, as suggested, no-fault accident compensation removes any financial incentive for people to take care? Does the existence of a no-fault system take away the subjective sense of entitlement to redress?[70] More particularly, to what extent is a no-fault statutory scheme premised on a construction of financial loss that is more appropriate to men than women? What compensation, if any, is available for women who have not suffered loss of earnings, since they may not have been working outside the home?[71]

In the remainder of this chapter, we examine the specific injury of rape or sexual assault. We start by looking at criminal law responses and then move on to consider the increasing use (at least in some jurisdictions) of civil actions to respond to this kind of harm.

RAPE

There has been a vast amount of feminist research, lobbying and other political activity directed at effecting changes in the law of rape or sexual assault since the 1970s. This is because it is the most obvious injury that occurs to women because they are women.

Within the women's movement, at least in America, rape in the early 1970s was *the* feminist issue. It symbolised women's unique vulnerability to attack from men at any time and an attack involving a fundamental violation of their physical and sexual being.[72]

Further, although rape has long been officially recognised as an injury by the criminal law, feminists have also recognised that it is an area where the law's own response to rape has itself further injured women. Much of the feminist work has centred on the criminal justice system's response to the treatment of rape, but there has also been increasing attention in recent years given to civil responses to rape or sexual assault.

'Real rape' [73]

One of the most important issues for feminists is the question of the extent to which the law's definition of what amounts to rape was, and despite feminist

---

70 Note here Judge Cartwright's comment: 'Not one patient told me she wanted financial redress': Cartwright Report, at 172. Manning notes that the plaintiff in *A v Bottrill* 'conceded from the outset that exemplary damages do not play a compensatory role, that she was not bringing her claim for money, but rather for vindication, condemnation, and accountability. In addition, civil proceedings for exemplary damages offered her the only way for her claim to be aired in court': Manning, 'The Story of a Screening Programme', at 231.
71 For a related discussion in the context of the NSW recommendations flowing from the NSWLRC's report: *A Transport Accident Scheme for NSW*, see Graycar, 'Non-Earners and Accident Compensation: Women Sold Out Again' (1985) 10 *Legal Service Bulletin* 86. See Lucinda M Finley, 'Female Trouble: The Implications of Tort Reform for Women' (1997) 64 *Tennessee Law Review* 847; and see the discussion of some of these questions in Chapter 5 where we consider the valuation of women's work in the home in the context of accident compensation.
72 Anne Edwards, 'Male Violence in Feminist Theory: an Analysis of the Changing Conceptions of Sex/Gender Violence and Male Dominance' in Jalna Hanmer and Mary Maynard (eds), *Women, Violence and Social Control*, Macmillan, London, 1987, at 18.
73 This is the title of Susan Estrich's book which in full is *Real Rape: How the Legal System Victimizes Women Who Say No*, Harvard University Press, Cambridge MA, 1987. What she means by 'real rape' is described in the short extract below from her article 'Rape'

activity, to a large extent still is, a masculinist definition. Law professor Susan Estrich captured this some years ago in the introduction to her article through the notion of 'real rape'.

Susan Estrich, 'Rape'
(1986) 95 *Yale Law Journal* 1087

[1087] I. INTRODUCTION

Eleven years ago, a man held an ice pick to my throat and said: "Push over, shut up, or I'll kill you." I did what he said, but I couldn't stop crying. A hundred years later, I jumped out of my car as he drove away.

I ended up in the back seat of a police car. I told the two officers I had been raped by a man who came up to the car door as I was getting out in my own parking lot (and trying to balance two bags of groceries and kick the car door open). He took the car, too.

They asked me if he was a crow. That was their first question. A crow, I learned that day, meant to them someone who is black.

They asked me if I knew him. That was their second question. They believed me when I said I didn't. Because, as one of them put it, how would a nice (white) girl like me know a crow?

Now they were on my side. They asked me if he took any money. He [1088] did; but while I remember virtually every detail of that day and night, I can't remember how much. But I remember their answer. He did take money; that made it an armed robbery. Much better than a rape. They got right on the radio with that.

We went to the police station first, not the hospital, so I could repeat my story (and then what did he do?) to four more policemen. When we got there, I borrowed a dime to call my father. They all liked that.

By the time we went to the hospital, they were really on my team. I could've been one of their kids. Now there was something they'd better tell me. Did I realize what prosecuting a rape complaint was all about? They tried to tell me that "the law" was against me. But they didn't explain exactly how. And I didn't understand why. I believed in "the law", not knowing what it was.

Late that night, I sat in the Police Headquarters looking at mug shots. I was the one who insisted on going back that night, my memory was fresh. I was ready. They had four or five to "really show" me; being "really shown" a mug shot means exactly what defense attorneys are afraid it means. But it wasn't any one of them. After that, they couldn't help me very much. One shot looked close until my father realized that the man had been the right age ten years before. It was late. I didn't have a great description of identifying marks, or the like: No one had ever told me that if you're raped, you should not shut your eyes and cry for fear that this really is happening. You should keep your eyes open focusing on this man who is raping you so you can identify him when you survive. After an hour of talking, I left the police station. They told me they'd be back in touch. They weren't.

A clerk called me one day to tell me that my car had been found minus tires and I should come sign a release and have it towed – no small matter if you don't have a car to get there and are slightly afraid of your shadow. The women from the rape crisis center called me every day, then every other day, then every week. The police detectives never called at all.

I learned, much later, that I had "really" been raped. Unlike, say, the woman who claimed that she'd been raped by a man she actually knew, and was with voluntarily. Unlike, say, women who are "asking for it," and get what they deserve. I would listen as seemingly intelligent people explained these distinctions to me, and marvel; later I read about them in books, court opinions, and empirical studies. It is bad enough to be a "real" rape victim. How terrible to be – what to call it – a "not real" rape victim.

Even the real rape victim must bear the heavy weight of the silence that surrounds this crime. At first, it is something you simply don't talk about. Then it occurs to you that people whose houses are broken into or who [1089] are mugged in Central Park talk about it all the time. Rape is a much more serious crime. If it isn't my fault, why am I supposed to be ashamed? If I shouldn't be ashamed, if it wasn't "personal", why look askance when I mention it?

As this introduction makes clear, I talk about it. I do so very consciously. Sometimes I have been harassed as a result. More often it leads women I know to tell me they too are victims, and I try to help them. I cannot imagine anyone writing an article on prosecutorial discretion without disclosing that he or she had been a prosecutor. I cannot imagine myself writing on rape without disclosing how I learned my first lessons or why I care so much.[74]

Notes

1. Survey data consistently show that women are much more likely to be raped by someone they know than by a total stranger. For example, in the Australian Bureau of Statistics' 1996 Women's Safety survey, only some 22.3% of sexual violence described to the survey was committed by a man who was a stranger to the victim-survivor.[75]

   However, Fox and Freiberg, in their first study of sentencing in Victoria, suggest that, at least up to the 1980s, the rape of a stranger was viewed more seriously by the judiciary than the rape of a friend or acquaintance.[76] There is some evidence that this attitude is changing: 'There is a trend for more recent

---

74   For an analysis of the reproduction of 'real rape' in newspapers, television and film, see Alison Young, 'Violence as Seduction: Enduring Genres of Rape' in Adrian Howe (ed), *Sexed Crime in the News*, Federation Press, Sydney, 1998.
75   ABS, *Women's Safety Australia*, Cat No 4128.0, 1996, Table 3.18, at 23. This figure is likely to overestimate the proportion of sexual violence which was committed by a stranger as the ABS only counts a woman who had experienced violence from more than one known perpetrator once in the total. Sexual violence was defined as '[s]exual assaults' which included 'acts of a sexual nature carried out against a woman's will through the use of physical force, intimidation or coercion, or any attempts to do this. Unwanted sexual touching is excluded from sexual assault'. Threats of sexual assault are included in the statistics on sexual violence; these are defined as 'the threat of an act of a sexual nature which the woman believes is able and likely to be carried out' (at 4; cf 82). Relationships classified were current partner, previous partner, boyfriend/date, family member, friend, boss/co-worker and 'other' including 'professionals' (notes to Table 3.18). See also, Department for Women, *Heroines of Fortitude: The Experiences of Women in Court as Victims of Sexual Assault*, 1996, which examined all sound-recorded sexual assault trials in NSW in 1994-95: only 10% of the accused were strangers to the victim-survivor (at 57); cf Melanie Heenan and Helen McKelvie, *Evaluation of the Crimes (Rape) Act 1991, Executive Summary*, Department of Justice, Vic, 1997, at 17.
76   Richard Fox and Arie Freiberg, *Sentencing: State and Federal Law in Victoria*, Oxford University Press, Melbourne, 1985, at 514: 'Reference is often made in the cases to the fact that the rape has been committed upon a complete stranger. This is treated as an aggravating factor'. See also Charlotte L Mitra, 'Judicial Discourse in Father-Daughter Incest Appeal Cases' (1987) 15 *International Journal of the Sociology of Law* 121 at 143-4 where Mitra quotes from a sentencing judge in 1982 in Chester Crown Court (UK): 'If this girl had not been your daughter this would have been a very serious matter because she at the time was fifteen and you were forty-six'; and Renate M Mohr, 'Sexual Assault Sentencing: Leaving Justice to Individual Conscience' in Julian V Roberts and Renate M Mohr (eds), *Confronting Sexual Assault: A Decade of Legal and Social Change*, University of Toronto Press, Toronto, 1994, at 178-81.

appellate decisions to reject the general proposition that a more lenient view should be taken of rapes which are committed within or against a background of a sexual relationship with the victim'.[77] However, Warner also points out that there are 'specific factors which are commonly regarded as mitigating relationship rape', including 'the wishes of the victim'.[78] Here Warner discusses the decision in *H*.[79] The decision concerned three counts of sexual offences, including oral and anal penetration of a woman by her husband, together with non-sexual violence. The accused was sentenced to two years and 11 months' imprisonment on each of the three charges, all to be served concurrently. The trial judge stated that he had taken into account the views of the wife – who urged that her husband not be imprisoned, indeed, had sought to have the charges dropped – and consequently imposed a lesser sentence than he otherwise would have (indicating that he would have otherwise imposed a sentence of seven to eight years). On appeal, it was argued that the trial judge had not given sufficient weight to the victim's views. A majority of the WA Court of Appeal agreed and imposed a non-custodial sentence. Malcolm CJ stated:

> In my opinion, the result of the imposition of the prison sentence in the present case has been to inflict a significant punishment upon the victim by depriving her of the support and assistance she needs from him as the mother of young children.[80]

Kennedy J, in agreeing with the Chief Justice, emphasised that the case was not about a failure to take account of the victim's wishes, but the impact of the sentence on the victim.[81] In his dissenting judgment, Murray J drew attention to the severity of the assaults in question and the fact that they were committed in the presence of a baby-sitter and the children. He noted:

> [T]he prosecution of a criminal offence by a public prosecuting authority is not in any sense an action brought on behalf of the victim. That person has, and should have, no ownership of the process of prosecution, and that person can have no capacity to dictate to the court what he or she desires should be the outcome of the sentencing process.[82]

Should the wishes of the victim or, indeed, the effect of the sentencing of an accused on that victim, ever be relevant to a sentence? Do you agree that a criminal prosecution is in no sense 'an action brought on behalf of the victim'?

2. One of the most controversial sentencing decisions in the 1990s was that in the Victorian case of *Hakopian*.[83] In that case, Judge Jones of the Victorian

---

77   Kate Warner, 'Sentencing in Rape' in Patricia Easteal (ed), *Balancing the Scales: Rape, Law Reform and Australian Culture*, Federation Press, Sydney, 1998, at 175. See also Fox and Freiberg, who in their more recent work state that '[t]he relevance to sentencing of the fact that the offender and the victim had a prior relationship ... [is] not ... settled. On the one hand, breach of trust is regarded as an aggravating factor. On the other hand, the level of fear or terror may be less in the case of a rape by a stranger', Richard Fox and Arie Freiberg, *Sentencing: State and Federal Law in Victoria*, 2nd ed, Oxford University Press, Melbourne, 1999, at 923 (para 12.407).
78   Warner, 'Sentencing in Rape', at 176.
79   (1995) 81 A Crim R 88.
80   *Ibid*, at 104.
81   *Ibid*, at 105.
82   *Ibid*, at 106.
83   *R v Hakopian* (unreported, VCC, 8 August 1991). For commentary on the case, see Michelle Fisher and Fahna Ammett, 'Sentencing of Sexual Offenders When Their Victims are Prostitutes and Other Issues Arising Out of *Hakopian*' (1992) 18 *Melbourne University Law Review* 683; and Deborah Z Cass, '*R v Hakopian*' (1993) 1 *Feminist Legal Studies* 203.

County Court sentenced Heros Hakopian to three years and four months' imprisonment, with a minimum of 16 months, for the kidnapping, aggravated rape and aggravated indecent assault of a sex worker. Hakopian had forced his victim to continue oral intercourse by the use of a knife. In sentencing Hakopian, Judge Jones said it was reasonable to presume that a prostitute suffered less psychological harm because she 'would have been involved in sexual activities on many occasions with men she had not met before, in a wide range of situations'.[84] Judge Jones was applying a previous decision of the Victorian Supreme Court, *Harris*, which involved the sexual assault of two women, one who was currently engaged in sex work and one who had previously worked as a prostitute. In *Harris*, Starke J had said that rape 'when committed against prostitutes ... is not as heinous as when committed, say, on a happily married woman living in a flat in the absence of her husband when the miscreant breaks in and commits rape on her'.[85] He also stated that 'the forcible sexual act itself would not cause a reaction of revulsion' in a sex worker 'which it might cause in a chaste woman'.[86]

While the sentence in the *Hakopian* case was increased on appeal,[87] the Court of Criminal Appeal did not have 'to address directly the relevance, or otherwise, of the victim's status as a prostitute',[88] as the DPP did not pursue this issue on appeal.[89]

Is the logical implication of the courts' decisions in *Harris* and *Hakopian* that all victim/survivors of convicted rapists should be asked how active a (consensual) sex life they have had: if they have had an active sex life, then presumably the sentence of their rapist should be reduced?[90] What data have the judges relied on to reach their conclusions about the effect of rape on sex workers?

The Victorian Law Reform Commission, in reviewing *Hakopian*, accepted that the harm suffered by the victim was a relevant factor in sentencing but continued:

---

84 *Hakopian*, at 8.
85 *Attorney-General v Harris* (unreported, VCCA, 11 August 1981), at 7 per Starke J. Cf the then *Victorian Sentencing Manual*, which is described by Fisher and Ammett as providing that there were a series of factors said to be relevant to assessing the gravity of an offence including 'whether the offence was committed in the presence of others, the age of the victim, the relationship between the offender and the victim, the vulnerability of the victim, the harm to the victim ..., prostitution, and the conduct of the victim prior to the offence' (Fisher and Ammett, 'Sentencing of Sexual Offenders', at 684).
86 *Harris*, at 6.
87 To four and a half years, with a minimum of two and a half years: *R v Hakopian* (unreported, VCCA, 11 December 1991).
88 Law Reform Commission of Victoria, *Report No 46, Rape: Reform of Law and Procedure, Supplementary Issues*, July 1992, at 4.
89 As explained by the Commission: 'However, in handing down the decision of the Court, Crockett J (who had been on the bench in *Harris*) observed that counsel for the Crown had conceded that "the judge correctly applied what this Court had to say in similar circumstances in the case of *R v Harris*". Rightly or wrongly, this was ready [*sic*] by many people as indicating that the Court still regarded *Harris* as "good law"'(*ibid*).
90 See Greg Craven, 'Hookers Hurt Less', *Herald-Sun*, 7 January 1992, at 12, who argued: 'it seems most likely that an individual who regularly sells sex would feel less violated than the average person by forcible sexual intercourse. ... Would we not all agree that some rapes are so horrific for their victims that extra-heavy, rather than lighter sentences should be imposed? Examples could include the rape of young people unused to sexual activity, or religious women vowed to chastity, or – for that matter – lesbians to whom the idea of any heterosexual activity is abhorrent'.

If sentences are to be differentiated on the basis of the psychological effect of the crime on the victim, these assessments must be based on information about the actual impact of the offence on that particular victim, not simply on the fact that the victim comes from a particular social or occupational group, or that she or he has more or less sexual experience than other victims. Regrettably, the decisions in *Harris*, and by the trial judge in *Hakopian*, failed to satisfy this basic requirement.

... [F]or the most part researchers have not found clear differences in the degree of trauma experienced by various classes of victim – such as young as opposed to older victims, or victims who were acquainted with the offender as compared to victims of 'stranger rapes'. Moreover, the one known study dealing specifically with the psychological impact of rape on prostitutes reports that:

> The emotional trauma experienced by rape victims in general appears to be compounded by several factors in the case of street prostitutes. The informal code of the street prostitute precludes a display of hurt or emotional upset or the leaning on personal or societal supports for assistance in emotional trauma. Most of the prostitutes felt that they could not break the code and, therefore, dealt with their feelings alone and/or suppressed them ... Another factor compounding the negative impact of rape on prostitutes was their general sense of powerlessness. This helplessness usually experienced as a result of rape is exacerbated in the case of street prostitutes by their pervasive feelings of impotence in life.[91]

The Commission's major recommendation in response to the criticisms of the *Harris* and *Hakopian* decisions was for judicial education and review of the sentencing manual, to be undertaken by the Judicial Studies Board. In a submission to the Commission, the Women's Legal Resource Group had suggested radical changes to sentencing legislation. These included making it a relevant factor in sentencing that rape was a gendered crime and that sentencing should be 'directly proportional to the disparity of power and/or extent of trust operating between the offender and the victim'.[92] This proposal focuses on the actions of the accused, or the relationship between the accused and his target, rather than on the reactions of the victim. Is this a more useful focus?

The construction of heterosexuality

Catharine MacKinnon has also challenged the law's definition of rape, urging us to reconsider the continuum of heterosexual sex and rape.

Catharine A MacKinnon, 'Feminism, Marxism, Method, and the State: Toward Feminist Jurisprudence'
(1983) 8 Signs: *Journal of Women in Culture and Society* 635

[646] II
Feminists have reconceived rape as central to women's condition in two ways. Some see rape as an act of violence, not sexuality, the threat of which intimidates all women. Others see rape, including its violence, as an expression of male sexuality,

---

91 *Ibid*, at 5-6. The Commission is quoting from M Silbert, 'Compounding Factors in the Rape of Street Prostitutes' in AW Burgess (ed), *Rape and Sexual Assault II*, Garland, New York, 1988.
92 Cited in Fisher and Ammett, 'Sentencing of Sexual Offenders', at 687.

the social imperatives of which define all women. The first, formally in the liberal tradition, comprehends rape as a displacement of power based on physical force onto sexuality, a pre-existing natural sphere to which domination is alien. ... The more feminist view to me, one which derives from victims' experiences, sees sexuality as a social sphere of male power of which forced sex is paradigmatic. Rape is not less sexual for being violent; to the extent that coercion has become integral to male sexuality, rape may be sexual to the degree that, and because, it is violent.

The point of defining rape as "violence not sex" or "violence against women" has been to separate sexuality from gender in order to affirm sex (heterosexuality) while rejecting violence (rape). The problem remains what it has always been: telling the difference. The convergence of sexuality with violence, long used at law to deny the reality of women's violation, is recognized by rape survivors, with a difference: where the legal system has seen the intercourse in rape, victims see the rape in intercourse. ... Instead of [647] asking, what is the violation of rape, what if we ask, what is the nonviolation of intercourse? To tell what is wrong with rape, explain what is right about sex. If this, in turn, is difficult, the difficulty is as instructive as the difficulty men have in telling the difference when women see one. Perhaps the wrong of rape has proven so difficult to articulate because the unquestionable starting point has been that rape is definable as distinct from intercourse, when for women it is difficult to distinguish them under conditions of male dominance.

... [651] The law distinguishes rape from intercourse by the woman's lack of consent coupled with a man's (usually) knowing disregard of it. A feminist distinction between rape and intercourse, to hazard a beginning [652] approach, lies instead in the *meaning* of the act from women's point of view. What is wrong with rape is that it is an act of the subordination of women to men. Seen this way, the issue is not so much what rape "is" as the way its social conception is shaped to interpret particular encounters. Under conditions of sex inequality, with perspective bound up with situation, whether a contested interaction is rape comes down to whose meaning wins. If sexuality is relational, specifically if it is a power relation of gender, consent is a communication under conditions of inequality. It transpires somewhere between what the woman actually wanted and what the man comprehended she wanted. ... The problem is this: the injury of rape lies in the meaning of the act to its victims, but the standard for its criminality lies in the meaning of the same act to the assailants. Rape is only an injury from women's point of view. It is only a crime from the male point of view, explicitly including that of the accused.

... [T]he legal problem has been to determine whose view of that meaning constitutes what really happened, as if what happened objectively exists to be objectively determined, thus as if this task of determination is separable from the gender of the participants and the gendered nature of their exchange. Thus, even though the rape law oscillates between subjective tests and more objective standards invoking social reasonableness, it uniformly presumes a single underlying reality, not a reality split by divergent meanings, such as those inequality produces. Many women are raped by men who know the meaning of their acts to women and proceed anyway. But women are also violated [653] everyday by men who have no idea of the meaning of their acts to women. To them, it is sex. Therefore, to the law, it is sex. That is the single reality of what happened. When a rape prosecution is lost on a consent defense, the woman has not only failed to prove lack of consent, she is not considered to have been injured at all. Hermeneutically unpacked, read: because he did not perceive she did not want him, she was not violated. She had sex. Sex itself cannot be an injury. Women consent to sex every day. Sex makes a woman a woman. Sex is what women are *for*.

Notes

1. Is MacKinnon arguing that all heterosexual sex is rape? Or is she challenging, as Liz Kelly suggests, 'the assumption that all sexual intercourse that is not defined as rape is, therefore, consensual'?[93] Liz Kelly interviewed 60 women about their experiences of sexual violence.[94] She found that:

    > [W]omen's experiences of heterosexual sex are not either consenting or rape, but exist on a continuum moving from choice to pressure to coercion to force. ... [T]he categories I have used to record women's experiences, pressure to have sex, coercive sex and rape, shade into one another ... 'Coercive sex' is the term used in this research to cover experiences women interviewed described as being "like rape".
    >
    > ... One group of women recalled that saying 'no' to sex had been a problem in the past, but described how they developed a belief in their right to say no and a commitment to themselves only to have sex when they desired it. This was not an easy process for any of these women. In this group, women currently involved in a heterosexual relationship were more likely to feel sex was consensual:
    >
    >> I think this is probably the first sexual experience where I've felt equal and I haven't felt used because I've definitely said no if I haven't wanted to.
    >
    > A larger group of women felt that saying no, particularly in an ongoing relationship, was not something they found easy to do. Many of these women referred to occasions when they had sex when it was not what they wanted. They clearly felt that they "owed" sex to their partners regardless of their own feelings. ...
    >
    > Most women's initial response to the question "Have you ever felt pressured to have sex when you didn't want to?" was to say that this had happened but that physical force was not used. The presence of physical coercion clearly made it easier for women to define their experience as abusive. ...
    >
    > Pressurised sex seems to cover situations in which women chose not to say no, but in which they were not freely consenting.
    >
    > The term coercive sex covers experiences of forced sex which women discussed either in response to the question about pressure to have sex or the question about rape. The responses were more likely to refer to particular experiences in which there was explicit pressure from the man, often including the threat of some physical force. Women's consent was overtly coerced. At the time of the interviews, women did not define these experiences as rape:
    >
    >> I couldn't call that rape. ... I mean there was that one *bad* case of it, he's forced sex on me a number of times, that's what I would call a woman being taken for granted. We'd had a row and I'd gone to sleep in the other room and he came and got me by the arm and he dragged me into the bedroom and said 'you will remember this when you're old' – meaning I will remember this wonderful sexy scene where this guy is

---

93 Liz Kelly, 'The Continuum of Sexual Violence' in Hanmer and Maynard (eds), *Women, Violence and Social Control*, Macmillan, London, 1987, at 46; cf Catharine A MacKinnon, *Feminism Unmodified*, Chapter 3, 'Sex and Violence'.

94 The sample included women who were asked to participate because of their specific experience of rape, incest or domestic violence (30 women). The others participated regardless of their experiences of sexual violence (*ibid*, at 47). Kelly in her analysis is building on work by Pauline Bart, 'Women of the Right: Trading for Safety, Rules and Love: Review of A Dworkin, *Right Wing Women*', *The New Women's Times Feminist Review* (November/December 1983), 9-11.

> showing me his wonderful masculine strength and desire and passion – I wasn't turned on by it at all.
>
> ... One of the ways in which the concept of the continuum is useful is that it can allow for definitions of experience to change over time. The following quotes illustrate how, in retrospect, women made explicit links between pressurised or coerced sex and rape:
>
>> I didn't say to him I didn't want to, I didn't dare to [pauses] you know you don't want to, but you are still doing it. That's why in my eyes now it's rape with consent. It's rape because it's pressurized but you do it because you feel you can't say no, for whatever reason.
>>
>> Where do you define rape? The pressure to have sex was overwhelming. ... I was made to feel guilty. It isn't rape but *incredible* emotional pressure was put on and I wanted that man out of my room as soon as possible.
>
> She added later in the interview:
>
>> I remember an occasion where he wouldn't let me get up, and he was very strong. He pulled my arms above my head, I didn't put up much of a *struggle*. I mean I wouldn't have seen that as rape because I associated rape with strangers, dark, night and struggle. I didn't put up much of a struggle, but *I didn't want to*, so in a sense that was rape, yes. ...
>
> The examples demonstrate that many women experience non-consensual sex which neither they nor the law and, even more unlikely, the man, define as rape. Women do, however, feel abused by such experiences and a number of women recalled short-term and long-term effects that were similar to those experienced by women who defined their experiences as rape at the time. There is no clear distinction, therefore, between consensual sex and rape, but a continuum of pressure, threat, coercion and force. The concept of a continuum validates the sense of abuse women feel when they do not freely consent to sex and takes account of the fact that women may not define their experience at the time or over time as rape.

Can the criminal law capture this continuum experience?[95]

2. Do you agree with MacKinnon that rape is mischaracterised if it is described as a crime of violence?[96] Sharon Marcus argues, by contrast, that legislation that treats sexual offences separately from assault 'separates sexual parts from the person and views them as objects which have been violated'.[97] She argues that assault is more readily seen as 'subject-subject violence against persons'?[98] Do you agree? Marcus goes on to argue:

> For definitional purposes, however, rape is clearly neither sex nor simply assault. Rape could best be defined as a sexualized and gendered attack which imposes sexual difference along the lines of violence.[99]

Is Marcus here saying something very similar to MacKinnon?

3. Angela Harris has criticised MacKinnon's understanding of rape for excluding the experiences of African-American women:

---

95 See Gail Mason, 'Reforming the Law of Rape: Incursions into the Masculinist Sanctum' in Diane Kirkby (ed), *Sex, Power and Justice: Historical Perspectives on Law in Australia*, Oxford University Press, Melbourne, 1995, at 66.
96 See also Carol Smart, *Feminism and the Power of Law*, Routledge, London, 1989, at 43-4.
97 Sharon Marcus, 'Fighting Bodies, Fighting Words: A Theory and Politics of Rape Prevention' in Judith Butler and Joan W Scott (eds), *Feminists Theorize the Political*, Routledge, New York, 1992, at 397.
98 *Ibid.*
99 *Ibid.* See also Vikki Bell, '"Beyond the 'Thorny Question'": Feminism, Foucault and the De-sexualisation of Rape' (1991) 19 *International Journal of the Sociology of Law* 83.

This analysis, though rhetorically powerful, is an analysis of what rape means to white women masquerading as a general account; it has nothing to do with the experience of black women. For black women, rape is a far more complex experience, and an experience as deeply rooted in color as in gender.

For example, the paradigm experience of rape for black women has historically involved the white employer in the kitchen or bedroom as much as the strange black man in the bushes. During slavery, the sexual abuse of black women by white men was commonplace. Even after emancipation, the majority of black women were domestic servants for white families, a job which made them uniquely vulnerable to sexual harassment and rape.

Moreover, as a legal matter, the experience of rape did not even exist for black women. During slavery, the rape of a black woman by any man, black or white, was simply not a crime. Even after the Civil War, rape laws were seldom used to protect black women against either white or black men, since black women were considered promiscuous by nature. In contrast to the partial or at least formal protection white women had against sexual brutalization, black women frequently had no legal protection whatsoever. "Rape", in this sense, was something that only happened to white women; what happened to black women was simply life.

Finally, for black people, male and female, "rape" signified the terrorism of black men by white men, aided and abetted, passively (by silence) or actively (by "crying rape"), by white women. ...

Thus, the experience of rape for black women includes not only a vulnerability to rape and a lack of legal protection radically different from that experienced by white women, but also a unique ambivalence. Black women have simultaneously acknowledged their own victimization and the victimization of black men by a system that has consistently ignored violence against women by perpetrating it against men. The complexity and depth of this experience is not captured, or even acknowledged, by MacKinnon's account.[100]

Harris's comments resonate with the experiences of indigenous women in Australia. Raymond Evans described the 'sexual relations' between white men and indigenous women in Queensland in the late 19th and early 20th century as 'fall[ing] mainly into the patterns of outright capture and rape, prostitution and concubinage. All have features in common of male aggression and domination, as well as human degradation'.[101]

---

100 Angela Harris, 'Race and Essentialism in Feminist Legal Theory' (1990) 42 *Stanford Law Review* 581 at 598-601.
101 Raymond Evans, '"Don't You Remember Black Alice, Sam Holt": Aboriginal Women in Queensland History' (1982) 8 *Hecate* 6 at 12. He reports 'From Burketown, a certain IS Swan observed in 1892: I seen them chain up ... [*an Aboriginal woman*] to a tree – one leg on each side ... then a pair of handcuffs on her ancles [*sic*] for being too long looking for horses. I went and looked at her – the ants were running all over her person ... [*one man*] sent ... [*an Aboriginal woman*] with the mail man to Burketown to be sent south to some of his friends as a slave ... She went through Burketown while I was there ... consigned to a publican ... She knew nothing of where she was going (*ibid*)'. See also Raymond Evans, 'Harlots and Helots: Exploitation of the Aboriginal Remnant' in Raymond Evans, Kay Saunders and Kathryn Cronin, *Exclusion, Exploitation and Extermination: Race Relations in Colonial Queensland*, Australian and New Zealand Book Co, Sydney, 1975; Su-Jane Hunt, 'Aboriginal Women and Colonial Authority: Northwestern Australia 1885-1905 in Judy MacKinolty and Heather Radi (eds), *In Pursuit of Justice: Australian Women and the Law 1788-1979*, Hale and Iremonger, Sydney, 1979, at 32-40: see especially Hunt's description of Aboriginal women's attempts to seek redress for sexual assault and other violence against them (at 39-40).

And Jill Bavin-Mizzi found in her study of some 1300 sexual assault trials in 'the Supreme Courts of Victoria, Queensland and Western Australia between 1880 and 1900 only six [*complainants*] were Aboriginal'.[102] She concludes her examination of 'European-Aboriginal Sexual Assaults' with the following observations:

> It would seem that, while sexual assaults on Aboriginal women were barely recognised in late-nineteenth-century Australia, sexual assaults committed by Aboriginal men on European women were disproportionately feared. Yet, the press did not necessarily deliberately play down the one act and embellish the reports of the other. Like the people judging cases of European-Aboriginal sexual assault, the press held 'commonsense' assumptions about the character of Aboriginal women and men: Aboriginal women were promiscuous and Aboriginal men were savages. While there were exceptions based on close personal knowledge of Aboriginal complainants and assumptions about 'loose' European women, late-nineteenth-century Australians generally believed ... that Aboriginal women could not be raped and that all but the most 'wanton' of European women would never consent to sexual intercourse with an Aborigine. These beliefs found expression in the courts in the low conviction rate in sexual assault cases involving Aboriginal complainants and the high conviction and execution rates in cases involving Aboriginal defendants.

But these conclusions about European-Aboriginal sexual assaults describe the stereotypes and assumptions of late-nineteenth century European Australians. It is far more difficult to identify Aboriginal understandings of European-Aboriginal rapes.[103]

In 1995, the Australian government asked the Human Rights and Equal Opportunity Commission to inquire into 'the past laws, practices and policies which resulted in the separation of Aboriginal and Torres Strait Islander children from their families by compulsion, duress or undue influence, and the effects of those laws, practices and policies'.[104] The 'Stolen Generation' inquiry, as it became known, found that the children who were taken away and placed in foster homes and children's homes, were commonly the victims of sexual abuse:

> Nationally at least one in every six (17.5%) witnesses to the Inquiry reported such victimisation. A similar proportion (13.3%) reported sexual abuse to the WA Aboriginal Legal Service: 14.5% of those fostered and 10.9% of those placed on missions.[105]

---

102 Jill Bavin-Mizzi, *Ravished: Sexual Violence in Victorian Australia*, UNSW Press, Sydney, 1995, at 170.
103 *Ibid*, at 195-6. Cf Carmel Harris, 'The "Terror of the Law" As Applied to Black Rapists in Colonial Queensland' (1982) 8 *Hecate* 22; Susan Jane Hunt, *Spinifex and Hessian: Women's Lives in North-Western Australia*, UWA Press, Perth, 1986 at 104-10; Heather Goodall, '"Saving the Children": Gender and the Colonisation of Aboriginal Children in NSW, 1788 to 1990' (1990) 2 (44) *Aboriginal Law Bulletin* 6.
104 HREOC, *Bringing Them Home: National Inquiry into the Separation of Aboriginal and Torres Strait Islander Children from Their Families*, Commonwealth of Australia, Sydney, 1997. The terms of reference, from which the above quote is taken, are reproduced at the front of that report. We have extracted some of that report in Chapter 9. See also HREOC, *Racist Violence: Report of National Inquiry into Racist Violence in Australia*, Canberra, 1991, which reports a series of allegations made to it of abuse (including rape) of Aboriginal women by police officers, especially in Queensland (at 88-9).
105 *Bringing Them Home*, at 194.

In *Heroines of Fortitude*, the 1996 study undertaken by the NSW Department for Women on sexual assault trials, of the 150 cases studied, 11% 'involved an Aboriginal woman complainant. This means that Aboriginal women were ten times more likely to be complainants in ... [*the*] study than non-Aboriginal women. There were also 18 accused that were of Aboriginal descent. In 11 of the 17 cases involving an Aboriginal woman complainant (61%), the accused was an Aboriginal man'.[106] While these figures indicate a much greater recognition of sexual violence against Aboriginal women than in colonial and early post-colonial times, they also mark publicly an alarming incidence of sexual violence against Aboriginal women and a very high incidence of sexual violence by Aboriginal men against Aboriginal women. Greer has suggested that the latter is at odds with pre-colonial experience:

> It would seem that in traditional Aboriginal communities sexual assault was practically unknown. Aboriginal people had a clear guide about good and bad behaviour, with discipline being strictly maintained by tribal elders. However, the colonisation of Australia by the British in 1788 caused significant changes in gender relationships amongst Aboriginal men, women and children and inflicted a standard of violence that has gradually increased with time.[107]

Given this information on the incidence of violence against indigenous women, do you think MacKinnon's account of rape is useful for understanding sexual assault against Indigenous women?

4. John McInnes and Christine Boyle ask:

> Can a feminist reconstruction of sexual assault law ... truly promote egalitarian aims if other disadvantaged groups continue to form a disproportionately large percentage of those who get charged with sexual assault, and if the result of conviction is that they are incarcerated?[108]

How would you answer their question?

Proving rape

Lord Hale, a 17th century English jurist, stated, in his *Pleas of the Crown*, that 'it must be remembered, that it [rape] is an accusation easily to be made and hard to be proved, and harder to be defended by the party accused, tho' never so

---

106 *Heroines of Fortitude: The Experiences of Women in Court as Victims of Sexual Assault*, Gender Bias and the Law Project, Department for Women, Sydney, 1996, at 97.
107 Pam Greer with Jan Breckenridge, '"They Threw the Rule Book Away": Sexual Assault in Aboriginal Communities' in Jan Breckenridge and Moira Carmody (eds), *Crimes of Violence: Australian Responses to Rape and Child Sexual Assault*, Allen and Unwin, Sydney, 1992, 189. Greer here cites Judy Atkinson, who wrote a report for the federal government in 1990 on Aboriginal women and violence. Atkinson surveys some of the anthropological and historical data on violence in traditional communities, as well as documenting the effect of colonisation: see 'Violence in Aboriginal Australia: Colonisation and Gender' (1990) 14 (2) *Aboriginal and Islander Health Worker* 5 and 'Violence in Aboriginal Australia: Part 2' (1990) 14 (3) *Aboriginal and Islander Health Worker* 4.
108 John McInnes and Christine Boyle, 'Judging Sexual Assault Law Against a Standard of Equality' (1995) 29 *University of British Columbia Law Review* 341 at 348. Their answer to that question is 'No': '[W]e wonder if sex equality could ever truly be promoted by a system that, however transformed in the way it views women, still resorts to the barbarity of "correction" – which really means punishment, depersonalisation and stigmatization – as the means by which the harm of forced sex can be acknowledged. Nevertheless, we maintain that the law must evolve so as to make it far clearer that rape is seriously harmful and profoundly unacceptable in a society committed to the equality of all its citizens' (*ibid*).

innocent'.[109] Presumably, because Lord Hale's views were or became so persuasive, the law developed technical rules requiring corroboration of women's evidence in rape cases before it was accepted. These included a 'fresh complaint' rule which provided that, if there was evidence of the woman victim complaining soon after the rape, the complaint was more likely to be true[110] and rules allowing the history of the woman's prior sexual activity to be given in open court.[111] Although these rules of evidence have been modified in most jurisdictions as a result of feminist pressure, there seems little doubt that these rules developed because of a widespread belief that women lie, particularly about rape.[112]

In 1979, the Chief Justice of the South Australian Supreme Court, stated:

> The reasons for requiring a trial judge, as a matter of practice, to warn the jury in a sexual case of the danger of convicting on uncorroborated evidence, are well understood. It is sufficient to quote from the judgment of Salmon J in *R v Henry and R v Manning* ((1968) 53 Cr App R 150 at 153) where he said:
>> What the judge has to do is to use clear and simple language that will without any doubt convey to the jury that in cases of alleged sexual offences it is really dangerous to convict on the evidence of the woman or girl alone. This is dangerous because human experience has shown that in these courts girls and women do sometimes tell an entirely false story which is very easy to fabricate, but extremely difficult to refute. Such stories are fabricated for all sorts of reasons, which I need not now enumerate, and sometimes for no reason at all.
>
> Such considerations are by no means confined to cases in which the alleged victim is female and the warning is also given where the alleged victim is male. The danger of fabrication in sexual cases is greater than in other cases precisely because the allegations are sexual in character. Sex is prone to excite the imagination and the emotions, thereby creating a danger of false accusation resulting from hysterical or vindictive motives. Furthermore a person who has engaged in sexual conduct may be tempted to protect his or her own reputation or

---

109 Sir Matthew Hale, *Pleas of the Crown* Vol 1, at 635. The debate about Hale's contribution to the development of the marital immunity for rape is discussed in Chapter 5. Hale's statement continues to be cited with approval in Louis Waller and CR Williams, *Criminal Law: Text and Cases*, 9th ed, Butterworths, Sydney, 2001, at 92.

110 For a discussion of the fresh complaint rule, see Model Criminal Code Officers Committee, *Chapter 5: Sexual Offences Against the Person Report*, May 1999, at 257-61.

111 The Model Criminal Code Officers Committee notes that there appeared to be two 'justifications' for allowing information on prior sexual activity to be presented: one, that it went to consent, apparently on the presumption that, if a woman had had consensual sexual activity with one man, she was likely to do so with another and, second, that a woman who was sexually active was more likely to lie (*ibid*, at 217).

112 In 1978, the late Glanville Williams, one of the world's best known criminal law writers, stated: 'Many complaints of rape are false, since the woman in fact consented' (*Textbook of Criminal Law*, Stevens and Sons, London, 1978, at 196). By the second edition (1983), this had become 'Some (we do not know how many) complaints of rape are false, since the woman in fact consented' (Glanville Williams, *Textbook of Criminal Law*, 2nd ed, Stevens and Sons, London, 1983, at 238). The leading US evidence textbook, *Wigmore on Evidence*, contained the following passage in the 1970 edition: 'Modern psychiatrists have amply studied the behaviour of errant young girls and women coming before the courts in all sorts of cases. Their psychic complexes are multifarious, distorted partly by inherent defects, partly by diseased derangements or abnormal instincts, partly by bad social environment, partly by temporary psychological or emotional conditions. One form taken by these complexes is that of contriving false charges of sexual offences by men. *No judge should ever let a sex offense charge go to the jury unless the female complainant's social history and mental make-up have been examined and testified by a qualified physician*' (3A Wigmore, *Evidence* para 924a (Chadbourn rev, 1970), Little Brown and Co, Boston, 1970). For a critique, see Leigh Bienen, 'A Question of Credibility: John Henry Wigmore's Use of Scientific Authority' (1983) 19 *California Western Law Review* 235.

position by alleging that he or she has been subject to force. The motives for false accusation in a particular case may be difficult to discover. It seems to me that these considerations apply, not only to the question whether the accused has had sexual relations with the alleged victim, but also, and with at least equal force, to the question whether the alleged victim consented to such relations. It is not difficult to think of reasons why a person who has consented to sexual activity might allege subsequently that the activity was without his or her consent.[113]

Although King CJ's formulation is 'gender-neutral', most victims of sexual assault under gender-neutral laws continue to be women. For example, in the Victorian Community Council Against Violence study of all rapes reported to the police between 1987-90, 93.6% of victim/survivors were women and 98.9% of alleged perpetrators were men.[114]

Various Australian studies have indicated that in more recent times the rate of complaints classified by police as false is quite low.[115] And data indicate that rape is not a complaint easily made. The 1996 ABS Women's Safety Survey indicated that only some 15% of rapes are reported to the police.[116]

Notes

1. Much of the feminist legal work around rape has focused on the rules of evidence that governed sexual assault trials. Most jurisdictions have enacted a variety of reforms including restrictions on sexual history evidence and abolition of the common law rule requiring a corroboration warning. However, more recent feminist work has questioned the usefulness of these reforms. Some of that questioning has been at the level of demonstrating the degree of lack of compliance by lawyers and judges with the new restrictive rules.[117] Others have examined the reintroduction of something similar to the old laws by appellate court interpretation.[118] Yet other scholars have argued that the experiences of rape victim/survivors in the court room are governed by much deeper structures than can be addressed by restrictive rules of evidence.[119] Alison Young argues:

   > [I]f context and content were all that dictated the generation of narrative, then we could be sure that once certain procedures were agreed upon, once certain topics were accepted as permissible and other topics outlawed, then rape trials could proceed in ways that inflicted no further suffering upon the victim. However, I would argue that such suffering is produced as much by the process of law's storytelling itself, as through the substantive detail of defence questioning. It is not enough for the victim to be vilified according

---

113 *R v Sherrin (No 2)* (1979) 21 SASR 250 at 254.
114 Victorian Community Council Against Violence, *A Profile of Rapes Reported to Police in Victoria 1987-90*, 1991, at v and 16.
115 See, for example, *ibid*, at vii and 64, indicating a rate of 4.9%.
116 ABS *Women's Safety Australia*, December 1996, Cat No 4128.0: only 14.9% of women who had been sexually assaulted in the past 12 months reported the matter to the police: see Table 4.7, at 32.
117 For an overview of the relevant empirical studies focusing on the restrictions on sexual history and sexual reputation evidence, see Therese Henning and Simon Bronitt, 'Rape Victims on Trial: Regulating the Use and Abuse of Sexual History Evidence' in Patricia Easteal (ed), *Balancing the Scales*, at 76.
118 See, for example, Kathy Mack's discussion of the High Court's decision in *Longman* (1989) 168 CLR 79, '"You should scrutinise her evidence with great care": Corroboration of women's testimony about sexual assault' in Easteal (ed), *Balancing the Scales*, at 59.
119 See, for example, Ngaire Naffine, 'Possession: Erotic Love in the Law of Rape' (1994) 57 *Modern Law Review* 10.

to received ideas about dress or drink, she must also be made to rub up against the fantasy that informs the defence account, made to perform as a character in its narrative.

The *insinuation* strategies ... operate from within the victim's own narrative. If the victim argues that she went to a nightclub with a friend for fun, or drank a certain number of beers, or wore a bikini because she was at a beach party, the strategy of insinuation works to coat that activity with moral opprobrium. The questions, however, do not take issue with those facets of the victim's narrative; instead, they seek to vary the evaluative emphasis that is placed on those narrative components. The victim will be asked questions in direct examination by the Crown, questions which allow her to elaborate her story within the legal frame. Insinuative questioning by the defence will pose questions to which her own answers may constitute the damaging information. Thus in *R v P* the defence asks, 'When you left the party you'd had a good time, is that right?', and the victim answers, 'Yes, I had'. This obviates the need for the defence to attempt any obvious strategies of character smearing with questions such as 'Are you a good time girl?', which might well meet with objections from opposing counsel.

However, *implication* of the victim in the defence narrative works by challenging the very foundation of the victim's narrative. The defence counsel inserts into the cross-examination a series of questions which are designed for the victim to answer only briefly, usually in the form of 'yes' or 'no', or a short phrase. These questions are structured in two alternating forms: first, a prefacing phrase such as 'I suggest to you that' followed by the defence version of what happened; or second, the defence version of events followed by the suffix 'what do you say to that?' Juries are told ... that the evidence is constituted by the answer to the question, rather than the question itself. It is, of course, ludicrous to think that juries either ignore the question and focus on the answer (a notion that denies the self-proclaimed dialogism of trial discourse), or are unaffected by the barrage of suggestions that defence counsel lay out before them. Some examples from the transcripts may serve to demonstrate the techniques.

In *R v N-T*, the following exchange took place:

Q: I will tell you what I suggest happened to you. As you were walking in the street outside the area where the vacant land is, you were kissing each other.
A: I don't think so. ...
Q: And I suggest to you that you decided the grassed area was, well, about as good a spot as you were going to get to lie down together, because it was a bit soft, isn't that right?
A: No, that's not right. ...
Q: And I suggest to you that you voluntarily had sex with him?
A: No, I didn't.
Q: And I suggest to you that what happened was he got up and left you like, if I could use the term, a shag on rock, just left you, after sex. Left you, didn't he? Is that right?
A: I beg your pardon?
Q: He got up and just left you after he had had sex with you, didn't he?
A: What do you want me to say? That ...
Q: Isn't that right? He didn't spend any time with you immediately after the sex act, did he?
A: Well, I didn't – wouldn't hope so.
Q: But look, he just got up and left, didn't he?
A: That's right.

Q: And I suggest to you that that insulted you. Is that right?
A: No.
Q: And I suggest to you that you felt that you had been abandoned and I suggest to you you thought that the best way to get back at him was to say that you had been raped. Isn't that right?
A: No, that's not right.

There are a number of devices at work here. First, the use of 'And' at the outset of five of the questions creates a connection to the previous question and erases the answer given by the victim between questions. The victim answers in the negative, yet the defence lawyer's 'And' flattens out her denial, and creates a narrative building block from one question to the next in his construction of an exculpatory explanation. Second, phrases such as 'I suggest to you that' and 'isn't that right' constitute affirmative frames in which the mini-narrative of the question is lent a positive evaluative aura. Third, the victim is encouraged to give only very brief answers, which merge and become numbly repetitive. In contrast, the jury hear brisk and authoritative explanations using commonsense terms and folkloric notions in which to situate the disputed events.

... Victims occasionally attempt to challenge the implicative mode of questioning, by confronting the logic of the questions or demanding further logic or proof than the defence has offered. The following two excerpts show this being done unsuccessfully by one woman and successfully by another (successfully in that her case was the only one examined which resulted in a conviction). In *R v O*, the defence counsel was repeatedly asserting that the victim consented to various acts with the defendant. Her response was to demand why, if this was so, the defendant fired a gun over her head in the bedroom. Her reward for raising this point of narrative logic was to be reprimanded in front of the jury for non-cooperation:

Q: I suggest to you that you and he kissed and cuddled and you allowed him to touch you in various parts of your body without protest?
A: And if I let him then why did he produce a gun? ...
His Honour: No, just answer the question.
A: If I wanted him to, then he didn't have to use a gun ...
His Honour: Just a moment, please excuse me. Excuse me, madam, would you be good enough to answer the question?
A: That's true, he wouldn't have had to ... use a gun ... if I'd wanted him to ...
His Honour: Do you want a short break? You've got to answer questions, you can't simply volunteer information, he's entitled to ask you questions.
A: He wasn't the one that sat there and got shot near the (indistinct). [Witness distressed.] ...
His Honour: No, you've got to listen to me, madam. If you are not distressed, you have got to grapple with his questions ... I think you had better have a short time but when you return to the witness box you must behave in a manner that's expected of all witnesses in this court.

At this point the victim was sent out of the courtroom and the jury addressed by the judge:

You are to judge these matters on the evidence. I do not wish to comment any further than that except to say that you must perform your task objectively ... having regard to the evidence ... which you accept or reject, which is indeed entirely a matter for you.

On the one hand, this exchange demonstrates the all-too-familiar asymmetry of power in legal discourse. ... The excerpt also illustrates the power of law as a peculiarly monologic form of dialogue, in which the right to question is authorised at the expense of the right to answer. Legal discourse cannot bear to be questioned without an answer being given. Thus the situation is represented as a problem of an uncooperative witness rather than a question which, in endorsing an act of violence by the accused against the woman, repeated it. Further repetition of law's violence occurred as, after a short break, the victim was addressed by the judge in the absence of the jury: 'I know it's an ordeal for you, but it's going to be necessary for you to be more responsive in answering the questions. If I have to declare this a mistrial you'll have to come back on another occasion, do you follow?' The defence counsel and judge in this case also engaged at several points in describing the victim in a derogatory fashion. For example, the defence counsel described the victim as 'confused and disoriented', to which the judge replied, '[i]t isn't the first time she has appeared not to be entirely *au fait* with matters'. The victim was then admonished in the presence of the jury to 'maintain your concentration'. An act of resistance to law's monologic dialogue thus led to the public shaming of the victim and the demolition of her attempted autonomy as a participant in the trial process.

Greater success in resisting the strategy of implication in the defence narrative is found in the case of *R v K*. The victim had been abducted by her ex-boyfriend and taken to his house, where she was beaten by him, gagged, spat on, and subject to a number of indecent assaults and acts of sexual penetration. The defence argument was that she consented to the sexual acts and to being beaten and humiliated because their conventional sexual practices during their relationship had been sado-masochistic in nature. The victim engages with the illogic of the questions, and pushes the defence counsel as to the substance of his allegations against her:

Q: I suggest to you that you were very interested in sado-masochistic practices ... that's why the word 'slave' appears in one of your letters [to K] ...?
A: I disagree with you. ...
Q: I suggest to you ... that you used to go places where you could buy magazines and clothes and videos related to sado-masochism ...?
A: No I didn't.
Q: I suggest to you that you, yourself, obtained sado-masochistic magazines and you produced them or were very interested in them?
A: I disagree. My house was actually searched for that kind of stuff and nothing – nothing was found. ...
Q: I suggest to you that you had a number of articles that related to sado-masochism but you – you kept them hidden.
A: I disagree. I assume they would find them if I did keep them hidden, if they searched. ...
Q: I suggest to you that you bought [articles] and took [them] to K's place. I suggest you bought this video and took it to K's place?
A: That is such a lie. That is such a lie. That is such a lie ... What video store did I get it? Where did I get it? Do I have a video card for this? ...
Q: I suggest to you that you bought him for his 21st birthday a set of handcuffs?
A: That's a lie. ...

> Q: I suggest to you the reverse, that in fact the position is that your evidence about all this is a big lie?
> A: No, you're wrong. You can suggest whatever you want; you're wrong and K's a big liar.
> Q: Why then did you say these things in the letters to him that are plainly about sado-masochism?
> A: Did I – did I mention any type of video; did I mention any type of book; that's such a lie.

At times the technique of insinuation combines with the strategy of implication, as can be seen in another excerpt from *R v K*:

> Q: What I suggest to you is that you commonly, both of you, commonly used to have a choker, a buckle or a belt or a choker around your neck for the purpose of heightening enjoyment during sex. ...
> A: Wrong, I never did that. You're insinuating that – I don't know what the correct wording for it? What, what word was it that you used for those sex games?
> Q: I said sado-masochism?
> A: Correct, that's what you were insinuating.

In the first example, we see the victim demand evidence to back up the story being told ('Do I have a video card for this?, 'did I mention any type of video?').

She also counterposes incontrovertible components from the prosecution narrative against the defence counsel's suggestion ('My house was actually searched for that kind of stuff and nothing was found'). She also rejects the defence version of events in extremely strong terms, repeating the phrases 'that's a lie' and 'you're wrong' many times over. In the second excerpt, her two responses begin with the words 'wrong' and 'correct' respectively. This represents one of the main differences between her evidence and that given by other victims in the cases examined. The usual response from victims is 'yes' or 'no': defence counsel often ask questions which demand alternating 'yes' and 'no' answers. These function as simple rejections of a proposition, one opinion against another. They also allow the jury to hear, repeatedly and in alternation, 'yes, yes, no, no' and so on, with the effect that 'yes' and 'no' blur into that notorious commonplace: 'yes means no'. The victim in *R v K* takes a different tack, answering 'wrong' and 'correct' in place of 'yes' and 'no'. She thus draws attention to the hermeneutic processes underlying the defence construction of events, and simultaneously invests her own narrative with further weight. This victim's striking determination of response and resistance to both insinuation and implication will have contributed to the defendant being convicted by the jury.[120]

What does Young's analysis suggest about feminists' work in trying to reform the 'special' rules of evidence that have applied in sexual assault trials? How is it possible to intervene in the defence's creation of narratives in rape trials? One persistent recommendation for dealing with 'gender bias' in sexual

---

[120] Alison Young, 'The Waste Land of the Law, The Wordless Song of the Rape Victim' (1998) 22 *Melbourne University Law Review* 442 at 456-62; the references for the cases in the above extracts are *R v P* (unreported, VCC, Melbourne, Wodak J, April 1997); *R v N-T* (unreported, VCC, Melbourne, Crossley J, November 1996); *R v O* (unreported, VCC, Melbourne, Walsh J, February 1997); *R v K* (unreported, VCC, Melbourne, Gebhardt J, September 1996). Cf John M Conley and William M O'Barr, *Just Words: Law, Language and Power*, University of Chicago Press, Chicago, 1998; and Rae Kaspiew, 'Rape Lore: Legal Narrative and Sexual Violence' (1995) 20 *Melbourne University Law Review* 350.

assault cases has been education of the judiciary. What would be the value of asking judges to read and discuss Young's article? Do you think judges would see it as part of their role to intervene in the 'implication' or 'insinuation' of the victim/survivor into the narratives about rape that Young argues are created in a rape trial? How useful would it be to give Young's article to targets of sexual abuse who are about to give evidence in a criminal trial?[121]

2. Australia's public debate on 'gender bias' in the law was (re)ignited in early 1990 by the reporting of the statements of Bollen J, a Supreme Court judge in South Australia, presiding over a trial of rape in marriage. He suggested that a measure of 'rougher than usual handling' was justified by a husband in seeking consent from his wife. However, what was in fact more concerning was the 'anecdote' he relayed to jurors in the same case to 'assist' in their weighing of the evidence as to whether the woman had consented. At the time of the decision, South Australia's evidence law provided that in sexual offence proceedings 'the judge is not required by any rule of law or practice to warn the jury that it is unsafe to convict the accused on the uncorroborated evidence of the alleged victim of the offence'.[122] In his summing up to the jury, Bollen J told the story of 'the "respectable married business man" on the train'. This gentleman caught an old-fashioned English train with carriages divided into small areas. He was there alone. A 'respectably dressed' woman entered the part of the carriage he was travelling in:

> The woman approached the man; sat near him; tore at her dress to expose her chest; knocked her head hard against the wooden side of the train and scratched herself, thus producing bruising and bleeding; and pulled the communication cord.
>
> The train stopped; the guard came running. "He tried to rape me" she said. The guard said he would have to call the police, and did. With the woman making this allegation, the police felt it their duty to charge the respectable businessman. So he was arrested, brought before a magistrate and released on bail. It was a shocking thing for him to have to face. It was too much for him. He took his own life. Soon after that, the same sort of incident happened on the same run, at the same spot, with the same woman. Further investigation showed that she was mentally deranged and it turned out that she had been doing this quite a bit. So you can see how careful we have to be about false allegations of rape.
>
> This is a dramatic story of course, far removed from the facts here, but it is just an illustration of the need to scrutinise all the evidence very, very carefully, bearing in mind all the time that it is possible for a woman to manufacture a false allegation that it has happened.[123]

All members of the Full Court of the Supreme Court on appeal[124] held that this anecdote was inappropriate: 'It could only have conveyed to the jury that complainants in sexual cases generally are to be viewed with suspicion and

---

121 In this context, see Alison Young, 'Cross-examination tactics in rape trials' in CASA House, *Who's On Trial? A Training Manual for Sexual Assault Support Workers*, Melbourne, 1998.
122 *Evidence Act* 1929, s 34I(5). That is, a corroboration warning was optional and the situations where it should be given were governed by the High Court decision in *Longman v Queen* (1989) 168 CLR 79.
123 Cited in the appeal court decision *Question of Law Reserved on Acquittal Pursuant to Section 351(1A) Criminal Law Consolidation Act* (1993) 59 SASR 214 at 216.
124 Though note that this 'appeal' was not against the jury acquittal – such appeals are not available; it merely functioned as guidance for future courts and the accused's acquittal stood.

that is not legally permissible'.[125] A majority of the court also held that Bollen J's comments on 'rougher than usual handling' were unlawful.

A Senate Committee examined sexual assault cases in the light of the furore surrounding Bollen J's comments (and the reported comments of other judges). It found that a corroboration warning was given in 45% of the sample of South Australian cases and in some 30% of Western Australian cases. It concluded that:

> [A] significant number of the cases examined demonstrate the resilience in some jurisdictions of certain unconscious beliefs and stereotypes in cases of alleged sexual assault. The belief that women, for various reasons, concoct incidents of sexual assault, still seems to be common among some judges. By adhering to these traditional statements, the rationale for which other judges have questioned, judges are potentially influencing the outcome of cases.[126]

3. One comparatively recent technique used by defence counsel in both Canada and Australia, perhaps in response to the recent evidentiary restrictions mentioned above, has been to seek access to rape victim/survivors' counselling records.[127] This came to public attention in Australia when an ACT sexual assault counsellor refused to produce a client's records in response to a court subpoena. She was (briefly) jailed for contempt of court.[128] The Model Criminal Code Officers Committee (MCCOC)[129] considered the reasons why access to counsellors' records should be restricted:

> Whilst there does not appear to be any empirical evidence to support the claim that sexual assault complainants will not seek counselling if confidentiality cannot be assured, it is not an unreasonable conclusion to draw. It has generally been accepted that the number of sexual assault complaints to the police and sexual assault prosecutions have risen in response to improved services to complainants, including in large measure a heightened awareness on the part of police and prosecution personnel of the need to minimise the "re-victimisation" of the complainant by the criminal justice process. The most obvious of these is that some restrictions on cross-examination of the complainants have been legislatively introduced in all Australian jurisdictions. Sexual assault counselling services have been significant agents of change in the treatment of the complainant

---

125 *Ibid*, at 219 per King CJ. However, King CJ also quoted from his previous decision in *R v Pahuja* (1987) 49 SASR 191 where he said 'Acts of Parliament do not and do not purport to, change human nature. There are aspects of human nature and behaviour, such as sexual appetite, certain motives for making false complaints and proneness to certain types of fantasies, which have a peculiar bearing upon sexual cases and which may be important in certain factual situations (*Pahuja*, at 199, cited in *Question of Law*, at 217-18).

126 Senate Standing Committee on Legal and Constitutional Affairs, *Gender Bias and the Judiciary*, Canberra, May 1994, at 55.

127 In Canada, see *R v O'Connor* [1995] 4 SCR 411.

128 See Margo Kingston, 'Privacy issue as rape therapist jailed' *Sydney Morning Herald*, 15 December 1995, at 1. In response, NSW, Victoria and South Australia legislated to restrict, but not prohibit, access to counsellor records: see *Evidence Amendment (Confidential Communications) Act 1997* (NSW); *Evidence (Confidential Communications) Act 1998* (Vic); and *Evidence (Confidential Communications) Amendment Act 1999* (SA).

129 The Committee has endeavoured to draft a national criminal law code (criminal law currently being a matter within the purview of each of the States and Territories of Australia), which it is hoped that all States and Territories will adopt, to introduce a level of uniformity to Australian criminal law.

> by the criminal justice system. It is not unrealistic to assume that if those same counselling services come to be seen by complainants as sources of information with which the complainant may be publicly humiliated, complainants may refrain from seeking counselling altogether. ...
>
> Independently of the effect of disclosure of counselling communications from the complainants' perspective, there is empirical evidence of quite adverse effects on the counselling relationship from the counsellors' perspective. Faced with the prospect of compulsory disclosure in respect of potentially every counselling relationship, sexual assault counselling services are adopting counter-measures which include the creation of "dummy" files, encrypted files and/or minimal record keeping. These practices not only inhibit the counselling relationship, but they militate against the accountability of the counsellor. ...
>
> ... Sexual assault services argue that their records are not forensically relevant at all. The focus of counselling is the emotional and physical health of the complainant, not the investigation of the alleged assault. The exploration of a multitude of complex emotional and psychological responses to an assault through counselling in fact undermines the reliability of much, if not all, of the content of the communication.[130]

Despite these arguments, the MCCOC did not support a complete ban on access to counsellors' records, but rather recommended restricted access. They rejected an argument that there should be a counsellor privilege parallel to client legal privilege, where communications between a lawyer and a client for the purposes of legal proceedings are 'absolutely protected':[131]

> This analogy with client legal privilege is problematic because it ignores the foundations of that class of privilege, namely that legal practitioners are officers of the court, bound by complex and strict rules of professional practice. The paramountcy of the public interest in protecting the confidentiality of the client/lawyer relationship springs from its rationale, namely the "furtherance of the administration of justice through the fostering of trust and candour in the relationship between lawyer and client". While Cossins and Pilkington have argued that anything less than a similar absolute privilege dissuades complainants from reporting sexual assaults, thereby "impairing the administration of justice by preventing the apprehension and conviction of offenders", the argument is misconceived because in the absence of client legal privilege the operation of the rule of law itself is jeopardised. This is not so if a client/counsellor privilege does not exist, albeit the consequences may be regrettable in terms of not bringing to justice as many offenders as would otherwise be the case.[132]

The MCCOC also suggested 'that a blanket prohibition would promote stay applications and substantially increase the prospects of a successful appeal against conviction on the unsafe and unsatisfactory ground'.[133]

Are you convinced that the 'rule of law' requires a different rule for lawyers and their clients as opposed to counsellors and their clients? If it is correct to say that more trials would be stayed with a blanket prohibition on access to counsellor records, what does that tell us about traditional notions of

---

130 MCCOC, *Chapter 5: Sexual Offences Against the Person: Report*, May 1999, at 277-9.
131 *Ibid*, at 281.
132 *Ibid*.
133 *Ibid*, at 283.

a 'fair trial'? How could details of a counselling session ever be relevant to a criminal trial?[134]

Neutralising rape

A number of jurisdictions have replaced the common law's gender-specific crime of rape with gender-neutral offences that expand the range of activities covered by rape law and some have also replaced the crime of rape altogether with gender-neutral graded offences of sexual assault. In her 'Sexual Assault and the Feminist Judge', Christine Boyle addressed the issue of gender-neutral rape laws.[135] In making the argument that gender-neutrality hides the gender-specificity of the crime, she posed an analogy outside sexual assault:

> A possible analogy would involve a crime of lynching Black people, which enabled judges to treat it more seriously than ordinary homicide. Imagine that this crime was reformed to make it race-neutral. The new crime would be labelled racial homicide, rather than lynching Black persons. The courts would have to come up with a meaning for racial in a legal context in which a racial homicide could be committed by a white on a Black, or a Black on a Black, or any combination, without any assistance from our understanding of the oppression of Blacks by whites. There may have been very good reasons for making the change, but it would be evident that the term racial would be difficult if not impossible to define, especially if we could not take the historical oppression of Blacks into account in interpreting the term.[136]

However, Gail Mason has noted:

> Feminist arguments in favour of sex-neutrality have asserted that it will assist in eroding women's mythical status as a (the only) sexed and rapeable subject and as a consequence reduce the focus on consent and corroboration during rape trials.[137]

Clearly, Boyle has grave doubts as to whether this has been achieved. Or, in Naffine's words:

> The liberal solution to equal sexual rights for women has been to effect a crude reversal and reciprocity of sex rights and responsibilities – to make women the same as men. The modern grant of sexual subjectivity to women, taken to its logical liberal end, as Australia has done, seems to entail the legal recognition of women's sexual ability to rape. Women are now seen to have so much potency to do what it was once thought only men could do to women that there now needs to be a law to prevent us from doing this to men. What this neatly steps around is the nature of the male violence which (ostensibly) rape laws were designed to punish. The sexual democratisation of rape has changed neither the possessive form nor direction of sex – in which a man takes a woman for use. This is still how it is supposed to happen. Nor have the new liberal laws extinguished the economic and

---

134 For other discussions of this issue, see Annie Cossins and Ruth Pilkington, 'Balancing the Scales: The Case for the Inadmissibility of Counselling Records in Sexual Assault Trials' (1996) 19 *University of New South Wales Law Journal* 222; and Annie Cossins, 'Tipping the Scales: The Need to Protect Counselling Records in Sexual Assault Trials' in Easteal (ed), *Balancing the Scales*; Marilyn T MacCrimmon, 'Trial by Ordeal' (1996) 1 *Canadian Criminal Law Review* 31.
135 Christine Boyle, 'Sexual Assault and the Feminist Judge' (1985) 1 *Canadian Journal of Women and the Law* 93. See also Catharine A MacKinnon, 'Feminism, Marxism, Method and the State: Toward Feminist Jurisprudence' (1983) 8 *Signs* 635 (parts of which are extracted above).
136 Boyle, 'Sexual Assault', at 103-4.
137 Mason, 'Reforming the Law of Rape' in Kirkby (ed), *Sex, Power and Justice*, at 54.

social disadvantages suffered by women ... which diminish their ability to make uncoerced sexual choices.[138]

Note

1. One other way to recognise the gendered nature of rape is via the use of a preamble in rape legislation. The preamble to the Canadian sexual assault legislation (Bill C-49) acknowledges 'grave concern about the incidence of sexual violence and sexual abuse' and the 'prevalence of sexual assault against women and children'.[139] The MCCOC did not recommend the adoption of a preamble. Their report stated: '[R]ecasting the basic offence in gender neutral terms recognises that both females and males may be the victims or perpetrators of sexual assault. The law should offer equal protection and impose punishment'.[140] Is the preamble model a useful one to follow? What other arguments can you suggest in favour of a gender neutral law?

Moving beyond consent?

Definitions of rape in almost all jurisdictions as well as that in the MCCOC's proposals maintain consent as a central element of the offence. Consent is essential to both the mental element of the offence – whether the accused knew she was not consenting – and the external element of the offence – whether sexual penetration without consent occurred. Such a focus has been strongly criticised, criticisms which are summarised by the MCCOC. They note that it has been argued that to retain consent as a vital element leads to an 'excessive focus on the complainant at trial'.[141] A focus on her conduct and state of mind allows stereotypes to influence the thinking of the jury:

> Researchers have found, for instance, that where consent is an issue, jurors are adversely affected by evidence about a victim's lifestyle such as whether she drank, took drugs, had sexual relations outside of marriage or had prior acquaintance with the accused. Stereotyped notions of how women might behave

---

138 Ngaire Naffine, 'Possession: Erotic Love in the Law of Rape' (1994) 57 *Modern Law Review* 10 at 24-5. Cf Margaret Thornton, 'Feminism and the Contradictions of Law Reform' (1991) 19 *International Journal of the Sociology of Law* 453 at 463: 'Reformist moves towards sex-neutral sexual assault laws were thought to be a positive step in jettisoning the entrenched medico-legal-popular mythology which stigmatised women as sex-crazed, venal and untrustworthy. However, insufficient cognizance was taken of the fact that the neutrality prescript within law operates to occlude the dominant values, not to guarantee substantive fairness'.
139 Bargen and Fyshwick recommended the adoption of this sort of preamble in Australian jurisdictions: see Jenny Bargen and Elaine Fyshwick, *Sexual Assault Law Reform: A National Perspective*, Office of the Status of Women, 1995, at 66. They include the full Canadian preamble, at 67. And note the wording of early drafts of a preamble prepared by a coalition of women's groups centrally involved in consultation around the new Canadian sexual assault law which would have recognised racism in the operation of sexual assault laws; these early drafts are discussed in Sheila McIntyre, 'Redefining Reformism: The Consultations that Shaped Bill C-49' in Julian V Roberts and Renate M Mohr (eds), *Confronting Sexual Assault: A Decade of Legal and Social Change*, University of Toronto Press, Toronto, 1994; the legislation is reproduced in an Appendix B to that book. See also the objects section of Part 15A of the NSW *Crimes Act* 1900 which 'recognises that domestic violence is predominantly perpetrated by men against women and children' (s 562AC(3)(b)).
140 MCCOC, *Model Criminal Code: Chapter 5: Sexual Offences Against the Person Report*, May 1999, at 13.
141 MCCOC, *Sexual Offences*, 21.

during sexual encounters (most notably, that "No" really means "Yes") present further difficulties.

A fourth concern turns upon the strength and power imbalances which may exist between the attacker – whether a stranger or, more typically, an acquaintance – and the victim. These imbalances may account for any lack of struggle on the victim's part. However, this apparent submission on the part of the victim may be wrongly interpreted to mean consent was present.

Fifthly, the offence as presently constructed effectively assumes that the complainant consented, unless the prosecution is able to prove 'lack of consent' beyond reasonable doubt. This is the case even where there is evidence that force or violence was used against the complainant [142]

More radically, Wendy Brown has argued that:

> Insofar as consent involves agreeing to something the terms of which one does not determine, consent marks the subordinate status of the consenting party. Consent in this way functions as a sign of legitimate subordination.
> … If in rape law, men are seen to *do* sex while women *consent* to it, if the measure of rape is not whether a woman sought or desired sex but whether she acceded to it or refused it when it was pressed upon her, then consent operates both as a sign of subordination and a means of its legitimation. Consent is thus a response to power – it adds or withdraws legitimacy – but is not a mode of enacting or sharing in power. Moreover, since consent is obtained or registered rather than enacted, consent is always mediated by authority – whether in a second or third person – and is thus both constitutive of that authority and legitimated by it. In these two respects, consent would appear to be profoundly at odds with radical democratic forms of equality and autonomy.[143]

A number of jurisdictions have attempted to remove the focus on consent. Perhaps the best known example is that of the American state of Michigan. The Law Reform Commission of Victoria summarised the Michigan approach as

> focus[ing] on the *circumstances* in which the sexual penetration was alleged to have taken place. Under this new approach, the prosecution has to prove only that there was sexual penetration, or some other form of sexual contact, in "coercive circumstances". The prosecution does not have to prove that there was also a lack of consent on the part of the complainant, although the defence can still raise consent as a defence.[144]

However, the Law Reform Commission did not adopt this approach given that 'research has found that, even though the statute no longer makes reference to consent, in practice this has remained the key issue in many rape trials. … More generally, studies of the Michigan reforms have concluded that the reform package did not have a major effect on reporting or arrest rates, and had only a limited impact on prosecution practices and trial outcomes'.[145]

Peter Rush and Alison Young have proposed a new approach to defining rape that they argue can decrease the emphasis on consent. They have suggested defining rape in the following way:

---

142 *Ibid*, at 23.
143 Wendy Brown, *States of Injury: Power and Freedom in Late Modernity*, Princeton University Press, Princeton, 1995, at 163.
144 Law Reform Commission of Victoria, *Rape: Reform of Law and Procedure*, Appendixes to Interim Report No 42, July 1991, at 13-14 (emphasis added).
145 *Ibid*, at 16. The major study of the Michigan reforms referred to by the Commission is JC Marsh, A Geist and N Caplan, *Rape and the Limits of Law Reform*, Auburn House, Boston, 1982.

A person who:
   (a) voluntarily engages in sexual penetration of another person, and
   (b) voluntarily causes that other person serious injury
   (c) with the intention of causing serious injury or with recklessness as to causing serious injury,
is guilty of the offence of rape.[146]

At the structural level, the difference between their approach and that in Michigan is that under their approach rape is defined as a 'crime of consequences' – the consequence of serious injury – rather than a 'crime of circumstances' – for example, sexual penetration which occurs in the circumstances of force, fear etc, the traditional definition. Rush and Young state they 'do this in order to legally take account of the fact that the primary problem of sexual offences is the trauma suffered by the victim of the offence. ... A definition which identifies the primary problem of sexual offences in the *circumstance* of consent does not establish injury *to the victim* as relevant to the determination of criminal liability'.[147] The authors do not explicitly define injury, but note that it is intended to cover both 'physical and affective consequences'.[148]

As suggested, one of the reasons for developing their proposal was to move away from the centrality of consent. They argue:

> To the extent that consent may intrude, [*in their proposed offence*] it will only do so as *evidence* relevant to the physical element of the definition (specifically para (b)) and will definitely *not* be definitionally or evidentially relevant to the mens rea or fault element of the definition.[149]

In relation to para (b), they posit two scenarios: one, where the 'the acts of sexual penetration are alleged to be the cause of the serious injury' and the second, where 'the acts of sexual penetration provide the setting in which other acts are alleged to be the cause of the injury'.[150] In the first scenario:

> [D]efence counsel might argue that the acts of sexual penetration took place but that the defendant did not cause serious injury because the complainant consented – or, in briefer terms, that the complainant did not suffer serious injury because she was consenting. Our proposed definition would permit such an argument being made. However, we emphasise ... that consent has a precise and limited role, namely –
>
> One, it is *not* a part of the legal *definition* – it is only *evidence* going to disprove the prosecution's allegation that the victim suffered the serious injury caused by the sexual penetration. ...
>
> Two, this claim of consent is only relevant evidence going to the physical element and defendants will not be able to attach such evidence to a denial of mens rea. ... [O]ur proposed definition does not include a mens rea as to the circumstances of consent. Thus ... there is no dual inquiry as to consent, but only an actus reus inquiry; as such our proposal goes some way to reducing the importance of consent but without eliminating it.

---

146 Peter Rush and Alison Young, 'A Crime of Consequence and A Failure of Legal Imagination: The Sexual Offences of the Model Criminal Code' (1997) 9 *Australian Feminist Law Journal* 100 at 106.
147 *Ibid*, at 108.
148 *Ibid*. They also note their preference to define the crime in terms of causing injury, rather than serious injury, but persisted with the latter in order to encourage readers to take the proposal seriously (at 107).
149 *Ibid*, at 109.
150 *Ibid*, at 107.

Three, given that consent is only evidence, whether or not the claim is believed is a matter for the jury. ...

Taking the second scenario (where the acts of sexual penetration provide the setting in which other acts are alleged to be the cause of the serious injury), the issue of consent has a different place. Whether or not the victim consented *to sex* would be totally irrelevant to the determination of guilt or innocence. The only role of consent would be that the defence might attempt to argue that the victim consented *to the serious injury*. ... [I]n logic, the defence claim by itself is admission of the prohibited consequence, and whether or not the victim consented to serious injury does not change the fact that serious injury was caused.[151]

As well as reducing the focus on consent, Rush and Young argue that their proposal puts the focus of the trial on the defendant, rather than the victim. 'That focus asks whether the acts of the defendant caused serious injury and whether these causative acts support an inference as to the mentality of the defendant'.[152]

Notes

1. Do you agree that Rush and Young's proposal limits the role of consent? Is it likely to put the focus on the defendant rather than the victim? Although the proposal was originally put in a submission to the MCCOC, the Committee did not engage with it in any detail. While they summarise the proposal,[153] and describe it as a 'striking alternative',[154] the MCCOC merely states, 'the view of the Committee is that it is very difficult indeed to conceive of a structure of sexual offences that is not founded on the absence of consent on the part of the victim'. Does this mean that they think the Rush and Young proposal is not founded on the absence of consent? Do you agree? The MCCOC goes on to say:

    > After all, with regard to sexual contact between adults, it is the absence of consent on the part of one of the parties that determines at the most basic level whether that contact should be permissible or not.
    >
    > The Committee does not consider that attempting to reformulate the sexual offences without reference to lack of consent is the most effective way of responding to the undoubted problems with consent. Although the offences could be drafted so as to remove direct emphasis upon consent, in most cases the issue will of necessity arise. As noted above, that may well reflect the fact that the essential difference between the act of rape and lawful sexual intercourse is indeed the lack of consent.[155]

    Assuming that the MCCOC is correct and the 'essential difference' between rape and lawful sexual intercourse is lack of consent, does this mean it also needs to be a defining element of the *legal* definition of rape?
2. Do you think Rush and Young's proposal meets Wendy Brown's critique of a rape law based on consent?

---

151 *Ibid*, at 110-11.
152 *Ibid*, at 116.
153 MCCOC, at 27-9.
154 *Ibid*, at 27.
155 *Ibid*, at 29.

CIVIL ACTIONS FOR SEXUAL ASSAULT

Introduction

Elizabeth Sheehy argues:

> A woman who has been raped may have many reasons to pursue compensation. It may be the most empowering action available to her, especially if the criminal process has derailed, as it so often does. Compensation may be the only process which *she* gets to drive, instead of respond to; it may be the only time when the legal system focuses on *her* needs; and it may be the only state acknowledgment of a wrong against her that she will receive.[156]

Compensation can be pursued through a variety of forums and against a variety of parties. It may be possible to sue the perpetrator directly, for example for battery/trespass to the person; alternatively, a third party, such as a landlord or police department could be sued for negligence; and most jurisdictions have statutory schemes that provide compensation to victims of crime.[157] These latter provide a (usually small token) payment from the state and have been described as the 'proffering of a gesture of concern and solidarity with the person offended against ... [*as*] part of a process that has the potential to reintegrate the victim/survivor into the community – to the benefit of both the individual wronged and the community generally. It goes beyond the mere affording of medical or therapeutic services'.[158]

Bruce Feldthusen has described the relatively recent Canadian trend to use tort law to respond to sexual assault:

> Something new and provocative is happening in the law of torts. Victims of rape, other sexual assaults, incest, and other forms of child sexual abuse are using the civil justice system to sue the perpetrators in numbers and in circumstances never seen before. Although some courts have referred to these as "new" tort actions for "sexual assault", in fact the action is none other than the traditional action in battery. What is new is the growing tendency for sexual battery victims to exercise the long available, but largely ignored, civil option.
>
> In addition, at least two truly "new" avenues of civil relief appear to be developing in the area of sexual wrongdoing. The first deals with "sexual exploitation" in power-imbalanced relationships. The second consists of negligence claims against third parties.
>
> In the exploitation cases, the defendant, typically a male professional, employs his relative power to secure the victim's apparent "consent" to sexual conduct. Courts [*in Canada*] are beginning to take the power imbalance seriously and to invalidate on that ground what might have been accepted as the plaintiff's consent. ...
>
> The new negligence claims are based on an allegation that the third party breached a legal duty to protect the victim from a sexual battery by another. Defendants in third party negligence claims have included landlords, child welfare agencies, school boards, and police officials. Negligence actions have also been brought against mothers for failing to protect their daughters from sexually abusive fathers and stepfathers.

---

156 Elizabeth A Sheehy, 'Compensation for Women Who Have Been Raped' in Julian V Roberts and Renate M Mohr (eds), *Confronting Sexual Assault: A Decade of Legal and Social Change*, at 205.
157 See, for example, *Victims Support and Rehabilitation Act* 1996 (NSW); *Victims of Crime Assistance Act* 1996 (Vic).
158 Ian Freckelton, 'Compensating the Sexually Assaulted' in Easteal (ed), *Balancing the Scales*, at 194.

It is too early to predict whether the trend to employ the civil action in sexual battery cases will continue. If it does, it may have interesting implications for the entire law of torts. Today, tort law has little direct impact on individuals. Few individuals, unless backed by a subrogating insurer, can afford to invoke the tort process. Fewer still are willing and able to bring an action against an effectively judgment-proof individual defendant. The true parties to most tort litigation are large enterprises, insurers, and governments. ...

What is striking about the sexual battery actions, or at least many of them, is that they appear far more consistent with the corrective justice model than with any instrumentalist notion of tort law. Most sexual battery actions are brought by individual women standing alone, and against individual defendants. Moreover, damages do not always seem central to the action. Frequently, plaintiffs have litigated sexual battery actions knowing in advance there would be virtually no prospect of collecting on the judgment.

Instead of the prospect of financial gain, many sexual battery plaintiffs have reported therapeutic motivations for suing. By therapeutic, I mean only that some aspect of the litigation – the complaint, the process, or the outcome – is expected to, or does, assist the victim along the path to recovery. For some plaintiffs, the sexual battery action was perceived as part of the healing process. Others have indicated that they brought suit to punish their assailant. Still others claim they sought public vindication. At least one plaintiff hoped her suit would encourage other victims. Taken together, these constitute an unusual modern manifestation of the original justifications of tort law: corrective justice, vindication, appeasement and even retribution.[159]

Notes

1. In the following chapter, we discuss some criticisms of the use of tort law to respond to sexual harassment. For example, some commentators have argued that tort law individualises the harm of sexual harassment and that discrimination law is a more effective way to respond to that harm. Do you think the same critique can be made of using tort to respond to sexual assaults? Alternatively, does the suggestion by Feldthusen about the traditional functions of tort law – 'corrective justice, vindication, appeasement and ... retribution' – indicate that tort law has a clear role in cases of both sexual assault and sexual harassment?
2. The extract from Feldthusen refers to Canadian cases where the focus has been the imbalance of power between the abuser and his target. In *Norberg v Wynrib*,[160] a woman sued her doctor for sexual assault. She was addicted to pain killers and when the doctor became aware of this, he agreed to continue supplying them in exchange for sexual contact. In the Supreme Court of Canada, three of the judges allowed her action in battery, deciding that 'consent' had been induced by the abuse of an unequal power relationship. However, L'Heureux-Dubé and McLachlin JJ, while agreeing with the result, preferred to characterise the situation as a breach of fiduciary duty. That is,

---

159 'The Civil Action for Sexual Battery: Therapeutic Jurisprudence?' (1993) 25 *Ottawa Law Review* 203 at 205-12. See also Bruce Feldthusen, 'The Canadian Experiment with the Civil Action for Sexual Battery' in Nicholas J Mullany (ed), *Torts in the Nineties*, LBC, Sydney, 1997; and Nathalie Des Rosiers, Bruce Feldthusen and Oleana AR Hankivsky, 'Legal Compensation for Sexual Violence: Therapeutic Consequences and Consequences for the Judicial System' (1998) 4 *Psychology, Public Policy and Law* 433.
160 [1992] 2 SCR 226.

they decided that the relationship between a doctor and patient was fiduciary in nature. They stated:

> Dr Wynrib was in a position of power vis-à-vis the plaintiff; he had scope for the exercise of power and discretion with respect to her. He had the power to advise her, to treat her, to give her the drug or to refuse her the drug. He could unilaterally exercise that power or discretion in a way that affected her interests. And her status as a patient rendered her vulnerable and at his mercy, particularly in light of her addiction. ... All the classic characteristics of a fiduciary relationship were present. Dr Wynrib and Ms. Norberg were on an unequal footing. He pledged himself – by the act of hanging out his shingle as a medical doctor and accepting her as his patient – to act in her best interests and not permit any conflict between his duty to act only in her best interests and his own interests – including his interest in sexual gratification – to arise.[161]

And, in *M(K) v M(H)*,[162] a majority of the Supreme Court of Canada characterised the parent-child relationship as fiduciary in nature. In this case, the appellant was a victim of incest who brought an action against her father for abuse perpetrated by him against her from the time she was eight until she left home at 17. The court said:

> It is intuitively apparent that the relationship between parent and child is fiduciary in nature, and that the sexual assault of one's child is a grievous breach of the obligations arising from that relationship. Indeed, I can think of few cases that are clearer than this. For obvious reasons society has imposed upon parents the obligation to care for, protect and rear their children. The act of incest is a heinous violation of that obligation. Equity has imposed fiduciary obligations on parents in contexts other than incest, and I see no barrier to the extension of a father's fiduciary obligation to include a duty to refrain from incestuous assaults on his daughter.[163]

Do you think breach of fiduciary duty is a useful way of envisaging abuse by a doctor of a patient or a father of his child or step-child?[164] Is assault by a brother or step-brother necessarily an abuse of trust or power? Would it be helpful to envisage the relationship between academic staff and students as fiduciary in nature? While a person can consent to breach of a fiduciary relationship,[165] in order for that consent to be valid, the person must know the other's responsibility is fiduciary in nature. Does knowing that the breach of a fiduciary relationship can be consented to encourage you to see the academic/student relationship as fiduciary in nature?

Apart from the possible conceptual attraction of the fiduciary concept,[166] being able to envisage the legal harm as breach of fiduciary duty may in some jurisdictions have the additional advantage of avoiding difficulties that strict

---

161 *Ibid*, at 275.
162 [1992] 3 SCR 3
163 *Ibid*, at 61-2.
164 Adrian Howe has argued that the concept of breach of fiduciary duty better captures injuries of this nature than does tort, which she also claims has a tendency to individualise such injuries and mask their social nature: Adrian Howe, 'Fiduciary Law meets the Civil Incest Suit: Re-Framing the Injury of Incestuous Assault – A Question of Visibility' (1997) 8 *Australian Feminist Law Journal* 59 esp at 73 et seq.
165 Roderick Meagher, William Gummow and John Lehane, *Equity Doctrine & Remedies*, 3rd ed, Butterworths, 1992 at 143-4.
166 It should be noted that the High Court has expressly disapproved of the expansive approach taken by the Canadian courts to the concept of fiduciary duty: see *Breen v Williams* (1996) 186 CLR 71.

application of limitation periods can cause for such claims.[167] Generally, a tort claim must be made within a limited time from a cause of action 'accruing'.[168] This time may be clear when a person is injured in a car accident – the cause of action accrues from the time of the accident – but many women who are sexually abused as children have suppressed their memories of that abuse and do not realise that the symptoms they are suffering from are related to the abuse until after the limitation period has expired.[169]

Difficulties caused by limitation periods that barred claims for dust related diseases suffered by men at work led to statutory changes in the 1960s that provided for the extension of those periods in certain cases for people whose injuries did not manifest any symptoms until many years later.[170] For some types of action, generally personal injury damages arising from 'negligence, nuisance or breach of duty', limited extensions of time are available from the time a person knew (or, in some cases, ought to have known) that they have been injured by the defendant.

This type of statutory amendment was put to the test in England in relation to sexual abuse in *Stubbings v Webb*, which concerned a claim by a woman against her step-father and step-brother for damages flowing from sexual abuse in childhood.[171] The issue before the court was whether she had brought her action too late. She had not sued within six years of the original injury (or, in her case as a minor, from her majority), but she tried to rely on the amendments. The House of Lords held that these did not apply to child sexual assault, since her action was a 'trespass to the person', not personal injury caused by 'negligence, nuisance or breach of duty'. As Lord Griffiths explained the distinction: 'If I invite a lady to my house one would naturally think of a duty to take care that the house is safe but would one really be thinking of a duty not to rape her?'[172] He also said:

> The plaintiff's case was that although she knew she had been raped by one defendant and had been persistently sexually abused by the other she did not realise that she had suffered sufficiently serious injury to justify starting proceedings for damages until she realised that there might be a causal link between psychiatric problems she had suffered in adult life and her sexual abuse as a child. ... If it was necessary to decide the point I should not have found it easy to agree with the Court of Appeal. Personal injury is defined [*under the Act*] as including 'any impairment of a person's physical or mental condition' and I have the greatest difficulty in accepting that a woman who knows that she has been raped does not know that she has suffered a significant injury.[173]

---

167 See *Williams v Minister Aboriginal Land Rights Act* (1994) 35 NSWLR 497 esp per Kirby P; but compare the approach taken by the Full Federal Court in *Paramasivan v Flynn* (1998) 160 ALR 203.
168 See, for example, *Limitation of Action Act* 1958 (Vic), which provides for a limitation period of six years, though for a minor this period runs from the age of majority (18). For the classic exposition of this approach, see *Cartledge v Jopling* [1963] AC 758.
169 See Graycar and Morgan, 'Disabling Citizenship: Civil Death for Women in the 1990s?' (1995) 17 *Adelaide Law Review* 49 at 63 et seq.
170 For a discussion of these provisions (in the context of the Queensland legislation), see the decision of the High Court in *Brisbane South Regional Health Authority v Taylor* (1996) 186 CLR 541.
171 [1993] AC 498.
172 *Ibid*, at 508. However, see the Court of Appeal decision in the same case where all three judges readily accepted that there had been a breach of duty: *Stubbings v Webb* [1991] 3 All ER 949.
173 [1993] AC 498 at 505-6. See also Graycar and Morgan, 'Disabling Citizenship', and Joanne Conaghan, 'Tort Litigation in the Context of Intra-familial Abuse' (1998) 61 *Modern Law Review* 132.

3. It will be recalled that in New Zealand, the Accident Compensation scheme bars actions for compensation for personal injury although it remains possible to pursue an action for exemplary damages. The rationale for this is that exemplary damages are not designed to compensate the plaintiff for her injury, but rather to punish the defendant. In the 1990s, a number of New Zealand women were awarded exemplary damages for sexual assault. Joanna Manning suggests that plaintiffs who bring these actions are 'motivated by the non-instrumental objectives of tort law, such as punishment, the desire for revenge, vindication by a symbolic victory, appeasement, accountability, and to assist the plaintiff psychologically in recovering' and that this has particularly been the case in the sexual assault cases.[174] A debate developed in New Zealand over whether or not exemplary damages were available in situations where a perpetrator had been convicted (or indeed, charged and acquitted) for the offence to which the action related.[175] What are the arguments for and against retaining a limited right of action for exemplary damages where compensatory damages are no longer available? Does permitting a person to claim exemplary damages where a defendant has been convicted (or indeed, acquitted) constitute 'double punishment'? Why might survivors argue that they should retain the right to sue the perpetrator, even if he has been convicted of an offence?

Tort law and equality

A landmark Canadian civil action for sexual assault combines an equality-based understanding of sexual assault with the traditional tort of negligence. Jane Doe, the victim of a serial rapist, sued the police for negligence *and* a breach of her constitutional right to equality.[176] It took over 10 years for her case to be decided, but in 1998 it was finally resolved.

Jane Doe v Metropolitan Toronto (Municipality) Commissioners of Police
(1998) 160 DLR (4th) 697

MacFarland, J ... [701] [Jane Doe] was raped and otherwise sexually assaulted at knife point in her own bed in the early morning hours of August 24, 1986 by a stranger subsequently identified as Paul Douglas Callow. [Jane Doe] then lived in a second floor apartment at ... in the City of Toronto; her apartment had a balcony which was used by the rapist to gain access to her premises. At the

---

174 See Joanna Manning, 'The Story of a Screening Programme' (2001) 9 *Torts Law Journal* 229 at 231.
175 See John Smillie, 'Exemplary Damages for Personal Injury' [1997] *New Zealand Law Review* 140; Joanna Manning, 'Professor Smillie's 'Exemplary Damages for Personal Injury'' [1997] *NZ Law Review* 176. See also *Daniels v Thompson* [1998] 3 NZLR 22 (Thomas J dissenting); affirmed by the Privy Council in *W v W* [1999] 2 NZLR 1. The decision in *Daniels v Thompson* was effectively overruled by Parliament: see *Accident Insurance Act*, s 396. See also Joanna Manning, 'Exemplary Damages and Criminal Punishment in the Privy Council' (1999) 7 *Torts Law Journal* 129.
176 Section 15(1) of the *Canadian Charter of Rights and Freedoms* provides 'Every individual is equal before and under the law and has the right to the equal protection and equal benefit of the law without discrimination, and, in particular, without discrimination based on race, national or ethnic origin, colour, religion, sex, age or mental or physical disability'.

time, [Jane Doe] was the fifth known victim of Callow who would become known as "the balcony rapist".

[Jane Doe] brings a suit against the Metropolitan Toronto Police Force (hereafter referred to as MTPF) on two bases; firstly, she suggests that the MTPF conducted a negligent investigation in relation to the balcony rapist and failed to warn women who they knew to be potential targets of Callow of the fact that they were at risk. She says, as the result of such conduct, Callow was not apprehended as early as he might have been and she was denied the opportunity, had she known the risk she faced, to take any specific measures to protect herself from attack. Secondly, she said the MTPF being a public body having the statutory duty to protect the public from criminal activity, must exercise that duty in accordance with the *Canadian Charter of Rights and Freedoms* and may not act in a way that is discriminatory because of gender. She says the police must act constitutionally, they did not do so in this case and as the result, her rights under sections 15 and 7 of the *Charter*, have been breached. She seeks damages against the MTPF under both heads of her claim.

... It is necessary when considering claims under section 15 of the *Charter* that they be considered in relation to the larger social, political and legal context. ...

[702] The evidence establishes beyond peradventure that among adults, the perpetrators of sexual violence are overwhelmingly male and the victims overwhelmingly female. It is not disputed that this was known to the MTPF in 1986.

... It is also proved on the evidence, that the majority of sexual assaults committed against women are not reported to the police, a fact of which the MTFP was also aware in 1986. The evidence establishes ... that a reason many sexual assault victims do not report to the police is because they have concerns about the attitudes of the police or courts to this type of incident and this fact has been recognised by the Supreme Court of Canada, see *R v Osolin*, [1993] 4 SCR 595, at 628 ....

[MacFarland J here outlined a series of reports undertaken from the mid-1970s indicating problems with the way the MTFP handled sexual assault complainants; she also examined the way this particular investigation was undertaken. In relation to the failure to warn, MacFarland J concluded:]

[729] ... Sgts Cameron and Derry *[the investigating officers]* determined that this investigation would be "low key" compared to the investigation conducted into the "Annex Rapist" *[another serial rapist operating in Toronto some months earlier; that investigation had been the subject of much media coverage]* and no warning would be given to the women they knew to be at risk for fear of displacing the rapist leaving him free to re-offend elsewhere undetected.

I am not persuaded that their professed reason for not warning women is the real reason no warning was given.

... [730] I find that the real reason a warning was not given in the circumstances of this case was because Sgts Cameron and Derry believed that women living in the area would become hysterical and panic and their investigation would thereby be jeopardized. In addition, they were not motivated by any sense of urgency because Callow's attacks were not seen as "violent" as *[the earlier serial rapist's]* by comparison had been.

I am satisfied on the evidence that a meaningful warning could and should have been given to the women who were at particular risk. That warning could have been given by way of a canvass of their apartments, by a media blitz – by holding widely publicized meetings or any one or combination of these methods. Such a warning should have alerted the particular women at risk, and advised them of suggested precautions they might take to protect themselves. The defence experts, with the exception of [*one*] agreed that a warning could have been given without compromising the investigation on the facts of the case. ...

[731] ... I am satisfied on Ms [Jane Doe's] evidence that if she had been aware a serial rapist was in her neighbourhood raping women whose [732] apartments he accessed via their balconies she would have taken steps to protect herself and that most probably those steps would have prevented her from being raped.

... It is no answer for the police to say women are always at risk and as an urban adult living in downtown Toronto they have an obligation to lookout for themselves. Women generally do, every day of their lives, conduct themselves and their lives in such a way as to avoid the general pervasive threat of male violence which exists in our society. Here police were aware of a specific threat or risk to a specific group of women and they did nothing to warn those women of the danger they were in, nor did they take any measures to protect them.

Discrimination

The plaintiff's argument is not simply that she has been discriminated against, because she is a woman, by individual officers in the investigation of her specific complaint – but that systemic discrimination existed within the MTPF in 1986 which impacted adversely on all women and, specifically, those who were survivors of sexual assault who came into contact with the MTPF – a class of persons of which the plaintiff was one. She says, in effect, the sexist stereotypical views held by the MTPF informed the investigation of this serial rapist and caused that investigation to be [733] conducted incompetently and in such a way that the plaintiff has been denied the equal protection and equal benefit of law guaranteed to her by s. 15(1) of the *Charter*.

The MTPF has since at least 1975 been aware of the problems it has in relation to the investigation of sexual assaults.

Among those problems:

- survivors of sexual assault are not treated sensitively.
- lack of effective training for officers engaged in the investigation of sexual assault including a lack of understanding of rape trauma syndrome and the needs of survivors.
- lack of co-ordination of sexual assault investigations.
- some officers not suited by personality/attitude to investigation of sexual assault.
- too many investigators coming into contact with victims.
- lack of experienced investigators investigating sexual assault.
- lack of supervision of those conducting sexual assault investigations.

The force has conceded in public documents as well as in internal documents at least since 1975, that it has difficulties in these areas, that it will take immediate steps to remedy these shortcomings – yet the problems continued through to 1987 and beyond.

... [734] The problems continued and because among adults, women are overwhelmingly the victims of sexual assault, they are and were disproportionately impacted by the resulting poor quality of investigation. The result is, that women are discriminated against and their right to equal protection and benefit of the law is thereby compromised as the result.

In my view the conduct of this investigation and the failure to warn in particular, was motivated and informed by the adherence to rape myths as well as sexist stereotypical reasoning about rape, about women and about women who are raped. The plaintiff therefore has been discriminated against by reason of her gender and as the result the plaintiff's rights to equal protection and equal benefit of the law were compromised. ...

[*Doe was awarded some Can$220,000, including an amount of $175,000 for general damages. In making this award, MacFarland J cited the judgment of Cory J in the Supreme Court of Canada in Osolin, who stated:*]

> It cannot be forgotten that a sexual assault is very different from other assaults. It is true that it, like all other forms of assault, is an act of violence. Yet it is something more than a simple act of violence. Sexual assault is in the vast majority of cases gender based. It is an assault upon human dignity and constitutes a denial of any concept of equality for women [*R v Osolin* [1993] 4 SCR 595 at 669].[177]

Notes

1. MacFarland J also found that Doe's constitutional right to security of the person had been breached by the police action[178] and that they had been negligent in their investigation. The finding that a duty of care is owed by the police in these circumstances contrasts with the decision of the House of Lords in *Hill v Chief Constable of West Yorkshire*.[179] That case concerned 'the Yorkshire Ripper', perhaps the most notorious killer of women in Britain since Jack the Ripper. Between July 1975 and November 1980, Peter Sutcliffe murdered 13 women and attempted to murder eight others, all in the area of West Yorkshire. He was arrested in 1981 and confessed to the crimes. In *Hill*, the mother of Sutcliffe's last victim sued the Chief Constable of West Yorkshire for negligence (on behalf of her daughter's estate). As in *Doe*, the police applied to strike out the statement of claim, arguing that it disclosed no cause of action. The police had been successful in the lower courts[180] and Ms Hill appealed to the House of Lords. The House of Lords held that the statement of claim was rightly struck out:

    > Sutcliffe was never in the custody of the police force. Miss Hill was one of a vast number of the female general public who might be at risk from his activities, but was at no special distinctive risk in relation to them. ... [T]he identity of the wanted criminal was at the material time unknown and it is not averred that any full or clear description of him was ever available. ... Hill cannot ... be regarded as a person at special risk simply because she was young and female. Where the class of potential victims of a particular habitual criminal is a large one the precise size of it cannot in principle affect the issue. All householders are potential victims of a habitual burglar, and all females those of an habitual rapist.[181]

    Lord Keith would also have dismissed the appeal on the additional ground that, for public policy reasons, an action should not lie against the police in circumstances such as these. And Lord Templeman pointed out that Mrs Hill proposed that any damages awarded would be donated to charity. The purpose of her action was to obtain an investigation 'so that lives shall not be lost in the future'.[182] What effect, if any, might this fact have had on the outcome of the case?

---

177 Cited in *Jane Doe*, at 746.
178 Section 7 of the *Canadian Charter of Rights and Freedoms* provides 'Everyone has the right to life, liberty and security of the person and the right not to be deprived thereof except in accordance with the principles of fundamental justice'.
179 [1989] AC 53.
180 For the Court of Appeal's decision, see [1988] QB 60.
181 [1989] AC 53 at 62.
182 *Ibid*, at 64.

The police in *Doe* had also tried to have the case dismissed before trial,[183] but the court rejected the challenge, stating that the principle of public policy relied on in *Hill* to exempt the police from liability was not part of Canadian law.[184]

Contrast this with the view of Lord Templeman in *Hill*:

> [I]f this action lies, every citizen will be able to require the court to investigate the performance of every policeman. If the policeman concentrates on one crime, he may be accused of neglecting others. If the policeman does not arrest on suspicion, a suspect with previous convictions, the police force may be held liable for subsequent crimes. The threat of litigation against a police force would not make a policeman more efficient. The necessity for defending proceedings, successfully or unsuccessfully, would distract the policeman from his duties.[185]

What other policy arguments can you see for and against exempting the police from liability in such cases?[186]

2. The House of Lords in *Hill* gives us no facts concerning the police investigation of Sutcliffe. Joan Smith has pointed out that Sutcliffe was finally arrested by police from a different police force (that is, not the West Yorkshire police who were conducting the investigation).

> Sutcliffe, a married man living in a semi-detached house in a good suburb of Bradford, was simply not what anyone had expected. ... Sutcliffe had been interviewed not once but *nine* times. He wore the same size boots as the murderer (indeed, the boot which had left an impression on a sheet in the flat of one of the victims, and on the thigh of another, was standing in Sutcliffe's garage as he was interviewed). His only alibi for the murder was given, contrary to police procedure, by close relatives, including his wife. He had a previous conviction, ... as a result of being found in a woman's garden with a knife and hammer – the very weapons used by the Ripper. ... His appearance matched fairly closely photofit pictures created by two of his surviving victims. His various cars, which had left tyre prints at the scene of some of the murders, were frequently logged by police in red light districts in Bradford, Leeds and Manchester. ...[187]

Smith describes the course of the investigation: the series started with three attacks on women who survived. In all three cases, serious head wounds had been inflicted, probably by a hammer, and at least two of the women had also been slashed with a knife. These three women, although they all lived in the same area (Bradford-Lees), varied substantially in age – from 14 to 46. However, Smith argues that '[t]here should have been every reason for police to link the cases, at least tentatively, as the work of the same man, and a man whose motive was an overwhelming hatred of women – any women'.[188] The next two attacks involved murders; one of the women was working as a

---

183 *Jane Doe v Police Board of Commissioners (Metropolitan Toronto)* (1989) 58 DLR (4th) 396. For a discussion of this case see Mayo Moran, 'Case Comment' (1993) 6 *Canadian Journal of Women and the Law* 491.
184 The main authority relied on was *Neilsen v City of Kamloops* [1984] 2 SCR 2.
185 [1989] AC 53 at 65.
186 Note that the House of Lords has modified its approach to the policy issue somewhat: see *Barrett v Enfield London Borough Council* [1999] 3 All ER 193 and see also the decision of the European Court of Human Rights in *Osman v United Kingdom* (1998) 29 EHHR 245.
187 Joan Smith, *Misogynies: Reflections on Myth and Malice*, Faber and Faber, London, 1989, at 118.
188 *Ibid*, at 121.

sex-worker at the time of the attack and the other was assumed to be so working.[189] The police saw a link in the two murders and identified the killer as a prostitute killer.

> Three major errors flowed from the acceptance of this hypothesis. First, genuine Sutcliffe victims were excluded from the list of his crimes because they were the wrong 'type' of woman, while a murder ... he did not commit *was* included on grounds of the ... woman's character and habits. Second, the police fell into the trap of expecting the killer to behave like the nineteenth-century Ripper. Third, they convinced themselves that they 'knew' the killer in some mysterious and undefined way; that, if they were suddenly confronted by him, they would recognize him at once. ...
>
> What did they expect? Someone slavering at the mouth who would throw back his cloak and flourish a blood-stained knife? Obviously not; what [*the police*] were expressing was actually no more than a vague expectation of *difference*, that there would be something – a nervous gesture, a manner of speaking, staring eyes, a careless remark about prostitutes – that would single him out. Whoever he was, whatever his background, this man would be different from the rest, and from them. They were wrong, of course .... One of the chief ironies of the whole Yorkshire Ripper case is that the police spent millions of pounds fruitlessly searching for an outsider when the culprit was just an ordinary bloke, a local man who shared their backgrounds and attitudes to a remarkable degree.[190]

Does this information about the police investigation of the case explain more clearly why Ms Hill might have brought her action? Why do none of these facts appear in the House of Lords' judgment?

3. In 2001, the Constitutional Court of South Africa overturned a decision rejecting a claim against the police brought by a woman who had been sexually assaulted. She argued that, in failing to take steps to prevent the man who attacked her from doing so, the police had breached their duty to ensure that she enjoyed her constitutional rights, inter alia, to equality and freedom and security of the person. The court held that, in developing the common law, account must be taken of the Bill of Rights: '[T]he courts must remain vigilant and should not hesitate to ensure that the common law is developed to reflect the spirit, purport and object of the Bill of Rights'.[191]

The court noted that the police had positive obligations to prevent crime and, in addressing those obligations:

> [F]ew things can be more important to women than freedom from the threat of sexual violence. As it was put by counsel for the amicus curiae,[192]
>
> 'Sexual violence and the threat of sexual violence goes to the core of women's subordination in society. It is the single greatest threat to the self-determination of South African women'.[193]

---

189 '[E]leven more women were to die and five more to survive horrific assaults before he was brought to justice (*ibid*, at 122).
190 *Ibid*, at 123-4.
191 *Carmichele v Minister for Safety and Security and Minister of Justice and Constitutional Development*, Constitutional Court of South Africa, CCT 48/00, 16 August 2001, para 36. The court added that this obligation applied in both civil and criminal cases, and whether or not the parties expressly requested the court to do so.
192 The Gender Research Project of the Centre for Applied Legal Studies at the University of the Witwatersrand.
193 *Carmichele v Minister for Safety and Security and Minister of Justice and Constitutional Development*, Constitutional Court of South Africa, CCT 48/00, 16 August 2001, at para 62.

The court continued:

> South Africa also has a duty under international law to prohibit all gender-based discrimination that has the effect or purpose of impairing the enjoyment by women of fundamental rights and freedoms and to take reasonable and appropriate measures to prevent the violation of those rights.[194]

It will be recalled that *Jane Doe* was decided on both tort law and constitutional (equality) law grounds (though MacFarland J made it clear that the damages to be awarded were the same for both actions). How likely is it that the existence of the *Charter of Rights and Freedoms* (and the absence of a comparable document in England)[195] affected the outcomes in *Jane Doe* and *Hill?* What does this, and the reliance on the Constitution in developing South African tort law in *Carmichele*, suggest about the likelihood of Australian courts taking an expansive role of the duty of public bodies such as the police to protect women from sexual violence?

4. Some common law civil actions have also been pursued in Australia. For example, in *S v S*,[196] Ms S successfully sued the host of a party she attended after one of the other guests raped her. The NSW Court of Appeal confirmed the trial judge's finding that the defendant had ignored the plaintiff's absence after seeing her followed to the bathroom by the perpetrator and, when the defendant entered the bedroom where the rape occurred, probably in response to cries for help, 'it was inconceivable that ... the defendant could have formed a genuine view that nothing untoward was happening in the bedroom'.[197] The defendant in this case had conceded that a duty of care was owed to the plaintiff; the court was prepared to accept the concession in this case but stated that '[t]his is *not* a pronouncement that it is my considered view that there was a duty of care in this case .... . [I]n general social hosts do not owe duties to social guests, but that circumstances may arise where the foreseeability of harm and the capacity of the host to prevent it combine to bring a duty of care into existence'.[198] When should social hosts owe a duty to guests? Are foreseeability of harm and the capacity to prevent it appropriate criteria for determining a duty of care in these circumstances? Assuming they are, what circumstances would you see as giving rise to this duty? Should such a duty arise for a bar manager who observes a group of men sexually harassing a woman?

Conclusion

This chapter has raised a series of questions about the role of law in responding to violence against women. In some circumstances, law has explicitly sanctioned violent abuses, as it has done in relation to the sterilisation of women thought to have an intellectual disability. In more recent times, tort law has provided some redress for some of the harms we have discussed in this chapter. The New Zealand cervical cancer 'experiment' and its aftermath raises the question of the extent to which the absence of traditional legal redress has encouraged the abuse of

---

194 *Ibid.*
195 Cf *Human Rights Act* 1998 (UK), which came into effect in 2000.
196 *S v S* (unreported, NSWCA, 17 July 1998).
197 *Ibid*, typescript, at 8 (citing the trial judge's findings).
198 *Ibid*, typescript, at 11-12.

women's bodies. The material on rape in turn allows us to consider the different roles of criminal and civil law in responding to this pervasive legal harm, and more broadly the role of law in both contributing to and ameliorating harm. The theme of the role of law is continued in the next chapter in this part (dealing with sexual harassment and pornography), and returned to in the final chapter, a chapter explicitly considering strategic questions about engaging with law.

Chapter Twelve

Sexual Harassment and Pornography

Introduction

This chapter concerns gendered injuries which are both more common and more recently recognised as injuries than either medical abuses of women or rape, the subject of the previous chapter. Whilst its central focus is sexual harassment, particularly sexual harassment in the workplace, we also examine pornography.

The focus in this chapter thus shifts from gendered harms that have an individual woman as their immediate target to harms that are more generally directed at all women. Sexual harassment provides the link between those harms that are directly invasive of an individual woman's body and those that on their face are directed to 'all women' because of the varied ways in which sexuality can invade a workplace. The cases we discuss in the following section range from direct sexual assault to pornography on the workplace walls. Sometimes these sexual acts are directed towards individual women, while sometimes they are directed towards women more generally.

Sexual harassment has only relatively recently been recognised as a legal wrong as well as a gendered harm and we examine the success of the creation of a cause of action for this type of harm. Legal responses to pornography are both less well-developed and more controversial, especially within feminism. There is no clear consensus on whether pornography is harmful to women (and men) and, assuming that it is, whether a legal response is appropriate. We briefly canvass these debates.

SEXUAL HARASSMENT

Tort or discrimination law?

The prevalence of sexual harassment in the workplace is a constant reminder to women that their experiences of paid work are often quite different from those of men. In her landmark 1979 book, *Sexual Harassment of Working Women*,[1] Catharine MacKinnon persuasively argued that sexual harassment constitutes a form of sex discrimination. MacKinnon has subsequently described the development of sexual harassment doctrine as 'sexual politics as feminist jurisprudence',[2] that is, using law to create a cause of action to deal with injuries to women, designed from the standpoint of women's experience. MacKinnon analyses the experience of sexual harassment in the following way:

---

1 Yale University Press, New Haven, 1979.
2 Catharine A MacKinnon, *Feminism Unmodified*, Harvard University Press, Cambridge, MA, 1987, Chapter 9. This aspect is explored in more detail in Chapter 13 of this book.

> Sexual assault as experienced during sexual harassment seems less an ordinary act of sexual desire directed towards the wrong person than an expression of dominance laced with impersonal contempt, the habit of getting what one wants, and the perception (usually accurate) that the situation can be safely exploited in this way – all expressed sexually. It is dominance eroticized. The sense that emerges from incidents of sexual harassment is less that men mean to arouse or gratify the women's desires, or often even their own, and more that they want to know that they can go this far this way any time they wish and get away with it. The fact that they can do this seems itself to be sexually arousing. The practice seems an extension of their desire and belief that the woman is there *for them*, however they may choose to define that.[3]

MacKinnon argued that discrimination law was better able to respond to women's experience of the injury of sexual harassment than tort law which, as we have seen, has been used (in limited ways) to respond to other forms of violence against women, including rape. MacKinnon stated:

> Most broadly considered, tort is conceptually inadequate to the problem of sexual harassment to the extent that it rips injuries to women's sexuality out of the context of women's social circumstances as a whole. ...
>
> The essential purpose of tort law ... is to compensate individuals one at a time for mischief which befalls them as a consequence of the one-time ineptitude or nastiness of other individuals. The occurrence of such events is viewed more or less with resignation, as an inevitability of social proximity, a fall-out of order which can be confronted only probabilistically. Sexual harassment as understood in ... [*Sexual Harassment of Working Women*] is not merely a parade of interconnected consequences with the potential for discrete repetition by other individuals, so that a precedent will suffice. Rather, it is a group-defined injury which occurs to many different individuals regardless of unique qualities or circumstances, in ways that connect with other deprivations of the same individuals, among all of whom a single characteristic – female sex – is shared. Such an injury is in essence a group injury. The context which makes the impact of gender cumulative – in fact, the context that makes it injurious – is lost when sexual harassment is approached as an individual injury, however wide the net of damages is cast. ... [T]he purpose of discrimination law is to change the society so that this kind of injury need not and does not recur. Tort law considers individual and compensable something which is fundamentally social and should be eliminated. ...
>
> All of this is not to say that sexual harassment is not both wrong and a personal injury, merely that it is a social wrong and a social injury that occurs on a personal level. To treat it as a tort is less simply incorrect than inadequate. The law recognizes that individual acts of racism could be torts in recognizing that the dignitary harm of racist insults can be compensated like any other personal injury. This does not preclude a finding that the same acts of racial invective on the job are race discrimination. Although racial insults impact upon blacks on a personal level, they are systematically connected to the "living insult" of segregation. Although reparations may be due, the stigma is not eradicable by money damages to one black person at a time. As with sexual harassment, the reason these acts can occur and recur, and the source of their sting, is not the breaking of a code of good conduct, but the relegation to inferiority for which they stand.
>
> To see sexual harassment as an injury to morality is to turn it into an extreme case of bad manners, when the point is that it is the kind of bad manners almost exclusively visited upon women by men with the power to get away with it. One

---

3   *Sexual Harassment of Working Women*, at 162.

can see the social invisibility of blacks as white rudeness, but it makes more sense to see it as racism. The major difference between the tort approach and the discrimination approach, then, is that tort sees sexual harassment as an illicit act, a moral infraction, an outrage to the individual's sensibilities and the society's cherished but unlived values. Discrimination law casts the same acts as economic coercion, in which material survival is held hostage to sexual submission.[4]

Notes

1. MacKinnon argues that sexual harassment is a group or social injury.[5] One of the problems she sees in using tort remedies is that tort individualises the experience of injury, thereby hiding its gendered nature. In Chapter 11 we referred to class actions in the United States brought by women against manufacturers of harmful products such as the Dalkon Shield and DES. Does the fact that these tort actions were brought by groups of women, rather than by individual women, address some of MacKinnon's concerns about tort as an individualised remedy? Can the criticisms MacKinnon develops of the inadequacy of tort law to respond to the injury of sexual harassment be applied to the use of tort remedies for the crime of rape described in the previous chapter? Is the criminal law a group or individual-based response to harms to women? MacKinnon points out that many acts of sexual harassment are technically crimes and yet she also rejects criminal law as the appropriate legal response to sexual harassment.[6] What problems do you perceive in using the criminal law to respond to sexual harassment? Are there, by contrast, problems in pursuing cases of sexual assault as acts of discrimination (rather than through the criminal law)?[7]
2. Joanne Conaghan, while remaining skeptical about the potential of tort law, is also less sanguine than MacKinnon about the potential of discrimination law for addressing the wrong of sexual harassment, at least in the United Kingdom.

> [T]he legal conception of sex discrimination is equally individualistic. Addressing a wrong perpetrated against an individual by an individual, it takes little practical account of the wider social context within which discrimination takes place. Secondly, by addressing *sex* discrimination rather than discrimination against women, sex discrimination law is just as guilty as the law of tort of ignoring the power dimension in sexual harassment. Most fundamentally though, sex discrimination law proscribes *differential* treatment rather than the treatment itself. This diverts legal attention away from the fact that the harassing behaviour is objectionable and offensive, whether or not it is motivated by any discriminatory intent. Moreover, it reinforces a conception of sexual inequality based on discrimination rather than subordination, on difference rather than dominance. If sexual harassment is about the abuse of power in a gendered context why present it simply as differential treatment? This does not absolve the tort system from MacKinnon's critique but it does demonstrate that both

---

4   *Sexual Harassment of Working Women*, at 171-3.
5   See the discussion of Adrian Howe's article, '"Social Injury" Revisited: Towards a Feminist Theory of Social Justice' in the introduction to Chapter 10.
6   *Sexual Harassment of Working Women*, at 161-4.
7   See Krista Schoenheider, 'A Theory of Tort Liability for Sexual Harassment in the Workplace' (1986) 34 *University of Pennsylvania Law Review* 1461.

approaches – tort and sex discrimination law – possess the same fundamental flaws.[8]

Would you make the same criticism of anti-discrimination law in your jurisdiction? In Australian jurisdictions, while sexual harassment can be encompassed within the general sex discrimination provisions, it is separately dealt with as a distinct legal harm. Does this help avoid the general comparative or differential treatment approach of sex discrimination laws? Conaghan argues that the differential model obscures the fact that sexual harassment is 'objectionable and offensive' regardless of the discriminatory intent with which it is performed. Does Conaghan's argument in turn support an understanding of sexual harassment as being about morality or offensiveness, rather than about abuse of power in the workplace?[9]

3. In some jurisdictions, the debate about whether tort law is an inadequate remedy is somewhat moot, as there may be no alternative. Until September 1995, in the Australian State of Tasmania,[10] there was no State-based anti-discrimination legislation. In some contexts, the Commonwealth *Sex Discrimination Act* 1984 could be invoked in Tasmania. However, it did not apply to local councils so when Karina Barker claimed to have been sexually harassed in her local government employment, she brought a civil action alleging, inter alia, negligence, assault and battery, and defamation.

> During the course of her employment Barker was subjected to a variety of sexual advances by her male co-workers and by her immediate superior. These included conduct which could have formed the basis for a rape complaint, repeated and persistent fondling about the breasts and buttocks, and confinement within a motor vehicle by one of the defendants. In addition, the defendants uttered repeated slurs, concerning Ms Barker's mode of dress, her conduct and her sexual proclivities, which were found to be defamatory.[11]

The defendant council was held liable both directly, for failing to provide a safe system of work, and vicariously, for the actions of its employees. A jury awarded her $120,000 in a verdict in July 1993.[12] Berns points out that the case does not extend the conceptual boundaries of any of the tort actions relied on. However, it remains significant, Berns argues, for a number of reasons. In relation to defamation, the case 'emphasised that the law was prepared to take seriously women's interests in being free from sexual innuendoes and demeaning sexual remarks. No longer were these to be treated as normal or as harmless good natured fun'.[13] And with respect to the torts of assault, battery and false imprisonment:

> First, it makes it clear that torts such as assault, battery and false imprisonment have the capacity to protect women's rights to dignity, autonomy and

---

8   Joanne Conaghan, 'Gendered Harms and the Law of Tort: Remedying (Sexual) Harassment' (1996) 16 *Oxford Journal of Legal Studies* 407 at 430. Cf Joanne Conaghan and Wade Mansell, *The Wrongs of Tort*, Pluto Press, London, 1993, at 128.
9   The extent to which sexual harassment is 'about morality' is discussed further below.
10 See now *Sex Discrimination Act* 1994 (Tas), s 17.
11 Sandra S Berns, 'The Hobart City Council Case: A Tort of Sexual Harassment for Tasmania?' (1994) 13 *University of Tasmania Law Review* 412 at 412.
12 *Barker v Lord Mayor, Alderman and Citizens of the City of Hobart, Barrat, Gentile and Stacey* No 1501/1990, Hobart Registry, Supreme Court of Tasmania (unreported jury decision; reported in the *Sunday Tasmanian*, 11 July 1993).
13 Berns, 'The Hobart City Council Case', at 413.

personal security. Conventionally, the torts of assault and battery in particular have often been associated in the minds of lawyers and lay people alike with hostile, aggressive, or physically threatening conduct. Often, this constellation of images has been interpreted from a male point of view as conduct which the reasonable man would understand as hostile, aggressive, or physically threatening. The *Hobart City Council* case is significant because it disrupts and extends these meanings. It establishes beyond doubt that both the threat of unwanted sexual contact and the actualisation of that threat violate the dignity, the autonomy and the personal security of those individuals (primarily women) who are subjected to them. The core value protected by tort actions in assault, battery and false imprisonment is the entitlement of all individuals to dignity, autonomy and personal security. Any contact which threatens the personal dignity, autonomy and security of the individual is potentially within the scope of the tort action.[14]

Do you think that tort law may have become more open to recognising sexualised injuries because of developments in anti-discrimination law? MacKinnon developed her equality claim for sexual harassment (as well as her critique of tort law) in the 1970s. Do you think the same critique would be made today?[15] Conaghan and Mansell also warn about the limitations of tort actions: they suggest that the legal formulations of the traditional torts are likely to pose severe barriers in many cases of sexual harassment.[16] For example, the tort of assault, which may provide a remedy where a battery is threatened, carries the constraint that 'threats, however violent or intimidating, are not necessarily assaults unless they pose an imminent danger'.[17] It may be difficult to establish, in some circumstances, that the sexual harassment imposes an 'imminent danger'.

4. One of the causes of action pursued in *Barker* was that of defamation. In 1991, well-known NSW footballer Andrew Ettingshausen instigated proceedings against Australian Consolidated Press for defamation after a magazine published by the company published a photograph of him in which an outline of his (unclad) penis was visible.[18] In 1993, a jury awarded him $350,000. On appeal, this amount was reduced to $100,000.[19] How do the damages awarded in this case compare to those awarded in sexual harassment cases?[20]

The development of a legal doctrine

None of the early sex discrimination statutes originally mentioned sexual harassment expressly as a particular form of actionable sex discrimination but

---

14　*Ibid*.
15　See Morgan, 'Sexual Harassment and the Public/Private Dichotomy: Equality, Morals and Manners' in Margaret Thornton (ed), *Public and Private: Feminist Legal Debates*, Oxford University Press, Melbourne, 1995.
16　Joanne Conaghan and Wade Mansell, *The Wrongs of Tort*, Pluto Press, London, 1993, Chapter 7: 'Feminist Perspectives on Tort Law: The Example of Sexual Harassment'.
17　*Ibid*, at 138.
18　*Ettingshausen v Australian Consolidated Press Ltd* (1991) 23 NSWLR 443, in which Hunt J ruled that the matter could go before a jury.
19　An account of the case can be found in 'Latest Developments' (1993) 18 *Gazette of Law and Journalism* 16.
20　For a table of those awards, see *Australian and New Zealand Equal Opportunity Law and Practice*, ¶89-960.

MacKinnon's argument that sexual harassment is sex discrimination came to be accepted in courts and tribunals in many jurisdictions.[21]

O'Callaghan v Loder was the first Australian case to hold that sexual harassment was sex discrimination.[22] In that case, Ms Sue O'Callaghan, a lift driver in the NSW Department of Main Roads, alleged that she had been sexually harassed by Loder, the Commissioner for Main Roads. In the hearing dealing with the legal question of whether the alleged sexual harassment could amount to sex discrimination under the NSW *Anti-Discrimination Act* 1977, Mathews J defined sexual harassment in the following way:

> [A] person is sexually harassed if he or she is subjected to unsolicited and unwelcome sexual conduct by a person who stands in a position of power in relation to him or her.[23]

In deciding whether this could amount to sex discrimination, the Tribunal held that:

- Sexual harassment could amount to less favourable treatment of a woman than a man on the ground of sex: it took judicial notice of the fact that heterosexual people were more common in the community than bisexuals, therefore it was likely that a male would not have been similarly treated by Loder. However, it also noted that men could be sexually harassed by other men.
- The Act prohibited discrimination in the 'terms or conditions of employment' and an employer's sexual advances, where they were made a condition of continuing in the employment or where the victim lost her job or suffered some other direct employment detriment, could amount to such discrimination.
- It was not necessary to find that there had been the loss of a 'tangible job benefit'; the existence of sexual harassment in the workplace could, of itself, amount to discriminatory terms and conditions of employment.
- In all cases:

    > The employer must either know that his conduct is unwelcome, or the circumstances must be such that he should know it. In other words, conduct which is persisted with in the face of rejection from the employee is capable of being unlawful under this head. Conduct which is continued in the face of an equivocal response may or may not be so. In all cases it is a pre-condition of liability that the complainant show both that the conduct was unwelcome in fact and that the employer either knew or ought to have known of this.[24]

- Although the Tribunal did not decide the point, it expressed some doubt as to whether an employee could claim she had been discriminated against if she had been motivated to comply with her employer's demands by a desire for advancement.

---

21 See, for example, *Meritor Savings Bank v Vinson* 477 US 57 (1986) (US); *Janzen et al v Platy Enterprises Ltd; Women's Legal Education and Action Fund (LEAF), Intervener* [1989] 1 SCR 1252 (Canada); *O'Callaghan v Loder* (1984) EOC ¶92-023 (cf (1984) EOC ¶92-022 and (1984) EOC ¶92-024) (NSW)); *R v Equal Opportunity Board; Ex parte Burns* (1984) EOC ¶92-122 (Vic).

22 (1984) EOC ¶92-023. However, the NSW *Anti-Discrimination Act* 1977 has been amended to explicitly cover sexual harassment with a definition the same as the Commonwealth Act: see *Sex Discrimination Act* 1984 (Cth), s 28A; and *Anti-Discrimination Act* 1977 (NSW), s 22A.

23 (1984) EOC ¶92-023, at 75,496.

24 *Ibid*, at 75,506.

Sexual harassment is now specifically included as an actionable form of discrimination in all Australian State and Territory legislation.[25]

While most provinces in Canada have specifically legislated to make sexual harassment an actionable form of sex discrimination, the Supreme Court of Canada has also confirmed that, even without such specific legislation, sexual harassment amounts to sex discrimination. In *Janzen v Platy Enterprises Ltd; Women's Legal Education and Action Fund (LEAF), Intervener*,[26] the Supreme Court overturned a decision of the Manitoba Court of Appeal[27] that sexual harassment does not amount to sex discrimination. The case concerned allegations by two waitresses that they had been sexually harassed by a fellow employee, the cook. They alleged he had touched them on their breasts, buttocks and abdomen and, when he had ceased the sexual touching, proceeded to harass them through delaying the filling of their orders, etc. Huband JA commenced his judgment with these words: 'I am amazed to think sexual harassment has been equated with discrimination on the basis of sex. I think they are entirely different concepts'. He continued:

> Sexual harassment is not socially acceptable conduct. Depending on the nature of it, it might constitute a criminal offence or a civil wrong under the common law. But I cannot understand how it can be equated with sexual discrimination.
>
> I suppose it is conceivable to conjure up a hypothetical situation where the two would merge into one. Suppose that an employer wants to hire men only, but in ostensible compliance with the Act he hires women as well as men. Having done so he then decides to make working conditions so miserable for the women that they will resign. His tactic is to use sexual harassment to achieve his discriminatory purpose. Such a scenario may be conceivable, but it did not happen that way in the present case and, short of that sort of format, the two concepts do not coincide. ...
>
> I am conscious, of course, that it is within the power of the legislative body to say that black is white, or that day is night, or that harassment is discrimination. At least one legislative body, namely the Parliament of Canada, has done so, but not Manitoba.[28]

The Supreme Court of Canada rejected this analysis, quoting from the LEAF factum presented in the case:

> [S]exual harassment is a form of sex discrimination because it denies women equality of opportunity in employment because of their sex.[29]
>
> To argue [*as the Manitoba Court of Appeal did*] that the sole factor underlying the discriminatory action was the sexual attractiveness of the appellants and to say that their gender was irrelevant strains credulity. Sexual attractiveness cannot be separated from gender. The similar gender of both appellants is not mere coincidence, it is fundamental to understanding what they experienced. All female employees were potentially subject to sexual harassment

---

25 In addition to the NSW and Commonwealth legislation noted above, see, for example, *Equal Opportunity Act* 1995 (Vic), ss 85-95.
26 [1989] 1 SCR 1252.
27 [1987] 1 WWR 385; 43 Man R (2d) 293 (Man CA).
28 *Ibid*, at 396. For commentaries on this case see Mariann Burka, 'Sexual Harassment: Manitoba's Step Backward – A Case Comment on *Govereau and Janzen v Platy Enterprises Ltd*' (1987) 16 *Manitoba Law Journal* 245; MA Hickling, 'Employer's Liability for Sexual Harassment' (1988) 17 *Manitoba Law Journal* 124. In fact, before the case reached the Canadian Supreme Court, Manitoba had enacted legislation making sexual harassment an actionable form of sex discrimination.
29 *Janzen v Platy* [1989] 1 SCR 1252 at 1290-1 (quoting the LEAF factum).

by the respondent Grammas. ....Because they were women, the appellants were subject to a disadvantage to which no man at the restaurant would have been subject.[30]

The US Supreme Court has similarly confirmed the position reached in other courts and tribunals that sexual harassment is a form of sex discrimination. In *Meritor v Vinson*,[31] the court held that sexual harassment was actionable sex discrimination even if no direct tangible job detriment had been suffered and decided that consent, or 'voluntary' participation, was not a defence under American discrimination law (Title VII) (though the advances must be 'unwelcome').[32]

The following section looks at how these legislative and judicial understandings have worked in practice.

Whose perspective?

Notwithstanding the judicial recognition that sexual harassment amounts to sex discrimination, successfully establishing a case has not proved easy. In the trial of *O'Callaghan v Loder*, the plaintiff failed to make good her claim as the Tribunal held that Ms O'Callaghan had not communicated to her employer that his advances were unwelcome to her. The Tribunal recognised that:

> Persons in positions of power in the employment sphere must be aware of the ramifications of their positions: That employees of lower status might well be reluctant to voice their true feelings for fear of employment-related repercussions. Accordingly, the higher the disparity between the status of the parties involved, the greater the obligation on the part of the employer to observe and respect any unwillingness or reluctance shown by the employee.[33]

However, despite this recognition, the Tribunal insisted that:

> [T]here is also an onus on the employee to make her unwillingness known to the employer. One can entirely sympathise with an employee, such as the complainant, who has reservations about expressing her true feelings as she genuinely, if unnecessarily, fears for her job. An employee should not be placed into a situation where she feels constrained to endure her employer's continued advances because she fears employment-related retaliation if she expresses her resistance. That should be one of the evils sought to be remedied if one is to have effective laws against sexual harassment in the workplace. On the other hand, one cannot have workable laws which proscribe activities solely upon the basis of the attitude of the recipient of those activities. There must also be a requirement that the recipient – in this case, Miss O'Callaghan – took some steps to make her attitude known to the employer. The onus of showing that she did so in this case rests upon her.[34]

And, on the evidence available to the Tribunal, it concluded:

> In the event, we cannot be satisfied that Mr Loder should have been aware that his conduct would be unwelcome to Miss O'Callaghan. The fact is that we are

---

30 *Ibid*, at 1290.
31 *Meritor Savings Bank v Vinson* 477 US 57 (1986).
32 However, the Supreme Court went on to hold that it did not follow from their finding that consent was irrelevant, 'that a complainant's sexually provocative speech or dress is irrelevant as a matter of law in determining whether he or she found particular sexual advances unwelcome' (*ibid*, at 69).
33 *O'Callaghan v Loder* (1984) EOC ¶92-024 at 75,514.
34 *Ibid*, at 75,514-15.

unable to reach any degree of satisfaction as to the nature of any sexual activity which preceded this incident, or as to what took place during it. We do know that it caused considerable distress to Miss O'Callaghan. But we cannot infer merely from the fact of her distress that Mr Loder's conduct must have been so extreme that he should have been aware of its unwelcome nature. To do so would be far too speculative in relation to a matter which she must prove. This is particularly so in the light of the fact that Miss O'Callaghan was apparently more upset by the rumours than she was by any conduct of Mr Loder's on this occasion.[35]

Note

1. Helen Mills has criticised the Board's insistence on the requirement that the employer knows that his sexual advance is unwelcome and unsolicited.[36] She argues that this is importing a requirement of intention to discriminate which, at least at the time she was writing, was not required to establish a successful sex discrimination claim when sexual harassment was not involved.[37] Furthermore, she argues that this test substitutes the perspective of the harasser for that of the victim. Mills suggests that, on the Board's own understanding of sexual harassment, the correct test is 'whether the sexual conduct creates an unwelcome feature of the employment'.[38] The Board does appear to be aware of the difficulty of telling an employer that his sexual advances are unwelcome when the employee fears loss of her job. However, it is not prepared to consider only the perspective of the victim. Would it be a more useful approach to the development of 'workable' laws on sexual harassment to consider only the victim's perspective?

    Alternatively, is the Board's approach, which envisages liability for sexual harassment not only when an harasser subjectively knows his approaches are unwelcome, but also where he ought to have known they were unwelcome, a more appropriate middle ground? Recall that, when the Board applied this more objective test, it was not prepared to find that Mr Loder, the Commissioner for Main Roads, should have known that his advances were unwelcome to Ms O'Callaghan, a lift-driver in the department. Given this, perhaps an objective test is, in practice, of limited assistance. If a victim-focused test is rejected and the traditional objective test envisaged by the Board is also seen as inappropriate, might a more appropriate test be to focus attention not so much on whether the advance was unwelcome or should have been seen as unwelcome, but rather on whether the employment relationship between the perpetrator and the target of the alleged harassment was such that the sexual relationship could never be consented to? Does this sort of approach imply that women are always already victims and incapable of consent?

---

35 *Ibid*, at 75,515.
36 Helen Mills, 'Sexual Harassment as Sex Discrimination' (1984) 9 *Legal Service Bulletin* 5 at 6.
37 She cites the unreported case of *Harrison v Watson*, noted in the 1979 Annual Report of the NSW Anti-Discrimination Board at 10-11. But see now the Victorian cases of *Chief General Manager, Department of Health v Arumugam* (1987) EOC ¶92-195 and *Teed v Mount Alexander Hospital* (1987) EOC ¶92-211.
38 Mills, 'Sexual Harassment as Sex Discrimination', at 6.

The 'reasonable victim/person/woman/employee'

Effectively, there are two forms of sexual harassment cognisable by sex discrimination law. These were described in *O'Callaghan v Loder* above. The first is where the sexual harassment leads to loss of a job or some other direct tangible job benefit, known in the United States, as quid pro quo discrimination. The second is where there is no loss of a tangible job benefit but the sexual harassment or the atmosphere created by it becomes such a feature of the job that it amounts to a term or condition of the employment – in the United States, known as hostile work environment discrimination. Both forms of sexual harassment have been successfully litigated in Australia.[39] The recognition of a 'hostile work environment' by courts and tribunals, particularly if that hostility is not solely directed towards an individual woman, raises the issue of the reasonableness of women's reactions in acute form.

In *Rabidue v Osceola*,[40] Vivienne Rabidue alleged that she was discriminated against by her employer, Osceola Refining Company, in that she was exposed to a hostile work environment. Ms Rabidue was employed as a credit and office manager. According to Keith J, on appeal (and it is interesting to note that more details of the work situation appear in this dissenting appeal judgment than in the trial court's decision):

> In common work areas plaintiff and other female employees were exposed daily to displays of nude or partially clad women belonging to a number of male employees at Osceola. One poster, which remained on the wall for eight years, showed a prone woman who had a golf ball on her breasts with a man standing over her, golf club in hand, yelling "Fore." And one desk plaque declared "Even male chauvinist pigs need love." Plaintiff testified the posters offended her and her female co-workers.
>
> In addition, Computer Division Supervisor Doug Henry regularly spewed anti-female obscenity. Henry routinely referred to women as "whores," "cunt", "pussy" and "tits." *See Rabidue v Osceola*, 584 F Supp 419, 423 (ED Mich 1984). Of plaintiff, Henry specifically remarked "All that bitch needs is a good lay" and called her "fat ass." Plaintiff arranged at least one meeting of female employees to discuss Henry and repeatedly filed written complaints on behalf of herself and other female employees who feared losing their jobs if they complained directly.[41]

Rabidue failed in her action, both at trial court level and on appeal. The trial court held that the vulgarity of Henry was annoying but minor and, in relation to the posters, held:

> The Court believes that the posters had but a negligible effect in this case. No evidence was offered indicating that the plaintiff had any especial sensitivity to erotic pictures. Furthermore, as the Court has mentioned the ... [*Equal Employment Opportunity Commission*] standard pertains to the average female employee. In other words the test is an objective one.
>
> For better or worse, modern America features open displays of written and pictorial erotica. Shopping centers, candy stores and prime time television regularly display pictures of naked bodies and erotic real or simulated sex acts.

---

39 For a case of hostile work environment harassment, see, for example, *Horne and McIntosh v Press Clough Joint Venture and the Metals and Engineering Workers' Union (WA)* (1994) EOC ¶92-556.
40 584 F Supp 419 (1984) (District Court, Michigan); 805 F 2d 611 (6th Cir 1986).
41 805 F 2d 611 at 623-4.

Living in this milieu, the average American should not be *legally* offended by sexually explicit posters.[42]

Rabidue appealed to the US Court of Appeals, Sixth Circuit. The court dismissed her appeal, with Keith, Circuit Judge, dissenting.

Vivienne Rabidue, Plaintiff-Appellant v Osceola Refining Company, A Division of Texas-American Petrochemicals, Inc, Defendant-Appellee
805 F 2d 611 (6th Cir 1986)

KEITH, Circuit Judge, concurring in part, dissenting in part.

[626] [T]he reasonable person perspective fails to account for the wide divergence between most women's views of appropriate sexual conduct and those of men. ... I would have courts adopt the perspective of the reasonable victim which simultaneously allows courts to consider salient sociological differences as well as shield employers from the neurotic complainant. ... Moreover, unless the outlook of the reasonable woman is adopted, the defendants as well as the courts are permitted to sustain ingrained notions of reasonable behavior fashioned by the offenders, in this case, men. ...

[627] I conclude that for actionable offensive environment claims, the relevant inquiry is whether the conduct complained of is offensive to the reasonable woman. Either the environment affects her ability to perform or it does not. The backgrounds and experience of the defendant's supervisors and employees is irrelevant.

Nor can I agree with the majority's notion that the effect of pin-up posters and misogynous language in the workplace can have only a minimal effect on female employees and should not be deemed hostile or offensive "when considered in the context of a society that condones and publicly features and commercially exploits open displays of written and pictorial erotica at newsstands, on prime-time television, at the cinema and in other public places." At 622. "Society" in this scenario must primarily refer to the unenlightened; I hardly believe reasonable women condone the pervasive degradation and exploitation of female sexuality perpetuated in American culture. In fact, pervasive societal approval thereof and of other stereotypes stifles female potential and instills the debased sense of self worth which accompanies stigmatization. The presence of pin-ups and misogynous language in the workplace can only evoke and confirm the debilitating norms by which women are primarily and contemptuously valued as objects of male sexual fantasy. That some men would condone and wish to perpetuate such behavior is not surprising. However, the relevant inquiry at hand is what the reasonable woman would find offensive, not society, which at one point also condoned slavery. I conclude that sexual posters and anti-female language can seriously affect the psychological well being of the reasonable woman and interfere with her ability to perform her job. ...

Notes

1. MacKinnon has noted in *Feminism Unmodified*: 'She [Rabidue] did not say she was offended, she said she was discriminated against based on her sex'.[43] Has the legal claim of sexual harassment been adequately understood as a

---

42 584 F Supp 419 at 433. See also the majority judgment in the Court of Appeals (805 F 2d 611 at 622), referred to by Keith J in the extract quoted below.
43 *Feminism Unmodified*, Harvard University Press, Cambridge, MA, 1987, at 115.

claim of discrimination rather than one of offensiveness (or bad manners)?[44] Note that the amendments to the Commonwealth sexual harassment provisions enacted in 1992 continue to define sexual harassment as an unwelcome request for sexual favours, an unwelcome sexual advance or engaging in other unwelcome conduct of a sexual nature but this is unlawful only if 'a reasonable person, having regard to all the circumstances, would have anticipated that the person harassed would be *offended*, humiliated or intimidated'.[45] Does this legislative definition entrench the understanding of sexual harassment as merely a breach of good manners? On the other hand, does a target of sexual harassment necessarily want to describe her experience as one of being humiliated or intimidated?

Frances Olsen has suggested that one reason for the comparative success of sexual harassment claims is because of an unconscious invocation of the public/private distinction. It is seen as inappropriate that a quintessentially 'private' activity, sexuality, which should be kept in the family, is brought into the public world of work.[46] Do you agree that this perception, rather than an understanding of the subordination suffered by women due to sexual harassment in the workplace, is more likely to have informed tribunal, judicial and now legislative understandings of the sexual harassment action?[47] Note that Conaghan, in the passage cited above describing the limitations of understanding sexual harassment as sex discrimination, stated: 'This [*the proscription in sex discrimination law of differential treatment rather than proscribing the treatment itself*] diverts legal attention away from the fact that the harassing behaviour is objectionable and offensive, whether or not it is motivated by any discriminatory intent'. Does this suggest an understanding of sexual harassment as 'about morality' rather more than 'about equality'?

2. How differently might claims of sexual harassment (or indeed, other legal claims) be dealt with were Keith J's standard of the 'reasonable woman' to be adopted? The standard has in fact been adopted in a number of US jurisdictions.[48] In the 1988 *Sheiban* case,[49] three women receptionists employed by Dr Sheiban alleged that he had sexually harassed them, both in their interviews for the job (by, for example, asking whether they had sex with their boyfriends) and while they were employed. The harassment during employment included touching, lowering the zips on their uniforms and sexualised comments, including protestations of his love for them. In relation to the employment harassment, Einfeld J found that harassment had occurred, but

---

44 For an argument that sexual harassment should be understood as a breach of good manners, see Jeffrey Minson, *Questions of Conduct: Sexual Harassment, Citizenship, Government,* MacMillan, Hampshire, 1993; cf, in response, Morgan, 'Sexual Harassment and the Public/Private Dichotomy'.

45 *Sex Discrimination Act* 1984 (Cth), s 28A(1) emphasis added; see also *Anti-Discrimination Act* 1977 (NSW), s 22A; *Anti-Discrimination Act* 1991 (Qld), s 119; *Equal Opportunity Act* (1984) (SA), s 87(11); *Equal Opportunity Act* 1995 (Vic), s 85; *Discrimination Act* 1991 (ACT), s 58; *Anti-Discrimination Act* (NT), s 22: all State and Territory legislation is now in the same or similar terms.

46 Frances Olsen, 'The Family and the Market: A Study of Ideology and Legal Reform' (1983) 96 *Harvard Law Review* 1497 at 1551, note 207.

47 See Morgan, 'Sexual Harassment and the Public/Private Dichotomy'.

48 See Kathryn Abrams, 'The Reasonable Woman: Sense and Sensibility in Sexual Harassment Law' [1995] *Dissent* 48 and Caroline A Forell and Donna M Matthews, *A Law of Her Own: The Reasonable Woman as a Measure of Man,* New York University Press, New York and London, 2000.

49 *Hall, Oliver and Reid v Sheiban* (1988) EOC ¶92-227.

that it was trivial and did not warrant an award of damages. Einfeld J found that 'a reasonable woman' would not have taken the respondent seriously, and that any 'sensible woman' would have reacted with humour or pity to the respondent's alleged professing of love to the complainant and his desire to have a relationship with her some time in the future. Whose standard is being applied here? The decision was overturned by the Full Federal Court.[50] How does such an approach fit within the 'equal treatment/special treatment' debate discussed in Chapter 3 above? What advantages or disadvantages do you perceive for women in courts' adopting different standards according to the sex of the plaintiff?

3. Lucinda Finley has taken issue with a reasonable woman standard. She argues:

> While victims should have the perspectives and experiences of people like themselves taken into account in evaluating their situations, the "reasonable woman" standard does not fully solve the problems at hand. What does a reasonable woman standard do for a man who finds the conduct at a place such as Osceola offensive and painful? What about a man who works in the home and reacts as a reasonable mother would? In other words, substituting a reasonable woman standard to judge the conduct of women, but not going further to question the inclusiveness of the norms informing the reasonable person standard, implies that women's experiences and reactions are something for women only, rather than normal human responses. Since women are a significant proportion of persons, their experiences should count as the experiences of a reasonable person, not merely as the experiences of a reasonable woman.
>
> A reasonable woman standard may also create the perception that the law allows "special" treatment for women – that it lets them off the hook with regard to expected normal, (that is, "male") behavior.[51]

4. Kathryn Abrams has expanded this critique.

> The first goal of the "reasonable woman" standard was to emphasize the gendered character of sexual harassment and prevent resort to a "common sense" that was likely to preserve the status quo. The second goal was to permit access to a distinct set of perspectives that would open the way for a transformation of workplace norms. ... This second, and arguably more important, task can still be performed under a "reasonable person" standard.
>
> My own argument begins with the anti-essentialist insight that neither modes of knowing nor particular bodies of knowledge are inextricably linked to biological or social gender. There are things that women are more likely to know by virtue of having lived as women. There are practices – such as those involving devaluation or sexualization – to which they are likely to have a heightened sensitivity by virtue of having experienced them, heard about them repeatedly, or seen them applied to other women. But this likelihood cannot be collapsed into inevitability: some women have had few of the experiences that produce such sensitivity; others respond with indifference or denial; women who are aware of discriminatory practices may perceive them in different ways. Just as being female does not guarantee transformative perceptions of sexual conduct in the workplace, being male does not exclude the possibility of having, or developing, them. If perceptions of sexual harassment do not depend solely

---

50 *Hall v Sheiban Pty Ltd* (1989) EOC ¶92-250.
51 Lucinda Finley, 'A Break in the Silence: Including Women's Issues in a Torts Course' (1989) 1 *Yale Journal of Law and Feminism* 41 at 64.

on biology, life experience, or gender-specific modes of knowing, but rather on varied sources of information regarding women's inequality – if such perceptions, in other words, are a matter not of innate common sense but of informed sensibility – then they can be cultivated in a range of women and men. The "reasonable person" standard, properly elaborated, might be a vehicle for the courts to play a role in this educative process.[52]

Abrams goes on to suggest four types of information that 'could be offered by expert testimony or by counsel in framing their clients' claims.[53] The first is information about 'barriers that women have faced, and continue to face in the workplace' including that they are new to many workplaces, much of the work they do is underpaid and undervalued, they have been met with hostility when entering many non-traditional jobs, glass ceilings, and failure to accommodate their disproportionate parenting responsibilities:

> As a result, many women feel they are marginal participants in the workplace, that their hold on their job or on the respect of their superiors is tenuous and subject to factors not within their control. Sexualised conduct in the workplace may interact with all of these factors, inducing a sense of precariousness or professional threat that it would not necessarily induce in a man.[54]

Secondly, information on 'the role of sexualized treatment in the workplace' is required. While recognising that women do see sex as pleasurable, '[y]et among the most familiar meanings, themes of intimidation, objectification, and devaluation are readily discernible. High rates of sexual assault by strangers and acquaintances have led many women to feel that their sexuality makes them physically vulnerable. The "myth of the black rapist" has produced a complicated legacy for black women, in which fears about physical security vie with suspicions of racial exploitation'.[55] This kind of information, she argues, is required as a backdrop to sexualised treatment in the workplace 'so that professedly well-intentioned men who defend sexual talk as harmless humour can understand that it may have connotations they do not see'.[56] Thirdly, information on the effects of sexual harassment on women and other co-workers is required and, finally, information on the variety of ways women respond to harassment should also be available. She concludes:

> The court's embrace of the "reasonable person" standard is not an unequivocal step forward. It avoids promulgating falsely unifying images of women. But it also fails to jolt judges into recognition that their intuitive perspectives are not the only, or the preferable, vantage point on the claims before them. The challenge confronting feminist advocates is to provide this jolt by other means; not through the jarring, but so far unelaborated, mechanism of a gendered referent, but through illumination of those factors that have shaped women's responses to sexual harassment. If viewed as an invitation to offer concrete information about women's lives, the "reasonable person" standard may yet help legal decision makers to create a less oppressive workplace.[57]

---

52   Abrams, 'The Reasonable Woman', at 51-2.
53   *Ibid*, at 52.
54   *Ibid*.
55   *Ibid*.
56   *Ibid*, at 53.
57   *Ibid*, at 54.

Do you agree with these critiques of the reasonable woman standard? Do you think if tribunals and courts were presented with the kind of information Abrams has suggested, they would receive the kind of 'jolt' she says is required? Would this information be admissible in proceedings in your jurisdiction? Is there other information that would be useful (and admissible)?

5. As noted, Abrams suggests that the experience of sexual harassment for African-American women involves 'fears about physical security' vying with 'suspicions of racial exploitation'. Is the experience necessarily one of rivalry between these two perspectives? Consider the relevance of this description in the context of a non-English speaking background woman sexually harassed in Australia. Ekaterina Djokic made complaints of racial and sex discrimination and sexual harassment during her employment as a packer in a meatworks.[58] Under the heading of 'sex discrimination and race discrimination', the HREOC found that she was described by fellow workers, both women and men, as a 'wog bitch' or a 'Greek bitch' in part because she refused to take unauthorised breaks with her fellow workers, but rather kept on working, and had made complaints about the shoddy work of her fellow workers.[59] Under the heading of sexual harassment, the Tribunal discussed a series of complaints. It rejected a complaint that the first respondent, Mr Sinclair, a foreman in the meatworks, had 'flick[ed] the back of her bra strap and touch[ed] the top of her trousers'.[60] She had also alleged 'that the first respondent would refer to her on a regular basis as a "fucking wog bitch", "stupid wog bitch" when she commenced working on his chain'. No specific findings of fact were made on this and other allegations, but the Tribunal found 'that his general demeanour towards the complainant over a sustained period, described by the complainant as "pushing her", reflected a hostility, based on her sex, that was oppressive to her and such as to constitute sexual harassment'.[61] The final allegation of sexual harassment related to the events which led to her sacking. The Tribunal accepted the complainant's version of what happened:

> She said that she was approached by the first respondent at about 7:00am [*on the morning she was sacked*] ... and was asked by him whether she was available to do overtime that day. She replied "No". She then alleges that Mr Sinclair pressed her for a reason why she wasn't available to do overtime. When she refused to tell him he allegedly said to her "Fuck you woman. I'll bring you to your knees." She explained that a heated argument ensued in which she swore at Mr Sinclair, and as a result she was told by him to leave the boning room. At approximately 8:30am, the complainant was taken to a meeting for the purpose of investigating the dispute. Mr Malone [*the boning room superintendent*] was present at this meeting to represent the second respondent and three union members were present to represent the AMIEU and the complainant. The outcome of the meeting was that the complainant was dismissed. The reason for dismissal was because the complainant swore at a foreman.

The Tribunal concluded:

> I have no hesitation in characterising such behaviour [*the behaviour of Mr Sinclair*] as sexual harassment. It was a serious abuse of power. ...

---

58 *Djokic v Sinclair* (1994) EOC ¶92-643 (a partial report).
59 *Djokic v Sinclair*, HREOC transcript, at para 31.
60 *Ibid*, at para 32.
61 *Ibid*.

> I view this episode as the culmination of a history of discrimination of the complainant in the workplace on the ground of both her sex and her race and therefore characterise it as unlawful conduct for which the second respondent [*the company running the meatworks*] is responsible.[62]

Ms Djokic had sought reinstatement but, as the second respondent no longer operated the meatworks, the Commission decided it was not able to do this. Instead, it awarded a sum of $11,000 under each of the Acts, with Mr Sinclair ordered to pay $2000 and the company $20,000. At one point the Tribunal describes the allegations made in this case as one of 'intertwined' race and sex discrimination. Is this an adequate description of the complaints described? Did the Tribunal deal with them as 'intertwined'? Why were separate awards made in relation to sex discrimination and race discrimination? Do you think the allegations dealt with by the tribunal explicitly as sexual harassment should be described as 'intertwined' race and sex discrimination? Do you think these allegations should be dealt with as *sexual* harassment?

6. In a discussion of anti-lesbian harassment,[63] Celia Kitzinger addresses the issue of 'intersectional' harassment. She counsels against a focus on the intention of the harasser, and instead advocates a focus on the target of the harassment:

> We are harassed as whole people: we don't ever stop being all of whom we are. When anti-semitic comments are made because of my surname, being lesbian may not be irrelevant: I have retained my 'maiden' name and my heterosexual sister, who took her husband's non-Jewish name, is not subjected to such comments. My friend who is subjected to racist taunt as she walks through a hostile neighbourhood late at night is certainly harassed because she is black, but the opportunity for the harassment arises as she returns home late at night from a lesbian bar. We do not experience our oppressions as fragmented according to discrete identity categories, nor should we have to label what happens to us as though it could be neatly categorised into mutually exclusive or competing oppressions.
>
> The notion of anti-lesbianism which is separate and clearly distinguishable from any other form of oppression can only be a 'prototypical' white, middle-class, able-bodied, gentile concept of what anti-lesbianism is and how it works. *All* lesbians suffer from anti-lesbianism, although the form it takes varies depending on the race/ethnicity, class, age and disability status of the lesbian at whom it is directed. For example, the same man who, drawing on racial and class stereotypes of British women, taunts a middle-class white lesbian with frigidity or sexual inexperience, may assume that a working-class black lesbian is sexually promiscuous, has extensive experience of sex with men, and is continually ready and willing for sexual encounters. The black woman's experience is not anti-lesbianism *plus* racism, but anti-lesbianism *structured by* racism, or racism *structured by* anti-lesbianism. The emphasis she chooses to give this may depend on her audience and her intentions: with black heterosexual women, it may be necessary to speak of the former, in order that they notice her oppression *as a lesbian*; with white lesbians, it may be necessary to speak of the latter, in order that they may notice her oppression *as a black woman*. ... The

---

62　*Ibid*, at paras 36-38. There was also a further finding of sex discrimination in the company's failure to train her as a slicer. All the slicers in the workplace were men and they had refused to train any women. This refusal 'was meekly accepted by management' (at para 39).

63　Celia Kitzinger, 'Anti-lesbian Harassment' in Clare Brant and Yun Lee Too (eds), *Rethinking Sexual Harassment*, Pluto Press, London, 1994.

question 'Was it anti-lesbianism, or was it racism?' sets up a false dichotomy. There is no 'prototypical' lesbian, harassed 'purely' for her lesbianism, against which all other lesbians' oppression can be compared in order to determine the extent to which their victimisation can be said to be 'additional' to hers. Oppressions are not additive, but interactive.

... [T]here is much to be gained from the assumption that any incident of harassment .... is directed at the whole person and can be appropriately labelled anti-lesbian *and* racist *and* disableist *and* ... whatever other aspects of our identity are routinely under attack.[64]

Would it be possible for, say, a Greek-Australian lesbian to take this approach in a legal forum?

Gender neutrality

Most sexual harassment laws are expressed in gender-neutral terms; that is, the law says that both men and women can (equally) be subject to sexual harassment. Because the Commonwealth Constitution only allows the Commonwealth to enact laws on specific matters (reserving a general and residual law-making power to the States), the Commonwealth has only limited powers with respect to sex discrimination. The Commonwealth's power to enact laws to eliminate discrimination against women arises from s 51(xxix) of the Constitution, the external affairs power. This power allows the Commonwealth to enact laws that give domestic force to international agreements to which Australia is a party.[65] The sexual harassment provisions in the *Sex Discrimination Act* in so far as they apply to women generally (that is, other than those who could be covered under other provisions of the Constitution, because, for example, they work in corporations: see s 51(xx)) are based on the international Convention on the Elimination of All Forms of Discrimination Against Women. To be valid, the legislation needs to conform reasonably closely to the terms of the Convention.[66]

In 1988 a Federal Court judge upheld the constitutional validity of the sexual harassment provisions.[67] Spender J was faced with an argument that, insofar as the sexual harassment provisions of s 28 dealt only with sexual harassment of women, they did not implement Art 15(1) of the Convention on the Elimination of All Forms of Discrimination Against Women and were thus unconstitutional. That Article provides that 'State Parties shall accord to women equality with men before the law'. Spender J stated:

> To give effect to the Convention, the legislation must be directed at the elimination of discrimination against women. Legislation which was directed at the elimination of discrimination generally could not fairly be characterized as "legislation giving effect to the Convention". The argument of the respondents assumes that one cannot promote the exercise and enjoyment of rights "on the basis of equality with men" by prohibiting discrimination against women. There is implicit in this argument a necessity for a legislative prohibition of sexual harassment of men to be in existence.

---

64 *Ibid*, at 132-3.
65 See *Koowarta v Bjelke-Petersen* (1982) 153 CLR 168 and *Commonwealth v Tasmania* (1983) 158 CLR 1 (*Tasmanian Dams* case).
66 See *Tasmanian Dams* case.
67 *Aldridge v Booth* (1988) EOC ¶92-222.

I reject this argument. It would seriously restrict the operation of the Convention, and its implementation. It puts an unwarranted premium on the existence of legislation, which may or may not reflect the true position in fact.

If this argument of the respondent be right, legislation prohibiting the killing of young girls would be inconsistent and contrary to the terms of the Convention, unless there was in existence legislation prohibiting the killing of young boys, even though, in fact, the killing of young girls was widespread, and the killing of young boys non-existent or rare.[68]

Notes

1. What model of equality, of those described in Chapter 3, is Spender J adopting here? What model was adopted by the respondent?
2. Another variation on the gender-neutral theme is what MacKinnon has described as the bisexual defence.[69] This is the argument (rejected in *O'Callaghan v Loder*) that a harasser could be found to be 'bisexual', thereby harassing men and women equally, and thus not subjecting a woman to treatment on the ground of her sex, different from that to which a man would be subjected. MacKinnon noted in 1987 that this argument had been raised in the United States, but was met with the response that the issue was a question of fact (rather than law) and had not subsequently been used.[70] That the argument still has some rhetorical force is indicated by Wilcox J's judgment in *Hall, Oliver and Reid v Sheiban*, where he was not prepared to find that Sheiban would not have treated a male applicant for a receptionist's job in the same way as he treated the women complainants.[71]
3. Drucilla Cornell has developed a new and gender-neutral definition of sexual harassment. She suggests that sexual harassment should be redefined as:

   a) unilaterally imposed sexual requirements in the context of unequal power, or
   b) the creation and perpetuation of a work environment which enforces sexual shame by reducing individuals to projected stereotypes or objectified fantasies of their "sex" so as to undermine the primary good of self-respect, or
   c) employment-related retaliation against a subordinate employee or, in the case of a university, a student, for a consensually mutually desired sexual relationship.[72]

What advantages and disadvantages, if any, flow from a definition of sexual harassment which is gender-neutral? How does Cornell's definition compare to the definition in the *Sex Discrimination Act* (and essentially reproduced in all States and Territories) noted above?

---

68 *Ibid*, at 77,095.
69 *Feminism Unmodified*, at 108.
70 *Ibid*.
71 (1989) EOC ¶92-250 at 77,406. Wilcox J was here discussing whether Dr Sheiban's behaviour could be described as sex discrimination.
72 Drucilla Cornell, *The Imaginary Domain: Abortion, Pornography and Sexual Harassment*, Routledge, New York, 1995, at 170.

Sexual harassment beyond the workplace: Feminists create 'victims'?

Sexual harassment is obviously not something that happens only in the workplace. Towards the end of 1991 two students alleged that they were sexually harassed by the Master of Ormond College at a student party after the formal valedictory dinner. The college is a prestigious residential institution for students at Melbourne University. One student alleged that the master squeezed her on the breast twice while dancing with her; the other alleged that the Master had invited her into his office, locked the door, admitted that he had 'indecent' thoughts about her, told her she was beautiful, touched her hands and breasts and asked for a kiss.[73] The students (in fact it appears that there were initially five students alleging that they were sexually harassed that night) originally tried to pursue an informal complaint with the then Chairman of the College Council, Sir Daryl Dawson, then a High Court judge. Sir Daryl later resigned from the Council. Some three months later the College set up a committee of three to 'formalise' the complaints (of the two women who persisted). The sub-committee reported to the Council that the women had made their complaints in good faith, but indicated its confidence in the Master.[74] The two students then made complaints to the police. The Master of the College was charged with two counts of indecent assault. In relation to the first complaint, he was found guilty by a magistrate. This decision was appealed and he was acquitted, the judge saying that the complainant was 'an excellent witness' but the charge had not been proved 'beyond reasonable doubt', the requisite criminal standard of proof.[75] On the second charge, he was acquitted, the magistrate saying that, although he believed something had happened in the study, he could not determine what and the Master should receive the benefit of the doubt.[76] The Master resigned from the College. The two complainants had also pursued a discrimination complaint against the College with the Victorian Equal Opportunity Commission. These were conciliated and the settlement included a public apology to the two young women:

(i) 'the College acknowledges that the complaints could have been handled differently by the Ormond College Council and ... with more sensitivity and with a greater degree of apparent impartiality'; and that
(ii) 'it did not have in place an adequate policy and procedure which may have enabled the complaints to be resolved within the college'.
(iii) The College also accepted that 'the students had acted honourably and brought the matter to the attention of the appropriate persons in a discreet manner'.
(iv) 'The College regrets any hurt and distress suffered by the students'.[77]

The criminal proceedings were reported in the media. Helen Garner, a well-known Australian author, on seeing a newspaper report of the criminal proceedings, wrote to the Master describing the actions of the young women as 'punitive', 'appallingly destructive, priggish and pitiless'.[78] Garner then proceeded to write a

---

73 See Helen Garner, *The First Stone: Some Questions About Sex and Power*, Picador Pan Macmillan, Sydney, 1995, at 1-13.
74 See Jenna Mead, 'Sexual Harassment and Feminism: Jenna Mead talks to Amanda Lohrey' (1995) 2 *Republica* 166.
75 See *The First Stone*, at 36.
76 *Ibid*, at 19.
77 Mead, 'Sexual Harassment and Feminism', at 173.
78 *The First Stone*, at 16. See Morgan, 'The Power of Storytelling: A quest for a public discourse on sexual harassment', in Phillip Tahmindjis (ed), *The Law and Sexual Harassment: International, Domestic and Comparative Aspects*, Kluwer, forthcoming 2002.

book about the case, *The First Stone,* published in March 1995. The book persisted with this theme, arguing that the young women 'over-reacted' in going to the police with their complaint.

Given that Garner's book is written in a fictional or story-telling style, it is often difficult to analyse precisely her argument. Annie Cossins has proposed the following possibilities:

> Garner's primary focus in *The First Stone* [*TFS*] is on the *nature* of Gregory's [*the Master's*] alleged sexual behaviour and its apparent harmlessness. Since the students' response to his sexual behaviour is the subject of a considerable amount of scorn and invective on the part of Garner, it is important to examine what it is about the *nature* of Gregory's alleged sexual behaviour that made her decide that the criminal justice system is the inappropriate site for resolution and redress. Is it because
>
> - [1][79] the alleged acts of sexual assault were really 'clumsy passes' [*TFS*, at 101], 'hapless social blunders' [*TFS*, at 101], and 'foolish things' [*TFS*, at 93] done at a party which every woman, at some time or other, is required to deal with as a natural part of heterosexual relations and should just be put up with as a 'minor unpleasantness'? [*TFS*, at 40]. In other words, are uninvited sexual advances an inherent expression of masculinity which should be accommodated by women who are charged with protecting men's egos: to be 'cool enough to ... ask for an acknowledgment and an apology' [*TFS*, at 92], to be forgiving and protect them from the consequences of their behaviour?
> - [2] physical harm is more serious than psychological harm and there was no physical force which caused the two women demonstrable harm?
> - [3] Garner believes that the two young women *attracted* the alleged uninvited sexual advances because of their physical attributes and/or style of dress?
> - [4] the alleged offender was well-educated with a prestigious academic position and, on those grounds, should have been protected from the consequences of his behaviour? Would Garner's concern have been as great if the alleged offender was, say, the gardener of Ormond College?
>
> [5] Or does Garner have an unstated belief that women's bodies are *acceptable* sites for playing out male desire (up to the point where no demonstrable physical harm occurs) because men 'who behave as Colin Shepherd [*this is the pseudonym given to the Master of Ormond College by Garner*] was accused of doing' are 'just poor bastards' who 'aren't scary or powerful' [*TFS*, at 99] and are merely responding to eros (the essential ingredient in heterosexual relations) which must never be sacrificed?

Notes

1. Is it possible to provide support in *The First Stone* (and subsequent statements by Garner on her position) for all these alternative theses? Cossins has clearly supported her suggestive analysis in relation to alternatives [1] and [5] by citation to *The First Stone*. In relation to alternative [2], Garner states:

   > I know that between 'being made to feel uncomfortable' and 'violence against women' lies a vast range of male and female behaviours. If we deny this, we enfeeble language and drain it of meaning. We insult the suffering of

---

79 We have added the numbers to Cossins' points for ease of reference.

women who have met real violence, and we distort the subtleties of human interaction into caricatures that can only serve as propaganda for war.[80]

Morgan has responded to this analysis:

> Obviously there's a scale from discomfort to violence, a scale that focuses on the extent of physical invasion, but we might also want to think about the links between the harm of rape and sexual harassment and uncover the commonalities between them. As ... Carol Smart has suggested 'they are both demonstrations of the same problem of women being constituted as sexualized bodies' [Smart, *Law, Crime and Sexuality,* Sage, London, 1995, at 223]. I'm not suggesting they are 'the same' but I am suggesting that they call on similar cultural sources for their effect. To take sexual harassment seriously is not to 'insult the suffering of women who have met real violence', but rather to try to understand the way in which harm is done, and the many ways in which women are created as second-class citizens.[81]

What advantages or risks are there in connecting sexual harassment and rape?

2. In relation to alternative [3] (the suggestion that Garner might be arguing that the women attracted the attention because of their physical appearance or clothing), it can be observed that Garner includes a detailed description of one of the complainants wearing a revealing dress in her college photo[82] and refers to the need for her to take 'the responsibility of learning to handle the effects, on men, of her beauty and her erotic style of self-presentation'.[83]

And, in her speech to the Sydney Institute some months after *TFS* was published, Garner stated:

> It is an article of faith amongst some young feminists that a woman can go about the world dressed in any way she pleases. They think for a man to respond, and I don't mean threaten or touch or attack, for a man to respond to what he sees as a statement of her sexuality and her own attitude to it, is some sort of outrage. ... Sexy clothes are part of the wonderful game of life, but to dress to display your body, and then to project all the sexuality of the situation onto men and then blame them for it just so you can continue to be innocent and put upon, is not at all responsible, and what is more it is a relinquishing of power.[84]

Mark Davis responded to this passage:

> It seems odd that, twenty-five years after the second wave of feminism, we are still hearing that women should take responsibility for men's desires and are misbehaving if they don't.[85]

---

80   *The First Stone,* at 221. See also *ibid,* at 100-1 and 150.
81   Morgan, 'Sexual Harassment: Where Did It Go in 1995?' in Jenna Mead (ed), *Bodyjamming: Sexual Harassment, Feminism and Public Life,* Random House, Sydney, 1997, at 109.
82   *The First Stone,* at 58-9.
83   *Ibid,* at 89.
84   *Sydney Morning Herald,* August 9, 1995 at 8. And in the same piece, though not included in the *Herald* version, Garner said, if a 'woman dresses to captivate, she'd better learn to keep her wits about her for when the wrong fish swims into her net': Helen Garner, 'The Larry Adler Lecture 1995 – The Fate of the First Stone' [1995] *The Sydney Papers* at 37 and quoted in Mark Skulley and Jane Freeman, 'Speech by Garner pours fat on the fires of feminism', *Sydney Morning Herald,* 10 August 1995, at 6.
85   Mark Davis, *Gangland: Cultural Elites and the New Generationalism,* Allen and Unwin, Sydney, 1997, at 86.

3. In relation to alternative [4], Garner recounts an interview with a friend who said:

> "A man in Shepherd's position must not do the things he was accused of."
>
> "It's terrible to me," I *[Garner]* said, disconcerted, "to see the effects of this on his life – on his family."
>
> "Oh," she said, "I don't believe he *deserved* what's happened to him. He may be 'innocent' – but he's paying for many, many other men who have *not* been caught. It's the irony of things, that sometimes the innocent or nearly-innocent pay for what the guilty have done."
>
> Yes, and you can't make an omelette without breaking eggs: what a cruel and ethically rotten argument.[86]

If Garner's position was influenced by the Master's loss of his position in the aftermath of the students' complaints, is there still not a further question of who should be fixed with responsibility for this? Does it rest with the students, the police, the college, the university or somewhere else? If the responsibility is seen as that of the complainants, is it ever possible for women to complain of sexual harassment against a man who holds a position of (public) importance?

4. As Mark Davis, and Morgan, have suggested, *The First Stone* resonates very strongly with the American critique of so-called 'victim-feminism'.[87] Garner laments 'this determination to cling to victimhood at any cost, which seems to have become the loudest voice of feminism today'.[88] In relation to the story in *The First Stone*, this lament appears to relate to the complainants' willingness to go to the police. However, as we have noted in Chapter 10, there is also a growing critique within feminism of a relentless depiction of women's victimisation that fails to recognise simultaneously the agency women exercise. This critique accepts that some feminist work seems to represent women as always, already and only victims but, rather than suggesting that women have adopted this role, takes a more critical stance in trying to highlight, as Abrams has described it, agency within victimisation.[89] Thus, it is possible to examine Garner's own story about the complainants in the Ormond case with a different focus, and notice instead the considerable agency the young women exercised:

> One of the major themes of Garner's book, *The First Stone*, was that the young women who took their complaints of assault to the police (and the state Equal Opportunity Commission) had overreacted. Their actions were overreactions in Garner's view, because, they had all sorts of other options. These included 'get[ting] her mother or her friends to help her sort him out later, if she couldn't deal with it herself at the time' [*TFS*, at 15]; 'standing up and fighting back with their own weapons of youth and quick wits' [*TFS*, at 40]; 'tak[ing] the responsibility of learning to handle the effects, on men, of her beauty and her erotic style of self-presentation [*TFS*, at 89]; or 'ask[ing] for an acknowledgment and an apology' [*TFS*, at 92].[90]

---

86 *TFS*, at 181; see also, *ibid*, at 79, 136 and 187.
87 See Davis, *Gangland*, Chapter 4 'Stoned again: the victim feminism scare', 75-98. See also Morgan, 'The Power of Storytelling'. This issue is discussed in more detail in Chapter 10.
88 *Sydney Morning Herald*, 9 August 1995, at 8.
89 Kathryn Abrams, 'Sex Wars Redux: Agency and Coercion in Feminist Legal Theory' (1995) 95 *Columbia Law Review* 304.
90 Morgan, 'The Power of Storytelling'.

Garner's argument appears to be that by making a complaint to the police the young women were adopting the victim role, refusing to recognise their own power, having been duped (probably by feminists) into only being able to define themselves as victims and incapable of looking after themselves. This seems to me to underestimate the difficulties of making a report to the police – although one defines oneself as a victim to make a report of a possible crime, it requires considerable agency to do so – and, as well, considerably underplays the independent discretion of the police. Most particularly, the book (and much of the debate afterwards), largely ignored what the young women in this case actually did, prior to going to the police. For example, in relation to "deal[ing] with it herself at the time", the young woman who alleged that the Master had squeezed her breast on the dance floor, said that the first time he did this she removed his hand and placed it back on her waist [*TFS*, at 27]. After the second time, she excused herself and found her friends [*TFS*, at 25]. She asked one of her friends, who had been dancing (safely) with the Master earlier to do so again.[91]

We have noted above the more formal attempts made by the complainants, separate from their report to the police, to resolve the complaint informally.[92] How important is it to explore the agency women often exercise when sexually harassed? Can you see any risks in emphasising women's agency in cases of sexual harassment?

PORNOGRAPHY

The regulation of pornography has become a site of conflict between feminists and civil libertarians and amongst feminists themselves. This section of the chapter considers traditional modes of pornography regulation and feminist interventions into state regulation of obscenity and pornography, as well as some of the feminist criticism of those interventions.

An obscenity approach

Pornography in Australia is currently regulated through the law on obscenity, though what is obscene is not necessarily equivalent to what is pornographic.[93] At common law, it was a crime to publish an 'obscene libel', that is, material which had a tendency 'to deprave and corrupt those whose minds are open to such immoral influences and into whose hands a publication of this sort may fall'.[94]

More recently, Australian courts moved to assess whether the material 'by reason of the extent to which and the manner in which it deals with sexual matters, transgress[es] the generally accepted bounds of decency'.[95] The question of

---

91 Morgan, 'The Power of Storytelling'.
92 See also Cossins, who notes that Garner's 'opinion of the actions of the two students after the two trials remains the same [*as that expressed in the letter to the Master, noted above*]; to her they are involved in an 'absurd, hysterical tantrum' [*TFS*, at 39] despite evidence of the College's obstruction of their attempts to resolve their complaints of sexual harassment informally' ('On Stone Throwing', at 538).
93 According to Andrea Dworkin, pornography literally means the 'graphic depiction of whores': Andrea Dworkin, *Pornography: Men Possessing Women*, Perigee Books, New York, 1981, at 199-201.
94 *R v Hicklin* (1868) LR 3 QB 360 at 371 per Cockburn CJ; and in Australia, see *Ex parte Collins* (1899) 9 LR (NSW) 497.
95 *Crowe v Graham* (1968) 121 CLR 375 at 395 per Windeyer J.

whether something is indecent or obscene must be assessed in the light of 'contemporary' or 'community standards':

> Contemporary standards are those currently accepted by the Australian community. ... And community standards are those which ordinary decent-minded people accept. They are not what those who peddle obscenities and indecencies urge should be accepted.[96]

In other words, as Butler and Rodrick described it, 'the test for obscenity has moved away from being one based on morality and is now one based on society's manners'.[97]

The States and the Commonwealth have a cooperative scheme for the classification of films and other publications.[98] The *Classification (Publications, Films and Computer Games) Act* 1995 (Cth) provides that, in making a classification decision, the Classification Board must have regard to 'the standards of morality, decency and propriety generally accepted by reasonable adults'.[99] The Board can refuse classification to a film or other publication; the consequences of classification are governed by complementary State legislation, for example, the *Classification (Publications, Films and Computer Games) Enforcement Act* 1995 (Vic). This Act provides, among other things, that it is an offence to exhibit in a public place a film that is not classified.[100]

The Commonwealth also regulates the importation of obscene images. The *Customs (Prohibited Imports) Regulations* 1956 (Cth) regulate the importation of films, computer games or other publications which:

> describe, depict, express or otherwise deal with matters of sex, drug misuse or addiction, crime, cruelty, violence or revolting or abhorrent phenomena in such a way that they offend against the standards of morality, decency and propriety generally accepted by reasonable adults to the extent that they should not be imported.[101]

Such goods cannot be imported into Australia unless the Attorney-General or other authorised person has given permission for their importation in writing.[102] In considering whether to grant this permission, the decision-maker should take account of the extent to which the permission seeker conducts artistic, educational, cultural or scientific activities to which the goods relate,[103] and the reputation of the permission-seeker both generally and in relation to their educational and other related activities.[104]

Catharine MacKinnon has described the obscenity approach to the regulation of pornography as 'enforc[ing] morals':

---

96 *Ibid*, at 399.
97 Des Butler and Sharon Rodrick, *Australian Media Law*, LBC, Sydney, 1999, at 321. Note that obscenity law is now usually in statutory form: see, for example, *Crimes Act* 1900 (NSW), s 578C.
98 However, not all States and Territories have agreed to all parts of the scheme. For example, Queensland can classify or reclassify computer games (see *Classification of Computer Games and Images Act* (1995) (Qld)) and classifies publications: see *Classification of Publications Act* 1991 (Qld).
99 The *Classification (Publications, Films and Computer Games) Act* 1995 (Cth), s 11(a); other matters that must be taken into account include the literary, artistic and educational merit, the general character of the film, publication etc and the audience to whom it is to be published.
100 Section 6.
101 *Customs (Prohibited Imports) Regulations* 1956 (Cth), reg 4A(1A)(a).
102 Regulation 4A(2).
103 Regulation 4A(2AA)(b).
104 Regulation 4A(2AA)(c).

In practice, it prohibits depictions of sex that some men find offensive – that is, the public showing of sex that some men want to say they do not want other men to see. It takes the view that sex is dirty, women are dirty, and homosexuality is bad .... It cares more about whether men blush than whether women bleed. It is designed to suppress not eradicate; does nothing to hold pornographers accountable for promoting aggression, bigotry, and discrimination; and cannot empower pornography's victims. Virtue and vice are its concerns; women and children are not.[105]

Pornography and equality

The United States: The ordinance approach

Andrea Dworkin and Catharine MacKinnon have argued that a more productive way of approaching the suppression of pornography is to treat the injury of pornography as an injury to women's claims to equality. MacKinnon contrasts their approach to the traditional obscenity approach:

> From the feminist perspective, obscenity is a moral idea; pornography is a political practice. Obscenity is abstract; pornography is concrete. Obscenity conveys moral condemnation as a predicate to legal condemnation. Pornography identifies a political practice that is predicated on power and powerlessness – a practice that is, in fact, legally protected. The two concepts represent two entirely different things. ... Men treat women as whom they see women as being. Pornography constructs who that is. Men's power over women means that the way men see women defines who women can be. ... The feminist critique of pornography ... proceeds from women's point of view, meaning the standpoint of the subordination of women to men.[106]

Dworkin and MacKinnon drafted an ordinance that treats the issue of the production and distribution of pornography as a matter of sex discrimination. In it they argue that:

> Pornography is a systematic practice of exploitation and subordination based on sex that differentially harms and disadvantages women. The harm of pornography includes dehumanization, psychic assault, sexual exploitation, forced sex, forced prostitution, physical injury, and social and sexual terrorism and inferiority presented as entertainment. The bigotry and contempt pornography promotes, with the acts of aggression it fosters, diminish opportunities for equality of rights in employment, education, property, public accommodations, and public services; create public and private harassment, persecution, and denigration; promote injury and degradation such as rape, battery, sexual abuse of children, and prostitution, and inhibit just enforcement of laws against these acts; expose individuals who appear in pornography against their will to contempt, ridicule, hatred, humiliation, and embarrassment and target such women in particular for abuse and physical aggression; demean the reputations and diminish the occupational opportunities of individuals and groups on the basis of sex; contribute significantly to restricting women in particular from full exercise of citizenship and participation in the life of the community; lower the human dignity, worth, and civil status of women and damage mutual respect

---

105 'Pornography's Empire', Paper presented to the 9th Commonwealth Law Conference, 16-20 April 1990, Auckland, New Zealand.
106 Catharine A MacKinnon, *Toward a Feminist Theory of the State*, Harvard University Press, Cambridge, MA, 1989, at 196-7.

between the sexes; and undermine women's equal exercise of rights to speech and action ....[107]

Pornography is defined in the ordinance as:

> [T]he graphic sexually explicit subordination of women through pictures and/or words that also includes one or more of the following: (a) women are presented dehumanized as sexual objects, things or commodities; or (b) women are presented as sexual objects who enjoy humiliation or pain; or (c) women are presented as sexual objects experiencing sexual pleasure in rape, incest or other sexual assault; or (d) women are presented as sexual objects tied up or cut up or mutilated or bruised or physically hurt; or (e) women are presented in postures or positions of sexual submission, servility or display; or (f) women's body parts – including but not limited to vaginas, breasts, or buttocks – are exhibited such that women are reduced to those parts; or (g) women are presented being penetrated by objects or animals; or (h) women are presented in scenarios of degradation, humiliation, torture, shown as filthy or inferior, bleeding, bruised or hurt in a context that makes these conditions sexual.[108]

The ordinance allows women to bring a claim of sex discrimination if they have been assaulted in a way that is directly caused by pornography, if they are defamed in pornography, if they have pornography forced on them or if they are coerced into performing pornography. Probably the most controversial part of the ordinance is that which provides that trafficking in pornography is sex discrimination and allows a court to order cessation of trafficking via an injunction.

A version of the ordinance was enacted in Indianapolis and immediately (and successfully) challenged as being in violation of the First Amendment to the United States Constitution.[109] This provides (in part) that 'Congress shall make no law ... abridging the freedom of speech or of the press'. The court in *Hudnut* found that the controls on pornography went beyond the regulation of obscenity that the US Supreme Court had accepted was not protected by the First Amendment and stated:

> Under the ordinance graphic sexually explicit speech is "pornography" or not depending on the perspective the author adopts. Speech that "subordinates" women and also, for example, presents women as enjoying pain, humiliation, or rape, or even simply presents women in "positions of servility or submission or display" is forbidden, no matter how great the literary or political value of the work taken as a whole. Speech that portrays women in positions of equality is lawful, no matter how graphic the sexual content. This is thought control. It establishes an "approved" view of women, of how they may react to sexual encounters, of how the sexes may relate to each other. Those who espouse the approved view may use sexual images; those who do not, may not.
>
> Indianapolis justifies the ordinance on the ground that pornography affects thoughts. Men who see women depicted as subordinate are more likely to treat them so. Pornography is an aspect of dominance. It does not persuade people so much as change them. It works by socializing, by establishing the expected

---

[107] Section 1(2) of the Model AntiPornography Civil-Rights Ordinance in Andrea Dworkin and Catharine A MacKinnon, *Pornography and Civil Rights: A New Day for Women's Equality*, Organizing Against Pornography, Minneapolis, 1988, at 138. The ordinance is also reproduced in full in the first edition of *The Hidden Gender of Law*, at 376-9.

[108] Section 2(1) of the ordinance, in *Pornography and Civil Rights*, at 138-9.

[109] *American Bookseller Association, Inc v Hudnut, Mayor, City of Indianapolis* 771 F 2d 323 (7th Cir 1985).

and the permissible. In this view pornography is not an idea; pornography is the injury. ...

... [W]e accept the premises of this legislation. Depictions of subordination tend to perpetuate subordination. The subordinate status of women in turn leads to affront and lower pay at work, insult and injury at home, battery and rape on the streets. ...

Yet this simply demonstrates the power of pornography as speech. All of these unhappy effects depend on mental intermediation. Pornography affects how people see the world, their fellows, and social relations. If pornography is what pornography does, so is other speech. Hitler's orations affected how some Germans saw Jews. ...

Racial bigotry, anti-semitism, violence on television, reporters' biases – these and many more influence the culture and shape of our socialisation. None is directly answerable by more speech, unless that speech too finds its place in the popular culture. Yet all is protected as speech, however insidious. Any other answer leaves the government in control of all of the institutions of culture, the great censor and director of which thoughts are good for us.[110]

Notes

1. Drucilla Cornell disagrees with MacKinnon and Dworkin. She claims that the notion that pornography directly causes harm to women is simplistic:

   > I question the appropriateness of the causal model which treats rape as the direct effect of pornography. Thus, I do not simply reject MacKinnon's causal analysis because social-scientific studies are inconclusive as to the relationship between pornography and rape. I question the very use of the cause-and-effect model. It is difficult to use such a model in the complex, symbolically-driven world of sexuality. The model, however, is crucial for the structure of the Dworkin/MacKinnon ordinance.[111]

2. Although the approach adopted in the MacKinnon/Dworkin ordinance was rejected as unconstitutional in the United States, such an approach – that pornography is a harm to women's claims to equality – has been influential in Canada.

Canada: Interpreting obscenity law

The decision of the Supreme Court of Canada in *Butler*[112] concerned the constitutionality of the Canadian *Criminal Code* provision making it an offence to make, distribute, possess, etc, obscene material.[113] Butler, who ran a video store selling and renting 'hard core' videos, was charged, together with an employee, with a series of offences involving the sale of, possession of and exposing to public view, obscene material. The Code provided that 'any publication the dominant characteristic of which is the undue exploitation of sex, or of sex and any one or more of the following subjects, namely, crime, horror, cruelty and

---

110 *Ibid*, at 328-30. *Hudnut* was summarily affirmed by the US Supreme Court (475 US 1001 (1986)); that is, the case was not argued before the court and no reasons for the decision were produced, yet the decision was approved.
111 Drucilla Cornell, *The Imaginary Domain: Abortion, Pornography and Sexual Harassment*, Routledge, New York, 1995, at 101.
112 *R v Butler* [1992] 1 SCR 452.
113 See *Criminal Code*, RSC, 1985, C-46, s 163(1).

violence, shall be deemed to be obscene'.[114] The accused argued that these provisions interfered with their freedom of expression, protected under the *Canadian Charter of Rights and Freedoms*.

The Supreme Court analysed three tests which had been used in recent times by courts to determine whether a publication was obscene: the 'community standards of tolerance test', the 'degradation or dehumanisation test' and the 'artistic defence'. The first test, developed in Australia in *R v Close*,[115] and adopted in Canada in *Brodie*,[116] provides that obscenity is to be judged by the standards of the community – what members of the jury believe other members of the community would tolerate:[117]

> There does exist in the community at all times – however the standard may vary from time to time – a general instinctive sense of what is decent and what is indecent, of what is clean and what is dirty ....[118]

This test does not require expert evidence to establish the standards of the community.[119] In relation to the second test, the court said:

> There has been a growing recognition in recent cases that material which may be said to exploit sex in a "degrading or dehumanizing" manner will necessarily fail the community standards test. ...
>
> Among other things, degrading or dehumanizing materials place women (and sometimes men) in positions of subordination, servile submission or humiliation. They run against the principles of equality and dignity of all human beings. In the appreciation of whether material is degrading or dehumanizing, the appearance of consent is not necessarily determinative. Consent cannot save materials that otherwise contain degrading or dehumanizing scenes. Sometimes the very appearance of consent makes the depicted acts even more degrading or dehumanizing.[120]

Finally, there is a third test, or defence, which is used to determine that the exploitation of sex is 'not undue' 'if there is no more emphasis on the theme than is required in the serious treatment of the theme of a novel with honesty and uprightness'.[121]

> Accordingly, the "internal necessities" test or what has been referred to as the "artistic defence", has been interpreted to assess whether the exploitation of sex has a justifiable role in advancing the plot or the theme, and in considering the work as a whole, does not merely represent "dirt for dirt's sake" but has a legitimate role when measured by the internal necessities of the work itself.[122]

The court went on to consider the interrelationship of these three tests and divided pornography[123] into three categories:

> (1) explicit sex with violence, (2) explicit sex without violence but which subjects people to treatment that is degrading or dehumanizing, and (3) explicit sex without violence that is neither degrading nor dehumanizing. ...

---

114 Section 163(8).
115 [1948] VLR 445. See also *Crowe v Graham* (1968) 121 CLR 375.
116 [1962] SCR 681.
117 *Butler*, at 478.
118 *R v Close* [1948] VLR 445 at 465, cited in *Butler*, at 476.
119 *Butler*, at 476-7.
120 *Ibid*, at 478-9.
121 *Brodie* [1962] SCR 681 at 704-5, cited in *Butler* at 481.
122 *Butler*, at 482-3.
123 The court appears to use the term interchangeably with 'obscenity'.

> The courts must determine as best they can what the community would tolerate others being exposed to on the basis of the degree of harm that may flow from such exposure. Harm in this context means that it predisposes persons to act in an anti-social manner as, for example, the physical or mental mistreatment of women by men, or, what is perhaps debatable, the reverse. Anti-social conduct for this purpose is conduct which society formally recognizes as incompatible with its proper functioning. The stronger the inference of a risk of harm the lesser the likelihood of tolerance. ...
>
> In making this determination with respect to the three categories of pornography referred to above, the portrayal of sex coupled with violence will almost always constitute the undue exploitation of sex. Explicit sex which is degrading or dehumanizing may be undue if the risk of harm is substantial. Finally, explicit sex that is not violent and neither degrading nor humanizing is generally tolerated in our society and will not qualify as the undue exploitation of sex unless it employs children in its production.[124]

Finally, the court factored in the third test noted above and affirmed that, if the work does contain undue exploitation of sex under the first two of the above tests, it may still be found not to be obscene if 'this portrayal of sex [*is*] essential to a wider artistic, literary, or other similar purpose'.[125]

The court concluded that the *Criminal Code* provision did interfere with freedom of expression, a right protected under s 2 of the Charter. It then went on to consider whether this interference could be justified under s 1 of the Charter. Section 1 of the Charter states: 'The Canadian Charter of Rights and Freedoms guarantees the rights and freedoms set out in it subject only to such reasonable limits prescribed by law as can be demonstrably justified in a free and democratic society'. The court found that the obscenity provision was justified under s 1. In doing so, it emphasised that the justification for the regulation of pornography had to be on the basis of harm to society rather than morality:

> To impose a certain standard of public and sexual morality, solely because it reflects the conventions of a given community, is inimical to the exercise and enjoyment of individual freedoms, which form the basis of our social contract. ... The prevention of "dirt for dirt's sake" is not a legitimate objective which would justify the violation of one of the most fundamental freedoms enshrined in the Charter.[126]
>
> [T]here is a growing concern that the exploitation of women and children, depicted in publication and films, can in certain circumstances, lead to "abject and servile victimization" [*R v Red Hot Video Limited* (1985) 45 CR (3d) 36 at 43-4, per Nemetz CJBC]. As Anderson JA also noted in that same case, if true equality between male and female persons is to be achieved, we cannot ignore the threat to equality resulting from exposure to audiences of certain types of violent and degrading material. Materials portraying women as a class as objects for sexual exploitation and abuse have a negative impact on "the individual's sense of self-worth and acceptance".[127]

---

124 *Butler*, at 484-5.
125 *Butler*, at 486.
126 *Butler*, at 492-3. Cf: 'The objective of maintaining conventional standards of propriety, independently of any harm to society, is no longer justified in the light of the values of individual liberty which underlie the *Charter*' (at 498).
127 *Butler*, at 497.

Notes

1. The proposition that the harm of pornography is the harm to women's claims to equality was the position argued by the Women's Legal Education and Action Fund (LEAF) in the *Butler* case.[128] After the decision in *Butler*, Karen Busby maintained:

> LEAF, like many organizations which view violence against women as a measure and agent of women's inequality, count the Court's decision in *Butler* as a feminist breakthrough. It marks an extraordinary shift in the traditional rationale for obscenity laws from a community standard based on a general instinctive sense of what is decent and indecent (the *Brodie* standard) to an obscenity law premised on sex inequality and harms to women. While *Butler* still refers to a "community standard", the test has been so altered that resemblance to the pre-*Butler* standard is in name only. The Court explicitly recognized that the pre-*Butler* "community standards" test did little to elucidate the underlying question as to why some exploitation of sex falls on the permitted side and some on the prohibited side. The law no longer retains one universal standard of morally acceptable sexual representations.[129]

Are there differences in pursuing an equality approach via the ordinance model and advocating an equality approach in the interpretation of criminal obscenity laws as was pursued in *Butler*? Ann Scales argues:

> *Butler* interprets a section of the *Criminal Code*, in contrast to the MacKinnon-Dworkin ordinance, which in creating a civil action for sex discrimination, places the first interpretive moves in the hands of victims of pornography, to identify what is pornographic, and to demonstrate the harms therefrom. In criminal prosecutions of customs seizures, the first interpretive moves are in the hands of public officials: that is, those invested by the status quo with a uniquely legitimated authority to use physical force, which force is usually deployed to protect the *status quo*, to wit, the persecution of women in pornography.[130]

Is who takes those 'first interpretive moves' important? Can a focus on equality come in at any stage in the process? MacKinnon, in the extract from *Towards a Feminist Theory of the State* noted above, argued that 'the two concepts' – pornography and obscenity – 'represent two entirely different things'. Is it therefore possible to graft a feminist understanding of pornography onto a traditional understanding of obscenity? Interestingly, Andrea Dworkin apparently opposed any engagement by feminists with obscenity laws:

> Obscenity law is a total dead-end in dealing with the pornography industry. The whole idea of obscenity law is based on the idea that women's bodies are filthy and disgusting and shouldn't be seen. I think obscenity laws are real censorship laws, easy to use against literature that should be protected, and hard to use against what really harms women.[131]

---

128 See Karen Busby, 'LEAF and Pornography: Litigating on Equality and Sexual Representations' (1994) 9 *Canadian Journal of Law and Society* 165. MacKinnon was one of the authors of LEAF's factum. Busby notes that LEAF was the only participant in the case to make an argument based on equality (at 172).
129 Busby, 'LEAF and Pornography', at 176.
130 Ann Scales, 'Avoiding Constitutional Depression: Bad Attitudes and the Fate of *Butler*' (1994) 7 *Canadian Journal of Women and the Law* 349 at 362-3.
131 From an interview with Andrea Dworkin, in *The New Yorker*, 3 October 1994, cited in Scales, 'Avoiding Constitutional Depression', at 363, note 38.

Could you make the argument, by contrast, that if obscenity laws continue to exist, feminists should work to promote feminist interpretations of these laws? Scales suggests: 'The value of *Butler* will be in whether it can bridge the gap between obscenity and pornography regulation'.[132] Some of the perceived risks in feminist engagement with obscenity laws are explored below.

2. Scales, however, also notes criticisms of the civil action approach:

> I am aware that some anti-pornography feminist lawyers believe the civil action is the wrong way to go, because it "privatizes" the harms, that is, makes the harms of pornography into a set of personal problems, privately realized and privately pursued.[133]

Do you agree with this criticism? Scales does not, arguing that 'civil rights claims, though brought by private persons, represent a public commitment to equality, as opposed to mere compensation'.[134] This argument is reminiscent of the debate raised above in relation to sexual harassment. Does the 'equality context' transform the debate about pornography in the same way MacKinnon suggested it might transform the understanding of sexual harassment? Alternatively, do the same limitations that Conaghan suggested inhere in a sex discrimination approach to sexual harassment, also inhere in the ordinance approach to pornography?

3. The intervention by LEAF in *Butler*, and the *Butler* decision itself, have been subject to extensive criticism by some Canadian feminists. Cossman et al argue:

> We do not believe that the *Butler* decision is an unequivocal victory for feminism – indeed, we do not see it as a victory at all. Nor do we see the *Butler* decision as representing a fundamental transformation in the law of obscenity. The language has changed, but the moral regulation has not.[135]

Cossman argues that the *Butler* decision continues to be imbued with notions of morality:

> [T]he underlying sexual morality [*of the Court in Butler*], and its assumption of sexual negativity, sexual essentialism, and sexual monism, can be seen to leave s 163 transformed in language alone. The classification of sexual representations into one of the three categories of pornography according to the community-standards test of harm can only be done by an implicit reliance on an underlying sexual morality. The very concept of sex that is or could be degrading only makes sense through the underlying discourses on sexuality – of good sex/bad sex, mind/body distinctions, and the assumptions of sexual negativity, essentialism, monism, and hierarchy on which those distinctions are based. Similarly, community standards only make sense in relation to a prevailing, and generally accepted, understanding of sexual morality in which some sex is good and some sex is not.[136]

For example, Cossman argues that the Court in *Butler*, by persisting with a 'community standards' test for determining what is obscene, and citing *Close* to do so,[137] casts obscenity

---

132 Scales, 'Avoiding Constitutional Depression', at 363.
133 *Ibid*.
134 *Ibid*.
135 Brenda Cossman and Sharon Bell, 'Introduction' in Brenda Cossman, Sharon Bell, Lise Gotell and Becki L Ross, *Bad Attitude/s on Trial: Pornography, Feminism and the Butler Decision*, University of Toronto Press, Toronto, 1997, at 20.
136 Brenda Cossman, 'Feminist Fashion or Morality in Drag? The Sexual Subtext of the *Butler* Decision' in Cossman et al, *Bad Attitude/s on Trial*, at 127.
137 *R v Close* [1948] VLR 445 at 465, cited in *Butler*, at 476.

in the language of indecency and dirt. Not all sexual representations are obscene, only indecent or dirty sexual representations are obscene. Within this framework, there is a distinction made between good and bad sex – a binary opposition between clean and dirty, decent and indecent. Bad sex is dirty sex. There is no positive theory of sexual expression that tells us what makes sex good.[138]

While the second test used to determine what is obscene, the 'degrading and dehumanising test', focuses more clearly on harm to women, it continues, according to Cossman, to rest on a dichotomy between good sex and bad sex. And in the third test, '[w]e again see the view that sex is dirt – it is dirty, it is bad. Within this vision, art cannot be sex for sex's sake. By definition, sex is not art. Sex is not a legitimate focus for art. It can at most be part of the larger artistic purpose, but sexuality in and of itself is not art. Within the court's view, this is one area of activity (or subhuman activity) that is inappropriate for artistic portrayal'.[139]

Cossman concludes:

> In this reading of the *Butler* decision, the sexual subtext can be seen to inform the Court's decision of the objective of the legislation, and indeed the discussion of the constitutionality of the law as a whole. Notwithstanding the Court's best efforts to cast the objective of the law as the prevention of harm, particularly of harm towards women, the underlying sexual morality continues to infuse and shape the discourse of the decision. We do not have to look very far to find the continued references to morality, to sexual morality, to good sex and bad sex, to sex being of the body and thus bad, unless it can be made something more, and thereby good. Yet, there is no explicit articulation of what makes sex good. Rather, good sex is simply implied as that which bad sex is not: not base, not physical, not violent, not degrading or dehumanizing, not involving children. The sexual subtext of the *Butler* decision is informed by the discourses that have dominated Western thought since the nineteenth century: sexual negativity <sex is bad>, sexual essentialism <sex is biological>, sexual monism <sex is singular>, and sexual hierarchy <some sex is better than other>.
>
> ... In *Butler*, these assumptions interact in seemingly multiple and highly contradictory ways to constitute sex as a highly unstable character – yet not so unstable as to be easily displaced. This unstated sexual morality remains powerfully entrenched as the ideologically dominant discourse of sexuality.[140]

Do you agree that these dichotomies are relied on in the Supreme Court's decision? If you accept Cossman's position that the *Butler* decision, while expressed in terms of harm to women, continues to be imbued with traditional notions of morality, does that lead to the conclusion that the decision is not a feminist victory?[141]

Similar criticisms were made of the alliances formed between the Christian right and radical feminists in campaigns in the United States to get the MacKinnon/Dworkin anti-pornography ordinance passed. West describes the danger in the following way:

---

138 Cossman, 'Feminist Fashion or Morality in Drag?', at 109.
139 *Ibid*, at 113.
140 *Ibid*, at 127-8.
141 Note that the Supreme Court of Canada explicitly rejects the charge that *Butler* was 'morality in disguise' in *Little Sisters Book and Art Emporium v Canada (Minister of Justice)* [2000] 2 SCR 1120, esp at paras 61-64.

The syllogism is not hard to work out: pornography endangers women's physical safety, security, and freedom (the feminist premise); pornography also endangers the family, marriage, monogamy, and virtue (the conservative premise); *therefore, women's physical security, safety, and freedom must depend on the stability of the family, marriage and sexual virtue* – just as conservatives have always claimed.[142]

Is West's syllogism logically flawed?

4. Cossman et al also argue that the so-called anti-pornography feminists (and indeed the courts) assume that pornographic images have one 'unequivocal meaning that can be interpreted objectively',[143] a proposition they believe is unsustainable:

> Building on the insights of postmodernism that meaning is historically and contextually specific and contingent, *Bad Attitude/s on Trial* challenges this unidimensional approach to representation and meaning. We challenge the idea that pornography has only one meaning, ... the idea that the meaning of lesbian and other sexual representations can be determined objectively without reference to the specific communities within which those representations are produced, exchanged, and consumed. ...
>
> [We] are united in ... [the] insistence that subjectivity and context matter in the interpretation of sexual imagery, and that images can be simultaneously subject to multiple interpretations. We believe that anti-pornography feminism's approach to representation is flawed in its denial of the multiplicity of meaning and the relevance of context in the production of meaning. An image may be offensive to some, challenging to others, and sexually arousing to yet others. ... Rather than being clear and unequivocal, the meaning of sexual representations is a site of political and discursive struggle.[144]

Or, as Becki Ross puts it, also in *Bad Attitude/s*:

> [N]o pornographic text (s/m or other) operates as a site of singular, univocal meaning: textualized fantasy does not supply a single point of identification for viewers. As such, women (lesbian and non-lesbian) are and can be agents of pornographic fantasy. Whoever she is, the woman pictured in erotic texts is not *fixed in meaning* as an injured, assaulted object; her subject position as unilaterally oppressed victim is not stable. Once we accept this, we then recognize that there can be no definitive acts of harm that flow from exposure to sexual images, s/m or not.[145]

Think about some image or piece of writing that you have found obscene or pornographic. Could you articulate why you found it so? Do you think all of your friends, particularly your feminist friends, would also find it similarly pornographic? Can the exploitation of women, at least in heterosexual pornography, or pornography produced for the heterosexual market, be defined with sufficient specificity to authorise its banning? Is a legal forum the place in

---

142 Robin West, 'The Feminist-Conservative Anti-Pornography Alliance and the 1986 Attorney-General's Commission on Pornography Report' [1987] *American Bar Foundation Research Journal* 681 at 700. Cf Lisa Duggan, 'Censorship in the Name of Feminism' in Gail Chester and Julienne Dickey (eds), *Feminism and Censorship: The Current Debate*, Prism Press, Dorset, 1988.
143 Cossman and Bell, 'Introduction' in Cossman et al, *Bad Attitude/s*, at 25.
144 *Ibid*, at 25-6.
145 Becki L Ross, ' "It's Merely Designed for Sexual Arousal": Interrogating the Indefensibility of Lesbian Smut' in Cossman et al, *Bad Attitude/s*, at 183.

which to explore the different meanings of (allegedly) pornographic images, that is, a place to have that 'political and discursive struggle'? Gotell, also in *Bad Attitude/s*, argues it is not:

> What grounds LEAF's factum in *Butler*, ... is indeed a preference for incontestable legal 'Truth' over unstable politics, for discoveries over decisions, and for stable subjects armed with established rights over unwieldy pluralities adjudicating for themselves on the basis of argument and persuasion.[146]

Ann Scales, a supporter of the MacKinnon/Dworkin ordinance, thinks a legal forum has more potential. Writing in support of the *Butler* decision, she argues:

> Even when most exercised in the US debate over the civil pornography ordinance, I would not have asserted that it would unproblematically *work*. Effectiveness is a long-term question. If such ordinances were in effect long enough in enough places, then one could assess whether the pornography industry would be forced to change, or whether women would be differently empowered in the ongoing struggle for other than pornographically defined selves. Of more immediate importance, had such ordinances gone into effect, a long *interpretive competition* would have ensued. An inevitable part of that competition would have been the attempted co-optation of the ordinance by a conspiracy of pornographers and their apologists.[147]

Is there more room for an 'interpretive competition' in an ordinance-based approach than in the application of obscenity laws or does the legal nature of the forum in each case preclude such a competition?[148]

5. Some of the opposition to anti-pornography feminists' engagement with the law is that it will have the effect of interfering with the exploration of sexualities that challenge traditional mainstream heterosexual imagery – that further empowering the state by feminist support for censorship regulation will lead to increased surveillance of 'other' sexualities. Cossman et al argue: 'We believe that state censorship of pornography stifles women's own search for ways of expressing the complexities of our sexual lives and serves to inhibit women's sexual agency and power'.[149]

There is some evidence that gay and lesbian images have been particularly targeted since the decision in *Butler*.[150] For example, Little Sisters Bookstore, a well-known lesbian and gay book shop in Vancouver, argued that imports to that bookstore had been subjected to heightened inspections for no principled reason and thus that the administration of customs regulations interfered with their equality rights. As described by the Supreme Court:

---

146 Lise Gotell, 'Shaping *Butler*: The New Politics of Anti-Pornography' in Cossman et al, *Bad Attitude/s*, at 52.
147 Ann Scales, 'Avoiding Constitutional Depression', at 360.
148 Mariana Valverde suggests that the meaning of 'harm' in *Butler* is very open. She argues '[m]aking judgements about harm and about risks is not the sort of activity that can be easily monopolized by the organs of sovereign state power': Mariana Valverde, 'The Harms of Sex and the Risks of Breasts: Obscenity and Indecency in Canadian Law' (1999) 8 *Social and Legal Studies* 181 at 195.
149 Cossman and Bell, 'Introduction', in Cossman et al, *Bad Attitude/s*, at 31. Cf Becki Ross, '"It's Merely Designed for Sexual Arousal": Interrogating the Indefensibility of Lesbian Smut' in Cossman et al, *Bad Attitude/s*.
150 Although the targeting had commenced before the *Butler* decision: see Scales, 'Avoiding Constitutional Depression', at 359, note 28.

While Little Sisters and its suppliers are routinely targeted, mainstream bookstores receive more favourable treatment. For example, the operator of Duthie Books, a general interest bookstore in British Columbia, testified that at the request of Little Sisters they ordered a number of books that had been prohibited when destined for Little Sisters. The shipping instructions were intentionally made identical to those given by Little Sisters. In spite of the fact that Customs inspected the books, they arrived without incident. Similarly, books that were prohibited when destined for Little Sisters were widely available at other general interest bookstores in Vancouver, and even at the Vancouver Public Library.[151]

Cossman suggests that it could well be argued that the *Butler* framework should be restricted to heterosexual pornography, or 'that courts at least address the question of how the understanding of harm could be applied to gay and lesbian sex'.[152] She points out that:

> Many gay men and lesbians have argued that gay or lesbian sexual representations have absolutely nothing to do with the harm towards women associated with heterosexual pornography. Carl Stychin has contended, for example, that the sexually explicit images of gay male pornography do not reinforce patriarchal male sexuality, but, rather, directly challenge dominant constructions of masculinity by displacing the heterosexual norm [Carl Stychin, 'Exploring the Limits: Feminism and the Legal Regulation of Gay Male Pornography' (1992) 16 *Vermont Law Review* 857]. ...
> How does men watching pictures of men having sex with men, or women watching pictures of women having sex with women, contribute to the type of harm to women identified in *Butler*?[153]

Cossman continues:

> In the case law that followed on the heels of the *Butler* decision, however, the courts have neither limited the *Butler* test to heterosexual materials nor explored how this heterosexually defined concept of harm can be applied to gay and lesbian imagery.[154]

And she goes on to suggest that this is not surprising given the court's reliance, as noted above, on dichotomies of good sex and bad sex: indeed, she argues that the condemnation of gay and lesbian imagery under the *Butler* test reveals the decision's clear reliance on notions of morality and immorality.

By contrast, Scales argues:

> Within this radical feminist analysis, the fact that sexually explicit materials are gay and lesbian does not automatically exempt them from regulation under *Butler*. Pornography exists only in the context of a gendered society, which equates maleness with domination and femaleness with subordination, maleness with objectification and femaleness with the-objectified [*sic*]. Though the genders may be rearranged in gay and lesbian pornography, if the turn-on requires domination and subordination, then those materials affirm the social hatred of women. ... The value enacted, therefore, in some gay and lesbian materials, is that it is socially acceptable,

---

151 *Little Sisters Book and Art Emporium v Canada*, at para 188.
152 Cossman, 'Feminist Fashion or Morality in Drag', at 129.
153 *Ibid*, at 128-9.
154 *Ibid*, at 129.

indeed, desirable, to turn women (or their surrogates) into things, to deprive us of ourselves, and to screw us to death.[155]

In the *Little Sisters* litigation, LEAF argued:

> [T]hat sado-masochism performs an emancipatory role in gay and lesbian culture and should therefore be judged by a different standard from that applicable to heterosexual culture. In support of this position LEAF points out that, by definition, gender discrimination is not an issue in "same-sex erotica". On the other hand, the intervener Equality Now took the view that gay and lesbian individuals have as much right as their heterosexual counterparts to be protected from depictions of sex with violence or sexual conduct that is dehumanizing or degrading in a way that can cause harm that exceeds community standards of tolerance.[156]

The court concluded in *Little Sisters*:

> LEAF's argument seems to presuppose that the *Butler* test is exclusively gender-based. Violence against women was only one of several concerns, albeit an important one, that led to the formulation of the *Butler* harm-based test, which is itself gender neutral. While it would be quite open to the appellants to argue that a particular publication does not exceed the general community's tolerance of harm for various reasons, gay and lesbian culture as such does not constitute a general exemption from the *Butler* test.[157]

Scales' argument in support of the application of the *Butler* test to gay and lesbian pornography appears to rely on a cultural identification of subordinating images of sex with heterosexuality – that is, notwithstanding that the images used are of same-sex sexual activity which is subordinating, they rely on cultural images of heterosexual subordination for their effect. The court's approach, by contrast, appears to rely on the fact that the *Butler* approach was gender (and sexuality) neutral and same-sex images that involve subordination have a direct effect on lesbian and gay sexuality. Which approach do you find more convincing? Why do you think LEAF argued that sado-masochism means something different in the lesbian and gay community than it might in the heterosexual world?

6. Cornell has argued that an approach to the regulation of pornography that focuses on the use of law to restrict the distribution of pornography 'treats the women in the industry as if they were incapable of asserting their own personhood and, in this way, assumes that others need to act on their behalf. ... [P]orn workers have become the ultimate figuration of the victim who

---

155 Scales, 'Avoiding Constitutional Depression', at 365; see also Christopher Kendall, '"Real Dominant, Real Fun!": Gay Male Pornography and the Pursuit of Masculinity' (1993) 57 *Saskatchewan Law Review* 21 at 22-3: 'Gay male pornography epitomizes what it means to be "male" as socially defined. It offers gay men a choice: one can be violent and aggressive, hence masculine (read "male") or one can be the person over/upon whom that power should be exercised (read "female as socially defined"). The resulting gender/power hierarchy, rather than challenging compulsory heterosexuality and male dominance, reinforces social norms that make compulsory heterosexuality and male dominance the interconnected and oppressive constructs that they are. The result for gay men is self-hate and internalized homophobia. The result for society at large is but one more medium that goes a long way in maintaining systematic inequality because it promotes rather than undermines a gender hierarchy in which "male" is top and "female" (read all women and those gay men who fail to conform to the "male" construct and who are thus socially feminized) is bottom. This hierarchy depends on the homophobic rejection of gay male sexual "difference" and in turn permits sex discrimination'.
156 *Little Sisters*, at para 63.
157 *Ibid*, at para 64.

needs to be rescued. But this is certainly not how porn workers see themselves'.[158] And as Cornell later argues: '[W]e must not entrench stereotypes of femininity as the basis of discrimination law. We do not, in other words, want law to endorse the culturally encoded femininity that, in the work of Catharine MacKinnon reduces woman to the "fuckee", or the victim, and demands her protection as such'.[159] Does the ordinance approach and/or an equality approach to understanding obscenity construct women as always already victims?

7. Annalise Acorn has argued that feminists abandoned the terrain of the legal regulation of pornography and sexual performance in the wake of *Butler*, an abandonment which has led, in her view, to the explicit (re)instatement of a conservative understanding of the harm of pornography in *Mara*.[160] In *Mara*,[161] the Supreme Court of Canada concluded that the performance of 'table-top' dancers, a performance which involved 'sexual contact between dancers and audience members',[162] was indecent. Acorn suggests that the court showed no interest in properly utilising the harm principle enunciated in *Butler* – there was no discussion of 'women's statements, views, theories or experience in the Court's analysis of the question of whether the performances in question were harmful to women'.[163] In her view:

> [The decision] is concerned with keeping orthodox boundaries of the private in place and is more driven by an abhorrence of the "publicization" of the private than it is by a concern with the equality analysis set out in *Butler*.[164]

Acorn argues that LEAF, and the court in *Butler*, failed to differentiate their analysis of the harm of pornography from a traditional one, such as Devlin's well-known 1965 argument that assumes a shared community morality.[165]

> Instead of effecting a necessary break from this form of analysis – fixation on the sensibility of the community as the standard – *Butler* grafted the notion of harm to women onto the existing referent of the community standard. Rather than jettisoning the argumentative structure of Devlin's justification for the prohibition of the "immoral", the Court preserved it but held it was to be understood in terms of feminist analysis of pornography that highlights violence, degradation, dehumanization, and the perpetuation of women's inequality as the relevant social harm. ...
> ... What was not sufficiently clarified or stressed by the Court was that the harm LEAF was trying to identify and make salient was the sort of identifiable harm to individuals that would take the court beyond the need

---

158 Drucilla Cornell, *The Imaginary Domain: Abortion, Pornography and Sexual Harassment*, Routledge, New York, 1995, at 96; cf Ross, in *Bad Attitude/s*, at 185.
159 Cornell, *The Imaginary Domain*, at 99.
160 Annalise Acorn, 'Harm, Community Tolerance, and the Indecent: A Discussion of *R v Mara*' (1997) 36 *Alberta Law Review* 258: 'The prosecutorial targeting of gay and lesbian pornography after *Butler*, along with the lack of impact the decision has had on the marketing of hard core violent heterosexual pornography, has left many feminists who were previously strong supporters of criminal sanctions in this area feeling chastened, embarrassed and willing to delete pornography from the feminist agenda' (at 264).
161 [1997] 2 SCR 630.
162 Acorn, 'Harm, Community Tolerance', at 259.
163 *Ibid*.
164 *Ibid*, at 260.
165 See Patrick Devlin, *The Enforcement of Morals*, Oxford University Press, Oxford, 1965, discussed by Acorn, 'Harm, Community Tolerance', at 268.

for finding some kind of nebulous social harm understood in terms of anxiety around the disintegration of society. Here the feminist ambivalence toward the type of harm to women they are concerned with is significant: was the concern with harm to individual and identifiable women or were feminists identifying a new species of social harm that could be linked to the orthodox anxiety around the dissolution of shared values?[166]

Acorn suggests feminists were concerned with the former harm – harm to individual and identifiable women. Do you agree? Do you think that a sufficient emphasis on this sort of harm does break the connection with more conservative discourses on the harm of obscenity?

The role of law?

This whole discussion raises profound questions about the role of law in the regulation of pornography or obscenity. If the 'message' of images is not unequivocal, it would be much more difficult to justify their regulation through criminal law or, indeed, civil law. Let us assume that most viewers or readers could agree that some particular material was obscene or pornographic, including most feminist consumers. Does this mean you would support the state banning its distribution? Is the state likely to consistently apply a feminist definition of pornography? Is there *a* feminist understanding of pornography? Are there ways to think more creatively about the role of law in the regulation of pornography?

Many feminists have suggested that one role for law in the sex industry generally is to ensure 'that performers and models involved in the production of pornography are provided with adequate working conditions and are both entitled to and able to realise in practice the rights, remedies, and benefits available to workers generally'.[167] Hence, many would support the ordinance's provisions for a civil cause of action for those coerced into the production of pornography.[168]

Cornell goes further and, while strongly opposed to most aspects of the MacKinnon/Dworkin ordinance, in particular, the regulation of the distribution

---

166 Acorn, 'Harm, Community Tolerance', at 269.
167 Sandra Berns, 'Pornography, Women, Censorship and Morality' (1989) 7 *Law in Context* 30 at 61. Cf Cossman and Bell, 'Introduction' in Cossman et al, *Bad Attitude/s*, at 44: 'The complex relationship between sexual representations and sexual acts is further obscured in the argument that obscenity law is intended to address the coercive conditions under which women in the mainstream pornography industry may work. Although we may have reason to be concerned about the conditions under which sexual images are produced, these conditions are not the appropriate focus of obscenity law. Repressing the representation does nothing to address the underlying material conditions under which these representations may have been produced. Employment conditions should be the focus of employment laws. Women in the sex industry – be it prostitution or the production of pornography – should be entitled to the same kind of employment protection that other workers are afforded. They should not have to work in conditions that are hazardous. They should not have to work in conditions against their will. Taking prostitution and pornography out of the criminal code would be the first step towards a restructuring of the legal regulation of sex work. A second step would then be to enforce the range of laws that otherwise apply to employment. Employment-standards law, human-rights law, occupational-health-and-safety law, and workers-compensation law could all substantially improve the conditions under which sex work occurs. Such legal regulation could directly address the coercive conditions under which some women in the mainstream pornography industry may work. Obscenity legislation cannot'. Cf Cornell, *The Imaginary Domain*, esp at 97.
168 See, for example, Susan Etta Keller, 'Viewing and Doing: Complicating Pornography's Meaning' (1993) 81 *Georgetown Law Journal* 2195 and Cornell, *The Imaginary Domain*, at 102: 'I would allow someone like Linda Lovelace, if she could show that she was indeed raped in the production of a pornography film, to enjoin its circulation'.

of pornography, she does support zoning laws to control the display of pornography:[169]

> We should use zoning to prevent enforced viewing of pornography. ... I would limit zoning to display regulation, ie, the outward appearance of video stores and what is displayed in their windows. I do not, however, premise my defence of zoning on the concept of public decency. Instead, it is the possible encroachment upon a woman's imaginary that justifies the zoning. No woman should be forced to view her own body as it is fantasized as a dismembered, castrated other, found in bits and pieces. She should also not be forced to see her "sex" as it is stereotypically presented in hardcore porn through explicit depiction of sex acts. In hardcore porn the woman is only there as her "sex". She should not, in other words, be forced to see her "self", her "sexed self" since a woman's self is always sexed, as reducible to an object, and thus as inherently unworthy of personhood. The kind of imagery I am describing clearly violates the degradaton [sic] prohibition if one is forced to confront it. Of course, not all women find exposure to these images an encroachment on their imaginary domain, or more precisely, on their ability to construct such a domain in the first place. For some women, exploration of hard-core pornography is crucial to their sexual imaginary. My argument is only that no one should be an enforced viewer to the degree that these images do infringe on some women's imaginary domain.
>
> ... Unlike MacKinnon, I justify zoning not on the basis of what pornography does to its male viewers, but because of the wrong it can impose on women in its enforced viewing. Feminism must not focus solely on what men have done to women. Rather, feminism must continuously seek ways in which women can unleash their own imaginary from the constraints that have been imposed upon them through rigid definitions of femininity. The purpose of zoning is precisely to keep pornography safely resting in its jackets, out of the view of those who seek to inhabit or construct an imaginary domain independent of the one it offers. If we are to value the proliferation of imaginaries, we must protect the psychic space for their creation and expression.[170]

Note

1. Does the shift in focus from pornography's effect on men to its effect on women in Cornell's support of zoning regulation avoid the entrenchment of women as victims that, it is suggested, is inherent in the MacKinnon/Dworkin ordinance approach? Can Cornell's approach avoid confusion with other attempts at conservative regulation of morality?

Conclusion

This part of the book has allowed us to raise complex questions about the appropriate role of law in responding to harms against women and, indeed, the understanding of what is or might be harmful. We have considered a broad array of injuries, trying to move beyond those traditionally recognised as harms by the criminal law, to consider medical abuses, sexual harassment and pornography.

---

169 Cornell also supports a civil rights action for those harmed in the pornography industry: see *The Imaginary Domain* at 102-3.
170 *Ibid*, at 103-4. Cornell also proposes a new definition of pornography and she would restrict the regulation she proposes to heterosexual pornography: see *ibid*, at 106-8.

This array of harms has allowed us to consider in some depth the way law can or could be used to respond to gendered injuries, and the effect of legal engagement. Some of these issues are revisited in the next (and concluding) chapter.

PART FIVE

AN AGENDA FOR GENDER?

Chapter Thirteen

Strategies in Law

Introduction

This chapter brings together some broad questions about feminist strategies for engaging with the legal system. We commence, and conclude, the chapter by considering whether there is any point engaging with law – that is, we ask the question of whether law is a likely site for generating progressive political change on behalf of women. In order to consider that question, we spend the bulk of the chapter examining a range of different forms of engagement with law. We start by examining some aspects of women's lower status within the legal profession, and then discuss and evaluate a range of ways in which women might engage with law. But first, we return to issues of legal method, which we explored in detail in Chapter 4.

Is there any point engaging with law?

In Chapter 4 we raised a series of questions about legal method, including law's tendency to make claims to truth and thus to discount the validity of knowledges outside law's own frame of reference. A question we raised there was whether law (or legal method) were amenable to feminist challenges. For example, in her book, *Feminism and the Power of Law*, Carol Smart argued that we needed to 'marginalize law and to challenge law's over-inflated view of itself'.[1] Her aim was to 'create a greater space for feminism as a form of knowledge which has until now been continuously disqualified by law'.[2] Smart expressed a concern that 'within the development of feminist jurisprudence there may be a tendency to accept parameters already laid down by law and positivist social science'.[3] This concern informs our consideration of a series of strategies and we return to it at the end of this chapter.

Adding women (and stirring): Will more women make a difference?

It is still common to hear suggestions that the under-representation of women in senior positions in the legal profession (for example, senior counsel, partners in law firms and the judiciary) is a function of history – 'it's only a matter of time' – and that as more women graduate from law schools, this will change. However, women have been well represented in law schools for some considerable time and,

---

1 *Feminism and the Power of Law*, Routledge, London, 1989, at 3.
2 *Ibid*.
3 *Ibid*. Smart is particularly concerned about the use of rights discourse, which she suggests has become 'more of a weapon against women than in favour of feminism'. For a discussion of rights discourses, see Morgan, 'Equality Rights in the Australian Context: A Feminist Assessment' in Phillip Alston (ed), *Towards an Australian Bill of Rights*, HREOC/CIPL, Canberra, 1994.

while the number of 'handmaidens' in law, as Thornton has described them[4] may have increased, the number of women who are partners in law firms, for example, has actually declined over the past 10 years, at least in NSW.[5] Reports of inquiries such as *Equality of Opportunity for Women at the Victorian Bar*[6] and the Keys Young report in NSW[7] suggest that the climate for women barristers and women solicitors remains a chilly one. It is still the exception, rather than a matter of routine, for judges to be women, so much so that a NSW Court of Appeal full bench constituted solely by women received a prominent photograph in the newspaper (a page three photograph of a different kind).[8] And to the extent women are appointed to the bench, not only are they still seen as oddities, but perhaps because they are extraordinary, they may also be the subject of challenges to their impartiality, that is, simply challenged on the basis that they are women.[9]

When the Australian Women Lawyers Association was launched in 1997, Justice Mary Gaudron, the first (and by 2001, still the only) woman to have been a member of the High Court of Australia, said:

> It has been said for many years, that it is only a matter of time until women are properly represented in the various fields of legal endeavour. Well, how much time? It is close on 100 years since we've had women lawyers, since the doors have been formally open. It's 45 years since we had a women lawyers' association in New South Wales; for over 30 years we've had women silks, with Roma Mitchell's appointment in South Australia in 1962 and Joan Rosanove's in Victoria in 1965; we've had anti-discrimination legislation in three States for 20 years and at a national level since 1984. For the past 20 years women have represented in excess of 30% of all law graduates and now represent more than half.
>
> In the life of the Supreme Court of New South Wales, just over 180 justices have been appointed to it. Only three of those have been women. The last 5 appointees have been men. I have, I confess, heard many explanations for the under-representation of women in the ranks of leading advocates. I have, for example, been told that women with merit will inevitably be granted silk and get the briefs they deserve. This is a theory I might accept if there were evidence that merit is the universal yardstick for the granting of silk to men or, even, for the success of male barristers.
>
> A more recent theory, and one propounded by the New South Wales Bar Association in its dissenting report on Recommendations on Judicial Appointment to the Ministerial Committee on Gender Bias and the Law is not that there is discrimination at the Bar, but that women are making decisions early in their careers not to pursue the opportunities available. In other words, they are deciding not to go to the Bar. Could it be that the work practices at the Bar are not congenial to women? Could it be that the cost of establishing chambers has a different impact on women who may need to interrupt their careers by reason of

---

4   Margaret Thornton, *Dissonance and Distrust*, Oxford University Press, Melbourne, 1996, at 8.
5   Law Society of NSW, *Profile of the Solicitors of NSW 1998*, Research Report 2, 1998, Table 7.
6   Victorian Bar Council, 1998. See Rosemary Hunter and Helen McKelvie, 'Gender and Legal Practice' (1999) 24 *Alternative Law Journal* 57.
7   Keys Young, *Research on Gender Bias and Women Working in the Legal Profession*, Report Prepared for the Department for Women, 1995; and NSW Ministry for the Status and Advancement of Women, *Gender Bias and the Law: Women Working in the Legal Profession in NSW*, summary report, March 1995.
8   Claire Harvey, 'All Rise, Women in the Law Set a New Benchmark', *Australian*, 16 April 1999, at 3
9   See, for example, *Bird v Free* (1994) 126 ALR 475. We have discussed this at some length in Chapter 4 above and see, more generally, Graycar, 'The Gender of Judgments: Some Reflections on "Bias"' (1998) 32 *UBCLR* 1.

motherhood? Could it be that the system of patronage, which, after all, is about maintaining the status quo, is inimical to women? Could it be that the environment that men have created is hostile?

> Worse, by far, than the under-representation of women is the fact that notwithstanding the progress that has been made by women in the law and notwithstanding the existence of anti-discrimination legislation, the law is no more accessible than it was, say, 30 years ago, no more affordable, no more efficient and barely more responsive to the needs of women and minorities.[10]

In her speech, Justice Gaudron referred to a note that she had written to a colleague on the court in which she commented:

> The trouble with the women of my generation is that we thought if we knocked the doors down, success would be inevitable: the trouble with the men of your generation is that so many still think that, if they hold the doors open, we will be forever grateful.

Also, in 1997, Federal Court Justice Catherine Branson discussed women's more limited access to the senior echelons of the legal profession in a speech to the NSW Women Lawyers Association.

> Studies concerned with gender bias and the law have identified the culture of the legal profession, both in the private law firms and at the bar, as an impediment to women's success in the law. ... [A]n increasing proportion of women lawyers in NSW is working in private corporations and a decreasing proportion of women lawyers in NSW is working in the private sector of the legal profession. This may well ... raise questions as to the respective capacities of the corporate sector and the private legal sector to make cultural changes in response to the increasing numbers of professional women in the workplace.[11]

After outlining data about the paucity of women judges in Australia, Justice Branson told the following story:

> The remarks that I wish to juxtapose to the statistics with which I opened were made at a recent NSW Bar Association function. What was said on the occasion to which I am referring was something to this effect:
>
> "X's appointment to the Supreme Court, whilst most welcome, took us all by surprise: after all he is a male, heterosexual, came from the inner-bar and he knows something about the law having practiced it for many years".

Notes

1. As Justice Branson went on to point out, the inference that was intended to be drawn from this 'jocular' remark is that judicial appointments are now overwhelmingly made from the ranks of outsiders: that is, women, gay men or lesbians, non-barristers and (perhaps most disturbingly) people unskilled in the law. Of course, as the data she cited (and Justice Gaudron referred to)

---

10 Justice Mary Gaudron, 'Speech to launch Australian Women Lawyers', 19 September 1997, available on <http://www.hcourt.gov.au/speeches/gaudronj/gaudronj_wlasp.htm>. See also Justice Branson's speech to NSW Women Lawyers Association, 'Running on the Edge', October 1997, who said that it 'is important to challenge the notion that time alone will fix the problem, or that it will be sufficient for individual women to be seen to practise the law with a high degree of competence. These things we now know cannot alone achieve significant change': <www.wlansw.asn.au/branson.htm>.

11 Justice Catherine Branson, speech to NSW Women Lawyers Association, 'Running on the Edge', October 1997, available at <www.wlansw.asn.au/branson.htm>.

show, nothing could be further from the truth. How then do we account for the power and persistence of such a myth?

2. Is it clear that having more women judges will improve women's position in law, both as members of the legal community and as people whose legal problems are resolved by courts (or by negotiation in the 'shadow of the law')? What arguments support having more women? Is it an issue of representation – that is, since women constitute over half the population, they should be represented in a substantial manner? If the argument is simply one of representation, then should the judiciary be constituted to reflect the general spread of the population in all ways?[12] What do the bias challenges discussed in Chapter 4 tell us about what knowledges or common senses judicial decision-makers bring (or are expected to bring) to decision-making? Are these knowledges impaired or enhanced by membership of, or experience within, some group or experience not commonly shared by white able-bodied heterosexual men? Does a woman who comes to the bench cease to see the world through the lens of her various experiences as a woman, as a mother, as a (potential) target of male violence, etc? Does a black judge learn to disavow knowledge of the existence of racism?

3. Might arguments about increasing the number of women judges imply that it is not the responsibility of the existing white male judges to take on board feminist and other critiques of the legal system? One alternative, or additional, strategy to increasing the responsiveness of the judiciary is to ensure that the current judges are made aware of the gendered (and racialised) partiality of many legal doctrines. To this end, various courts, especially the Family Court, and other bodies such as the Australian Institute of Judicial Administration (AIJA), have undertaken programs on issues such as gender awareness and cultural diversity.[13] Canadian Sherene Razack has pointed out that since, according to Homi Bhabha, '"multiculturalism must be seen to be done, as noisily and publicly as possible", white judges are being urged to be culturally sensitive'.[14]

> Judges begin to practice what Dwight Greene has described for the American context as a kind of "pluralistic ignorance": "Mostly affluent white males talking among themselves about what are the reasonable choices for poor people of color to be making in situations virtually none of the judges have ever been in". ... In Canada white judges have been

---

12 For discussion of this issue in relation to juries, see Martha Minow, 'Stripped Down Like a Runner or Enriched by Experience: Bias and Impartiality of Judges and Jurors' (1992) 33 *William & Mary Law Review* 1201. Cf the decision of the US Supreme Court in *JEB v Alabama ex rel TB* 511 US 127 (1994); and see *Biddle v The Queen* [1995] 1 SCR 761 (Supreme Court of Canada).

13 Compare the comment by North J in *Sun Zhan Qui v Minister for Immigration and Ethnic Affairs*: A decision-maker may not be open to persuasion and, at the same time, not recognise that limitation. Indeed, a characteristic of prejudice is the lack of recognition by the holder. Some judges, including myself, who have in recent years attended gender and race awareness programmes, have been struck by the unrecognised nature of the baggage which we carry on such issues. Decisions made upon assumptions or prejudgments concerning race or gender have been made by many well-meaning judges, unaware of the assumptions or preconceptions which, in fact, governed their decision-making: (1997) 151 ALR 505 at 563-4 (Federal Court, Full Court).

14 Sherene Razack, 'What is to be Gained by Looking White People in the Eye? Culture, Race, and Gender in Cases of Sexual Violence' (1994) 19 *Signs* 894 at 898, citing Homi Bhabha, 'A Good Judge of Character: Men, Metaphors, and the Common Culture' in Toni Morrison (ed), *Race-ing Justice, En-Gendering Power: Essays on Anita Hill, Clarence Thomas, and the Construction of Social Reality*, Pantheon, New York, 1992.

discussing Aboriginal culture and its relevance to the sentencing of Aboriginal males convicted of sexual assault, among other offenses. At least three judicial education programs have been undertaken to "sensitize" judges to issues of cultural diversity among immigrant as well as aboriginal communities (projects conceived of as entirely separate from gender sensitivity training, thereby rendering racialized women invisible).[15]

Does this suggest that such programs should be abandoned? How might we respond constructively to such critiques?[16]

4. In her speech extracted above, Justice Branson suggested that judges and others with power and privilege in the legal profession should use that power for progressive ends.

> [T]here is, I think, a special role that those of us whose political authority is greater than average can play. Included in that class are all those who hold positions of authority in Bar Associations, Law Societies, legal firms and of course, those who hold judicial office. All of us in these positions enjoy the privileges, and share the responsibilities, of leadership. We can, if we choose to do so, exert particular influence within our own legal institutions in an endeavour to make them places in which all lawyers, female and male, can feel comfortable and find support and encouragement. We can do all of this whilst at the same time seeing to protect that which is positive in our legal traditions. We can, in short, seek to expose attempts, conscious and unconscious, to maintain as part of the law, a male-based culture already passed its use-by-date.
>
> ... [T]his might well involve a measure of what is currently fashionable to describe as "political correctness". As I understand the notion of "political correctness", it involves an eschewing of language which, either implicitly or explicitly, excludes from a group those who have a legitimate claim to be part of it; and it further involves not articulating those judgments based on prejudices that cannot withstand intellectual scrutiny. So understood, I am happy to say that I am a supporter of political correctness. So understood, more, not less of it, it seems to me, would be in the public interest.[17]

What are some of the ways that judges might proactively engage with social justice issues?[18] Might doing this raise concerns about them being 'political'?[19]

---

15 Razack, 'What is to be Gained', at 898-9, citing John O Clamore, 'Critical Race Theory, Archie Shepp, and Fire Music: Securing an Authentic Intellectual Life in a Multicultural World' (1992) 65 *Southern California Law Review* 2129.

16 For another critical discussion, see Sonia N Lawrence, 'Cultural (In)sensitivity: The Dangers of a Simplistic Approach to Culture in the Courtroom' (2001) 13 *Canadian Journal of Women and the Law* 107 at 130-2.

17 Justice Catherine Branson, 'Running on the Edge', Address to the Women Lawyers Association of NSW, 15 October 1997, available at <http://www.wlansw.asn.au/branson.htm>.

18 In 2001, two lesbian judges in South Africa brought actions alleging that their treatment denied them their constitutional right to equality. In the first, Judge Kathleen Satchwell challenged the regulation dealing with allowances payable to judges (for example, travel allowance) on the ground that, while heterosexual spouses were recognised, her same sex partner was not. In the second case, Suzanne Du Toit and her partner, Judge Anna-Maria De Vos, challenged provisions of the *Child Care Act* and *Guardianship Act* that did not recognise same sex partners as joint adoptive parents. Both succeeded: see <http://www.suntimes.co.za/business/legal/2001/09/30/carmel01.asp>.

19 Recall the discussion in Chapter 4 where a feminist legal scholar was described under the rubric 'Legal Scholarship for a Cause', while a tax lawyer was described as undertaking 'conventional legal research'. See Christine Boyle, 'Sexual Assault and the Feminist Judge' (1986) 1 *Canadian Journal* 93 at 102, note 39.

5. In her 1987 book, *Feminism Unmodified*, Catharine MacKinnon also addressed the question of whether the increased participation of women, both as lawyers and as judges, will bring about any effective change in the structure and values of the legal system. In 'On Exceptionality: Women as Women in Law', a speech to mark the elevation of two women to the Supreme Court of Minnesota, she asked:

> When I think about Rosalie and Mary Jean on this Court, I ask myself: will they use the tools of law as women, for all women. I think that the real feminist issue is not whether biological males or biological females hold positions of power, although it is utterly essential that women be there. ... My issue is what our identifications are, who our community is, to whom we are accountable. [20]

Is the issue, then, not so much how many women there are on courts, but how many feminists?[21]

6. Early in 1999, the Supreme Court of Canada, in a 9-0 decision, overturned a judgment of the Alberta Court of Appeal in a sexual assault case.[22] While all members of the court found that it was wrong for the Court of Appeal to have adopted a concept of 'implied consent' to sexual assault, L'Heureux-Dubé J, one of two women on the court, issued a separate judgment, with which one other (male) judge expressly concurred. She addressed some of the myths and stereotypes in the judgment of McClung JA in the court below, who had said, inter alia, that 'the complainant did not present herself ... in a bonnet and crinolines'[23] and who said of the perpetrator, his 'advances to the complainant were far less criminal than hormonal'.[24] The day after the Supreme Court's judgment, Justice McClung wrote a letter to a national newspaper attacking Justice L'Heureux-Dubé, and linking the male suicide rate in Quebec with her judgment.[25] What followed was a national 'debate' over a period of weeks about whether 'feminism had gone too far', coupled with calls for Justice L'Heureux-Dubé's resignation.[26] In April 1999, the Canadian Judicial Council dismissed REAL Women's complaint against Justice L'Heureux-Dubé[27] and,

---

20 *Feminism Unmodified*, at 77.
21 Cf Justice Maryka Omatsu, 'On Judicial Appointments: Does Gender Make a Difference?' in Joseph Fletcher (ed), *Ideas in Action: Essays on Politics and Law in Honour of Peter Russell*, University of Toronto Press, Toronto, 1999; Ontario Law Reform Commission, 'Gender Representation in the Canadian Judiciary' by Isabel Grant and Lynn Smith in *Appointing Judges: Philosophy, Politics and Practice*, OLRC, Toronto, 1991; Clare McGlynn, 'Judging Women Differently: Gender, the Judiciary and Reform' in Susan Millns and Noel Whitty (eds), *Feminist Perspectives on Public Law*, Cavendish, London, 1999; Sean Cooney, 'Gender and Judicial Selection: Should there be More Women on the Courts?' (1993) 19 *Melbourne University Law Review* 20.
22 *R v Ewanchuk* [1999] 1 SCR 330.
23 Cited by L'Heureux-Dubé J in *Ewanchuk*, at para 88.
24 *Ibid*, at para 92.
25 The letter was published in the *National Post*, 26 February 1999; and see also *National Post*, 27 February 1999: 'Judge Reiterates Belief That Teen Wasn't Assaulted'.
26 REAL Women (Realistic, Effective and Active for Life), a well-known conservative group, lodged a complaint against her to the Canadian Judicial Council. In our first edition, we extracted a speech given by former Supreme Court Justice Justice Bertha Wilson, now published as 'Will Women Judges Make a Difference?' (1990) 28 *Osgoode Hall Law Journal* 507. When she first made that speech, REAL Women also called for her resignation. For just one example of some of the hostile press Justice L'Heureux-Dubé received, see (syndicated columnist) Barbara Amiel, 'Feminists, Fascists and Other Radicals: Claire L'Heureux-Dubé opposes the ideas for which we fought WWII and the Cold War', *National Post*, Commentary, 6 March 1999.
27 Canadian Judicial Council, News Release, 'Council releases response to REAL Women of Canada', available at <http://www.cjc-ccm.gc.ca/english/news_releases/1999_04_01.htm>.

in May 1999, the Council issued its determination on the 24 complaints it had received about Justice McClung, expressing 'strong disapproval' of his conduct.[28] In its letter to him, the Council noted that it was 'simply unacceptable conduct for a judge' to imply, as he did in the *Ewanchuk* judgment, that the complainant was not a 'nice girl' or that she could have resolved any difficulties with a 'slap in the face' or a 'well placed knee'. The panel also disapproved of what they described as his 'gratuitous observations' about gays and lesbians in his reasons for judgment in *Vriend*.[29]

Do you think an attack like that made by Justice McClung against Justice L'Heureux-Dubé would have been made had the latter been male? What does an incident like this tell us about the place of women in law, even those who, like Justice L'Heureux-Dubé, serve on their country's highest judicial body?[30]

Intervening in litigation

There are obviously ways for the perspectives of women to be presented in court without their being judicial decision-makers. It is often suggested that a Bill of Rights opens up courts to challenges by disadvantaged groups and that perhaps, if Australia had a Bill of Rights, women would be able to use it as yet another legal strategy to advance women's rights.[31] Yet, as Canadian researchers Gwen Brodsky and Shelagh Day have demonstrated, in the first three years after the Canadian Charter of Rights and Freedoms came into force, only '17 of 591 cases were argued by or on behalf of "disadvantaged" groups'.[32] That is, to the extent that women's groups do participate in Charter litigation, it will often be in the role of intervener in someone else's litigation. In her discussion of *R v Seaboyer; R v Gayme*,[33] the Supreme Court of Canada's 1991 decision about the rape shield statute, Liz Sheehy notes:

> The prohibitive costs of Charter litigation and the survival needs of those who have suffered discrimination (who are therefore reluctant to take on the social consequences of assuming the legal status of 'victim') are continuing obstacles to women's participation in Charter litigation.[34]

Sheehy points out that, while there are difficulties that confront feminists attempting to engage in any litigation, there are particular issues that arise when the litigation involves criminal law, such as the challenge to the rape shield law brought by the defendants in *R v Seaboyer* and *R v Gayme*.

---

28 See Canadian Judicial Council, News Release, 'Panel Expresses Strong Disapproval of McClung Conduct', available at <http://www.cjc-ccm.gc.ca/english/news_releases/1999_05_21.htm>.
29 *Ibid*. In *Vriend v Alberta* [1998] 1 SCR 493, the Supreme Court of Canada overturned a judgment of the Alberta Court of Appeal ((1996) 181 AR 116) which had held that the *Individual's Rights Protection Act* 1980 (Alberta) did not apply to discrimination on the grounds of sexuality.
30 For a review of Justice L'Heureux-Dubé's work, see Mimi Liu, 'A "Prophet With Honour": An Examination of the Gender Equality Jurisprudence of Madam Justice Claire L'Heureux-Dubé of the Supreme Court of Canada' (2000) 25 *Queen's Law Journal* 417.
31 See the discussion by Hilary Charlesworth, and other presentations to the Women's Constitutional Convention, at <http://www.womensconv.dynamite.com.au/charles3.htm> and <http://www.womensconv.dynamite.com.au/prgoram5.htm> (January 1998).
32 Gwen Brodsky and Shelagh Day, *Women and the Canadian Charter of Rights and Freedoms: One Step Forward or Two Steps Back?* Canadian Advisory Council on the Status of Women, Ottawa, 1989.
33 [1991] 2 SCR 577.
34 Elizabeth Sheehy, 'Feminist Argumentation before the Supreme Court of Canada in *R v Seaboyer; R v Gayme:* The Sound of One Hand Clapping' (1991) 18 *Melbourne University Law Review* 450 at 456.

> Women are infrequently in the position of accused and women in the role of 'complainant' do not have legal status as parties. A 'complainant' will not ordinarily have her own lawyer ... and, even if she retains counsel, it is questionable whether that lawyer would have standing to interfere in the conduct of a criminal trial. ...
>
> A feminist organisation could have perhaps gone on the offensive and sought out a woman testifying as the primary witness in a particular rape trial in order to create a test case. However ... how can feminists in good faith ask a woman who has survived a rape to sacrifice herself by shouldering a lengthy and painful litigation process ...?[35]

As we noted above, Sheehy points out that litigation is rarely initiated by feminists who instead tend to be responding to someone else's case. One consequence of this is that the first time a feminist organisation may be involved is at the appellate stage, by which time it is no longer possible to adduce evidence, including statistical or expert evidence, that might help to elucidate the context; and the structure and content of the argument has, especially in a criminal case, already been set by the accused, requiring feminist lawyers to make what may be particularly conservative arguments. Sheehy suggests that this latter tendency is very common:

> [L]awyers, including feminist lawyers, often 'hedge their bets' by offering alternative, less radical positions. For example, in an effort to have some influence upon the outcome in *Seaboyer*, I have used this form of argument in my own writing by arguing that: first, sexual history evidence is never 'relevant'; second, even if considered 'relevant', its exclusion does not offend section 7 because 'fundamental justice' must also include women's interests in bodily security; third, if section 7 were said to be violated, such violation must be offset against women's equality rights in section 15 ...; and fourth, even if a section 7 charter violation were found, the law should be saved under section 1 as 'demonstrably justified in a free and democratic society'.[36]

Sheehy points out that arguing in this way leaves it open for judges to ignore the more radical arguments in favour of the least radical.

Even without a Charter or Bill of Rights, litigation does sometimes raise issues of central concern to women. In Chapters 7 and 8, we discussed aspects of the litigation that flowed from *CES v Superclinics*,[37] a case that involved the failure by a medical centre to diagnose a young woman's pregnancy. CES sued the centre, seeking, inter alia, the costs of bringing up her child. After the trial judge had found against her on the ground that had she terminated the pregnancy, it would have been 'illegal', the High Court granted leave to appeal against a somewhat inconclusive decision of the NSW Court of Appeal.

We argued prior to the High Court's hearing the appeal that this case was basically a medical negligence case and that the judges who had focused their attention on the legality or otherwise of what was a purely hypothetical abortion were going beyond what was necessary or relevant for them to decide the case.[38]

However, the approach we had taken did not anticipate the intervention of the Catholic Church. In a surprising decision, the Catholic Bishops Conference and the Catholic Health Care Providers' Federation were granted leave by the High

---

35 Sheehy, at 457-8.
36 *Ibid*, at 460.
37 (1995) 38 NSWLR 47.
38 Graycar and Morgan, '"Unnatural Rejection of Womanhood and Motherhood": Pregnancy, Damages and the Law – A Note on *CES v Superclinics*' (1996) 18 *Sydney Law Review* 323.

Court to participate in the case as amicus curiae.[39] The application for amicus curiae standing was itself contested: it was decided by a vote of 3:3 of the members of the High Court, the casting vote being that of the Chief Justice.[40] Once the church was allowed to participate, the nature of the case was set to change dramatically into what became known as the first major 'abortion test case'. At that stage, women's organisations had no option but to try to respond.[41] The Abortion Providers' Federation, however, was granted amicus curiae standing[42] and the Women's Electoral Lobby (WEL) later announced its intention to seek leave to participate as well. In the event, the case settled before the application by WEL could be decided.[43]

Notes

1. In her discussion on *Seaboyer*, Sheehy also suggests that:

   [I]t is neither simple nor certain that we can articulate a 'women's' position on many issues involving claims to equality. Women of colour, white women and First Nations women may start with different understandings of their oppression; white women may stand in relations of dominance and racism with respect to non white women; and we may have political priorities which are not identical. It may also be difficult to prepare a 'women's' position in the context of litigation given class differences and competing feminist visions.[44]

   Suppose WEL's application to participate in *CES* had been upheld: how would an intervention by 'women' have taken account of such concerns? As we noted in Chapter 4, it may be difficult in a litigation context to reflect a more nuanced understanding of the recent challenges to 'white' feminism by Aboriginal women and women of non-English speaking background. In Chapter 8, we discussed some of the different ways in which women experience their reproductive lives and raised the concern about the difficulties of

---

39 See *Superclinics Australia Pty Ltd v CES*, High Court of Australia, No S88 of 1996, Transcript of Proceedings, 11 September 1996.
40 There were only six members hearing the application as Kirby J did not sit: he had been a member of the NSW Court of Appeal when it considered the matter. When the application for leave to intervene was made, Brennan CJ said: 'I have asked the Senior Registrar to inform counsel that I know Father McKenna, a deponent to one of the affidavits in support of the application to intervene, or to appear amicus curiae, and a number of members of the Australian Catholic Bishops' Conference': Transcript of Proceedings, 11 September 1996, at 4.
41 The decision to respond was made even though there is no organised women's litigation group. This contrasts quite sharply with the situation in Canada where the Women's Legal Education and Action Fund (LEAF) has intervened in a series of cases, including before the Supreme Court of Canada, on behalf of women. Some of this work is described in Sherene Razack, *Canadian Feminism and the Law*, Second Story Press, Toronto, 1991; and see LEAF, *Equality and the Charter: 1985-1995*, Emond Montgomery, Toronto, 1996.
42 *Superclinics Australia Pty Ltd v CES*, High Court of Australia, No S88 of 1996, Transcript of Proceedings, 12 September 1996.
43 See Jo Wainer, 'Abortion before the High Court' (1997) 8 *Australian Feminist Law Journal* 133. For more general discussion of the role of amicus curiae in the context of this litigation, see Rosemary Owens, 'Interveners and Amicus Curiae: The Role of The Courts in a Modern Democracy' (1998) 20 *Adelaide Law Review* 193. See also The Hon Justice Susan Kenny, 'Interveners and Amici Curiae in the High Court' (1998) 20 *Adelaide Law Review* 159 esp at 162-5; and Warwick Neville, 'Abortion Before the High Court – What Next? Caveat Interventus: A Note on Superclinics Pty Ltd v CES' (1998) 20 *Adelaide Law Review* 183. Neville was the solicitor for the Catholic Bishops Conference and the Catholic Health Care Providers in the case.
44 Sheehy, 'The Sound of One Hand Clapping', at 456.

conveying some of these differences to a court, while in Chapter 11, we discussed other aspects of women's reproduction, particularly injurious interferences such as eugenic sterilisation. It is unclear whether there would have been an opportunity, even if WEL were granted amicus curiae status,[45] to include in argument any of this diversity of experience. In Australia, there is virtually no history of women making equality arguments, or arguments about reproductive freedom, in the higher courts. Does that mean that we would be constrained to make the most simplistic of arguments about 'women'? By contrast, could it be argued that we have a clean slate and therefore a clear opportunity to construct the most nuanced arguments available in a way that might be constrained by precedent in other jurisdictions?[46]

2. Following the decision of the Canadian Supreme Court in *R v Seaboyer, R v Gayme*, a coalition of women formed to work on redrafting new legislation. The legislation which ensued survived a challenge in the Supreme Court in *Darrach v R*.[47] The process leading to its drafting is described by Sheila McIntyre:

> My hope is that the story of the coalition will provoke new thinking about old debates concerning whether and how women and other historically disempowered groups should pursue egalitarian social change through law. I argue for a particular model of feminist law reform whose measure of achievement is not the reform's particular substantive legal yield or its potential as a building block for changing other laws, but the degree to which it translates principles of accountability to, inclusion of, and genuine power sharing among the broad women's community into feminist legal practice.[48]

What does a focus on process, rather than outcome, imply for legal change? Do you agree with McIntyre that the most appropriate measure of success of a law reform effort is the extent to which the process includes traditionally excluded groups of women (rather than the substantive change achieved)? Apart from monitoring the diversity of groups represented in law reform consultations, how would you assess the success of feminist law reform efforts according to McIntyre's criteria?

Initiating litigation

The discussion of *Seaboyer* and *CES* relates to the most common way in which women's groups are involved in litigation – intervening in cases initiated by others. On occasion women are the primary parties or initiators of the litigation. A good example of this is the case we extracted in Chapter 11 involving Jane Doe, a Toronto rape victim so incensed by the police failure to warn women at risk of attack by a serial rapist that she brought a civil action against the police for negligence.[49] After a 10-year battle, her action was finally heard in 1998 and she was successful.

---

45   There was a suggestion at the time that the Abortion Providers Federation would be raising the same issues as WEL and therefore their application might have been refused.
46   There is a certain irony in the fact that the Catholic Church's successful application for amicus standing in CES is widely considered to have paved the way for a broader range of groups to participate in litigation. In Chapter 8, we discuss the church's involvement in the McBain litigation, concerning access to assisted reproduction services.
47   *Darrach v R* [2000] 2 SCR 443.
48   Sheila McIntyre, 'Redefining Reformism: the Consultations that Shaped Bill C-49' in Julian V Roberts and Renate M Mohr (eds), *Confronting Sexual Assault: A Decade of Legal and Social Change*, University of Toronto Press, Toronto, 1994, at 293-4.
49   *Jane Doe v Metropolitan Toronto (Municipality) Commissioners of Police* (1998) 160 DLR (4th) 697.

However, there are a number of reasons why test cases initiated by and on behalf of women are likely to be extremely rare. The most mundane (but perhaps the most critical) is the barrier of cost – litigation is very expensive and legal aid is sparse and unlikely to be available for test case litigation. Generally speaking, the majority of Australian legal aid funds go to criminal defendants.[50] In 1992, the High Court of Australia decided in *Dietrich v R*[51] that, in a trial for a serious criminal offence, a person's right to a fair trial may require the state to provide the person with legal representation. The court said:

> [N]o argument was put ... that recognition of such a right for the provision of counsel at public expense would impose an unsustainable financial burden on government. In these circumstances, we should proceed on the footing that if a trial judge were to grant an adjournment to an unrepresented accused on the ground that the accused's trial is likely to be unfair without representation, that approach is not likely to impose a substantial financial burden on government and it may require no more than a re-ordering of the priorities according to which legal aid funds are presently allocated.[52]

In 1994, the Commonwealth Attorney General's Department published a paper on the gendered effects of (then current) legal aid policies.[53] The data referred to in the paper pre-dated the decision in *Dietrich*. It was pointed out that, since the vast majority of criminal defendants are men, while women are more likely to be seeking legal aid funds for family law or civil actions,[54] legal aid funds are increasingly being spent on crime and therefore are less available for the types of cases women might be involved with. It was anticipated that the decision in *Dietrich* would significantly exacerbate that situation.[55]

Notes

1. The High Court made the point that no-one presented an argument in the *Dietrich* case as to any financial implications the case might have. Who might have made such an argument? What assumptions underpin the primacy given to funding criminal cases? What other types of cases might raise issues that go to interests analogous to loss of liberty?[56]
2. Even if funding is available for test case litigation, there are a series of tactical and ethical issues raised by such actions. For example, whose case is it? Who

---

50 See Legal Aid and Family Services, *Gender Bias in Litigation Legal Aid*, Issues Paper, Attorney General's Department, February 1994; ALRC, *Equality Before the Law: Justice for Women*, Report No 69 Part 1, 1994, Chapter 4, 'Access to Justice: Legal Aid'.
51 (1992) 177 CLR 292.
52 *Dietrich v R* (1992) 177 CLR 292 at 312 per Mason CJ and McHugh J. The High Court noted that, while the Commonwealth and all States were given notice of the issues to be argued, only the Commonwealth and South Australian governments had participated in the case.
53 *Gender Bias in Litigation Legal Aid*.
54 For some discussions of legal aid funding in the context of family law, see Rosemary Hunter et al, *Legal Services in Family Law*, Law and Justice Foundation, 2001; John Dewar, Barry Smith and Cate Banks, *Litigants in Person in the Family Court of Australia*, Family Court of Australia, Research Report No 20, 2000. See also Billi Clarke and Helen Matthews, *Trial by Legal Aid: A Legal Aid Impact Study*, Crossroads Family and Domestic Violence Unit and Victorian Women's Refuges and Associated Domestic Violence Services Legal Sub Group, 1999.
55 The detailed findings are discussed in Graycar and Morgan, 'Disabling Citizenship: Civil Death for Women in the 1990s?' (1995) 17 *Adelaide Law Review* 49.
56 See Mary Jane Mossman, 'Gender Equality and Legal Aid Services: A Research Agenda For Institutional Change' (1993) 15 *Sydney Law Review* 30; Mary Jane Mossman, 'Gender Equality, Family Law and Access to Justice' (1994) 8 *International Journal of Law and the Family* 357.

has control? What are the consequences of a successful (or unsuccessful) action? What constitutes a 'precedent'? For example, will other (Canadian) trial judges be bound by the decision in *Jane Doe*? It will be recalled that, in Australia in 2000, the federal government vigorously defended a test case brought by Lorna Cubillo and Peter Gunner, members of the 'stolen generations'; indeed, the government is reported to have spent $11.5m defending the case at trial.[57] The government's resistance to an apology or any kind of group response to the 'stolen generations' suggests that, even had they been successful, the government may still have defended claims brought by other individuals.

3. What other constraints might attach to pursuing social change through litigation? In Chapter 8, we explored a variety of legal strategies used by feminists to ensure access to safe, publicly funded abortion. We speculated on the advantages and disadvantages of various approaches. Similar questions can be raised about many areas of women's lives. For example, in the context of campaigns for recognition of gay and lesbian relationships, Graycar and Millbank have argued that, in jurisdictions where constitutional litigation has led to legislation recognising same sex relationships, the resulting legislation may be constrained by the form of the legal challenge.[58] They argue that relationship recognition legislation that has been developed outside a litigation context may be more likely to recognise a more flexible range of relationships (such as non-sexual and non-cohabiting relationships) than legislation that is enacted to respond to a successful court challenge. For example, following the decision of the Supreme Court of Canada in *M v H*,[59] the province was required to amend all relevant statutes to ensure that same sex couples were treated the same as heterosexual couples.[60] By contrast, in NSW, the ACT and Victoria, the law now recognises (albeit in limited circumstances) some relationships that are not sexual or cohabiting relationships, moving beyond the 'comparator' of the heterosexual cohabiting couple.[61] Is this an argument for NOT pursuing a Bill of Rights or some other form of constitutional guarantee of equality in Australia? Alternatively, or additionally, is it an argument for an understanding of equality that moves beyond strict equal treatment? While the Supreme Court of Canada has understood equality in a contextualised fashion, does the comparator model of equality – is this group treated the same as that group – continue to dominate constitutional litigation?

---

57 *Cubillo and Gunner v Commonwealth* (2000) 174 ALR 97. Bob McMullan, then Shadow Minister for Aboriginal Affairs, commented: 'This litigation has cost taxpayers over $11.5 million to date and there are more costs to come. These costs, when broken down, include over $1 million for one lawyer alone and $770,000 spent on private investigators', at <http://www.humanrights.gov.au/movingforward/speech_mcmullan.html> (16 August 2001). These costs relate only to the trial: the (unsuccessful) appeal would have involved considerable additional costs.

58 See Reg Graycar and Jenni Millbank, 'The Bride Wore Pink ... To the Property (Relationships) Legislation Amendment Act 1999: Family Law Reform in NSW' (2000) 17 *Canadian Journal of Family Law* 227 at 273-4.

59 *M v H* [1999] 2 SCR 3.

60 The title of the ensuing statute explains its origins: *Amendments Because of the Supreme Court of Canada Decision in M v H 1999* (Ontario), SO 1999, c 6.

61 See for discussion of the NSW and ACT legislation, Graycar and Millbank, 'The Bride Wore Pink'; and Graycar, 'Concept of Family Under Review' (2001) 39(3) *Law Society Journal* 64; for a discussion of the Victorian legislation, see Miranda Stewart, 'Victoria: Same Sex Domestic Partnerships Now Law' (2001) 26 *Alternative Law Journal* 261.

Creating new legal claims

Sexual harassment

As we noted in Chapters 10 and 12 above, 'sexual harassment' is a recently developed legal name for a practice of long standing. The first comprehensive legal response to this form of injury was developed by Catharine MacKinnon[62] and 10 years on she reflected on the development of this legal claim:

> ### Catharine A MacKinnon, 'Sexual Harassment: Its First Decade in Court'
> in *Feminism Unmodified*, Harvard University Press, Cambridge MA, 1987
>
> [103] Sexual harassment, the event, is not new to women. It is the law of injuries that it is new to. ... Sexual harassment, the legal claim – the idea that the law should see it the way its victims see it – is definitely a feminist invention. Feminists first took women's experience seriously enough to uncover this problem and conceptualize it and pursue it legally. ...
>
> The law against sexual harassment is a practical attempt to stop a form of exploitation. It is also one test of sexual politics as feminist jurisprudence, of possibilities for social change for women through law. The existence of a law against sexual harassment has affected both the context of meaning within which social life is lived and the concrete delivery of rights through the legal system. The sexually [104] harassed have been given a name for their suffering and an analysis that connects it with gender. They have been given a forum, legitimacy to speak, authority to make claims, and an avenue for possible relief. Before, what happened to them was all right. Now it is not.
>
> This matters. ...
>
> ... The legal claim for sexual harassment made the events of sexual harassment illegitimate socially as well as legally for the first time. Let me know if you figure out a better way to do that.
>
> At this interface between law and society, we need to remember that the legitimacy courts give they can also take. Compared with a possibility of relief where no possibility of relief existed, since women started out with nothing in this area, this worry seems a bit fancy. ... With sexism, there is always a risk that our demand for self-determination will be taken as a demand for paternal protection and will therefore strengthen male power rather than undermine it. ...
>
> Institutional support for sexual self-determination is a victory; institutional paternalism reinforces our lack of self-determination. ... Ultimately, though, the question of whether the use of the state for women helps or hurts can be answered only in practice, because so little real protection of the laws has ever been delivered.
>
> The legal claim for sexual harassment marks the first time in history, to my knowledge, that women have defined women's injuries in a law. ... When the design of a legal wrong does not fit the wrong as it happens to you, as is the case with rape, that law can undermine your social and political as well as legal legitimacy in saying that what happened was an injury at all – even to yourself.
>
> It is never too soon to worry about this, but it may be too soon to know whether the law against sexual harassment will be taken away from us or turn into nothing or turn ugly in our hands. The fact is, this law is working surprisingly well for women by any standards, particularly when compared with the rest of sex discrimination law. If the question is whether a law designed from women's

---

62 See *Sexual Harassment of Working Women*, Yale University Press, New Haven, CT, 1979.

standpoint and administered through this legal system can do anything for women – which always seems to me to be a good question – this experience so far gives a qualified and limited yes. ...

[116] ... For feminist jurisprudence, the sexual harassment attempt suggests that if a legal initiative is set up right from the beginning, meaning if it is designed from women's real experience of violation, it can make some difference. To a degree women's experience can be written into law, even in some tension with the current doctrinal framework. Women who want to resist their victimization with legal terms that imagine it is not inevitable can be given some chance, which is more than they had before. Law is not everything in this respect, but it is not nothing either. Perhaps the most important lesson is that the mountain can be moved. When we started, there was absolutely no judicial precedent for allowing a sex discrimination suit for sexual harassment. Sometimes even the law does something for the first time.

Notes

1. In an omitted section of her discussion of sexual harassment, MacKinnon states: 'Whether the possibility of relief alters the terms of power that gives rise to sexual harassment itself, which makes getting away with it possible, is a different problem'. Do you agree that creating new claims from the standpoint of women is a matter about which feminists should be optimistic? Is it possible for new legal claims to take a specifically feminist perspective, or is it inevitable that the approach will need to be modified in order to be effective?
2. In our discussions of violence, and of sexual harassment (Chapters 10 and 12), we drew attention to the increasing tendency for women to disparage women's claims of violence or sexual harassment as manifestations of 'victim feminism' (for example, Helen Garner's *The First Stone*). In Chapter 12 we were critical of Garner's approach. Nevertheless, could it be argued that the cause of action for sexual harassment amounts to a 'demand for paternal protection' which 'strengthen[s] male power rather than undermine[s] it'?

The Violence Against Women Act

Building on the establishment of the claim for sexual harassment, feminists in the US campaigned over many years to have federal Congress enact a national *Violence Against Women Act*. The Act created a civil right of action for women harmed by violence against them – they could bring an action for sex discrimination directly against the perpetrator. In 2000, a majority of the Supreme Court of the United States held that the Act was beyond the scope of Congress's legislative power.

Catharine A MacKinnon, 'Disputing Male Sovereignty: On United States v Morrison'
(2000) 114 *Harvard Law Review* 135

[135] [*In 2000*] in *United States v Morrison* [120 S Ct 1740 (2000)], the Violence Against Women Act (the VAWA) became one of only two federal laws against discrimination to be invalidated by the United States Supreme Court since Reconstruction. In passing the VAWA, Congress sought to remedy well-documented inadequacies in existing laws against domestic violence and sexual

assault – acts of which women are the principal victims and men the principal perpetrators – by providing a federal civil cause of action for sex discrimination that victims could use directly against perpetrators in state or federal court. Congress passed the statute under both the Commerce Clause and the ... Fourteenth Amendment. ... [T]he 5-4 Morrison majority held that neither clause authorized the VAWA. Congress's commerce power, the Court said, reaches only those private acts that are "economic in nature," which violence against women, despite its impact on interstate commerce, was deemed not to be. Congress's equality power, the Court ruled, is limited to addressing state [136] acts, a limit the VAWA, in reaching what were termed private actors and private acts, was found to transgress. ...

[137] ... I. Background

The Morrison majority did not contest what Congress found during its four years of hearings on the VAWA: violence against women is a sex-based abuse that states have long failed adequately to address. "Violence against women," a phrase used by the women's movement since the 1970s, became in the VAWA a shorthand for the legal term of art "gender-motivated violence," encompassing violent acts directed against men as well as women that are based on gender, the social meaning of sex. In passing the VAWA, Congress intended to put the ability to address sex-based violence into the hands of survivors, in order more effectively to stop violence against them.

Crucially, for the first time in United States history, the VAWA established "zero tolerance" for sex-based violence as a matter of public policy in providing that "[a]ll persons within the United States shall have the right to be free from crimes of violence motivated by gender." Existing laws against gender-motivated violence, by omission as well as by pattern of practice, embody a margin of toleration, project an aura of lassitude, exude a sense in enforcement that some aggression against women by men is inevitable. Legal institutional processes are so imprinted with denial of sexual abuse – both its normality and effective impunity, especially when committed by men [138] with power among men – that it is as if the laws do not mean what they say. The VAWA openly repudiated such systemic habits.

Congress further perceived that the body of law that had pervasively and dramatically failed women subjected to violence by men needed not only a national floor of effectiveness, a uniform standard below which it could not fall, but also a conceptual overhaul from the ground up. Law defined the crime of rape long before women were permitted to vote or to serve on juries. Members of the group more likely to perpetrate sexual assault than be victimized by it have written its legal rules, excluding from that process those more likely to be victimized. To be effective as well as democratic, the VAWA could not simply federalize preexisting criminal or tort law.

In a new departure, the VAWA's civil rights remedy placed violence against women within the law of sex discrimination, recognizing that violence against women is gender-based: it happens because those who do it, and those who have it done to them, are members of social groups defined by sex. The VAWA was the first legislation anywhere to recognize that rape may be an act of sex inequality, its injury a violation of human status on the basis of membership in a gender group. Locating acts of gender-based violence under the rubric of civil rights, identifying the group grounds of a socially based injury, freed survivors from the acontextualized and stigmatic standards of prior criminal and tort law – laws enacted and interpreted when women had no public voice. After an extensive and detailed empirical investigation, Congress produced legislation against battering and rape that began to fit the facts of violence against women for the first time.

Because it was civil, the VAWA by design placed state power into the hands of those victimized by sex-based violence. ... [I]t made perpetrators directly accountable to survivors, potentially intervening in the balance of power between the sexes by empowering rather than protecting the victims of sex-based violence. The civil remedy allowed survivors to initiate and control their own litigation against sex-based violation rather than leaving them at the mercy of police or prosecutorial discretion. Moving beyond incarceration as an outcome – which typically accomplishes little beyond the brutalization (much of it sexual) of perpetrators, promoting more brutality rather than change – the VAWA's civil remedy offered injunctive relief and damages: levers, resources, and authoritative findings to alter perpetrators' behavior and to value and restore survivors.

In all these respects, the Violence Against Women Act took an historic stand and hopeful step toward free and safe lives for women as equal citizens of this nation.

As MacKinnon goes on to note, the Act was invalidated when the action brought by a woman who had been raped at a college which had failed to respond effectively to the injury she experienced tried to seek redress under the Act. She points out:

[144] In receiving no relief from the criminal justice system, Christy Brzonkala's case was typical of most rape cases. Although social attitudes toward rape victims may have improved subtly beginning in the 1970s, rape law reform efforts in the US in the 1970s and 1980s produced little or no detectable improvement in reporting, arrest or conviction rates. ... It was this entrenched lack of progress that the VAWA sought to address, this tide that Christy Brzonkala was swimming against, this system that Chief Justice Rehnquist evoked ... when he wrote, in denying her access to a remedy, "[i]f the allegations here are true, no civilized system of justice could fail to provide her a remedy" [*Morrison*, at 1759].

[145] II. The Decision
... The Morrison majority analyzed violence against women as noneconomic, in the language of commerce, and as local, in the language of federalism, hence constitutionally inappropriate for federal legislation. ... The Court expressed repeated concern for the fate of other laws and the governmental balance if the VAWA was upheld but no concern at all for the fate of violated women if it was invalidated.

Notes

1. The court's invocation of the public/private distinction builds upon the traditional 'state action' doctrine discussed in Chapter 2 above. Indeed, in her critique, MacKinnon suggests that the 'Morrison majority does not simply respect a preexisting line between what is private and what is public. It draws that line by abandoning women wherever violence against them takes place'.[63] She points out:

> Christy Brzonkala was away at school when she was raped, paying to attend a public educational institution. She was gang-raped by men she had barely met in a room not her own. Public officials effectively condoned her violation through public legal processes. In what sense was her rape private?[64]

How would you respond to that question?

---

63 (2000) 114 *Harvard Law Review* 135 at 170.
64 *Ibid*, at 171.

2. In his dissenting judgment, Souter J questioned the majority view that gender motivated crimes were not 'economic in nature' and lacked 'commercial character'.[65] As MacKinnon notes, 36 of the 50 American States supported the enactment of the VAWA, clearly providing some support for the view that they believed it was legitimate for Congress to use its commerce power to pass the law. How would you argue that such violence is economic and has clear financial implications both to the individual and the community?

Developing evidentiary strategies: The example of 'battered woman syndrome'

As we noted in Chapter 10, a small number of women who have experienced violence from their partner respond by using lethal force. In defending a murder charge, many of these women may face difficulties in resorting to traditional defences such as self-defence[66] and provocation. Some feminists wanted to introduce evidence aimed at explaining the behaviour of women who had been living in situations of domestic violence, especially the behaviour of those who responded with lethal violence, most particularly to explain the behaviour as action in self-defence. This strategy became one of introducing evidence from experts, usually psychiatrists or psychologists, who testified that women who killed in such circumstances suffered from 'battered woman syndrome'.[67] King CJ in *R v Runjanjic and Kontinnen*, the first Australian case to accept expert evidence of BWS, articulated this view when he stated:

> It emerges from the literature that methodical studies by trained psychologists of situations of domestic violence have revealed typical patterns of behaviour on the part of the male batterer and the female victim, and typical responses on the part of the female victim. It has been revealed, so it appears, that women who have suffered habitual domestic violence are typically affected psychologically to the extent that their reactions and responses differ from those which might be expected by persons who lack the advantage of an acquaintance with the result of those studies.
>
> Repeated acts of violence, alternating very often with phases of kindness and loving behaviour, commonly leave the battered woman in a psychological condition described as "learned helplessness". She cannot predict or control the occurrence of acute outbreaks of violence and often clings to the hope that the kind and loving phases will become the norm. This is often reinforced by financial dependence, children and feelings of guilt. The battered woman rarely seeks outside help because of fear of further violence. It is not uncommon for such women to experience feelings for their mate which they describe as love. There is often an

---

65 There were two dissenting opinions. Souter J filed a dissenting opinion, which Stevens, Ginsburg and Breyer JJ joined; and the dissenting opinion of Breyer J was joined by Stevens J, while Souter and Ginsburg JJ joined in part.

66 The current common law of self-defence is governed by *Zecevic v DPP* (1987) 162 CLR 645, which on its face, should be responsive to the situation of women who kill violent men. The basic test is whether what the accused did was reasonably necessary in the circumstances. There is no separate requirement that the accused was responding to an imminent attack or that the response was proportionate.

67 Lenore Walker, *The Battered Woman Syndrome*, Springer Publishing Co, New York, 1984; and for a critique, see Ian Leader-Elliott, 'Battered but not Beaten: Women who Kill in Self Defence' (1993) 15 *Sydney Law Review* 403. Expert evidence on BWS has been accepted in every jurisdiction in Australia: Julie Stubbs and Julia Tolmie, 'Falling Short of the Challenge? A Comparative Assessment of the Australian Use of Expert Evidence on the Battered Woman Syndrome' (1999) 23 *Melbourne University Law Review* 709 at 721.

all-pervasive feeling that it is impossible to escape the dominance and violence of the mate. There is a sense of constant fear with a perceived inability to escape the situation.[68]

The strategy of using BWS evidence has been strongly criticised by some feminists. In a 1992 article, Elizabeth Sheehy, Julie Stubbs and Julia Tolmie raised a number of concerns about the use of such evidence:

> First, the issue is constructed as being beyond the understanding of the lay juror. This is ironic, given that domestic violence is so widespread in the community. ...
>
> Secondly, the voice of an expert is preferred to that of a woman herself. This reinforces the notion that a woman is not a reliable witness, that her account needs to be buttressed by that of an expert.
>
> Thirdly, the threshold for the admission of expert evidence ... effectively requires the reconstruction of her experience in a way which is consistent with scientific or medical discourse. The resort to a 'syndrome' to explain the experiences of a battered woman is a response to this requirement. What might be useful in describing the experiences of, and responses by, some battered women is reified as a syndrome used to proscribe typical responses by battered women.
>
> Fourthly, the fact that it is usual that expert evidence concerning the battered woman syndrome is given by a psychiatrist or psychologist reinforces notions of irrationality or disorder on the part of the woman. Rather than suggest that her conduct is rational, reasonable and comprehensible, the introduction of psychiatric or psychological evidence implies the opposite. Would psychological or psychiatric testimony be necessary otherwise?
>
> Fifthly, the characterisation of women who resort to violent self-help as helpless is lacking in logic. Learned helplessness does not assist in explaining a woman's resort to killing her abuser. It is also at variance with the help-seeking behaviour of some women to characterise them as helpless. ...
>
> Sixthly, a reliance on expert testimony concerning the psychological reactions by battered women also shifts the focus from the myriad of reasons why a woman may remain in a violent relationship: always implicit is the assumption that if not for her psychological state it was both reasonable and possible to leave. ...
>
> The focus on why a woman *didn't* leave a violent relationship presumes several things. It presumes that she hasn't left – but many women do leave and are coerced into returning by further violence and or threats. It presumes that the violence ceases if a woman leaves the relationship —but the homicide statistics indicate otherwise: many women are killed by spouses either soon after leaving their relationships or whilst in the process of leaving. It fails to address the fact that threats and violence may act to keep women in violent relationships. It fails to acknowledge what research demonstrates about the lack of assistance from police or other agencies for women who are the victims of domestic violence. And, importantly, it fails to acknowledge the limited opportunities for women attempting to leave violent relationships – the lack of affordable housing, childcare, employment and the poverty which awaits many women and children who leave violent men. ...
>
> Choices about staying or leaving, where they can be characterised as choices given the limited options available, may be made with the interests of the children, rather than her own interests, given priority.
>
> A seventh concern ... is that it does not confront the narrow male standard on which reasonableness is constructed. ... Rather, the narrow reasonable standard remains undisturbed, with expert evidence being necessary to explain the departure. ...

---

68   *R v Runjanjic, R v Kontinnen* (1991) 53 A Crim R 362 at 366.

The possibility arises that a battered woman who does not conform to the necessary criteria for the battered woman's syndrome may be disadvantaged for failing two tests of reasonableness – the allegedly neutral male standard and the "reasonable battered women" stereotype. ...

A final concern with the use of battered woman syndrome evidence is that whilst the number of women who kill abusive men is small, such cases have a huge impact on both cultural and legal understandings of women-battering. The focus which the syndrome accords to the psychological characteristics of the woman on trial obscures the social and political dimensions of domestic violence. ... The question which needs to be asked is not 'why didn't she leave', but rather, 'why weren't effective protective mechanisms and social supports in place to make it possible for this woman to escape the violence?'[69]

Notes

1. King CJ referred in his judgment to the decision of Wilson J in *R v Lavallée*,[70] where the Supreme Court of Canada held that evidence of BWS was admissible at the trial of a woman charged with murdering her partner. King CJ described the judgment of Wilson J as a 'strongly, at times passionately, expressed judgment'.[71] Wilson J clearly recognised the gendered nature of violence:

    > If it strains credulity to imagine what the "ordinary man" would do in the position of a battered spouse, it is probably because men do not typically find themselves in that situation. Some women do, however. The definition of what is reasonable must be adapted to circumstances which are, by and large, foreign to the world inhabited by the hypothetical "reasonable man".[72]

    In more recent work, Stubbs and Tolmie suggest that the use of BWS in the US and Canada developed out of a clear recognition of the gendered nature of defences. By contrast:

    > The Australian decisions do not start by recognising limitations in the manner in which the law is applied. In particular, they do not recognise the manner in which existing legal defences have been interpreted to exclude the experiences of many women. Instead Australian decisions tend to proceed on the basis that BWS evidence is useful in explaining the allegedly different perceptions of a woman who has been battered and has developed the symptoms of the syndrome.[73]

---

69 Elizabeth Sheehy, Julie Stubbs and Julia Tolmie, 'Defending Battered Women on Trial: The Battered Woman Syndrome and its Limitations' (1992) 16 *Criminal Law Journal* 369 at 384-7. See also Kirby J in *Osland v R* (1998) 197 CLR 316. For some early critical work, see Elizabeth Schneider, 'Describing and Changing: Women's Self-Defense Work and the Problem of Expert Testimony on Battering' (1986) 9 *Women's Rights Law Reporter* 195; and Elizabeth Schneider, 'Particularity and Generality: Challenges of Feminist Theory and Practice in Work on Woman Abuse' (1992) 67 *New York University Law Review* 520.
70 [1990] 1 SCR 852.
71 *Runjanjic and Kontinnen* (1991) 53 A Crim R 362 at 369.
72 *R v Lavallée* [1990] 1 SCR 852 at 874.
73 Julie Stubbs and Julia Tolmie, 'Falling Short of the Challenge? A Comparative Assessment of the Australian Use of Expert Evidence on the Battered Woman Syndrome' (1999) 23 *Melbourne University Law Review* 709 at 711. Note that Stubbs and Tolmie recognise that the North American experience is not 'uniform, unproblematic or ideal'. Rather they focus on what they describe as 'best practice' in those countries (at note 2).

What are the implications of such an Australian failure? Why might the different jurisdictions have developed such varied approaches to the situation of battered women defendants who kill?

2. *Lavallée* was decided in 1990. The issue came before the Supreme Court of Canada again in 1998 in *Malott*.[74] In a concurring judgment, L'Heureux-Dubé J (with whom McLachlin J agreed) acknowledged the concern that the use of 'syndrome' evidence might lead to a woman being required to show either that she was 'reasonable "like a man" or reasonable like a "battered woman"'.[75]

> It is possible that those women who are unable to fit themselves within the stereotype of a victimized, passive, helpless, dependent, battered woman will not have their claims to self defence fairly decided. For instance, women who have demonstrated too much strength or initiative, women of colour, women who are professionals, or women who might have fought back against their abusers on previous occasions, should not be penalized for failing to accord with the stereotypical image of the archetypal battered woman. ...
>
> How should the courts combat the 'syndromization' ... of battered women who act in self defence? The legal inquiry into the moral culpability of a woman who is, for instance, claiming self defence must focus on the reasonableness of her actions in the context of her personal experiences, and her experiences as a woman, not on her status as a battered woman and her entitlement to claim that she is suffering from 'battered woman syndrome'. ...
>
> To fully accord with the spirit of *Lavallée*, where the reasonableness of a battered woman's belief is at issue in a criminal case, a judge and jury should be made to appreciate that a battered woman's experiences are both individualized, based on her own history and relationships, as well as shared with other women, within the context of a society and a legal system which has historically undervalued women's experiences.[76]

Wilson J, who wrote the leading judgment in *Lavallée*, was the first woman appointed to the Supreme Court of Canada. The dissenting member of the Ontario Court of Appeal, whose judgment was affirmed in *Malott*, Justice Abella, is also a woman, as are Justices L'Heureux-Dubé and McLachlin (now Chief Justice of the Supreme Court of Canada). What relevance, if any, do you consider this might have?

3. In their 1999 article, Stubbs and Tolmie suggest that:

> Recent US and Canadian legal developments have recognised that, where relevant, what is required to assist judges and juries is not so much expert testimony about whether or not a woman might have BWS but rather broad 'social framework evidence' to provide the context within which to understand the issues in a given case.[77]

---

74 [1998] 1 SCR 123.
75 *Malott* [1998] 1 SCR 123 at para 40, citing Isabel Grant, 'The "Syndromization" of Women's Experience' in Donna Martinson et al, 'A Forum on Lavallée v R: Women and Self Defence' (1991) 25 *University of British Columbia Law Review* 23; and Julie Stubbs and Julia Tolmie, 'Race, Gender, and the Battered Woman Syndrome: An Australia Case Study' (1995) 8 *Canadian Journal of Women and the Law* 122.
76 *Malott* [1998] 1 SCR 123 at paras 40-43.
77 Stubbs and Tolmie, 'Falling Short of the Challenge?' (1999) 23 *Melbourne University Law Review* 709 at 711.

It follows from this that the range of experts called on to give evidence in North America is likely to be broader than the psychologists and psychiatrists who typically give evidence in Australia.[78] What kinds of expertise would be relevant? What kind of material would constitute 'social framework evidence'? Are there other ways, apart from listening to experts, for judges to know about the context in which women are battered?

4. Stubbs and Tolmie make the point that there are now Australian cases where women who kill their battering spouses have been acquitted – that is, have successfully raised self-defence – without invoking BWS evidence.[79] Do you think it is likely that this would have happened without the introduction of BWS evidence in earlier cases?[80]

Legislative initiatives/law reform

We mentioned earlier the arguably limited role played by litigation in a jurisdiction that does not have a Bill of Rights. Historically, feminist activism in Australia has focused on the legislative arena far more than on the courts. For example, in Chapter 8, we discussed the changes to the abortion laws in WA that followed the charging of a medical practitioner. In that situation, the WA legislature proved responsive to changes that were led by women.[81] In the 1970s and 1980s, it was common to refer in Australia to the 'femocracy', a term coined to acknowledge the role of feminists in working with the government sector in achieving change for women.[82] There are also other ways in which feminist concerns may be seen to have moved into the 'mainstream' reform agenda. Some examples include the establishment of government units, such as the Violence Against Women unit of the Attorney General's Department in NSW and comparable units in other jurisdictions.

Another way in which feminist concerns can be placed on mainstream agendas is via institutional (or ad hoc) law reform processes, such as law reform commission inquiries or via participation in parliamentary inquiries or other forms of public debate. In the early 1990s, the federal government asked the Australian Law Reform Commission to inquire into *Equality Before the Law*.[83]

---

78   *Ibid*, at 730-1. Here Stubbs and Tolmie discuss some Australian cases where social workers, for example, gave evidence.
79   *Ibid*, at 739-41.
80   There are also particular barriers for racialised women: see Julia Tolmie, 'Pacific-Asian Immigrant and Refugee Women Who Kill their Batterers: Telling Stories that Illustrate the Significance of Specificity' (1997) 19 *Sydney Law Review* 472; and see Linda Ammons, 'Mules, Madonnas, Babies, Bath Water, Racial Imagery and Stereotypes: The African American Woman and the Battered Woman Syndrome' [1995] *Wisconsin Law Review* 1003. In Chapter 3, we discuss Stubbs and Tolmie's analysis of *R v Hickey*, a case involving an Aboriginal woman who killed her Aboriginal male partner: see Julie Stubbs and Julia Tolmie, 'Race, Gender and the Battered Woman Syndrome: An Australian Case Study' (1995) 8 *Canadian Journal of Women and the Law* 122.
81   Lisa Teasdale, 'Confronting the Fear of Being 'Caught': Discourses on Abortion in Western Australia' (1999) 22 *University of New South Wales Law Journal* 60. See also the success of gay and lesbian relationship recognition activism, discussed above.
82   See Sophie Watson (ed), *Playing the State: Australian Feminist Interventions*, Verso, London, 1990; Hester Eisenstein, *Inside Agitators: Australian Femocrats and the State*, Allen and Unwin, Sydney, 1996.
83   The Commission published three reports as part of this inquiry: Report No 67 (Interim): *Women's Access to the Legal System*; and Report No 69 Part I: *Equality Before the Law: Justice for Women*; Report No 69 Part II: *Equality Before the Law: Women's Equality*.

The Commission's publications drew attention to a large number of issues that women in Australia felt denied them equality before the law. A significant number of submissions focused on violence against women and, in particular, the impact of violence in the context of family law.[84] As we noted in our discussion of 'equality' in Chapter 3, three of us dissented from the majority in the view we took about how the Commission's proposed *Equality Act* should operate. While the majority supported a gender neutral Act, we argued that legislation designed to respond to women's inequality should be directly addressed at the problem and therefore any such Act should apply only to women.

Notes

1. It is sometimes suggested that the recommendations made by the ALRC in its *Equality* reports were not implemented because there was not unanimity among the Commissioners. Assume for the sake of argument that this is the case: does this mean that it is always necessary to compromise on outcomes in order to achieve a result? What other impediments might there have been to implementation of a number of the recommendations of the inquiry?[85]
2. Much of the early activist work done by feminists in Australia was concerned with violence against women, in recognition of the fact that many aspects of criminal law, while not necessarily perceived as issues of 'women's equality', are of central relevance to women. A recent example is provided by the inquiry undertaken by the NSW Law Reform Commission into what was then s 409B of the *Crimes Act* 1900, the provision that deals with sexual history and reputation evidence.[86] In 1996, a report called *Heroines of Fortitude* documented 'the experiences of women in court as victims of sexual assault' in NSW.[87] The report painted a bleak picture of those experiences. Amongst other findings, half of the complainants in the study were accused in court of having made false reports and there was widespread questioning which the researchers found relied on stereotyped views of 'appropriate' behaviour of women complainants in sexual assault. Shortly after the report was released, the Attorney General of NSW asked the State's Law Reform Commission to 'review the operation of s 409B of the *Crimes Act* 1900 (NSW) taking into account the purpose for which it was enacted and recent case law'. In its 1998 report, the Law Reform Commission recommending relaxing the restrictions on the provisions, that is, introducing a discretion into the legislation permitting a wider range of evidence to be adduced (with the court's consent). The Commission's report refers a number of times to the *Heroines* report in somewhat dismissive terms, for example, suggesting that summaries of the evidence are presented in 'quite subjective and emotive terms'.[88] While the

---

84 We have discussed this in more detail in both Chapters 5 and 9.
85 Note that to some degree, several of the recommendations in the Family Law chapter (Report No 69 Part I, Chapter 9) have been implemented, though their impact has been undercut by the other contemporaneous changes, such as introduction of a 'right to contact': see Rhoades, Graycar and Harrison, *The Family Law Reform Act: The First Three Years*, 2000 (discussed in Chapter 9).
86 Section 409B of the *Crimes Act* 1900 (NSW), as it then was, is now s 105 of the *Criminal Procedure Act* 1986 (NSW).
87 Department for Women, *Heroines of Fortitude: The Experiences of Women in Court as Victims of Sexual Assault*, 1996 (also discussed in Chapter 11).
88 NSWLRC, *Review of Section 409B of the Crimes Act, Report No 87*, 1998, at para 6.54, referring to *Heroines*, at 246. See generally, the discussion of the report at paras 6.51-6.54.

Commission's report makes clear that the vast majority of submissions argued for the maintenance of the strict statutory limits (which *Heroines* demonstrated were being regularly ignored),[89] the Commission focused on the submissions from the defence bar and the interests of the defendant. For example, under the heading, 'The Commission's response', it was stated:

> 6.9 It is integral to the fairness of a trial that the accused has an opportunity to cross-examine and lead evidence on matters of substantial relevance to his or her defence. Protecting that right is not a question of favouring the accused over the complainant, or of weighting the system to protect the "criminal". It is surely a matter of public interest that our criminal justice system remain centred on the presumption of innocence and the right of every person charged to be tried fairly.

To what extent should law reform bodies be required to reflect in their recommendations the majority of the submissions made? How should law reform commissions be constituted? The report on s 409B was undertaken by four commissioners, all of whom were (or in one case, had been) judicial officers. Are judges always the best placed to address law reform issues that affect the community? Would there be dangers in requiring bodies such as Law Reform Commissions or parliamentary inquiries to reflect in their recommendations the position that can garner most supporters?[90] How might we balance the concerns of representativeness?[91]

3. In 2000, a report was published documenting the outcome of three years' research on the 1996 introduction of amendments to the *Family Law Act 1975* (Cth).[92] The report was widely publicised and its executive summary was reproduced in a number of publications.[93] Shortly after its release, it

---

89   For a list of the submissions that supported maintaining the strict exclusion of evidence, rather than moving toward a discretion, as supported by the defence bar (and the Commission), see NSWLRC, Report No 87, Chapter 4, fn 55. These included the Department for Women, the Office of the Status of Women, Department of Prime Minister and Cabinet, various regional sexual assault services and hospital services. A number of submissions, including that of the Health Department, and some from academic lawyers, proposed that, while some changes might be warranted, a 'rules based' approach should be maintained (that is, they also opposed the introduction of a discretion): see NSWLRC, Report No 87, Chapter 4, fn 57.

90   Note, by contrast, that the majority of those who made submissions to the 1992 Joint Select Committee on the Family Law Act were men or women who supported men's groups: see Linda Hancock, 'Reforming the Child Support Agenda: Who Benefits?' (1998) *Just Policy* No 12, March 1998, 20 at 28-30, for an analysis of how the majority of views put to parliamentary committees such as the 1992 Joint Select Committee come from non-resident parents. On the broader issue of the impediments to women's (especially custodial parents') participation in public processes see also Martha Fineman, 'Illusive Equality: On Weitzman's Divorce Revolution' [1986] *American Bar Foundation Research Journal* 781 at 787-8; Ruth Lister, 'Women, Economic Dependency and Citizenship' [1990] *Journal of Social Policy* 445. Compare the 2000 Senate report on superannuation where a majority of government senators chose to rely extensively on the (small number of) submissions from groups such as the Festival of Light to reject a proposal to extend partner benefits to those in same-sex relationships: Senate Select Committee on Superannuation and Financial Services, *Report on the Provisions of the Superannuation (Entitlements for Same-Sex Couples) Bill 2000* (April 2000). Of the 41 submissions received, only five opposed the Bill. However, the Committee received many more letters and emails in support of the legislation, but these were not treated as submissions: see Report, Chapter One.

91   Note that the Commission's report has not been implemented and the government delayed for some considerable period after receiving the report before tabling it in parliament.

92   Helen Rhoades, Reg Graycar and Margaret Harrison, *The Family Law Reform Act: The First Three Years*, 2000 (discussed in Chapter 9).

93   See *Australian Family Lawyer*, December 2000; and (2001) 58 *Family Matters* 80-3.

was the subject of some critical responses in *Family Matters*.[94] One of these suggests that 'great caution should be exercised before treating some of [the research's] conclusions as valid research findings' and describes the report as 'an articulate representation of one point of view' about the impact of the new legislation.[95] Parkinson also suggests that 'there is much that we can learn from the report ... particularly where it is possible to disentangle the evidence from the authors' interpretations of it'.[96] After suggesting that we 'need to move beyond the gender war and produce a body of research which by its rigour and balance provides a base of undisputed knowledge upon which sound policy can be developed', he remarks that the criticism is not intended to be directed to 'feminist legal scholarship'.[97] Why do you think it was considered relevant to refer to 'feminist legal scholarship' or the 'gender wars'?

The other critical response starts by questioning the researchers' assessment of the context in which the reforms were enacted and suggests that, by stating (the empirical fact) that the majority of calls for reform came from 'aggrieved non-custodial parents and in particular fathers' rights groups', this challenges 'the legitimacy of concerns expressed by non-resident parents'.[98] What is the significance of the fact that studies undertaken by other non-feminist identified researchers have come to identical conclusions as the 2000 research, yet have not received the same response?[99] What does this say about the place of research conducted by feminists? What do you think Parkinson has in mind in referring to 'rigour and balance'? What is 'undisputed knowledge'? Refer back to some of the epistemological issues explored in Chapter 4 in thinking about these questions.[100]

An alternative feminist process? The Grandview Agreement

In the first edition of this book, we explored the increasing attention being paid to non-litigious forms of dispute resolution, which, in the early 1980s, were being heralded by some feminists as more appropriate ways of dealing with legal issues. As Hilary Astor described what she called the 'honeymoon period':

> There was a period in the mid 1980s when feminist writers were enthusiastic about the potential of ADR. It was argued that the courts are not a hospitable environment for women. Litigation is imbued with patriarchal values and does not take into account women's needs and interests. It was suggested

---

94 Lawrie Moloney, 'Researching the Family Law Reform Act: A Case of Selective Attention?'(2001) 59 *Family Matters* 64; and see letter from Patrick Parkinson, 'A Plea for Greater Rigour in Socio-Legal Research' (2001) 59 *Family Matters* 77.
95 Parkinson, at 77.
96 *Ibid*, at 78.
97 *Ibid*.
98 Moloney, at 64.
99 John Dewar, Stephen Parker et al, *Parenting, Planning and Partnership: The impact of the new Part VII of the Family Law Act 1975 (Cth)*, Family Law Research Unit Working Paper No 3, Griffith University, 1999; John Dewar and Stephen Parker, 'The Impact of the New Part VII' (1999) 13 *Australian Journal of Family Law* 96.
100 For the authors' response, see Rhoades et al, 'Researching Family Law Reform: The Authors Respond' (2001) 59 *Family Matters* 68.

that mediation and other alternative methods might be better suited to women's needs.[101]

Astor then turned to consider the 'sceptical period' in which a somewhat more sanguine approach was taken and concerns were raised about the impact of violence in particular, and inequalities in bargaining power more generally, on women's capacity to participate effectively in mediation.[102] More recently, enthusiasm for ADR as 'the' feminist alternative has become even more tempered and attention has focused on finding different ways to respond to harm that do not draw exclusively either on 'traditional' litigation or on 'alternative' dispute resolution but, rather, might have the capacity to recast or reshape legal responses more effectively for women or others who have historically been marginalised by the legal system.[103]

One illustration is the establishment of the *Grandview Tribunal* or *Grandview Healing Package*, a Canadian response to one instance of 'institutional abuse'. The term 'institutional abuse' is often used to describe a range of situations in which children have been removed from their families (as were members of the 'stolen generations', discussed in Chapter 9 above) and placed in institutional care. It is now becoming increasingly apparent that, instead of looking after these children appropriately, many of them were subjected to a range of types of abuse, including psychological, emotional, physical and sexual.[104] Attempts to bring civil actions for damages about such injuries have almost invariably failed, on one or more grounds. These include limitation of actions rules,[105] evidentiary issues,[106] problems in attributing responsibility[107] and occasionally jurisdictional problems.

---

101 Hilary Astor, 'Civil Procedure' in Graycar and Morgan (eds), *Work and Violence Themes: Including Gender Issues in the Core Law Curriculum*, 1996, available at <http://pandora.nla.gov.au/ tep/10029>). The work she was referring to here includes the classic Carrie Menkel-Meadow, 'Portia in a Different Voice: Speculations on a Women's Lawyering Process' (1985) 1 *Berkeley Women's Law Journal* 39 (drawing in turn on Carol Gilligan, *In a Different Voice, Psychological Theory and Women's Development*, Harvard University Press, Cambridge MA, 1982); Janet Rifkin, 'Mediation from a Feminist Perspective: Promise and Problems' (1984) 2 *Law and Inequality* 21.
102 See, for example, 'Feminist Issues in ADR' (1991) 65 *Law Institute Journal* 69; Hilary Astor, 'The Weight of Silence: Talking About Violence in Family Mediation' in Margaret Thornton (ed), *Public and Private: Feminist Legal Debates*, Oxford University Press, Melbourne, 1995 for some examples. On dispute resolution more generally, see Hilary Astor and Christine Chinkin, *Dispute Resolution in Australia*, 2nd ed, Butterworths, Sydney, 2002.
103 For a moving account of South Africa's Truth and Reconciliation Commission, a pioneering attempt to respond to the systemic harms perpetrated by apartheid, see Antjie Krog, *Country of My Skull*, Vintage, London, 1999.
104 See Law Commission of Canada, *Restoring Dignity: Responding to Child Abuse in Canadian Institutions*, 2000.
105 See Graycar and Morgan, 'Disabling Citizenship: Civil Death for Women in the 1990s?' (1995) 17 *Adelaide Law Review* 49; Queensland Law Reform Commission, *Review of the Limitation of Actions Act 1974 (Qld)*, Report No 53, 1998.
106 A clear example is *Cubillo and Gunner v Commonwealth* (2000) 174 ALR 97 (and see Jennifer Clarke, 'Casenote: Cubillo v Commonwealth' (2001) 25 *Melbourne University Law Review* 218). See also *Williams v Minister Aboriginal Land Rights Act 1983 and New South Wales* [2000] NSWCA 255.
107 The issue of vicarious liability has been reconsidered by the highest courts in Canada and England respectively in the context of institutional abuses of children: see *Bazley v Curry* [1999] 2 SCR 534; *Lister v Hesley Hall Limited* [2001] UKHL 22 (3 May). In 2001, the High Court of Australia reconsidered its approach to the doctrine of vicarious liability, though the case involved responsibility for injuries caused by the negligence of bicycle couriers rather than perpetrators of sexual abuse: see *Hollis v Vabu* [2001] HCA 44 (9 August).

One such institution was the Grandview Training School for Girls in Ontario Canada. Feldthusen, Hankivsky and Greaves describe the institution and its history in their article.[108]

> The Grandview Training School for Girls was a custodial institution for girls between the ages of twelve and eighteen years ... open from ... 1933 until ... 1976. While some girls who attended Grandview had committed minor crimes, such as shoplifting, many were sent to Grandview because they were found to be "unmanageable" under the *Juvenile Delinquents Act*. They were often sent to the school simply because their parents or guardians could not or would not provide for [73] their social, emotional and educational needs. ... [T]hese girls became wards of the province of Ontario upon entering Grandview. Many experienced physical, sexual and psychological abuse while in custody.[109]

They go on to explain how the Grandview 'Healing Package' came about:

> In 1991, former residents of Grandview formed the Grandview Survivors Support Group, which, by 1994, had successfully negotiated the terms of the Grandview Agreement. The first paragraph of the overview to the agreement states:
>> [S]ociety has a direct responsibility to provide the support necessary to facilitate the healing process of survivors of sexual and institutional abuse. ... It also recognizes that current individual-based solutions offered by the civil justice system are inadequate responses to institutionalized and sexual abuse.
>
> The Grandview agreement provided for a compensation process markedly and deliberately different from either civil litigation or [*criminal injuries compensation*] claims. It permitted all former Grandview residents to apply for specific medical and other benefits. Additional financial and other benefits, such as vocational and educational training and therapy, tattoo removal, scar reduction programs, and access to a crisis line were available to those women who had their claims of abuse "validated" through an alternative dispute resolution process. An award for direct financial support to a maximum of $60,000 was also available. ... Although it is not used in the settlement itself, the term Grandview "healing package" is commonly used by government officials and claimants in reference to this complicated agreement.
>
> There were six adjudicators appointed to hear and validate the claims. They were all mutually agreed upon by the parties to the agreement. All six were female; five were law professors and one was a practising lawyer. Hearings were private and were held in public buildings or, occasionally, in hotel rooms. It was not the purpose of the process to allocate blame to individual perpetrators. ... The subjects all had legal assistance in preparing their documentation [*paid for under the agreement*] but only rarely did the claimants appear for adjudication represented by counsel.
>
> ... The Grandview Agreement process was consensual and was negotiated by a victim support group. The focus of the Grandview Agreement was explicitly therapeutic. An alternative dispute resolution process was adopted in part to avoid the perceived anti-therapeutic aspects of civil litigation. The adjudicators were exclusively women with expertise in, and sensitivity to, female sexual abuse. One was an Aboriginal woman who specialised in adjudicating claims from Aboriginal survivors. The adjudicators were chosen

---

108 Bruce Feldthusen, Olena Hankivsky and Lorraine Greaves, 'Therapeutic Consequences of Civil Actions for Damages and Compensation Claims by Victims of Sexual Abuse' (2000) 12 *Canadian Journal of Women and the Law* 66.

109 *Ibid*, at 72-3.

with the approval of the support group. Lawyers played a much different role in this process than they did in civil litigation.[110]

Notes

1. The maximum amount that could be claimed by any one person under the agreement was $60,000 and the agreement contained a table setting out examples of types of abuse and the likely range of the award. For example, an award in the highest range ($40,000 to $60,000) would be made for repeated serious sexual abuse and physical beating and threats causing continuing harm resulting in serious dysfunction. It is clear that, for some of the women, much larger awards might have been made had they pursued civil actions via the tort system. What would you see as the advantages and disadvantages of having a specially designed process of this nature, but with limited financial compensation available?
2. As another aspect of the agreement, the government of Ontario undertook to acknowledge the harm that occurred. The agreement provided:

   > 2.3.1 Each beneficiary will be entitled to receive an acknowledgement from the Government intended to reflect a recognition of the efforts of the GSSG [*Grandview Survivors' Support Group*] to bring to the attention of provincial authorities allegations of abuse and in the context of this Agreement to develop a non court based process designed to assist those who may have been abused in the circumstances reflected in this Agreement. Any process must be sensitive to the need to ensure the integrity of the criminal prosecution process and to respect the rights of those accused of crime. Any such acknowledgement will be in a general form.

   The agreement expressly said that 'at an appropriate time' an acknowledgement was to be read out by the Attorney General in the legislature. Even though the government changed (a progressive government which had signed the agreement was replaced by a conservative government), the (conservative) provincial government did in fact publicly apologise in November 1999.[111]
3. How likely is it that other groups of women who have suffered forms of institutional abuse will be able to design their own framework and process for the hearing of their claims and insist upon feminist adjudicators? Does the Grandview Healing Package open up the possibilities for further exploration of feminist forms of resolving disputes? What effect, if any, will the fairly pervasive backlash against feminism have on the development of such processes? Can you suggest why the Ontario government might have chosen to sign this agreement?

Is there any point engaging with law?

In 1989, Mari Matsuda articulated the dilemma faced by feminists and other outsiders engaging with law.

---

110 *Ibid*, at 73-4. In one of the omitted footnotes, the authors explain the fact that 'tattoo removal' was one of the items for which compensation could be claimed by noting that many of the residents had tattooed themselves using sewing needles and India ink and that those tattoos were a constant reminder of the abuse and therefore removal was an important part of the healing process.
111 Feldthusen et al, *Postscript*, at 116.

Outsider scholars have recognised that their specific experiences and histories are relevant to jurisprudential inquiry. They reject narrow evidentiary concepts of relevance and credibility. They reject artificial bifurcation of thought and feeling.
...

And what of procedure, of law? Here outsiders respond with characteristic duality. On the one hand, they respond as legal realists, aware of the historical abuse of law to sustain existing conditions of domination. Unlike the postmodern critics of the left, however, outsiders ... have embraced legalism as a tool of necessity, making legal consciousness their own in order to attack injustice. Thus, to the feminist lawyer faced with pregnant teenagers seeking abortions, it would be absurd to reject the use of an elitist legal system or the use of the concept of rights when such use is necessary to meet the immediate needs of her client. There are times to stand outside the courtroom door and say, "This procedure is a farce, the legal system is corrupt, justice will never prevail in this land as long as privilege rules in the courtroom." There are times to stand inside the courtroom and say, "This is a nation of laws, laws recognizing fundamental values of rights, equality and personhood." Sometimes, ... there is a need to make both speeches in one day. [112]

Mary Heath and Ngaire Naffine undertook a review of the record of South Australia in relation to rape law reform in 1994, which revealed that South Australia had lagged behind other States in its reform efforts.[113] They concluded their review, relying on Matsuda, as we also conclude this book, with two alternative feminist conclusions:

(a) One Feminist Conclusion: "there are times to stand outside the courtroom door"
Rape laws in South Australia do not work. The chances of a woman seeing her rapist convicted in court are negligible and thus the very presence of rape law on the books is fraudulent to women. MacKinnon has said that rape is only regulated not prohibited: In South Australia it is difficult to see that it is even regulated. The women of South Australia would be better served without a law of rape which fosters the myth that rape and sexual assault are criminal acts in this State. The maintenance of the current regime merely serves to encourage women to report rape and to participate in rape prosecutions that are in fact damaging to them personally.

(b) Another Feminist Conclusion: "there are times to stand inside the courtroom"
Feminist lawyers have an ethical obligation to engage with the law which affects the lives of women. To abandon the attempt to create a law of rape that might be useful for women is to abandon women to the rapists and to leave law reform in the hands of the state when it has been well established that the state does not work in our best interests. We feminists must work therefore to improve the law of rape while retaining an awareness of the poorness of its fit with the lives of women.[114]

---

112 Mari Matsuda, 'When the First Quail Calls: Multiple Consciousness as Jurisprudential Method' (1989) 11 *Women's Rights Law Reporter* 7 at 8 (reprinted in Mari J Matsuda, *Where is Your Body? And Other Essays on Race, Gender, and the Law*, Beacon Press, Boston, 1996).
113 Mary Health and Ngaire Naffine, 'Men's Needs and Women's Desires: Feminist Dilemmas about Rape Law Reform' (1994) 3 *Australian Feminist Law Journal* 30.
114 *Ibid*, at 51.

Bibliography

Abel, Richard, 'Law Books and Books About Law' (1973) 26 *Stanford Law Review* 175

Aboriginal and Torres Strait Islander Women's Task Force on Violence, *Aboriginal and Torres Strait Islander Women's Task Force on Violence Report*, Queensland Department of Aboriginal and Torres Strait Islander Policy and Development, Brisbane, 2000

Abrams, Kathryn, 'Sex Wars Redux: Agency and Coercion in Feminist Legal Theory' (1995) 95 *Columbia Law Review* 304

Abrams, Kathryn, 'The Reasonable Woman: Sense and Sensibility in Sexual Harassment Law' [1995] *Dissent* 48

Acorn, Annalise, 'Harm, Community Tolerance, and the Indecent: A Discussion of *R v Mara*' (1997) 36 *Alberta Law Review* 258

Adelson, Pamela, Michael Frommer and Edith Weisberg, 'Termination of Pregnancy in New South Wales, 1990' (1996) 20 *ANZ Journal of Public Health* 64

Albiston, Catherine, 'The Social Meaning of the Norplant Condition: Constitutional Considerations of Race, Class, and Gender' (1994) 9 *Berkeley Women's Law Journal* 9

Albury, Rebecca, 'Abortion: But I Thought That Was Settled Years Ago' (1989) 31-32 *Refractory Girl* 12

Albury, Rebecca, *The Politics of Reproduction: Beyond the Slogans*, Allen and Unwin, Sydney, 1999

Allars, Margaret, *Introduction to Australian Administrative Law*, Butterworths, 1990

Allen, Judith A, 'Octavius Beale Re-considered: Infanticide and Abortion in NSW 1880-1939' in Sydney Labour History Group, *What Rough Beast? The State and Social Order in Australian History*, George Allen and Unwin, Sydney, 1982

Allen, Judith A, *Sex & Secrets: Crimes Involving Australian Women Since 1880*, Oxford University Press, Melbourne, 1990

Ammons, Linda, 'Mules, Madonnas, Babies, Bath Water, Racial Imagery and Stereotypes: The African American Woman and the Battered Woman Syndrome' [1995] *Wisconsin Law Review* 1003

Annas, George, 'Forced Cesareans: The Most Unkindest Cut of All' (1982) 12 *Hastings Center Report* 16

Anon, 'Lesbian Custody – A Personal Account' (1980) 20 *Refractory Girl* 2

Arditti, Rita, Renate Duelli Klein and Shelley Minden (eds), *Test-Tube Women: What Future for Motherhood*, Pandora Press, London, 1984

Arthur, Stacey L, 'The Norplant Prescription: Birth Control, Woman Control, or Crime Control?' (1992) 40 *UCLA Law Review* 1

Ashe, Marie, 'Law-Language of Maternity: Discourse Holding Nature in Contempt' (1988) 22 *New England Law Review* 521

Astor, Hilary, 'A Question of Identity: The Intersection of Race and Other Grounds of Discrimination' in Race Discrimination Commission, *Racial Discrimination Act 1975: A Review*, AGPS, Canberra, 1995

Astor, Hilary, 'Feminist Issues in ADR' (1991) 65 *Law Institute Journal* 69

Astor, Hilary, 'The Weight of Silence: Talking About Violence in Family Mediation' in Margaret Thornton (ed), *Public and Private: Feminist Legal Debates*, Oxford University Press, Melbourne, 1995

Astor, Hilary, 'Civil Procedure' in Graycar and Morgan (eds), *Work and Violence Themes: Including Gender Issues in the Core Law Curriculum*, 1996, available at <http://pandora.nla.gov.au/tep/10029>

Astor, Hilary, 'Elizabeth's Story: Mediation, Violence and the Legal Academy' (1997) 2 *Flinders Journal of Law Reform* 13

Astor, Hilary and Christine Chinkin, *Dispute Resolution in Australia*, 2nd ed, Butterworths, Sydney, 2002

Atkinson, Judy, 'Violence in Aboriginal Australia: Colonisation and Gender' (1990) 14(2) *Aboriginal and Islander Health Worker* 5

Atkinson, Judy, 'Violence in Aboriginal Australia: Part 2' (1990) 14(3) *Aboriginal and Islander Health Worker* 4

Atkinson, Judy, 'A Nation is Not Conquered' (1996) 3(80) *Aboriginal Law Bulletin* 4

Attorney General's Department, *Property and Family Law: Options for Change*, Commonwealth of Australia, Canberra, July 1999

Attorney General's Department, *Superannuation and Family Law: A Position Paper*, Commonwealth of Australia, Canberra, 1998

Atwood, Barbara, 'Ten Years Later: Lingering Concerns About the Uniform Premarital Agreements Act' (1993) 19 *Journal of Legislation* 127

Austen, Siobhan E and Elisa R Birch, *Family Responsibilities and Women's Working Lives*, Women's Economic Policy Analysis Unit (WEPAU), Curtin University of Technology, Discussion Paper Series 00/9, August 2000

Australian Banking Industry Ombudsman Ltd, *Report on Relationship Debt*, Bulletin No 22, September 1999

Australian Broadcasting Commission, 'The Unfortunate Experiment', *Four Corners* documentary, screened on 8 August 1988

Australian Bureau of Statistics (ABS), *Women in Australia*, Cat No 4113.0, 1993

Australian Bureau of Statistics (ABS), *How Australians Use Their Time*, Cat No 4153.0, 1994

Australian Bureau of Statistics (ABS), *Women's Safety Australia*, Cat No 4128.0, 1996

Australian Bureau of Statistics (ABS), *Australian Standard Classification of Occupations*, 2nd ed, Cat No 1220.0, 1997

Australian Bureau of Statistics (ABS), *Time Use Survey, 1997*, Cat No 4150.0, 1998

Australian Bureau of Statistics (ABS), *Labour Force, Australia*, February 1999, Cat No 6203.0, 1999

Australian Bureau of Statistics (ABS) *Australia Now – A Statistical Profile*, July 1999, Cat No 6203.0, 1999

Australian Bureau of Statistics (ABS), *Australian Social Trends 1999*, Cat No 4102.0, 1999

Australian Bureau of Statistics (ABS), *Housing: Special Article: Value and equity in the family home*, Year Book Australia, 1999

Australian Bureau of Statistics (ABS), *Australian Social Trends 2000*, Cat No 4102.0, 2000

Australian Bureau of Statistics (ABS), *Unpaid Work and the Australian Economy 1997*, Cat No 5240.0, 2000

Australian Bureau of Statistics (ABS), *Labour Force Status and Other Characteristics of Families Survey*, June 2000, Cat No 6224.0, 2000

Australian Bureau of Statistics (ABS), *Employee Earnings, Benefits and Trade Union Membership*, August 2000, Cat No 6310.0, 2001

Australian Bureau of Statistics (ABS), *Australian Social Trends 2001*, Cat No 4102.0, 2001

Australian Institute of Health and Welfare, *Adoptions in Australia, 1998-1999*, available at <http://www.aihw.gov.au/publications/welfare/aa98-9/index.html>

Australian Law Reform Commission (ALRC), *Matrimonial Property*, Discussion Paper 22, 1985

Australian Law Reform Commission (ALRC), *Standing in Public Interest Litigation*, Report No 27, AGPS, Canberra, 1985

Australian Law Reform Commission (ALRC), *Child Custody, Fostering and Adoption; The Recognition of Aboriginal Customary Laws*, Research Paper No 4, Report No 31, AGPS, Canberra, 1986

Australian Law Reform Commission (ALRC), *Loss of Consortium: Compensation for Loss of Capacity to do Housework*, Report Number 32 (Community Law Reform for the ACT), AGPS, 1986

Australian Law Reform Commission (ALRC), *Equality before the Law: Women's Access to the Legal System*, Report No 67 (Interim), Commonwealth of Australia, 1994

Australian Law Reform Commission (ALRC), *Equality before the Law: Justice for Women?* Report No 69 Part I, Commonwealth of Australia, 1994

Australian Law Reform Commission (ALRC), *Equality before the Law: Women's Equality*, Report No 69 Part II, Commonwealth of Australia, 1994

Bacchi, Carol Lee, *The Politics of Affirmative Action: 'Women', Equality and Category Politics*, Sage, London, 1996

Backhouse, Constance, 'Desperate Women and Compassionate Courts: Infanticide in Nineteenth Century Canada' (1984) 34 *University of Toronto Law Review* 447

Backhouse, Constance, 'Bias in Canadian Law: A Lopsided Precipice' (1998) 10 *Canadian Journal of Women and the Law* 170

Bagshaw, Dale and Donna Chung, 'Gender Politics and Research: Male and Female Violence in Intimate Relationships' (2000) 8 *Women Against Violence: An Australian Feminist Journal* 4

Baker, Arthur, 'Post-divorce parenting – Rethinking Shared Residence' (1996) 8 *Child and Family Law Quarterly* 217

Bargen, Jenny and Elaine Fyshwick, *Sexual Assault Law Reform: A National Perspective*, Office of the Status of Women, 1995

Baron, Paula, 'The Free Exercise of Her Will: Women and Emotionally Transmitted Debt' (1995) 13 *Law in Context* 23

Barrett, Michele, *Women's Oppression Today: Problems in Marxist Feminist Analysis,* Verso, London, 1986

Bart, Pauline, 'Women of the Right: Trading for Safety, Rules and Love: Review of A Dworkin, *Right Wing Women*', *The New Women's Times Feminist Review,* November/December, 1983

Bateman, Margaret, 'Lesbians, Gays and Child Custody: An Australian Legal History' (1992) 1 *Australian Gay and Lesbian Law Journal* 47

Bavin-Mizzi, Jill, *Ravished: Sexual Violence in Victorian Australia*, UNSW Press, Sydney, 1995

Baxter, Janeen, 'Why Don't Men Do More Housework?' (1994) 4(9) *Eureka Street* 37

Baxter, Janeen, 'Marital Status and the Division of Household Labour: Cohabitation vs Marriage' (2001) 58 *Family Matters* 16

Beggs, John and Bruce Chapman, *The Foregone Earnings from Child-Rearing in Australia*, ANU Centre for Economic Policy Research, Discussion Paper No 190, June 1988

Behrendt, Larissa, 'Aboriginal Women and the White Lies of the Feminist Movement: Implications for Aboriginal Women in Rights Discourses' (1993) 1 *Australian Feminist Law Journal* 27

Behrens, Juliet, 'Domestic Violence and Property Adjustment: A Critique of 'No Fault' Discourse' (1993) 7 *Australian Journal of Family Law* 9

Behrens, Juliet, 'Violence in the Home and Family Law: An Update' (1995) 9 *Australian Journal of Family Law* 58

Behrens, Juliet and Bruce Smyth, *Spousal Support in Australia*, Working Paper No 16, Australian Institute of Family Studies, 1999

Behrens, Juliet and Kim Bolas, 'Violence and the Family Court: Cross Vested Claims for Compensation' (1997) 11 *Australian Journal of Family Law* 164

Bell, Christine, 'Case Note: *Planned Parenthood of Southeastern Pennsylvania, et al v Robert P Casey, et al*' (1993) 1 *Feminist Legal Studies* 91

Bell, Diane and Renate Klein (eds), *Radically Speaking: Feminism Reclaimed*, Spinifex Press, Melbourne, 1996

Bell, Vikki, '"Beyond the 'Thorny Question'": Feminism, Foucault and the Desexualisation of Rape' (1991) 19 *International Journal of the Sociology of Law* 83

Bender, Leslie, 'A Lawyer's Primer on Feminist Theory and Tort' (1988) 38 *Journal of Legal Education* 3

Bennett, Belinda, 'Reproductive Technology, Public Policy and Single Motherhood' (2000) 22 *Sydney Law Review* 625

Bennett, Laura, 'Women and Enterprise Bargaining: The Legal and Institutional Framework' (1994) 36 *Journal of Industrial Relations* 191

Berns, Sandra, 'Pornography, Women, Censorship and Morality' (1989) 7 *Law in Context* 30

Berns, Sandra, 'The Hobart City Council Case: A Tort of Sexual Harassment for Tasmania?' (1994) 13 *University of Tasmania Law Review* 412

Bhabha, Homi, 'A Good Judge of Character: Men, Metaphors, and the Common Culture' in Toni Morrison (ed), *Race-ing Justice, En-Gendering Power: Essays on Anita Hill, Clarence Thomas, and the Construction of Social Reality*, Pantheon, New York, 1992

Bickenback, JE, 'Damages for Wrongful Conception: *Doiron v Orr*' (1980) 18 *University of Western Ontario Law Review* 493

Bienen, Leigh, 'A Question of Credibility: John Henry Wigmore's Use of Scientific Authority' (1983) 19 *California Western Law Review* 235

Bittman, Michael, *Juggling Time: How Australian Families Use Their Time*, OSW, Department of the Prime Minister and Cabinet, 1991

Bittman, Michael and Jocelyn Pixley, *The Double Life of the Family*, Allen and Unwin, Sydney, 1997

Blagg, Harry, *Crisis Intervention in Aboriginal Family Violence*, Summary Report, Commonwealth of Australia, 2000

Blewett, Jill, 'The Abortion Law Reform Association of South Australia: 1968-1973' in Jan Mercer (ed), *The Other Half: Women in Australian Society*, Penguin, Melbourne, 1975

Bordo, Susan, 'Feminism, Postmodernism, and Gender-Scepticism' in Linda Nicholson (ed), *Feminism/Postmodernism*, Routledge, London, 1990

Bordow, Sophy, 'Defended Custody Cases in the Family Court of Australia: Factors Influencing the Outcome' (1994) 8 *Australian Journal of Family Law* 252

Boreham, Paul, Richard Hall, Bill Harley and Gillian Whitehouse, 'What Does Enterprise Bargaining Mean for Gender Equity? Some Empirical Evidence' (1996) 7 *Labour and Industry* 51

Boris, Eileen, 'Looking at Women Historians Looking at "Difference"' (1987) *Wisconsin Women's Law Journal* 213

Borland, Jeff, 'The Equal Pay Case – Thirty Years On' (1999) 32 *Australian Economic Review* 265

Bottomley, Anne (ed), *Feminist Perspectives on the Foundational Subjects of Law?* Cavendish, London, 1996

Bottomley, Anne, Susie Gibson and Belinda Meteyard, 'Dworkin; Which Dworkin? Taking Feminism Seriously' (1987) 14 *Journal of Law and Society* 47

Bouchard, Josée, Susan B Boyd and Elizabeth A Sheehy, 'Canadian Feminist Literature on Law: An Annotated Bibliography' (1999) 11(1&2) *Canadian Journal of Women and the Law* 1

Bourke, Joanna, 'Women's Business: Sex, Secrets and the Hindmarsh Island Affair' (1997) 20 *University of New South Wales Law Journal* 333

Boyd, Susan, 'Ideologies in Canadian Child Custody Law' in Carol Smart and Selma Sevenhuijsen (eds), *Child Custody and the Politics of Gender*, Routledge, London, 1989

Boyd, Susan, '(Re)Placing the State: Family, Law and Oppression' (1994) 9 *Canadian Journal of Law and Society* 39

Boyd, Susan, 'Challenging the Public/ Private Divide: An Overview' in Susan Boyd (ed), *Challenging the Public/Private Divide: Feminism, Law, and Public Policy*, University of Toronto Press, Toronto, 1997

Boyd, Susan (ed), *Challenging the Public/ Private Divide: Feminism, Law, and Public Policy*, University of Toronto Press, Toronto, 1997

Boyd, Susan, 'Family, Law and Sexuality: Feminist Engagements' (1999) 8 *Social and Legal Studies* 369

Boyd, Susan B, Helen Rhoades and Kate Burns, 'The Politics of the Primary Caregiver Presumption: A Conversation' (1999) 13 *Australian Journal of Family Law* 233

Boyd, Susan and Elizabeth Sheehy, 'Feminist Perspectives on Law: Theory and Practice' (1986) 2 *Canadian Journal of Women and the Law* 1

Boyle, Christine LM et al, *A Feminist Review of Criminal Law*, Minister of Supply and Services, Ottawa, 1985

Boyle, Christine, 'Sexual Assault and the Feminist Judge' (1985) 1 *Canadian Journal of Women and the Law* 93

Boyle, Christine, 'Publication of Identifying Information About Sexual Assault Survivors: *R v Canadian Newspapers Co Ltd*' (1990) 3 *Canadian Journal of Women and the Law* 602

Brady, Susan M and Sonia Grover, *The Sterilisation of Girls and Young Women in Australia: A legal, medical and social context*, HREOC, Sydney, 1997

Brady, Susan, John Briton and Sonia Grover, *The Sterilisation of Girls and Young Women: Issues and Progress*, 2001, available at <www.humanrights.gov.au//disabilityrights/sterilisation/index.html>

Branson, Catherine, speech to NSW Women Lawyers Association, 'Running on the Edge', October 1997, available at <www.wlansw.asn.au/branson.htm>

Brett, Peter and Louis Waller, *Criminal Law: Text and Cases*, 4th ed, Butterworths, Sydney, 1977

Brod, Gail Frommer, 'Premarital Agreements and Gender Justice' (1994) 6 *Yale Journal of Law and Feminism* 229

Brodsky, Gwen and Shelagh Day, *Canadian Charter Equality Rights for Women: One Step Forward or Two Steps Back?* Canadian Advisory Council on the Status of Women, Ottawa, 1989

Brookes, Barbara, *Abortion in England 1900-1967*, Croom Helm, London, 1988

Brown, Thea et al, *Violence in Families – Report No 1: The Management of Child Abuse Allegations in Custody and Access Disputes before the Family Court of Australia*, Monash University, Melbourne, 1998

Brown, Wendy, 'Reproductive Freedom and the Right to Privacy: A Paradox for Feminists' in Irene Diamond (ed), *Families, Politics and Public Policy: A Feminist Dialogue on Women and the State*, Longman, New York, 1983

Brown, Wendy, *States of Injury: Power and Freedom in Late Modernity*, Princeton University Press, New Jersey, 1995

Bryson, John, *Evil Angels*, Viking, Melbourne, 1985

Bunkle, Phillida, *Second Opinion: the Politics of Women's Health in New Zealand*, Oxford University Press, Auckland, 1988

Burgmann, Meredith, 'Women and Enterprise Bargaining in Australia' in Suzanne Hammond (ed), *Equity Under Enterprise Bargaining*, ACIRRT Working Paper No 33, Australian Centre for Industrial Relations Research and Teaching, University of Sydney, 1994

Burka, Mariann, 'Sexual Harassment: Manitoba's Step Backward – A Case Comment on *Govereau and Janzen v Platy Enterprises Ltd*' (1987) 16 *Manitoba Law Journal* 245

Burns, Ailsa, Kate Burns and Karen Menzies, 'Strong State Intervention: The Stolen Generations' in JM Bowes and A Hayes (eds), *Children, Families and Communities*, Oxford University Press, Melbourne, 1999

Burton, Clare, *Gender Bias in Job Evaluation*, Affirmative Action Agency, Monograph No 3, Canberra, 1988

Burton, Clare, *Redefining Merit*, Monograph No 2, Affirmative Action Agency, AGPS, Canberra, 1988

Burton, Clare, Raven Hag and Gay Thompson, *Women's Worth: Pay Equity and Job Evaluation*, AGPS, Canberra, 1987

Burton, Clare, *The Promise and the Price: The Struggle for Equal Opportunity in Women's Employment*, Allen and Unwin, Sydney, 1991

Busby, Karen, 'LEAF and Pornography: Litigating on Equality and Sexual Representations' (1994) 9 *Canadian Journal of Law and Society* 165

Butler, Des and Sharon Rodrick, *Australian Media Law*, LBC, Sydney, 1999

Butler, Judith, *Gender Trouble: Feminism and the Subversion of Identity*, Routledge, New York, 1990

Butler, Judith, 'Contingent Foundations: Feminism and the Question of "Postmodernism"' in Judith Butler and Joan Scott (eds), *Feminists Theorize the Political*, Routledge, New York, 1992

Cabinet Sub-Committee on Maintenance, *Child Support: A Discussion Paper on Child Maintenance*, AGPS, Canberra, 1986

Calabrese, Guido, *Ideals, Beliefs, Attitudes and the Law*, Syracuse University Press, Syracuse, 1985

Cameron, Edwin, 'Sexual Orientation and the Constitution: A Test Case for Human Rights' (1993) 100 *South African Law Journal* 450

Cannold, Leslie, *The Abortion Myth: Feminism, Morality, and the Hard Choices Women Make*, Allen and Unwin, Sydney, 1998

Carcach, Carlos and Marianne James, *Homicide Between Intimate Partners in Australia*, Australian Institute of Criminology, Trends and Issues Paper No 90, Canberra, 1998

Carlin, Tyrone M, 'The Contracts Review Act 1980 (NSW)' (2001) 23 *Sydney Law Review* 125

Carney, Terry and David Tait, *The Adult Guardianship Experiment: Tribunals and Popular Justice*, Federation Press, Sydney, 1997

Carter, John and David Harland, *Contract Law in Australia*, 3rd ed, Butterworths, Sydney, 1996

Carter, Meredith, Ariel Couchman, Kim Windsor and Jocelynne Scutt, 'Women, Reform and the Law', *Australian Society*, April 1986

Cartwright, Silvia, *The Report of the Committee of Inquiry into Allegations Concerning the treatment of Cervical Cancer at National Women's Hospital and into Other Related Matters*, Government Printing Office, Auckland, 1988

Cashman, Peter, 'The Dalkon Shield' in Peter Grabosky and Adam Sutton (eds), *Stains on a White Collar*, Federation Press, Sydney, 1989

Cass, Bettina, 'Rewards for Women's Work' in Carole Pateman and Jacqueline Goodnow (eds), *Women, Social Science and Public Policy*, Allen and Unwin, Sydney, 1985

Cass, Bettina, 'Gender in Australia's restructuring labour market and welfare state' in Anne Edwards and Susan Magarey (eds), *Women in a Restructuring Australia: Work and Welfare*, Allen & Unwin, Sydney, 1995

Cass, Deborah Z, '*R v Hakopian*' (1993) 1 *Feminist Legal Studies* 203

Caulfield, Timothy and Gerald Robertson, 'Eugenic Policies in Alberta: From the Systematic to the Systemic' (1996) 35 *Alberta Law Review* 59

Chammalas, Martha and Linda K Kerber, 'Women, Mothers and the Law of Fright: A History' (1990) 88 *Michigan Law Review* 814

Charlesworth, Hilary and Christine Chinkin, *The Boundaries of International Law: A Feminist Analysis*, Manchester University Press, Manchester, 2000

Chasnoff, Ira J, Harvey J Landress and Mark E Barrett, 'The Prevalence of Illicit Drug or Alcohol Use During Pregnancy and Discrepancies in Mandatory Reporting in Pinellas County, Florida' (1990) 322 *New England Journal of Medicine* 1202

Chisholm, Richard, 'Case Note: Marriage of Goudge' (1985) 13 *Aboriginal Law Bulletin* 9

Chisholm, Richard, 'Assessing the Impact of the *Family Law Reform Act 1995*' (1996) 10 *Australian Journal of Family Law* 177

Clamore, John O, 'Critical Race Theory, Archie Shepp, and Fire Music: Securing an Authentic Intellectual Life in a Multicultural World' (1992) 65 *Southern California Law Review* 2129

Clare, Ross, *Equity and Retirement Income Provision in Australia*, The Association of Superannuation Funds of Australia, February 2001

Clarke, Adele, 'Subtle Forms of Sterilization Abuse: A Reproductive Rights Analysis' in Rita Arditti, Renate Duelli-Klein and Shelley Minden (eds), *Test Tube Women: What Future for Motherhood?*, Pandora, London, 1984

Clarke, Billi and Helen Matthews, *Trial by Legal Aid: A Legal Aid Impact Study*, Crossroads Family and Domestic Violence Unit and Victorian Women's Refuges and Associated Domestic Violence Services Legal Sub Group, 1999

Clarke, Jennifer, 'Casenote: Cubillo v Commonwealth' (2001) 25 *Melbourne University Law Review* 218

Code, Lorraine, 'Epistemology' in Alison M Jaggar and Iris Marion Young (eds), *A Companion to Feminist Philosophy*, Blackwell Publishers, Malden, MA, 1998

Coleman, Karen, 'The Politics of Abortion in Australia: Freedom, Church and the State' (1988) 29 *Feminist Review* 75

Colker, Ruth, 'Feminism, Sexuality, and Self: A Preliminary Inquiry into the Politics of Authenticity' (1988) 68 *Boston University Law Review* 217

Colker, Ruth, *Abortion and Dialogue: Pro-Choice, Pro-Life, and American Law*, Indiana University Press, Bloomington and Indianapolis, 1992

Collier, Richard, *Masculinity, Law and the Family*, London, Routledge, 1995

Collier, Richard, '"Nutty Professors", "Men in Suits" and "New Entrepreneurs": Corporeality, Subjectivity and Change in the Law School and Legal Practice' (1998) 7 *Social and Legal Studies* 27

Collins, Hugh, 'The Decline of Privacy in Private Law' (1987) 14 *Journal of Law and Society* 91

Comment, 'Litigating Incest Torts Under Homeowner Insurance Policies' (1988) 18 *Golden Gate University Law Review* 539

Community Law Reform Committee of the Australian Capital Territory (ACTCLRC), *Loss of Consortium; Loss of Capacity to do Housework*, Report No 4, 1991

Conaghan, Joanne, 'The Invisibility of Women in Labour Law: Gender-Neutrality in Model-Building' (1986) 14 *International Journal of the Sociology of Law* 377

Conaghan, Joanne, 'Gendered Harms and the Law of Tort: Remedying (Sexual) Harassment' (1996) 16 *Oxford Journal of Legal Studies* 407

Conaghan, Joanne, 'Tort Litigation in the Context of Intra-familial Abuse' (1998) 61 *Modern Law Review* 132

Conaghan, Joanne, 'Reassessing the Feminist Theoretical Project' (2000) 27 *Journal of Law and Society* 351

Conaghan, Joanne and Wade Mansell, *The Wrongs of Tort*, Pluto Press, London, 1993, 384

Coney, Sandra, *The Unfortunate Experiment*, Penguin, Auckland, 1988

Conley, John M and William M O'Barr, *Just Words: Law, Language and Power*, University of Chicago Press, Chicago, 1998

Cook, Rebecca J and Bernard M Dickens, *Issues in Reproductive Health Law in the Commonwealth*, Commonwealth Secretariat, London, 1986

Cooney, Sean, 'Gender and Judicial Selection: Should there be More Women on the Courts?' (1993) 19 *Melbourne University Law Review* 20

Corea, Gena et al, *Man-Made Woman: How New Reproductive Technologies Affect Women*, Hutchinson, London, 1985

Cornell, Drucilla, *The Imaginary Domain: Abortion, Pornography and Sexual Harassment*, Routledge, New York, 1995

Cossins, Anne, 'On Stone Throwing from the Feminist Sidelines: A Critique of Helen Garner's Book, *The First Stone*' (1995) 20 *Melbourne University Law Review* 528

Cossins, Annie, 'Tipping the Scales: The Need to Protect Counselling Records in Sexual Assault Trials' in Patricia Easteal (ed), *Balancing the Scales: Rape, Law Reform and Australian Culture*, Federation Press, Sydney, 1998

Cossins, Annie and Ruth Pilkington, 'Balancing the Scales: The Case for the Inadmissibility of Counselling Records in Sexual Assault Trials' (1996) 19 *University of New South Wales Law Journal* 222

Cossman, Brenda and Sharon Bell, 'Introduction' in Brenda Cossman, Sharon Bell, Lise Gotell and Becki L Ross, *Bad Attitude/s on Trial: Pornography, Feminism and the Butler Decision*, University of Toronto Press, Toronto, 1997

Cossman, Brenda, 'The Precarious Unity of Feminist Theory and Practice: The Praxis of Abortion' (1986) 44 *University of Toronto Faculty Law Review* 85

Crenshaw, Kimberlé, 'Demarginalizing the Intersection of Race and Sex: A Black Feminist Critique of Antidiscrimination Doctrine, Feminist Theory and Antiracist Politics' [1989] *University of Chicago Legal Forum* 139

Crenshaw, Kimberlé, 'Mapping the Margins: Identity Politics, Intersectionality, and Violence Against Women' (1991) 43 *Stanford Law Review* 1241

Dahl, Tove Stang, 'Women's Rights to Money' (1984) 12 *International Journal of the Sociology of Law* 137

Daly, Anne and Anne Hawke, 'The Impact of the Welfare State on the Economic Status of Indigenous Australian Women' (1995) 28 *Australian Economic Review* 29

Davies, Margaret, *Asking The Law Question*, Law Book Co, Sydney, 1994

Davis, Mark, *Gangland: Cultural Elites and the New Generationalism*, Allen and Unwin, Sydney, 1997

Davis, Robyn and Judith Dikstein, 'It Just Doesn't Fit' (1997) 22 *Alternative Law Journal* 64

Daws, Leonie, Jillian Brannock, Ross Brooker, Wendy Patton, Georgia Smeal and Shane Warren, *Young People's Perceptions of and Attitudes to Sexual Violence*, National Youth Affairs Research Scheme, National Clearinghouse for Youth Studies, Hobart, 1995

Dawson, T Brettel, 'First Person Familiar: Judicial Intervention in Pregnancy, Again: G(DF)' (1998) 10 *Canadian Journal of Women and the Law* 213

Delgado, Richard, 'Story-Telling for Oppositionists and Others: A Plea for Narrative' in Richard Delgado (ed), *Critical Race Theory: The Cutting Edge*, Temple University Press, Philadelphia, 1995

Delorey, Anne Marie, 'Joint Legal Custody: A Reversion to Patriarchal Power' (1989) 3 *Canadian Journal of Women and the Law* 33

Dempsey, Ken, *Inequalities in Marriage: Australia and Beyond*, Oxford University Press, Melbourne, 1997

Des Rosiers, Nathalie, Bruce Feldthusen and Oleana AR Hankivsky, 'Legal Compensation for Sexual Violence: Therapeutic Consequences and Consequences for the Judicial System' (1998) 4 *Psychology, Public Policy and Law* 433

Devlin, Patrick, *The Enforcement of Morals*, Oxford University Press, Oxford, 1965

Devlin, Richard, 'We Can't Go On Together With Suspicious Minds: Judicial Bias and Racialised Perspective in *R v RDS*' (1995) 18 *Dalhousie Law Journal* 408

Dewar, John, 'Indigenous Children and Family Law' (1997) 19 *Adelaide Law Review* 217

Dewar, John, 'Reducing Discretion in Family Law' (1997) 11 *Australian Journal of Family Law* 309

Dewar, John, Barry Smith and Cate Banks, *Litigants in Person in the Family Court of Australia*, Family Court of Australia, Research Report No 20, 2000

Dewar, John and Stephen Parker, 'The Impact of the New Part VII' (1999) 13 *Australian Journal of Family Law* 96

Dewar, John, Grania Sheehan and Jody Hughes, *Superannuation and Divorce in Australia*, Working Paper 18, AIFS, Melbourne, 1999

Dewar, John, Stephen Parker et al, *Parenting, Planning and Partnership: The impact of the new Part VII of the Family Law Act 1975 (Cth)*, Family Law Research Unit Working Paper No 3, Griffith University, 1999

Dicey, AV, *Lectures on the Relation between Law and Public Opinion in England During the Nineteenth Century*, London, Macmillan, 1920

Diduck, Alison and Helena Orton, 'Equality and Support for Spouses' (1994) 57 *Modern Law Review* 681

Dixon, Owen, 'The Survival of Causes of Action' (1951) 1 *University of Queensland Law Journal* 1

Donnelly, Hugh, Stephen Cumines and Ania Wilczynski, *Sentenced Homicides in NSW 1990-1993: A Legal and Sociological Study*, Judicial Commission of NSW, Sydney, 1995

Du Bois, Ellen et al, 'Feminist Discourse, Moral Values and the Law – A Conversation' (1985) 34 *Buffalo Law Review* 11

Duclos, Nitya, 'Disappearing Women: Racial Minority Women in Human Rights Cases' (1993) 6 *Canadian Journal of Women and the Law* 25

Duden, Barbara, *Disembodying Women: Perspectives on Pregnancy and the Unborn*, Harvard University Press, Cambridge, MA, 1993

Duffy, Ailsa, Druiscilla Barrett and Maire Duggan, *Report of the Ministerial Inquiry into the Under-Reporting of Cervical Smear Abnormalities in the Gisborne Region*, April, 2001 (available at <http://www.csi.org.nz>)

Duggan, Lisa, 'Censorship in the Name of Feminism' in Gail Chester and Julienne Dickey (eds), *Feminism and Censorship: The Current Debate*, Prism Press, Dorset, 1988

Dunn, Kristie, 'Splitting the Difference: Superannuation, Equality and Family Law' (1998) 12 *Australian Journal of Family Law* 214

Dunn, Kristie, 'Yakking Giants: Equality Discourse in the High Court' (2000) 24 *Melbourne University Law Review* 427

Dworkin, Andrea, *Pornography: Men Possessing Women*, Perigee Books, New York, 1981

Dworkin, *Intercourse*, Arrow Books, London, 1987

Dworkin, Andrea and Catharine A MacKinnon, *Pornography and Civil Rights: A New Day for Women's Equality*, Organizing Against Pornography, Minneapolis, 1988

Easteal, Patricia (ed), *Balancing the Scales: Rape, Law Reform and Australian Culture*, Federation Press, Sydney, 1998

Eaton, Mary, 'Abuse by Any Other Name: Feminism, Difference and Intralesbian violence' in Martha Albertson Fineman and Roxanne Mykitiuk (eds), *The Public Nature of Private Violence: The Discovery of Domestic Abuse*, Routledge, New York, 1994

Edmond, Gary, 'Azaria's Accessories' (1998) 22 *Melbourne University Law Review* 396

Edwards, Anne, 'Male Violence in Feminist Theory: an Analysis of the Changing Conceptions of Sex/Gender Violence and Male Dominance' in Jalna Hanmer and Mary Maynard (eds), *Women, Violence and Social Control*, Macmillan, London, 1987

Edwards, Anne and Susan Magarey (eds), *Women in a Restructuring Australia: Work and Welfare*, Allen and Unwin, Sydney, 1995

Edwards, Meredith, *The Income Unit in the Australian Tax and Social Security Systems*, AIFS, Melbourne, 1984

Edwards, Meredith, 'Individual Equity and Social Policy' in Jacqueline Goodnow and Carole Pateman (eds), *Women, Social Science and Public Policy*, Allen and Unwin, Sydney, 1985

Eekelaar, John, *Family Security and Family Breakdown*, Penguin, Harmondsworth, 1971

Eisenstein, Hester, *Inside Agitators: Australian Femocrats and the State*, Allen and Unwin, Sydney, 1996

Eisenstein, Zillah R, *The Female Body and the Law*, University of California Press, Berkeley, 1988

Estrich, Susan, 'Rape' (1986) 95 *Yale Law Journal* 1087

Estrich, Susan, *Real Rape: How the Legal System Victimizes Women Who Say No*, Harvard University Press, Cambridge, 1987

Ettelbrick, Paula, 'Who is a Parent? The Need to Develop a Lesbian Conscious Family Law' (1993) 10 *New York Law School Journal of Human Rights* 513

Evans, Raymond, 'Harlots and Helots: Exploitation of the Aboriginal Remnant' in Raymond Evans, Kay Saunders and Kathryn Cronin, *Exclusion, Exploitation and Extermination: Race Relations in Colonial Queensland*, Australian and New Zealand Book Co, Sydney, 1975

Evans, Raymond, '"Don't You Remember Black Alice, Sam Holt": Aboriginal Women in Queensland History' (1982) 8 *Hecate* 6

Eveline, Joan, 'The Politics of Advantage' (1994) 19 *Australian Feminist Studies* 129

Expert Group on Family Financial Vulnerability, *Good Relations, High Risks: Financial Transactions within Families and Between Friends*, Report, 1996

Family Law Council, *Sterilisation and Other Medical Procedures on Children*, AGPS, Canberra, 1994

Family Law Council, *Violence and the Family Law Act: Financial Remedies*, AGPS, Canberra, 1998

Fehlberg, Belinda, 'Surety Wives and Australian Law: Akins v National Australia Bank' (1997) 11 *Banking and Finance Law Review* 423

Fehlberg, Belinda, *Sexually Transmitted Debt: Surety Experience and English Law*, Clarendon Press, Oxford, 1997

Fehlberg, Belinda and Bruce Smyth, 'Pre-Nuptial Agreements for Australia: Why Not?' (2000) 14 *Australian Journal of Family Law* 80

Feldthusen, Bruce, 'The Civil Action for Sexual Battery: Therapeutic Jurisprudence?' (1993) 25 *Ottawa Law Review* 203

Feldthusen, Bruce, 'The Canadian Experiment with the Civil Action for Sexual Battery' in Nicholas J Mullany (ed), *Torts in the Nineties*, LBC, Sydney, 1997

Feldthusen, Bruce, Olena Hankivsky and Lorraine Greaves, 'Therapeutic Consequences of Civil Actions for Damages and Compensation Claims by Victims of Sexual Abuse' (2000) 12 *Canadian Journal of Women and the Law* 66

Ferrante, Anna, Frank Morgan, David Indermaur and Richard Harding, *Measuring the Extent of Domestic Violence*, Hawkins Press, Sydney, 1996

Field et al, 'Maternal Brain Death During Pregnancy: Medical and Ethical Issues' (1988) 260 *Journal American Medical Association* 816

Fincher, Ruth, 'Women, immigration and the state: Issues of social difference and justice' in Anne Edwards and Susan Magarey (eds), *Women in a Restructuring Australia: Work and Welfare*, Allen and Unwin, Sydney, 1995

Fineman, Martha, 'Implementing Equality: Ideology, Contradiction and Social Change. A Study of Rhetoric and Results in the Regulation of the Consequences of Divorce' (1983) *Wisconsin Law Review* 789

Fineman, Martha, 'Illusive Equality: On Weitzman's *Divorce Revolution*' [1986] *American Bar Foundation Research Journal* 781

Fineman, Martha, *The Neutered Mother, the Sexual Family and Other Twentieth Century Tragedies*, Routledge, New York, 1995

Fineman, Martha Albertson and Roxanne Mykitiuk (eds), *The Public Nature of Private Violence: The Discovery of Domestic Abuse*, Routledge, New York, 1994

Finley, Lucinda, 'Transcending Equality Theory: A Way Out of the Maternity and the Workplace Debate' (1986) 86 *Columbia Law Review* 1118

Finley, Lucinda, 'A Break in the Silence: Including Women's Issues in a Torts Course' (1989) 1 *Yale Journal of Law and Feminism* 41

Finley, Lucinda, 'The Pharmaceutical Industry and Women's Reproductive Health: The Perils of Ignoring Risk and Blaming Women' in Elizabeth Szockyj and James G Fox (eds), *Corporate Victimisation of Women*, Northeastern University Press, Boston, 1996

Finley, Lucinda, 'Female Trouble: The Implications of Tort Reform for Women' (1997) 64 *Tennessee Law Review* 847

Fisher, Michelle and Fahna Ammett, 'Sentencing of Sexual Offenders When Their Victims are Prostitutes and Other Issues Arising Out of *Hakopian*' (1992) 18 *Melbourne University Law Review* 683

Flood, Michael, 'Claims about Husband Battering', available at <http://www.anu.edu.au/~a112465/XY/husbandbattering.htm>

Forell, Caroline A and Donna M Matthews, *A Law of Her Own: The Reasonable Woman as a Measure of Man*, New York University Press, New York and London, 2000

Fortin, Jane ES, 'Can You Ward a Foetus?' (1988) 51 *Modern Law Review* 768

Fox, Richard and Arie Freiberg, *Sentencing: State and Federal Law in Victoria*, Oxford University Press, Melbourne, 1985

Fox, Richard and Arie Freiberg, *Sentencing: State and Federal Law in Victoria*, 2nd ed, Oxford University Press, Melbourne, 1999

Freeman, Michael, 'Doing his best to sustain the sanctity of marriage' in Norman Johnson (ed), *Marital Violence*, Routledge, London, 1985

Freeman, Michael, 'Contracting in the Haven: *Balfour v Balfour* Revisited' in Roger Halson (ed), *Exploring the Boundaries of Contract*, Dartmouth, Aldershot, 1996

Freeman, Michael, 'Family Values and Family Justice' (1997) 50 *Current Legal Problems* 315

Fried, Marlene Gerber (ed), *From Abortion to Reproductive Freedom: Transforming a Movement*, South End Press, Boston, MA, 1990

Frug, Mary Joe, 'Rereading Contracts: A Feminist Analysis of a Contracts Casebook' (1985) 34 *American University Law Review* 1065

Funder, Kathleen, 'Australia: A Proposal for Reform' in Lenore J Weitzman and Mavis McLean (eds), *Economic Consequences of Divorce: The International Perspective*, Clarendon Press, Oxford, 1992

Funder, Kathleen; Margaret Harrison and Ruth Weston, *Settling Down: Pathways of Parents After Divorce*, AIFS, Melbourne, 1993

Gallagher, Janet, 'Prenatal Invasions and Interventions: What's Wrong with Fetal Rights?' (1987) 10 *Harvard Women's Law Journal* 9

Gallagher, Janet, 'Fetus as Patient' in Sherrill Cohen and Nadine Taub (eds), *Reproductive Laws for the 1990's*, Humana Press, Clifton, NJ, 1989

Garner, Helen, *The First Stone: Some Questions About Sex and Power*, Picador Pan Macmillan, Sydney, 1995

Gatens, Moira and Alison MacKinnon (eds), *Gender and Institutions: Welfare, Work and Citizenship*, Cambridge University Press, Melbourne, 1998

Gaudron, Mary, 'Speech to launch Australian Women Lawyers', 19 September 1997, available at <http://www.hcourt.gov.au/speeches/gaudronj/gaudronj_wlasp.htm>

Gaudron, Mary and Michal Bosworth, 'Equal Pay?' in Judy Mackinolty and Heather Radi (eds), *In Pursuit of Justice: Australian Women and the Law 1788-1979*, Hale and Iremonger, Sydney, 1979

Gavigan, Shelley, 'The Criminal Sanction as it Relates to Human Reproduction: The Genesis of the Statutory Prohibition of Abortion' (1983) 3 *Journal of Legal History* 20

Gilligan, Carol, *In a Different Voice: Psychological Theory and Women's Development*, Harvard University Press, Cambridge MA, 1982

Gilligan, Carol, 'Feminist Discourse, Moral Values and the Law' (1985) 34 *Buffalo Law Review* 11

Ginzberg, Janet, 'Compulsory Contraception as a Condition of Probation: The Use and Abuse of Norplant' (1992) 58 *Brooklyn Law Review* 979

Glen, Kristin Booth 'Abortion in the Courts: A Laywoman's Guide to the New Disaster Area' (1978) 4 *Feminist Studies* 1

Glen, Kristin Booth, 'Understanding the Abortion Debate: A Legal, Constitutional and Political Framework' [1986] *Socialist Review* 51

Glendon, Mary Ann, *Abortion and Divorce in Western Law*, Harvard University Press, Cambridge, MA, 1987

Glucksman, Miriam A, 'Why "Work"? Gender and the "Total Social Organization of Labour"' (1995) 2 *Gender, Work and Organization* 63

Gluckstern, Helen and Pauline Presland, *Divorce for Mature Age Women: Why Now?* Family Court Research Report No 11, June 1993

Goldhar, Jeff, 'The Sterilisation of Women with an Intellectual Disability' (1991) 10 *University of Tasmania Law Review* 157

Goldsworthy, Kerryn, 'Martyr to her sex', *The Age Saturday Extra*, 15 February 1986

Gomez, Laura E, *Misconceiving Mothers: Legislators, Prosecutors and the Politics of Prenatal Drug Exposure*, Temple University Press, Philadelphia, 1997

Goodall, Heather, '"Saving the Children": Gender and the Colonisation of Aboriginal Children in NSW, 1788 to 1990' (1990) 2 (44) *Aboriginal Law Bulletin* 6

Goodman, Janice, Rhonda Copelon Schoenbrod and Nancy Stearns, 'Doe and Roe: Where Do We Go From Here?' (1971-1973) 1 *Women's Rights Law Reporter* 20

Goodzeit, Carolyn, 'Rethinking Emotional Distress Law: Prenatal Malpractice and Feminist Theory' (1994) 63 *Fordham Law Review* 175

Gordon, Linda, *Women's Body, Women's Right: A Social History of Birth Control in America*, Penguin, New York, 1977

Gotell, Lise, 'Litigating Feminist 'Truth': An Antifoundational Critique' (1995) 4 *Social and Legal Studies* 99

Granberg, Donald, 'The Abortion Activists' (1981) 13 *Family Planning Perspectives* 157

Grant, Isabel, 'The "Syndromization" of Women's Experience' in Donna Martinson et al, 'A Forum on *Lavallée v R*: Women and Self Defence' (1991) 25 *University of British Columbia Law Review* 23

Grant, Isabel and Judith Mosoff, 'Hearing Claims of Inequality: *Eldridge v British Columbia (A-G)*' (1998) 10 *Canadian Journal of Women and the Law* 229

Grant, Isabel and Lynn Smith, 'Gender Representation in the Canadian Judiciary' in *Appointing Judges: Philosophy, Politics and Practice*, OLRC, Toronto, 1991

Gray, Matthew and Bruce Chapman, 'Foregone Earnings from Child Rearing' (2001) 58 *Family Matters* 4

Graycar, Regina, 'Non-Earners and Accident Compensation: Women Sold Out Again' (1985) 10 *Legal Service Bulletin* 86

Graycar, Regina, 'Review of Katherine O'Donovan, *Sexual Divisions in Law*' (1987-88) 26 *Journal of Family Law* 265

Graycar, Regina, 'Family Law and Social Security: The Child Support Connection' (1989) 3 *Australian Journal of Family Law* 70

Graycar, Regina, 'Women's Work: Who Cares?' (1992) 14 *Sydney Law Review* 86

Graycar, Regina, 'Love's Labour's Cost: The High Court Decision in *Van Gervan v Fenton*' (1993) 1 *Torts Law Journal* 122

Graycar, Regina, 'Legal Categories and Women's Work: Explorations for a Cross-Doctrinal Feminist Jurisprudence' (1994) 7 *Canadian Journal of Women and the Law* 32

Graycar, Regina, 'Sterilisation of Young Women with Disabilities: Towards a New Regulatory Framework' (1994) 1 *Australian Journal of Human Rights* 380

Graycar, Regina, 'Damaged Awards: The Vicissitudes of Life as a Woman' (1995) 3 *Torts Law Journal* 160

Graycar, Regina, 'Matrimonial Property and Models of Equality: Discourses in Discord?' (1995) 25 *Victoria University of Wellington Law Review* 9

Graycar, Regina, 'The Relevance of Violence in Family Court Decision Making' (1995) 9 *Australian Journal of Family Law* 58

Graycar, Regina, 'Telling Tales: Legal Stories about Violence Against Women' (1996) 7 *Australian Feminist Law Journal* 79

Graycar, Regina, 'Hoovering as a Hobby and Other Stories: Gendered Assessments of Personal Injury Damages' (1997) 31 *University of British Columbia Law Review* 17

Graycar, Regina, 'Compensation for the Stolen Children: Political Judgments and Community Values' (1998) 21 *University of New South Wales Law Journal* 253

Graycar, Regina, 'The Gender of Judgments: Some Reflections on "Bias"' (1998) 32 *University of British Columbia Law Review* 1

Graycar, Reg, 'Law Reform by Frozen Chook: Family Law Reform for the New Millennium?' (2000) 24 *Melbourne University Law Review* 737

Graycar, Reg, 'Concept of "Family" under Review' (2001) 39(3) *Law Society Journal* 64

Graycar, Reg and Jenni Millbank, 'The Bride Wore Pink . . . to the *Property (Relationships) Legislation Amendment Act 1999*: Family Law Reform in NSW' (2000) 17 *Canadian Journal of Family Law* 227

Graycar, Regina and Jenny Morgan, 'Disabling Citizenship: Civil Death for Women in the 1990s?' (1995) 17 *Adelaide Law Review* 49

Graycar, Reg and Jenny Morgan, 'Legal Categories, Women's Lives and the Law Curriculum OR: Making Gender Examinable' (1996) 18 *Sydney Law Review* 431

Graycar, Reg and Jenny Morgan, '"Unnatural Rejection of Womanhood and Motherhood": Pregnancy, Damages and the Law – A Note on *CES v Superclinics*' (1996) 18 *Sydney Law Review* 323

Graycar, Reg and Jenny Morgan (eds), *Work and Violence Themes: Including Gender Issues in the Core Law Curriculum*, 1996, available at <http://pandora.nla.gov.au/tep/10029>

Graycar, Reg, Robyn Johansson and Jenny Lovric, 'Third Party Guarantees' (2001) 12 *Journal of Banking and Finance Law and Practice* 181

Greer, Pam with Jan Breckenridge, '"They Threw the Rule Book Away": Sexual Assault in Aboriginal Communities' in Jan Breckenridge and Moira Carmody (eds), *Crimes of Violence: Australian Responses to Rape and Child Sexual Assault*, Allen and Unwin, Sydney, 1992

Gregory, Bob, 'Labour Market Institutions and the Gender Pay Ratio' (1999) 32 *Australian Economic Review* 273

Grieve, Norma and Ailsa Burns (eds), *Australian Women: New Feminist Perspectives*, OUP, Melbourne, 1986

Grillo, Trina, 'Anti-Essentialism and Intersectionality: Tools to Dismantle the Master's House' (1995) 10 *Berkeley Women's Law Journal* 16

Grosz, Elizabeth and Gayatri Spivak, 'Criticism, Feminism and the Institution: An Interview with Gayatri Chakravorty Spivak' (1984/85) 10/11 *Thesis Eleven* 175

Hall, Richard, *Gender Equity and Enterprise Bargaining*, Australian Centre for Industrial Relations Research and Training, (ACIRRT), Working Paper No 57, June 1999, Sydney, 1999

Hancock, Linda, 'Reforming the Child Support Agenda: Who Benefits?' (1998) *Just Policy* No 12, March 1998

Handsley, Elizabeth, 'Mental Injury Occasioned by Harm to Another: A Feminist Critique' (1996) 14 *Journal of Law and Inequality* 391

Harris, Angela, 'Race and Essentialism in Feminist Legal Theory' (1990) 42 *Stanford Law Review* 581

Harris, Carmel, 'The "Terror of the Law" As Applied to Black Rapists in Colonial Queensland' (1982) 8 *Hecate* 22

Harrison, Kate, 'Child Custody and Parental Sexuality: Just Another Factor?' (1980) 20-21 *Refractory Girl* 7

Harrison, Margaret, 'Family Law, Recent Issues and Initiatives' (1999) 52 *Family Matters* 61

Harrison, Margaret and Regina Graycar, 'The Family Law Reform Act: Metamorphosis or More of the Same?' (1997) 11 *Australian Journal of Family Law* 327

Harrison, Margaret, Patricia Harper and Meredith Edwards, *Child Support – Public or Private?* Paper presented to Family Law Conference, Hobart, 1984

Hartsock, Nancy, 'Foucault on Power: A Theory for Women' in Linda Nicholson (ed), *Feminism/Postmodernism*, Routledge, London, 1990

Haskell, Thomas and Sanford Levinson 'Reply to Alice Kessler-Harris' (1989) 67 *Texas Law Review* 1591

Haskell, Thomas and Sanford Levinson, 'Academic Freedom and Expert Witnessing and the *Sears* Case' (1987) 66 *Texas Law Review* 1629

Headey, Bruce, Dorothy Scott and David de Vaus, 'Domestic Violence in Australia: Are women and men equally violent?' (1999) 2 *Australian Social Monitor* 57

Heath, Mary and Ngaire Naffine, 'Men's Needs and Women's Desires: Feminist Dilemmas about Rape Law Reform' (1994) 3 *Australian Feminist Law Journal* 30

Heenan, Melanie and Helen McKelvie, *Evaluation of the Crimes (Rape) Act 1991*, Executive Summary, Department of Justice, Vic, 1997

Henning, Therese and Simon Bronitt, 'Rape Victims on Trial: Regulating the Use and Abuse of Sexual History Evidence' in Patricia Easteal (ed), *Balancing the Scales: Rape, Law Reform and Australian Culture*, Federation Press, Sydney, 1998

Herman, Didi and Carl Stychin (eds), *Legal Inversions: Lesbians, Gay Men and the Politics of Law*, Temple University Press, Philadelphia, 1995

Hickling, MA, 'Employer's Liability for Sexual Harassment' (1988) 17 *Manitoba Law Journal* 124

Himmelweit, Susan, 'More Than "A Woman's Right to Choose"' (1988) 29 *Feminist Review* 38

Hocking, Barbara Ann and Alison Smith, 'From *Coultas* to *Alcock* and Beyond: Will Tort Law Fail Women'? (1995) 11 *Queensland University of Technology Law Journal* 120

Holcombe, Lee, *Wives and Property: Reform of the Married Women's Property Law in Nineteenth Century England*, Martin Robertson, Oxford, 1983

Horder, Jeremy, *Provocation and Responsibility*, Clarendon Press, Oxford, 1992

Hore, Elizabeth, Janne Gibson and Sophy Bordow, *Domestic Homicide*, Family Court of Australia, Research Report No 13, March 1996

Horwill, Frank and Sophy Bordow, *The Outcome of Defended Custody Cases in the Family Court of Australia*, Research Report No 4, Family Court of Australia, 1983

Howe, Adrian, '"Social Injury Revisited": Towards a Feminist Theory of Social Justice' (1987) 15 *International Journal of the Sociology of Law* 423

Howe, Adrian, 'Chamberlain Revisited: The Case Against The Media' (1989) 31-32 *Refractory Girl* 2

Howe, Adrian, 'Sweet Dreams: Deinstitutionalising Young Women' in Graycar (ed), *Dissenting Opinions: Feminist Explorations in Law and Society*, Allen and Unwin, Sydney, 1990

Howe, Adrian, 'The Problem of Privatised Injuries: Feminist Strategies for Litigation' in Martha Fineman (ed), *At the Boundaries of Law: Feminism and Legal Theory*, Routledge, New York, 1990

Howe, Adrian, 'Provoking Comment: The Question of Gender Bias in the Provocation Defence – A Victorian Case Study' in Norma Grieve and Ailsa Burns (eds), *Australian Women: Contemporary Feminist Thought*, Oxford University Press, Melbourne, 1994

Howe, Adrian, *Punish and Critique: Towards a Feminist Critique of Penality*, Routledge, London, 1994

Howe, Adrian, 'Fiduciary Law meets the Civil Incest Suit: Re-Framing the Injury of Incestuous Assault – A Question of Visibility' (1997) 8 *Australian Feminist Law Journal* 59

Howe, Adrian, 'Imagining Evidence, Fictioning Truth – Revisiting (Courtesy of OJ Simpson) Expert Evidence in the Chamberlain Case' (1997) 3 *Law Text Culture* 82

Howell, Nicola, 'Sexually Transmitted Debt: A Feminist Analysis of Laws Regulating Guarantors and Co-Borrowers' (1995) 3 *Australian Feminist Law Journal* 93

HREOC, *Racist Violence: Report of National Inquiry into Racist Violence in Australia*, Canberra, 1991

HREOC, *Bringing Them Home: National Inquiry into the Separation of Aboriginal and Torres Strait Islander Children from Their Families*, Commonwealth of Australia, Sydney, 1997

Huggins, Jackie, 'A Contemporary View of Aboriginal Women's Relationship to the White Women's Movement' in Norma Grieve and Ailsa Burns (eds), *Australian Women: Contemporary Feminist Thought*, Oxford University Press, Melbourne, 1994

Hughes, Jody, 'Repartnering After Divorce: Marginal Mates and Unwedded Women' (2000) 55 *Family Matters* 16

Hughes, John, 'Case and Comment: The National Women's Case in the Court of Appeal' [1990] *New Zealand Law Journal* 114 April, 1990

Hunt, Su-Jane, 'Aboriginal Women and Colonial Authority: Northwestern Australia 1885-1905 in Judy MacKinolty and Heather Radi (eds), *In Pursuit of Justice: Australian Women and the Law 1788-1979*, Hale and Iremonger, Sydney, 1979

Hunt, Susan Jane, *Spinifex and Hessian: Women's Lives in North-Western Australia*, UWA Press, Perth, 1986

Hunter, Rosemary, 'Representing Gender in Legal Analysis: A Case/Book Study in Labour Law' (1991) 18 *Melbourne University Law Review* 305

Hunter, Rosemary, *Family Law Case Profiles*, Justice Research Centre, Sydney, June 1999

Hunter, Rosemary, *The Beauty Therapist, the Mechanic, the Geoscientist and the Librarian: Addressing the Undervaluation of Women's Work*, ATN, Wexdev, University of Technology, Sydney, 2000

Hunter, Rosemary, 'The Mirage of Justice: Women and the Shrinking State', Paper presented at Feminist Legal Academics Workshop (FLAW), Brisbane, February 2001

Hunter, Rosemary and Helen McKelvie, 'Gender and Legal Practice' (1999) 24 *Alternative Law Journal* 57

Hunter, Rosemary and Julie Stubbs, 'Model Laws or Missed Opportunity?' (1999) 24 *Alternative Law Journal* 12

Hunter, Rosemary et al *Legal Services in Family Law*, Law and Justice Foundation, 2001

Ikemoto, Lisa C, 'Furthering the Inquiry: Race, Class, Culture in the Forced Medical Treatment of Pregnant Women' in Adrien Katherine Wing (ed), *Critical Race Feminism: A Reader*, New York University Press, New York, 1997

Innes, Jane, 'Equal Pay and the *Sex Discrimination Act* 1984' (1986) 11 *Legal Service Bulletin* 254

Jessep, Owen and Richard Chisholm, 'Children, The Constitution and the Family Court' (1985) 8 *University of New South Wales Law Journal* 152

Johnson, Dianne, 'From Fairy to Witch: imagery and myth in the Chamberlain case' (1984) 2 *Australian Journal of Cultural Studies* 90

Joint Select Committee on the Family Law Act (the 'Ruddock Committee'), *Family Law in Australia*, AGPS, Canberra, 1980

Joint Select Committee, *The Family Law Act 1975: Aspects of its Operation and Interpretation*, AGPS, Canberra, 1992

Jordan, Emma Coleman, 'The Power of False Racial Memory and the Metaphor of Lynching' in Anita Fay Hill and Emma Coleman Jordan (eds), *Race, Gender and Power in America: The Legacy of the Hill-Thomas Hearings*, Oxford University Press, New York, 1995

Jordan, Peter, *The Effects of Marital Separation on Men: 'Men Hurt'*, Family Court Research Report No 6, 1985

Jukic, Radmila, *Till Debt us do Part*; Melbourne, Consumer Credit Legal Service, 1994

Karpin, Isabel, 'Legislating the Female Body: Reproductive Technology and the Reconstructed Woman' (1992) 3 *Columbia Journal of Gender and Law* 325

Karst, Kenneth, 'Woman's Constitution' [1984] *Duke Law Journal* 447

Kaspiew, Rae, 'Rape Lore: Legal Narrative and Sexual Violence' (1995) 20 *Melbourne University Law Review* 350

Katzen, Hayley, 'It's a Family Matter, Not a Police Matter: The Enforcement of Protection Orders' (2000) 14 *Australian Journal of Family Law* 119

Katzen, Hayley, *How do I prove I saw his shadow? Responses to breaches of Apprehended Violence Orders: A Consultation with Women and Police in the Richmond Local Area Command of NSW*, 2000

Kaye, Miranda, 'Equity's Treatment of Sexually Transmitted Debt' (1997) 5 *Feminist Legal Studies* 35

Kaye, Miranda and Julia Tolmie, 'Discoursing Dads: The Rhetorical Devices of Fathers' Rights Groups' (1998) 22 *Melbourne University Law Review* 162

Kaye, Miranda and Julia Tolmie, 'Fathers' Rights Groups in Australia' (1998) 12 *Australian Journal of Family Law* 19

Keller, Susan Etta, 'Viewing and Doing: Complicating Pornography's Meaning' (1993) 81 *Georgetown Law Journal* 2195

Kelley, Jonathan and MDR Evans, 'Attitudes toward abortion: Australia in comparative perspective' (1999) 2 *Australian Social Monitor* 83

Kelley, Jonathan and MDR Evans, 'Should abortion be legal?: Australians' opinions and their sources in ideology and social structure' in Jonathan Kelley and Clive Bean, *Australian Attitudes: Social and political analysis from the National Social Sciences Survey*, Allen and Unwin, Sydney, 1988

Kelly, Jonathan, MDR Evans and Bruce Headey, 'Moral Reasoning and Political Conflict: The Abortion Controversy' (1993) 44 *British Journal of Sociology* 589

Kelly, Liz, 'The Continuum of Sexual Violence' in Jalna Hanmer and Mary Maynard (eds), *Women, Violence and Social Control*, Macmillan Press, London, 1987.

Kelly, Liz, *Surviving Sexual Violence*, Polity Press, Cambridge, 1989

Kendall, Christopher, '"Real Dominant, Real Fun!": Gay Male Pornography and the Pursuit of Masculinity' (1993) 57 *Saskatchewan Law Review* 21

Kenney, Sally, 'Reproductive Hazards in the Workplace: The Law and Sexual Difference' (1986) 14 *International Journal of the Sociology of Law* 393

Kenney, Sally, *For Whose Protection? Reproductive Hazards and Exclusionary Policies in the United States and Britain*, University of Michigan Press, Ann Arbor, 1992

Kenny, Susan, 'Interveners and Amici Curiae in the High Court' (1998) 20 *Adelaide Law Review* 159

Kessler-Harris, Alice, '*EEOC v Sears Roebuck and Company*: A Personal Account' (1987) 25 *Feminist Review* 46

Kessler-Harris, Alice, 'Response to Haskell and Levinson' (1988) 67 *Texas Law Review* 429

Keys Young, *Research on Gender Bias and Women Working in the Legal Profession*, Report Prepared for the Department for Women, New South Wales, 1995

Kidd, Michael P and Xin Meng, 'Trends in the Australian Gender Wage Differential over the 1980's: Some Evidence on the Effectiveness of Legislative Reform' (1997) 30 *Australian Economic Review* 31

Kingdom, Elizabeth, 'Legal Recognition of a Woman's Right to Choose' in Julia Brophy and Carol Smart, *Women in Law*, Routledge, London, 1985

Kitzinger, Celia, 'Anti-lesbian Harassment' in Clare Brant and Yun Lee Too (eds), *Rethinking Sexual Harassment*, Pluto Press, London, 1994

Kline, Marlee, 'Race, Racism and Feminist Legal Theory' (1989) 12 *Harvard Women's Law Journal* 115

Kline, Marlee, 'Child Welfare Law, "Best Interests of the Child" Ideology, and First Nations' (1992) 30 *Osgoode Hall Law Journal* 375

Kline, Marlee, 'Complicating the Ideology of Motherhood: Child Welfare Law and First Nation Women' (1993) 18 *Queen's Law Journal* 306

Koenig, Thomas and Rustad, Michael, 'His and Her Tort Reform: Gender Injustice in Disguise' (1995) 70 *Washington Law Review* 1

Kolder, Veronika EB, Janet Gallagher and Michael T Parsons, 'Court-Ordered Obstetrical Interventions' (1987) 316 *New England Journal of Medicine* 1192

Koshan, Jennifer, 'Sounds of Silence: The Public/Private Dichotomy, Violence, and Aboriginal Women' in Susan B Boyd (ed), *Challenging the Public/Private Divide: Feminism, Law, and Public Policy*, University of Toronto Press, Toronto, 1997

Kramarae, Cheris and Paula A Treichler, *A Feminist Dictionary*, Pandora Press, Boston, 1985

Krieger, Linda J and Patricia N Cooney, 'The Miller-Wohl Controversy: Equal Treatment, Positive Action and the Meaning of Women's Equality' (1983) 13 *Golden Gate University Law Review* 513

Krog, Antjie, *Country of My Skull*, Vintage, London, 1999

L'Heureux-Dubé, Claire, 'Recent Developments in Family Law' (1993) 6 *Canadian Journal of Women and the Law* 269

L'Heureux-Dubé, Claire, 'Making Equality Work in Family Law' (1997) 14 *Canadian Journal of Family Law* 103

Lacey, Nicola, 'Theory into Practice? Pornography and the Public/Private Dichotomy' (1993) 20 *Journal of Law and Society* 93

Lader, Lawrence, *Abortion II: Making the Revolution*, Beacon Press, Boston, 1973

Lahey, Kathleen, '"...until women themselves have told all that they have to tell ..."' (1985) 23 *Osgoode Hall Law Journal* 519

Lake, Marilyn, 'Dealing with Sexual Difference' (1999) 24 *Alternative Law Journal* 265

Laster, Kathy, 'Infanticide: A Litmus Test for Feminist Criminological Theory' (1989) 22 *ANZ Journal of Criminology* 151

Law Commission of Canada, 'Recognizing and Supporting Close Personal Relationships Between Adults', Discussion Paper, May, 2000

Law Commission of Canada, *Restoring Dignity: Responding to Child Abuse in Canadian Institutions*, 2000

Law Reform Commission of British Columbia, *Report on Interspousal Immunity in Tort*, LRC 62, Vancouver, 1983

Law Reform Commission of Victoria, *Homicide Prosecutions Study*, Report No 40

Law Reform Commission of Victoria, *Rape: Reform of Law and Procedure*, Report No 42, July, 1991

Law Reform Commission of Victoria, *Rape: Reform of Law and Procedure, Supplementary Issues*, Report No 46, July, 1992

Law Society of NSW, *Profile of the Solicitors of NSW 1998*, Research Report 2, 1998

Law, Sylvia, 'Rethinking Sex and the Constitution' (1984) 132 *University of Pennsylvania Law Review* 935

Lawrence, Sonia N, 'Cultural (In)sensitivity: The Dangers of a Simplistic Approach to Culture in the Courtroom' (2001) 13 *Canadian Journal of Women and the Law* 107

Lazarus, S, J Trucano and K McCarthy, 'Young Women and the Penal System in Victoria', paper delivered to Australian Law and Society conference, 6 December, 1987

Leader-Elliott, Ian, 'Battered but not Beaten: Women who Kill in Self Defence' (1993) 15 *Sydney Law Review* 403

LEAF, *Equality and the Charter: 1985-1995*, Emond Montgomery, Toronto, 1996

Legal Aid and Family Services, *Gender Bias in Litigation Legal Aid*, Issues Paper, Attorney General's Department, Canberra, February, 1994

Lessard, Hester, 'The Idea of the "Private": A Discussion of State Action Doctrine and Separate Spheres Ideology' (1986) 28 *Dalhousie Law Journal* 107

Lessard, Hester, 'The Construction of Health Care and the Ideology of the Private in Canadian Constitutional Law' (1993) 2 *Annals of Health Law* 121

Lindsay, Jo, 'Diversity but not Equality: Domestic Labour in Cohabiting Relationships' (1999) 34 *Australian Journal of Social Issues* 267

Lipman-Blumen, Jean, 'Toward a Homosocial Theory of Sex Roles: An Explanation of the Sex Segregation of Social Institutions' in Martha Blaxall and Barbara Reagan (eds), *Women and the Workplace*, University of Chicago Press, Chicago, 1976

Lister, Ruth, 'Women, Economic Dependency and Citizenship' [1990] *Journal of Social Policy* 445

Littleton, Christine, 'Reconstructing Sexual Equality' (1987) 75 *California Law Review* 1279

Littleton, Christine, 'Book Review; Feminist Jurisprudence: The Difference Method Makes' (1989) 41 *Stanford Law Review* 751

Liu, Mimi, 'A 'Prophet With Honour': An Examination of the Gender Equality Jurisprudence of Madam Justice Claire L'Heureux-Dubé of the Supreme Court of Canada' (2000) 25 *Queen's Law Journal* 417

Lock, Jennifer, *The Aboriginal Child Placement Principle*, NSWLRC, Research Report No 7, 1997, 278

Lücke, HK, 'The Intention to Create Legal Relations' (1967-70) 3 *Adelaide Law Review* 419

Luker, Kristin, *Abortion and the Politics of Motherhood*, University of California Press, Berkeley, 1984

Luntz, Harold, *Assessment of Damages for Personal Injury and Death*, 3rd ed, Butterworths, Sydney, 1990

MacCrimmon, Marilyn T, 'Trial by Ordeal' (1996) 1 *Canadian Criminal Law Review* 31

MacDermott, Therese, 'Linking Gender and Superannuation' (1997) 2 *International Journal of Discrimination and the Law* 271

McDonald, Peter (ed), *Settling Up: Property and Income Distribution on Divorce in Australia*, Australian Institute of Family Studies (AIFS) and Prentice-Hall of Australia, Melbourne, 1986

McDonnell, Kathleen, *Not an Easy Choice: A Feminist Re-Examines Abortion*, South End Press, Boston, 1984

McGlynn, Clare, 'Judging Women Differently: Gender, the Judiciary and Reform' in Susan Millns and Noel Whitty (eds), *Feminist Perspectives on Public Law*, Cavendish, London, 1999

McInnes, John and Christine Boyle, 'Judging Sexual Assault Law Against a Standard of Equality' (1995) 29 *University of British Columbia Law Review* 341

McIntosh, G, 'Childcare in Australia: Current Provision and Recent Developments', *Background Paper 9*, Social Policy Research Group, Parliament of Australia, Parliament Library, Canberra, 1997/98

McIntyre, Sheila, 'Redefining Reformism: The Consultations that Shaped Bill C-49' in Julian V Roberts and Renate M Mohr (eds), *Confronting Sexual Assault: A Decade of Legal and Social Change*, University of Toronto Press, Toronto, 1994

MacKenzie, Catriona, 'Abortion and Embodiment' (1992) 70 *Australian Journal of Philosophy* 136

MacKinnon, Catharine A, *Sexual Harassment of Working Women*, Yale University Press, New Haven, CT, 1979

MacKinnon, Catharine A, 'Feminism, Marxism, Method and the State: An Agenda for Theory' (1982) 7 *Signs* 515

MacKinnon, Catharine A, 'Feminism, Marxism, Method and the State: Toward Feminist Jurisprudence' (1983) 8 *Signs* 635

MacKinnon, Catharine A, 'The Male Ideology of Privacy: A Feminist Perspective on the Right to Abortion' (1983) 17 *Radical America* 23

MacKinnon, Catharine A, *Feminism Unmodified: Discourses on Life and Law*, Harvard University Press, Cambridge, MA, 1987

MacKinnon, Catharine A, *Toward a Feminist Theory of the State*, Harvard University Press, Cambridge, MA, 1989

MacKinnon, Catharine A, 'Pornography's Empire', Paper presented to the 9th Commonwealth Law Conference, 16-20 April 1990, Auckland, New Zealand, 1990

MacKinnon, Catharine A, 'Reflections on Sex Equality Under Law' (1991) 100 *Yale Law Journal* 1281

MacKinnon, Catherine A, 'Disputing Male Sovereignty: On United States v Morrison' (2000) 114 *Harvard Law Review* 135

MacKinnon, Catharine A, 'Points Against Postmodernism' (2000) 75 *Chicago-Kent Law Review* 687

Mahoney, Joan, 'Death With Dignity: Is There An Exception for Pregnant Women?' (1989) *University of Missouri-Kansas City Law Review* 221

Mahoney, Martha, 'Legal Images of Battered Women: Redefining the Issue of Separation' (1991) 90 *Michigan Law Review* 1

Mahoney, Martha 'Victimization or Oppression? Women's Lives, Violence, and Agency' in Martha Albertson Fineman and Roxanne Mykitiuk (eds), *The Public Nature of Private Violence: The Discovery of Domestic Abuse*, Routledge, New York, 1994

Mahowald, Mary, 'Beyond Abortion: Refusal of Caesarean Section' (1989) 3 *Bioethics* 106

Maine, Henry Sumner, *Ancient Law*, OUP, London, 1931

Manning, Joanna, 'Exemplary Damages and Criminal Punishment in the Privy Council' (1999) 7 *Torts Law Journal* 129

Manning, Joanna, 'Professor Smillie's 'Exemplary Damages for Personal Injury'' [1997] *NZ Law Review* 176

Manning, Joanna, 'Exemplary Damages in Negligence: The Story of A Screening Programme' (2001) 9 *Torts Law Journal* 229

Marcus, Isabel, 'Reframing "Domestic Violence": Terrorism in the Home' in Martha Albertson Fineman and Roxanne Mykitiuk (eds), *The Public Nature of Private Violence: The Discovery of Domestic Abuse*, Routledge, New York, 1994

Marcus, Sharon, 'Fighting Bodies, Fighting Words: A Theory and Politics of Rape Prevention' in Judith Butler and Joan W Scott (eds), *Feminists Theorize the Political*, Routledge, New York, 1992

Marsh, JC, A Geist and N Caplan, *Rape and the Limits of Law Reform*, Auburn House, Boston, 1982

Mason, Gail, 'Reforming the Law of Rape: Incursions into the Masculinist Sanctum' in Diane Kirkby (ed), *Sex, Power and Justice: Historical Perspectives on Law in Australia*, Oxford University Press, Melbourne, 1995

Matheson, Clare, *Fate Cries Enough*, Spectre, Auckland, 1989

Matsuda, Mari, 'Affirmative Action and Legal Knowledge: Planting Seeds in Plowed-Up Ground' (1988) 11 *Harvard Women's Law Journal* 1

Matsuda, Mari, 'When the First Quail Calls: Multiple Consciousness as Jurisprudential Method' (1989) 11 *Women's Rights Law Reporter* 7

Matsuda, Mari, 'Pragmatism Modified and the False Consciousness Problem' (1990) 63 *Southern California Law Review* 1763

Matsuda, Mari, *Where is Your Body? And Other Essays on Race, Gender, and the Law*, Beacon Press, Boston, 1996

Mead, Jenna, 'Sexual Harassment and Feminism: Jenna Mead talks to Amanda Lohrey' (1995) 2 *Republica* 166

Meagher, Roderick, William Gummow and John Lehane, *Equity Doctrine & Remedies*, 3rd ed, Butterworths, 1992

Memmott, Paul, Rachael Stacy, Catherine Chambers and Catherine Keys, *Violence in Indigenous Communities: Full Report*, Report to Crime Prevention Branch of the Attorney-General's Department, Commonwealth of Australia, January 2001

Menkel-Meadow, Carrie, 'Portia in a Different Voice: Speculations on a Woman's Lawyering Process' (1985) 1 *Berkeley Women's Law Journal* 39

Menon, Nivedita, 'Abortion and the Law: Questions for Feminism' (1993) 6 *Canadian Journal of Women and the Law* 103

Meteyard, Belinda, "Review of Weitzman's The Divorce Revolution" (1986) 14 *International Journal of Sociology of Law* 435

Milkman, Ruth, 'Women's History and the Sears Case' (1986) 12 *Feminist Studies* 108

Mill, John Stuart, 'The Subjection of Women' in JS Mill and Harriet Taylor, *Essays in Sex Equality* (A Rossi ed), University of Chicago Press, Chicago, 1970

Millbank, Jenni, 'Lesbian Mothers, Gay Fathers: Sameness and Difference' (1992) 2 *Australian Gay & Lesbian Law Journal* 21

Millbank, Jenni, 'Hey Girls, Have We Got a Super Deal for You' (1993) 7 *Australian Journal of Family Law* 104

Millbank, Jenni, 'Every Sperm is Sacred?' (1997) 22 *Alternative Law Journal* 126

Millbank, Jenni, 'Lesbians, Child Custody and the Long, Lingering Gaze of the Law' in Susan Boyd (ed), *Challenging the Public/Private Divide: Feminism, Law and Public Policy*, University of Toronto Press, Toronto, 1997

Millbank, Jenni, 'Same Sex Couples and Family Law', http//www.familycourt.gov.au/papers/html/millbank.html (October 1998)

Millbank, Jenni, *Meet the Parents: A Review of the Research on Lesbian and Gay Parenting*, Gay and Lesbian Rights Lobby, Sydney, 2002

Miller, John, 'The Accident Compensation Act and damages claims' [1987] *New Zealand Law Journal* 159

Mills, Helen, 'Sexual Harassment as Sex Discrimination' (1984) 9 *Legal Service Bulletin* 5

Milroy, Stephanie, 'Maori Women and Domestic Violence: The Methodology of Research and the Maori Perspective' (1996) 4 *Waikato Law Review* 58

Minow, Martha, 'Consider the Consequences' (1986) 84 *Michigan Law Review* 900

Minow, Martha, 'Stripped Down Like a Runner or Enriched by Experience: Bias and Impartiality of Judges and Jurors' (1992) 33 *William & Mary Law Review* 1201

Minsk, Morton, *At Any Cost: Corporate Greed, Women and the Dalkon Shield*, Pantheon, NY, 1985

Minson, Jeffrey, *Questions of Conduct: Sexual Harassment, Citizenship, Government*, MacMillan, Hampshire, 1993

Mitra, Charlotte L, 'Judicial Discourse in Father-Daughter Incest Appeal Cases' (1987) 15 *International Journal of the Sociology of Law* 121

Mnookin, Robert and Lewis Kornhauser, 'Bargaining in the Shadow of the Law: The Case of Divorce' (1979) 88 *Yale Law Review* 950

Model Criminal Code Officers Committee (MCCOC), *Sexual Offences Against the Person Report*, May 1999

Mohr, Renate M, 'Sexual Assault Sentencing: Leaving Justice to Individual Conscience' in Julian V Roberts and Renate M Mohr (eds), *Confronting Sexual Assault: A Decade of Legal and Social Change*, University of Toronto Press, Toronto, 1994

Moloney, Lawrie, 'Researching the Family Law Reform Act: A Case of Selective Attention?' (2001) 59 *Family Matters* 64

Monture, Patricia, 'A Vicious Circle: Child Welfare and First Nations' (1989) 3 *Canadian Journal of Women and the Law* 1

Moran, Mayo, 'Case Comment' (1993) 6 *Canadian Journal of Women and the Law* 491

Moreton-Robinson, Aileen, 'Masking Gender and Exalting Race: Indigenous Women and Commonwealth Employment Policies' (1992) 15 *Australian Feminist Studies* 5

Moreton-Robinson, Aileen, *Talking Up to the White Woman: Indigenous Women and Feminism*, University of Queensland Press, Brisbane, 2000

Morgan, Jenny, 'Controlling Minors' Fertility' (1986) 12 *Monash University Law Review* 161

Morgan, Jenny, 'Feminist Theory as Legal Theory' (1988) 16 *Melbourne University Law Review* 743

Morgan, Jenny, 'Equality Rights in the Australian Context: A Feminist Assessment' in Phillip Alston (ed), *Towards an Australian Bill of Rights*, HREOC/CIPL, Canberra, 1994

Morgan, Jenny, 'Sexual Harassment and the Public/Private Dichotomy: Equality, Morals and Manners' in Margaret Thornton (ed), *Public and Private: Feminist Legal Debates*, Oxford University Press, Melbourne, 1995

Morgan, Jenny, 'Provocation Law and Facts: Dead Women Tell No Tales, Tales Are Told About Them' (1997) 21 *Melbourne University Law Review* 237

Morgan, Jenny, 'Sexual Harassment: Where Did It Go in 1995?' in Jenna Mead (ed), *Bodyjamming: Sexual Harassment, Feminism and Public Life*, Random House, Sydney, 1997

Morgan, Jenny, 'Foetal Imaginings: Searching for a Vocabulary in the Law and Politics of Reproduction' (2000) 12 *Canadian Journal of Women and the Law* 371

Morgan, Jenny, 'The Power of Storytelling: A quest for a public discourse on sexual harassment', in Phillip Tahmindjis (ed), *The Law and Sexual Harassment: International, Domestic and Comparative Aspects*, Kluwer, forthcoming 2002

Morgan, Derek, 'Foetal Sex Identification, Abortion and the Law' (1988) 18 *Family Law* 355

Morgan, Wayne, 'Identifying Evil for What It Is: Tasmania, Sexual Perversity and the United Nations' (1994) 19 *Melbourne University Law Review* 740

Morris, Anne and Susan Nott, 'The Law's Engagement With Pregnancy' in Jo Bridgeman and Susan Millns (eds), *Law and Body Politics: Regulating the Female Body*, Dartmouth, Aldershot, 1995

Morris, Anne and Therese O'Donnell (eds), *Feminist Perspectives on Employment Law*, Cavendish Press, London, 1999

Morrison, Toni, *Beloved*, Picador, London, 1988

Mossman, Mary Jane, "Review of Weitzman's The Divorce Revolution" (1986) 5 *Canadian Journal of Family Law* 341

Mossman, Mary Jane, 'Feminism and Legal Method: The Difference it Makes' (1986) 3 *Australian Journal of Law and Society* 30

Mossman, Mary Jane, 'Gender Equality and Legal Aid Services: A Research Agenda For Institutional Change' (1993) 15 *Sydney Law Review* 30

Mossman, Mary Jane, 'Gender Equality, Family Law and Access to Justice' (1994) 8 *International Journal of Law and the Family* 357

Mouzos, Jenny, *Femicide: An Overview of Major Findings*, Trends and Issues Paper, No 124, Australian Institute of Criminology, Canberra, 1999

Mouzos, Jenny, *Femicide: The Killing of Women in Australia 1989-1998*, Research and Public Policy Series, No 18, Australian Institute of Criminology, Canberra, 1999

Mouzos, Jenny, *Homicidal Encounters: A Study of Homicide in Australia 1989-1999*, Research and Public Policy Series, No 28, Canberra, 2000

Mouzos, Jenny, *Indigenous and Non-Indigenous Homicides in Australia: A Comparative Analysis*, Trends and Issues Paper No 210, Australian Institute of Criminology, 2001

Naffine, Ngaire, *Domestic Violence and the Law: A Study of s.99 of the Justices Act (SA)*, Women's Adviser's Office, Department of Premier and Cabinet, Adelaide, 1985

Naffine, Ngaire, 'Possession: Erotic Love in the Law of Rape' (1994) 57 *Modern Law Review* 10, 356

Naffine, Ngaire and Rosemary J Owens (eds), *Sexing the Subject of Law*, LBC, Sydney, 1997

National Committee on Violence Against Women, *National Strategy on Violence Against Women*, October 1992

Naylor, Bronwyn, 'Pregnant Tribunals' (1989) 14 *Legal Service Bulletin* 41

Neave, Marcia, 'Private Ordering in Family Law: Will Women Benefit?' in Margaret Thornton (ed), *Public and Private: Feminist Legal Debates*, Oxford University Press, Melbourne, 1995

Nedelsky, Jennifer, 'The Practical Possibilities of Feminist Theory' (1993) 87 *Northwestern University Law Review* 1286

Neely, Richard, 'The Primary Caretaker Parent Rule: Child Custody and the Dynamics of Greed' (1984) 3 *Yale Law and Policy Review* 168

Neville, Warwick, 'Abortion Before the High Court – What Next? Caveat Interventus: A Note on Superclinics Australia Pty Ltd v CES' (1998) 20 *Adelaide Law Review* 183

Note, 'Maternal Rights and Fetal Wrongs: the Case Against the Criminalization of Fetal Abuse' (1988) 101 *Harvard Law Review* 994

Nsiah-Jefferson, Laurie, 'Reproductive Laws, Women of Color, and Low-Income Women' in Sherrill Cohen and Nadine Taub (eds), *Reproductive Laws for the 1990s*, Humana Press, Clifton, NJ, 1989

NSW Department for Women, *Heroines of Fortitude: The Experiences of Women in Court as Victims of Sexual Assault*, Gender Bias and the Law Project, Department for Women, Sydney, 1996

NSW Law Reform Commission, *Accident Compensation Working Paper 1: A Transport Accidents Scheme For New South Wales*, Working Paper 22, 1983

NSW Law Reform Commission, *Accident Compensation: A Transport Accidents Scheme for NSW*, Report No 43, 1984

NSW Law Reform Commission, *Provocation, Diminished Responsibility and Infanticide*, Discussion Paper No 31, 1993

NSW Law Reform Commission, *Review of the Adoption of Children Act 1965 (NSW)*, Report No 81, March, 1997

NSW Law Reform Commission, *Review of s 409B of the Crimes Act 1900 (NSW)*, Report No 87, 1998

NSW Law Reform Commission, *Guaranteeing Someone Else's Debts*, Issues Paper No 17, 2000

NSW Law Reform Commission, *Surveillance: An Interim Report*, Report No 98, 2001

NSW Ministry for the Status and Advancement of Women, *Gender Bias and the Law: Women Working in the Legal Profession in NSW*, Summary Report, March, 1995

NSW Ombudsman, *Policing Domestic Violence in NSW: A Special Report to Parliament under s.31*, December, 1999

NSW Pay Equity Inquiry, *Appendices to the Report to the Minister*, 14 December 1998, Matter No IRC6320 of 1997, Industrial Relations Commission of NSW, Sydney, 1998

Nygh, Justice Peter, 'Sexual Discrimination in the Family Court' (1985) 8 *University of New South Wales Law Journal* 62

O'Donovan, Katherine, 'Should all Maintenance of Spouses be Abolished?' (1982) 45 *Modern Law Review* 424

O'Donovan, Katherine, *Sexual Divisions in Law*, Weidenfeld and Nicolson, London, 1985

O'Donovan, Katherine, 'Review of Weitzman's *The Divorce Revolution*' (1987) 14 *Journal of Law and Society* 273

Office of the Status of Women, *Community Attitudes to Violence Against Women: Detailed Report*, AGPS, Canberra, 1995

Olsen, Frances E, 'The Family and the Market: A Study of Ideology and Legal Reform' (1983) 96 *Harvard Law Review* 1497

Olsen, Frances E, 'The Myth of State Intervention in the Family' (1985) 18 *Journal of Law Reform* 835

Olsen, Frances E, 'Feminism and Critical Legal Theory: An American Perspective' (1990) 18 *International Journal of the Sociology of Law* 199

Olsen, Frances E, 'Constitutional Law: Feminist Critiques of the Public/Private Distinction' (1993) 10 *Constitutional Commentary* 319

Omatsu, Maryka, 'The Fiction of Judicial Impartiality' (1997) 9 *Canadian Journal of Women and the Law* 1

Omatsu, Maryka, 'On Judicial Appointments: Does Gender Make a Difference?' in Joseph Fletcher (ed), *Ideas in Action: Essays on Politics and Law in Honour of Peter Russell*, University of Toronto Press, Toronto, 1999

Outshoorn, Joyce, 'Abortion Law Reform: A Woman's Right to Choose?' in Mary Buckley and Malcolm Anderson (eds), *Women, Equality and Europe*, MacMillan Press, Hampshire, 1988

Owens, Rosemary, 'Women, "Atypical" Work Relationships and the Law' (1993) 19 *Melbourne University Law Review* 399

Owens, Rosemary, 'Interveners and Amicus Curiae: The Role of The Courts in a Modern Democracy' (1998) 20 *Adelaide Law Review* 193

Paglia, Camille, *Sex, Art and American Culture*, Vintage Books, New York, 1992

Pahl, Jan, 'Household Spending, Personal Spending and the Control of Money in Marriage' (1990) 24 *Sociology* 119

Pahl, Jan, *Money and Marriage*, St Martins Press, NY, 1989

Palmer, Geoffrey, *Compensation for Incapacity*, Oxford University Press, Wellington, 1979

Parkinson, Patrick, 'Custody, Access and Domestic Violence' (1995) 9 *Australian Journal of Family Law* 41

Parkinson, Patrick, 'A Plea for Greater Rigour in Socio-Legal Research' (2001) 59 *Family Matters* 77

Partnerships Against Domestic Violence, Attitudes to Domestic and Family Violence in the Diverse Australian Community, Commonwealth of Australia, June 2000

Pateman, Carol, 'Women and Consent' (1980) 8 *Political Theory* 149

Pateman, Carol, 'The Shame of the Marriage Contract' in Stiehm, Judith (ed), *Women's Views of the Political World of Men*, Transnational Publishers, New York, 1984

Pateman, Carole, 'The Marriage Contract' in Norma Grieve and Ailsa Burns (eds), *Australian Women: New Feminist Perspectives*, Oxford University Press, Melbourne, 1986

Pateman, Carole, *The Sexual Contract*, Polity Press, Cambridge, 1988

Patterson, Charlotte and Raymond Chan, 'Families Headed by Lesbian and Gay Parents' in Michael Lamb (ed), *Parenting and Child Development in 'Nontraditional' Families*, Erlbaum, New Jersey, 1999

Paul, Charlotte, 'The New Zealand cervical cancer study: Could it happen again?' (1988) 297 *British Medical Journal* 533

Petchesky, Rosalind Pollack, *Abortion and Women's Choice: The State, Sexuality and Reproductive Freedom*, Northeastern University Press, Boston, 1985

Petchesky, Rosalind Pollack, 'Foetal Images: The Power of Visual Culture in the Politics of Reproduction' in Michelle Stanworth (ed), *Reproductive Technologies: Gender, Motherhood and Medicine*, Polity Press, Cambridge, 1987

Petersen, Kerry, 'The Public Funding of Abortion Services: Comparative Developments in the United States and Australia' (1984) 33 *International and Comparative Law Quarterly* 158

Petersen, Kerry, *Abortion Regimes*, Dartmouth, Aldershot, 1993

Pettman, Jan, *Living in the Margins: Racism, Sexism and Feminism in Australia*, Allen and Unwin, Sydney, 1992

Pocock, Barbara, 'All Change, Still Gendered: The Australian Labour Market in the 1990s' (1998) 40 *Journal of Industrial Relations* 580

Pocock, Barbara, 'Equal Pay Thirty Years On: The Policy and the Practice' (1999) 32 *Australian Economic Review* 279

Policy Discussion Paper (Green Paper), *Affirmative Action for Women*, Vol 1

Polikoff, Nancy, 'The Deliberate Construction of Families Without Fathers: Is it an Option for Lesbian and Heterosexual Mothers?' [1996] *Santa Clara Law Review* 375

Polikoff, Nancy, 'Recognizing Partners But Not Parents/Recognizing Parents But Not Partners: Gay And Lesbian Family Law In Europe And The United States' (2000) 17 *New York Law School Journal of Human Rights* 711

BIBLIOGRAPHY

Polk, Ken, *When Men Kill: Scenarios of Masculine Violence*, Cambridge University Press, Melbourne, 1994

Polk, Ken and David Ranson, 'Patterns of Homicide in Victoria' in Duncan Chappell, Peter Grabosky and Heather Strang (eds), *Australian Violence: Contemporary Perspectives*, Australian Institute of Criminology, Canberra, 1991

Preston, Alison C, *Deregulation and Relative Wages: Stability and Change in Australia*, Women's Economic Policy Analysis Unit (WEPAU), Curtin University of Technology, Discussion Paper Series 00/04, August, 2000

Preston, Alison C and Geoffrey V Crockett, *Effects of Labour Market Regulation on the Gender Pay Gap*, Women's Economic Policy Analysis Unit (WEPAU), Curtin University of Technology, Discussion Paper Series 99/5, October, 1999

Public Policy Research Centre, *Community Attitudes Towards Domestic Violence in Australia*, 1988

Queensland Law Reform Commission, *Review of the Limitation of Actions Act 1974 (Qld)*, Report No 53, 1998

Radi, Heather, 'Whose Child?' in Judy Mackinolty and Heather Radi (eds), *In Pursuit of Justice: Australian Women and the Law 1788-1979*, Hale and Iremonger, Sydney, 1979

Ralph, Stephen, 'Working with Aboriginal Families' (1997) 46 *Family Matters* 46

Rathus, Zoe, 'Inroads into the Rights of Married Women' (1989) 14 *Legal Service Bulletin* 184

Raymond, Janice G, *Women as Wombs: Reproductive Technologies and the Battle Over Women's Freedom*, Harper, San Francisco, 1993

Razack, Sherene, *Canadian Feminism and the Law*, Second Story Press, Toronto, 1991

Razack, Sherene, 'What is to be Gained by Looking White People in the Eye? Culture, Race, and Gender in Cases of Sexual Violence' (1994) 19 *Signs* 894

Read, Peter, *The Stolen Generations: The Removal of Aboriginal Children in New South Wales 1883 to 1969*, NSW Ministry of Aboriginal Affairs, Occasional Paper No 1

Rhoades, Helen, 'Intellectual Disability and Sterilisation – An Inevitable Connection?' (1995) 9 *Australian Journal of Family Law* 234

Rhoades, Helen, 'Child Law Reforms in Australia – A Shifting Landscape' (2000) 12 *Child and Family Law Quarterly* 117

Rhoades, Helen, 'Posing as Reform: The Case of the Family Law Reform Act' (2000) 14 *Australian Journal of Family Law* 142

Rhoades, Helen, 'The No-Contact Mother: Reconstructions of Motherhood in the Era of the "New Father" ' (2002) 16 International *Journal of Law, Policy and the Family* (forthcoming)

Rhoades, Helen, Reg Graycar and Margaret Harrison, *The Family Law Reform Act: The First Three Years*, University of Sydney and Family Court of Australia, 2000

Rhoades et al, 'Researching Family Law Reform: The Authors Respond' (2001) 59 *Family Matters* 68

Rifkin, Janet, 'Mediation from a Feminist Perspective: Promise and Problems' (1984) 2 *Law and Inequality* 21

Riseley, AC, 'Sex, Housework and the Law' (1981) 7 *Adelaide Law Review* 421

Roberts, Dorothy, 'Punishing Drug Addicts who have Babies: Women of Colour, Equality and the Right of Privacy' (1991) 104 *Harvard Law Review* 1419

Roberts, Julian V and Renate M Mohr (eds), *Confronting Sexual Assault: A Decade of Legal and Social Change*, University of Toronto Press, Toronto, 1994

Robertson, John A, 'Procreative Liberty and the Control of Conception, Pregnancy, and Childbirth' (1983) 69 *Virginia Law Review* 405

Robertson, John, 'Reconciling Offspring and Maternal Interests during Pregnancy' in Sherrill Cohen and Nadine Taub (eds), *Reproductive Laws for the 1990's*, Humana Press, Clifton, NJ, 1989

Robertson, John and Lynn Paltrow, '"Fetal Abuse": Should We Recognize it as a Crime?' (1989) 75 *ABA Journal* 38-9 (August)

Robson, Ruthann, 'Lavender Bruises: Intra-Lesbian Violence, Law and Lesbian Legal Theory' (1990) 20 *Golden Gate University Law Review* 567

Robson, Ruthann, 'Lesbian Jurisprudence?' (1990) 8 *Law and Inequality* 443

Robson, Ruthann, *Lesbian (Out)Law: Survival Under the Rule of Law*, Firebrand Books, Ithaca, New York, 1992

Robson, Ruthann, 'To Market, To Market: Considering Class in the Context of Lesbian Legal Reforms' (1995) 5 *Review of Law and Women's Studies* 173

Robson, Ruthann, *Sappho Goes to Law School: Fragments in Lesbian Legal Theory*, Columbia University Press, New York, 1998

Robson, Ruthann, 'Making Mothers: Lesbian Legal Theory and The Judicial Construction Of Lesbian Mothers' (2000) 22 *Women's Rights Law Reporter* 15

Roche, Jeremy, 'The Children Act 1989: Once a Parent Always a Parent?' (1991) 5 *Journal of Social Welfare and Family Law* 345

Rodgers, Bryan and Jan Pryor, *Divorce and Separation: The Outcomes for Children*, Joseph Rowntree Foundation, York, 1998

Rodgers, Sanda, 'Fetal Rights and Maternal Rights: Is There a Conflict?' (1986) 1 *Canadian Journal of Women and the Law* 456

Rodgers, Sanda, '*Winnipeg Child and Family Services v DFG*: Juridical Interference with Pregnant Women in the Alleged Interest of the Fetus' (1998) 36 *Alberta Law Review* 711

Rodgers, Sanda and Caroline Andrew (eds), *Women and the Canadian State*, McGill/Queens University Press, Montreal, 1996

Roiphe, Katie, *The Morning After: Sex, Fear, and Feminism on Campus*, Little, Brown and Co, Boston, 1993

Ronalds, Chris, *Affirmative Action and Sex Discrimination*, 2nd edition, Pluto Press, Sydney, 1991

Rothman, Barbara Katz, *The Tentative Pregnancy*, Viking, New York, 1986

Rush, Peter and Alison Young, 'A Crime of Consequence and A Failure of Legal Imagination: The Sexual Offences of the Model Criminal Code' (1997) 9 *Australian Feminist Law Journal* 100

Russo, Laura, *Date Rape: A Hidden Crime*, Australian Institute of Criminology, Trends and Issues Paper No 90, Canberra, 2000

Sandor, Danny, 'Same-Sex Couples Can Adopt in Ontario: The Canadian Case of *Re K* and its significance to Australian Family Law' (1997) 11 *Australian Journal of Family Law* 23

Sarmas, Lisa, 'A Step in the Wrong Direction: The Emergence of Gender 'Neutrality' in the Equitable Presumption of Advancement' (1994) 19 *Melbourne University Law Review* 758

Sarmas, Lisa, 'Storytelling and the Law: A Case Study of *Louth v Diprose*' (1994) 19 *Melbourne University Law Review* 701

Sawyer, Phillipa, ' "Naming Whiteness": An Inquiry into Lindy Chamberlain's *Through My Eyes* and Australian Nationalist Discourses' (1997) 3 *Law Text Culture* 107

Scales, Ann 'Towards a Feminist Jurisprudence' (1980-81) 56 *Indiana Law Journal* 375

Scales, Ann, 'The Emergence of Feminist Jurisprudence: An Essay' (1986) 95 *Yale Law Journal* 1373

Scales, Ann, 'Avoiding Constitutional Depression: Bad Attitudes and the Fate of *Butler*' (1994) 7 *Canadian Journal of Women and the Law* 349

Scales-Trent, Judy, 'Women in the Lawyering Process: The Complications of Categories' (1990) 35 *New York Law School Law Review* 337

Scheppele, Kim Lane, 'Facing Facts in Legal Interpretation' (1990) 30 *Representations* 42

Scheppele, Kim Lane, 'Just the Facts Ma'am: Sexual Violence, Evidentiary Habits, and the Revision of Truth' (1992) 37 *New York Law School Law Review* 123

Scheppele, Kim Lane, 'Manners of Imagining the Real' (1994) 19 *Law and Social Inquiry* 995

Schneider, Elizabeth, 'Describing and Changing: Women's Self-Defense Work and the Problem of Expert Testimony on Battering' (1986) 9 *Women's Rights Law Reporter* 195

Schneider, Elizabeth, 'Particularity and Generality: Challenges of Feminist Theory and Practice in Work on Woman Abuse' (1992) 67 *New York University Law Review* 520

Schoenheider, Krista, 'A Theory of Tort Liability for Sexual Harassment in the Workplace' (1986) 34 *University of Pennsylvania Law Review* 1461

Scott, Joan, 'Deconstructing Equality-Versus-Difference: Or the Uses of Poststructuralist Theory for Feminism' (1988) 14 *Feminist Studies* 33

Scott, Joan Wallach, *Only Paradoxes to Offer: French Feminists and the Rights of Man*, Harvard University Press, Cambridge, 1996

Scutt, Jocelynne 'Going Backwards: Law Reform and Women Bashing' (1986) 9 *Women's Studies International Forum* 49

Seaman, Nicola, *Fair Shares? Barriers to Equitable Property Settlements for Women*, Women's Legal Services Network/National Association of Community Legal Centres, Canberra, 1999

Senate Legal and Constitutional Legislation Committee, *Provisions of the Family Law Amendment Bill 1999*, December 1999

Senate Legal and Constitutional Legislation Committee, *Inquiry into the Provisions of the Sex Discrimination Amendment Bill (No 1) 2000*, 2000

Senate Select Committee on Superannuation and Financial Services, *Report on the Provisions of the Superannuation (Entitlements for Same-Sex Couples) Bill 2000*, April, 2000

Senate Standing Committee on Legal and Constitutional Affairs, *Gender Bias and the Judiciary*, May, 1994

Seymour, John, 'A Pregnant Woman's Decision to Decline Treatment: How Should the Law Respond?' (1994) 2 *Journal of Law and Medicine* 27

Seymour, John, *Childbirth and the Law*, Oxford University Press, Oxford, 2000

Shanner, Laura, 'Pregnancy Intervention and Models of Maternal-Fetal Relationship: Philosophical Reflections on the *Winnipeg CFS* Dissent' (1998) 36 *Alberta Law Review* 751

Shapiro, Julie, 'A Lesbian Centred Critique of Second Parent Adoptions' (1999) 14 *Berkeley Women's Law Journal* 17

Shaw, Josephine, 'Wrongful Birth and the Politics of Reproduction: West German and English Law Considered' (1990) 4 *International Journal of Law and the Family* 52

Shea, Goldie M, *Redress Programs Relating to Institutional Child Abuse in Canada*, background paper for the Law Commission of Canada, October 1999, available at <http://www.lcc.gc.ca/en/themes/mr/ica/shea/redress/index.html>

Sheehan, Grania and Bruce Smyth, 'Spousal Violence and Post Separation Financial Outcomes' (2000) 14 *Australian Journal of Family Law* 102

Sheehan, Grania and Jody Hughes, *Division of Matrimonial Property in Australia*, Research Paper No 25, AIFS, March, 2001

Sheehy, Elizabeth A, *Personal Autonomy and the Criminal Law: Emerging Issues for Women*, Background Paper, Canadian Advisory Council on the Status of Women, Ottawa, September, 1987

Sheehy, Elizabeth, 'Feminist Argumentation before the Supreme Court of Canada in *R v Seaboyer; R v Gayme*: The Sound of One Hand Clapping' (1991) 18 *Melbourne University Law Review* 450

Sheehy, Elizabeth A, 'Compensation for Women Who Have Been Raped' in Julian V Roberts and Renate M Mohr (eds), *Confronting Sexual Assault: A Decade of Legal and Social Change*, University of Toronto Press, Toronto, 1994

Sheehy, Elizabeth A, Julie Stubbs and Julia Tolmie, 'Defending Battered Women on Trial: The Battered Woman Syndrome and its Limitations' (1992) 16 *Criminal Law Journal* 369

Sheldon, Sally, *Beyond Control: Medical Power and Abortion Law*, Pluto Press, London, 1997

Shepela, Sharon Toffey and Ann T Viviano, 'Some Psychological Factors Affecting Job Segregation and Wages' in Helen Remick (ed), *Comparable Worth and Wage Discrimination: Technical Possibilities and Political Realities*, Temple University Press, Philadelphia, 1986

Sherry, Suzanna, 'Civic Virtue and the Feminine Voice in Constitutional Adjudication' (1986) 72 *Virginia Law Review* 543

Siegel, Reva, 'Reasoning from the Body: A Historical Perspective on Abortion Regulation and Questions of Equal Protection' (1992) 44 *Stanford Law Review* 261

Silbert, M, 'Compounding Factors in the Rape of Street Prostitutes' in AW Burgess (ed), *Rape and Sexual Assault II*, Garland, New York, 1988

Singer, Peter and Deane Wells, *Making Babies: The New Science and Ethics of Conception*, Scribners Sons, NY, 1985

Singh, Supriya, *For Love Not Money: The Stories of Women in Family Business*, Consumer Advocacy and Financial Counselling Association of Victoria, Melbourne, 1995

Singh, Supriya, *Women, Information and the Family Business*, Consumer Advocacy and Financial Counselling Association of Victoria, Melbourne, 1995

Singh, Supriya, *Marriage Money: The Social Shaping of Money in Marriage and Banking*, Allen and Unwin, Sydney, 1997

Smart, Carol, 'Review of Weitzman's The Divorce Revolution' (1987) 26 *Journal of Family Law* 261

Smart, Carol, *Feminism and the Power of Law*, Routledge, London, 1989

Smart, Carol, 'Law's Power, the Sexed Body, and Feminist Discourse' (1990) 17 *Journal of Law and Society* 194

Smart, Carol, 'Law's Truth: Women's Experience' in Regina Graycar (ed), *Dissenting Opinions: Feminist Explorations in Law and Society*, Allen and Unwin, Sydney, 1990

Smart, Carol, 'Law, Feminism and Sexuality: From Essence to Ethics?' (1994) 9 *Canadian Journal of Law and Society* 15

Smart, Carol and Bren Neale, *Family Fragments?* Polity Press, Cambridge, 1999

Smillie, John, 'Exemplary Damages for Personal Injury' [1997] *New Zealand Law Review* 140

Smith, Diane, 'Towards an Aboriginal Household Expenditure Survey: Conceptual, Methodological and Cultural Considerations', Discussion Paper No 10/1991, Centre for Aboriginal Economic Policy Research, Canberra, 1991

Smith, Joan, *Misogynies: Reflections on Myth and Malice*, Faber and Faber, London, 1989

Smith, Lynn, 'An Equality Approach to Reproductive Choice: *R v Sullivan*' (1991) 4 *Yale Journal of Law and Feminism* 92

Smith, Philippa, *Superannuation – Sisters Start Doin'It for Themselves!*, ASFA Media Release, November, 2000

Smyth, Ailbhe, 'The "X" Case: Women and Abortion in the Republic of Ireland, 1992' (1993) 1 *Feminist Legal Studies* 163

Snider, Gregg, 'Measuring the Cost of Children' (1995) 40 *Family Matters* 44

South Australian Council on Reproductive Technology, *Quarterly Bulletin*, No 10, March, 2000

Spelman, Elizabeth V, *Inessential Women: Problems of Exclusion in Feminist Thought*, Beacon Press, Boston, 1988

Spender, Peta, 'Corporations Law: Women as Directors of Companies' in Graycar and Morgan (eds), *Work and Violence Themes: Including Gender Issues in the Core Law Curriculum*, 1996, available at <http://pandora.nla.gov.au/tep/10029>

Spiegelman, Paul J, 'Integrating Theory and Practice in the Law School Curriculum: The Logic of Jake's Ladder in the Context of Amy's Web' (1988) 38 *Journal of Legal Education* 243

Spivak, Gayatri Chakavorty (with Ellen Rooney) 'In a Word, *Interview*' (1989) 1(2) *Differences* 124

Statham, Bronwyn, ' (Re)producing Lesbian Infertility: Discrimination in Access to Assisted Reproductive Technology' (2000) 9 *Griffith Law Review* 112

Stefan, Susan, 'Whose Egg is it Anyway? Reproductive Rights of Incarcerated, Institutionalized and Incompetent Women' (1989) 13 *Nova Law Review* 405

Sternhell, Carol, 'Life in the Mainstream: What Happens when Feminists Turn up on Both Sides of the Court Room?' *Ms Magazine*, July, 1986

Stewart, Miranda, 'Victoria: Same Sex Domestic Partnerships Now Law' (2001) 26 *Alternative Law Journal* 261

Streeton, Julie Dodds, 'Feminist Perspectives on the Law of Insolvency' in Dodds Streeton & Langford, *Aspects of Real Property and Insolvency Law* (1994) Research Paper No 6, *Adelaide Law Review*, Adelaide

Strimling, Wendy S, 'The Constitutionality of State Laws Providing Employment Leave for Pregnancy: Rethinking *Geduldig* After *Cal Fed*' (1989) 77 *California Law Review* 171

Stubbs, Julie, 'Domestic Violence Reforms in NSW: Policy and Practice' in Suzanne Hatty (ed), *National Conference on Domestic Violence, Vol 2*, Australian Institute of Criminology, Canberra, 1986

Stubbs, Julie and Sandra Egger, *The Effectiveness of Protection Orders in Australian Jurisdictions*, AGPS, Canberra, 1993

Stubbs, Julie and Julia Tolmie, 'Race, Gender and the Battered Woman Syndrome: An Australian Case Study' (1995) 8 *Canadian Journal of Women and the Law* 122

Stubbs, Julie and Julia Tolmie, 'Falling Short of the Challenge? A Comparative Assessment of the Australian Use of Expert Evidence on the Battered Woman Syndrome' (1999) 23 *Melbourne University Law Review* 709

Sturgess, Robert H, '*In Re AC*: A Court-Ordered Cesarean Becomes Precedent for Nonconsensual Organ Harvesting' (1989) 13 *Nova Law Review* 649

Stychin, Carl and Didi Herman (eds), *Sexuality in the Legal Arena*, Athlone Press, London, 2000

Sullivan, Maureen, 'Rozzie and Harriet: Gender and Family Patterns of Lesbian Co-Parents' (1996) 10 *Gender and Society* 747

Sunday Times Insight Team, *Suffer the Children: The Story of Thalidomide*, Andre Deutsch, London, 1979

Sussex, Lucy, 'Portrait of a Murderer in Mixed Media: Cultural Attitudes, Infanticide and the Representation of Frances Knorr' (1995) 4 *Australian Feminist Law Journal* 39

Sutherland, Edwin, *White Collar Crime*, Holt, Rinehart and Winston, New York, 1949

Swain, Shurlee and Renate Howe, 'Death: a very army of murderesses within our midst' in Shurlee Swain and Renate Howe, *Single Mothers and their Children: Disposal, Punishment and Survival in Australia*, Cambridge University Press, Cambridge, 1995

Swanton, Jane, 'Damages for "wrongful birth" – *CES v Superclinics (Aust) Pty Ltd*' (1996) 4 *Torts Law Journal* 1

Sykes, Edward I and Michael C Pryles, *Conflict of Laws: Commentary and Materials*, Law Book, Sydney, 3rd ed, 1988

Teasdale, Lisa, 'Confronting the Fear of Being 'Caught': Discourses on Abortion in Western Australia' (1999) 22 *University of New South Wales Law Journal* 60

Temkin, Jennifer, *Rape and the Legal Process*, London, Sweet and Maxwell, 1987

Thompson, Judith Jarvis, 'A Defence of Abortion' (1971) 1 *Philosophy and Public Affairs* 47

Thomson, Michael, 'After *Re S*' [1994] *Medical Law Review* 127

Thornton, Margaret, 'Affirmative Action, Merit and the Liberal State' (1985) 2(2) *Australian Journal of Law and Society* 28

Thornton, Margaret, 'Feminism and the Contradictions of Law Reform' (1991) 19 *International Journal of the Sociology of Law* 453

Thornton, Margaret, 'The Public/Private Dichotomy: Gendered and Discriminatory' (1991) 18 *Journal of Law and Society* 448

Thornton, Margaret, 'Discord in the Legal Academy: The Case of the Feminist Scholar' (1994) 3 *Australian Feminist Law Journal* 53

Thornton, Margaret (ed), *Public and Private: Feminist Legal Debates*, Oxford University Press, Melbourne, 1995

Thornton, Margaret, *Dissonance and Distrust: Women in the Legal Profession*, Oxford University Press, Melbourne, 1996

Todd, Stephen, 'Privatisation of Accident Compensation: Policy and Politics in New Zealand' (2000) 39 *Washburn Law Journal* 404

Tolmie, Julia, 'Pacific-Asian Immigrant and Refugee Women Who Kill their Batterers: Telling Stories that Illustrate the Significance of Specificity' (1997) 19 *Sydney Law Review* 472

Trebilcock, Michael and Stephen Elliott, 'The Scope and Limits of Legal Paternalism: Altruism and Coercion in Family Financial Arrangements' Unpublished paper, University of Toronto, February, 1999

Tribe, Laurence, *Constitutional Choices*, Harvard University Press, Cambridge, MA, 1985

Tribe, Laurence, *Abortion: The Clash of Absolutes*, WW Norton and Co, New York, 1990

Trimboli, Lily and Roseanne Bonney, *An Evaluation of the NSW Apprehended Violence Order Scheme*, NSW Bureau of Crime Statistics and Research, Sydney, 1997

Trindade, Francis and Peter Cane, *The Law of Torts in Australia*, Oxford University Press, Melbourne, 1985

UN Human Rights Committee, 'Equality of Rights Between Men and Women', General Comment No 28, 68th Session, March, 2000

Valverde, Mariana, 'The Harms of Sex and the Risks of Breasts: Obscenity and Indecency in Canadian Law' (1999) 8 *Social and Legal Studies* 181

VandenHeuvel, Audrey and Mark Wooden, *Non-English-Speaking Background Immigrant Women and Part-Time Work*, AGPS, Canberra, 1996

Vennell, Margaret, 'Informed Consent or Reasonable Disclosure of Risks: The Relevance of an Informed Patient in the Light of the New Zealand Accident Compensation Scheme' [1987] *Recent Law* 160 (June)

Vennell, Margaret, 'Medical misadventure in a no fault society' in Ronald D Mann and John Havard (eds), *No Fault Compensation in Medicine*, Royal Society of Medicine Services Ltd, London/New York, 1989

Vennell, Margaret, 'Medical injury compensation under the New Zealand Accident Compensation Scheme: an assessment compared with the Swedish Medical Compensation Scheme' (1989) *Professional Negligence* 141 (September/October)

Victorian Bar Council, *Equality of Opportunity for Women at the Victorian Bar*, Melbourne, 1998

Victorian Community Council Against Violence, *A Profile of Rapes Reported to Police in Victoria 1987-90*, 1991

Vogler, Carolyn and Jan Pahl, 'Social and Economic Change and the Organisation of Money within Marriage' (1993) 7 *Work, Employment and Society* 71

Wainer, Jo, 'Abortion before the High Court' (1997) 8 *Australian Feminist Law Journal* 133

Walker, Kristen L, '1950s Family Values vs Human Rights: In Vitro Fertilisation, Donor Insemination and Sexuality in Victoria' (2000) 11 *Public Law Review* 292

Walker, Kristen L, 'Equal Access to Assisted Reproductive Services: The Effect of *McBain v Victoria*' (2000) 25 *Alternative Law Journal* 288

Walker, Kristen, 'Should there be Limits on Who May Access Infertility Services? A Legal Perspective', 2002 (forthcoming)

Walker, Lenore, *The Battered Woman Syndrome*, Springer Publishing Co, New York, 1984

Wallace, Alison, *Homicide: The Social Reality*, Research Study No 5, Bureau of Crime Statistics and Research, Attorney General's Department, Sydney, 1986

Waller, L and CR Williams, *Criminal Law: Text and Cases*, 9th ed, Butterworths, Sydney, 2001

Warner, Kate, 'Sentencing in Rape' in Patricia Easteal (ed), *Balancing the Scales: Rape, Law Reform and Australian Culture*, Federation Press, Sydney, 1998

Watson, Sophie (ed), *Playing the State: Australian Feminist Interventions*, Verso, London, 1990

Watts, Garry, 'Family Law: Super Becomes Family Property' (2001) 39(9) *Law Society Journal* 54

Weedon, Chris, *Feminist Practice and Post-Structuralist Theory*, Blackwell, Oxford, 1987

Weedon, Chris, *Feminism, Theory and the Politics of Difference*, Blackwell, Oxford, 1999

Weitzman, Lenore, *The Divorce Revolution: The Unexpected Social and Economic Consequences for Women and Children in America*, Free Press, NY, 1985

Wells, Celia, 'On the Outside Looking in: Perspectives on Enforced Caesareans' in Sally Sheldon and Michael Thomson (eds), *Feminist Perspectives on Health Care Law*, Cavendish, London, 1998

West, Robin, 'The Difference in Women's Hedonic Lives: A Phenomenological Critique of Feminist Legal Theory' (1987) 3 *Wisconsin Women's Law Journal* 81

West, Robin, 'The Feminist-Conservative Anti-Pornography Alliance and the 1986 Attorney-General's Commission on Pornography Report' [1987] *American Bar Foundation Research Journal* 681

West, Robin, 'Jurisprudence and Gender' (1988) 55 *University of Chicago Law Review* 1

Weston, Ruth and Bruce Smyth, 'Financial Living Standards After Divorce' (2000) 55 *Family Matters* 10

Wigmore, *Evidence*, Little Brown and Co, Boston, 1970

Wilczynski, Ania, 'Child-Killing by Parents: Social, Legal and Gender Issues' in R Emerson Dobash et al (eds), *Gender and Crime*, University of Wales, Cardiff, 1995

Williams, Patricia, 'On Being the Object of Property' (1988) 14 *Signs* 5

Williams, Wendy W, 'Equality's Riddle: Pregnancy and the Equal Treatment/Special Treatment Debate' (1984-85) 13 *New York University Review of Law and Social Change* 325

Wilson, Bertha, 'Will Women Judges Make a Difference'? (1990) 28 *Osgoode Hall Law Journal* 507

Wilson, Bertha, 'Women, the Family and the Constitutional Protection of Privacy' (1992) 17 *Queen's Law Journal* 5

Winder, Chris and Neil Gunningham, 'Protective Legislation and Discrimination in Employment in the Australian Lead Industries: The Reproductive Effect of Inorganic Lead' (1988) 4 *Australian and New Zealand Journal of Occupational Health and Safety* 9

Wirth, Linda, *Breaking Through the Glass Ceiling: Women in Management*, International Labour Organisation, Geneva, 2001

Wolcott, Ilene and Jody Hughes, *Towards Understanding the Reasons for Divorce*, AIFS, Working Paper no 20, June, 1999

Wolf, Naomi, *Fire with Fire: The New Female Power and How it Will Change the 21st Century*, Random House, New York, 1993

Women's Policy Co-ordination Unit, Department of Prime Minister and Cabinet, *Criminal Assault in the Home: Social and Legal Responses to Domestic Violence Discussion Paper*, Victoria, July, 1985

Wood, Briar, 'The Trials of Motherhood: the case of Azaria and Lindy Chamberlain' in Helen Birch (ed), *Moving Targets; Women, Murder and Representation*, Virago, London, 1993

Wooden, Mark, 'Enterprise Bargaining and the Gender Earnings Gap' (1997) 23 *Australian Bulletin of Labour* 214

Wootten, Hal, 'The Alice Springs Dam and Sacred Sites' (1993) 65 *Australian Quarterly* 8

Working Group, *Model Domestic Violence Laws: Report*, Partnerships Against Domestic Violence, Canberra, 1999

Young, Alison, 'Cross-examination tactics in rape trials' in CASA House, *Who's On Trial? A Training Manual for Sexual Assault Support Workers*, Melbourne, 1998

Young, Alison, 'The Waste Land of the Law, The Wordless Song of the Rape Victim' (1998) 22 *Melbourne University Law Review* 442

Young, Alison, 'Violence as Seduction: Enduring Genres of Rape' in Adrian Howe (ed), *Sexed Crime in the News*, Federation Press, Sydney, 1998

Young, Claire, 'Child Care – A Taxing Issue?' (1994) 39 *McGill Law Journal* 539

Young, Claire, 'Child Care and the Charter: Privileging the Privileged' (1994) 2 *Review of Constitutional Studies* 20

Young, Claire, 'Public Taxes, Privatizing Effects, and Gender Inequality' in Susan Boyd (ed), *Challenging the Public/Private Divide: Feminism, Law, and Public Policy*, University of Toronto Press, Toronto, 1997

Young, Lisa, 'Sissinghurst, Sackville-West and Special Skill' (1997) 11 *Australian Journal of Family Law* 268

Young, Margot, 'Change at the Margins: *Eldridge v British Columbia (A-G)* and *Vriend v Alberta*' (1998) 10 *Canadian Journal of Women and the Law* 244

Young, Margrette, Julie Byles and Annette Dobson, *The Effectiveness of Legal Protection in the Prevention of Domestic Violence in the Lives of Young Australian Women*, Trends and Issues Paper No 148, Australian Institute of Criminology, Canberra, 2000

Index

Aboriginal and Islander Child Care Agency 282
Aboriginal legal services 282-283
Aboriginal women *see* Indigenous women
Abortion 2-3, 183-189, 199-222, 429-431
    Australia
        Australian Capital Territory 206
        criminal law 200-202, 205-206, 221
        defence of necessity 201
        Levine ruling 201-202, 205
        Lusher amendment 214
        Medicare 214
        Menhennit ruling 200-201, 205
        Simon amendment 214
        South Australia 204-205, 207
        Western Australia 205-206, 207, 212
    amicus curiae briefs 251, 430-431
    anti-choice protesters 207, 215-217
    Canada 23, 203-204, 215-217, 221-222
    connection and 222
    constitutional law 202-204
    equality 209-212, 217, 252
    family law 220-222
    father's rights 218-222
    foetal development 203
    hospital autonomy 215-217
    'informed consent' 206
    injunctions 219-221
    legal history 200
    legal status 184
    medical model 206-207, 211
    morality 212-213
    public funding 213-214
    public opinion 217-218
    public/private dichotomy 23, 208-209
    religion 218
    rights and 212-213
    sexuality 218
    tort 183-189
    UK 207, 208, 214, 219
    USA
        anti-choice protesters 207
        constitutional law 202-203, 207
        Hyde Amendment 213-214
        Missouri statutes 219
        subordination principle 209
    see also Foetal rights; Privacy
Abrams, Kathryn 212, 322-323, 393-394
ACT Law Reform Commission 131-132
ACTU (Australian Council of Trade Unions) 160
Administrative law 194, 219-221, 316
Adoption 187-188, 286

ADR (alternative dispute resolution) 445-446
Affirmative action laws 156-159
African-American women 49, 50
    death of children 297-298
    eugenic sterilisation 329, 332-333
    foetal rights 225-227
    rape 49, 351-352
    sexual harassment 395-396
    victim-agency debate 323
    see also Indigenous women
AH Robins company 335, 336
ALRC *see* Australian Law Reform Commission
Amicus curiae briefs 251, 430-431
Anti-discrimination laws
    categorisation of groups 55
    legal discourses 153
    public/private dichotomy 23-24
    racial minority women (Canada) 51-53
    racism 48, 50, 59-60, 63, 285, 396-397
    sexual harassment 384-388
    victim-agency debate 325
    wages for women 151-156
    see also Equal opportunity laws
Apprehended violence orders (AVOs) 318-319, 321
Army of Men 265-266
ART (assisted reproductive technology) services 253
Artificial insemination by donor (AID) 39-40, 249-257
Assisted reproduction 249-257
Astor, Hilary 52, 76-77, 112, 445-446
Australian Divorce Transitions Project (ADTP) 101
Australian Institute of Family Studies (AIFS) 98, 264
Australian Iron and Steel 151-152
Australian Law Reform Commission (ALRC)
    ACT Law Reform Commission 131-132
    domestic violence 109
    Equality Act 32, 40, 163, 443
    Equality Before the Law: Justice for Women 99-101, 275-277, 442-445
    Equality Before the Law: Women's Equality 28-30, 442-445
    Status of Women Act 40-43
Australian Women Lawyers Association 423-424
AVOs (apprehended violence orders) 318-319, 321
Backhouse, Constance 58, 65
Bar Association, NSW 423

INDEX

Battered women 312-313, 324, 369
   'battered woman syndrome' 53-54, 438-442
   see also Domestic violence; Rape; Sexual assault
Baxter, Janeen 89, 166-168
Bias, doctrine of 57-65, 192-194, 360-362, 422-428
Bill of Rights 2, 22, 33, 373-379, 407-418, 428-431, 433
Binary oppositions 8-9, 156 see also Public/private dichotomy
Biology as destiny 192-194
Bisexual defence in sexual harassment 398
Black women see African-American women; Indigenous women
Boyd, Susan 22, 267-273
Boyle, Christine 76-77, 364-365
Branson, Justice Catherine 424-426
Breadwinner/dependant model 169, 259
Breast implant litigation 336-337
Bringing Them Home (report) 20, 64, 278-283, 285, 373
Brown, Wendy 78, 366, 368
Burns, Kate 267-273, 283-284
Burton, Clare 157-159, 161
Butler, Judith 79-80, 301
Caesarean sections, forced 236-243
Cannold, Leslie 167, 213
Care, costs of 133-138, 183-192
Cass, Bettina 149, 168-169
Catholic Church 40, 251-253, 429-430
CEDAW (Convention on the Elimination of All Forms of Discrimination Against Women) 41, 252, 397-398
Cervical cancer study (NZ) 337-343
Child abuse
   foetal rights 223
   institutional abuse 446-448
   sexual 353
   violence against children 276-277
Child care 18-20
   Aboriginal and Islander Child Care Agency 282
   allowance for vicissitudes 140-141
   breadwinner/dependant model 169, 259
   distribution in families 88-89, 138, 260, 274
   formal 142
   lesbian households 89
   primary caregivers 267-277, 283-284
   workers 162
Child custody 258-277
   'best interests' principle 261, 263, 273, 284-285
   consent agreements 265-266
   contact 259, 262-263, 276-277
   custody law 260-267
   disparate rates of repartnering 264-265, 267
   domestic violence 271-272, 276-277
   existing arrangements 272-273
   extended family 285-286
   Family Law Act 1975 (Cth) 259-260
   'friendly parent rule' 262-263
   gender neutrality 260-267
   indigenous families 277-287
   institutional abuse 446-448
   legal discourses 260-267
   legal history 258-259
   mothers who work outside the home 263-264
   National Committee on Violence Against Women 275-276
   parental responsibility 259
   parental worthiness 270-272
   primary caregivers 267-277, 283-284
   residence orders 259, 270-272, 274-275
   same sex couples 287-292
   shared parental responsibility 274-275
   specific issues orders 259
   status quo principle 277, 284
   'tender years' doctrine 258-259, 260
   unequal expectations 273
   violence against children 276-277
Child welfare legislation 281-283, 287
Children
   adoption 187-188, 286
   child support 334
   costs of care 183-192
   death of 291-296, 297-298
   economic value of 299
   incest and fiduciary duty 371
   parenthood of 182, 183-192
   parenting styles 284
   same sex couples 89, 290
   sexual abuse of stolen generation 353
   tort law 298-299
   women's work 107
   see also Child care; Child custody
Civil wrongs, law of see Tort law
Class discrimination 48, 210-211, 227-228
Code, Lorraine 56, 81
Cohabitation rule 14-15
Colonisation 53-54, 81-84, 278, 314
Colour, women of see African-American women; Indigenous women
Commercial law
   domestic violence 124-125
   relationship debt 114-115
   'sexually transmitted debt' 114-115
Community legal centres 105
Compensation
   accident 132
   Grandview Agreement (Canada) 446-448
   no-fault accident compensation legislation (NZ) 132, 340-343, 373
   sexual assault 369-380
   solatium 298-299
   see also Damages; Injuries; Tort law

INDEX

Conaghan, Joanne 1, 145, 372, 383-384
Conflict Tactics Scale (CTS) 309-310
Connection
    abortion and 222
    indigenous women and 63-64, 198
    thesis 195-196
Consciousness-raising 54, 71-74
Consortium 126-132
Continuum of sexual violence 327-328
Contraception
    class and race issues 210-211, 227-228
    Dalkon Shield 335-336
    depo provera 211
    Norplant 227-228, 333
'Contract marriage' 112
Convention on the Elimination of All Forms of Discrimination Against Women 41, 252, 397-398
Cornell, Drucilla 398, 407, 418-419
Cossman, Brenda 411-415
Criminal law
    abortion 200-202, 205-206, 221
    Chamberlain trial 291-296
    fact-finding methodologies 67-69
    foetal rights 244-249
    gendered harms 301-302
    infanticide 296-297
    legal aid 432
    Model Criminal Code Officers Committee 362-364, 365, 368
    protection orders 317-319
    provocation, defence of 67-69, 197-198, 311
    rape 343-368, 443-444
    sexual harassment 383
    violence against women 316-317
    Violence Against Women Act (US) 435-438
Custody law *see* Child custody
Dahl, Tove Stang 85-86, 90-91
Dalkon Shield 335-336
Damages
    costs of care 133-138
    domestic violence 316
    economic and non-economic losses 130-131
    'nervous shock' 173-174, 179-183
    personal injury damages 126-138, 139-145
    wrongful birth 183-192
    see also Compensation; Injuries; Tort law
Davenport, Cheryl 205
Davies, Margaret 57, 80-81
Deconstruction of subjecthood 57, 79, 301, 324-325
Defamation 385
Defences
    necessity 201
    provocation 67-69, 197-198, 311
    self-defence 53-54, 324, 442

DES (diethylstilbestrol) 336
Dichotomies 8-9, 10-11, 336-337, 412 *see also* Public/private dichotomy
Differences approach 29-30, 48-55, 153-156, 325-326
Disabilities, women with 13, 50, 268, 328-332
Discourses *see* Legal discourses
Discrimination
    bias and 58-59
    CEDAW 41, 252, 397-398
    child custody 291
    class 48, 210-211, 227-228
    'equal pay' cases 150-151
    ethnicity 52-53
    indirect 29
    infertility treatment services 250-257
    intersectionality in 50-54, 196, 396-397
    male challenges to women-only programs 35-44
    marital status 252-253
    men's claims of in Family Court 265-266
    racism 48, 50, 59-60, 63, 285, 396-397
    same sex couples 287-292
    sex 31, 33-35, 151-156, 252-257
    sexual assault 375-376
    see also Anti-discrimination laws
Discrimination law, sexual harassment in 370, 381-383, 383-384
Divorce 97, 98-108, 264-265, 267
Doctrine of dependent domicile 94
Domestic violence
    attitudes to violence against women 306-308
    AVOs and DVOs 318-319, 321
    'battered woman syndrome' 53-54, 438-442
    against care givers 137-138
    child custody 271-272, 276-277
    commercial law 124-125
    Conflict Tactics Scale (CTS) 309-310
    decriminalisation 317-318
    definition of family violence 111, 314
    family law 108-111, 271-272, 275-277
    forfeiture rule 315-316
    gender neutrality and language of 308-314
    homicidal 304-306, 311, 438-442
    incidence of 304
    indigenous women 314, 320-321
    interspousal immunity 94-95
    intervention and non-intervention 12-13, 18
    intra-lesbian 312-313
    IsssA survey 310-311
    legal storytelling 76-77
    lesbians 320
    National Committee on Violence Against Women 275-276

INDEX

protection orders 317-319
self-defence claims 324, 438-442
separation assault 324
spousal violence 109-110
terminology 313-314
victim-agency debate 322-326
Violence Against Women Act (US) 435-438
Western Australia 312
see also Rape; Social injury to women
Dominance feminism, theory of 30-32, 37-44, 322-324
Drugs
unsafe 334-337
use in pregnancy 223-228
Duty of care 369-380
DVOs (domestic violence orders) 318-319
Economic (in)dependence of women 98-108
child custody 267
economic and non-economic losses 130-131
equal pay 150-151
feminisation of poverty 105-106
'Women's Rights to Money' 85-86
see also Women's work
Enterprise-based wages 163-165
Epistemologies 56-84, 393-394, 444-445 see also Feminist methodologies; Legal methodologies
'Equal Access to Assisted Reproductive Services' 250-251
Equal opportunity laws
affirmative action laws 156-159
male challenges to women-only programs 35-44
pregnancy 34-35, 37
sexual harassment 399
wages for women 151-156
see also Anti-discrimination laws
Equality
abortion 209-212, 217, 252
child rearing 43-44
comparable worth and job evaluation 163
constitutional basis 33, 63, 202-204, 207, 373-379, 406-418, 428-431, 433
differences amongst women 48-55
differences approach 29-30, 48-55, 153-156, 325-326
Equality Act 32, 40, 163, 443
Equality Before the Law: Justice for Women 275, 442-445
Equality Before the Law: Women's Equality 28-30, 442-445
in family law 99-101
foetal rights 235
formal or rule 26, 28-29
Hindmarsh Island Bridge dispute 81-84
maternity leave 33-35
models
comparator 433
male challenges to women-only programs 35-44
pregnancy 33-35, 37
presumption of advancement 44-48
pornography and 405-419
privacy rights 26-27
public/private dichotomy 32
relational losses 299
special treatment 29-30
subordination principle 30-32, 37-44
tort law 373-379
'women' as category 54-55, 78-81, 300-301
women in law 427-428
Essentialism, gender 48, 54, 73-74, 80, 195-198, 258-259, 393-394
Ethics
abortion 221, 222
of care and connection 194-195
foetal rights 242-243
test case litigation 432-433
Ethnicity 52-53
Eugenic sterilisation 328-334
Evidentiary strategies 438-442
Fact-finding methodologies 67-71, 120, 254-255
Families
family violence 276-277, 314, 320-321
'family wage' 147-149, 150
impact on paid work 144-145
intervention and non-intervention 12-13, 17-20, 96-97, 254, 437
meaning of 97
presumption of advancement 47
primary caregivers 267-277, 283-284
public/private dichotomy 10-12
unregulated 11-12
women's unpaid work 87-88
work in 87-138
work policies 168
see also Child care; Child custody; Family law
Family Court see Family law
Family law
abortion 220-222
child custody 263-264
community legal centres 105
contact 276-277
domestic violence 108-111, 271-272, 275-277
equality 99-101
eugenic sterilisation 329-331
extended family 286
families, meaning of 97
Family Law Council 330-331
family relationships 96-97
fathers as full-time carers 264

Family law (*cont*)
    financial aspects 98-138
    indigenous families 277-287, 283-284
    interspousal immunity 94-95
    law reform 443-445
    matrimonial property 91-92, 98-108, 102-103, 114
    men's claims of discrimination 265-266
    National Committee on Violence Against Women 275-276
    obligation to support 147-148
    primary caregivers 269
    racism 285
    rape 93
    reported cases in disputes 104
    residence orders 270-272, 274-275
    same sex couples 287-292
    spousal maintenance 106
    superannuation 107-108, 146-147
    violence against children 276-277
    violence against women 316-317
    violence in disputes 275-277
    Women's rights to money 85-86
    work in families 87
    see also Child custody; Divorce; Domestic violence; Economic (In)dependence of women; Maintenance
Fathers
    abortion 218-222
    child custody 258-259, 260-262
    claims of discrimination in Family Court 265-266
    as full-time carers 264
    rights groups 266
Fehlberg, Belinda 1, 113, 115, 121, 122, 125
Feldthusen, Bruce 369-370, 446-447
Female plaintiffs 132
Feminisation of poverty 105-106
Feminism
    anti-pornography 413-414
    cultural 195-196
    deconstruction of subjecthood 57, 79, 301, 324-325
    domestic violence 312-313
    dominance theory 30-32, 37-44, 322-324
    epistemologies 56-84, 393-394, 444-445
    family violence 314
    'femocracy' 442
    Grandview Agreement (Canada) 448
    ideologies 208
    post-modern 78-81, 300-301
    sexual difference 325-326
    sexual harassment 399-403
    see also Feminist methodologies
Feminist jurisprudence 72
    connection thesis 195-198
    criminal law 428-429
    initiating litigation 431-433

    legal method 56-70, 422-428
    obscenity laws 410-411
    pornography 405-407
    rape and rules of evidence 356-361
    sexual assault law 354
    sexual harassment 381-383, 434-435
    strategies in law 227, 422-449
    victim-agency debate 301-302, 322-326, 402-403, 435
    violence against women 317-321
    Violence Against Women Act (US) 435-438
    women in law 427-428
    see also Feminist litigation; Legal methodologies
Feminist methodologies 56-84
    abortion 211
    'battered woman syndrome' 439-440
    claims to truth 72-74, 78-81, 156, 422
    consciousness raising 71-74
    evidentiary strategies 438-442
    gender and cultural awareness education 425-426
    Grandview Agreement (Canada) 445-448
    humourlessness 1-449
    initiating litigation 431-433
    intervening in litigation 428-431
    law reform 431, 442-445
    legal storytelling 66-67, 71, 74-77, 154-155, 157-159, 356-361
    pornography 405-407
    women in law 427-428
    see also Legal methodologies; Sexual harassment
Fiduciary duty, breach of 370-371
Finley, Lucinda 94-95, 334-335, 393
First Stone (Garner) 399-403, 435
Foetal rights 222-249
    African-American women 225-227
    Australia 231
    Canada 221-222, 229-230, 232-236, 245-249
    child abuse 223
    civil actions: court-ordered treatment 236-243
    civil actions: wardship 228-236
    criminal law 244-249
    'duty to rescue' 242-243
    equality 235
    ethics 242-243
    family law 221
    forced caesarean sections 236-243
    medical research 223-225
    relationship between woman and foetus 245-248
    UK 228-229, 244-245
    unborn child 236
    USA 207, 223-228, 242
    and women's rights 212-213, 219, 230-236

INDEX

Forfeiture rule 315-316
Foundationalism 73-74, 78, 300-301 *see also* Essentialism, gender
Frug, Mary Joe 171
Fruitpickers judgment 148
Garner, Helen 399-403, 435
Gaudron, Justice Mary 423-424
Gay men
    anti-pornography and 414-416
    family law 97, 287-290
    right of privacy 24-26
    South Africa 26-27
    Tasmania 24-26, 77
Gender neutrality 28-29, 42, 45-48
    bisexual defence 398
    in custody law 260-267
    Equality Act 32, 40, 163, 443
    forfeiture rule 316
    language of domestic violence and 308-314
    in rape laws 364-365
    and sexual assault victims 356
    sexual harassment 397-398
    see also Gender
Gender-specific injury 300-326 *see also* Domestic violence; Social injury to women
Gendered harms 300-326
Gendered wage gap 145-147
Gilligan, Carol 6, 194-195, 222
Gotell, Lise 73-74, 212
Government action 23
Grandview Agreement (Canada) 445-448
Grillo, Trina 48-49, 54
Harris, Angela 48, 351-352
Hartsock, Nancy 79, 301
Harvester judgment 147-149
Health
    Medicare 214
    National Women's Health Program 36
    specific services for women 38
    unsafe drugs and medical devices 334-335
Heroines of Fortitude (report) 345, 354, 443-444
Heterosexuality
    infertility treatment services 249
    and rape 348-354
Hill, Anita 69-71
Hindmarsh Island Bridge dispute 81-84
Homemakers *see* Women's work
Homosexuality 24-26, 77, 287-292, 433 *see also* Gay men; Lesbians
Homosocial reproduction 157-159
Howe, Adrian 291-296, 300-302, 311
Hughes, Jody 98, 102-103
Hunter, Rosemary 149, 153, 161-163
ICCPR *see* International Covenant on Civil and Political Rights

Impartiality 61-64
Incest 371
Independent legal advice 114, 124
Indigenous women
    Aboriginal Child Placement Principle 282-283, 286-287
    Aboriginal legal services 282-283
    'Aboriginality' 280
    adoption 286
    affirmative action laws 159
    assimilation policies 280-282
    'best interests' principle 285
    Bringing Them Home (report) 20, 64, 278-283, 285, 354
    Chamberlain trial 295
    child custody 277-287
    child welfare legislation 281-282
    colonisation 53-54, 81-84
    connection to community 53-54, 198, 442
    contraception 210-211
    extended family 285-286
    family violence 314, 320-321
    forcible removal of children 20, 64, 279-280, 281-282, 283, 353
    gender and race 49, 63, 285
    Hindmarsh Island Bridge dispute 81-84
    homicidal violence 304-305
    judicial education programs 425-426
    labour force participation 146
    Link-Up 282
    litigation 430-431
    primary caregivers presumption 268, 283-284
    protection and segregation 278-279
    public/private dichotomy 20-21
    rape 352-354
    relationships with children 298-299
    self-determination 282-283
    sexual abuse of stolen generation children 353
    sexual assault trials study 354
    see also African-American women
Infanticide 296-297
Infertility treatment services 39-40, 249-257
Injunctions
    abortion 219-221
    violence against women 316
Injuries
    see Compensation; Contraception; Damages; Domestic violence; Medical; Pornography; Rape; Sexual Harassment; Social Injury to women; Tort law; Violence against women
International Covenant on Civil and Political Rights 24-26
International law 6, 24-25
International Social Science Survey Australia (IsssA) 310-311
Intersectionality in discrimination 50-54, 196, 396-397

Interspousal immunity 94-95
Intervention and non-intervention 12-13, 17-20, 96-97, 254, 437
Intrauterine devices 335-336
IVF (in vitro fertilisation) 39-40, 249-251
Judicial notice 106, 128-129
Judiciary
  gender and cultural awareness education 425-426
  and legal doctrine 425
  representation in the 425
  women in the 424-425
  women judges 441
Kingdom, Elizabeth 208, 214
Kline, Marlee 277-278
Labour law 85-86, 145-147
Labour market institutions 163-165
Labour force participation 89-90, 143, 149, 165-166
Lacey, Nicola 18, 20, 22, 24
Lake, Marilyn 325-326
Language 54-55, 182, 208, 211-212, 308-314, 426
Leadership, responsibilities of 426
LEAF (Canada) *see* Women's Legal, Education and Action Fund
Legal aid 432
Legal discourses
  anti-discrimination laws 153
  asymmetry of power in 359
  child custody 260-267
  constructing relationships 171-172
  differences approach 29-30, 48-55, 153-156, 325-326
  distributive justice 190
  expert evidence 439-440
  gender neutrality 260-267
  human subjectivity 324-325
  implication of victim in rape trials 357-360
  insinuation strategies in rape trials 357, 360
  intersectionality 51
  language 54-55, 182, 208, 211-212, 308-314
  'policy' arguments 188, 190
  public/private dichotomy 11
  reasonableness 255-256, 390-395, 438-442
  right to question 359
  separation thesis 195-196
  violence against women 314-316
  see also Legal methodologies
Legal education
  absence of 5
  feminist jurisprudence and 422-428
  gender and cultural awareness 425-426
  violence against women 316
Legal methodologies
  the Bar 423-424
  bias, doctrine of 57-65, 192-194, 360-362, 422-428
  claims to objectivity 56-65
  claims to truth 65-74, 78-81, 156, 422
  epistemic privilege 56
  fact-finding methodologies 67-71, 120, 254-255
  feminist jurisprudence and 422-428
  impartiality 61-64
  judging, nature of 62-63, 438-442
  judiciary 424-426
  legal aid 432
  'merit', use of term 157-158, 423
  necessity to marginalise 422
  neutrality, baseline definition of 60-64
  pecuniary losses 299
  selecting precedents 56, 432-433
  separation thesis 195-196
  see also Feminist jurisprudence; Feminist methodologies; Legal discourses
Legal storytelling 66-67, 71, 74-77, 154-155, 157-159, 356-361
Lesbians
  anti-lesbianism 396-397
  anti-pornography and 414-416
  domestic violence 312-313, 320
  IVF 250-257
  as mothers in family law 287-292
  primary caregivers 269
  Property (Relationships) Act 1984 114
  stranger violence 320
  Tasmania 24-26, 77
  work in families 89
Lessard, Hester 22-23, 215
Link-Up 282
Litigation, test case 431-433
MacKinnon, Catharine 30-31, 48, 56-57, 71-73, 80-81, 195, 208, 213-214, 267, 322, 348-350, 381-383, 391-392, 404-407, 427, 434-438
Maintenance, spousal 106
Mandela, Nelson 43
Marriage
  consortium 126-132
  'contract' 111-114
  divorce 97, 98-108, 264-265, 267
  financial guarantees 125
  interspousal immunity 94-95
  joint bank accounts 123
  legal consequences 91-96
  marital discord 305-306
  marital rape exemption 13
  marital status 252-253
  matrimonial property 91-92, 98-108, 102-103, 114
  prenuptial agreements 114
  spousal maintenance 106
  women's work 90-91
  see also Domestic violence
Maternity leave 33-35, 140

INDEX

Matsuda, Mari 55, 448-449
Media, trial by 291-296
Medical abuse
    New Zealand cervical cancer study 337-343
    sexual assault 370-371
Medical and other injuries to women 328-343 see also Medical abuse; Medical negligence; Social injury to women
Medical devices 334-335
Medical negligence 183-192
    cervical cancer screening 342-343
    feminist jurisprudence 429-430
    indigenous women 298-299
    no-fault accident compensation legislation (NZ) 132, 340-343, 373
Men
    Army of Men 265-266
    as breadwinners 169, 259
    challenges to women-only programs 35-44
    claims of discrimination in Family Court 265-266
    defence of provocation 67-69, 197-198, 311
    experience of violence 111, 308-314
    forced sterilisation 331-332
    gender neutrality and language of domestic violence 308-314
    as plaintiffs 35-44, 197-198
    Status of Women Act 41
    work in families 88-89
    see also Fathers; Gay men
'Merit', use of term 157-158, 423
Methodologies see Feminist methodologies; Legal methodologies
Mill, John Stuart 93
Millbank, Jenni 254, 287-290, 433
Model Criminal Code Officers Committee 362-364, 365, 368
Money and relationships 87
Morality 195, 212-213, 382-383, 403-405
Morgan, Wayne 25-26, 77
Motherhood 183-192, 291-296 see also Children; Fathers
Naffine, Ngaire 364-365, 449
National Committee on Violence Against Women 275-276
National Network of Women's Legal Services 105
National Women's Health Program 36
'Natural justice' 57-65
Negligence 173-192, 342-343, 369, 373-379, 429-430 see also Injuries; Tort law
'Nervous shock' 173-183 see also Tort law
NESB women 52-53, 146, 395-396
Neutrality, baseline definition of 60-64
New Zealand cervical cancer study 337-343
Ngarrindjeri people 81-84

No-fault accident compensation legislation (NZ) 132, 340-343, 373
Norplant (contraceptive) 227-228, 333
Nursing and 'comparable worth' 160
Objectivity
    claims to 56-65
    and subjecthood of women see Subjecthood of women
Obscenity approach to pornography 403-405, 407-418
Olsen, Frances 8-9, 17-18, 96-97, 153, 392
Orchidectomies 331-332
Outworkers 162
Parental responsibility for children see Child custody
Parenthood see Children; Fathers; Motherhood
'Partial agency' 212
Pay Equity Inquiry, NSW 160-163
Personal injury damages 126-138, 139-145
Persons cases 42
Pocock, Barbara 149-151, 157, 160
Point of view see Epistemologies
Police liability in sexual assault 373-379, 431
Political correctness, notion of 426
Pornography 403-419
    artistic defence 408-409, 412
    community standards 403-405, 408-409, 410
    degradation test 408-409, 412
    equality and 405-419
    first interpretive moves 410
    homosexuality 414-416
    obscenity approach 403-405, 407-418
    ordinance approach 405-407, 410-414
    privatised harms 411
    public/private dichotomy 417
    role of law in regulation 418-419
    and speech 406-407
    trafficking in 406
    zoning regulation 418-419
Post-modern feminism 78-81, 300-301
Power, distribution of 65-66, 359, 405-407, 426, 435 see also Subordination principle
Precedents 56, 432-433
Pregnancy
    assisted reproduction 249-257
    bias and 58, 192-194
    DES 336
    equality 210, 212
    as equality model 33-35, 37
    medical model 243-244
    medical negligence 183-192
    Thalidomide 336
Pregnant tribunals 192-194
Premarital agreements 113-114
Presumption of advancement 44-48
Primary caregivers 267-277, 283-284
Private ordering of marriage contract 111-114
Procedural fairness 57-65, 194

INDEX

Property ownership 91-92, 98-108, 102-103, 114
Protection orders 317-319
Provocation, defence of 67-69, 197-198, 311
Psychological injuries *see* Injuries
Public/private dichotomy 10-27
    abortion 23, 203, 208-209, 211-212, 215-217, 222
    anti-discrimination laws 23-24
    cohabitation rule 14-15
    construction of 'the private' 15-17
    dichotomies 8-9, 10-11, 336-337, 412
    equality 32
    families 10-12
    Hindmarsh Island Bridge dispute 81-84
    indigenous women 20-21
    intervention and non-intervention 12-13, 17-20, 96-97, 254, 437
    legal discourse 11
    marital rape exemption 13
    pornography 417
    privacy 20-21, 24-27
    sexual harassment 392
    sterilisation of minors 13-14
    Violence Against Women Act (US) 437
    what is 'public'? 22-24
Racism 48, 50, 59-60, 63, 285, 396-397
Rape
    African-American women 49, 351-352
    civil actions for 369-380, 431
    consent, moving beyond 365-368
    construction of heterosexuality 348-354
    continuum in heterosex 350-351
    corroboration warning 355-356, 361-362
    counsellors' records 362-364
    definition of 348-350, 365, 367-368
    fresh complaint rule 355
    and gender 349, 360-362
    immunity from prosecution 13, 93-94
    law reform 365, 449
    legal storytelling 67, 356-361
    Michigan reforms 366
    neutralising 364-365
    post-modern feminism 79-80
    proving 354-364
    psychological effect of 348
    rape shield law 428-429
    'real' rape 344-345
    relationship 345-346
    rules of evidence 356-361
    sentencing legislation 348
    and sex 347, 349
    sex workers and 347-348
    and sexual harassment 401
    stolen generation children 353
    by stranger 345-346
    subordination principle 349
    tort law 317
    Violence Against Women Act (US) 435-438
    wishes of victim 346
    see also Sexual assault
'Real' rape 344-345
'Reasonable victim' standard 255-256, 390-395, 438-442
'Reasonableness' 255-256, 390-395, 438-442
Relationships
    comparator model of equality 433
    connection thesis 196-198
    death of children 298-299
    ethic of care and connection 194-195
    indigenous women 298-299
    male plaintiffs 197-198
    and money 87
    'nervous shock' 173-192
    relationship debt 114-115
    woman and foetus 244-249
    wrongful birth 183-192
Religious beliefs 218
Reproduction 199-257, 249-257 *see also* Abortion; Foetal rights
Rhoades, Helen 267-273, 277, 329, 444-445
Rights
    abortion 212-213
    privacy 24-27
    see also Foetal rights
Sameness/difference debate 29-30, 48-55, 153-156, 325-326
Sarmas, Lisa 45-48, 74-76
Scales, Ann 410-411, 414-416
Scheppele, Kim Lane 69-71
Scott, Joan 8, 155-156, 325
Separation assault 324
Separation thesis 195-196
Sex discrimination 31, 33-35, 151-156, 252-257
    legislation 151, 153
    pornography 405-407
    see also Sexual harassment
Sexual assault
    civil actions for 369-380, 431
    common law 379
    compensation 369
    constitutional law 373-379
    criminal law 443-444
    discrimination 375-376
    equality and 373-379
    fiduciary duty 370-371
    imbalance of power 369-370
    limitation periods 372
    medical abuse 370-371
    negligence 369, 376-379
    police liability 377
    privacy 21
    therapeutic motivation for suing 370
    tort law 369-370, 373-379
    Violence Against Women Act (US) 435-438
    see also Rape; Sexual harassment

Sexual harassment 381-403
   African-American women 395-396
   anti-discrimination laws 384-388
   bisexual defence 398
   defamation 385
   discrimination law 370, 381-383, 383-384
   as dominance eroticised 382
   fact-finding methodologies 69-71
   feminism 399-403
   gender neutrality 397-398
   group or social injury 382
   hostile work environment 390-391
   LEAF (Canada) 387-388
   legal claim of 434-435
   male perspectives on 388-389
   NESB women 395-396
   public/private dichotomy 392
   Rabidue appeal 391-392
   and rape 401
   'reasonable victim' standard 255-256, 390-395, 438-442
   redefinition of 398
   sex discrimination 31, 385-388, 397-398
   Status of Women Act 40
   tort law 370, 381-383
   victim-agency debate 322-326, 402-403
   see also Sex discrimination
Sexual violence 327-328 *see also*
   Pornography; Sexual harassment; Social injury to women
sexuality
   abortion 218
   Chamberlain trial 291-296
   as an issue of privacy 24-26
   lesbians 287-292
   morality 412
   pornography 404-405
   public/private dichotomy 392
   rape and 349-351
'Sexually transmitted debt' 114-115
Sheehan, Grania 98, 102-103, 109-110
Sheehy, Elizabeth 28-29, 31, 369, 428-429, 430
Sick leave 33-35
Small businesses 114-115
Smart, Carol 65-66, 73, 79-80, 171, 257, 422
Smyth, Bruce 102, 109-110, 113
Social injury to women
   anti-choice protesters 215-217
   attitudes to violence against women 306-308
   breast implant litigation 336-337
   cervical cancer screening 342-343
   concept of 300-302
   continuum of sexual violence 327-328
   criminal law 301-302
   Dalkon Shield 335-336
   DES (diethylstilbestrol) 336
   disabilities, women with 328-332
   eugenic sterilisation 328-334
   gendered harms 300-326
   incidence of violence 303-306
   indigenous women 304-305
   New Zealand cervical cancer study 337-343
   no-fault accident compensation legislation (NZ) 132, 340-343, 373
   separation assault 324
   Thalidomide 336
   unsafe drugs and medical devices 334-337
   victim-agency debate 322-326
   see also Domestic violence; Pornography; Rape; Sexual assault; Sexual harassment
Social justice issues 426
Social security law 14-15, 85-86, 168-170
Solatium (compensation for loss) 298
Sporting activities, notions of 38-39
State action *see* Intervention and non-intervention
Status of Women Act 40-43
Sterilisation
   in Canada 331-332
   eugenic 328-334
   of minors 13-14, 183-192
   wrongful birth 183-192
'Stock story' 66-67, 71, 74-77
'Stolen generations' 20, 278-285, 433
Subordination principle
   abortion 209
   approach to equality 30-31, 40, 43-44
   child rearing 43-44
   comparable worth and job evaluation 163
   consent and 366
   pornography 405-407
   power, distribution of 65-66, 359, 405-407, 426, 435
   rape and 349
   Status of Women Act 40
   see also Equality; Power, distribution of
Superannuation 107-108, 146-147
Surrogacy 6
Tasmanian Gay and Lesbian Rights Group 24-26, 77
Tax 12, 18-20, 116-119, 123, 141, 142, 147, 168
Terminations *see* Abortion
Test case litigation 431-433
Thalidomide (drug) 336
Thomas, Clarence 69-71
Thornton, Margaret 1, 9, 23, 157-159, 194, 423
Torres Strait Islander women *see* Indigenous women

INDEX

Tort law 126, 132
    anti-discrimination laws 384-385
    death of children 298-299
    equality and 373-379
    foetal rights 230-231
    Grandview Agreement (Canada) 448
    limitation periods 372
    'nervous shock' 173-183
    sexual assault 369-370
    sexual harassment 370, 381-383
    solatium 298
    violence against women 316-317
    Violence Against Women Act (US) 435-438
    wrongful birth 183-192
Trust devices 93
Truth, claims to 65-74, 78-81, 156, 422
Union membership 163-165
United Nations Human Rights Committee 6, 24-26
Universalism *see* Essentialism, gender; Foundationalism
Unregulated family 11-12
Vasectomies 331-332
Vicissitudes, allowance for 140-141
Victim-agency debate 212, 301-302, 322-326, 402-403, 435
Violence against women 275-276, 303-308, 316-321, 435-438, 442 *see also* Domestic violence; Social injury to women
Violence Against Women unit (NSW) 442
Wages for women
    abortion 210
    affirmative action laws 156-159
    anti-discrimination laws 151-156
    comparable worth and job evaluation 159-163
    'equal pay' cases 150-151
    'family wage' 147-149
    Fruitpickers judgment 148
    gendered wage gap 145-147
    Harvester judgment 147-149
    labour market institutions 163-165
    'merit' 157-158
    Pay Equity Inquiry, NSW 160-163
    Sears case 153-156
    wage-fixing judgments 147-149
    see also Women's work
Walker, Kris 250-251, 256
Wallace, Alison 304-306
West, Robin 195, 412-413
'Women' as category 54-55, 78-81, 300-301

Women of colour *see* African-American women; Indigenous women
Women's bodies, invading 327-380
Women's Electoral Lobby (WEL) 430-431
Women's Legal Education and Action Fund (LEAF) 42, 51, 73-74, 387-388, 430
    abortion 210, 212
    harm of pornography 410-411, 416-418
    relationship between woman and foetus 245-248
Women's work
    ACT Law Reform Commission 131-132
    child care 259, 261-262
    child custody 263-264
    children 107
    consortium 126-132
    damages for costs of care 133-138
    domestic distribution 88-89, 128-129, 166-167
    economic or non-economic loss 130-132
    equity measures 164-165
    feminisation of poverty 105-106
    financial institutions 119-120
    household income 123, 148
    labour force participation 89-90, 143, 149, 165-166
    legal consequences of marriage 91-96
    marriage and family 90-91
    marriage 'contract' 111-114
    maternity leave 33-35, 140
    matrimonial property 91-92, 98-108, 102-103, 114
    no-fault accident compensation legislation (NZ) 132, 340-343, 373
    paid workforce 89-90, 143-145
    personal injury damages 126-138, 139-145
    primary caregivers 267-277, 283-284
    same sex couples 89, 290-291
    sex workers 347-348, 378
    small businesses 114-115
    superannuation 107-108, 146-147
    trading while insolvent 125-126
    vertical segregation 143
    whose loss? 129-130
    work in families 87-138
    see also Sexual harassment; Wages for women
Wrongful birth 183-192
Wrongful conception 183-192
Young, Alison 356-361, 366-368
Zoning regulation in pornography 418-419